T0361537

ENZO FERRARI

ENZO FERRARI

THE DEFINITIVE BIOGRAPHY OF AN ICON

LUCA DAL MONTE

First published in Great Britain in 2024 by Cassell, an imprint of
Octopus Publishing Group Ltd
Carmelite House
50 Victoria Embankment
London EC4Y 0DZ
www.octopusbooks.co.uk

An Hachette UK Company
www.hachette.co.uk

Original title: *Ferrari Rex. Biografia di un grande italiano del Novecento – Nuova edizione* by Luca Dal Monte

Photo credits: Archivio Giorgio Nada Editore

Distributed in the US by
Hachette Book Group
1290 Avenue of the Americas
4th and 5th Floors
New York, NY 10104

Distributed in Canada by
Canadian Manda Group
664 Annette St.
Toronto, Ontario, Canada M6S 2C8

ISBN (hardback): 978-1-78840-471-6
ISBN (paperback): 978-1-78840-472-3

A CIP catalogue record for this book is available from the British Library.

Printed and bound in Great Britain

Typeset in 11.25/14.5pt Garamond Premier Pro by Jouve (UK), Milton Keynes

10 9 8 7 6 5 4 3 2 1

This FSC® label means that materials used
for the product have been responsibly sourced.

MIX
Paper | Supporting
responsible forestry
FSC® C104740

To Lodovica and Nicolò

Contents

Modena

The precise date of Enzo Ferrari's birth is still a matter of dispute. Official documents show his birth date as 20 February 1898, but Ferrari himself always claimed that he was born on 18 February – the day his mother, until her death in 1965, habitually sent him a birthday telegram signed 'Your loving mom.'[1] In his autobiography he attributes the discrepancy of two days between his birth and its registration to very heavy snowfall that had prevented his father from reaching the registry office in the city of Modena, Italy.[2] This was the accepted version during Ferrari's lifetime.

However, if you go and check the records, you will discover that there is no mention, anywhere, of particularly heavy snow in Modena during those days in February 1898. The city weather bulletin for 18 February recorded 'cold and rain', but no snow. In fact, the winter of 1898 was one of the very few in the 19th century when snow did not fall at all upon Modena.[3]

And then there is the fact that Enzo's father never reached the city registry office. The birth of Enzo Anselmo Giuseppe Maria Ferrari was registered by midwife Teresa Allegretti. That the registration took place in the early afternoon of 24 February rather than in the first hours after the birth is most likely the reason behind the date error.[4]

The true question, then, is why the registration – in the absence of heavy snow – was done six days after Enzo was born, when the law of the land required it to be done immediately after the birth. The answer is right there on the birth certificate itself, handwritten by the clerk of the registry office and overlooked by all for so many years. After 'having verified the birth', the clerk wrote, he exempted the midwife from 'show[ing] me the baby because of his health'.[5] Baby Enzo was registered six days after his birth because, until then, his survival was uncertain. This should not come as a surprise in a nation where, at that time, one baby in every four died before their fifth birthday, and the death of a newborn in the first hours or days after birth was all too common.

The story of the heavy snowfall sounds like one that loving parents may have fabricated to explain to their son why he was celebrating his birthday on 18 February while official papers read 20 February, to protect him from the naked truth. It is possible that, once he was older, Enzo might have been told the true story, but by that time the tale of the snowfall with its romantic implications and the two birth dates were already part of his personal legend, and he may have simply preferred to leave things the way they were.

Thus, in the presence of an official document stating his time of birth as 3am on Sunday 20 February, it is safe to assume that Enzo Ferrari was born at 3am on Friday 18 February 1898.

Enzo was christened in the small church of Santa Caterina, not far from his home, on the other side of the railroad tracks.[6] He was given the name Enzo Anselmo, though the second name in Italy is usually dropped and lives only in official paperwork. His middle name, Anselmo, was to honour his godfather, Anselmo Chiarli, a friend of his father's and the owner, with his brothers, of a successful Modena winery.[7]

His father was a metalworker from the nearby village of Carpi, where Enzo's grandfather owned a small family-run drugstore under the Portico del Grano colonnade overlooking the central square.[8] Born on 15 July 1859,[9] the year Modena and its territory were annexed to the Kingdom of Italy, Alfredo Ferrari had first worked as an apprentice in a metal shop in Carpi, then moved to the city right after his wedding. In Modena he was hired by the Rizzi Foundry, where he was quickly named technical director. With the little money he was able to put aside, a few years before Enzo was born he opened his own shop.[10]

Alfredo was an austerely dressed man with a big moustache, according to the fashion of the time. Though his work absorbed most of his attention, he also liked to take his family to the theatre and had a taste for music. He had played the cello in his youth, and kept a piano at home.[11] He was 'a man of good culture',[12] sending letters to his business contractors in clear, firm handwriting, mimicking the way the *literati* had written in the century that had just come to a close in a rather ingenious way using '7mber' in place of 'September' – in Italian, 'sette' is 'seven' and forms the beginning of the month name 'Settembre' (because September used to be the seventh month of the year, which is where its name comes from).[13]

By the time Enzo was born, Alfredo was a well-to-do middle-class entrepreneur who built bridges and canopies for the state railways. Forty years after the unification of the Kingdom of Italy, the country's railway network was undergoing rapid and constant expansion, and Alfredo Ferrari – a tireless worker and careful administrator – was prospering. His company employed ten to thirty workers, depending on the work it managed to win.[14]

The shop was next to the house where Alfredo lived with his family, a rectangular building about 90m (100yd) long, with a corrugated iron roof and dirt floor.[15] On its redbrick facade a sign read Costruzioni Meccaniche Alfredo Ferrari (Alfredo Ferrari Mechanical Constructions). A few large doors opened onto a grassy courtyard, and a double row of windows carried the day's light inside the otherwise unlit shop.

Alfredo turned his hand as needed to every task his company required: manager, designer, accountant, typist . . .[16] Enzo would never forget this lesson. From his father young Enzo learned the importance of the 'order of things' and of 'diligently keeping a record of everything that went on'.[17] For the boy, the father was a living example of devotion to duty, and a strong individualist – no more so than in his approach to business. Alfredo preferred working alone with complete autonomy, rather than in a joint partnership, even though that would have shared the risk as well as the reward. His philosophy was emphasized in the business credo that he taught his son, which Enzo would never forget: to be successful, one should not have to answer to any partner, and should be independent. So when the time came to create his own company, Enzo would remember what his father had taught him, in slightly playful terms, perhaps, yet with dead-serious intent: that the number of partners of any firm should always be an odd number and, preferably, 'inferior to three' – meaning only one: himself – but that was the precise way his father chose to word it.

His mother had been born Adalgisa Bisbini. She was a beautiful woman with long dark hair and striking features. Friendly and charming, she was appealing to men, whose attention did not diminish even after her wedding.[18] She was born in the village of Marano sul Panaro near Modena on 3 June 1872.[19]

She taught Enzo simple life lessons: 'A person who is healthy,' she used to tell him, 'is rich without knowing it.'[20] But more important, she instilled in him the firm principle of never giving up, of always finding in one's work a shelter from life's setbacks, of invariably seeing in tomorrow a new beginning.[21] Theirs would be a difficult and bumpy relationship, but for 67 years Adalgisa would be Enzo's truest point of reference.

Harmony was not a trait in the family. The 12-year age difference between Alfredo and Adalgisa produced continuous tumult inside and outside the 4 walls of the house. Both were gifted with a distinct and strong personality, and they argued often and ferociously. They argued about almost anything, and theatrically so. By his own admission, his parents' continuous disputes and foul language had an impact on Enzo's own nature and the person he became.[22]

Enzo's elder brother had been born a year and a half earlier, on 7 August 1896. He was named Alfredo, like his father, and nicknamed Dino to prevent confusion.

The two brothers shared an unheated bedroom on the second floor of the house that their father had built next to the workshop. The house itself was made up of four rooms above a large storage area for tools and objects that came in handy in a life that, despite its setting on the outskirts of a northern Italian city of fifty thousand people, still retained a strong country flavour.

The house was spartan in terms of both layout and furniture. The only luxury that Alfredo had allowed himself – apart from his beloved piano – was the red marble staircase. The memory of the 'pink' marble staircase would always remain with Enzo.[23]

While Enzo was by no means a difficult boy, he certainly wasn't as disciplined and obedient as his brother. For example, Enzo showed no interest in, nor patience for, those Sunday school lessons which he, like all his peers in Catholic Italy, was obliged to attend in preparation for the sacraments of first communion and confirmation.

Father Morandi, the old priest who taught Sunday school in the rectory of the parish church of Santa Caterina, was irritated by Enzo's lack of attention during lessons.[24] Adalgisa's religious conviction was deep and sincere – despite the fact that Modena was already surrounded by early manifestations of the socialist scepticism that would soon envelop the whole Emilia-Romagna region – and she had a tough time compelling Enzo to finish the preparatory course so that he could receive his first communion and be confirmed.

She managed it, however, and Enzo's first communion and confirmation ceremony was held on Whit Sunday 1903, officiated by monsignor Natale Bruni, who was in his fourth year as Bishop of Modena.[25] The two brothers, Enzo (five) and Dino (seven), had attended confession the previous day. This would be, by his own admission, the first and last confession of Enzo's life. Certain of having nothing to fear, Enzo confessed all those innocent weaknesses that, in the mind of a boy on his first real contact with the mysteries of religion, he considered sins. The priest gave him such a harsh penance that Enzo abandoned any future desire or need for confession.[26]

Each morning the two brothers walked to their elementary school, located on Via Camurri, not far from their house. The principal was a tiny white-haired old lady who constantly reprimanded Enzo for his inattentiveness. She could not understand how two brothers, so close in age and so attached to each other, could be so different in their approach to school. Enzo sat at his desk, bored, waiting for the bell announcing the end of the day's classes. Relief came in the familiar form of Dick, the family's enormous Great Dane, who waited outside the school building to walk back home with the two brothers.[27]

Of the many sports practised by Enzo, his favourite was track and field, a discipline that was enjoying a wave of popularity in Italy thanks to the evolution of the modern Olympic Games. Dino and Enzo had their own personal track and invited their school friends to train on it. The Ferrari home, situated alongside Via Camurri, between fields and the railway line, was accessed by a dirt track about 180m (200yd) long that ran along the wooded edge of a ditch of stagnant water. Using a tape measure taken from their father's workshop, Dino and Enzo measured the exact distance of 100m, planting two wooden poles to mark the start and finish lines at the beginning and end of the track.

The Ferrari brothers had their own private long-distance track, too, created on the dirt roads ringing the winery that belonged to the Chiarli brothers. Dino easily beat his younger brother, over long and short distances.

Enzo was better than all the rest at just one activity; even better than his beloved brother Dino and their group of friends, which included Peppino, the son of the grocer; another Enzo, the son of the school janitor; Luciano, the best student in his class; and Carlo, the son of the barber. Enzo excelled at clay pigeon shooting. After much insistence, he had managed to convince his father to buy him a Flobert rifle, which he used to shoot at targets made of clay pipes. To have more fun, Enzo and Dino often mischievously practised by shooting at the mice that infested the ditch leading to their house.

At one point their father saw Enzo's interest in clay pigeon shooting as a way of making him study harder at school, and invented a scheme entitling Enzo to a certain number of cartridges depending on his grades. If it had not been for the kind mediation of Toni, a 14-year-old boy who was an apprentice metalworker in his father's workshop but was also entrusted with the boys' care, Enzo would have had very few cartridges to shoot.[28]

Adversaries in all sorts of athletic events, Dino and Enzo were allies in an activity that was then very fashionable because of the still rudimentary nature of communications in Italy: pigeon keeping. Their father had assigned them the care of his carrier pigeons, and while Dino trained them, ten-year-old Enzo assumed responsibility for the organizational aspects of the birds' participation in competitions in Modena and throughout its territory.[29] With hindsight, it is all too easy to identify in this organizational activity the seeds of Enzo's future vocation, which would initially take the form of Scuderia Ferrari and, subsequently, of the company that would bear his name.

Enzo's life may (arguably) not have contained enough studying, but he certainly participated in a lot of sports and had a clear passion for clay pigeon shooting and a growing interest in organization. He also loved music – or, to be precise, the theatre.

Despite the fact that their father had played the cello in his youth and the presence of a piano in their home, neither boy ever learned to play an instrument. But both loved to go to the theatre on Saturday nights with their parents.

Enzo had a passion for operettas, traditionally staged at Teatro Storchi, just outside Porta Bologna: *The Merry Widow, Geisha, Eva, The Princess of Dollars*. In his heart he hoped to become a famous tenor. More than by the music itself, young Enzo was attracted by the 'extravagant and fatuous world' of the performing arts, and especially by the actresses.[30] It was indeed the 'show girls who were, along with the catchy melodies, the reason' for his love of operettas.[31] 'Lack of voice and of talent' ended his career long before it ever had a chance to begin, however.[32]

After the theatre, the family loved to dine out. They would often go to a little cosy family-run restaurant in the back of the Giusti grocery store in downtown Modena, 'where the food was delicious'.[33] Though his father never said so, Enzo suspected that his dad's choice of a restaurant run by a grocer was sentimental, 'remembering that he himself was the son of a grocer from Carpi'.[34]

By all accounts, Enzo's life in the first decade of the 20th century was a tranquil one. Though not particularly privileged, Enzo certainly lived more comfortably than most of his peers in Modena. His father Alfredo would work each day from well before dawn to way past dusk, but would end earlier on Saturdays to spend time with his family. 'Those were happy times,' Enzo would write over half a century later, which 'seemed as though they would never end.'[35]

The Spark

In 1903, with his business flourishing, Alfredo Ferrari decided to buy his first car.[1] He chose a vehicle built by one of the 30 or so French manufacturers, a single-cylinder De Dion-Bouton, built in 1898. Enzo and his brother, dressed alike by their mother (as was fashionable at the time) in shorts, striped shirt under a light jacket and braces (suspenders), rode next to their father and experienced a tremendous outburst of emotion.[2] The De Dion-Bouton of Alfredo Ferrari was the 28th car registered in the Province of Modena, and the first car that Enzo, then aged 5, saw at close quarters.

The first automobile had been spotted in Modena eight years earlier, in September 1895, three years before Enzo's birth.[3] On 24 September, 'an automatic chariot by Benz' had made its way into town, having travelled from Milan to Modena the day before. Four Modena citizens had experienced the emotion of their first short ride in an automobile to Rubiera, a village on the Via Emilia roughly halfway between Modena and Reggio Emilia. Their journey had lasted only 28 minutes, but the echo of that first ride would fill countless conversations that fall and winter.

Little by little, not knowing that it would one day be considered the cradle of sports cars, Modena came to terms with this new means of transportation.

On 6 September 1908, when Enzo was ten years old, his father took him to see his first automobile race. It produced an indelible 'spark' in his heart.[4] This early excitement kindled an eternal fire in him, a passion to which Enzo would dedicate the rest of his life. Later, Ferrari recalled the thrill of one race in particular, the Florio Cup, a classic of the Bologna area, which was held on country dirt roads linked to the Via Emilia, the old consular road from the Adriatic Sea to Milan where the troops of the Roman Republic had marched, centuries before the birth of Christ. It was there, while watching the dust-covered race cars of Felice Nazzaro and Vincenzo Lancia – the first champions of a sport still in its youth – roaring through the sunbaked countryside amid rows of poplar trees, that young Enzo began to dream of one day *becoming* Ferrari.

By 1908 motor racing had entered its second decade of life in Italy, but it was still a rough sport. The roads were not paved, and the races were usually extremely long, lasting many hours – often far too many for the cars and the physical stamina of the drivers. Races were not held on specially designed tracks equipped with appropriate facilities. The concept of motor-racing tracks was still undeveloped. Instead, races were generally held on regional or provincial roads linking several towns, which would be closed along certain stretches. The word *circuit* was used only because the drivers covered a course that was normally 20, 30 or 40 miles in length, time and time again.

There were no proper protective barriers for the spectators, whose number increased each year. Curiously enough, it was the lack of this rudimentary safety precaution that remained imprinted in Enzo's mind at the end of that first race he attended.

On the most challenging bend on the course, the organizers of the Florio Cup had flooded the fields on the outside of the road with 25.5cm (10in) of water. The intention was that if any car went off the road, the water would stop it as quickly as possible, to protect the spectators who, one assumes, were crowded on dry ground at a distance of about 35–40m (40–50yd) from the dirt track. At just ten years old, Enzo was fascinated by the 'innocuous excitement, with unexpected splashes and soakings for spectators and drivers'.[5]

Enzo, however, also took in information of a more sporting nature. The winner of this first race he'd attended was Felice Nazzaro, at an average speed of almost 130km/h (80mph), completing the 533km (331 miles) of the race in 8 hours. Vincenzo Lancia, who had just founded the car-manufacturing factory that bore his name, set the fastest lap.

The following year, 1909, Enzo attended a second race, which won him over definitively. He did not even have to travel far, but simply cross the railway line behind his home and walk 3.5km (2 miles) across the fields to reach the seemingly endless stretch of Navicello, the provincial road that was the setting for a local race with a pretentious name: the *Record del Miglio* – Record of the Mile (1 mile is 1.6km).

Lancia and Nazzaro, the two top drivers of the 1908 Florio Cup, were prestigious names in Italy in the first decade of the 20th century, but the drivers taking part in Modena's Record del Miglio were far less known. Although Ceirano, Gioia, Scipioni, Carminati and Da Zara have long been forgotten, with their participation in this particular race they indirectly affected the world of motor racing more than they ever could have imagined.

The organizing committee – the local Associazione Modenese Automobilistica

(AMA) – had received 30 entries. The city was frenzied, the excitement palpable. On Friday 7 June 1909, men arrived from Milan to lay asphalt on the long stretch that would host the race the following Sunday. All week long the citizens of Modena visited the headquarters of the AMA and the shops of Stanguellini and Palmieri to buy tickets for the race. On Saturday, the whole city stopped to silently witness the scrutineering of each car.

On Sunday morning, a few hours before the start of the race, it began to rain. Excited to attend the second race of his life, Enzo didn't let this ruin his plans, leaving his house early to reach Nonantola on foot. Later that morning, the citizens of Modena who owned a car left the city to reach the site of the race, which, at 1pm, 2 hours before the start, would be closed to normal traffic. Those who didn't own a car (the overwhelming majority) and who didn't want to walk, as Enzo and his brother Dino had done, took advantage of the transport offered by the organizers and reached Nonantola for the modest price of one lira each.

The rain quit a few hours before the start of the race. Organizers then dampened the quickly drying road with buckets and barrels of water in an attempt to reduce dust.

The winner's average speed was 145km/h (90mph) – it seemed like each competitor's race lasted for the blink of an eye. Da Zara, speeding past Enzo and his brother, covered the distance of 1.6km (1 mile) in 41 seconds on his best attempt (out of 2). For Enzo the races stirred violent emotions within him, thrills that flared and died with a speed matched only by their intensity.

After that first running of the race, Modena was consumed by a deeply felt motoring fever. Everyone in town was eagerly awaiting the 1910 event, especially after the news broke that famed Felice Nazzaro would be among the contenders.[6] Despite its short history – only a single running! – in the absence of international races the Record del Miglio had quickly become one of the most anticipated events of the Italian motoring season. The nation's largest daily newspapers sent their reporters to Modena to cover the race this time.[7]

Enzo's excitement must have been tangible: Nazzaro, the greatest of all Italian drivers, and the winner of the first race he had attended two years earlier, would now speed by again before his very eyes. So would Vincenzo Lancia, another of the great names of the infant sport whom he had seen race in Bologna in September 1908. Though he left no record of it, Enzo cannot have missed the second run of the Record del Miglio. Unfortunately for him and his fellow citizens, the 1910 running of the mile-long speed attempt was also going to be the last.

An accident involving two cars, two drivers and their two mechanics put an end to an event that had produced such great enthusiasm in a very short time.

The following year a more modest regularity contest – where the winner is not the fastest, but the one who comes closest to a time set in advance – was staged in Modena. All five legs started and ended in the city, the first on 23 April 1911 and the last on 29 April. Twenty-five cars entered, with no driver of national fame. Only Ernesto Ceirano was there to remind the speed-hungry *Modenesi* of the Record del Miglio.

As his passion for cars and races grew, Enzo found it more difficult than ever to concentrate on school. He simply had no interest in his studies. If his performance in elementary school was bad, things only worsened when he started the *istituto tecnico* vocational school, which he would attend for three years. School felt like a waste of time for a boy who could not be like his brother, no matter how hard he tried, even though he desperately wanted to emulate his father.

Papà Alfredo and *mamma* Adalgisa kept telling him that studying was fundamental to one's life, but it was no use. His father, with whom Enzo became more and more argumentative as he grew older, would incessantly push him to finish his studies and earn the degree that he, Alfredo, had never obtained. He wanted Enzo to become an engineer and continue the family business with his brother. Unfortunately, maths may have been Enzo's worst subject. He had only a superficial interest in geography, though he did enjoy history and clearly loved writing compositions and essays. Although he hadn't received any particular training in writing, he thought he 'was not bad at it at all'.[8] Thus, finding a genuine pleasure in the field, Enzo began to dedicate himself to a semi-professional practise of journalism, the second of his youthful passions.

In 1914, the year World War I broke out in Europe, 16-year-old Enzo, now enrolled in the city vocational school, began an after-school internship with *Provincia di Modena*, the town's conservative daily newspaper. The paper had been run a few years earlier by novelist Luciano Zuccoli, who had so captured Enzo's imagination with his dual careers as journalist and author that Enzo confessed his dream of one day becoming the editor in chief of his hometown newspaper.

In this last year of peace in Italy, Enzo spent more and more time in the paper's newsroom, where he typically tried to absorb the various techniques of newspaper reporting. He didn't have much responsibility – he was little more than the paper's gofer – but it was a beginning. He was never given the honour of a byline, even when he got a chance to write a story.

In November 1914, however, his name finally appeared in print, in the pages of the Milan-based *La Gazzetta dello Sport* national sports newspaper. In fact, that month young Enzo had three of his stories published, all with his byline. All three articles were next-day reports of the Sunday major league soccer matches played in Modena. The first story was printed on Monday 2 November and the others appeared on 16 and 23 November.

Having first fallen hopelessly in love with motor racing and the thrills that speed could provide, then added 'aspiring journalist' to his list of interests, Enzo now began to pay attention to a different and more ordinary attraction. Like his friends, he had started to notice the opposite sex. At 16, he fell in love with a 14-year-old girl. Despite Enzo's best efforts, however, the girl would have none of it. He would walk by and she wouldn't even look over. They never spoke. All of his attentions were met with 'indifference', which Enzo described as 'the most terrible of all weapons'.[9]

Then, one summer night infested by mosquitoes, Enzo made his real-life hopes known for the first time.[10] It was the summer of 1915, and Enzo was by now 17. He was with his great childhood friend Peppino, the grocer's son, who lived in a fine house on the other side of his father's workshop. The two boys were at the Modena customs barrier, in the flickering light of a gas lamp. Killing time in the heat of a steamy night, Peppino asked Enzo what he wanted to do when he grew up, and Ferrari found himself confessing what until then had only been a secret passion.

Enzo was holding an illustrated magazine open to page 9 – *La Stampa Sportiva*, which had been printed in Turin every week since 1901, and had helped to nurture the sports ambitions of Enzo and his brother over the years.

The issue that Enzo had in his hands was number 26, published on Sunday 27 June 1915. About mid-page, the smallest of three photographs featured Ralph DePalma, a driver virtually unknown to the Italian public. The magazine reported that he was the winner of that year's Indianapolis 500, held on the 4km (2.5-mile) oval-shaped track in Indiana.

'I'm going to be a racing driver,'[11] Enzo said, in answer to his friend's question, boldly pointing at the magazine and at the small picture of DePalma, apparently at the wheel of a racing car but wearing a dress shirt and a necktie. What Enzo kept to himself were the thoughts behind his conviction: 'If DePalma could do it,' he had thought, 'why couldn't I?'[12]

'Good,' said his friend. 'If you can make it, it's got to be a wonderful job.'

It was the summer of 1915. Italy had entered the war on 24 May, seven days before the Indianapolis 500 was won by Ralph DePalma. The country was swept up in a strong and genuine nationalistic passion.

Enzo did not appear particularly attracted by the opportunity to win glory on the battlefield, however, but the same could not be said of his brother. At home, discussions soon arose between Dino and his father, with his mother acting as peacemaker in a desperate attempt to dissuade him from joining the fight. At last Dino prevailed and was allowed to leave as a volunteer.[13]

Thanks to the family's Diatto, his father's third car, Dino was assigned to the Corps of the Red Cross. He took the 3.0-litre, 4-cylinder car, which was transformed into an ambulance, to the front, shuttling between the first line and the hospitals in the rear.

For the moment, Enzo's age (17) shielded him from the call to arms. But if the war didn't end soon – at the time, very few people believed that it would last more than a few months – he too would have to join in the following year.

Meanwhile, having failed the third class at the Technical Institute, his studies were finally over.[14] In October, thanks to the experience he'd gained in his father's workshop, he found a job in the machine shop of the Modena fire department. He was hired as an instructor to teach those who had been drafted but, 'because of their age, if employed in auxiliary workshops, could obtain exemption from military service'.[15] Each course lasted three months. After this period they were all sent to the ammunition factory in Modena, one of countless Italian companies converted for wartime production.

A couple of nights before the end of the year, Alfredo Ferrari went to bed with a high fever. It started off as bronchitis, but quickly turned into severe pneumonia. Within three days he was dead.[16] It was 2 January 1916, and he was not quite 57 years old.

With the death of his father, Enzo lost a precise reference point. The severity of Alfredo's illness and his precipitous decline had struck without warning, a little over a month before Enzo's 18th birthday.

The sudden loss of his father was the first great sorrow in Enzo Ferrari's life – the first of many, and perhaps the one that began to shape the man he would become. The memories – not only of his father, but also of his sudden death – would never leave him.

Before the year ended, however, Enzo would be devastated by a second tragedy. On 16 December, in Sondalo, in the mountain province of Sondrio, his brother Dino died, too. After a year of war he had contracted pneumonia, which, because of the precarious conditions in which soldiers lived, had quickly killed him.[17] He was just 20 years old.

In less than 12 months, Enzo's life had been turned upside-down. Father and brother were gone. The sudden death of his father had, among other things, put at risk the Ferrari family's welfare – they could not live off the small salary Enzo was earning as a wartime instructor. Moreover, precious machinery from his father's workshop had been requisitioned by the army to be used in war production.

Five months before the death of his brother, in July 1916, Enzo had received his driver's licence. It was one of the few joys of that tragic, fateful year, and something he'd looked forward to with great anticipation. In the midst of so many miseries and fears, driver's licence number 1363 gave him at least the pleasure of sitting from time to time at the wheel of a car, the Caesar that his father had bought after Dino had left for the war with the family Diatto. Perhaps it was at this moment that Enzo Ferrari began to see cars as a means to freedom – not only freedom of movement, but also freedom from the uncertainties and anxieties of life.

On a beautiful summer day in 1917, Enzo drove his Caesar from Modena up the Apennines hills. When he arrived in the town of Sestola, he decided to test himself and measure the time it would take him to reach the village of Pavullo along a winding road comprising a seemingly endless series of slow bends and fast straights – difficult, but also fun. He was 19 years old and, despite the war and the loss of his father and brother, his passion for racing an automobile had not faded. Life could still be beautiful.

When he reached Pavullo, a small group of onlookers, a few men and boys, gathered around the car and its driver. Enzo looked almost as elegant as a city chauffeur rather than a racing pilot in the fashion of his childhood heroes, Nazzaro and Lancia. The moment was captured in a photograph. Enzo, with flying goggles raised on his floppy hat, reflected the pride of being one of the lucky and talented few to master an automobile, a device still shrouded in mystery to most. On the back of the photograph, in his own hand, Enzo wrote:

Sestola–Pavullo
After the Raid

Then he added the length and characteristics of the 'course' and the time taken to cover it. The road he described as '26 kilometres and 475 metres, with gradients of up to 12 per cent'; the time it took him to travel: '36 minutes and 12 seconds'.[18] It was Thursday 19 July 1917.

Enzo was still serving as an instructor at the Modena fire department school. The conflict was in a stalemate, and seemed no nearer an end. Then, on the night of 24 October, the Austrians broke the front near the town of Caporetto, and what had become an exhausting war of containment suddenly became a struggle to push back the invaders.

The general mobilization assumed levels never seen before. Boys born in 1899 were called to arms. In the meantime, those who, for one reason or another, had not been drafted in the previous three years were now called to arms. More stringent measures for exemption from military service for health reasons were immediately adopted. And many of those who had until then participated in the conflict by working in services related to the war effort but far from the theatre of operations were now drafted.

Enzo was ordered to give up his post of instructor and join the army. He was assigned to the Third Regiment of the Alpine Artillery, stationed in the Val Brembana area – north of Bergamo, far from Caporetto and the front. Despite his rudimentary skills as a mechanic and being one of the few with a driver's licence, he found himself shoeing mules.[19] Perhaps not the most fitting occupation given his past experience, but at least he was spared the misery of the trenches. After a few months he contracted pneumonia. Fearing he would end up like his father and brother, Enzo managed to get himself quickly sent to a military hospital in Brescia. Then, thanks to his mother, who was not about to lose the only remaining member of her family, he moved to a hospital in Bologna, close to home. While he had been spared the fighting and had not suffered the psychological and physical attrition of the trench, the long convalescence in two hospitals affected him deeply. His survival was at one time in question. Surrounded by the hopeless, he spent 'terrible days' and feared he was near the end.[20]

The environment in which Enzo found himself fighting for his life bore a resemblance to the one described in *A Farewell to Arms*, but without the poetry and sensuality of Hemingway's prose. Enzo later recalled: 'There was a shaded avenue that I could see from my room's window: the people, the world seemed to me so far away, almost out of reach.'[21] This was by day; at night he would hear hard blows resounding in the otherwise silent hospital hallways. Perhaps already knowing the answer, for a long time he didn't dare ask what the sound was. Then he braced himself. The nurse caring for him, a young war widow, at first gave him evasive answers. Then she told him the truth: what he was hearing echoing, night after night, was the sound of workers' hammers as they built the wooden coffins in which were laid to rest those of his fellow soldiers who had died that day.[22]

It took him two operations and a long hospital stay before he recovered and returned to Modena. But he never forgot.

The Dream Comes True

World War I, the 'Great War', ended in Italy on 4 November 1918.

With the conflict finally over, the automobile suddenly found scores of enthusiasts. Those who had profited from the war and were now rich longed for the new mode of transportation. The youth eyed it as a symbol of modernity. There were more than 100,000 enlisted men who had used cars, trucks and ambulances in war operations: drivers, mechanics and technicians who left the war theatre with a deep disgust for atrocity, but also with a profound fondness for cars. In their own way they had been the protagonists of the beginning of a new era – the era of the internal-combustion engine. Now they were all looking for peacetime jobs that would allow them to continue driving automobiles. The most daring ones began to think of themselves as racing drivers.[1]

Enzo Ferrari was one of them.

By the autumn of 1918, Enzo was ready to start anew. The war had taken its toll on his family: his father and brother were gone. Their company was all but crushed. All he had left was his loving but possessive mother. It did not take him long to realize that, notwithstanding his love for her and his affection for his hometown, his future lay elsewhere.

Ironically, it was his mother who pushed him away from Modena when she got him an interview with Diego Soria, the commercial director of Fiat in Turin.[2] Before the war, Fiat had already employed four thousand people. By the end of the war the company ranks had more than quadrupled.[3] With a little luck, Enzo would find a job there.

To prevent him from becoming a racing driver – Enzo had expressed his intention to sell the house in which they were living to buy a racing car – his mother was willing to do all she could to buy him access to an automotive company, convinced that Enzo would accept any position as long as it gave him the chance to work in the industry. Enzo gladly accepted his mother's help, but took the train to Turin hoping to get a job with Fiat as a tester. His intuition told him this would be the first step towards a career as a racing driver. After all, he had a driver's licence and a rudimentary knowledge of the mechanics of a car.

It was November,1918. The war had ended only a few weeks before.

In Turin Enzo was received by *Ingegner* (engineer) Diego Soria in the Corso Dante Fiat headquarters. He went to the meeting 'full of hopes'.[4] Soria was one of Fiat's top executives. His office had wooden furniture and green curtains. The man himself had short red hair. Half a century later Enzo would still remember every detail of that fateful interview.[5]

But the meeting, as cordial as it was, ended up a total disappointment. Very politely Soria told him that unfortunately Fiat was not able to hire all war veterans.[6] Instead of Enzo, Fiat actually hired Carlo Salamano, who shortly afterwards became one of the Fiat racing-team drivers, proving Enzo's intuition correct.[7]

Enzo had sincerely, though somewhat naively, hoped to find a job at Fiat. For this reason Soria's polite but negative answer left him distraught. He had no money, no job and no intention of going back to Modena. While walking through the Valentino Castle park along the banks of the Po River, he was overwhelmed. He brushed the snow off a park bench, sat down and wept.[8] Although it was a rare moment of true despair in his life, he was determined not to give up, and remained in Turin.

The first peacetime Christmas in four years found Enzo living alone in Turin, existing on his ever-decreasing savings. Early in January 1919, he found a job in a workshop in Via Ormea in Turin. A man named Giovannoni, an acquaintance of Enzo's father, who had himself come to Turin from Bologna, had opened a small repair shop in which a handful of people worked on small wartime trucks, transforming their chassis so they could become automobiles thanks to the precious hands of these first coachbuilders.

Enzo's task was to fine-tune the converted chassis, which he would then personally deliver to the Carrozzeria Italo-Argentina body shop in Milan. Although the workshop at Via Ormea was not comparable to the environment and motivations that he would have found at Fiat, young Enzo was happy at Giovannoni's. From the outset he realized that 'the role of the employee', all in all, 'was not that bad'. And 'even if the cold, the little knowledge and the modest pay' gave him 'at times physical and emotional pain', Enzo faced all with enthusiasm as he realized that he was doing the kind of work that he had 'always wanted' to do.

Enzo's days were now spent between Turin and Milan. Because of the terrible so-called Spanish influenza which in those winter months still claimed 450 deaths per day, bars and cafés were deserted all over Italy. In Turin the two cafés where automotive enthusiasts had convened before the war – Burrello and Allaria – were now empty. Only the Bar del Nord, near the Porta Nuova train station, was crowded. Here motor-racing enthusiasts from all over town gathered to rejoice in their common passion. Enzo was a regular. In the company of prewar racing drivers and World War I aviation aces, he felt in his element. He even had a chance to meet and get to know Felice Nazzaro – the hero of his youth, the winner of the first race he ever attended – and his brother, Biagio.[9]

Those afternoons and evenings at the Bar del Nord café fascinated and excited Enzo. Because of his passion and his competence, his opinion was soon sought after and appreciated. In those animated discussions, the step from converted chassis to racing cars seemed a small one, and Enzo soon found himself wondering, together with the rest of the crowd, when motor racing would resume. His dream of becoming a racing driver, confessed to his boyhood friend back in the first summer of the war, acquired new strength now, in the first winter after the conflict.

Each time he went to Milan, after delivering the converted chassis to Carrozzeria Italo-Argentina Enzo would stop at another café, the centrally located Bar Vittorio Emanuele. The clientele here were athletes. A few of them had even been racing drivers before the war. One day he met a former bicycle racer, Ugo Sivocci, whose brother Alfredo was still active in cycling.

Having switched to motor racing, Ugo, too, had made a small name for himself, finishing sixth in the 1913 Targa Florio won by Felice Nazzaro. Ugo was an employee of CMN – Costruzioni Meccaniche Nazionali – a minor car company that had recently been formed. Right after the war CMN had taken over the Milan plants of the De Vecchi car company, for whom Sivocci had raced the Targa Florio. Won over by Enzo's knowledgeable enthusiasm, Ugo spoke of him to his boss at CMN, a young engineer named Piero Combi. An interview was quickly arranged, at the end of which Enzo was offered a job.

Right before Easter 1919, Enzo thus left Turin and moved to Milan. The salary was good, almost 400 lire a month – twice as much as the pay of a regular mechanic. With this hiring, his 'hunger problems' came to an end.[10]

Alongside components from car manufacturer Isotta Fraschini, CMN mounted three-litre engines on brand-new chassis. The four-cylinder monobloc engines were the first ones that Enzo saw up close, and so began his enduring love affair with engines.[11] As well as assembling cars from parts coming from other manufacturers, Combi was planning to start an in-house CMN production programme to meet the rising demand for brand-new automobiles.[12]

In the first days of June excitement filled the café. News had reached the car-frenzied customers that French car manufacturer Peugeot had won the first Indianapolis 500 held after the end of the war. It had been DePalma's Indianapolis win that won Enzo over to car racing. Only four short years had passed since that night in the summer of 1915 when he had confessed to his friend Peppino his dream of becoming a racing driver.

To the disappointment of all café regulars, however, there were still no motor-racing events planned in Italy. The same was true for most of war-torn Europe. Then, in the summer, they heard that tiny but war-spared Denmark was organizing the first race in Europe since the outbreak of the Great War. The race was scheduled for 24 August on the small island of Fanø. No newspapers carried this information. Café customers found out about it directly from driver Ferdinando Minoia, one of the regulars, who was the only Italian invited to the event. At the wheel of a 130hp Fiat, Minoia went on to win the race.[13]

Spurred on by the excitement over Minoia's win, Enzo, working with Sivocci, 'for the first time sensed the early symptoms of a small vocation'[14] for racing. He bought his first racing car from CMN, at a good discount. As a guarantee he pledged his salary for the next few months. When news spread in Modena that he had spent all his money on a racing car, people called him 'mad', and the nickname stuck for a long time. The car was a CMN 15/20 – it had a 2.3-litre, 4-cylinder, 36hp engine with a top speed of 80km/h (50mph).[15] Not the paragon of speed, but a beginning nonetheless.

September brought the news that Enzo and his café associates had been waiting for: at last, the first postwar race in Italy was scheduled, for 5 October – the Parma–Poggio di Berceto hillclimb. All Italian car manufacturers, racing drivers and aspiring drivers – Enzo included – received a personal letter from the secretary of the organizing committee. Because of a wartime restriction that had not yet been repealed, manufacturers were still banned from entering motor-racing events, but the prohibition did not apply to individual drivers, who could bypass the restriction by entering the event independently.[16]

Enzo was understandably excited. His dream was about to come true. He was 21 years old and about to compete in the first race of his life. What he lacked in experience he could make up for in terms of knowledge. Parma was only 40km (25 miles) from Modena, and the twisty roads climbing up the Apennines behind Parma were not so different from the familiar roads that ascended the Apennines south of Modena.

The 1919 Parma–Poggio di Berceto was the third running of a race first contested in 1913 as part of the celebrations for the hundredth anniversary of the birth of opera composer Giuseppe Verdi. The national press pompously described the 1919 event as the 'automotive rebirth' of Italy.[17] A total of 38 entries were received by the organizers, including Enzo's. In a detailed story introducing the race, Italy's largest sports daily listed Enzo Ferrari as one of the favourites in his class – odd, given that he was a rookie.[18]

On the Saturday, drivers practised in heavy rain. By Sunday morning the rain had stopped, but the day dawned cold and foggy. Despite the weather, thousands of racing fans climbed the hills from Parma to Poggio to watch their heroes. The long absence of events had only made their appetite for motor racing stronger. Some drove hundreds of miles to watch the race, leaving five hundred cars neatly parked on both sides of the road.[19]

The first driver, Carlo Alberto Conelli in an Aquila car, drove off at 8.30am. By this time rain had started to fall again over the second half of the track, from the village of Fornovo to the finish line. Enzo took the start at 10.55am. His CMN of 'indecipherable colour' had number 22 painted on the front radiator.[20]

Enzo's performance may not have been memorable, but it was wholly acceptable for a 21-year-old amateur in his first racing attempt. Next to him sat a complete stranger, bystander Nino Berretta, who had volunteered to take the role of passenger, the 'riding mechanic', to comply with race regulations.[21] Enzo drove his CMN to a fifth-place finish in his class, twelfth overall. After one driver was disqualified, he moved up one place both in the overall and the class standings. Bringing home the small prize money for his fourth-place finish also somehow earned his mother's blessing to continue his motor-racing efforts. The winner was, as predicted, Antonio Ascari.

In the newspapers' race reports the following day there was no mention of Enzo's performance. Ignored by the press but evidently pleased with his own performance, and eager to test his talent on higher grounds, Enzo next accepted an invitation to compete in the famed Targa Florio, scheduled for 23 November.[22]

Enzo left for Sicily at the wheel of the same CMN, which he would use in the race. All his possessions amounted to no more than 450 lire. Alongside him, in another CMN vehicle, was friend and colleague Ugo Sivocci. Their mechanics, Nino Conti and Ripamonti, also travelled with them.

The four men drove down the Via Emilia to reach the Adriatic, where they turned and headed south along the coastal road flanking the sea. They kept the Adriatic on their left until they reached the city of Pescara, where they began their westward crossing of the Italian peninsula through the Abruzzi plateau. One night, on the Cinquemiglia highlands, they found themselves trapped in the snow and surrounded by starving wolves. Before rangers could come to their aid with firearms and torches to disperse the beasts, Enzo himself protected his travelling companions by firing shots with the pistol that he always kept under the seat of his automobile.[23] His youthful passion for clay pigeon shooting was evidently coupled with a heartfelt need for personal security in the troubled Italy of 1919.

They reached Naples just in time to board the Città di Siracusa ferry.[24] After a stormy night at sea the four men and the two cars landed in Palermo, where the Targa Florio was headquartered. Enzo and his companions found hospitality at the permanent sports village built expressly for the race at Floriopolis, near the tiny village of Cerda, some 65km (40 miles) east of Palermo.[25]

The 1919 Targa Florio was the tenth running of a race first contested in 1906. Because of the many challenges it posed to both cars and drivers, it had quickly made a name for itself. Long before the now-famous Mille Miglia was conceived, the Targa Florio had acquired a status shared by no other race in Italy, and only a handful of others in Europe. The flamboyant personality of organizer Vincenzo Florio did the rest, ensuring the enthusiastic participation of the best drivers at the wheel of the most powerful racing cars.

On Saturday morning, the day before the race, Enzo drove his CMN for the first time on the trying Targa Florio course. But his only day of practice came to an abrupt end about halfway through the first lap when a violent downpour forced all activities to end.

Autumn in Sicily can be warm and sunny, but this year it was cold and wet. The Sunday weather forecast predicted more rain.[26] On Saturday night a prolonged thunderstorm disturbed the sleep of all the drivers. Rain fell on the coast and snow on the mountains. As Sunday morning dawned, a strong wind started to blow in off the sea. When Enzo awoke, he was welcomed by dark clouds and soaked roads. Sivocci, who had raced here before, knew that he and his fellow drivers were likely to face rain, fog and mud in the part of the circuit that climbed up the Madonie hills.[27]

Eager with anticipation, Enzo moved his car up near the starting line a few minutes before 8am. At 7.59am, he saw Indy winner André Boillot dash off. His thoughts must have gone to Ralph DePalma and to the magazine picture that had made him dream of becoming a racing driver. But there was no time to dwell on these thoughts; three minutes later, his turn came. At 8.02, with mechanic Nino Conti sitting next to him, Enzo took the start of the second race of his new career, the celebrated and perilous Targa Florio.[28]

Speeding past ancient lemon and orange trees and the elegant ladies who lined both sides of Cerda's mud-covered straight, Enzo had a monumental task ahead of him. His only previous race had been a 51km (32-mile) affair. On this day he was setting out to drive a menacing 107km (67-mile) course that he and the rest of the pack had to repeat four times, for a total distance of nearly 435km (270 miles). If the Parma–Poggio di Berceto had been a graceful climb, every turn, straight, bump, slope and descent of the Targa Florio hid vicious traps.

Enzo soon started to experience problems. After only a few miles, his car's gas tank began to shake loose. He nervously kept an eye on it until he had no choice but to stop and, with the help of his mechanic, physically strap the tank back to the body of the car with a piece of rope. Forty precious minutes went by as they worked on it, and by the time Enzo drove for the first time past the finish line, he had lapped in 3 hours, 4 minutes and 50 seconds.[29] Not surprisingly, he was in 16th (and last) place. Determined to make up at least some of the time he had lost, he concluded his next lap in 2 hours, 18 minutes and 34 seconds – setting the 8th-fastest time. But in spite of his effort, halfway through the event he was still in last place.[30]

Despite the worsening weather and the consequent deterioration of the road, on lap three Enzo was even quicker. If it hadn't been for the gas tank problem on lap one, Enzo would have been right behind the best that day. But because of the 40-minute stop, he was now in danger – he had to complete his run within the 10-hour limit or he would be excluded from the final classification.[31] So, on he went, taking risks at every turn of a road that the rain had by then transformed into a river of mud. All in vain: when he finally arrived at the finish line, the place was deserted. Everyone had already returned to Palermo. Enzo found only a *carabiniere* waiting for him. The policeman had a big watch in his hand and dutifully jotted down the time of his arrival, rounding it to the nearest minute.[32] The race time limit had expired and all race officials, including timekeepers, had caught the last train back to the city, leaving the lone uniformed man behind to wait for latecomers, Enzo being the first of them.

Newspapermen, too, had already gone to Palermo to send their stories to newsrooms across Italy. Consequently, in the papers the next day there was no mention of Enzo's performance. All the fanfare was for Indy winner André Boillot, who had won the race.[33] The rest of the coverage was of the crash that had ended Antonio Ascari's race, and the death of a spectator who had inadvertently crossed the finish line just as Boillot's Peugeot was speeding by. The death of the bystander made an impression on Enzo, as it was 'the first time' he had felt 'the presence of death on race tracks'.[34]

Not finding his name on the official race classification, the next day the 21-year-old unknown amateur from Modena went to see organizer Vincenzo Florio to complain. The self-confident and charming 36-year-old gentleman politely listened to Enzo, then scornfully asked why he was complaining: Enzo had arrived shamefully late, had not taken any risk (!) and now he, *Don* Vincenzo Florio, was gratifying him with a ninth place overall and third in class.[35]

Easily won over by Florio's irresistible charm, Enzo was placated. For him the inclusion in the official classification, which also meant minor prize money, was a 'small success',[36] and this was the beginning of a long-lasting friendship with one of the 'pioneers' of Italian motorsports.

Before the year was out, Enzo would see his name 'in lights' for the first time. On Monday 8 December, sports magazine *Paese Sportivo* ran a story on his first two racing feats: 'The Youngest Survivor of the Targa Florio', featuring a photo of the young driver. Enzo was not yet 22, and had proven his talent in a race that was known for being both demanding and dangerous.

The profile of Enzo was brief but flattering. 'He is a young man from Modena who has a glowing future in motor racing ahead of him,' the magazine predicted. 'Born in 1898, tall, very strong, audacious, prompt and confident at the wheel, a perfect and tested driver, Ferrari, haunted by *guigne*' – French for 'bad luck' – 'has successfully performed in both the Targa Florio and the Parma–Poggio di Berceto hillclimbs.'[37] Flattered by this attention from the press, and pleased with himself for what he had been able to achieve in such a short time, Enzo started to look for a more powerful and reliable car than his CMN. His attention was soon captured by a name with an exotic and somewhat aristocratic sound: Isotta Fraschini (IF).

Enzo learned that three of the six 1914 Isotta Fraschini Grand Prix cars produced before the war were still in Italy. The other three were in the United States, where they had been raced, without much success, at Indianapolis. He quickly came to the conclusion that this was the car that could make the difference to his still-young racing career. A 7.0-litre car with 100hp more than his CMN, and with a top speed of over 145km/h (90mph), could propel him to greater recognition and fame.

With virtually no money in his pocket and only his old CMN 15/20 to trade in, Enzo set about purchasing an Isotta Fraschini 100/110 IM Corsa in Cliente configuration ('Cliente' designated it as a 'customer car' rather than a current 'works' race car, campaigned by the manufacturer). It was indeed a powerful car – but it was also seven years old, having being produced in 1913. Enzo knew that car manufacturers would soon put out new racing cars and all prewar units would become obsolete. Pooling his resources with friend Guglielmo Carraroli,[38] whose goal was to become his race mechanic, Enzo used his best charm; after some negotiation, based on the assumption that soon this car would no longer find any potential buyers, he persuaded the car manufacturer to essentially swap cars with him.[39]

It was a big personal victory for Enzo. Of course, one should not forget that the relationship between Isotta Fraschini and CMN was very tight, and that Enzo was no stranger to the IF executives with whom he negotiated.

After purchasing the new car without asking for his mother's blessing (something she would throw back in his face time and time again throughout her long life),[40] the next money that came out of Enzo's virtually empty pockets was the 150-lire entry fee for the 30 May Parma–Poggio di Berceto hillclimb, the first race that he chose to enter in the 1920 racing season. Besides a new car, Enzo now had a new race mechanic as well in Carraroli, who owned half of the car.[41]

Giuseppe Campari won the race with a time that was four seconds faster than Count Giulio Masetti's. Enzo was 2 minutes and 21 seconds slower than Campari, but a whole 10 minutes faster than he had been in 1919. It was the third-fastest time of the day, the second in his class.[42] It was also his first podium finish. At the wheel of a more-competitive car, and despite problems with the tyres in the second part of the climb, Enzo had shown that he could easily be among the top drivers.

Oddly enough, in the aftermath of the race, the only one not happy with his performance was Enzo himself. Perhaps sensing that he could have done better than third, he got out of his car and wept.[43] Although very much taken with Campari's first career success, the press diligently took note of Enzo's third-place finish: 'valiant, and unlucky', they wrote of him the day after the race.[44]

Once the emotion wore off, however, Enzo was electrified by his strong showing, and chose next to enter the Circuito del Mugello race, scheduled for 13 June. The entry fee was enormous, but part of the 500 lire was destined for a good cause – a fund for the reconstruction of the Mugello area, which had been destroyed the year before by a violent earthquake. At any rate, the huge prize money balanced the expensive entry fee: 50,000 lire, to be split among the drivers in the top four positions.[45]

This year's race was the second running of an event first held in 1914, albeit in a different format. The race length was nearly 320km (200 miles) over five laps of 64km (40 miles) each. After his showing at Parma, Enzo was among the favourites. According to the press, he was one of five drivers who could aim for the grand prize, the other four being Campari, Meregalli, Brilli-Peri and Osella.[46]

The first driver dashed off at 7.04am; Ascari, at 7.29; Brilli-Peri, at 7.56; Enzo, at 8.02. Of the 30 entrants, 24 took the start. Only five finished the race. The difficult course relentlessly took its toll. Most cars experienced technical failures of one kind or another. Several drivers crashed, including Ascari, who had to be rushed to the hospital along with his race mechanic.[47]

With friend Guglielmo Carraroli again at his side, Enzo drove 'a beautiful and very smooth' race, but he too was unable to finish. At the end of the fourth lap he was in third place, but the burning of a fuse forced him to retire before he could launch his final assault on Masetti and Campari. His first reaction was one of anger and frustration, with tears coming to his eyes.[48] Then, despite the huge missed opportunity, he took it gamely, parked his car on the side of the road and stood there watching the rest of the race, good-naturedly talking to the spectators who had crowded around him.[49] The winner was once again Campari, who was trailing Masetti when the latter violently left the road after a tyre blew up.[50]

The next race was scheduled for the following Sunday, 20 June. Since this too was held in Tuscany, Enzo stayed in the area to better prepare for it. The Coppa della Consuma was one of the oldest racing events in Italy, and one of the shortest, only 16km (10 miles) in total.

By the time Enzo took the start, rain had begun to fall. As had happened on the previous Sunday, Count Masetti was stunningly fast – so fast that he lowered the record time that Vincenzo Lancia had set in 1904. But when the crowd was already hailing him as the winner, another Tuscan nobleman, Marquis Niccolini, did even better, taking four seconds off Masetti's record time. At this point only Campari and Enzo, who were still on the course, could take victory away from Niccolini. But while rain damaged the last miles of Campari's run, on the finish line spectators and race officials waited in vain for Enzo's car to show up. A puncture had forced him to stop in the first part of the climb to replace the damaged tyre. Engine troubles had subsequently forced him to abandon the race completely.[51]

The first races of the 1920 season had taught Enzo two lessons: at the wheel of a decent car he was almost as fast as the best of the lot. But as powerful as the Isotta Fraschini undoubtedly was, it was also unreliable. He had by now convinced himself that he could have a future in motor racing, but he had also learned something that he would never forget: not even the best driver had any chance of victory if he was not at the wheel of the best car.

And it didn't take him long to realize that the best cars available were being produced in Milan by Alfa Romeo.

First Love

Propelled by the success and reputation of Antonio Ascari and Giuseppe Campari, by the summer of 1920 Alfa Romeo was extremely popular with well-to-do amateur drivers. In August Enzo Ferrari, one of the best amateurs on the scene, made an appointment with Alfa Romeo's sales and racing manager, Giorgio Rimini.[1]

Enzo was cordially received at the factory's headquarters in the Portello suburb of Milan. Rimini, seeing Enzo's potential and impressed by his determination, decided to give him a chance and hired him as the third driver of an Alfa Romeo works team alongside the two best professional Italian racing drivers, Antonio Ascari and Giuseppe Campari.[2] Thus, after only five races and a single podium finish, Enzo was offered a chance that only twelve short months before would have seemed impossible.

Talent certainly played a role in this first tangible achievement of his racing career; otherwise, Rimini would have simply sold him a car and not hired him. But the key factors were Enzo's perseverance, a stubborn faith in himself and an insatiable thirst for success – not simply in motor racing, but in life.[3] These were all qualities that would never abandon Enzo, eventually shaping him into the automotive giant he became.

Little by little, Enzo was putting his life together. CMN had been a springboard. Now that he was an official Alfa Romeo racing driver, he left his old job without much regret. By contrast, he held on to the commercial representation of CMN for his native Emilia-Romagna region, which he had obtained some time before.

However, he had more in mind.

In a building at 5 Via Jacopo Barozzi, just outside the medieval city centre of Modena, in that same month of August Enzo opened Carrozzeria Emilia, his first entrepreneurial activity. On the one hand Carrozzeria Emilia was the most obvious of things: a CMN showroom. But on the other – and this was Enzo's grand plan – it was an independent coachbuilder.

For in addition to selling CMN models and repairing and repainting cars of any brand, he planned to build bodies for those customers who, as was standard then, bought chassis, radiator, hood and dashboard from car manufacturers and then counted on one of the many coachbuilders to complete the car.[4] The idea was not revolutionary, of course, since it was precisely what Carrozzeria Italo-Argentina did in Milan with the chassis that Enzo personally took there from the Giovannoni workshop in Turin. But it was a demonstration that Enzo was learning fast and eager to expand his horizons.

Enzo Ferrari was the general manager of Carrozzeria Emilia. To fund it he had sold the Villa Santa Caterina house, what little remained of his father's metal workshop and whatever was left of his inheritance.[5] With 37,500 lire, he held 75 per cent of the total share capital of 50,000 lire. The remaining 12,500 lire had been supplied by Pietro Casalegno, a man Enzo had met the previous year in Turin.

Casalegno's title was 'chief engineer' when Carrozzeria Emilia E. Ferrari and C. was incorporated on Sunday 1 August 1920, in the presence of attorney Camillo Donati. His responsibilities were to design and build the bodies that would suit the chassis that customers would buy from them – those made by CMN – or from other retailers. Enzo kept for himself the commercial, PR and administrative roles. From a legal standpoint, Enzo Ferrari was 'legally responsible without limitation' for Carrozzeria Emilia. The company was registered on Friday 6 August. The agreement would expire on 31 December 1926.[6] After less than two years in the automotive world, Enzo Ferrari thought he knew enough to start his own business. Thanks to his motor-racing activities, especially now that he was racing for Alfa Romeo, he counted on having the contacts to find enough customers.

His mother had been against this bold move. Like many people in those days, she still did not understand the enormous potential of the automobile, and found it senseless to sell most of the family's properties to start Carrozzeria Emilia. But in the end Enzo was all that she had left in life, and she couldn't help but go along with his decision.

Enzo's first engagement with Alfa Romeo was the Targa Florio. The participants were once again welcomed by cold and rain. Underneath a thick layer of mud, sharp stones emerged here and there as deadly hazards for the 16 drivers and their cars. Against one such stone during practice Campari destroyed one of the tyres of his Alfa Romeo Grand Prix car. While he managed to keep his car on the road, the wrecked tyre disappeared into a gorge.[7]

On race day the weather was as bad as it had been in the previous days, but Giuseppe Merosi had had the foresight to place gauze screens and mud flaps on the three Alfa Romeos. The first driver took the starter's flag at 7am. After him, drivers dashed off six minutes apart. Campari started his race at 7.06, Enzo, wearing a scarf his mother had given him as a good luck charm,[8] exactly one hour later.[9]

On his first passage across the finish line Enzo was informed that he was in fifth position, almost eight minutes behind race leader Airoldi, driving an Itala. Enzo led teammate Campari by one second. With water fouling the spark plugs of his engine, Campari had experienced problems throughout the whole lap; his four-cylinder engine was now running on three.[10] It later turned out that Enzo had been mistakenly misinformed by his team, however: although he was more than eight minutes behind the leader of the race, he was, in fact, in second position – not fifth.[11]

With three laps remaining, the weather worsened further, and the road came to resemble a river of moving mud, hiding thick stones. A few miles into the second lap, Campari was forced to retire and Enzo became Alfa Romeo's only hope to save the day. Despite the rain and the mud, he drove a superb second lap, setting the second-fastest time of the day and securing second place, behind Meregalli's Nazzaro, the new leader.[12] By the beginning of the third lap the sun had started to dry some of the mud that covered the entire course. But by now, with some 225km (140 miles) behind them, all drivers were fatigued. Meregalli's third lap was two minutes slower than his second; Enzo's, three minutes slower. When both drivers started their fourth and final lap, Enzo trailed Meregalli by eleven minutes and twenty-six seconds.

Suddenly, halfway through the final lap, Meregalli slowed considerably. The challenging course was taking its toll. Overwhelmed with fatigue, Meregalli was struggling to keep his car on the road.[13] Sensing that the leader was having problems, despite the weariness of a long and demanding race Enzo knew that the moment had arrived to give all that he had left. Racing at 'unheard-of speed',[14] he skilfully narrowed Meregalli's lead. But despite a final lap in which he took seven minutes off Meregalli's performance and recorded the fastest overall lap time of the race, Enzo could only claim second place.[15]

Although it was a terrific result for a 22-year-old at his first event with a new car, the final outcome could have been even better had Enzo been informed at the end of lap one that he was in fact in second position and not in fifth. With that knowledge, his attack on the leader would probably have started sooner, and with much better odds.[16] Feeling that he had just narrowly missed a great opportunity for which he had no direct responsibility, Enzo was so overcome with frustration that he began to weep 'like a child', somewhat immaturely swearing that he 'would never race again'.[17]

Speaking to a reporter at the end of the race, Enzo spoke of 'animals and trees and big rocks scattered on the course' slowing down his final rush to the finish. Somewhat maliciously the same reporter told his readers that Enzo had been damaged more by Campari's reckless race conduct than by whatever objects the young driver had found in front of his car: by not abandoning the race once he realized that his car was not functioning properly, the journalist wrote, Campari only played Meregalli's game, damaging whatever chances his teammate had of catching him.[18]

By evening Enzo's rage had disappeared. Flattered by reporters, complimented by the Alfa Romeo team manager, hailed by spectators and pleased with the 12,000-lire second-place prize, the magnitude of his performance finally settled in, his pledge never to race again all but forgotten.[19]

Enzo returned from Sicily with something more precious than the considerable prize money: the first seeds of a long-lasting friendship with teammate Giuseppe Campari. A generous and talented man who could never quite decide whether he wanted to be a motorsports ace or an operatic tenor, Campari would soon become instrumental in Enzo's growth within the Alfa Romeo ranks. For his part, Enzo reciprocated with unconditional affection and unwavering admiration for the champion.

The Targa Florio was the last significant race of the season. Alfa Romeo nonetheless entered cars for its works drivers in Gallarate's Chilometro Lanciato speed attempt, scheduled for 14 November. Campari competed in the 'racing cars' class, Antonio Ascari and Enzo in the 'production cars' category.[20]

Enzo set the fastest time of his class. His recorded speed was 120km/h (74mph) – faster than Ascari's, who was at the wheel of a more-powerful, brand-new 1921 Type 20/30 Sport model. Though this was an unconventional event, it was Enzo's first class win. The young understudy was learning fast.

Campari won his class, too, but it was Andrea Silvani at the wheel of a V12 Packard who won the race, reaching the notable speed of 157.894km/h (98mph). Enzo was impressed with the winner's car, particularly with its 12-cylinder engine. Having seen officers of the US Army drive Packards during and after the war, he had developed a curiosity about the V12 engine that powered them. Now his curiosity turned into a serious interest, which would soon become an unexpected obsession.[21]

The Targa Florio had been the backdrop of his first encounter with Campari. Gallarate would serve the same purpose for Enzo in becoming more familiar with another giant of motorsports: Antonio Ascari. Their friendship had a bit of a rocky start when, on the way back to Milan that afternoon, in the thick fog that had descended, Enzo accidentally bumped into the rear end of Ascari's car, which had come to an unexpected stop at a railroad crossing. Both men were driving back in the cars they had used in the race. Perhaps antagonized by the fact that Enzo had been quicker that day in the Chilometro Lanciato, Ascari became visibly and loudly irritated with his young and mortified teammate.[22] Fortunately, the accident was soon forgotten, and Ferrari and Ascari went on to develop a sincere friendship.

* * *

On 18 February 1921, Enzo Ferrari turned 23.

In little more than two years he had steered his life in the direction he had dreamed of since he was a boy. With the opening of Carrozzeria Emilia, he had started a business through which he was hoping to replicate the commercial success of his father. And thanks to Giorgio Rimini, he had realized his adolescent dream of becoming a racing driver – a good one, too, as his second-place finish at the Targa Florio proved. Not to mention that, working with superstar teammates of the calibre of Ascari and Campari, he could now learn the secrets of the trade.

For the third time in three years, on 8 May 1921, Enzo was at the start of the Parma–Poggio di Berceto hillclimb. While Campari was at the wheel of the 1914 Grand Prix, Ascari, Sivocci and Enzo were each entrusted with a Type 20/30 ES Sport. For Enzo, on a course that he knew well, with the exact same car as his teammates, this was a huge chance to prove his skill to the Alfa Romeo management. Instead, whereas Ascari and Sivocci dominated their class and Campari finished second overall, Enzo's race ended at Fornovo, about halfway through the climb, where a breakdown forced him to withdraw.[23]

Three weeks passed, and Enzo was once again to compete at the Targa Florio. The bad autumn weather of the past two years had convinced Vincenzo Florio to return to his prewar habit and hold the race in the spring.

With Campari to compete for the overall victory in the 1914 Grand Prix, Enzo and Sivocci would try to secure the grand prize in the 4.5-litre class in their 20/30 ES Sports.[24]

In a race won by Giulio Masetti for Fiat, with Max Seiler's Mercedes coming in second, despite a terrific fourth and final lap Campari finished only third overall. But the truly great result for Alfa Romeo was secured by Sivocci and Enzo, who finished first and second in their class and fourth and fifth overall – the first two drivers in regular production cars after three race cars.

Now almost a veteran of the race, Enzo's performance was a solid one. After a not particularly brilliant first lap, in the next round he handily lowered his previous lap time. Then, on lap three, Enzo set the race's third-fastest time and jumped to fourth place overall. After a puncture forced Sivocci to stop and replace a tyre, Enzo moved up to third place, first in his class. When he passed the Cerda finish line to start the final lap, after more than 320km (200 miles), only six short seconds separated the two Alfa Romeo drivers.

In the last lap, experience and perhaps sheer ability played a role as Sivocci made up the lost time and outpaced Enzo by more than two minutes. Enzo, who still lowered his previous record lap time by another 24 seconds, had nothing to regret. Although Sivocci had prevailed, Enzo had been almost as brilliant and certainly as reliable as his more-expert teammate.

Things were beginning to look good for 23-year-old Enzo. Not only was he greatly valued at Alfa Romeo, but he was also rising fast in the constellation of postwar racing drivers. Last but not least, he was in love.

From the summer of 1921, a young and attractive blonde was almost constantly at his side. He had met Laura Domenica Garello not long after arriving in Turin in the first months after the war. He spotted her one evening while taking a stroll beneath the porticos near the Porta Nuova train station.

She was 'a beautiful girl, blonde, elegant, lively, petite',[25] according to Ferrari's later autobiography. And she had gorgeous eyes.[26] Anxious as he was for some warmth and companionship, he immediately felt a natural attraction for the young woman. Their courtship had initially suffered from the opposition of Laura's parents, and then from Enzo moving to Milan to take the job with CMN,[27] but the love story had endured. By the summer of 1921, however, Laura had taken the bold step of moving into Enzo's small apartment in Modena.[28]

The young unmarried couple living together soon learned to coexist not so much with the subtle prejudices of a small town as with the open opposition of Enzo's mother. By nature overprotective, Adalgisa soon became exceedingly jealous of her son's girlfriend. The jealousy quickly gave way to daily and sometimes violent quarrels between the two women, with Enzo caught in the middle, unable or just reluctant to take sides. He was in that uncompromising phase of his life in which he still thought that love could overcome any obstacle.[29] After all, there were some in Modena who thought of Laura as the most beautiful girl in town.[30]

Perhaps to stay away from Adalgisa as much as possible, Laura began to accompany Enzo wherever he went. In mid-July she escorted him to Mugello, where Alfa Romeo had scheduled a few days of practice ahead of the 24 July race. With his mother at safe distance in Modena, and in the company of his pretty 21-year-old girlfriend, these were happy days for Enzo – perhaps the happiest of his entire life.

With Ascari forced to withdraw in the final lap and Sivocci out of the race as well, at Mugello Campari and Enzo finished first and second overall. The press praised his performance and 'his splendid, steady pace'.[31]

Enzo also received the Targa Masetti trophy, which was traditionally awarded to the driver who prevailed in the category reserved for regular production cars.[32] For Enzo this was a significant personal achievement. For Alfa Romeo, along with the grand prize won by Campari, it was an extra honour that sealed its domination of the race.

The unprofitability of Carrozzeria Emilia, however, was a personal problem that marred an otherwise perfect time for Enzo, who was learning the hard way that the work of coachbuilder could not be improvised. Lacking any specific business experience, he had delegated to minority shareholder Pietro Casalegno the technical aspects of their company. Because of his racing activity and trips that kept him away from Modena for days on end, it was clear that Enzo could not devote the time and attention that he should have to this side of his complex business.

The summer of 1921 was a steamy one. With an eye on September's Brescia race week, in the first days of August Enzo went to Milan to take delivery of a new Alfa Romeo Type 20/30 E S model, which he would drive in the upcoming Coppa delle Alpi event.[33]

This was quite an unusual competition, a 9-day, 5-stage regularity race up and down most of the Italian Alps that started in Turin and ended in Milan – two cities no more than 112km (70 miles) apart via normal roads – after more than 2,300km (1,430 miles). The driver who maintained an average speed of, or closest to, 48km/h (30mph) throughout the whole event would be declared the winner.[34]

Of the 30 drivers who had entered, 24 left the Turin Stadium early on the morning of Sunday 7 August. Enzo, the 14th to see the starter's flag, dashed off at 6.05am

For the following nine days Enzo cruised through the Alps at the wheel of his Alfa Romeo Type 20/30 E S.

Enzo was one of seven drivers who completed the long race at the required 30mph average speed. Penalized by an ambiguous set of rules that calculated the final results on the basis of the individual standings at the end of each of the five stints, plus eventual penalties picked up by drivers along the way, plus a clause benefiting less-powerful cars, Enzo was designated sixth place overall. However, Max Sailer refused to let the judges take a closer look at his Mercedes and was disqualified, so Enzo gained a position, ending up in fifth place.[35]

The media was once again impressed by Enzo's ability, although some maliciously noted that the 'very young driver from Modena sometimes is too impatient' in his racing conduct.[36]

Two weeks later, in the Aosta–Gran San Bernardo hillclimb, Enzo scored another fifth place overall, this time also winning his class. As uneventful as the race was for him on purely sporting terms, on this last Sunday in August Enzo met a man who, 30 years later, would play a large role in his becoming an automotive legend. Among the entrants was a young man from Turin at his maiden race. His name was Battista Farina. Like Enzo, he was trying to make a name for himself as a racing driver. And, just like Enzo, his gigantic role in the automobile world would not be as a racing driver.[37]

On 4 September, Brescia was going to host the first Grand Prix of Italy. Not having a car that qualified for the race, the Alfa Romeo drivers would sit out the event.

Enzo went to Brescia as a spectator, though he and his teammates were scheduled to take part instead in two other events in the Brescia area the week after the grand prix. The first was the Chilometro Lanciato speed attempt, a sort of qualifying round for the Gran Premio Gentlemen's Race, scheduled for the Sunday after the grand prix. The speed attempt was scheduled for Wednesday morning, 7 September, on a 1.6km (1 mile) stretch of unpaved road near the village of Montichiari, on the outskirts of Brescia.

Enzo did well. He came fifth overall and fourth in his class – the best of all the Alfa Romeo drivers.[38]

Sensing the opportunity at hand, Enzo decided to practise extra hard in the few days left before the race, but on Friday morning, driving at full speed on a seemingly deserted road, he narrowly survived his first race accident. A herd of cows unexpectedly emerged from the nearby meadows and crossed the road. Coolly assessing the situation, Enzo quickly downshifted while pressing the brake pedal hard. He was able to drastically reduce his Alfa Romeo's speed, but not enough to keep it on the road. The car plunged into a ditch and flipped onto one side. Enzo and mechanic Fugazza were thrown out of the car. Astonishingly, they both escaped with only minor bruises. The car was a different story, however: parts of it were scattered everywhere, in and around the ditch. Back on his feet and happy to be alive, it was immediately obvious to Enzo that no mechanic would be able to put the car back together for the Sunday race.[39]

All that he had left to do was to protest the dangerous conditions in which he had been allowed to practise, so he rushed to see race organizer Arturo Mercanti. Enzo was so distraught that he could not hold back the profanities. The verbal assault was so violent that he was not only officially thrown out of the race, but also banned for life from any Italian racing event. It took the personal intervention of the president of the Italian Automobile Club to reinstate him.[40]

Despite this, Enzo was confirmed as one of the four official Alfa Romeo drivers for the 1922 season alongside Ascari, Campari and Sivocci. Although he was perhaps the least talented of the four, the press made no distinction, labelling the Alfa Romeo squad the 'formidable quartet'. For his part, after two seasons Enzo was now unpretentiously confident in his qualities as a racing driver.[41]

Laura

If his racing career had taken a turn in the right direction, the same could not be said of Enzo's love life. The arrival of Laura in Modena had not brought the couple the serenity they both desired. The daily struggle with Adalgisa had soon exhausted the young woman, who had at first sought and found refuge in her fiancé's frequent trips. But come autumn, Laura raised the white flag and succumbed to a situation of enormous stress, suffering from an acute form of nervous breakdown.

The first measure taken by the doctor was to send her as far away from Modena and Enzo's mother as possible. Laura left for a period of rest in Santa Margherita Ligure, on the Italian Riviera. Here she began to receive, almost daily, long and thoughtful letters from Enzo. Written in black ink – his signature purple ink was yet to come – they were all recommending the same things: absolute tranquillity. In early December, to reassure her, he went so far as to talk of a future wedding.[1]

Was the wedding that hadn't happened yet the cause of Laura's depression, rather than her troubled relationship with Adalgisa? Or was the promise of a wedding that Enzo was now making only an encouragement to heal, a sort of light at the end of the tunnel?

Despite her severe depression and the stress that it caused him, Enzo was fond of Laura. In his letters to her – neatly written, rich with anecdotes, loving thoughts and words of hope – he was always affectionate.

The same could not be said of Laura, who wrote to him much less frequently, and much shorter letters. In her rare letters she would constantly complain about the time his letters took to reach her on the Riviera. And although the tone of his letters was always one of understanding, in her letters Laura was often negative and at times even aggressive.

Laura's real disease was jealousy. It was suspicion that consumed her, and for distrust there was no medicine or cure. He, of course, *was* cheating on her, but with his automobiles and his total commitment to what he by then saw as his chosen mission in life. Women were not part of the equation; not at this point, anyway.

What Laura did not understand was the complete – *total*, to use a word that Enzo would soon start to employ – devotion he had for sports cars.[2]

At any rate, the couple spent Christmas separately – he in Modena with his mother, she at the Hotel Regina Elena of Santa Margherita Ligure.

In the cold and fog of Modena, Enzo continued to pour all the energy that remained after dealing with his stressful long-distance relationship with Laura into the complex management of Carrozzeria Emilia. Although orders were coming in, the situation was not as good as Enzo might have wished.

*   *   *

The first race of the 1922 season was the 13th running of the Targa Florio, scheduled for 2 April. It was an event with a prodigious international flavour: 48 drivers at the wheel of cars made by 12 manufacturers from 4 different countries – France, Germany, Austria and Italy.[3] Alfa Romeo had at first planned to entrust Enzo with one of the two new Type R L s making their debut that day.[4] But in the end they sent only one R L to Sicily, for Augusto Tarabusi, while Enzo, together with teammates Ascari, Sivocci, Clerici and Lady Maria Antonietta Avanzo, was given the old and reliable 4500cc Type 20/30 E S.[5]

The race was a huge disappointment for the whole team. Enzo was never in the heat of the battle, and finished 16th overall, far from Giulio Masetti's privately entered Mercedes. Ascari, Sivocci and Enzo finished first, second and third in their class, however. At the end of the race they were awarded the Biglia Cup for the best overall team, but the trophy did little to brighten the day. For Alfa Romeo the 1922 Targa Florio was a total debacle.[6]

In mid-April Ferrari participated in the Milan Fair with a booth entirely dedicated to Carrozzeria Emilia. It was the first time that he had attended a public event as an independent coachbuilder. The local Modena press called his product 'a masterpiece'. According to the journalist who wrote the story, 'the discreet and elegant body, the fine finishing of all details, the ingenious application of folding seats [combine] two rare qualities: elegance with practicality'.[7]

Enzo enclosed the newspaper clipping in an envelope along with his most recent letter to Laura on 25 April. Always anxious for the fate of Carrozzeria Emilia, whose commercial success unfortunately did not match the description in the article, Ferrari wanted to see in the praise and enthusiasm of the journalist an encouraging sign. But his letter to Laura once again contained concerns for the young woman's health. Laura would need continued attention on her return from the Riviera, where she'd been since well before Christmas.

Laura returned to Modena in early May. She went to see the doctor and then left for the hills. But the cure would be long. And, to some degree, it would never end.

June brought no better luck to either Alfa Romeo or Enzo.

In mid-July Enzo received the news that racing driver and friend Biagio Nazzaro had died in an accident in the French Grand Prix at Strasbourg. The news was disturbing for a number of reasons. Biagio was one of the regulars at the Bar di Porta Nuova café in Turin, where Enzo had spent many an evening in the first months after the war, and the two had become good friends since.

But more disturbing than the death of a friend and colleague was the thought that Enzo had somehow sensed that Biagio's death was imminent three months before, when, after helping him out from under his flipped car at the Targa Florio, he'd had the distinct perception that while his friend may have cheated death that day, it would come soon – just three months later, as he now knew.[8]

The summer of 1922 was a trying time for both Alfa Romeo and Enzo Ferrari. While the car manufacturer was manifestly unable to close the gap to either Fiat or Mercedes, Enzo remained deeply touched by the death of Biagio Nazzaro.

Adding further tension was Laura's never-fading negative attitude and irritating suspiciousness, recovering on the hills south of Modena and still consumed by jealousy.[9] Making things worse was the precarious situation of Carrozzeria Emilia. Despite the quality of the work, the deep economic crisis that had engulfed Italy was killing small companies like Enzo's one by one. Always a realist, he reached the inevitable conclusion that he would have to give his lawyer friend Camillo Donati a mandate to liquidate the company if necessary.

Still, Enzo remained optimistic – perhaps not about the future of Carrozzeria Emilia, but certainly about his professional life in general. 'We'll get out of this somehow,' he wrote to Laura.[10] And although shaken by the demise of his friend Nazzaro, he decided to compete in the Aosta–Gran San Bernardo hillclimb scheduled for the last Sunday in July. He had sent his entry to the organizers, but had failed to mention the make of car that he intended to use. This seemed bizarre, since for the last two years Enzo Ferrari had raced solely and exclusively at the wheel of Alfa Romeos.[11]

The rumours and conjecture this led to turned out not to be without foundation. While the press speculated on his next moves, back in Modena Enzo was at work tuning a car built by a small Austrian manufacturer named Steyr. In fact, Enzo had wanted to drive the Steyr the previous Sunday, at the Susa–Moncenisio hillclimb, but a valve failure had forced him to postpone his debut with the Austrian manufacturer. At first, due to the severity of the problem, he had feared that he would have to send the car back to Austria. Then, in mid-July, he had received the necessary spare parts from Vienna and had been able to repair it and prep it in time for the race. Thus, on the morning of the race, Ferrari showed up on the starting line of the Aosta–Gran San Bernardo hillclimb at the wheel of the small Austrian race car.

Despite being only 24 years old, Enzo Ferrari was one of the best drivers on the scene. For a small Austrian manufacturer aiming to conquer the Italian market, his surprising signing – albeit for one race – was a great publicity move. On his part, by showing the Alfa Romeo management that other manufacturers were interested in him, Enzo could send the unequivocal message that, for all his devotion and gratitude, he should not be taken for granted.

The race was, however, once again a massive disappointment for Enzo. The car had technical problems throughout the climb – problems so severe that Enzo never had a real chance. 'My race,' he commented the day after, 'did not go so well; spark-plug problems made me lose precious minutes.' He finished eighth overall and second in his class. 'That's fine,' he said somewhat philosophically. 'The important thing is that my health is good.'[12] With Laura's nervous breakdown, the lack of luck in his races and the potential closing of Carrozzeria Emilia, his health was really the only thing that had not deserted him.

As soon as he returned to Modena, Ferrari met with his lawyer friend Donati to discuss the fate of Carrozzeria Emilia. Donati was a sharp attorney who knew his business, and by the end of August he told Enzo that he had a worthy solution to end the suffering and the financial bloodshed of Carrozzeria Emilia.[13] The company would indeed be liquidated, one of countless small businesses that were not going to survive the economic crisis of postwar Italy. Donati had managed to convince Renzo Orlandi, the owner of another coachbuilding shop in Modena, to purchase part of the equipment and materials from Enzo's company.

In late summer, like the previous year, Alfa Romeo again sat out the Grand Prix of Italy, held for the first time on the Autodromo Nazionale in Monza, a dozen miles or so from Milan. Enzo naturally went to Monza for the race weekend, and on race day, Sunday 10 September, was standing just a few feet away from the eight cars lined up on the starting grid.[14] The race was won by Pietro Bordino driving a Fiat, after almost six hours and 800km (500 miles).[15]

The year was almost over. In terms of racing results, 1922 had not been nearly as positive as 1921, but Enzo had once again proven himself to be a picture-perfect teammate for the most experienced members of the Alfa Romeo squad, and the press had never missed an opportunity to praise his racing skills.

Only the closing of Carrozzeria Emilia cast a shadow on an otherwise positive business year. Painful as it was, the drastic action had been necessary to halt the drift of money and avoid greater consequences. It had taken Adalgisa's intervention to help Enzo out. To pay off his son's debts Mrs Ferrari had sold personal property, including some of her furniture.

The humiliation of this colossal failure and the embarrassment he felt about his mother's life-saving aid served as a fundamental lesson in the life of Enzo Ferrari. If it is true that negative experiences often teach more than positive ones, in the indisputable disaster of his first entrepreneurial experiment – which he never forgot, though he always avoided mentioning it – is the key to the future success of the man and the company he would one day create.

That winter Enzo spent as much time as possible at the Alfa Romeo headquarters in Milan alongside engineers, technicians and mechanics – always curious and eager to lend a hand and learn. He felt the first symptoms of what he identified as an 'almost compulsive desire to do something for the automobile, this creature that I loved passionately'.[16]

Thus he became better acquainted with the company's management, especially with Giorgio Rimini and chief designer Giuseppe Merosi. Enzo tried to learn as much as possible from these experienced men to avoid a future repetition of the Carrozzeria Emilia fiasco.

Sensing his total availability, Rimini began to use him for commissions of increasing importance.[17] Whatever the task, Enzo was always available to do things and go places. Enzo was delighted by Rimini's 'intelligence and charm'.[18] And while he admired Merosi for his technical intuition, he closely observed Rimini in action, wanting to learn all he could about managing every aspect of the multifaceted life of a racing team.[19]

His frequent visits and extended stays in Milan also meant he could get to know his famous teammates better. Now one of them, Enzo was admitted to the exclusive club of the Alfa Romeo drivers. Campari began to invite him to dinners and parties, introducing him to the good life.[20]

But as time went by, Enzo also became more familiar with Antonio Ascari. A much more self-disciplined man when it came to his social life, Ascari was enormously generous. When in his company Enzo would hardly ever be allowed to pay for his own meals; although he may have felt some natural embarrassment over this, he must have greatly appreciated it after the forced and costly closing of Carrozzeria Emilia.[21] Soon Enzo realized that, despite Campari's easy charm, he was more attracted to Ascari, whom he called *Il Maestro*, as did everyone else in the business.[22] Ascari owned a small workshop in Milan, had recently become the Alfa Romeo sales agent for the Lombardy region and used his motorsport success to boost sales. He was also deeply involved in the technical decisions of the Alfa

Romeo management, playing a key role in the development of the Type 20/30 E S Sport, the first postwar Alfa Romeo model.

His friendship with Antonio Ascari would be one of the pillars on which Enzo would fashion not only his own racing career, but also much of what he would become as a man of sports – and as a human being.[23] Fascinated by Ascari's expanded role within Alfa Romeo, Enzo was unintentionally but fatefully distancing himself from his own future as a racing driver.[24]

Victory!

Friday 13 April 1923, wearing a brand-new crimson sweater that Alfa Romeo had provided its works drivers,[1] Enzo was the fastest of the team's drivers in practice for the Targa Florio, the season's opening event. His understandable enthusiasm for this great result vanished after an unexpected and apparently anomalous remark by Antonio Ascari: the Targa Florio, the *Maestro* said, was a long and difficult race, where speed itself was not necessarily the key to victory.[2]

Electrified by his great personal performance, Enzo took Ascari's words to be motivated by envy. And because the remark annoyed him tremendously, he did not take note of what was in reality precious advice. On Sunday Enzo began the race with great fervour. Taking risks at every turn, on the first lap he set the race's fifth-fastest time. Then, as Ascari had hinted at, early in the second lap Enzo was betrayed by his speed.

In an effort to keep up the pace he had set from the start, Enzo entered one of the first bends on the circuit too fast. He was fortunately still in the lower part of the route and his Alfa Romeo ended its run in a dry ditch instead of in a gorge, as would have been the case only a handful of miles later. Enzo came out of the accident without a scratch, but the car was wrecked beyond imagination – impossible to put back on the road.

He walked back to the pits cursing himself more than bad luck. Only now did he understand the true meaning of Ascari's words. Envy had nothing to do with it. Ascari's advice had been disinterested and loyal. The arrogance was all Enzo's, who, after three whole seasons, was still able to make rookie mistakes. He was furious with himself; with his irresponsible behaviour he had thrown to the wind the chance to do well in a race in which he had always acquitted himself with honour.[3]

Back in the pits, he regained his composure. He put down the racing goggles and offered to help the team as an extra mechanic. Generosity was a quality he had in abundance. Every time his teammates came in, Enzo personally helped with refuelling their cars.[4] And when Ascari, less than 185m (200 yards) from the finish line, suddenly stopped with his engine mute, Enzo instinctively ran towards his teammate to help jump-start the car.

Ferrari, Ascari, his race mechanic and a second mechanic who had followed Enzo out of the pits were busy around the Alfa Romeo for five minutes before they could restart it. Despite the valuable time lost, Ascari was still leading the race. He quickly jumped back behind the steering wheel and hurriedly drove the 200 yards that separated him from the finish line.

Unfortunately for Ascari, in the heat of the moment the two mechanics and Ferrari himself had jumped on the car as well. The race marshals immediately warned him that if he did not go back and drive the last 200 yards again, with only his race mechanic on board, he would be disqualified. Ascari turned the car around and drove back to where it had stopped. Not finding his own mechanic, he helped on board one of the onlookers. Then, for the second time, he crossed the finish line. But in the time it took the Maestro to complete the operation, Ugo Sivocci had crossed the finish line too. And all that Ascari was left with was the satisfaction of a 'moral victory'.[5]

Sivocci had finally taken his first career win. Enzo immediately ran to embrace him.[6] The two shared a profound friendship, and despite the fact that his own first win had been postponed once again, Ferrari was sincerely happy for his friend. While he admired Campari and worshipped Ascari, his friendship with Sivocci was genuine, born out of the hunger and deprivation of the first months after the war. Enzo had never forgotten the help he'd received from Ugo in early 1919, and although he had in effect returned the courtesy in 1921, when he had opened the door of Alfa Romeo to his friend, he still cherished Sivocci's altruistic generosity.

Back from Sicily, Enzo and Laura went to Turin, where on Saturday 28 April they were married. The notice of the upcoming wedding had been announced on 18 March in the city of the bride and on 25 March in that of the groom.[7]

The two had been living together – theoretically, at least – for almost two years, and although the situation had not been idyllic for at least the past year now, Enzo had in all probability wanted to believe that the wedding would fix many things, beginning with Laura's health. He presumably hoped that, their status legalized, Laura would lower the tone of her jealousy. After becoming Mrs Enzo Ferrari, she would see the situation from a different, more reasonable angle, including the complex relationship with her mother-in-law.

This was a huge miscalculation on Enzo's part.

Against his relationship with Laura from the very beginning, the *other* Mrs Ferrari, *mamma* Adalgisa, disdainfully chose to stay in Modena. Understandably upset by his mother's condemnation, Enzo made the best of a bad lot. He owed Laura a ceremony, and to a ceremony he agreed. But that the situation bothered him is confirmed by the fact that he did not invite a single one of his many friends in the motor-racing world[8] – not even his close friend Sivocci, who was like a brother to him.

The morning of the last Saturday in April 1923, Enzo and Laura first showed up at the *Casa Comunale* town hall in Turin for a civil ceremony. At 8.35am they were in front of the clerk of the wedding licence office. Then the time came for the religious ceremony. In a small church near Fiat's Lingotto factory, no more than 20 people assembled, only relatives and friends of Laura's. Enzo was by himself. The Mass was celebrated by Father Clerici. As a joint wedding gift, the Garello family gave the bride a gold-plated purse.[9]

The newlywed couple did not have time for a honeymoon. The motor-racing season was almost in full swing, and Enzo was by now completely absorbed in his multifaceted role within Alfa Romeo.

The following weekend, Enzo and Laura went together to Cremona, where on Sunday he officially 'opened' the track by cruising around a lap at the wheel of his Alfa Romeo.

Saturday 2 June, five weeks after his wedding, Ferrari returned to Turin. This time the reason was professional. Guglielmo Carraroli, the friend with whom he had pooled resources in 1920 to buy the Isotta Fraschini, had arranged a secret meeting with Luigi Bazzi, one of Fiat's most gifted technicians.[10] Enzo was on a mission on behalf of Alfa Romeo.

The development of the new Grand Prix Romeo (or, as it was commonly called, P1) was not proceeding as Rimini had hoped. The commercial director of Alfa Romeo had by now realized that Merosi and Santoni, a talented designer with a degree in chemistry, needed professional help. Merosi himself was not an engineer and, at 51, belonged to a generation that preceded the automobile. What Alfa Romeo needed was someone who had been immersed in the automotive environment from birth, somebody who would go further, a person who coupled mechanical intuition with technical courage.

So, one evening in late May, Rimini had assigned to Enzo this most delicate mission.[11] Rimini had been clear that night: 'Where there are competent people,' he told Enzo, 'get them any way you can – as long as you don't break any law.'[12]

Ferrari met Luigi Bazzi in elegant Corso Vinzaglio in Turin.[13] The envoy wasted no time in preliminaries. Alfa Romeo, he said, was looking for senior technicians to fill the gap to Fiat. And since the Fiat was the car to beat, the most logical step was to look for those talents within Fiat itself. This most brief of introductions was followed by a simple, direct question: was Bazzi interested in moving to Milan and joining Alfa Romeo?[14]

Bazzi was flattered by the offer, which he had not expected. He asked for time to think about it, which Ferrari correctly interpreted as a good sign. Despite the urgency that Rimini had stressed – the P1's race debut was scheduled for the European Grand Prix at Monza in early September – he wisely did not press Bazzi for an answer on the spot. He told him to take his time and think about it. He would be in touch soon.

For the fifth time in five years, on 10 June Ferrari was at the start of the Circuito del Mugello race. At the wheel of one of the five works Alfa Romeo R L s from the Targa Florio in 1923, he completed just one lap before withdrawing due to problems with the carburettor. The following Saturday Enzo went to Ravenna where, the next day, he was scheduled to compete in the first running of the Circuito del Savio.

This race was going to be contested on Sunday 17 June over a total distance of almost 273km (170 miles), six laps of a fast dirt track that ran between the salt marshes and pine forests close to the Adriatic Sea. The start and finish were placed in front of the Santa Apollinare in Classe *basilica*, a few miles from Ravenna: the word *Traguardo* (meaning 'finish line') appeared in black letters on a white cloth, strung between two telegraph poles on opposite sides of the road.[15]

The automobile event was preceded in the morning by a motorcycle race that saw the participation, on an Indian bike, of a skinny little man who would soon become the ace of aces of the next generation of motor-racing drivers – Tazio Nuvolari. The main event of the day, the automobile race, started at 4.30pm.

Despite the far from memorable opposition, Enzo's was a perfect race. His driving style aroused the crowd, which, at the end of the race, invaded the road to carry him in triumph. He had waited four long years to taste his first win, and now the flavour could not have been sweeter. There was nothing, Enzo recognized that day, that could compare to one's first victory.[16] Although the Circuito del Savio did not number among the most important races of the season, for a 25-year-old racing driver with clear ambitions, taking home the winner's cup – along with a cheque for 4,000 lire[17] – was nevertheless a great achievement.

The Circuito del Savio was run on country roads not far from Lugo di Romagna, the small town in which, in 1888, famous Italian air force ace Francesco Baracca had been born. Baracca was one of the few authentic Italian heroes of the Great War. His 34 kills had sparked the imagination of his countrymen, the vast majority of whom, Enzo included, had seen what we now know as World War I as a 4th war of independence that ideally completed the *Risorgimento* (the 19th-century movement that led to Italy's unification). And when Baracca was shot down in the waning months of the war, the whole of Italy had cried and honoured him.

At the end of the race, among those who came to congratulate Enzo on his win was Count Enrico Baracca, the father of Francesco.[18]

Count Baracca was an elegant country gentleman who in postwar Italy had become something of a celebrity, thanks to the heroic deeds and tragic death of his son. That afternoon, the count was the guest of honour at the event.[19] After the screams and excitement of the crowd finally subsided, Ferrari and the count had a pleasant conversation. Despite the miseries of the war and the sudden deaths in quick succession of his father and brother, Enzo remained at heart a sentimentalist, and the compliments and attention paid to him by the father of a great hero must have pleased him a great deal.

The joy over his first win soon faded in light of the serious concern that Ferrari found in Milan, however. The victory at Savio was perfect for an advertising page in a sports newspaper,[20] but Alfa Romeo was aiming at something else. The defeat suffered at Mugello had not been digested, and had only aggravated the ongoing state of tension arising from Alfa Romeo's manifest inferiority to Fiat. To add further stress, there was no news from Bazzi.

Ferrari was anxious. Although the decision now rested solely in the hands of Bazzi, Enzo had personally exposed himself in the mission to steal him away from Fiat. The success or failure of the assignment would inevitably have an impact on him and on his prestige in the eyes of Rimini.

On 2 July, exactly one month after the meeting in Turin, the Grand Prix of the Automobile Club of France was staged in Tours. At the end of the race Bazzi walked over to the Alfa Romeo pits and told Ferrari that he accepted his offer.[21]

Luigi Bazzi wasted no time, immediately going to work to complete the job started by Merosi. Meanwhile, Ferrari took part once again in the Coppa delle Alpi 3,000km (1,864 miles) race from Turin to Monza, scheduled for 5 to 15 August. At the wheel of an Alfa Romeo RL Sport, Enzo tied for first place in both the overall and the 3000cc class category, at an average speed of 49km/h (30 mph). Under the race rules, designed to favour the less-powerful cars, he was moved down to fourth place in the final classification, however.[22]

In the morning of 16 August, the P1 was ready for shakedown at Monza. The three drivers who would race it on this very track on 9 September in the European Grand Prix – Ascari, Campari and Sivocci – took turns at the wheel of the only P1 thus far finished, and not yet painted in the signature Alfa Romeo red.[23]

The only 'great' excluded was Enzo Ferrari, who, despite his recent win and the reputation he enjoyed with the press, was always the fourth element of a formation of four. For him it was no surprise, but, rather, a somewhat natural conclusion that he had pragmatically expected, knowing all too well that he did not possess the same level of talent as his three teammates. But since his mind was by now not necessarily set only on sitting behind the steering wheel of a racing car, he took Alfa's decision with poise.

Monday 27 August was the first day of open-to-all official tests for the European Grand Prix. Alfa Romeo brought to Monza three P1s: number 6 for Ascari, number 12 for Campari and number 17 for Sivocci. The latter had chosen not to paint on the hood of his car the green four-leaf clover that had brought him luck at the Targa Florio. With his racing suit on top of his shirt and tie, Ferrari hung around in the pits with his teammates.

Despite Bazzi's work and the encouraging indications of the mid-August test, the P1 did not look like the car that could end Fiat's supremacy. Rimini was already privately thinking that the European Grand Prix would be the P1's first and last race. Work should immediately start on a completely new car.

Saturday 8 September was the last day of testing before the grand prix. For Alfa Romeo it was also the last chance to find some practical solution to overcome the confirmed supremacy of Fiat.

At 9.35am Ugo Sivocci came out of the pits and launched his Alfa Romeo down the straight. The number 17 P1 ran full speed until it skidded as the driver was about to take the left turn at the end of the *sottopassaggio* (underpass) straight. Sivocci instinctively attempted to correct the trajectory of the car, but with no success. The Alfa Romeo went off the track and crashed at high speed against one of the ancient trees of the Villa Reale park.[24]

Immediately notified of the incident, Enzo was among the first to arrive on the scene. The smash against the tree had left the P1 horribly crumpled. The lifeless body of his dear friend Ugo was lying on the grass. Then he saw Guatta, the mechanic, who had only broken his shoulder in the accident but was crying despairingly next to the dead driver. Though he realized that there was nothing he could do for his friend, Enzo kept his cool, putting Ugo in the car of an Englishman who had been watching practice in that spot and had witnessed the whole incident. Then he rode with both of them to the hospital in downtown Monza.

On learning of Sivocci's death, Nicola Romeo immediately decided to withdraw the team from the race.[25] Ferrari and the other Alfa Romeo drivers spent the weekend at the Umberto I hospital in Monza at Sivocci's wake.

For Enzo the death of Sivocci was a big blow. Ugo was much more than a colleague – he was the closest of friends. In some ways it was like reliving the death of his own father and brother. To him, over the past four years, Sivocci had in fact been like an older brother. Feeling part of the family, Enzo did everything that he could that weekend to console Ugo's grieving wife Marcella and son Riccardo.

Because of Sivocci's fatal accident at Monza, no one had a clear idea of the true potential of the P1. But Fiat's stunning success – Carlo Salamano had dominated the race – left no doubt about the amount of work in store for the Alfa Romeo engineers. The day after the funeral, Rimini called a meeting with his closest aides to analyse the situation and decide how to proceed.[26] Invited to the meeting at Portello were Merosi, Bazzi, Ascari, Campari and Enzo, whose role as personal adviser to the commercial director had by now put him centre stage when it came to developing Alfa Romeo corporate strategies.

The meeting produced two decisions. One was that, for Alfa Romeo, the 1923 season was finished after the Monza incident and, for this reason, they should immediately set the programme for the following season. The second was that the P1 would be retired even before its debut, and all should concentrate on the development of a new car, which they began from that moment on to refer to as P2.[27]

Bazzi had been a great addition to the team from a technical point of view, said Rimini. But it was not enough. If they wanted to put an end to the supremacy of Fiat, it was necessary to travel once again to Turin in search of yet more talent – gifted engineers who would come to Milan to work with Bazzi.

With selfless honesty, Bazzi suggested the name of a person who, in his opinion, was the best technician at Fiat – not a man who would come from Turin to work *for* him or *with* him, but a man to whom he himself would report. His name, he said, was Vittorio Jano. He was a man of great quality, Bazzi explained, and at Fiat was not appreciated for what he was worth. Leveraging his latent dissatisfaction, Bazzi suggested, may persuade him to leave Fiat.[28] Rimini turned to Enzo and, for the second time in three months, asked him to go secretly to Turin.

Aside from the satisfaction of having been entrusted with another mission of the utmost importance, there was an even more intimate gratification in his return to Turin, 'not to look for a job', as he had done in October 1918, 'but to offer [one]'.[29] Five years earlier, Fiat had brusquely denied him a job, and now he was trying to deprive the automotive giant of one of its best men, having already convinced another one to follow him only a few months before. Beyond the service that he was unquestionably doing for Alfa Romeo, if on a personal level this was not revenge, it was certainly something that resembled it.

The first contact with Jano was a little bumpy, however.

The meeting with Bazzi in the first days of June had been agreed on by both parties. This time Ferrari and Rimini decided to base their first approach on the element of surprise. Ferrari went to Turin and climbed the three flights of stairs of a building on Via San Massimo. He knocked at the door of an apartment and was met by Jano's wife, Rosina. The woman looked at him, puzzled, and asked why he wanted to see her husband. Ferrari, who had never loved preliminaries, ostentatiously said that he had come to offer her husband a job as a designer at Alfa Romeo.[30] The lady grunted. Her reply left Enzo speechless: 'Mr Jano,' she said, 'is too much of a Piedmont man to move from Turin.'[31] Fortunately for Enzo, Jano himself appeared at the door and invited him in.

Although the two did not know each other, they conversed at length.[32] Jano said that he was flattered, but did not conceal some scepticism. If Alfa Romeo really wanted him so much, why had they sent a young driver who had no defined role within the company? Why hadn't an Alfa Romeo executive come to see him?[33]

Although his pride was wounded, Ferrari behaved as a perfectly trained diplomat. Jano was not saying No. His was not a flat refusal; in fact, he seemed interested. What seemed to confuse Jano was the rank of the envoy, a simple 'mediator' without 'the authority to conclude'.[34] So Enzo patiently explained that Alfa Romeo did not want to directly expose itself for fear of rejection, which could be embarrassing for both. But if he indeed was interested, Enzo said, he would report the outcome of their interview to Giorgio Rimini, who was the commercial director of Alfa Romeo. And, he assured him, the next time he would be visited by a senior Alfa Romeo executive.[35]

In the interview that followed, Enzo left the stage to Alfa Romeo vice president Fucito. It was him, a man with no knowledge of nor interest in motorsport, who actually formulated the proposal. At Fiat, Jano, who was the head of a team of designers, was making 1,800 lire a month. Fucito offered him 3,500 lire plus housing. The technician first had to convince his wife to move to Milan, but then accepted. And when he went to formally sign the contract in the presence of Nicola Romeo at the Alfa Romeo tycoon's villa, Ferrari was there.[36]

It was early October 1923.

The moment Jano signed, Romeo said to his new chief designer: 'Listen, I do not expect you to make me the car that beats all – but I would like one to make a good impression, to create a pedigree for this company.'[37] To Enzo these words sounded suspicious, confirming his personal conviction that the reasons for which Romeo wanted a winning car had little to do with motorsport.

Indeed, Enzo had reason to suspect that Romeo's 'desire for a great triumph' was aimed at having 'the door opened to a high form of recognition' on the part of the government.[38] For a man of sports such as Enzo, for whom motor-racing victory was a goal in life – a goal for which some of his friends had died – these words could even sound offensive.

Enzo spent the rest of that autumn going back and forth as usual between Modena and Milan, Laura, as was now customary for her in the winter season, and despite the wedding, convalescing in Santa Margherita Ligure on the warm Italian Riviera.

The Champ

Even though his finances were not particularly flush in light of the fiasco of his first entrepreneurial attempt – of which, away from Modena, little was known – at the dawn of 1924 Enzo Ferrari was still an accomplished man. He was about to turn 26, and could rightly be proud of what he had achieved in the short span of 5 years. He was one of Italy's most prominent sportsmen, one of the top racing drivers at Alfa Corse (Alfa Romeo's official racing team),[1] the right-hand man of Alfa Romeo's commercial director, and the owner of a car dealership in his hometown.

His private life was much less serene.

Despite the wedding, Laura, now his wife, was still at odds with Enzo's mother and physically distant from Enzo for most of the year. Her health was not improving, and Enzo by now believed that Laura's problem was Laura herself. Simply put, he felt she did not want to heal; because of the severe state of depression in which she constantly lived, she was content to make his life difficult. The medical treatments, which in the early part of 1923 had seemed to work, did nothing for her now. What was worse, Laura showed no real interest in building a life together with Enzo.[2]

With Laura on the Riviera, that winter Enzo spent a long time in Geneva, working with the Swiss importer of Alfa Romeo, Albert Schmidt.[3] He had of course been sent to Switzerland by Rimini. It was one of those missions of increasing importance that the commercial director of Alfa Romeo was now systematically assigning him. Switzerland was becoming a major automobile market, and Alfa Romeo did not want to miss out on the commercial opportunity. Rimini had therefore decided to support the Swiss importer by sending the versatile Ferrari.

On 14 March, the opening day of the Geneva Motor Show, wearing his elegant double-breasted suit that he customarily wore on these formal occasions, Enzo was in the Alfa Romeo booth. Two days later, he was at the start of the 'flying kilometre challenge', one of the show's fringe events.

Driving the same Alfa Romeo R L SS he had used in his last race of 1923, Enzo lived up to expectations, setting the fastest time in the 'Sport' class, the fourth overall.[4] Although the event was of little interest to Enzo, the Geneva Flying Kilometre is the only race of his entire career that Enzo Ferrari entered outside Italy. The Italian press applauded his performance, calling it 'remarkable', and again praised the driver as 'brave'.[5]

The following Sunday, once again at the wheel of the reliable RL SS, Ferrari took part in the Coppa Verona, which had a final speed test on the Torricelle climb. In a race that was in fact little more than a training session ahead of the races that really mattered, Enzo finished second overall.[6]

On 9 April Enzo made the acquaintance of Prime Minister Benito Mussolini. Personally driving his new three-seater Alfa Romeo convertible from Milan to Rome, Mussolini stopped in Modena to confer with Senator Vicini. Eager to capitalize on the presence of the head of the government, Vicini invited him to lunch in his home district of Sassuolo, a town about 25km (15 miles) from Modena. Enzo, a works Alfa Romeo racing driver of national fame, was commanded to lead the column of cars accompanying Mussolini's.[7]

At the wheel of his racing Alfa Romeo RL SS, Enzo led the way with the confident manner of the professional driver. Rain had fallen the night before and the road was still damp. Worried that he'd lose contact with Enzo's car, Mussolini began to press on the accelerator, going so fast around some corners as to skid perilously. Once the column reached Sassuolo, some in Mussolini's party hurried over to Enzo, begging him to slow down his pace after lunch.

Enzo did not attend the official luncheon, eating in the next room with Mussolini's personal driver, Ercole Boratto. In the afternoon he sat again behind the wheel of his Alfa Romeo escorting *Il Duce* along the twisty Apennines roads, this time, as promised, at a slower pace. When they reached the Abetone pass, the company broke up. Mussolini continued on to Rome, while Enzo returned to Modena. They would never meet again.

The Targa Florio was next. Alfa Romeo decided to field four cars in the first major event of the 1924 season, but chose both Giulio Masetti and Frenchman Louis Wagner over Enzo. The other two drivers were Ascari and Campari.[8] Enzo was kept on board only as a stand-in driver.[9]

Something was obviously changing in the team's hierarchy. The death of Sivocci should have promoted Enzo to the rank of third driver, but now Alfa Romeo had shown that they preferred Masetti over him, and had even hired a new driver. As he'd done the previous autumn, when he had been excluded from the drivers' lineup at the would-be debut of the P1 in Monza, Enzo once again made the best of the situation. He still enjoyed driving very much, but his real interest was shifting more and more concretely from the role of driver to that of manager. And if on the one hand Rimini was beginning to exclude Enzo with an irritating regularity from races of major prestige, on the other hand, he was appreciating Ferrari more and more in his other role – that of personal consultant to the commercial director, which Enzo had been brilliantly and relentlessly developing for himself.

Although Laura neither appreciated nor accepted Enzo's decision to go to Sicily on the first anniversary of their wedding, despite her complaints Enzo left with the rest of the Alfa Romeo team.[10] Once in Sicily, the tensions quickly disappeared. Smiling and generous as always, Ferrari put himself at the complete disposal of the team and his teammates. During some phases of the race he even acted as the team signalman, showing the information board to teammates speeding by the front of the pits.[11] It was during this stay in Sicily that his bond with Ascari turned into a real friendship.[12]

The race was won by Christian Werner in a Mercedes. Masetti took second place, Campari fourth. Wagner finished a distant ninth. Enzo, who had had a successful personal history at the Targa Florio, would probably have done better than all of them.

On the way back from Sicily, Enzo sought and obtained permission to display the Alfa Romeos that had raced the Targa Florio in downtown Modena. In the large rectangular square overlooking the military academy, a crowd of fans and onlookers gathered around the cars, still covered with dust and mud. Apart from the commercial aspect of the operation, the stop in Modena was a clear message to his wife, who could see firsthand the interest and enthusiasm stirred by what he did in life. But it was also a message, just as personal and direct, to his fellow Modena citizens.

Elegant, tanned and smiling among dozens of people, all curious and at the same time fascinated by the racing cars with the green cloverleaf emblem,[13] Enzo towered above them all. He obviously remembered the suspicion that only a handful of years earlier had greeted his decision to sell all that he owned to pursue a career in the automotive sector. This day he could prove to everyone that his had not been an irresponsible investment: despite the embarrassing Carrozzeria Emilia disaster, in the first-class world of Alfa Romeo, today, his was a respected name.

The Coppa Verona had been the 24th race of Enzo's career. Despite his exclusion from the Targa Florio, as a racing driver he was reaching peak performance. For this reason no one was surprised when, on 25 May, Ferrari took his second career win on that same Circuito del Savio where he had won the year before.

Before the start, Enzo found time to introduce himself to one of the most interesting emerging talents in motorsport – Tazio Nuvolari. He had seen Tazio race the year before, but they had not spoken then.

Today they spoke, albeit very briefly.[14] This year Nuvolari was going to participate in the automobile race at the wheel of a Chiribiri Monza. The second run of the Circuito del Savio started after a delay of 30 minutes, at 3pm. Like the year before, each pair of cars started 30 seconds apart. Enzo was at the wheel of his red V6 Alfa Romeo R L, with the number 26 hand-painted on the hood.[15] Next to the radiator, like on all works Alfa Romeos this season, a white triangle with a green cloverleaf was also painted, as a tribute to Ugo Sivocci. Eugenio Siena, Campari's cousin, sat next to Enzo as his race mechanic for the first time. Next to them dashed off the number 27 Isotta Fraschini driven by Alfieri Maserati,[16] the towering figure among the brothers who, 10 years earlier, had opened the workshop that bore their name in Bologna.

Well aware of being at the wheel of a car more powerful than those driven by most other competitors, Enzo simply controlled the situation in the first laps. On lap four he decided it was time to show the Alfa's speed and started to gain ground on Emilio Materassi, setting the race's fastest lap.[17] Informed of Ferrari's sweeping march, Materassi increased his own pace, pushing his car beyond its limits until it broke down. From that point, the race was virtually over.

Dozens of people rushed to congratulate Ferrari on his new victory. Enzo was pleasantly surprised to see Countess Paolina Baracca Biancoli, the mother of the Great War ace. Not long after his first victory at Savio and his conversation with the hero's father in June the year before, Enzo had been invited to the country estate of Count Baracca. Unable to attend the race in person this year, the count had asked his wife to represent him.[18] In the year since Enzo's maiden victory at Savio, both had grown fond of the youthful and well-mannered driver from Modena, who had frequently found the time to go and visit them. And it was from the hands of the countess that Enzo received the winner's cup.

Laura had not accompanied Enzo to Ravenna, but the following week she went with him to Rovigo, where he took first place in the first Circuito del Polesine. For the second time in seven days, Enzo Ferrari beat Tazio Nuvolari, who once again came in second.[19] Enzo's race, said the press, had been 'brilliant and smooth'.[20]

The next day, Monday 2 June, at Portello, the first P2 was finally ready. Campari was granted the honour of the first run, a low-speed cruise inside the factory. Half an hour later it was Ascari's turn to sit behind the wheel for a round of the courtyard. Enzo was, of course, in the group watching with Rimini, Bazzi and Merosi.

Two days later, the new Alfa Romeo two-seater was trucked to the Monza track for the first real test. On this occasion, Enzo also did some laps at the wheel.[21] Time was short: the P2's official international debut was just 60 days away. The car was here, but the Alfa Romeo management team needed to make sure it was ready to take on Fiat and Mercedes.

The P2 seemed to perform well. The team felt they now needed a more-severe test in a race environment. It was Thursday evening; after a quick glance at the calendar the P2 was entered, without fanfare, in the Circuito di Cremona scheduled for that Sunday.

Alfa Romeo took a single P2 to Cremona. Painted in red and with Sivocci's cloverleaf on the hood, it was assigned to Antonio Ascari. Beside him sat Bazzi himself, who wanted to make sure everything was working as smoothly as possible. On Sunday, Ascari won the race hands down.

Ferrari was naturally in Cremona with the rest of the team that day. On the occasions that counted, whether he was racing or not, he was always there. Although not part of the grand prix project as far as the driver lineup went, his was one of the voices most listened to by the executives at Alfa Romeo. Not to mention the fact that, by having personally helped to bring both Bazzi and Jano to Milan, his contribution to the project was anything but marginal.

In early July Enzo received a welcome and unexpected surprise: the call to drive the P2 at the season-opening race, the highly anticipated and prestigious European Grand Prix that would be run in Lyon at the beginning of August. Masetti's decision not to participate had made this summons to the most important European race of the season possible. Initially part of the quartet of drivers entered by Alfa Romeo, Masetti had subsequently and somewhat mysteriously declined Alfa Romeo's call,[22] and so the team was now offering Masetti's car to Enzo. The other three drivers, as at the Targa Florio, were Ascari, Campari and Wagner.

Just when Enzo was beginning to digest a painful exclusion – Alfa Romeo's decision not to count him as one of its grand prix programme drivers – this big opportunity came knocking on his door. The Alfa Romeo management knew what they were doing. Although Enzo had lately been more useful to Rimini off the track, his racing talent was familiar to all. In the first part of the season, moreover, Enzo had been the best of all the Alfa Romeo drivers, and so this was the most logical of choices. His two consecutive wins at Savio and Polesine also indicated that Enzo was in great form that summer.

Ironically, the person least convinced by the call was Enzo Ferrari.[23]

Lyon

Giorgio Rimini's decision to entrust Enzo Ferrari with the fourth P2 in the upcoming Grand Prix of Europe was brilliant. A few days after the official communication, Enzo won the Coppa Acerbo hands down against those same Mercedes that had crushed Alfa Romeo at the Targa Florio three months earlier. In a race seen by Alfa engineers as a last P2 test before the race in Lyon, Enzo won at the wheel of his modest 3.6-litre RL Targa Florio 1924.[1] Antonio Ascari had sat out of the race, and the only P2 available had been driven by Giuseppe Campari.

For the first – and only – time in his career, Enzo raced with the number '1' painted on his car. At 7am on a hot Sunday in mid-July, with Eugenio Siena again at his side, Enzo was the first to dash off past the starter's yellow flag.[2] Divided into classes according to engine capacity, the other 17 cars left the starting line after him at intervals of 3 minutes.

The Coppa Acerbo track was a challenging one: 27km in total (about 16.75 miles), divided into three lengths of almost equal distance to form a triangle, with the apex facing north.

Some coincidences contributed to Enzo's day of glory. First was the imperfect condition of the Mercedes that arrived on the Adriatic coast: Count Domenico Antonelli's could not even take the start and Giulio Masetti's was forced to retire before half distance. And then, of course, the still approximate tuning of Campari's P2 was a gigantic help. After completing the first lap in a stunning time, Campari mysteriously disappeared from sight.[3] According to the strategy designed by Rimini before the race, Enzo was supposed to play the part of the 'hare', then give way to Campari and his P2, working to protect his lead. But however much Enzo looked behind him on the circuit's two long straights, he could not spot his teammate,[4] who had gone out with a cracked gearbox. He had hidden his P2 in a side street to puzzle his opponents, who were left wondering where he was.[5] No longer worried about having to give way to Campari, Ferrari eventually pressed on the accelerator. A couple of laps and he began to savour the great feat: with Masetti's and his teammates' withdrawal, the only Mercedes driver left in the race was the least-experienced Bonmartini.

The duel went on for three laps amid the roars and applause of the spectators lining the route under the summer sun. Ferrari maintained his 'safe and smooth' pace.[6] Bonmartini persisted, despite a stop to change a tyre. Then on lap seven he was forced to stop for fuel. He lost a few precious minutes – enough for Enzo to continue 'inexorably' to the finish line.[7]

Ferrari had won again. It was his third victory in the last three races. Although helped by the withdrawal of both Campari and Masetti, his race conduct while Bonmartini's Mercedes surged was impeccable.

At the finish line Ferrari and Bonmartini embraced with warmth and posed for photographs. Enzo received from the hands of Giacomo Acerbo (undersecretary of state and patron of the race, named in memory of his brother, Tito) the huge bowl in which were set 'drops of lapis lazuli and malachite', the upper edge framed by a horizontal flight of four swallows in silver to symbolize speed.[8] With the trophy he also took home a cheque for 5,000 lire and a gold medal offered as a prize by the king of Italy.[9]

For Ferrari it was a memorable day. The victory at Coppa Acerbo, the fourth of his career and third consecutive in the season, was worth all the others put together. Maybe even more. He had got the better of the Mercedes and had proved himself as fast and as consistent as his Alfa teammates. This was no small feat, and it was reflected in enthusiastic race reportage throughout the country. Not surprisingly, in an article that reflected the rhetoric of the time, *Gazzetta dello Sport* headlined their piece: 'Italian Victory at Circuito dell'Aterno'.[10]

Enzo left Pescara that evening with 'unforgettable memories' of a day that he would long relive in all its colours: 'the beach of Pescara, the pine forest of Francavilla, the warm hospitality of Abruzzi, the generous applause'.[11]

There was no time to rest or celebrate, however. On Monday Enzo was in Modena and, at 11am on Wednesday, he left for Lyon, accompanied by his friend Ferruccio Testi.

Ferrari was the youngest and the least experienced of the team, but his three straight wins had made him the centre of attention. The status of Ascari as lead driver and the role of Campari as his equal were not questioned, naturally. But after Pescara there were many who saw Enzo as the true third force in the field – so much so that one writer stated: 'We believe that if Ferrari will have a good day and will resist feeling overwhelmed in the company of so many illustrious champions, he may do really well.'[12]

In the middle of the night on Friday 18 July Enzo Ferrari and his three teammates walked the short distance to the track. Practice started at 4.30am, half an hour earlier than scheduled. There were four hours allotted for testing. Then, at 8.30, the first day of practice would end and the circuit would reopen to public traffic. Because Ferrari's P2 had not yet arrived from Italy, Ascari, Campari and Wagner practised in their own race cars. As a substitute Ferrari sat behind the wheel of the spare car, on which had been painted the number 19, which he would use in the race.

When his turn came, Enzo started the engine of the red P2 that he had been assigned for the day, taking turns with a teammate, with Luigi Bazzi in the seat next to him. As a tactical move, in Pescara the previous Sunday, Alfa Romeo had been silent on the gearbox problems experienced by Campari's P2, but Bazzi did not want to leave anything to chance. He wanted direct evidence of how his new creation was functioning. At stake was motor-racing hegemony in Europe.

At the end of the first practice session, Giovanni Canestrini wired his newspaper in Milan: 'All drivers just got acquainted with the track today. Nobody wanted to show their cards.' Even so, there had been some remarkable times.[13] The fastest of the Alfa Romeo drivers was Campari, followed by Ascari. Enzo had used the first day to understand the potential of the most powerful car he had ever driven, and to learn the circuit.

That evening the atmosphere in the spacious villa of Mademoiselle Lane on the road that led from Brignais to Vourles was relaxed. The early indications from the track were positive. The Alfa Romeo drivers and engineers could look forward with optimism to the race, which would be held in two weeks. There remained only one day of practice, Tuesday 22 July, but to overcome the limited time on the race track Alfa Romeo and Fiat executives had agreed to split a long straight of open road not too far from the villa where, in turn, both manufacturers' racing cars could test privately. Only Enzo seemed – oddly enough – uncomfortable among such cheerful company.

No one had noticed, but, despite appearances, over the last few days Enzo Ferrari had been experiencing a wrenching dilemma. He had long since marked on his calendar the trip to Lyon, but he had expected to be in France as the team's all-purpose man, not as an official driver. Until recently he would have killed, so to speak, to be given the chance to defend the colours of Alfa Romeo, and Italy, in a big international event. But now something had changed.

He himself wasn't sure of exactly what had happened. Perhaps it was the death of Sivocci that had begun the first doubts – doubts that in all likelihood had by now been confirmed as certainties. Although he had learned a long time ago that death was always a possibility on race tracks, its presence had always seemed distant – until it had knocked on Ugo's door.

Ugo Sivocci had been killed at the wheel of the P1, a car Enzo had been spared driving. There was the sense that perhaps this had been providential. Now there was the P2, and he was one of the drivers designated to take her on the track. He knew he did not possess Sivocci's talent – not to mention the talent of Ascari and Campari. And he had realized long ago that his love for cars – which led him to respect them in a race rather than abusing them, as his teammates did – would never allow him to take the final step, the one that separated great drivers from champions. These doubts had been on his mind for a long time.[14] But it was the ferocious power of the P2 that made him confront the evidence.

Ferrari had tried to rationalize the situation, but the more he rationalized, the more the situation had appeared irrational. The P2 had outrageous power. Most of the development was still to be done. There were dozens of details that could fail, dozens of things that could go wrong. Today he had only tested the car, but next Tuesday he would have to come out in the open. The second day of practice would be a sort of dress rehearsal for the European Grand Prix[15] and there was no way to hide.

If on the one hand the situation that had occurred at Alfa Romeo in the spring – when he was forced to yield to both Masetti and Wagner – had irritated him, on the other it had in fact relieved him of a burden. Being certain that he would not have to drive the P2, he had given the best performances of his career. But then the weight of the decision had begun to settle on him and the effect had been devastating.

The moment of truth had finally come.

In what for him was a courageous acceptance of the truth, he went to Rimini and put an end to his career as a professional racing driver.

* * *

The next day he was on a train carrying him back to Italy: first to Milan, then on to Modena. He had not told Rimini that he was retiring altogether; he'd just asked to return home earlier than planned.[16] His car was not ready and, at any rate, before leaving for Lyon it had already been planned that he would go back to Italy to take delivery of the car at Portello and then drive it up to France. Enzo would miss a day of practice on Tuesday 22 July, but he still had time to come back for the race on Sunday 3 August. The press was not told much. Canestrini had heard Enzo's confession as he got out of his P2, but as an Alfa Romeo intimate, decided he did not have to write all he knew. Instead, he simply wrote: 'Ferrari is back in Modena after the first trial and is still in Italy.'[17]

While the power of the P2 was what triggered the crisis, there was more – much more. With a calm mind Enzo probably would have been able to focus on the new car. As a racing driver he knew his business. In the past five years he had constantly driven cars that were more and more powerful. It was his job. But he had to be able to concentrate only on what he had to do at the wheel. He couldn't afford to waste precious energy constantly quarrelling with his wife, shouting all the time that if she wanted a husband with a less dangerous profession and who came home on time every night, she should have married a bus driver, not a racing driver.[18] Before leaving for Lyon he had even reassured Laura in writing, something unique in their intense private correspondence, stating that everything would go well.[19]

Before he'd left for Pescara, Laura had ordered him not to go to Lyon.[20] She knew that the invitation to the Grand Prix of Europe could advance her husband's career to the next level, distancing him even further from Modena – and from her. To reiterate her opposition to Enzo's participation in the grand prix, she had sent him a telegram in France ordering him to return home.[21]

But by the summer of 1924 Enzo Ferrari had only his racing career left. The couple's relationship had exploded shortly after the start of their – for the times – scandalous living together. Theirs had become a tiring relationship in which Enzo at least made the effort to understand her anxieties, while Laura did little or nothing to understand her man. After more than five years of life together, one could use a single hand to count the *months* in which they had enjoyed the intensity and happiness of a real, functioning relationship.

His wife's interference irritated him and made him explode in scenes that were just as violent and futile.[22] But Laura, in her own way, wasn't necessarily wrong. And on certain issues he knew that Laura had a point. The constant travelling to racing events and to the Alfa Romeo factory at Portello kept him away from his dealership in Modena for too much time. The dealership required much more attention and presence than he could provide. Although the race prizes he won were an important economic encouragement for the dealership, as was the advertising guaranteed by his profession as a racing driver, Laura had become insistent that her husband devote more time to his Modena business.

And then there was the memory of the Carrozzeria Emilia failure. One thing Enzo Ferrari knew for sure: he would never, ever repeat the disastrous experience that had led to the sinking of his first entrepreneurial effort. Not only did he owe it to Laura, who had since become his wife, and to himself, but he also owed it to his mother. Although she had never publicly supported him, Enzo loved his mother more than he would ever confess. He never forgot that a few years before, she had sold some of her furniture to pay the debts he'd incurred during his unsuccessful management of Carrozzeria Emilia. That entrepreneurial disaster and the subsequent humiliation of having to accept maternal help had had two specific causes, in addition to the crisis experienced by the country, which certainly had not helped: his total lack of expertise, and the many driving commitments that took him far from Modena and the Carrozzeria. Thanks to his increasing role at Alfa Romeo over the past two years, he knew that he now had the necessary experience. The important thing was not to make the same mistake again. He had to run his business, as much as possible, directly. The conclusion was simple: he would have to give up, or at least limit as much as possible, his motor-racing career. The European Grand Prix was a breaking point. If he raced it, he would become a member of Alfa Romeo's official lineup in the international arena. With the P2, Alfa Romeo would set out to conquer the first Makes World Championship, which was then being planned and would be staged in 1925. If he became part of this high-level sports project, he would clearly have very little time to devote to his entrepreneurial activity.

Enzo needed time to think about what he wanted to do with his life. Races were an important component of his existence, but no longer the only one. Working with Rimini, having stolen first Bazzi and then Jano from Fiat, contributing to the development of the P2, were all things that possessed an undeniable appeal for Enzo. The role of technical and commercial adviser to Rimini would allow him to remain in an environment that he loved, but would at the same time give him the opportunity to devote more energy to his entrepreneurial activity as representative of Alfa Romeo for Emilia and Romagna.

In this state of mind, crowded with too many ideas often conflicting with each other, Enzo was not in a position to take on a race as demanding as the second European Grand Prix, at the wheel of a car like the P2.[23] Whether he knew it or not, he was on the verge of collapse.[24]

*   *   *

The tensions, considerations and doubts – the haunting memories, fears and concerns, along with his huge responsibilities – were by now an intolerable burden. The new disappointment of his P2's continued unavailability after the unexpected promotion of a few weeks earlier was probably the final straw. He would not race in Lyon, but the emotional struggle continued to preoccupy him. He vacillated in his thinking about retiring from racing. He knew the issue needed to be decided once and for all. He couldn't stand another two and a half months in this state.

Therefore, not knowing what life had in store, but knowing exactly what he was renouncing, he made a difficult but courageous decision. He telegraphed Giorgio Rimini and informed him that he would not return to Lyon. He would stay in Modena. 'I do not feel like coming,' he wired, postponing his explanations until Rimini's return from France.[25]

Enzo left Modena to rest for a few days in the Apennines, south of the city.[26] He went to Sestola to relax and think things through, which must have been difficult with Laura nearby, seeing that she held such a huge share of responsibility for what had happened.

It was in Sestola that Enzo learned from newspapers of the 'superlative' victory achieved by Campari in Lyon.[27] Campari's triumph in the Grand Prix of Europe at the end of a race dominated by teammate Ascari had consecrated the Alfa Romeo P2 as the fiercest racing car in Europe. Fiat's hegemony had come to an end. Enzo had contributed to this result immensely, thanks to the role he had played in convincing Bazzi and then Jano to leave Turin. But in the moment of triumph he was far away, alone with himself and his regrets.

Later, back from their glorious day in Lyon, Ascari and Campari went to visit Enzo in Sestola. The affection and respect they felt for him was authentic. They had been surprised by his abrupt exit and failure to return, and they now wanted to check in person the health of a mate with whom, over the previous four years, they had shared experiences and prepared for their international feat. With a frankness worthy of the sincere friendship that united them, Ascari said, 'You made a mistake by not coming to Lyon.' Ferrari was equally honest: 'I couldn't come; I didn't feel like I could make it,' he said,[28] confirming at the same time that his was not a temporary withdrawal, but a definitive one.

To replace him as the fourth driver of the works team, which in mid-October would enter the Italian Grand Prix at Monza, Alfa Romeo called in veteran Ferdinando Minoia, one of the most respected pros on the scene.[29] Such a prestigious choice for his replacement must have given Enzo further distress. Alfa Romeo had completed a striking team to whom it would entrust the best car in Europe – a team of which he was a legitimate member, and that he had voluntarily quit, throwing to the wind the sacrifices of the previous five years and the dreams of a lifetime.[30]

* * *

His appointment as Knight of the Crown following the victory achieved in mid-July at Coppa Acerbo must have boosted his morale a little. Before the race, Giacomo Acerbo had obtained from the king the right to bestow the knighthood on the winner of a race dedicated to the memory of his late brother. And so it was. Within a few weeks, the appointment had been accepted and the honour bequeathed. At 26, in a time when it was still rare for sportsmen to be honoured for their deeds, Enzo Ferrari became one of the youngest Knights of the Kingdom of Italy.

On the evening of 29 August a dozen Modenese friends and admirers organized a dinner at Hotel San Carlo in downtown Modena to celebrate the knighting. It was an evening of fun and joy, highlighted by an irreverent menu, with the names of dishes making fun of his teammates.[31]

It is unclear how many of those who organized the dinner knew what Ferrari was planning for his future. It is possible that, while they celebrated the victories of Enzo's best year yet, Enzo himself had a sense of a death in his heart, knowing that those wins were the last of a career that only a few weeks earlier had looked as though it was about to ignite.

In early September Enzo was at any rate operational again in the Alfa Romeo dealership located in Modena's Piazza del Carmine. From now on he would pour all his energies into it without any racing distraction. It had been a difficult decision, but a necessary one. Now he had to learn to live with it.

While being treated for what was, in effect, a nervous breakdown, on Sunday 19 October Enzo felt the desire – and had the strength – to show his face again in the world of motorsport, which he loved so deeply, even as only a spectator. The weekend of the Italian Grand Prix, he showed up in the Alfa Romeo pits at Monza,[32] from where he watched the P2's terrific race.

His friendship with the Earl and Countess Baracca continued and they never missed a chance to invite him to their homes in Lugo di Romagna and San Polito.[33] Ferrari, who regarded the earl as not just another Alfa Romeo customer, but as the father of one of the few true Italian heroes of the Great War, reciprocated their affection. A few months earlier the countess had handed him the winner's trophy of the second Circuit of Savio. In the fall of 1924 Lady Baracca had something even more precious to give him.[34]

Like many airmen in the Great War, as both a sign of distinction and a good luck charm, Francesco Baracca had painted a personal emblem on his combat biplane – a prancing black horse.[35] As a gesture to an esteemed young man whose reputation was growing – apart from insiders, nobody else was aware of why Enzo hadn't raced at Lyon or his subsequent personal crisis – and in all likelihood as another way to perpetuate the memory of her fallen son, Countess Paolina said with emotion: 'Ferrari, if you put my son's prancing horse on your car, it will bring you luck.'[36]

To formalize the gift, Baracca's parents gave Enzo a black-and-white photograph of their son posing in the official uniform of the Italian Royal Air Force and standing in front of his biplane, the prancing horse quite visible on the side of the aircraft.[37] By hand, on the photograph, the earl and the countess had penned:

> *To Mister Cav. Enzo Ferrari ~ [From] the parents of*
> *Francesco Baracca,*
> *Paola and Enrico Baracca.*[38]

Enzo accepted the gift, greatly moved by the kindness of their totally unexpected gesture. Little did he know that he would find a real use for it just eight years later.[39]

Meanwhile, on the wave of enthusiasm generated by the first comforting performance of the P2, Jano had been immediately entrusted with the design of a medium-powered touring car that guaranteed the brilliant performance customers had come to expect from an Alfa Romeo. The result was a dynamic, fast, easy-to-handle car, with an engine that, especially in the Sport and Super Sport versions, fully implemented the best factors of the P2. The new car was introduced at the Milan Auto Show in April 1925, with the name 6C 1500. It soon became a huge success, both from a commercial and a racing point of view. For once Enzo Ferrari, who would sell this car in his Modena dealership, would benefit from the quality of a car for its commercial value.

In that same month of April 1925, Enzo Ferrari once again changed the location of his business, moving the Alfa Romeo dealership and workshop from Piazza del Carmine to 5 Via Emilia Est – from just inside to just outside Porta Bologna. The name of the company was now Cav. (short for 'Cavaliere') Enzo Ferrari General Agent Emilia-Romagna.[40]

Exile

Following a proposal made by the Royal Automobile Club of Italy in February 1925, the first automobile World Championship was established. Alfa Romeo, now that it had a car that towered over national and continental competition, could not have asked for anything better to consecrate its name on the international scene.

The World Championship would be played in four rounds: three in Europe and one in the United States, included primarily to give a 'global' dimension to the series. So, in addition to the grands prix of the automobile clubs of France, Italy and Europe, to be raced on the Belgian track of Spa, the Indianapolis 500 was added to the championship – even though it was clear from the outset that drivers and cars from America would only participate in the Indiana classic, while the Europeans would never cross the Atlantic.

Manufacturers would take points in only three of the four races – another sign that Indianapolis was in reality a stand-alone event in what was in every way a European championship. As a tribute to the nation that had devised the series, participation in the Italian Grand Prix was mandatory. Those who did not participate in it would not qualify for the final prize – the title of world champion. Each race would be held over a minimum distance of 800km (about 498 miles).

The assignment of points was rather complex and based on a concept diametrically opposed to what would be devised in modern racing. At the end of the year the winner would be the manufacturer – not the driver! – which accumulated the *fewest* points. The winner of each race was awarded one point. Two points were awarded to the second, three to the third. A fourth place meant four points. Those who placed after fourth place or failed to end a race would earn five points. Not taking part in a race meant six points.

With a reliable and powerful car and experienced drivers, Alfa Romeo showed up at the start of that first World Championship as the manufacturer to beat. Three of the drivers were selected to chase the world title: acclaimed champions Antonio

Ascari and Giuseppe Campari, and Count Gastone Brilli-Peri, who was chosen by the Alfa Romeo management to fill the third driver's spot, which only a few months before had been within the reach of Enzo Ferrari.

While it had allowed Enzo to shed some light on his working future, his turning-point withdrawal from Lyon had not brought any real benefit to his private life. Quarrels, struggles, conflicts and misunderstandings with Laura – constantly living apart from him in search of the healing in which perhaps neither one of them believed any more – continued uninterrupted. Laura kept moving from one place of convalescence to the next, going from the seaside to the mountains according to the season. Her stays in Modena were brief and increasingly rare. When she was not recuperating in one of the by-now customary resort towns, she was back in Turin with her mother and sister.

In mid-April Enzo's patience finally reached its limit. He came to realize that the enormous personal sacrifice he'd made the previous summer – when he'd thrown away his racing career, in large part for Laura's benefit – had been pointless. Laura was, as usual, away, and with no apparent intention of returning to Modena. She was once again staying in Turin with her mother. Enzo took pen and paper and wrote without hesitation, almost ruthlessly, pointing to his wife's behaviour and the causes of her conduct, which he knew very well. Harsh words in a bitter outburst, crude, yet sincere. The long and vicious letter ended in a peremptory manner so as not to give her any excuse or way out. Enzo gave Laura a 24-hour ultimatum to return to him. They were husband and wife, and the law of the land allowed him to speak in this fashion.[1]

No one knows whether Laura complied with the ultimatum and returned to Modena within the 24 hours. What we do know is that a month and a half later, calm seemed to have returned to the couple.

*   *   *

Alfa Romeo did not take part in the first round of the newborn World Championship, the Indianapolis 500, run on 30 May. The only European manufacturer at Indianapolis, although it was not there in an official manner, was Fiat, with a car independently driven by Pietro Bordino. American manufacturers got a head start in the championship standings. By not having participated, Alfa Romeo was automatically awarded six points, as prescribed by the new international regulations.

A month after Indianapolis, participants in the first World Championship found themselves at Spa, in the Belgian corner of the Ardennes forest, for the

European Grand Prix, which was in fact the championship's real debut race. None of them had raced in Indianapolis, just like no one among those who had competed in America a month earlier was now in Belgium. Twelve cars were entered. Of them, only seven took the start: four blue Delages representing France and the three red Alfa Romeos in the hands of Ascari, Campari and Brilli-Peri. Enzo Ferrari had stayed back in Modena.

It was a complete triumph for Alfa Romeo, with Ascari and Campari taking first and second places. In the pits Rimini rejoiced. Only a few years ago he had almost single-handedly sustained the entire sports programme of Alfa Romeo, when the Milan-based manufacturer could count on his enthusiasm and little else. Now, thanks also to the tangible contribution of his friend Enzo Ferrari, who had hunted down men who had proved of invaluable help, his racing department had shown it could dominate the racing world.

With the single point received, Alfa Romeo took the lead in the World Championship standings, alongside Indy winner Peter DePaolo (racing for Duesenberg), who was scheduled to attended only the last of the two remaining races of the season. And it was against this background that Alfa Romeo proceeded to the next race in Montlhéry.

As in Belgium, in Montlhéry Alfa Romeo entrusted its three P2s to Ascari, Campari and Brilli-Peri. But this time there was animosity between its drivers. The championship would reward a manufacturer and not a driver. For this reason, Campari, who had witnessed in the last two races two wins by teammate Ascari, was convinced that this time it was up to him to lead the P2 to victory – such was the conviction inside the Alfa Romeo team of the superiority of the car designed by Jano. Ascari, of course, had a different opinion.

The situation could be resolved only by a resolute stance from Rimini or Jano. This never came. Had he been present in France, perhaps with his *savoir faire* Ferrari would have been able to tip the scales towards one of the two drivers. Or he would have at least convinced Rimini and Jano of the necessity of making a choice, however painful. But Ferrari had once again stayed behind in Modena.

As the starter lowered the flag, from the second row of the grid Ascari decisively took the race lead. After approximately one-quarter of the race, the Maestro stopped for fuel. He was leading with a good advantage over his pursuers, starting with teammate Campari, who was now second. Rimini and Jano advised him to control the situation without taking unnecessary risks. 'I hope that there will be no more discussions,' was Ascari's laconic reply. 'Rest assured,' he was told.[2]

But Ascari was an audacious racing driver who could not just sit back and relax. The rivalry with his teammate Campari was real. Ascari also knew that, despite their friendship and mutual admiration, Campari would never recognize him as the captain of the team – he had openly said so only days before – and would not easily give in. So, to avoid any surprise, back on the track Ascari started to drive at the same pace he had used to cancel out his opponents in the early laps.

At this point it started to rain.

Nine kilometres into the 24th lap, high speed made Ascari's car suddenly skid. The wheels touched the grass and the P2 hit the fence on the side of the track. The P2 violently struck the fence and flipped over at a speed of 180km/h (111mph).

The public was informed that car number 3 had been in an accident. Silence fell on the circuit. Then, after a few moments, car number 3, with Campari at the wheel, passed in front of the grandstand on the start/finish straight. The announcer immediately corrected the report, announcing that it was car number 8 that had suffered an accident. Car number 8 was Ascari's. The driver had been thrown from the car and was injured.

Antonio Ascari remained for half an hour on the turf on the outside of the track, next to the overturned P2, without any assistance. Only one Italian spectator managed to get close to Ascari, who was unconscious. When the ambulance finally arrived, the doctor gave him first aid. But there was little to do. Ascari was put into the ambulance and died less than a kilometre from the site of the accident.

The announcer told the crowd lined along the entire track that Antonio Ascari was dead. Responding to a collective impulse, on the stands thirty thousand people rose. Men took off their hats as a sign of respect. Ladies clutched their handkerchiefs.[3]

The race was not suspended. The other cars kept running, including Campari's, which had inherited the lead from Ascari. Campari quit the race about halfway through the total distance, however, when he stopped for a second refuelling. Informed of what had happened to his teammate, he immediately took his racing goggles off, put down his helmet and got out of the car. Brilli-Peri had done just that nine laps earlier.

The news of Ascari's death was a real punch in the gut for Enzo. Not quite two years after the death of Sivocci, here was another tragedy, with all the gloomy consequences it involved. If Enzo needed further rationalization for his escape from Lyon, fate had just served him another.

What was more, in some frightening way, Ferrari felt he had somehow foreseen the death of Ascari – exactly as he had with Biagio Nazzaro's. When he had bid Ascari farewell just before he'd left for Montlhéry, Enzo had instinctively felt as if it was not a goodbye, but an adieu – 'the adieu to a great friend'.[4]

For the second time in two years Ferrari had lost a friend as well as a colleague.

Always fascinated by the personality as well as by the talent of Ascari, Enzo had long looked to him as his personal role model. Most of what Enzo had done over the past four years had been a sort of emulation of what Ascari himself had accomplished.

And then, in the sophisticated world of motor racing, Ascari had remained a simple, sincere, open and generous man, so easy to love. In the complexity of the motorsport community, Ascari possessed the rare gift of frankness; he had no secrets and no prejudices. Their friendship had been real. As real as Enzo's pain was now.

If Enzo Ferrari had lost a friend and a precise point of reference, for Giorgio Rimini the death of Ascari, aside from the human tragedy, posed a significant problem from a sporting point of view. Paradoxically, the best choice to replace the fallen champion was Ferrari, even though he had not raced in a year; after all, it was exactly what had happened the year before, when Enzo had been summoned for the European Grand Prix to replace Masetti. But Enzo's withdrawal at Lyon and what followed had naturally sent a clear message to Rimini and the Alfa Romeo management, so if they ever thought of this solution, they never formulated any proposal.

Nothing prevented Rimini from asking Ferrari for advice regarding Ascari's replacement, however – advice that produced the name of Tazio Nuvolari, the Alfa Romeo agent for the province of Mantua. Tazio was best known for his victories on motorcycles, but Enzo respected him, having raced against him in a couple of events the year before. The idea appealed to Rimini, who intuitively trusted Ferrari. He dismissed it only after Nuvolari crashed during a test session in Monza.[5]

Ultimately, Ascari was replaced with the most improbable of choices, an American driver of Italian ancestry unknown to the European public – Peter DePaolo, who in May had won the Indianapolis 500 for Duesenberg.[6]

With DePaolo at Alfa Romeo, Duesenberg crossed the Atlantic with no real hope of defeating Alfa Romeo on its home track. The American manufacturer started the race with a deficit of one point. An Alfa Romeo success would give the world title to the Italian manufacturer. However, a Duesenberg win and a second-place finish for Alfa Romeo would create a sort of 'playoff' event contested by these two manufacturers alone – a repetition of the race on the shortened distance of 200km (124 miles).

Which was not necessary.

On Sunday 6 September Alfa Romeo dominated the Italian Grand Prix from start to finish. The Autodromo Nazionale was packed to capacity, and the heir to the throne of Italy, Umberto, and his wife, Princess Jolanda, sat in the grandstands.

Ferrari was naturally at Monza, too. For the whole weekend he was at the Alfa Romeo pits, exactly as in the old days, his racing suit worn over his dress clothes. Now that both Sivocci and Ascari were gone, Ferrari was the only member of the Old Guard left. And even if he wasn't racing, he knew that his presence would comfort Campari, still shaken by the death of Ascari, and not in perfect physical condition because of the after-effects of a minor crash suffered in practice.

Campari, the early favourite, pulled ahead at the start. Then the race unexpectedly shifted in the direction of a hero no one expected – Gastone Brilli-Peri, whose odds bookmakers had given at 20 to 1 before the start.[7] Brilli-Peri took the lead and maintained it until the end of the 5-hour and 14-minute marathon. Campari finished second, Bartolomeo Costantini of Bugatti, third, while Tommy Milton of Duesenberg came in fourth.

Alfa Romeo was world champion.

The whole country rallied around Alfa Romeo, which had in the brief passing of just one year – ironically, since Enzo Ferrari's escape from Lyon – become the symbol of work and success the Italian way, taking the place once held by Fiat in the hearts of Italians.

For Ferrari and his dealerships, the success of Alfa Romeo on the track proved to be a great stimulus to the sale of new cars and the fine-tuning of those that some of his customers used in less-prominent races. Business was good at Alfa Romeo's Cav. Enzo Ferrari, exclusive dealer for Emilia-Romagna. Twenty-seven-year-old Ferrari ran the dealership from his dual headquarters at 5 Via Emilia Est in Modena and 6 Via Montegrappa in Bologna. In little more than a year since retiring from racing, Enzo had managed to ward off the ghosts of the past and bring about a decisive turning point in his business activities, all the while managing to remain in the orbit of Alfa Romeo's commercial department and racing team.

But suddenly something cracked in the beautiful apparatus of World Champion Alfa Romeo. On 21 October 1925, six weeks after the triumph of Monza, the board of directors decided to retire from racing, preferring to invest the budget until then reserved for competition into the design and production of road cars. Bringing Alfa Romeos to the track would from now on be up to private drivers, to whom the manufacturer would sell cars through its dealerships, including Enzo Ferrari's.

Shortly afterwards, Nicola Romeo was forced to step aside. The subsequent purge removed Giorgio Rimini, the architect of Alfa Corse and Enzo Ferrari's mentor at Portello. Then it was the turn of Merosi. And soon, of the old management team, only Jano and Bazzi were left.[8]

Enzo Ferrari spent 1926 in Modena, mostly away from racing. Now that Alfa

Romeo was no longer officially racing, his trips to Milan became less frequent, and were almost exclusively oriented to commercial issues. He began instead to go more and more often to Bologna, where he had in the meantime been named director of Alfa Romeo's official branch for Emilia, Romagna and Marche.

The epicentre of his life was once again in Modena, where he never missed an opportunity to participate in, or just pop up at, sporting events, including many that were distant from his beloved world of car races. He was seen at football matches, cycling events and, in the winter months, even at ski events on the slopes of the Apennines. In Modena no one had forgotten his brilliant past as a racing driver, and so, from time to time, he was invited to attend motor-racing and even motorcycle events as a guest starter.

For Enzo, 1926, even more than 1925, when he'd still had an almost constant relationship with Alfa Corse, was a period of intense activity in which he learned a great deal about a variety of things. While he was seen as an organizer, manager and promoter, he was always involved in the Modena sports scene.[9]

If in 1925 he had managed to leave the Lyon episode behind him and continue to do most of the things he had always done, the following year Enzo was forced almost to reinvent himself to maintain an intimate managerial position within Alfa Romeo.

Those years after Lyon represented a time when, in addition to learning about people and situations, Ferrari also learned how to cultivate the acquaintance of those who truly counted and could be useful to his business. The lesson of the failure of Carrozzeria Emilia would never be forgotten.

But first and foremost, Ferrari was a motor-racing man, and when he had finally metabolized the death of Antonio Ascari, the desire to remain close to motor racing started to gain strength. He first had to come to terms with himself, and then with his wife. But by the spring of 1927 he had made the decision to return to racing cars, even if not in the same form and in the same categories where he had made a name for himself between 1919 and 1924.

The successful first running of the Mille Miglia, held on 27 March 1927, played a significant role in convincing Enzo to return to racing. What would become the signature Italian race was not only a new competition – it was a new way of racing. The Mille Miglia was not open to cars like the P2 Grand Prix, but rather to the type of sports passenger cars closest to the production cars that could be found and purchased at any dealership, including Enzo's, or in any of the several dealer points scattered throughout the Emilia-Romagna and Marche regions, coordinated from the Alfa Romeo branch office that Enzo ran from the building at 6 Via Montegrappa in Bologna.[10]

A detail of no small importance was the fact that Ferrari had demonstrated in the recent past that he could master like few others in Italy the type of cars – less powerful and more docile than the P2 Grand Prix – that were admitted to those competitions the Mille Miglia seemed to have given new life to, or perhaps even helped to create.

Back to the Future

The new chapter in Enzo Ferrari's racing activity began on 15 May 1927, in Alessandria. That day Ferrari did not attend the main race, but rather a supporting event open to sports and *granturismo* cars.[1] Considering his past as a professional racing driver, this may seem surprising. But it is necessary to keep in mind two things: first, his return to racing was (in smaller part) to satisfy his innate desire for speed; the second, larger motivation was that, from now on, Ferrari would race essentially to advertise and support his core business – his network of car dealerships. His race craft had at any rate not been tarnished by the two and a half years of inactivity. At the wheel of an Alfa Romeo R L Mille Miglia with number 7 painted on the hood, Ferrari, wrote the press, drove 'as a master'. He led the 'smooth race' from start to finish, increasing his lead over the chasers lap after lap. He clinched a 'wholly deserved win', obtained at an average speed of almost 88km/h (55mph).[2] Three weeks later he took another win in the first Circuito di Modena, one of those new races born on the enthusiasm generated by the Mille Miglia. The same type of cars that had participated in the marathon up and down the Italian peninsula would battle each other on a city circuit comprising 30 laps. The choice of car for this particular race betrayed – or, rather, explained – the commercial implications of the new course of Enzo Ferrari's racing career: a 6C 1500, the agile car introduced two years earlier, with which Alfa Romeo aimed to boost its sales in Italy. A victory in Modena, thought Ferrari, would be worth more than entire advertising pages in newspapers and magazines.

With Maggi forced to retire after five laps, halfway through the race Enzo was firmly in second place, one minute behind Pintacuda. Five laps later, when the Sicilian nobleman was forced to quit too, Ferrari had no more rivals. Despite the rain that had started to fall, he maintained the lead until the chequered flag. Behind him came the other 6C 1500 driven by Attilio Marinoni, the best works tester of Alfa Romeo, separated by just 1 second, but behind nonetheless.[3] Two wins in two races. Although the first race had been little more than a picnic, and the second win had been assisted by the retirement of the two most powerful cars, it was clear that Ferrari still knew his stuff.

On the finish line, among fans and journalists and the confusion unleashed by enthusiasm for the victory of the home driver, Enzo also found Laura.[4] Now that the danger of professional racing had been pushed away, perhaps she realized that a limited commitment to racing by her husband could actually benefit his business.

*   *   *

The year 1928 was a highly formative one for Enzo Ferrari.

That winter in Italy the first Scuderia racing teams were formed. Since the direct commitment of car manufacturers was becoming ever more limited, the best drivers on the scene decided to tackle the problem head-on. Tazio Nuvolari and Emilio Materassi fashioned two teams of which they would be both drivers and owners.

Nuvolari chose to buy cars from a single manufacturer, Bugatti. Materassi instead diversified his investment by purchasing three Talbots, two Bugattis, two Italas, an Amilcar and even a Chrysler. Nuvolari hired the strongest among his motorcycle rivals, a young man from Galliate by the name of Achille Varzi, in what Canestrini called the 'small Scuderia Bugatti', to distinguish it from the works team out of Molsheim. Materassi chose as his teammate Luigi Arcangeli, nicknamed by his fans the 'Lion from Romagna'.[5]

Ferrari knew both Nuvolari and Materassi well by this time, and they shared mutual respect, but despite the large fleet of cars at their disposal Ferrari did not allow himself to be tempted by the new experience. Rather, he remained in the sphere of Alfa Romeo, for which, at the age of 30, but with a bond that had begun 8 years earlier, he was a sort of old sage.

He had decided to race only in events of relative importance that could be useful to his business, and his relationship with Alfa Romeo remained firm. In fact, in addition to maintaining the commercial representation for three Italian regions, Enzo was still a trusted consultant for Alfa Romeo's racing department.[6] Alfa's top management was by now chiefly made up of technocrats appointed by the state, but Ferrari's experience and personal charm still had an impact on the newcomers.

On the last Sunday in April 1928, Ferrari again sat behind the wheel of a racing car. The event was the Alessandria Circuit, the same race that the previous spring had marked his return to competition. It was reserved for cars in the sport category; grand prix cars had competed the previous Sunday.

Ferrari won hands down in an Alfa Romeo 6C Mille Miglia over five laps for only 160km (99 miles). The press, which had always appreciated Ferrari, took the opportunity to stress his unchanged talent, talking directly about the 'wonderful skill of the driver'. His conduct of the race was judged 'safe, very consistent, impressive'. According to reporters, Ferrari had driven 'with proven expertise and audacity'.

On 20 May, Ferrari triumphed again on his home turf. The second running of the Circuito di Modena was his at the end of a race that he had controlled throughout, nearly 360km (224 miles). The new success was hailed by the irrepressible enthusiasm of his fellow Modenese citizens, an enthusiasm that had accompanied him from the moment he had aligned his number 18 Alfa Romeo 6C 1500 on the starting line. Always tormented by the fear of not being fully accepted by his fellow citizens, on this day Ferrari was 'beaming because of the victory and moved by the demonstration of enthusiasm offered by public and authorities'.

The press appreciated his performance just as much. Elegant in his now-traditional race attire – jacket, tie, waistcoat under the duster[7] – Ferrari had 'confirmed his great driving skills, cool and confident'. [8] There were those who termed him 'wonderful for [his] style and conduct of [the] race'.[9]

Peppino Verdelli[10] made his debut at Enzo's side as the onboard mechanic who would accompany him in most of the handful of races that he would enter before the end of his racing career, and who, a few years later, would become his personal chauffeur.

Two weeks later, for the first time since the 1924 Coppa Acerbo, Enzo faced the best Italian drivers of his generation. The scene of the encounter was the Mugello circuit, renamed this year in honour of Giulio Masetti, who had died three years earlier during the Targa Florio. Ferrari drew on 'that impeccable style of his'[11] that allowed him, once Campari retired, to stay in second place for quite a while, behind Materassi in a Talbot. He finished third after Bruno Presenti, in an Alfa Romeo similar to his, passed him on the final lap.

Mugello was the last race of 1928 in which Enzo Ferrari took part as a driver. With only three events contested, but with two first places in Alessandria and Modena, and a third place at Mugello, he had earned the respectable figure of forty-five thousand lire, which put him in tenth place, alongside Achille Varzi, in terms of earnings among the fifty-two Italian drivers who had raced during the season. Of course, most of his annual salary came from his dealership activity; race prizes were just a nice bonus.

On 9 September Ferrari was at Monza as a spectator for the Italian Grand Prix. Before the start, he exchanged jokes with friend Materassi, who was close to retirement as a driver and thrilled at the prospect of his new chosen activity of manager and owner of the racing team that bore his name. Fate did not give him the opportunity, however. On lap 18 his Talbot took off in the middle of the straight and flew into a grandstand crowded with spectators. It was a tragedy of vast proportions: 23 spectators were dead, and 40 others injured. Materassi himself had been killed.[12]

For the Scuderie, their first season had been an experience of contrasts. Organizational, logistical and financial problems had repeatedly emerged during the year. The teams of Nuvolari and Materassi had found themselves in trouble several times, and the reasons were simple: despite enthusiasm and passion, they lacked the staff and structure of a car manufacturer and, moreover, did not have access to the funds that a manufacturer had.

Ferrari, who had followed the unfolding of events with an interest much deeper than one might suppose, realized from the outset that a racing team should be able to plan long term and, to do so, needed to have access to capital made up of more than race prize money. To aspire to success, a racing team should have wealthy founding members and involve as much as possible a car manufacturer from which they could buy cars and the necessary spare parts, but with, above all, an established direct line.

Nuvolari financed his team almost exclusively through the race prizes won by the 'Flying Mantuan' (as Nuvolari was now known) himself; by contrast, Ferrari had been intrigued by Materassi's set-up, which could count on the fresh money of wealthy Florentine enthusiasts. In the approach devised by Materassi, Enzo began to see how teams could thrive. Unfortunately Materassi had been killed before he could prove Enzo right.

Ferrari, who had observed and analysed the endeavours of Nuvolari and Materassi for an entire season, did not think to follow suit. He had been burned in the past by experiences faced with too much enthusiasm and as much approximation, and had learned a valuable lesson. So he went on as a dealer and an Alfa Romeo local agent, selling cars to gentleman drivers who raced them on Sundays, and, of course, racing himself every now and then. After all, in those early months of 1929, the press continued to speak of him as 'a great racing driver'.[13] Not surprisingly, the Sports Commission of the Royal Automobile Club of Italy had just assigned him International Licence number 1 for the season about to begin.[14]

Ferrari raced the first event of his new season on 21 April 1929, at Alessandria on the track now named after Pietro Bordino, where he had raced in each of the previous three years. Ferrari's race was good; he was running fourth overall when it suddenly came to an abrupt end against a concrete wall, because of a flat tyre. However violent, the impact with the wall stopped the out-of-control car and avoided far worse consequences. Canestrini told his readers the next day that, at the time of the accident, Ferrari had been 'battling at the top'.[15] Filippini in *Littoriale* was even more congratulatory, describing Ferrari as the 'best of the chasers'. His race, he wrote, 'was beautiful, confident, worthy of a good placement'.[16]

Despite the acclaim of the press, Enzo was deeply disappointed by his race.[17] He was afraid he could no longer find the form and fortune that he had once enjoyed. It was not just a matter of racing glory. For Ferrari, in this phase of his life, successfully completing a race had greater importance from a commercial perspective than from a sporting point of view, for the publicity and advertising it could provide for his business.

Meanwhile, Laura was again geographically and emotionally distant.

After her father died, she had gone to Turin, where she was still living with her sister, with no apparent will to return to Modena. To convince her to come home, Enzo suggested she bring her sister with her to Modena.[18] But his offers, as well as his pleas to come home, seemed to fall on deaf ears.

The first Sunday in June, the Circuito del Pozzo in Verona proved to be yet another unlucky race for Enzo. This time his brakes betrayed him about halfway through, when he was in second place. He resisted as best as he could and, relying solely on the front brakes, succeeded in placing fifth overall.[19]

The following Sunday, for the sixth time in his career, Enzo was at the start of the Circuito del Mugello. In the company of so many established champions, it must have seemed to him as if he'd gone back in time. While the faces may have changed, the talent had not. If in the first half of the 1920s he had battled Ascari, Nazzaro, Bordino, Materassi, Sivocci and Masetti, today he was facing Nuvolari, Varzi, Borzacchini, Biondetti and even Hans Stuck, the prince of hillclimbers, arrived from Germany.[20] Only Campari and Ferrari represented a sort of bridge between the beginning and the end of that incredible decade of motor racing.

At the wheel of his 6C 1750 Enzo finished eighth, never in the heart of the fight partly because of new tyres that made their debut that day, but also due to an alarming sickness he had suffered during the race.[21] He was 31 years old, with a body that was not really athletic and a profession that saw him in constant motion. In the morning he regularly got up before sunrise to get to any of the cities in the three regions he ran by the time the people he was meeting arrived at work. He usually skipped lunch to travel to another city or to meet another client. By late afternoon he was back in Bologna to make sure that everything proceeded unhindered in the branch office. Then he would return to Modena, where he checked the workshop to ensure that the day's work had been carried out.[22] This, day after day, week after week, month after month. During the weekends, of course, he often went to events scattered all over Italy where, although he rarely raced in person, he kept busy strengthening existing relationships and forging new ones. His illness was in all probability caused by the great heat of the late-spring afternoon. But Enzo interpreted it as a warning and, for the rest of the year, stayed away from the wheel of a race car.

As she had done every year, Laura was spending the summer months in Sestola, in the Apennines south of Modena, where she was staying at the Hotel d'Italie. Her health had never really improved. Although neither of them openly said so, husband and wife had long since realized that she would never really heal.

Despite the passing of time and everything that had happened, the correspondence between Enzo and Laura remained constant, a frank exchange in which husband and wife invariably engaged in personal controversy but at the same time told each other all that they could possibly tell. Enzo's beautifully handwritten letters were neat, written in correct and rich Italian. Laura's letters were often disorganized, in almost illegible handwriting, with a poor mastery of the Italian language.

Laura seemed unable to overcome her jealousy and state of perpetual anxiety, that semi-permanent illness with which she had now been living for eight years, and of which jealousy was both cause and effect.

For his part, Enzo, who no longer saw Laura as the only woman in his life, still refused to break away from her. The signs of a troubled relationship had been there since the beginning of their life together. Laura's jealousy was nothing new; it had manifested itself, without reason, well before the wedding, when the young woman hadn't understood that if Enzo cheated on her, it was not with another woman, but rather with his total devotion to the automobile. Enzo should have understood this and found the courage to end their story before marrying her. By the summer of 1929, although he was leading a sufficiently uninhibited love life, he had met a much younger girl at Carrozzeria Orlandi. He was not indifferent to her charms, but remained, in a sense, an emotional hostage to Laura.

The Scuderia

On Saturday 5 October 1929, the Automobile Club of Bologna hosted a gala dinner to honour local hero Alfieri Maserati, the manufacturer of the 16-cylinder car that in Cremona, a week earlier, had set the new flying 10km (6-mile) world record on unpaved roads.[1] The dinner was held at the Bologna *Casa del Fascio*, the Fascist Party House. The political times required that meetings of this size be held in a house owned by the party so that they could be quietly kept under control. Some of the guests were racing drivers who had battled against each other in the decade that was drawing to an end.

Party and sports authorities had seized the opportunity and had come to the gala dinner en masse. There were five speeches and the public reading of various congratulatory telegrams.[2] After the toasts, once the tributes to Borzacchini and Maserati had ended and the cheers subsided, Alfredo Caniato, a hemp entrepreneur from Ferrara, expressed to his tablemates his concerns regarding the future of motor racing. Enzo Ferrari was sitting at his table. Caniato said that despite the fun he had enjoyed in the recent past, he would probably quit racing.[3] Mario Tadini, a hillclimb race specialist from Bergamo, echoed his thoughts. Racing was becoming increasingly expensive and although new races were created every year, the direct participation of car manufacturers was fading rapidly and would probably end in the new decade.

Both of these men were clients of Enzo's, having bought from his dealership the Alfa Romeos they drove on circuits throughout Italy. Ferrari – for whom racing was both a source of personal reward and income earned from the cars he sold to a generation of rich men, looking for a different class of thrill – shared the same doubts and uncertainty about the future of motor racing. But, typically, in the general distress he also saw an opportunity – and quickly seized the moment.

If automobile manufacturers were reducing their investments and participation, the moment could be ripe, Ferrari said, for a larger role to be played by Scuderie, the private and normally small racing teams that had already been operating, if not flourishing, in the 1920s. He, for one, was ready to take up where manufacturers like Fiat and Alfa Romeo had left off.[4] And although earlier experiments attempted by first-class drivers Emilio Materassi and Tazio Nuvolari had failed, he was sure that he knew enough about both organizational and technical matters to succeed.

Caniato, Tadini and their other dinner companions were listening to Enzo with much more than polite interest. If properly addressed, the experiment could work. Enzo Ferrari's reputation for organization was perhaps matched only by his charm when it came to persuading an interested audience. He anticipated possible reservations about the feasibility of the project, and volunteered that the direct involvement of Alfa Romeo in the new racing team was a prerequisite.[5] This he said to a delighted audience, and the party split that night on the promise that they would soon hear from Enzo.[6]

A few days later Ferrari went to Milan to follow up on the idea and to pursue his own plan that Alfa Romeo become a part of the private racing team in the making. The task could have discouraged many, but not Enzo Ferrari.

Enzo went to the Portello factory in Milan that he knew so well. Facing management who were not particularly interested in racing or in maintaining Alfa Romeo's presence in international competition, he talked and talked.[7] He vibrantly expounded upon his ideas, a managerial programme from which all would gain: Alfa Romeo would remain active in racing, a cutting-edge activity from which solutions for everyday cars would continue to come; drivers and clients would go on racing and buying Alfa's sports cars; and, ultimately, Italy would still be properly represented on international grounds. This was not the last time this chord would be touched upon during the chauvinistic years of the Fascist era, with a management that had been selected by, and reported to, the Mussolini government in Rome.

Because of the smaller-scale operations and the minor costs involved, he said, Ferrari's new racing team could guarantee the only thing that Alfa Romeo could not: continuity. He intended to offer a wheel to gentleman drivers on a scale that had not been matched by any manufacturer in the past, while at the same time providing direct assistance to Alfa Romeo's official drivers on Italian and continental circuits, where and when the company's racing department would not directly participate.

He saved the knockout punch for last: by having *his* racing team enter *their* cars, he said, if they won, it was Alfa Romeo that won; if they were defeated, the burden would be borne by his Scuderia. He offered shares in the new Modena-based racing team in exchange for first-rate technical assistance and demonstrated high-standard logistic support.[8]

Whether the management of Alfa Romeo was convinced by Enzo's long-range plans and personal charm, or by Vittorio Jano's endorsement, which was itself a personal victory, the response was positive. Alfa Romeo agreed to take part in the new racing activity promoted by their sales agent for the Emilia-Romagna and Marche regions, a brilliant 31-year-old part-time driver with ambitions that clearly went full circle. They would not take more than 5 per cent of the new company's stakes, but Enzo Ferrari could now count Alfa Romeo in, with all that this meant – first and foremost, direct access to buy the best materials available in motor racing.

A few days later Enzo Ferrari again headed in the direction of Milan. Having won over Alfa Romeo, he had to complete the operation by winning over tyre manufacturer Pirelli. As with Alfa Romeo, Enzo was not so much in search of capital, for that would be provided by his wealthy gentleman-driver partners, who were far more inclined to risk their own money than established companies were. He was more interested in making Pirelli part of the game, much as he had done with Alfa Romeo, to gain direct access to a tyre supplier with a precise interest in serving his Scuderia as best as it could.

This second trip to Milan in a few days was also fruitful. Pirelli would purchase half the stakes for which Alfa Romeo was willing to subscribe, and they too were in. Now it was time for Enzo to go back to Modena and finalize the constitution of his own racing team.[9]

On Saturday morning, 16 November, Enzo Ferrari and a handful of gentlemen with a common passion for motor racing met in the spacious Corso Umberto offices of Enzo Levi, a well-known and highly respected Modena attorney. In the presence of one of the partners of Levi's office, notary Alberto Della Fontana, they formalized their intentions to establish a racing team.[10] Enzo had an additional plan in mind, but had not bothered to write it down. The parallel hiring of professional drivers normally entering major events as Alfa Romeo's official drivers need not be put in writing at this time.

Under the supervision of Dr Della Fontana, they chartered a joint-stock company. There were 200 shares, each worth 1,000 lire – 200,000 lire the total capital, a fair amount of money in the Italy of 1929. Brothers Alfredo and Augusto Caniato held the absolute majority, with 130 shares. Enzo Ferrari kept 50 shares for himself. Alfa Romeo had 10, and 5 each went to Pirelli and Ferruccio Testi, a Modena veterinarian with a passion for automobiles and photography.[11]

When it came time to name the newly formed company, all present unanimously approved the name of Scuderia Ferrari. Though he was a minority partner of the company, Enzo was without question the central person of the whole endeavour, the originator and the brains of the operation, the energy behind the future activity and, given his privileged relationship with Alfa Romeo, the Scuderia's assurance of success. Oddly enough, the only one who resisted giving the Scuderia the Ferrari name was Enzo himself, who had wanted to name it Mutina, from the old Latin name for the city of Modena. It had taken all the persuasion of family friend Enzo Levi to convince Enzo Ferrari of the appropriate name for the new venture.[12] And so, Scuderia Ferrari it was.

The new company was registered at the Modena tribunal on 29 November. The legal contract would last for two years, from 16 November 1929 to 16 November 1931. Alfredo Caniato was appointed president; Enzo Ferrari, managing director.[13]

Six days before Scuderia Ferrari was registered, Enzo had struck a deal that was already going to give his racing team a connotation different from the one for which it had been created – at least, according to what the legal papers said. With Achille Varzi and Tazio Nuvolari still in the early stages of their automotive careers, Enzo had secured the services of a motor-racing veteran, an ace still alive and active, Giuseppe Campari.[14]

Campari was a consecrated champion with a ten-year career behind him, made special by several grand prix wins, two triumphs in a row at the Mille Miglia in 1928 and 1929 and a victory in the strenuous Targa Florio. To the experienced eyes of Enzo, Campari was a triple asset for young Scuderia Ferrari: great publicity, higher participation prizes from race organizers and, last but not least, huge and reliable chances of winning.

The deal with Campari was for five races. His own 1930 contract with Alfa Romeo as a works driver was for an additional four. Majority stakeholders Alfredo and Augusto Caniato were puzzled by the hiring of a champion of Campari's magnitude by a small racing team that had been created with the written purpose of entering cars for its gentleman-driver members. The only explanation Enzo gave them was that Campari's hiring served to attract media attention to the new team – attention that could easily mean more clients for the Scuderia, thus starting their collective business on a high note.[15]

In reality, the double path that Enzo had privately envisioned for his company was all too clear: on the one hand, the stated purpose of the enterprise: technical assistance to gentleman drivers who would buy Alfa Romeos from his dealership; on the other, much more important to him, and in part financed by the first: the establishment of a first-rate racing team that would, in time, take Alfa Romeo's place as Italy's representative in major continental motorsport events.

The headquarters of Scuderia Ferrari were to be, at least in the beginning, in the same Garage Gatti structure that had served Enzo well since 1925. Yet Enzo soon realized the old building was too small to serve the double purpose of his new activity. He therefore started to look around for new premises, and was soon eyeing a property just around the corner from Garage Gatti, a few hundred yards down Viale Ciro Menotti.

This new structure, Garage Italia, contained both a workshop and a showroom, and would be ideal for his twin activities of Alfa Romeo dealer and racing-team principal. Not to mention that on the second floor there was a one-bedroom apartment, where he could easily move in with Laura, replicating what his father had done in the last decade of the nineteenth century, when in the two-story redbrick building on Via Camurri he had installed the workshop on the ground floor and his living quarters on the first.

In January 1930, accompanied by the ever-present Enzo Levi, Ferrari asked for an interview with the managing director of the largest bank in Modena, Banca di San Geminiano. Enzo went to ask for a loan of one million lire, an incredibly large sum.[16] It took guts just to ask for a loan of that magnitude. He had no properties, no houses, no land to put down as a guarantee. All he had were long-range plans and a charm that he used to present those plans to the bank's top manager. Giuseppe Casoli listened to him almost casually, never asking any question, never pressing for any explanation. Enzo had the distinct feeling that the interview was not going to lead to a good result,[17] when suddenly Casoli turned to friend Enzo Levi and said: 'This young man has just told me a pleasant story. What shall we do, *Avvocato* [attorney]? Should we give him the million he asks for?'[18]

A few minutes later Enzo left Casoli's office with Levi and the sum he had dared to request. With this money he would buy the Liberty-style building on Viale Ciro Menotti and the workshop behind it, where he would soon start his audacious adventure. Whether the bank's managing director had been convinced by his plans and determination, or whether Levi had somehow provided some type of collateral for him, is unknown, but Enzo never forgot the faith Casoli had placed in him. For the rest of his life, he never used any bank but the Banca di San Geminiano.[19]

That winter Enzo bought the cars that Scuderia Ferrari would use in the 1930 racing season: four six-cylinder Alfa Romeos of 1.5 and 1.7 litres, and the eight-cylinder, 2.0-litre P2, currently being shipped back from South America, which Enzo had tracked down and procured so that Giuseppe Campari could compete on the same level as the official Alfa Romeo works team, with which he had openly said there would be no competition. The cars were at the Alfa Romeo factory in Milan, where the P2 was also scheduled to go once it reached Italian shores. They were being updated and prepped for the new season by Alfa Romeo technicians, dividing their time between the works team cars and the four destined for Scuderia Ferrari in Modena.[20]

Enzo was determined as never before in his life, and totally focused. His morale soared. This was no small thing for someone who, less than six months earlier, had been on the edge of a nervous breakdown.[21] For him, work had always been – and always would be – the best antidote.

On Saturday 12 April, Scuderia Ferrari was ready to participate in its first race. Now running for the fourth time, the Mille Miglia was already acclaimed by Italians as *The Race*. Hoping to repeat his two consecutive wins of 1928 and 1929, Campari, who at Monaco would have driven an Alfa entered by Scuderia Ferrari, would participate in the Mille Miglia driving a works Alfa Romeo. So would both Tazio Nuvolari and Achille Varzi.

Enzo was therefore left with his gentleman-driver clients and partners and little hope to do well. Tadini/Siena, Caniato/Sozzi, Scarfiotti/Carraroli and Corelli/ Lenti were the four pairings that would enter the first event ever in the history of Scuderia Ferrari. Tadini, Caniato and Scarfiotti were at the wheel of 1.7-litre Alfas; Corelli, a less-powerful 1.5-litre. Enzo would sit out this time. In this first official race of his Scuderia, he had chosen to concentrate on the organizational side of the operation, knowing well that the situation could be better kept under control from the sidelines than from behind a steering wheel on unpaved dusty roads up and down Italy.

Three of the four Scuderia Ferrari cars were unable to finish the race. For Enzo it was understandably a huge disappointment. He knew all too well that his amateurs could not compete with the best professional Italian drivers of the day, but he had nonetheless hoped for a better showing. Only the weakest of the four pairs, Corelli and Lenti, finished the race – with a respectable fourth place in class.

Yet, there were also some encouraging signs: Tadini had driven an impressive first half of the race, holding fifth place overall in Rome, where all participants had started their way back north; Scarfiotti had battled with the leaders for most of the race before being forced to retire in Bologna, 160km (100 miles) or so from the chequered flag.

Although disappointing in terms of final results, for Scuderia Ferrari this first trial was nonetheless reassuring. No particular emergency had troubled the largely untested organization during the 2-day, 1,600km (1,000-mile) race all the way through half of the Italian peninsula. And all of Enzo's merry drivers had very much enjoyed the opportunity and the ride. Pictures taken by the always-present Ferruccio Testi on the descent from the Futa Pass in the Apennines, in the initial stages of the race, showed all Scuderia drivers pleasantly smiling and waving at the camera.[22]

If Enzo was disturbed by the massive superiority shown by the works Alfa Romeos – four cars in the first four places in the final standing – he could rejoice in the pleasure that the members of his Scuderia had felt. A happy client was a client ready to return and race again. And as for his personal plan of competing at the same level with the works Alfas, he would soon play his new cards.

The following Sunday, 20 April, Scuderia Ferrari took part in its second race, the Circuito Pietro Bordino in Alessandria. On the eve of the race he was nervous, as always before a race,[23] and this was no ordinary race: for the first time Enzo took the start as a driver of his own racing team. Pietro Bordino had been a talented driver who had been killed in Alessandria two years earlier during practice for this very event that now bore his name. The morning of the race, Enzo and the other drivers walked together to the spot where Bordino had been killed, laid a wreath next to the small memorial and then went back to the starting grid.[24]

Scuderia Ferrari had taken two Alfa Romeos to Alessandria. The 1750 was for Enzo, the less-powerful 6C 1500 for Alfredo Caniato. The competition was tough this Easter day: Achille Varzi, in open war with the Alfa Romeo management because he thought Jano had favoured archrival Nuvolari during the previous week's Mille Miglia, and had openly said so, was at the wheel of the new works P2, finally ready after the massive tune-up. Two French-blue Bugatti 2300s were in Alessandria for Belgian Georges Bouriano and Chilean Juan Zanelli. Victory would be fought out between these three cars. As he prepared to start the race, Enzo knew that for him today it would be virtually impossible to do better than fourth place.

Despite the technical disadvantage, Enzo started the race with his usual brio. At the end of the first lap he was in second place, 26 seconds behind Bouriano in his Bugatti and 8 seconds ahead of Varzi in his P2. Varzi had started the race on the last row of the grid and had lost time in getting past several slower cars that had started ahead of him. When, on lap 2, Varzi was finally free to release all the monstrous power of his new P2, Enzo managed to keep the gap to him respectable.

About halfway through the race, the unstable spring weather broke into a violent storm. Rain fell all over the circuit, quickly transforming the unpaved dusty roads into rivers of water and mud. At this point Enzo's talent began to make a difference and he started to gain on the cars ahead. With Bouriano now out of the race, under the rain Enzo gained a remarkable one minute in four laps on the other Bugatti driven by Zanelli.[25]

Enzo finished third overall, behind the P2 of Varzi and the Bugatti of Zanelli. It was the first podium finish for Scuderia Ferrari. Afterwards, he was a bit tired because of what he himself identified as a lack of training. But privately he was proud of his performance: everyone was saying that his race had been quite good.[26]

Caniato finished tenth overall and fourth in his class. Both cars entered by the Scuderia had finished the race – a big improvement from their maiden race.

Enzo and Scuderia Ferrari decided to sit out the next event, the renowned Targa Florio. The race itself was one of the most prominent in Europe, but it was held in Sicily, over 1,000 miles from Modena, a distance not worth the trip given the cars and drivers Enzo could have counted upon; of the Scuderia P2 there was still no news from Alfa Romeo. But when, after the race, Alfa Romeo decided to celebrate its latest triumph in the Sicilian classic, Enzo made sure he was among those invited to the event.

He went to Milan and skilfully played the part of the devoted and admiring junior partner. Winner Varzi was naturally there. Campari was there, too, now almost set to race with Scuderia Ferrari. All the top managers of Alfa Romeo were present, from company boss Prospero Gianferrari to chief mechanic Rescalli. But the president of the Italian Automobile Club, Senator Silvio Crespi, also attended the event.[27] For Enzo, a natural in courting personal relations, it was a huge opportunity to see and be seen, to hear and be heard.

On 11 May in Ascoli, Mario Tadini scored a second place overall, with Alfredo Caniato coming in fourth.[28] The Ascoli–Castel di Lama race was not very important, but Scuderia Ferrari was quickly learning the necessary organizational skills, and Tadini was rapidly emerging as a fast and reliable driver. Tadini's second-place finish was the best result achieved by the Scuderia, improving on Enzo's own third place in Alessandria.

A week later, on 18 May, the true nature of Enzo's scheme emerged for all to see. At last the first established champion entered a race as an official driver of Scuderia Ferrari. Giuseppe Campari was temporarily free from obligations with the works Alfa Romeos and was now ready to fulfil the contract he had signed with Enzo the previous winter.

Campari's debut race with Scuderia Ferrari was at the Circuito di Caserta, not far from Naples. Enzo sat out the race but entered two Alfa Romeo 1750 GSs for Campari and Tadini. The race thrived on the competition between 30 or so cars, with engines ranging from 1.1 and 2.2 litres to the 7.0-litre Mercedes entered by a Neapolitan driver with a German name, Fritz Caflisch.

Despite the power of his car, Caflisch was only in second place when Luigi Fagioli's Maserati ran out of gas during the final lap. Caflisch inherited the lead and kept it until the end. Giuseppe Campari finished third, Tadini sixth.[29]

While Campari's debut was far from outstanding, the Scuderia kept showing consistency and their cars proved, once more, to be very reliable. For a young organization at only its fourth event, it was a remarkable step in the challenging learning curve.

Next was the Reale Premio in Rome, the first race with an international flavour that Scuderia Ferrari would enter. It was the small team's first test in a real grand prix environment. The competition was significant in the capital of the Kingdom of Italy on this Sunday in late May. A total of 21 cars would battle each other on the 12km (8-mile) laps, to be repeated 20 times, of the Tre Fontane Circuit. Maserati was there with a formidable trio: Arcangeli, Fagioli and Nenzioni. Bugatti had entered Monaco-born Louis Chiron and French driver Count Bouriat-Quintart. Alfa Romeo had P2s for Achille Varzi and Tazio Nuvolari.[30] Enzo entered the same 1750 GSs he had entered the week before in Caserta for the same pair, Campari and Tadini. He had no illusions: victory today would be a contest between the Maseratis, the Bugattis and the P2s. He was thus happily unprepared for what he experienced that day. For the first time since he had started operations on his own, his Scuderia saved the day for Alfa Romeo. Both Varzi and Nuvolari dropped out of the race. The new P2/1930 was a very powerful car, but clearly not yet reliable. And reliability was precisely what Scuderia Ferrari had. Campari and Tadini, with their smaller 1750 GSs, finished fifth and seventh – distant from Luigi Arcangeli's Maserati, but both concluded the race.[31]

The Reale Premio was the ultimate triumph for Maserati.[32] Luigi Arcangeli, in his signature white overalls, won a race that was the final consecration for the small-but-dynamic automobile maker from Bologna. But the 1930 Reale Premio was also the first demonstration of the good, solid work that Enzo Ferrari and his Scuderia had set out to do.

Coincidence or not, when Enzo Ferrari and his team came back from Rome, they found a pleasant surprise: their Alfa Romeo P2 had finally been updated at Portello and was on its way to Modena. It had been almost six months since Enzo had bought this car, which, at the moment of purchase, was in South America. After a long voyage by sea, the car had been prepped at Alfa Romeo under the supervision of Vittorio Jano. Soon Alfa would introduce a new 8C for their works drivers, but for Scuderia Ferrari the revised P2 was a giant step up.

Also, it was going to be driven by a first-rate ace, not by any of the happy-go-lucky gentleman drivers who crowded the Viale Ciro Menotti workshop of Scuderia Ferrari in Modena.

Winning

The announcement came from Modena and caught the whole world of motorsport by surprise: Tazio Nuvolari had signed with Scuderia Ferrari.

It was a stroke of genius. Nuvolari had just won his first Mille Miglia at the end of a duel with Achille Varzi that had lasted for the entire 16 hours of the race. It was the beginning of a rivalry that would for years to come divide Italians of all ages and walks of life. For weeks people had talked about nothing but the final stages of the Mille Miglia, when Nuvolari was said to have turned off the lights of his Alfa Romeo and overtaken Varzi in the dark. Whether that story was true or not, Varzi had not refuted it, and legend had immediately taken hold of that race – the duel, and its winner. Now, by joining the name of his Scuderia to Nuvolari's, Ferrari would automatically benefit from this interest.

First Campari, now Nuvolari – Ferrari had worked with the recognized champion of the 1920s, and now he had secured the services of the ace of the future. Six months into the life of his Scuderia, Enzo was rapidly bringing his own plan to fruition. In addition to keeping his commitment to those gentleman drivers who wanted to experience the thrill of speed, providing them with cars and assistance, Enzo was also working tirelessly to give his new organization a prominent place on the national motoring scene. At Scuderia Ferrari there would always be room for wealthy amateurs, but Enzo Ferrari's real objectives were now clear to all.

Nuvolari's first race with Scuderia Ferrari was scheduled for mid-June. It was the Trieste-Opicina hillclimb, held for the first time in 1911. This was a demanding race, in which the talent of Nuvolari at the wheel of a P2 made all the difference. Despite the fact that 23 of the 40 participants beat the previous year's race time, Nuvolari won hands down. He completed the 9km (5.5 miles) of the ascent in 5 minutes and 59 seconds, at an average speed of nearly 100km/h (62mph) – 2 minutes quicker than the time set by the winner in 1929. The public could only just be kept behind the barriers when the loudspeakers announced the name of the winner and his fantastic performance.[1]

For Ferrari and his Scuderia, it was the first win – their first encounter with success. All four cars entered by Scuderia Ferrari had finished the race: Siena, fourth; Caniato, twelfth; Sozzi – one of the few true gentleman drivers assisted by the Scuderia in this first phase of activity – twentieth. But the hero of the day was, of course, Tazio Nuvolari. Enzo, in Trieste with his mechanics and technicians, rejoiced. It had taken him only seven races to clinch his first win. He was justifiably proud of his organization and his vision.

Two weeks later, Scuderia Ferrari participated in the Cuneo–Colle della Maddalena, another hillclimb. The race was one of the toughest in its category and, at more than 60km (37 miles), one of the longest. As in Trieste, Ferrari gave the P2 to Nuvolari, who in the days before the race restlessly tested the course. In a single day Tazio climbed 12 times from Cuneo to Colle della Maddalena.[2] But Enzo, excited after his first win, had also entered Luigi Arcangeli, the winner of the Reale Premio of Rome, whom Maserati had chosen not to enter for this race. Ferrari gave Arcangeli the same 1750 GS with which Siena had raced in Trieste.

With Achille Varzi forced to withdraw less than 15km (9 miles) from the finish and German Hans Stuck out as well, Nuvolari faced no real competition. Not only did he win the race, giving Enzo and his Scuderia their second win, but he also lowered the race time by ten minutes. Arcangeli, in his first race with Scuderia Ferrari, finished third.

Two weeks later, Enzo Ferrari and Tazio Nuvolari won their third race together. The pair began to appear unbeatable, at least in a certain type of event. On 13 July, Tazio dominated the Vittorio Veneto–Cansiglio, another hillclimb – 15km (9 miles) of dirt road that climbed to the timber forests from which for centuries the Republic of Venice had harvested the wood for its formidable ships. Nuvolari once again lowered the previous race time, set by Campari in 1928.

In just one month Nuvolari had given Enzo and his Scuderia three wins. But all three successes had been in hillclimbs – a form of racing that put drivers and their cars to the test, but lacked the charm and reputation of events raced on the many road circuits and the one permanent race track in Italy.

The next road circuit race was scheduled for early August in Livorno, the tenth Coppa Ciano. For Enzo the time had come to show the world the true value of his organization. He therefore entered three cars for three extraordinary drivers. Luigi Arcangeli would take the race at the wheel of an Alfa Romeo 1750. A second unit of the same model would be entrusted to Baconin Borzacchini. As usual, Nuvolari would drive the more-powerful P2.[3]

The race on the Montenero Circuit was heralded by the Italian press as the latest chapter in the endless contest between Nuvolari and Varzi. Ever since that legendary last phase of April's Mille Miglia, newspapers and magazines had fuelled the competition between the two great rivals. Further enhancing the significance of the race, the event bore the Ciano family name, the most powerful household in Livorno, now known to the rest of Italy as well because of the wedding, back in the spring, between 27-year-old Count Galeazzo Ciano and 19-year-old Edda Mussolini, the Duce's favourite daughter.

Once again Ferrari decided not to sit behind the wheel of a racing car. He knew that the rivalry between Nuvolari and Varzi could lead to the first meaningful victory of his Scuderia, and did not want to leave anything to chance. But he had probably not considered the fact that, despite the superhuman quality of his driver, even Tazio was a man, and, like all human beings, prone to making mistakes when antagonism prevailed. Once the starter's flag was lowered, Nuvolari forgot any race strategy and furiously rushed to attack Varzi, showing no respect for the car with which he had been entrusted.

The race ended the way Ferrari must have sensed it would from the start. Nuvolari and Varzi were both forced to withdraw because of mechanical failures caused by their absurd race pace. The public clamoured their disappointment at seeing the two rivals bow out without a clear winner. The press also voiced their discontent. At least for that day, there would be no answer to the question all Italian motorsport fans were asking themselves. The most disappointed of all was probably Ferrari.

The following Sunday, for the first time since it was established, Scuderia Ferrari took part in two events on the same day. Nuvolari went to Switzerland to participate in the time trial at Klausen – incidentally, the first race in which Scuderia Ferrari participated outside Italy. Enzo and four other drivers took part in the Circuit of the Three Provinces, on the hills of Tuscany and Emilia.

Sunday afternoon, 10 August, despite the fact that he had last raced in April, Ferrari gave a great personal performance. Twenty-five minutes into the race, Arcangeli reached the tiny village of San Marcello Pistoiese with Enzo in second place, a single minute behind. By Pievepelago, Borzacchini had overtaken Arcangeli, and Enzo was now in third place.

The torrid weather of the mid-August afternoon and the intensity of a demanding race soon began to claim their first victims, however. Borzacchini and Ferrari had technical problems. While the former broke the suspension of his right rear wheel, the latter broke the fuel pump.[4] From Sestola onward Arcangeli had no rivals left, and cruised on with relative calm to the finish line, located in the village of Bagni. Behind him came Tadini, the most talented among the nonprofessional drivers of Scuderia Ferrari, save of course for Enzo himself. The fifth Ferrari driver, Eugenio Siena, finished in fifth place.

Despite the far from memorable field of opponents, the performance of Scuderia Ferrari impressed observers. If Borzacchini and Enzo had not been forced to withdraw, the Scuderia would have placed four cars in the top four places. Alfa Romeo could only be happy with the service that Ferrari was delivering, as promised. Without spending a single penny or moving one person from Portello, the Milan manufacturer had placed two cars in the top two places in the most important race held in Italy that Sunday – a supremacy that the press stressed and praised in the next day's race reports.

In only his second race of the season, Enzo had once again demonstrated his talent. Before the withdrawal he had passed both Borzacchini and Arcangeli, staying firmly in the lead for a few kilometres.[5] At the age of 32, and with more important projects in mind, he had proven that he was still one of the best drivers on the scene.

The news that came from Switzerland in the evening was not as good. At Klausen, Nuvolari had not been able to do better than seventh. But by having raced on the same day in two events in two different countries, Scuderia Ferrari had gained additional experience in terms of organization and, consequently, further respect from its opponents. Not to mention the fact that Ferrari was improving Alfa Romeo's image in the world of motorsport.

Four months had passed between Enzo's first and second races of the season. Now, having proven to himself that he could still produce remarkable performances – if not fortunate ones – Enzo entered his name in the following Sunday's race, the Coppa Acerbo in Pescara, the event in which he had scored the greatest triumph of his career, in 1924.

But the three Alfa Romeos of Scuderia Ferrari could do little this Sunday against the formidable Maseratis of Varzi, Arcangeli and Fagioli. And contrary to the previous weekend, Enzo's performance was quite anonymous this time, culminating with a withdrawal due to technical failures. With Enzo out of the race and Nuvolari fifth, Borzacchini scored a solid third-place finishing, somehow making Enzo's Sunday a little less disappointing.

Next up, Monza presented an immense opportunity for Enzo. Alfa Romeo's management had had hopes right up until a few days before the event that the new eight-cylinder single-seaters would be finished in time for the race. But the team of technicians headed by Vittorio Jano had not managed the miracle this time. Knowing all too well that participation in the home race could not be turned down, Alfa Romeo chairman Prospero Gianferrari could find no other feasible solution than to trust Enzo Ferrari's organizational skills and assign him two works P2s to officially represent the company in the grand prix.[6]

The call from Milan did not find Enzo unprepared. He had trained his people for five months, had been personally ready from the very beginning and knew he would not fail. He therefore accepted enthusiastically.

To the two factory-tuned cars Enzo added his own P2, lining up a formidable formation with the extraordinary talents of Tazio Nuvolari, Giuseppe Campari and Baconin Borzacchini. The opportunity was gigantic for Enzo: Monza was no ordinary race for Italian fans, and especially so for Alfa Romeo, whose global headquarters were less than ten miles from the Autodromo Nazionale permanent race track.

The opposition on this first Sunday in September was frightening: they faced the powerful and wholly reliable Maseratis driven by Achille Varzi and Luigi Arcangeli, who had dominated the Italian racing scene for the whole season, and had scrupulously prepared for the showdown.[7] The theme of the race was a familiar one: Tazio Nuvolari against Achille Varzi. But there was also a new one: Scuderia Ferrari against Maserati, the new racing team taking on the established one. The Bologna brothers had been racing since 1926, Enzo, for less than six months.

Despite all of the expectations and everyone's best efforts, the race was a total debacle for Scuderia Ferrari. The event involved three separate heats, followed by a final run with the best drivers from each heat. For Nuvolari and Campari, the Monza Grand Prix lasted for only six laps out of the fourteen of the second heat.

The Maseratis ran smoother from the very beginning. To worsen the situation, the tyres on the P2s started to deteriorate very quickly. By the end of lap six Enzo's best drivers were out of the race. The following lap Borzacchini was also forced back to the pits with his tyres completely worn out. After seven laps, there were no more Scuderia Ferrari Alfa Romeos on the track to slow Maserati's winning march.

To please the thousands of spectators who had come from all over Italy to see Nuvolari battle Varzi – in case either of them had not, for any reason, qualified for the final run – the organizers had agreed beforehand to the popular *repechage* formula, which allowed any of the drivers who had not automatically qualified for the final event to battle each other for a few extra spots. Nuvolari and Campari, taking first and second in the *repechage*, were both admitted to the final stint.[8] This was not the way Enzo would have wanted it to happen, but at least he hypothetically had his two best drivers in the running for the overall victory.

The final run started at 3.45pm and was going to be raced over 35 laps; the heats had been run on 14 laps each, and the *repechage* on 7. At the end of lap one Enzo's top driver was in second position. On lap three Nuvolari dropped back to third place, which still meant a podium finishing. Two laps later Nuvolari overtook Varzi to reclaim second place. But the following lap he crossed the finish line far behind the leading pair and, after one more lap, slowly made his way to the pits, his tyres destroyed.

Of the three cars that Enzo had entered, none finished the race. Borzacchini, Campari and Nuvolari all withdrew way before the end of the event. Monza was a complete Alfa Romeo and Scuderia Ferrari disaster in the face of a total Maserati success, with Varzi, Arcangeli and Ernesto Maserati finishing in the top three positions.[9] Two days later, in a letter to his wife, who was still visiting her sister in Turin, Enzo spoke without reticence of the 'tragedy of Monza', pointing out that the race had been 'the greatest misfortune'.[10]

Yet despite the fact that the outcome was certainly not the desired one, the Monza failure was also a sort of blessing in disguise. Enzo was able to demonstrate firsthand to Alfa Romeo's management how useful his organization could also be on bad days – or *especially* on bad days – which was precisely what he had told them the previous autumn when trying to convince them to get on board with his new racing team.

*   *   *

On 5 October Enzo signed a new contract with Tazio Nuvolari. With Alfa Romeo's blessing, it seemed only fitting that Enzo would secure the Mantuan's services beyond the few races for which he had signed Tazio earlier in the year. On this first Sunday in October, Enzo put pen to paper to extend Nuvolari's services until the end of the current season and all through the next.

Evidently pleased with what he had seen, Nuvolari had chosen to stay within the greater Alfa Romeo world that Ferrari was guaranteeing, and accepted not only the opportunity that the Scuderia offered him but also the economic conditions that Enzo set. Tazio had faith in the almost-ready new 2.3-litre Alfa Romeo V8 that Vittorio Jano had been working on at Portello and confidence in Enzo Ferrari's qualities as a racing-team organizer.

The first racing season of Scuderia Ferrari was officially over. It had been a long run since mid-April, but undeniably a good one.

Back in Modena, Enzo found himself alone – again. Laura was still in Turin with her sister. The relationship between husband and wife remained stormy. Enzo's patience had reached its limit. As usual, the only possible reaction to the status quo was in the form of a letter, this time filled with accusations, bitter thoughts and brave resolutions.[11]

The cause of Laura's wearisome behaviour was always the same – that complex form of jealousy mixed with hatred toward not so much (or at least, not only) the women Enzo knew and met in the racing environment, but the attitude toward life that her husband maintained. He was always looking forward to the future, invariably open to solutions, while she was always anchored to the fears that had long ago ruined their lives.

But this time Enzo was not willing to passively accept it all, as he had too often done in the past. He looked back at the 11 years of their relationship and at how Laura's erratic behaviour and tormented life had pushed them apart, despite his best efforts. He told her that he couldn't take it any longer, especially now that he was totally absorbed in an activity that would very likely allow him to fulfil his lifelong dream of becoming a significant player in the motor-racing world that he loved so much. At this point in his life and career, Enzo was ready to sacrifice all that was necessary to succeed with his Scuderia – even his marriage. It was up to Laura to decide.[12] In 11 tormented years, this was undeniably the lowest point in their never-simple relationship. He gave her a choice: Laura was free to stay with him, or go. She chose to stay, but, sadly, their relationship would never improve.

Enzo allowed himself a few days of rest and then plunged back into business. The 1931 season was only a few months away, the first race scheduled for mid-February. He had to cash in on the positive results of the first year of his racing team's activity. Pirelli, Shell and Bosch had to be kept on board and, possibly, convinced to contribute even more in terms of material and perhaps money. Alfa Romeo had to be courted to continue the relationship into the new season, with the new cars to which Jano was putting the finishing touches, and on 21 October Enzo was already at Portello to discuss the programme for the new season.[13]

But the times also called for a celebration and, less than a month after the last racing event of the season, Enzo invited to Modena all of those who had contributed to Scuderia Ferrari's first year.

At the San Carlo Hotel in downtown Modena, on 8 November, Enzo started one of his traditions: the end-of-season gala dinner. The event was as pompous as one would expect in those days, with government authorities and Fascist Party personalities all claiming their few minutes of glory. Before dinner, Enzo and all of his guests followed local Fascist leader Temistocle Testa to visit the recently completed Modena *Casa del Fascio* Party house. On the spur of the moment, someone suggested that they send a celebratory telegram to the chairman of the Italian Olympic Committee, Leandro Arpinati, and to the head of Alfa Romeo operations, Prospero Gianferrari, both high-ranking regime officials.[14] Party hysteria and mass hypocrisy had become a widespread syndrome by 1930 and Enzo could not but play along.

Despite all the regime-imposed rhetoric, this Saturday-night dinner in Modena was a special evening for 32-year-old Enzo, something much more meaningful than the mere celebration of a year's work. It was the realization of a vision – a personal victory. In many ways, it was a private vindication. A town that had called him 'mad' after the war for his blind love of speed and visceral attraction to cars was celebrating him. Here in his hometown, on this night, he had convened illustrious drivers and renowned engineers, top managers of some of the nation's leading manufacturing companies, and high-ranking government officials, not to mention some of the most influential reporters, in town to inform readers throughout Italy of the celebration. In the quick passing of just a few months, Enzo had become the sole symbol of the Scuderia bearing his name. The Caniato brothers still held the majority of the stakes, and Tadini, too, was holding on to his share. But nobody had been fooled by the legal structure of the company. Everyone knew by now what they had guessed all along: there was one undisputed leader at Scuderia Ferrari. Enzo was king. Enzo must have chuckled if he remembered, as he probably did, the story *Il Littoriale* had run in October the previous year, when the news had first broken about the new racing team in the making. That day the reporter, drawing from the places of origin of the three men behind it, had labelled the new racing team a '*modenese-bolognese-ferrarese* Scuderia'.[15]

For Enzo, on this November night in Modena, there were drivers to compliment and victories to celebrate. There were happy customers to woo and contracts to renew. There were sponsors to court and partners to flatter. There were 50 attendees in all.[16] Enzo sat at the head table with the mayor of Modena and the top pair of political guests: Console Testa and Senator Vicini, who had come all the way from Rome. At the same table sat two of Enzo's Scuderia partners, Alfredo Caniato and Ferruccio Testi, the latter responsible for the logistics of the evening.[17]

Drivers Giuseppe Campari, Tazio Nuvolari and Luigi Arcangeli were the centre of attention – with Campari at one point performing, as he often did on similar occasions, a few opera arias. Vittorio Jano and Luigi Bazzi, the technical geniuses of Alfa Romeo, were also there, along with the bosses of Pirelli, Bosch, Shell and Alfa Romeo itself.[18] There were speeches and toasts and prizes given to the drivers and to Bazzi and Jano.[19] And there was also a one-page pictorial recap of the 1930 season that had been prepared by Ferruccio Testi, whose camera had taken precious shots throughout that first racing season of Scuderia Ferrari. Together with Enzo, Testi had prepared and printed on the dinner menu a few dozen pictures illustrating various phases of the races and moments of relaxation before or after the events. Over the pictures Enzo had scattered logos of his commercial partners – Bosch, Shell, Champion – with Scuderia partners Alfa Romeo and Pirelli understandably receiving central attention. It was a way to thank them, but also a way to lure them to participate in the upcoming 1931 season. Never immune to the attraction represented by newspapermen, Enzo had wanted the most influential media players that covered motorsport included on the poster as well.[20]

At the conclusion of the dinner, Ferrari started yet another tradition. All seven partners of the Scuderia – Enzo included – received a pair of golden cufflinks with the Alfa Romeo logo that he had commissioned from a jeweller in Milan. The use of the prancing horse as a symbol of the Scuderia was yet to come. The gift came in a yellow-lined, dark-blue rectangular box with the words *Soc. An. Scuderia Ferrari Modena* engraved on top.[21] It was the first of a long series of end-of-season gifts that Enzo would present every autumn to those who had worked with him during the year.

From a driver's point of view, Enzo's 1930 had not been a year to remember, though his ambitions were by now clearly set on something very different. With his new tasks as the undisputed leader of Scuderia Ferrari keeping him busy, Enzo himself had entered only three races, as in the previous two seasons. He had finished only one, scoring a forgettable fifth place; in two events he had been forced to withdraw. His earnings as a driver had been insignificant, with only 15,000 lire to his credit. The top earner Achille Varzi had made over 340,000 lire, Luigi Arcangeli almost 300,000, and Tazio Nuvolari, the ace on the rise, over 200,000.[22]

By contrast, Scuderia Ferrari had paid Alfa Romeo more than 270,000 lire to buy the cars the team's drivers had used during the season, along with the necessary spare parts. The first season of the new racing team had been managed impeccably by the indefatigable Enzo and his handful of employees. The lesson learned from the failure of Carrozzeria Emilia, which was constantly in his mind, had directed all the decisions that he had made. At the end of the year Enzo could proudly say that 'the whole administration of the Scuderia is closed, with good results'.

But 1930 had also and primarily been the first year of his daring experiment at managing a racing team, and he had shown the world that the experiment could work. With the exception of Achille Varzi, that season the best Italian drivers had all at one point or another raced under the insignia of Scuderia Ferrari. Of the 22 races entered in 1930, Scuderia Ferrari drivers had won 9. There were five second-place finishes and seven class victories. In certain races toward mid-season, the Scuderia had saved the day for Alfa Romeo. At Monza in September, Enzo's team had in fact officially represented Alfa Romeo – a clear endorsement of his activity, and a prelude of things to come.

This celebratory evening for Enzo was a night to remember.

The Prancing Horse

Enzo Ferrari confirmed for the new 1931 season the dual activity that his Scuderia had successfully carried out the previous year. On the one side he would continue to provide cars and assistance to those gentleman drivers who were, at least theoretically, the justification for the existence of Scuderia Ferrari. On the other, he would go on fielding a strong team made up of the best drivers on the scene, to keep up with, or replace when needed, the Alfa Romeo works team.[1] Neither amateurs nor professional drivers would receive a fixed salary, but they would get a percentage of the prize and race money, the percentage varying according to the drivers and the events attended.[2] Of course, any private motorist who wanted to enjoy the thrill of speed and was able to meet the necessary costs could find in Ferrari and in his Scuderia a reliable means to exercise their passion for motorsport.[3]

Still uncertain of the performance level of the new car, but also aware that they could not miss the Mille Miglia, just like the previous September the Alfa Romeo management entrusted their brand-new cars to Scuderia Ferrari to officially represent them in the most famous of all Italian races.

On 11 April Enzo Ferrari lined up in Brescia under the yellow and blue colours of his Scuderia two Alfa Romeo-owned 8Cs for Nuvolari/Guidotti and Arcangeli/Bonini.[4] Scuderia Ferrari also fielded eight other cars of her own: two 1500SSs for the Caniato brothers, and six 1750GSs for Campari, Klinger, Scarfiotti, Tadini, Severi and Borzacchini.

Achille Varzi's 5.0-litre Bugatti failed the valiant driver from Galliate after only 12km (7 miles). But the other likely winner – Rudolf Caracciola, in the supercharged Mercedes SSK – dominated the race from start to finish. Nuvolari did what he could until just after mid-race and the Rome checkpoint. Then he lost time due to a number of technical problems and ten tyre changes, for an anonymous ninth-place finish.[5] Arcangeli, in the other 8C, persisted until his tyres deserted him, too. Despite a brilliant performance, driving a 1750, Campari could do no better than second place, a whole eleven minutes behind Caracciola.

If the 8C had shown its expected limits, Scuderia Ferrari had saved Alfa Romeo's honour by scoring two class victories, with Campari (1750cc) and Alfredo Caniato (1500cc). These feats did not bring the glamour of an overall victory, of course, but Scuderia Ferrari had once again fulfilled its task: the team gained valuable in-the-field experience for Alfa Romeo, while at the same time bringing home the best possible result.

The team's 1931 season had actually started two months earlier, on 15 February, when Tazio Nuvolari had won the Verona–Bosco Chiesanuova in a 1500 GS. The Sunday after the Mille Miglia, on 19 April, the Scuderia took the start of the Monaco Grand Prix with a single car for 30-year-old Goffredo Zehender, a Calabria gentleman driver not without talent who finished 5th.

Another week, and the season gathered momentum. The first race of the Italian Championship was at the Bordino Circuit in Alessandria. Maserati and Alfa Romeo looked at this race with both anticipation and concern. The Maserati brothers' racing team seemed to have lost the energy of the previous season. Alfa Romeo was struggling to find a new dimension. In the middle was Scuderia Ferrari, which decided to field five cars, including an 8C for Nuvolari, once again sent to Alessandria to gain experience with the car, which clearly was not yet in its final version.[6] It was a prototype on which Ferrari's own men in Modena had worked after the car had been delivered from Alfa Romeo.[7] The Flying Mantuan did not finish the race. Tadini, in a 1750 GS, suffered the same fate. With the other 1750 GSs Arcangeli and Boschi finished in fifth and tenth places. At the wheel of a 1500 SS, Alfredo Caniato placed ninth overall. The Maseratis did just as poorly. The winners were Varzi and Bugatti. Alfa Romeo trudged. Scuderia Ferrari did what it could.

Then at Monza on 24 May, the day of the Italian Grand Prix (as an exception, held in the spring this year), things started to change – at least for Alfa Romeo. That day the 8C Monza, the new Grand Prix model designed by Jano, made its debut. The race had a gruelling ten-hour duration, and drivers worked in pairs, taking turns at the wheel. Campari and Nuvolari finished first, Minoia and Borzacchini second.

Scuderia Ferrari had sat out the race this time. Enzo went to Monza as a spectator and watched helplessly as an accident took the life of one of his drivers, friend Luigi Arcangeli, who crashed in the same place where Ugo Sivocci had died eight years earlier. He was at the wheel of Jano's new Alfa Romeo Type A, with two 1750cc engines mounted side by side, in parallel.

In June Ferrari fielded Scuderia cars in four different races. The result was three wins, including one scored by Ferrari himself in the Bobbio–Penice hillclimb at the wheel of an 8C 2300. It was Sunday, 14 June, the first time this season that Enzo had taken part in a race in the role of racing driver, from which he was gradually distancing himself. But his form had remained intact.

To be sure, the Bobbio–Penice was a minor race, and the only prominent name was his. But Enzo's performance was flawless, as one would expect from a businessman who had once been one of the best drivers of his generation, and still loved to race from time to time. At any rate the press, which had always supported him, praised the 'skilled' way he handled his 8C, adding: 'The crowd that thronged the last corners of the climb praised the style of the Old Guard driver.'[8]

In minor races the power of Scuderia Ferrari in terms of organization, quality of cars and racing drivers was unrivalled in Italy. What at the time was still missing, and what Enzo longed for, was the possibility of fighting on equal terms with the big teams of Maserati, Bugatti and Mercedes in the grand prix category – a chance that would come his way sooner than Enzo realized.

Alfa Romeo had so far this year directly managed participation in grand prix events held with the ten-hour distance and valid for the European Championship title – Italy, France and Belgium, the latter held on 12 July. The following week, the only Alfa Romeo entered in the German Grand Prix was entrusted to Scuderia Ferrari. The car was of course an 8C Monza, and the driver, Tazio Nuvolari.

Nuvolari finished fourth, paying duty also to the choice of tyre supplier operated by Alfa Romeo – German manufacturer Continental, selected for clear commercial reasons with an eye toward the German car market.[9] For Scuderia Ferrari, despite the podium miss, the final result was more than acceptable.

All major European drivers showed up for the Coppa Ciano, with the exception of the Germans who, that same Sunday, were competing at Berlin's Avus. The prize money was lavish, with a cheque for 100,000 lire just for the winner. Nuvolari had initially entered the German race, but was later convinced by Ferrari to take the start of the race in Livorno instead. A crowd of a hundred thousand excited Italians witnessed this latest chapter in the ongoing duel between Nuvolari and Varzi – a duel that came to an early stop, however, when, on the third of ten laps, Varzi returned to the pits with a flat tyre. At the end of the 2 hours and 20 minutes of the event, Nuvolari took an important win for himself, for Alfa Romeo and for Scuderia Ferrari, which also placed Campari fourth, Cortese sixth, D'Ippolito seventh and Carraroli tenth, with another 1750 GS – that same Guglielmo Carraroli who a decade earlier had been race mechanic for Enzo Ferrari.

The week after Livorno, Enzo Ferrari participated in his last race as a racing driver. For several days – since June, to be precise – he had known that the following winter he would become a father. Laura had told him in her usual abrupt manner: 'Ferrari, you will be a father', she had told him one evening, presenting him with 'a fait accompli'.[10] They had known each other for 12 years, had lived together for 10 and had been married for 8. Because of Laura's illness, the subject of children had not really been brought up for years, to the point where, in 1931, Enzo had effectively dismissed the idea of becoming a father from his mind.

Perhaps he had come to terms with something he thought inevitable, believing that with a wife like Laura, children would never come, and maybe that was for the best. Years later he would write that 'a man dominated by a passion like mine, with the risks, with the time it requires, cannot be a good husband and, [above all], a good father'.[11] True. But it sounds very much like a rational justification typical of the older Ferrari, the man who looked back at his human journey and tried to give it an order that it often did not possess.

The tragic fate of Sivocci and Ascari, who had died leaving young children behind, must also have been a big deterrent. 'Maybe subconsciously I was fighting off this idea' – he would say years later – 'because I had assessed, through the experience of others, the enormous responsibility of giving birth to a creature and bringing him up: a responsibility that frightened me, as I was absorbed by my passion and my work.'[12]

But the fact remains that, in the back of his mind, the idea of one day becoming a father had never abandoned him. This was natural – so much so that he had for some time concluded that, if one day 'I should have a son, I would stop driving racing cars, and turn [solely] to organizational and commercial matters'.[13]

At any rate, on 9 August, Ferrari took the start of the Circuit of the Three Provinces, his second race of the 1931 season. The first had been little more than a walk. Today the competition was tough, and included the familiar faces of Tazio Nuvolari and Baconin Borzacchini – first-rate competition from inside Scuderia Ferrari. The Scuderia fielded four cars: two eight-cylinders for Ferrari and Borzacchini, and two six-cylinders for Nuvolari and Klinger. It was going to be a real fight. Ferrari was driving a more-powerful car, but Nuvolari had by now become the driver whom generations of fans would dream of for decades.

The race started at 4.30pm. Ferrari and Borzacchini, in more-powerful cars, were the first to dash off. While Nuvolari was patiently waiting for his turn, with Peppino Verdelli at his side Ferrari launched into the attack. His lead over the second – Nuvolari, of course – was thirty seconds at the first checkpoint. Then it narrowed to 14 seconds. In Sestola, in the heart of the Apennines, Nuvolari took the lead from Ferrari with half a minute over him. But the next checkpoint showed that Ferrari had halved his deficit.

Having crossed the finish line with the day's fastest time, and unaware of the time Nuvolari, still on the course, was setting kilometre after kilometre, Enzo patiently sat waiting for the arrival of all remaining participants. When the news came that Borzacchini had withdrawn, Enzo knew that the only real contender left was the unpredictable Nuvolari, in a less-powerful car than his. Despite Tazio's revolutionary driving style, Ferrari was reasonably sure that victory was within his reach. A big surprise and an even bigger disappointment awaited him.

Nuvolari set the race's fastest time, at 1 hour, 58 minutes and 46 seconds. He beat Enzo by 32.9 seconds – nothing on a race 128km (80 miles) long. Decimo Compagnoni, the mechanic aboard Nuvolari's car, later revealed that when Tazio crossed the finish line, Ferrari was stunned; he kept staring at the chronometer as if he could not believe his eyes.[14]

Nuvolari's driving style, impetuous and disrespectful of the laws of physics, had made all the difference and had prevailed over Ferrari's own style, unruffled and very respectful of the car. But the whole race had centred on their running around each other. And if it is true that Nuvolari won driving a less-powerful car, at the end of the race the winner genuinely and sincerely praised the runner-up. 'In order to beat you,' Tazio told Enzo that afternoon, 'I had to work [harder than I've ever] done before.'[15]

In the middle of the summer, as always, the motoring season reached its zenith.

On 16 August, Ferrari went to Pescara for the Coppa Acerbo. He had been asked to officially represent Alfa Romeo, for which he was entrusted with two Type As for Nuvolari and Campari. To them Ferrari added two of his own 8C 2300s for Borzacchini and Severi.[16] Bugatti fielded cars for Varzi and Chiron, Maserati, for Fagioli and Ernesto Maserati.

Campari dominated the early stages of the race. Then the lead passed to Nuvolari, but when he was forced to slow down when the gasket on the head of one of his two engines burned, Campari retook first place, which he kept all the way to the chequered flag. Slowed down by tyre problems, most of the Maseratis and Bugattis were never in the heat of the race. Despite the time lost, Nuvolari finished third. Between the two Alfa Romeos came Chiron's Bugatti.

The day's surprise was thus the Alfa Romeo Type A, with its first win after a long and troubled development. Not the fastest on the long straights, the Type A proved unbeatable in the mixed section of the circuit. Above all, it proved to be the most balanced car, the only one without serious tyre problems – Dunlops this time, the same for all entrants.[17] Once again, Scuderia Ferrari had served Alfa Romeo well, securing valuable experience and a prestigious win.

Later that month, the Alfa Romeo management decided to participate in the Monza Grand Prix of early September with their works team. Ferrari once again went to the Autodromo Nazionale as a spectator. Meanwhile, back in Modena, his men were at work preparing for the remaining races of the season.

Scuderia Ferrari won three of the remaining four races of the season and took a second and a third place in the last, the Coppa Pierazzi, held on 28 October. This last event saw the Scuderia debut for Baroness Maria Teresa Avanzo, the first woman ever to race a car for Ferrari.

Enzo's work did not end with the last race of the season. The autumn months were devoted to the courtship of new sponsors, to the flattering of old ones and to tests of cars and materials. Among the new partner companies that would from now on be at the Scuderia's side was a carburettor factory located in Bologna, founded and chaired by Edoardo Weber,[18] who would in time become one of Enzo's most trusted friends.[19] As always, Ferrari's days began early, ended late in the evening and included long car trips during which he would never give up the steering wheel to anyone else.

In early November Alfa Romeo announced their intention for 1932 to be present in a direct form more frequently than in the previous season. Nuvolari and Borzacchini therefore communicated to Ferrari that in the new season they would drive fewer races for his Scuderia. Given these arrangements, Canestrini commented in his daily sports newspaper: 'We do not precisely know Enzo Ferrari's programme, but we believe that he will exclusively devote himself to young talents and gentleman drivers.'[20]

But the 1932 season, like the one that had just ended, would be a long one. And Enzo Ferrari knew that a car manufacturer such as Alfa Romeo, despite its announcements to the press, could only participate in a handful of races. For the others, it would inevitably have to defer to his Scuderia, as in 1930 and especially in 1931.

Meanwhile, the time came once again for the end-of-year gala dinner, the event that had charmed all of the guests on its premier the previous year. Ferrari changed the restaurant, but not the street, the central Via San Carlo in the very heart of Modena.

They all gathered on the evening of Saturday 21 November 1931 for a 'huge and noisy banquet'[21] in the 'magnificent halls of the Boninsegna restaurant'.[22] On the invitation and menu the Alfa Romeo emblem was duly printed. Scuderia Ferrari provided this celebratory dinner 'for her drivers and associates'. *Associates* was the word that henceforth in Enzo Ferrari's lexicon would indicate those who, inside or outside the Scuderia, worked for the team's success.

To all the drivers who had raced with his cars during the season, Ferrari gave a gold chain with an enamelled plaque on which he had had the name of each engraved. Always respectful of hierarchy, he gave Alfa Romeo mechanics a pair of gold cufflinks, while Scuderia Ferrari's received silver ones. To his boys, however, he also gave a bonus cheque,[23] his way of thanking them for their commitment, proficiency and passion. By now a skilled diplomat, he asked Senator Vicini to present the awards to his employees.[24]

Ferrari himself was given two prizes. The first came from Alfa Romeo managing director Prospero Gianferrari who, on behalf of the company, presented him with the knighthood that he had been granted by a recent decree of the state for his activity. The second was handed to him by Nuvolari: a 'magnificent parchment inscribed and signed by all the drivers of the Scuderia for the work done and as an affectionate act of gratitude'.[25]

But there was more. Ferrari had a last gift, which he distributed to all present – at least one hundred and fifty guests,[26] including cycling ace Costante Girardengo.[27] With the help and advice of Ferruccio Testi, he had prepared an 'interesting booklet'[28] 80 pages long titled *Two Years of Racing*. It was a summary of the season that had just ended and, much more briefly, of the one before. This was the logical continuation of the photographic project born in the form of a menu for the convivial dinner in November 1930. Although it was not so identified then, it was the first yearbook, one of the dearest of all Ferrari traditions.

'This humble publication,' Ferrari explained in the preface, 'in addition to reporting the influential opinions of the heads of sports, politics and industry, who have wanted to honour us with their benevolent judgement, wants to make known to organizers, drivers and manufacturers, what our activity in these first two years of life has been.'[29] Indeed, as the habit of the time required, the first pages of the brochure were reserved for the congratulatory messages of Italian VIPs, first of all the head of the government, who, while he did not dedicate it expressly to Ferrari or his Scuderia, as others did on those same pages, had, at the request of Ferrari,[30] sent a photograph of himself behind the steering wheel of an Alfa Romeo, on which the Duce had penned in his own hand: 'Benito Mussolini – Rome, October 1931 – IX'.[31]

But once the extended tribute to Italian institutions and the sports, automotive and press worlds came to an end, the publication provided what Ferrari had promised in the first pages – the account of what Scuderia Ferrari had done in its first two years of existence. Portraits of the drivers were included, his only after Nuvolari's, along with photographs of numerous Alfa Romeo models in action, images from race courses and the names and logos of Alfa Romeo and Ferrari suppliers. And, of course, the full list of events in which the Scuderia had participated: 22 in 1930 and 23 in 1931.

All of the inside pages were framed by yellow and blue patterns – that is, the colours of Modena and Scuderia Ferrari: 'Yellow and blue are our colours,' wrote Ferrari, 'the Visconti family serpent, the brand of our red machines, white-red-green the heart of our drivers.'[32]

The most telling page, however, was the first one, in which Enzo Ferrari briefly reviewed his racing life and identified the man who had inspired him when he created the Scuderia that now bore his name: Antonio Ascari. 'Inexorable fate portended his death when the most deserved fame consecrated him champion among champions, but as the memory of his deeds remained and will remain immortal, so the sacrifice he made for Italian motorsport's honour in a foreign land was not to be forgotten. It was then that in my mind took shape the idea of creating a Scuderia: an idea that only three years later I could translate into reality.'[33]

Ascari's legacy, what Ferrari identified as 'the spiritual heritage of the *Maestro*', then, was the force behind the Scuderia, 'which wants to be the school of audacity and gymnasium of boldness for young talents; a judicious organization for the champions.'[34]

Ferrari had all the reason in the world to be happy.

In only two years his efforts had taken him very far. 'In motorsport,' wrote Filippini in those days, 'rare are the examples of such quick and steady growth.' He added: 'Scuderia Ferrari has established a role for itself. It is the best-suited technical, sporting, promotional and commercial organization.'[35]

Filippini was a friend of Ferrari's, but also a shrewd and careful observer, who thus continued: 'Those who follow motorsport recall the memorable days of Scuderia Ferrari, the days, that is, when cars and drivers of the Modena team played a leading role in Italy and abroad. The days of Monza 1930, of Pescara and Brno 1931, in which, beyond the result, appeared in its full extent the power and the flawless organization of Scuderia Ferrari, now famous in the homeland and appreciated and requested outside the borders.'[36]

Vincenzo Florio, the legendary Sicilian aristocrat who had always exerted a magnetic influence on Ferrari, recognized Enzo's merit of having revived with his work 'the interest in motorsport' and pushed 'technical progress'.[37]

And then there was always Ferrari, the racing driver, who continued to be appreciated despite his deliberately limited activity.

'Enzo Ferrari,' wrote *Auto Italiana*, 'was and still is a true champion and a motorsport artist. People think of him as an old man because he has been around since the days when his chin still grew no beard, and now that he is 33 and has a prosperous belly that no trouser belt can reduce in appearance or proportions, there are those who, by looking at him, would not give him the merest of chances. Belly or not, however, Ferrari, whose business activity does not allow him to line up at the start of more than two or three events a year, still wins his share of races.'[38]

If the respect for Enzo the driver was unchanged, Ferrari was also enjoying the reputation of an excellent businessman. 'When he raced assiduously,' *Auto Italiana* went on, 'he ended up earning good money; now that he races less, he still makes money,' concluding, 'Lucky, then? Skilled, rather, and balanced and a tactician and shrewd and energetic all at the same time . . . a man who knows what he wants, a real organizer; a practical value increaser of his abilities; a champion who never goes off the road, as [one who goes] off the road never ends up the manager and the businessman.'[39]

Not a bad profile for someone who had left Modena at a very young age, and who many in town still remembered as 'the crazy Ferrari', a young man 'ruthless when behind the steering wheel of a car, and who did not want to do anything in life except drive his automobile'.[40]

*   *   *

The year 1932 dawned in the Ferrari household with the happiest of events. On 19 January, at 3.25pm, a baby boy was born on the first floor of 11 Viale Ciro Menotti, where Scuderia Ferrari had been headquartered for more than two years. Enzo gave his son his father's and brother's name – Alfredo. Like his uncle before him, everyone would always call him Dino.

The birth of the baby convinced Ferrari to make a decision that he had been pondering since the previous summer, when Laura had told him that he would become a father. His analysis was simple: 'My son could count on a modest comfort, fruit of my complex activity. But my son had a right to expect even more from me.'[41] Specifically: a father who lived to be at his side as he grew up. The deaths of Ascari and Sivocci, as well as those of other drivers he had seen fall over the years, had never left him.

By now the race prize money represented only the crumbs of his revenue. In addition to being the fulcrum, the CEO and one of the shareholders of the Scuderia that bore his name, Ferrari was also the Alfa Romeo agent for Emilia, Romagna and Marche; he also had consulting contracts with Alfa Romeo, Pirelli and Nafta – the Italian oil company.[42] Even if he was not wealthy, he was definitely comfortable. He had long known he would never be a champion and, in any case, the age at which one would aspire to be a champion had passed. He still enjoyed racing every now and then, but clearly his interests now lay elsewhere.

Thus the decision: the Circuit of the Three Provinces of the previous August had been his last race, the exciting head-to-head with Nuvolari, his last duel. From now on, Enzo Ferrari was going to be just a businessman, and, more and more, a 'mover of men and ideas'. Just in case, however, he renewed his racing licence for one more year, number 16 in Italy.[43]

But there was more. After the birth of his first child and the decision to stop racing came a change in the company structure of Scuderia Ferrari. Scuderia president Alfredo Caniato had resigned. In just two seasons, Scuderia Ferrari had become a very different organization from the one that had been presented in 1929. The organization's motto remained the same – 'for participating in car races in Italy and abroad with Alfa Romeo cars'[44] – but the ever more professional side of the operation was now evident to all.

And nobody was more aware of the change than those gentlemen drivers who were among the founding members of the Scuderia, those people Enzo Ferrari had relied on two years earlier for financial stability, but who now clearly felt out of place racing elbow to elbow with the likes of Nuvolari, Campari and Borzacchini, or when their team was called to officially represent Alfa Romeo, something that occurred more and more frequently. Mario Tadini was already gone. Now it was time for the Caniatos to leave.[45]

Ferrari did not lose his composure. He offered all the shares of the Caniato brothers – 130,000 lire, representing 65 per cent of the total – to a talented gentleman driver from Biella. Count Carlo Felice Trossi bought out the Caniatos and replaced Alfredo as chairman of Scuderia Ferrari. He paid for his shares through Banco Sella, the family bank.[46] Alfredo Caniato remained as a member of the board, together with Marquis Antonio Brivio Sforza, Gino Malagoli and Ferruccio Testi. Enzo Ferrari was formally confirmed as chief executive officer, with increasingly plenipotentiary powers and ambitions more and more distant from the original declared purposes of Scuderia Ferrari.[47]

Enzo Ferrari had never had a personal interest in motorcycles, but he had always observed that world with great curiosity. Looking at Nuvolari, who had been a champion on two wheels before he became one on four, he believed the move from bikes to cars was possible. At the end of the previous season he had welcomed with enthusiasm into the ranks of his drivers one of the best bikers in Italy – Piero Taruffi, who with a Scuderia Ferrari Alfa Romeo 8C 2.3 MM had won, the last Sunday in September, the Coppa Frigo in Bolsena.

Ferrari had been watching Taruffi closely for some time and, in the autumn, to have him race with the Scuderia, had offered him a choice between an Alfa Romeo 1750 and a 2300.[48] Now, won over by Taruffi's enthusiasm for bike races and, of course, seeing his own advantage from an economic point of view, he decided to open a motorcycle department in Scuderia Ferrari, for which he would make use of bikes built by British manufacturer Rudge. The bike department shared the same space in the Viale Ciro Menotti workshop that had been home to Scuderia Ferrari since 1930.

That spring and again in the summer, Ferrari renovated part of the building. First he built a portico on the front, which at the same time became the wide terrace of his first-floor apartment. Then he asked permission to add an extra floor to the building, which allowed him to make two more bedrooms and an atrium for his apartment. Finally he embellished the facade overlooking Viale Ciro Menotti in the art nouveau style of the original, even if the design of the metal railing on the new terrace betrayed his desire for modernity because of its great simplicity.

The Scuderia motorcycle department made its debut with a win on 28 March. Guglielmo Sandri placed first overall on a Rudge in the Modena Grand Prix Primavera. On 3 April Eugenio Siena, with an Alfa Romeo 8C Monza 2.3, recorded a far from memorable fourth place in the Grand Prix of Tunis. But the mind of Ferrari, like the mind of all Italians, was on the sixth Mille Miglia, scheduled for the weekend of 9 and 10 April.

Alfa Romeo entered three 8C 2300s for Nuvolari, Borzacchini and Campari. The Alfa works team would also lend direct assistance to a fourth 8C 2300 driven by German Rudolf Caracciola. Against this impressive array of forces, Ferrari fielded five identical cars, entrusted to less-talented and -experienced drivers. The entry from Scuderia Ferrari was completed by a supercharged British-made Austin Seven, though the car did not start the race.[49]

The 1932 Mille Miglia was won by Borzacchini in the works Alfa Romeo. The Milan manufacturer placed seven cars in the first seven places, eleven in the first twelve. Although it missed first place, Scuderia Ferrari did not do badly. At the wheel of an 8C, Carlo Felice Trossi and Tonino Brivio finished second overall, first in the gentlemen's category, which, in a country where foreign words were less and less used for political reasons, had been renamed 'non-experts'. Luigi Scarfiotti and Guido D'Ippolito scored an equally valuable third place overall, first in their category (2000cc) at the wheel of a 1750 SS TF.

As Enzo had anticipated, Alfa Romeo was forced to choose the events in which it would compete directly. Having won the Mille Miglia and waiting now for the big international races, Alfa stayed out of the Targa Florio, where it was naturally represented by Scuderia Ferrari and Alfa's two best drivers – Nuvolari and Borzacchini. Ferrari gave the aces two of his 8C Monza 2.3 models. He gave the other two to Pietro Ghersi and Tonino Brivio. To Marquis D'Ippolito, he gave a 1750.

Nuvolari clinched an easy win; Borzacchini came in second. For Varzi and Chiron in Bugattis, and for all the Maseratis, the 1932 Targa Florio was a total debacle. For Ferrari it was the first victory in the Sicilian classic, a race which for him, having participated and performed well in it as a driver, maintained a special importance.

As spring wore on Scuderia Ferrari collected an uninterrupted string of victories in minor races. On weekends when the automobile department was resting, Ferrari followed the activity of the motorcycle department. The Scuderia was also dominating bike races: first place with Taruffi in the European Grand Prix in Rome, first place with Mario Ghersi at Circuito Pietro Bordino in Alessandria, first place with Guglielmo Sandri in Bologna, first in Verona, Ferrara, Lugo di Romagna and Faenza.

In mid-June Alfa Romeo won the 24 Hours of Le Mans.

Not intending to participate in the 24 Hours of Spa, scheduled for 9 and 10 July, Alfa Romeo delegated Scuderia Ferrari to represent them. Thirty-three cars entered the exhausting race. The participants may not have been first-class, as at Le Mans, but the field was filled with audacious and motivated competitors.

The Alfa Romeo 8C 2300 that had won in France was naturally the great favourite in Belgium. Two were entrusted to the pairs of Brivio and Siena, and Taruffi (who alternated as a driver and a biker for the Scuderia) and Marquis D'Ippolito. They finished in this order, a great triumph for the Italian automotive industry, for Alfa Romeo and, of course, for Scuderia Ferrari.

At Spa the prancing horse that Francesco Baracca's mother had given Enzo in 1924 made its first appearance on Ferrari's cars. 'It will bring you luck,' Countess Paolina had said that day. Enzo had accepted the unexpected gift, wondering if he would ever find a use for it.

Why Ferrari decided to adopt the prancing horse after eight years is not entirely clear. Certainly, it distinguished his cars from the works units entered by Alfa Romeo, which were identified by the four-leaf clover that Sivocci had conceived for the 1923 Targa Florio, an emblem that Alfa Corse drivers had voluntarily continued to use to commemorate their late teammate and, later, Alfa Romeo adopted as a symbol of her racing department.

But why now?

Ferrari had always been a loyal and faithful partner of Alfa Romeo, always staying wisely in the background – letterhead, invitations, communications, publications of Scuderia Ferrari had always given great prominence to the Alfa Romeo logo. But something had changed in the relationship, never equal, with Alfa Romeo. This year the Milan-based company called on Ferrari to represent them with less frequency than in the previous season, and Enzo was clearly not enjoying nurturing young talents while the Alfa works team triumphed in international events.

Ferrari had simply reached a point where he had become aware of his own strength and had decided to start distancing himself from the parent company. And although the car debut took place at Spa, the prancing horse had first adorned a Scuderia vehicle – a bike – 6 days before the Spa 24 Hours, on 3 July, in Pontedera.

Whatever the reasons, in July 1932 Enzo Ferrari finally adopted the great gift of Earl and Lady Baracca. The prancing horse that the countess had given him in 1924 was black, and black it remained – although it is likely that Baracca's horse was originally red, and had become black as a sign of mourning after the death of the hero. The Royal Piedmont Cavalry had as its symbol a white prancing horse – silver when painted – on a red field. For some reason, perhaps because it was more visible and recognizable when he was flying, it is probable that Baracca had reversed the colour scheme, painting the horse red.[50]

Inspired by the example set by Sivocci, who had placed the green four-leaf clover in a white diamond, Ferrari placed the horse against a yellow shield – yellow being one of the two colours of the city of Modena. Above the shield he placed the three colours of the Italian flag, a chromatic touch that spoke volumes about his ambitions.[51]

* * *

While Alfa Romeo scored the most important international wins with the new P3, Ferrari picked up what was left with the 8C. Naturally he yearned to put his hands on a P3, and the chance came on 14 August at the Coppa Acerbo. Ferrari entrusted it to Nuvolari on a day when Alfa Romeo fielded a similar works unit for Caracciola, the debonair German racer the Portello management liked so much. After Caracciola's initial outburst, Nuvolari took the lead and went on undisturbed until the chequered flag. For Ferrari a win at Pescara always held a special meaning.

The Masaryk Cup at Brno was the last significant race in which Scuderia Ferrari took part in 1932. In a season when Alfa Romeo had managed to win all the major races, Ferrari had to content himself with the opportunities he had been offered. The same was true of the use of professional drivers, too often directly employed by Alfa Corse and free to race for Ferrari only on rare occasions.

Despite these annoyances, Scuderia Ferrari had become increasingly popular with fans and motor-racing pros. In addition to responding every time Alfa Romeo called upon them, the Scuderia had become the launching pad for many young

Italian drivers. Trossi, Brivio and Taruffi were the new names on everyone's lips. And if Trossi – rich, elegant and detached – lived in a dimension apart, Brivio and Taruffi fought with no holds barred to become the Scuderia's top driver.[52] Ferrari, who had grown up at the school of Ascari, Campari and Sivocci, a school in which it was difficult to win space, and where every conquest had demanded a great deal of sweat, let his young talents fight it out, convinced, as he always would be, that healthy internal competition would benefit everyone involved and, naturally, his Scuderia.[53]

Over everything and everyone reigned Enzo Ferrari. At 34 he was finally fully aware of his personal and considerable sporting, commercial and managerial skills. For young drivers he was a fantasy, for the older, an example and a reference point. For race organizers he was an assurance. For motor-racing fans, now including bike fans, a benefactor. For Alfa Romeo, a reliable collaborator. For institutions, an instrument of promotion matched by few.

The year 1932 had not been the best one for his Scuderia, but the ambivalent attitude of Alfa Romeo had had the undeniable merit of opening his eyes. Alfa Romeo would always occupy a special place in his heart, and in his business, but from now on the romanticism in his relationship with the company would be confined to the faded memories of Antonio Ascari and Giorgio Rimini. At Portello the music had changed. Ferrari, a pragmatist by nature, took notice and adjusted. Therefore in the autumn, after the season had ended and in the absence of an official statement by Alfa Romeo, he anticipated everyone by announcing that he had plans to expand the activity of his Scuderia in 1933. In mid-November he stated that he was considering the purchase of one or two Duesenberg eight-cylinder models, the car that ruled at Indianapolis, the never-forgotten race of his youth. His declared aim was to use American cars 'in high-speed events'.[54]

Naturally enough this was primarily a message addressed to Alfa Romeo, which in 1932 had at first denied him, then made him crave, the use of the new P3. Not knowing what decisions Alfa Romeo would eventually make for the upcoming season, Ferrari wanted to ensure that he looked sufficiently independent. Alfa Romeo remained central to his business, but it was no longer the only technical partner, at least in public statements.

So no one was surprised when, on Saturday evening, 19 November, at the Boninsegna restaurant in Modena, at the end of the 'famous annual banquet of Scuderia Ferrari',[55] the new yearbook distributed to all of the guests looked somewhat revolutionary. On a cover dominated by the yellow and blue colours of Modena – this itself a clear message – the prancing horse that had belonged to Baracca was framed in the three colours of the Italian flag.

Scuderia Ferrari was shouting her independence. With 50 races contested in Italy and outside the national borders – 30 with cars and 20 with bikes, the latter all in Italy – with her 26 overall victories, her 25 car drivers and 11 riders,[56] it could aspire to an independent role in motorsport. The caution that until recently had dictated all of Ferrari's moves had been set aside. The Alfa Romeo emblem was there, too, to be sure, but only on the back cover.

Enzo Ferrari was *becoming* Ferrari.

Tazio and I

'Through the severe scrutiny of competition,' wrote Enzo Ferrari at the end of 1932, 'we were able to evaluate and train in difficult situations a considerable number of young drivers, so that today we are certain of having created, if not authentic "aces", solid "reserves" who are now more than just "promising".'[1] He was speaking of Antonio Brivio, Carlo Felice Trossi and Piero Taruffi – those young drivers whom his Scuderia, not having the chance to employ the great champions when Alfa Romeo was fielding them directly, had inevitably used in the course of the previous racing season. These were talented young people who had been given the opportunity to grow and make a name for themselves within the ranks of Scuderia Ferrari. It was an accurate statement, but also one that contained less pride and a lot more bitterness than the casual observer might suspect. Ferrari was genuinely interested in young drivers, if for no other reason than as a reservoir of future talent in a sport that was extremely dangerous, and where the tribute demanded by the sport in terms of lives remained high. But his main goal was to win now, not tomorrow. And to win, he knew that he needed two things: the same level of trust that Alfa Romeo had granted him in 1931; and the new P3, of which everyone continued to be annoyingly jealous at Portello.

Alfa Romeo was soon to lend a helping hand, although not in the way that Ferrari was thinking.

The news was in the air, but confirmation didn't come until early in 1933. Through the carefully crafted words of an official press release, Alfa Romeo announced its withdrawal from motorsport, for the time being. Alfa would sit out the 1933 season to prepare for 1934, when the new 750kg (1,653lb) weight formula would be implemented. At least, that's what Alfa Romeo's management was saying in private.[2] Italy's economic situation had also strongly influenced their decision. Financial preoccupations prevailed over the duty to defend Italy's honour in motorsport. Doing so from now on would be up to Enzo Ferrari and his Scuderia.

Alfa Romeo's decision brought back to Modena the great drivers who had raced with Ferrari in 1930 and 1931, and occasionally in 1932 – Baconin Borzacchini and Tazio Nuvolari. The Flying Mantuan had reached an agreement with Ferrari on 22 January 1933,[3] and then personally persuaded a reluctant Borzacchini to join the Scuderia. Ferrari met them both at a restaurant in San Damaso, a tiny village a couple of miles from Modena, a regular location for many of his business meetings. Nuvolari, who was usually quiet, enthusiastically listed the many advantages that Scuderia Ferrari could offer them. He claimed to be linked to Enzo Ferrari by a fraternal friendship and said he was willing to swear allegiance to his Scuderia.[4] Induced by Nuvolari's words, Borzacchini signed.

Probably because they were still planning, at least at this stage, to return to motorsport in 1934 – and, in any case, reasonably certain that the 8C was still competitive against the Maseratis and Bugattis – Alfa Romeo decided not to allocate to Scuderia Ferrari (despite Enzo's insistence) the P3s that had dominated the final events of the previous season.[5]

Ferrari was consequently left on his own and forced to enhance his Scuderia's fleet by raising the 11 8Cs he owned – 6 in Monza and 5 in Sport configurations – from 2300 to 2600cc.[6] The rest of their fleet for the 1933 season was made up of two Alfa Romeo 1750 models and, rumour had it, a soon-to-be-delivered 4.5-litre Duesenberg, strongly desired by Enzo and by Count Trossi, who had recently been confirmed as chairman of Scuderia Ferrari for 1933–1934.[7]

Perhaps to irritate Alfa Romeo, which did not want to sell him the P3, or maybe just to protect himself in case the old Alfas he owned were not up to the task this year, Ferrari also placed an order in Bologna with the Maserati brothers for two 8CM models, although in the end he never bought them.[8]

At any rate, in February, Alfa Romeo gratified Enzo with the renewal of his contract as 'racing and commercial adviser'. Under this agreement, Ferrari would receive from Alfa Romeo two thousand lire each month.[9] It was no small figure – four times the average pay and twice the salary of a manager; money that he added to the rest of his earnings from the complex activities of the Scuderia that bore his name.

The 1933 season started on 26 March in Tunis. With the P3s illogically stored in a Portello warehouse, Ferrari entered two 8C Monzas for Nuvolari and Borzacchini. Ferrari had remained in Modena, while sending Siena and Compagnoni along with Nuvolari and Borzacchini to Tunisia.[10] The two Scuderia Ferrari cars dominated from start to finish – the Grand Prix of Tunisia was won by Nuvolari, with Borzacchini in second place. The first Maserati came in third.

While his drivers were winning on the Carthage circuit, Ferrari was preparing for the next event – the Mille Miglia, scheduled for the second weekend in April. Now that Alfa Romeo was on the sidelines, the responsibility of maintaining their streak of victories – four in six races – fell on Enzo's shoulders. At the same time, this responsibility implied that, for the first time, Scuderia Ferrari stood a real chance of winning the most popular of Italian races. On 8 April six Scuderia Ferrari Alfas dashed off from Brescia.

Nuvolari took the victory, with Taruffi in third place; Scuderia Ferrari failed to clinch second place, however.

After the Tunis Grand Prix and the Mille Miglia, on Sunday 23 April Ferrari had the opportunity to seize a victory at the Monaco Grand Prix, another race whose reputation was growing year after year.

Once again the only 8C with displacement increased to 2.6 litres was given to Nuvolari, who, during the 99th of 100 laps, was leading the race ahead of Varzi, in his Bugatti. But as Tazio went for the last time up to the Casino, the engine of his Alfa Romeo blew. Nuvolari quickly got out of the car and tried to push it to the finish line,[11] but it was all in vain. The day was partially saved for Scuderia Ferrari and Alfa Romeo by Borzacchini's second place. Trossi finished in fifth place, but Siena's engine had blown up, too.

Nuvolari, Brivio and Trossi finished first, second and third in the next event at the Pietro Bordino Circuit. Then they sailed for Tripoli, where the grand prix was going to be held on the new and fast Mellaha circuit – and where, for the first time, the race was linked to a million-lire lottery.

Nuvolari finished second behind Varzi's Bugatti. Borzacchini and Tadini were forced to withdraw because of mechanical failures. Despite Alfa Romeo's boasting, the 8C was no longer the formidable car it had once been. Yet, all P3s remained locked at Portello, notwithstanding Ferrari's relentless efforts – including asking Pirelli for help with the Alfa Romeo management.[12]

For once in Tripoli, the sporting side of a race took a backseat to the substantial prize money up for grabs with the *Lotteria dei Milioni,* the millionaire lottery combined with the grand prix. It was no secret that Nuvolari, Varzi and Borzacchini had agreed with each other and with the holders of the three tickets with whom they were paired in the draw to divide the prize money, regardless of which of the three won the race. In the days immediately following the grand prix there were threats of scandal and even denunciations, although the deal did not breach any rules.[13]

A few days after the race Nuvolari issued a statement asserting that Scuderia Ferrari was not involved in any agreement between the drivers and the lottery ticket holders. To make sure there was no misunderstanding, he openly stated that neither the president of the Scuderia, Carlo Felice Trossi, nor the managing director, Enzo Ferrari, knew of the agreement or had received money from the prize pool.[14]

The technical inferiority of Ferrari's current Alfa Romeos was embarrassingly exposed in all its disgrace on 21 May on the ultra-fast Avus circuit in Berlin. The deficit was in the order of 15 seconds per lap – a huge gap. Although this was still not enough to convince Alfa Romeo's management to bring the P3s out of retirement, it was sufficient to spark a rebellion inside Scuderia Ferrari.

The more experienced drivers were complaining of the little weight that Ferrari seemed to have in his dealings with the Alfa Romeo management. The younger drivers feared that the lack of competitiveness of the Scuderia's cars this year would halt their career progress and relegate them to the role of supporting actors. Well knowing their worth, Nuvolari and Borzacchini were not willing to see their opponents win with such ease – and this was particularly true for Tazio, whose career seemed to be a continuous duel with Achille Varzi. But while the young drivers feared Enzo Ferrari, the older ones, who had shared a part of their lives and careers with Ferrari, had no such problems.

It was Tazio Nuvolari who set the place on fire. The Mantuan was six years older than Ferrari and had raced against him in the past. They knew and respected each other, but Nuvolari was not afraid of Ferrari. Tazio had valued him as an opponent on race tracks, but he had simply never fully understood his role as manager of an organizational machine such as Scuderia Ferrari.

With the consent of Borzacchini, the other half of the Old Guard duo, Nuvolari asked to speak with Ferrari.[15] Their meeting was frank and painful. Nuvolari meant not only to reexamine his position within Scuderia Ferrari, but also to discuss once again the very organization of the Scuderia[16] – beginning with the name.[17] Conscious of his own fame, Nuvolari had begun to long for independence, intolerant of discipline and 'of having to report to someone who oversees his plans and his activity'.[18] He told Ferrari that the team should from now on be named nothing less than Scuderia *Nuvolari*-Ferrari. 'Rather than a financial issue,' Giovanni Canestrini remarked many years later, 'it was a matter of prestige, perhaps of impatience.'[19]

But it was also proof that Nuvolari had understood little or nothing of the role that Enzo Ferrari had carved out for himself four years earlier, always in precarious but profitable equilibrium between the changing plans of Alfa Romeo, drivers' extravagances, technical suppliers' needs, race organizers' demands, sponsors' requests and pressure from the press. And it was, unintentionally, proof that Enzo Ferrari's role was of such paramount importance as to be difficult to define and understand.

For Nuvolari, as probably for the vast majority of public opinion, Scuderia Ferrari was simply an abstract entity providing professional racers, gentleman drivers and privateers with cars manufactured by Alfa Romeo or received in use by the drivers themselves. The Flying Mantuan, like the others, did not comprehend the intangible role played by Scuderia Ferrari, an organization that bought most of the cars it entrusted to its drivers and served as an experimental racing lab for Alfa Romeo; a company that maintained a first-class team of technicians and mechanics that it deployed on race tracks and circuits in Italy and abroad; and took upon itself all the logistics of participating in a race. For Nuvolari to go to Enzo Ferrari and demand that he rename his organization Scuderia Nuvolari-Ferrari meant that he did not clearly understand the full scope of duties performed by the 35-year-old former driver from Modena and his men.

Ferrari said no to the name change, but he did agree to Nuvolari's request to enter certain races with a Maserati.

Ferrari had made a choice. To accommodate Nuvolari – the only element that he believed indispensable for the Scuderia's success – he was willing to sacrifice 13 years of loyalty to Alfa Romeo.

It would not be enough.

Nuvolari was forced to withdraw from the Grand Prix of France due to another mechanical failure, first with his 2.6 8C Monza, and then again with Taruffi's identical car, which Tazio took over to replace his original. After yet another withdrawal for the same reason at the Grand Prix of the Marne on 2 July, that evening Nuvolari met with Ernesto Maserati at the Hotel du Lion D'Or in Reims. They discussed the possibility of racing with a Maserati 8CM in the Belgian Grand Prix, the following Sunday. The next day Nuvolari, an official Scuderia Ferrari driver, signed a contract with Maserati.[20]

The car that Nuvolari intended to race at Spa was an official Maserati, 'lent and entrusted' by the Bologna company to the Mantuan.[21] The car, however, would not be entered by Officine Alfieri Maserati. Nuvolari was furious with Ferrari, but he knew perfectly well that he was contractually bound to Enzo's organization. His entry in the Belgian Grand Prix had been made by Scuderia Ferrari, and he would race as an official Scuderia Ferrari driver – but he would do it at the wheel of a Maserati.

According to the terms of the contract he had signed on 3 March with Scuderia Ferrari, Nuvolari enjoyed 'absolute autonomy' in the selection of cars that he would use in the various races.[22] Ferrari naturally had not thought then that his best driver would choose a car from outside the Scuderia's fleet. Racing with his own Maserati would in itself have been a huge exception to the rule,[23] and a clear demonstration of how eager Ferrari was to please him. Choosing a Maserati supplied directly from the Bologna company was a declaration of war on Nuvolari's part.

'It seemed certain,' motorsport reporters wrote the day after the Belgian Grand Prix, 'that Nuvolari would race with his Alfa Romeo. Instead, after again testing a Maserati yesterday, Nuvolari was finally convinced that with some modifications, this car was preferable to the Alfa Romeo.'[24] The press played down the situation; we cannot be sure whether this obfuscation was designed to please the Fascist regime, which did not tolerate disharmony even in the world of sport, or was done out of respect for the two contenders. But in any case, the public was now aware of the odd situation.

Not only had Tazio Nuvolari raced and won the Belgian Grand Prix in a Maserati 8CM owned by the Bologna team – he and Compagnoni had modified the car, despite the express wishes of Ernesto Maserati that he not do so. Entered by Scuderia Ferrari, Nuvolari's Maserati had raced without the prancing horse on the hood.[25]

Borzacchini, who had competed with the usual 8C Monza 2.6, struggled again and withdrew. Siena, with a similar car, finished fifth.

After the betrayal and victory at Spa, Nuvolari was convinced he had assumed a position of advantage in his personal war with Enzo Ferrari. But he had not reckoned on the new Ferrari, who was no longer the brilliant but docile and complacent driver he had known years ago.

Ferrari had never lied to himself. He had known all along that he did not possess the talent of Nuvolari – or of Campari and Ascari before him – and had always acknowledged his limits, even stepping diligently aside when necessary. But in his new role as head of Scuderia Ferrari, he knew he had no rivals. Therefore, there was no way that he would compromise;[26] after Spa, he made several verbal and written reprimands to Nuvolari, demanding that he adhere to the terms of his contract with the Scuderia.[27]

The situation was about to explode.

The two met a few days before the Coppa Ciano at the Alfa Romeo headquarters in Milan. By the end of the meeting, Ferrari had capitulated, agreeing that his organization would change its name to Scuderia Nuvolari-Ferrari, even if only for the following season.[28] Maybe he was trying to buy time. Perhaps, instead, he was only waiting for a *casus belli* – an event that provokes a war – which Nuvolari would soon offer him on a silver platter.

After the Milan summit had seemed to produce a truce, Nuvolari let Ferrari enter him for the 30 July Coppa Ciano in an Alfa Romeo. Instead, in late July Nuvolari had purchased from the Maserati brothers an 8CM similar to the one he had driven at Spa. He took the Maserati to Livorno, hid it, painted on the hood the same number 40 that had been painted on the Scuderia Alfa Romeo and, with the help of Compagnoni, made the same technical changes that they had performed on the other car.[29]

On practice day, Scuderia Ferrari lined up in its pit position an Alfa Romeo 8C Monza 2.6 for its best driver. Nuvolari instead appeared pushing his brand-new Maserati down that same pit lane[30] – with which he won the race. At the wheel of an 8C Monza 2.6, Brivio came in second. Borzacchini, who had to pit for yet another mechanical failure, climbed into Tadini's Alfa and finished fourth.

That night Nuvolari and Ferrari finalized their separation. Exasperated by Nuvolari's most recent victory and by his deceptions, Ferrari declared himself free from any commitment made to the Nuvolari–Borzacchini duo. The coup de grâce had been the audacity of a 'legal admonishment to comply with the contract' with which the two racers had presented Ferrari. Nuvolari and Borzacchini had given him eight days to comply. Ferrari did not wait that long, and told them to go to hell that very night.[31]

Well knowing that Nuvolari was not a driver like any others, in the course of the year Ferrari had come to grant him 'an almost absolute autonomy, especially as far as racing conduct, car choice, event participation were concerned'.[32] But he was not willing to abdicate and share with others the management of his organization. 'He could not,' as Canestrini would remark a few days later, 'reduce his authority to the point of reaching a further agreement and a new contract.'[33] Until this point, Ferrari had made the best of a bad situation. Now he was no longer willing to accept Nuvolari's impertinence.

For the moment, only those within Scuderia Ferrari knew about the separation; no facts were disclosed, no statements issued. Before making it public, which would inevitably arouse a clamour, Enzo Ferrari wanted to hold a Scuderia board meeting.[34]

He wasted no time. On Monday he went to Portello to plead his case once again.[35] This time they listened. Frightened by the loss of the best Italian racer, and perhaps feeling some responsibility for what had happened, Alfa Romeo's management finally agreed to sell Scuderia Ferrari the six P3s that had remained inactive in a Milan warehouse since the previous autumn.

Ferrari also bought the related spare parts and 'acquired' an old acquaintance – Luigi Bazzi, who in the summer of 1923 he had personally stolen from Fiat. After ten years as director of the Alfa Romeo experimental department, Bazzi would now move to Modena to take on the role of technical director of Scuderia Ferrari. Attilio Marinoni would also go to Modena, as a test driver.[36] The whole operation cost Scuderia Ferrari nearly 1.7 million lire.[37]

The Nuvolari and Scuderia Ferrari split became public the following day, Friday

4 August. In a long story, Canestrini not only reported the news but also unveiled some background details, including the reconciliation attempted by Alfa Romeo in late July and the real reason for the dispute – namely the request by the Flying Mantuan to change the name of the organization to Scuderia Nuvolari-Ferrari.[38] All Ferrari did that day was place a quick phone call to the *Gazzetta* to deny the rumour that Nuvolari, after leaving Scuderia Ferrari, had directly purchased an Alfa Romeo from the Portello factory to race against those fielded by the Scuderia.[39]

The following Monday, however, Enzo Ferrari decided to 'tell his side of the story', with a letter personally addressed to *Gazzetta dello Sport*.[40] He started with a clarification, stating that 'no administrative disagreement existed between Scuderia Ferrari and *signori* Nuvolari and Borzacchini; no issue on the division of the prize money'. And the reason, Ferrari claimed, was very clear, 'Nuvolari having signed for acceptance, also on behalf of Borzacchini on March 3, 1933, the full list of participation and prize money for the whole season.'[41] It was the lesson learned a long time before from Rimini: Ferrari not only read contracts in their entirety, but with an intention to enforce them.

Having made it clear that administrative reasons – economic, that is – were, in his opinion, only a pretext, Ferrari shifted his explanation to a more personal level. 'The cause of these disagreements,' he stated bluntly, was 'the will of Nuvolari to take absolute preeminence within Scuderia Ferrari'. But the Scuderia, Ferrari revealed, 'has decided not to consider any agreement that tied the future of the Company to the name of an ace, as brilliant as it may be'. Hence the separation, desired and sought not by Ferrari but by the two drivers, to whom 'Count Carlo Felice Trossi and I and the other Scuderia managers would not permit the enslavement of the Company'.[42]

'This,' Ferrari said, 'is the substantial dissent, which led to the departure and the repudiation of the contract by Nuvolari and Borzacchini, regardless of their written commitment.'[43] A contract, the managing director of Scuderia Ferrari insisted, which Nuvolari and Borzacchini had 'arbitrarily decided to tear apart'.[44]

Nuvolari's response was not long in coming. It too was entrusted to the pages of a sports daily, printed the following day, Tuesday 8 August 1933. Nuvolari and Borzacchini (the statement was signed by both) offered Italian motorsport fans their point of view, which was naturally opposite to Ferrari's. The contract, they argued, had not been 'torn' by them, but by Scuderia Ferrari, who had responded to their request by 'breaking all relations with us and hiring new drivers'. And of course, according to them, the reason for the dispute was 'only administrative and not of a racing nature', as stated by Ferrari. 'It is not true,' they wrote, 'that Nuvolari tried to assume an absolute preeminence in the company.'[45]

'The real truth,' Nuvolari and Borzacchini insisted, 'is that Scuderia Ferrari owes much of what it has become to us,' because 'with words one does not win any race.' The accusation was direct and merciless: while Ferrari was a master with words, they were good behind the steering wheel. But the two had more in store: 'Nobody,' they said, 'will be so naive as to believe that Scuderia Ferrari exists for the magnanimity and the liberality of some naive and fanatic breeder of racing drivers.'[46]

No one had or would ever dare so much! Only Tazio Nuvolari could call Enzo Ferrari *naive* and a *fanatic*.

The controversy would grow in intensity in the weeks to follow, until it engaged the legal representatives of both drivers and Scuderia Ferrari. In private, for the inflexibility demonstrated against him, Nuvolari would come to refer to Ferrari as an Old West 'sheriff'.[47]

But the quarrel would soon disappear from media headlines.

The Fascist regime's desire not to fuel a controversy between such prominent public figures was in all likelihood the real reason why the press stopped providing details of the split, and what followed, to Italian fans. Whatever the reasons, Enzo Ferrari – the manager of a racing team, and not the owner or CEO of a car company, such as Alfa Romeo – was now implicitly considered equal to one of the most popular sportsmen in Italy. It was not insignificant that the unspoken recognition of his organization's importance and Enzo himself had been reached in just three years.

The confrontation with the immensely popular Tazio Nuvolari made Ferrari stronger – probably not in purely sporting terms, because he had lost the services of the best racing driver of his generation, but certainly from a professional point of view, for standing up to him and not giving in to his demands.

* * *

The first week in August, even before the news of the separation from Nuvolari had become public, Ferrari had hired Luigi Fagioli and Louis Chiron, who would start to race for Scuderia Ferrari in Marseille at the end of the month. If Nuvolari had decided to compete 'as if isolated',[48] Ferrari carried on as if Tazio had never existed.[49] And in Pescara, on 15 August, Ferrari could also count on the class of one of his oldest and dearest friends – Giuseppe Campari.

At first the duel between Ferrari and Nuvolari seemed to favour the latter. On 6 August, Tazio had won the first Grand Prix of Nice with his Maserati. Fagioli, making his debut with Scuderia Ferrari, had finished only fourth. But with the next race, the much more important Coppa Acerbo in Pescara, the duel began to turn decisively in Ferrari's favour.

During the previous years, the Abruzzi motoring weekend had gained importance as the number of its races had grown. Scuderia Ferrari triumphed this year in all of them: with Fagioli in the Coppa Acerbo, Trossi in the Targa Abruzzo and Aldrighetti in the motorcycle event named the Trofeo Acerbo.[50]

The following Sunday, Scuderia Ferrari won, in France, the Grand Prix of Comminges in Saint Gaudens: Fagioli finished first with the 2.6-litre P3. But the real success for Ferrari occurred away from the race track. Nuvolari and Borzacchini, who had been scheduled to race, cancelled their participation. Without an organization like Scuderia Ferrari behind them, they had been unable to tune their Maseratis in time to send them to France, arousing the 'resentment of the organizers', who characterized 'in a rather severe way the conduct of the two Italian drivers'.[51]

The last Sunday in August Ferrari won also in Marseille: Chiron first, Fagioli second. The Monegasque Chiron, taking his first victory with Scuderia Ferrari, had alternated in the lead of the race with Nuvolari until, on lap 76 of 100, the Mantuan was forced to withdraw for a broken ball bearing.[52] Luck seemed to have turned against Nuvolari since he had left Ferrari.

August, the first month after the separation from the best driver on the scene, had therefore been a month of enormous satisfaction for Ferrari: eight races, seven wins. But the mind of Ferrari was typically already on the next race, the new clash with Nuvolari, the Italian Grand Prix on 10 September at Monza. That day there were actually going to be two separate events: the Italian Grand Prix in the morning, and the Monza Grand Prix in the afternoon. Nuvolari would take part only in the first event, but Scuderia Ferrari would compete in both.

The first event ended in yet another win for Ferrari and his Scuderia. Fagioli won in his 2.6 P3 over Nuvolari's Maserati after a duel that lasted the entire race distance – 500km (311 miles) – and nearly 3 hours. The second event turned out to be one of the most dramatic races in the history of a sport still young, but not new to tragedy.

The first heat of the Monza Grand Prix started at 2pm. Scuderia Ferrari fielded Trossi in the new Duesenberg, which, despite its extraordinary top speed on the long straights of the Autodromo Nazionale, was forced to withdraw as early as the second lap. In the second heat, which started at 3pm, the Scuderia fielded the great Giuseppe Campari in the number 22 Alfa Romeo 2.6 P3. The car to beat was Borzacchini's 3.0-litre Maserati. It was the second act of the day in a long rivalry that had inflamed the summer and the morning race.

At the end of the first lap, only three cars out of the seven that had started the race passed in front of the grandstands. Campari's Alfa Romeo and Borzacchini's Maserati were both among those missing. Rumours immediately spread that there had been an accident at the ultra-fast Curva Sud, involving four cars. One of the drivers had not reported a scratch. The other three had been taken to the hospital, it was said, although there were no details about their condition.

The race continued. Enzo Ferrari waited in the Scuderia pits with his men. A few minutes went by. Then the announcement came: Borzacchini and Campari were dead. Ferrari immediately decided to retire in mourning, renouncing a possible *repechage* for Trossi's Duesenberg for the final stint.[53] At the time, it was not an obvious decision to make.

After a break of two hours, the third heat was contested. Then the final, during which another accident took the life of a third driver, French count Czaikowski. At the end of the day the crowd at Monza silently walked toward the point of the track where the three drivers had been killed.[54] Enzo Ferrari had left the circuit long before to go to the hospital and pay tribute to the fallen.

Campari had been a longtime friend, the only survivor of his Alfa Romeo teammates. When Enzo, after the split from Nuvolari, had needed a hand, Campari had come to his rescue. A photograph published in the *Littoriale* two days after the incident, taken shortly before the start of that last race, portrayed Giuseppe and Enzo together, smiling like in the old days.[55] And despite their differences that summer – for the most part, it must be said, orchestrated by Nuvolari – Borzacchini had been one of the first drivers to race with his Scuderia.

It was mid-September, which meant five races before the end of the season. The first, on 17 September, was held only five days after the funeral of the three drivers killed at Monza. Ferrari fielded three cars at the Masaryk Circuit in Brno: two 2.6 P3s for Fagioli and Chiron, and a 2.6 8C Monza for Brivio. Chiron won and Fagioli placed second. The memory of Campari was honoured in the best way possible.

Ferrari had stayed in Modena, and neither did he go to San Sebastian the following week for the Spanish Grand Prix. Chiron won again, but caused pandemonium when he ignored pit communications commanding him to let Fagioli pass. Without knowing it, the Monegasque nearly caused serious problems for his employer.

Sensitive to the wishes of an important supplier such as Pirelli, for whom the Spanish market was of paramount importance, before the race Ferrari had given instructions that, if the two P3s were in the lead, Fagioli, whose car was fitted with Pirellis, should win. Instead Chiron, whose car was mounted on Belgium's

Englebert tyres, ignored the signals from the pits and went on undisturbed to the chequered flag.

Chiron tried to justify himself by saying that he had not noticed any signs coming from the pits,[56] but his behaviour ended up embarrassing Ferrari, who was a paid consultant for Pirelli.[57]

The Spanish Grand Prix was the last significant race of 1933.

It had been a troubled and excruciating season with plenty of drama both on and off the track. 'The work done in this fourth year of our life,' commented Ferrari that autumn, 'was not without its complications; most varied problems, new tasks, unexpected situations, aching epilogues, that our organization' – and here the reference to Nuvolari's defection from the Scuderia was clear – 'faced with inflexibility and decision.'[58]

But it had also and above all been a winning season. The overall wins amounted to 26, inside and especially outside the borders of Italy. In addition, Scuderia's motorcycle department scored eight wins out of twelve races, even though the activity on two wheels had been diminishing. The number of riders was reduced to six – five after Taruffi left – and events were contested only in Italy. 'The function of our institution,' Ferrari could proudly state, 'continues to be incessant and fruitful.'[59]

It was, however, the harsh confrontation with Nuvolari that had made Ferrari great in the year that was coming to an end. By flatly refuting the Flying Mantuan's claims, Ferrari had become much stronger in the eyes of the world. He had stood up, had not given in, had not caused additional problems or shown any remorse in letting him go. And the results had proven him right, since the drivers with whom he had replaced Nuvolari – Fagioli and Chiron – had won six of the seven events they raced. In autumn 1933, Nuvolari remained the greatest driver of them all, but Enzo Ferrari was much more self-confident and respected than he had ever been.

So there were more than enough reasons for the usual gala dinner celebrating the end of the year, held on Saturday 2 December in Ferrari's favourite restaurant, Fratelli Boninsegna, in central Via San Carlo in Modena. The times had changed, as we have seen, and the festive banquet was given the more virile – more Fascist, that is – name of 'Mess of Honour'.[60] But what mattered most is that the invitation finally included Baracca's prancing horse, which had become to all intents and purposes the symbol of Scuderia Ferrari.

The black horse against a yellow rectangle topped by the three colours of the Italian flag – in a curious anticipation of the logo that he would create many years later when he started his car company – also dominated the cover of the yearbook, which, for the third consecutive year, Ferrari presented all his guests.

This publication, 'like a movie', showed the 'prodigious activity of the Scuderia and its successful presence in all major European and Mediterranean events.'[61]

Hosting the evening were Ferrari, Count Trossi and the unflagging Ferruccio Testi – or, in the words of the press, members of whom were also invited to the dinner – 'the trio that [the Scuderia] owes the strength of her bases, the bold decisions, the promptness of execution'.[62] More than two hundred guests attended the dinner, to which Ferrari and 'his associates' had devoted a great deal of time in the days before.[63] In addition to party VIPs and motor-racing professionals, Ferrari never missed a chance to recognize and thank everyone who had contributed, or could do so in the future, to the success of his organization. Among them, of course, were the drivers of the upcoming season and those of the season that had just ended. To no one's surprise, Nuvolari had not been invited.[64]

The Moll Affair

A few days before Christmas 1933, looking ahead to the new season that would start in Pau in February, Enzo Ferrari predicted the leading role that the new German teams would play in 1934. Both in public and in private, he spoke of a real 'German threat', explaining that, in Germany, automakers 'had been at work for some time now, and are committed, especially in light of favourable environmental conditions, to honour the good name of German industry'.[1] In the fine diplomatic language that Ferrari had learned to use when necessary, *favourable environmental conditions* meant the financial support that Adolf Hitler's new Reich had promised and begun to allocate to the automotive industry of that country.

Ferrari mainly feared Mercedes. From journalists and insiders he had learned that German engineers in Stuttgart had focused on the development of a cutting-edge chassis. He would not say much about Auto Union, the new consortium formed by a union of four small manufacturers, of which little was known. He did know that both companies enjoyed a huge advantage over the competition because, for at least a year, they had been working on cars specifically conceived for the new 750kg (1,653lb) weight formula that would take effect with the 1934 season.[2] This was a substantial reduction from the previous weight, which had been 900kg (1,985lb). The German car manufacturers would use completely new cars, entirely designed to abide by the new regulations; all other European manufacturers would simply adapt their old cars to the new formula. The future did not worry Ferrari, however; by the end of the previous season, pending Alfa Romeo's decision on whether to build new cars for the 1934 season, he had put his men to work in the Modena workshop to adapt at least half of the six P3s owned by the Scuderia to the new weight formula.[3] Everyone knew 'from the day Bazzi and Marinoni joined that the Scuderia Ferrari is not only a magnificent sporting organization', but also 'a first-class technical group'.[4] The adaptation work mainly consisted of a slight weight decrease and enlarging the P3 car body.[5]

On the first day of December, Alfa Romeo officially announced the construction of six new cars that would be delivered exclusively to Scuderia Ferrari.[6]

Enzo had already confirmed – the only one in Europe to do so – the driver lineup for the next season. Two were the leaders of the new formation: Louis Chiron and the great Achille Varzi.[7]

Chiron had signed with Ferrari on 20 November; Varzi, even earlier. Architect of the courtship of Varzi – the only major driver never to have raced for Scuderia Ferrari – was Count Trossi, who had approached Achille in August, in Pescara, at the time of the Coppa Acerbo, and, away from prying eyes, had made him try the P3.[8] Nuvolari had left, slamming the door less than two weeks earlier. Ferrari was already thinking in terms of revenge, bringing into his team, in Tazio's place, his archrival.

It had been five years since the founding of Scuderia Ferrari. When asked to make an assessment of that time, Ferrari would skirt the issue. Five years? 'Scuderia Ferrari was born *today*,' he would say with a grin.[9] The answer contained modesty – partly true, partly dictated by his desire not to overdo it, in an effort not to arouse jealousy in a country where individual merits were not necessarily appreciated by the regime. But the answer was in large part sincere. It implied above all a very personal attitude that Ferrari had begun to adopt when contemplating the achievements of his working life, where each victory or accomplishment was only the starting point for the next.

Scuderia Ferrari was born today, he would explain, because 'hasn't our organization changed her goals and widened her horizon year after year? We started out quietly,' he liked to recall later, strong from the team's many successes. 'Today we have come far beyond our greatest hopes. In part,' he added with measured pride, 'it is due to our merit. Also in part,' he would say, with more realism than false modesty, 'it is due to the circumstances that led us to this. Our merit,' he reserved the right to say, 'is perhaps to often have found the right interpretation of times and events.'[10]

It was not that simple, of course. The success of Scuderia Ferrari was thanks in large part to his clear-eyed passion, his strong will, his never-wavering determination. But it was also true, as he liked to point out, that having been able to predict what would happen – and here it was his intuition that had made the difference – was a key factor in the rise of Scuderia Ferrari. In this regard, he recalled that 'when Alfa Romeo announced her withdrawal from competition' at the end of 1932, 'we were not totally unprepared'.[11]

And it was true. But the credit was all Enzo's, who had predicted very early the outcome of Alfa Romeo's evasiveness and had acted accordingly.

By the winter of 1934 Enzo Ferrari had become the reference point in the world of Italian motorsport. Alfa Romeo remained on the sidelines; Fiat had not been fielding cars for ten years; Officine Maserati had never made that final step and was alternating between supplying cars to privateers and a limited direct participation in a few races per season. Scuderia Ferrari, instead, had been created with the sole purpose of racing – 'a mix of technical experience, motorsport achievement and astute propaganda',[12] as Ferrari liked to describe the Scuderia in public – and had occupied the void.

From his small office, the 'brain and heart of Scuderia Ferrari',[13] Enzo directed the activity of about 50 people divided into 2 business units: the automotive and the motorcycle departments. And if it was true that the two activities did not carry the same weight in the organization of Scuderia Ferrari and in the consideration of the owner, it was also true that efforts continued in both directions.

If with the outside world he had become a fine diplomat and a perfect host, Ferrari had by now turned his organization into an absolute monarchy, however mitigated by a robust paternalism. Exchanges of views, especially at the technical level, abounded – and often resulted in outbursts of animosity. An angry tone had become part of the modus operandi that Ferrari had shaped over the previous few years, although the aggression shown, and sometimes even sought, was never an end in itself. What is more, violent discussions never altered the personal and professional relationships between the king and his subjects once the argument was settled – usually with the monarch's point of view prevailing. But Enzo had also learned to listen and to change his opinion when he realized that the other party's view was better than his.[14]

For the past four years Scuderia Ferrari had occupied the same spacious building a few hundred metres from Via Emilia, near the bridge over the Pradella, a little stream of water running across the city, just outside the medieval centre of Modena. Although the building had not changed, the Scuderia HQ had in fact changed address. The Urban Plan of 1933 had altered the name of that section of road where the Scuderia was located, from Viale Ciro Menotti to Viale Trento Trieste. The number had remained the same – 11.

The art nouveau structure had grown in size and now sported a large portico that could house the four Fiat and Lancia trucks bodied by Cavalier Renzo Orlandi – who twelve years earlier had purchased what was left of Carrozzeria Emilia – that were used to transport the Scuderia's cars and bikes to national and European venues. The exterior walls were painted in that cold pastel yellow that characterized most buildings in the Modena city centre.

Enzo lived upstairs with Laura and Dino, who was now two years old. The first-floor apartment was just above the Alfa Romeo showroom. A row of windows looked out onto Viale Trento Trieste, and from the rooms at the back the view extended over the workshop roof. The apartment itself was relatively small: a hall, a dining room, a kitchen, a bedroom, a small room for Dino and a bathroom. The decor was modest and the apartment had no fine furniture or valuable paintings.[15]

The relationship between husband and wife remained tense. The birth of their son had not softened Laura. Quarrels were the order of the day over even the most trivial matters. On Enzo's part, the patience and understanding he'd exhibited during the early years had long since turned into resignation – which did not mean passive acceptance of the situation but, rather, the pursuit of a relatively independent life outside those walls. It was not uncommon for Enzo to prefer to sleep at his mother's house on Corso Canalgrande, to the understandable and ill-concealed satisfaction of Adalgisa, who had never accepted her daughter-in-law.[16]

*   *   *

Alfa Romeo's decision to provide new cars only to Scuderia Ferrari had unexpected international repercussions. Before taking the decision, Alfa Romeo had accepted orders from a couple of French drivers and an English driver, each for a P3. Now they were told that their orders would not be honoured.

It fell to the new Alfa Romeo president, Ugo Gobbato, to solve the situation before it became a diplomatic incident on a European level. But it was not as simple as the decision to reserve new cars only for Scuderia Ferrari (for an Italian team, that is); as one would expect, there were geopolitical reasons. Gobbato skilfully devised a compromise – or, to be precise, two.

Englishman Brian Lewis, who intended to race again with an Alfa Romeo at the Mannin Moar in June, on the Isle of Mann, would get to use a P3 in 1933 configuration by paying Scuderia Ferrari a usage fee of 2,500 lire, plus 3,500 lire for insurance. He would have it just for one race and would pay all round-trip travel expenses (which Alfa Romeo quantified as an additional £250). Last but not least, Lewis was told that his British mechanics were to speak only in Italian in communicating with those coming from Modena.[17]

With the two Frenchmen, a different solution was needed. Lewis was the typical gentleman driver, an aristocrat with a passion for racing. But Guy Moll and Marcel Lehoux were talented professional racers. If the first dispute had been solved on a monetary level, with the two French drivers the solution had to be a sporting one. Therefore, to get out of an awkward situation, Alfa Romeo imposed on Enzo Ferrari to hire the two Frenchmen as works drivers for the Scuderia.[18]

The forced signing of the very skilled Moll strengthened an already-strong team, adding to Varzi's class and Chiron's experience a talent that Ferrari sensed would be important. But it also expanded the number of drivers beyond Ferrari's original plans; in the autumn, he had let go the new Italian champions, Luigi Fagioli and Tonino Brivio. Fagioli had signed with Mercedes, of whom very little was known. Brivio had signed with Bugatti. Gone also was Piero Taruffi, whose contrast with Ferrari had not subsided, and who, like Nuvolari, would race in 1934 as a privateer at the wheel of a Maserati.[19]

The 1934 season, which had been due to open on 18 February – the day Enzo Ferrari turned 36 – with the Grand Prix of Pau, officially got going only on 2 April. For financial reasons, that spring a number of events were cancelled, including the race in Pau and the following Grand Prix of Tunis. The first race was therefore the Monaco Grand Prix, where Scuderia Ferrari showed up in force.

Ferrari himself travelled to the French Riviera, although to leave Italy he had had to apply for a National Fascist Party affiliation card, which was now required to renew one's passport.[20] The Fascist Party had been ruling Italy since October 1922, and the dictatorship was officially established in January 1925. Ferrari didn't acquire his card until 1934, when he was compelled by the new laws. Like him, everyone else on the team also had to get one if they wanted to go to European events – mechanics, technicians and, of course, drivers.

At Monaco Varzi and Trossi were entrusted with the new 2.9-litre P3s, just arrived from Portello.[21] During practice they were the fastest. But the race culminated in a big surprise, because the victory went to Guy Moll at the wheel of an old 2.6-litre P3. Moll had been imposed on the Scuderia by Alfa Romeo, but Ferrari immediately recognized his talent, which exploded in all its greatness in Monte Carlo. That day Ferrari was fascinated by the class of the Algeria-born Frenchman, dazzled by what he identified as 'the stuff of which the greatest aces are made'.[22]

The Monaco Grand Prix was held on Monday. The following weekend was the Mille Miglia. After racing in Monte Carlo with a Bugatti, Nuvolari showed up in Brescia with an Alfa Romeo fielded by the newly formed Scuderia Siena, and paired with the former Ferrari driver and new team owner. It was the latest chapter in the endless Nuvolari–Varzi rivalry, but also a new episode in the newer contention between Nuvolari and Enzo Ferrari.

Ferrari was awaiting his cars – five in all – in Imola. The weather was uncertain. Huge black clouds were hanging over the city, and they did not promise anything good. Ferrari had called his men and been informed that it was raining up north, and that the drivers would find the road wet all the way to the Brescia finish line. When Varzi, who was battling with Nuvolari for the lead, arrived, Ferrari gave orders to mount Pirelli Stella Bianca *ancorizzate* tyres on his car. Ferrari knew from experience that the *ancorizzate* could make the difference on wet roads.

Having dismounted from his car to let the Scuderia mechanics replace the tyres and refuel, however, Varzi was surprised to see the *ancorizzate* tyres ready to go on his Alfa. The track was dry and tyres with deep grooves would inevitably slow him down. Irritated, he asked Ferrari what he was doing. While the mechanics waited to know which tyres they should mount, Ferrari and Varzi began a heated discussion, to the disbelief of bystanders. The clock was ticking.

Concerned by the obvious waste of time and exasperated by Varzi's behaviour, to avoid compromising his chance of success Ferrari gave in. 'Do what you want,' he said angrily.[23]

At this point Varzi suddenly fell silent. He seemed to think for a few moments and then, unexpectedly, changed his mind. He looked at Ferrari and said: 'All right, if you say so – give me the *ancorizzate*.'[24] The mechanics immediately proceeded, quickly mounting the *ancorizzate* tyres on Varzi's car. The moment Achille dashed off, the first drops of rain started to fall. 'You were right!' Varzi said to Ferrari before disappearing.[25]

Varzi found the road wet all the way to Brescia and, thanks to Ferrari's intuition and forethought, won his first Mille Miglia. Nuvolari, without the *ancorizzate*, finished eight minutes behind him.[26]

On Sunday 22 April, at Circuito Pietro Bordino in Alessandria, Scuderia Ferrari placed Varzi and Chiron in first and second place. But the race, held in prohibitive weather conditions, is remembered for a serious crash involving Nuvolari. The episode left Tazio with a double fracture on his left leg. Nuvolari bluntly accused two Ferrari drivers, archrival Varzi and Count Trossi, of having deliberately obstructed him.

Nuvolari pointed his finger to two separate episodes. The first happened during the second lap: while overtaking Varzi's Alfa, Nuvolari's Maserati made contact with Achille's P3. His car slipped but remained on the track. Shortly thereafter, Nuvolari was trailing Trossi's Alfa Romeo when, to avoid getting knocked over, he was forced to violently apply the brakes. This time, Tazio's Maserati drifted, went off the road and ended its run against the trunk of a tree.

Perhaps exasperated by the defeats that he was accumulating in the duel with Varzi, and in his personal war with Ferrari, Nuvolari saw malice in the behaviour of the two Scuderia drivers. More likely, as the press stated afterwards, the two accidents were caused by the rain, and by the fact that Nuvolari's Maserati 'was equipped with unsuitable tyres for wet ground'.[27] Just as at the Mille Miglia, whereas Ferrari had equipped the cars of his Scuderia with *ancorizzate* tyres, Nuvolari had not.

On 15 May Nuvolari sent a registered letter to the Racing Commission of RACI (Royal Automobile Club of Italy) in which he accused Ferrari's drivers of having blocked him, 'apparently following Scuderia's orders'.[28] Despite the passionate written protest sent to the national body, however, the controversy was soon silenced.[29] As in the past, politics prevailed.

But if the new Nuvolari case quickly disappeared from the pages of sports newspapers, controversy involving Moll soon attracted attention. The catalyst was some statements the Algerian driver made while talking to French journalists after the Grand Prix of Tripoli. That day the superiority of Ferrari's Alfa Romeos had been overwhelming. Moll had finished second behind Varzi. He had closely followed the Italian for most of the race, and had tried to surprise him in the last turn. It was the same tactic he had used in Monaco against Chiron.

After the race Moll voiced his disappointment to French journalists, among them the influential Charles Faroux, the reporter from *L'Auto*. Despite his young age, Moll was fully aware of his talent. Convinced that he had suffered fraud on the part of Varzi, who, when attacked in the last turn, had blocked the road in an unorthodox manoeuvre, Moll was not willing to quietly accept second place. His cry, music to the ears of French journalists, made headlines in French newspapers the next day.

Moll's words sparked controversy in France. Enzo Ferrari was accused of having decided the result of the race beforehand to favour an Italian driver. Some wrote that the 2.9-litre engine mounted in Moll's P3 was less powerful than the similar units found in the Alfas raced by Varzi, Chiron and Trossi. And there were even those who accused Ferrari of having inserted a clause in Moll's contract obliging him to adhere to team orders.[30] The controversy soon crossed the border and arrived in Italy, although with a different tone. To explain 'Moll's lack of camaraderie with his fellow Scuderia teammates and his individualistic attitude and contempt for discipline',[31] the Italian press brought to the attention of the public an issue that had until then remained a secret, despite rumours. The press revealed that Scuderia Ferrari had been forced to hire Moll to repair a wrong done months before by Alfa Romeo, which had first sold a racing car to the French driver and then cancelled the order.

Ferrari, who had in the meantime won the race at Avus with Moll on the day Auto Union made her debut in the world of grand prix, and who had until then taken all accusations in silence, set out to defend himself in the usual way – namely, through a letter addressed to the media. This time he chose the Italian magazine

Auto Italiana, where a note appeared in which Ferrari, with the usual precision and meticulous reference to official contracts, stigmatized the behaviour of the French press.

'It has been written,' Ferrari said, 'that it is a habit of the Scuderia that bears my name and which is honoured to represent the famed Alfa Romeo make in all competitions, to decide beforehand the order of arrival of each race and force drivers to comply with that order. Absolutely false!' he thundered, adding that 'the drivers of Scuderia Ferrari are free by contract and perfectly able to defend their chances, always'. To give more weight to his statement, he called on all to consult the contracts of his drivers. And he authorized the three foreign drivers of his Scuderia – Moll, Chiron and Lehoux – 'to show theirs'.[32]

'It has also been written,' he went on, 'that in Tripoli I had decided Varzi first, Chiron second. Equally false – so much so that the only two Scuderia cars equipped with brand-new engines were entrusted to Guy Moll and Count Trossi.' Then he explained in detail the racing strategy adopted by Scuderia Ferrari in Tripoli when, during the race, 'Varzi and Chiron, clearly leading over all others, were prudently told to slow down the pace,' while 'Guy Moll was left free and therefore could make up the time lost in an unanticipated pit stop.'[33]

While he was at it, Ferrari took the opportunity for a jab at his new and talented driver. If he had done it the previous year with an established champion like Nuvolari, he would not have qualms now with a young man in his early twenties. 'It would have been the right of Scuderia Ferrari,' he pointed out, 'to ask *signor* Moll to conduct his race in a manner more consistent with the interests of the organization to which he belongs, ordering him to avoid the risks of a tumultuous arrival.'[34]

Ferrari's public response all but put an end to the Moll controversy, along with the fact that after explaining to the whole world that he had not intended in any way to penalize his young driver, Ferrari had sidelined him.

On 1 July was the Grand Prix of the Automobile Club of France, on the same Montlhéry circuit where Antonio Ascari had died nine years earlier. After the Eifel Grand Prix in early June, the new and powerful Mercedes and Auto Union had become the cars to beat. Scuderia Ferrari continued to compete against them with the P3s, which, no matter how much work the Alfa Romeo technicians put in, were still cars designed several years earlier. Three men were chosen to race them: Varzi, Chiron and Trossi. Ferrari gave Moll the role of reserve. The Frenchman was paying not only for the statements to the press that had sparked the controversy, but also the fact that he had never meshed well with his teammates.

The gap between the German cars and all the others was evident right from the first practice sessions. Concerned by the situation, the new Scuderia Ferrari team manager, Nello Ugolini, phoned Modena to ask for direction. Ferrari ordered him to get Moll on the track with the others. Despite the irritation about his public statements and the problem posed by his lack of integration with his peers, Ferrari knew that the young Algerian had a rare talent. Ugolini obeyed; Moll took the wheel and immediately began to go faster than his teammates. The German cars remained distant, but Moll had significantly reduced the gap.

At the end of the day Ferrari decided not to employ Moll in the race, leaving him in the pits, back in the role of reserve. Moll climbed into Trossi's car only in the final part of the race, and only after the Italian aristocrat had stopped with the gearbox in bad shape. Penalized by the blatant inferiority of the car that he had inherited, but thanks to his prodigious and instinctive gifts, Moll quickly climbed to second place behind Chiron. Despite their technical superiority, Auto Union and Mercedes had shown unexpected mechanical fragility and had all withdrawn. France was now looking surprisingly good for Scuderia Ferrari.

Complying with the directions received over the phone from Ferrari, Ugolini signalled Moll to slow down and let Varzi pass.[35] Moll obeyed and the Alfa Romeo P3s finished first, second and third. In a day of unexpected triumph for the Italian automotive industry, serenity seemed to have returned to Scuderia Ferrari.

Partial calm may have returned to the Scuderia, but Varzi's prickly nature caused even more problems for Ferrari than the difficult management of young Moll.[36] The technical superiority that emerged in the French Grand Prix was only accidental. The German threat that Enzo Ferrari had predicted the previous autumn had indeed materialized.

In those races where German cars, still short of development, were forced to retire, Scuderia Ferrari had no rival. But when Mercedes and Auto Union took to the track with no technical problems, Scuderia Ferrari trailed. At the Nürburgring, in mid-July, Auto Union took its first grand prix victory, with Stuck. Behind him came Fagioli's Mercedes. And although Chiron finished third, it was only because the other German cars had all fallen to mechanical problems.

A month later, in Pescara, Scuderia Ferrari faced the Germans in what the Italian press on the eve of the race called 'the battle of the Titans'.[37] In its tenth running, in 1934 the Coppa Acerbo had acquired an importance almost equal to some of the more-established international events. Mercedes and Auto Union went to Pescara in force. The former entrusted three cars to Fagioli, Henne and Caracciola. The latter assigned two cars to Stuck and Sebastian. Ferrari took to the Adriatic shore four P3s for Varzi, Chiron, Moll and Ghersi.

The battle between the Italians and the Germans set the public on fire along the fast track that wound between the Adriatic coast and the hills inland, where, exactly ten years earlier, Enzo Ferrari had clinched the most prestigious success of his racing-driver career. In the first third of the race, Varzi's Alfa Romeo battled repeatedly for the lead with Caracciola's Mercedes and Stuck's Auto Union. In the second part, the duel between Germany and Italy continued with the fight between the Mercedes of Fagioli and the Alfa Romeo driven by Moll.

Slowed in the first part of the race by spark-plug problems,[38] Moll took the lead during the tenth of the event's twenty laps. One more lap and he pitted for refuelling. When he returned to the track, he started a spectacular chase of Fagioli, who had in the meantime taken the lead. In the pits, Enzo Ferrari followed the fantastic run of his young protégé with approval. The victory at Monte Carlo had given him confidence in Guy and had persuaded him to tolerate the young man's summer insubordination. Now he knew that he had not been mistaken: the young Algerian had Nuvolari's talent.

Lap after lap, Moll lowered his time, set a new record lap and narrowed the deficit to Fagioli. He drove as if he were in a sort of racing trance, one of those rare moments in a driver's career when man sublimates his talent and his car seems to support him in every conceivable way. The exciting run, with Moll driving to his limit, brought the spectators to a state of collective exhilaration. Leaning on the pit wall, Ferrari recognized the risks that Moll's inspiring driving involved. But he also knew that, for a driver of Moll's talent, the only real danger could be posed by colleagues of inferior class.[39]

In the end the young champion was betrayed by a gust of wind and not by the lesser class of Hans Henne, who suddenly appeared in front of Moll on the high-speed straight at Montesilvano. It was the 17th lap, and Moll had further reduced the gap to Fagioli. A strong wind was blowing from the Adriatic and had not let up all day. At this moment a stronger gust lifted, or perhaps just imperceptibly moved, the red Alfa Romeo as Moll was about to pass Henne's Mercedes at 270km/h (168mph).

It was Henne's first race, and the point where Moll moved to pass him was relatively narrow. Moll's P3 flew off the track, knocking down a dozen trees, and plunged into the ground. Moll was thrown from the cockpit and found on the opposite side of the road.[40] By the time rescuers arrived, he was already dead. The race, though it did not matter much, was won by Fagioli.

With the tragic death of Guy Moll, Ferrari lost a driver for whom he had been making great plans for the future. As well as by his talent, he had been fascinated by Moll's great 'coolness' and his extraordinary 'poise', his ability 'to split in two the reasoning, also under the inhuman demands of danger'.[41] Their collaboration lasted only a single season and had been brutally interrupted, but Ferrari would never forget the enthusiasm of those few months. In his personal ranking of racing drivers, Moll would always occupy a special place.[42]

The rest of the racing season went by fast. A win with Varzi in Nice, some victories in hillclimbs and minor races, a third-place finish in a Grand Prix of Italy dominated by Mercedes and Auto Union, a complete setback in the Grand Prix of Spain . . . As summer gave way to autumn, the P3 seemed to have lost not only its competitiveness but also its legendary reliability. Chiron had seemed unable to find his driving class in the first half of the season and Varzi looked like he had lost all of his passion. Comotti and Ghersi and the others had simply not made that step up that Ferrari had wished for.

It may have made sense after the quarrel with Nuvolari, but working with Varzi had proven difficult. Achille was stubborn and proud. In his relations with Ferrari he was shrewder than Nuvolari, but equally frustrating. Moreover, his contribution in terms of development had been lower than expected – something that became evident in the last races of the season, when the P3 suddenly began to be defeated even by Maseratis and Bugattis.

Although without much enthusiasm, Ferrari embarked on negotiations with Varzi to renew his contract for the following season.[43] In November came the announcement that Achille had signed with Auto Union – a blessing in disguise. If on the one hand the loss of Varzi was a big blow, on the other Ferrari could breathe a sigh of relief. In late October he had confirmed the fast and reliable Chiron, had welcomed Tonino Brivio back to the Scuderia and had entered negotiations with Frenchman René Dreyfus.

To complete the lineup that in 1935 would take on the increasingly competitive German cars, he now only lacked the established champion. And with the death of Moll and the departure of Varzi, there was only one other ace around.

Fighting the Silver Arrows

If for Enzo Ferrari the return of Tazio Nuvolari was the most natural solution that existed on the face of the earth, the Flying Mantuan had different ideas. Just like Varzi, Nuvolari had been greatly impressed by the potential shown by Auto Union in 1934. And like Achille, Tazio too had offered his services to the Germans.

Although he was going to cost more than the Germans expected, his demands were considered fair and were accepted.[1] But then the plot thickened. The Germans became elusive on the date for the signing. Then came the cold shower.

On 4 December, the management of Auto Union informed Nuvolari that the programme had changed.[2] In a letter dated 7 December, Nuvolari told the Germans that he understood their reasons. And all of a sudden, on the horizon appeared the familiar figure of Enzo Ferrari.

For Enzo Ferrari the return of Tazio Nuvolari had long been the only way to remain at the top. The Mantuan was the only driver in whom he saw the talents of Antonio Ascari and of the early Campari. He was the man who could enable Ferrari's Scuderia to face the German threat, if not on equal terms, at least with some chance of winning. The previous year the personal confrontation between the two had been rough. Each had accused the other, both in public and in private. At one point lawyers had taken over though, in the end, wisdom had prevailed.

For weeks on end in the autumn, and then into the early winter, patient negotiations continued, but always without direct contact. Ferrari would open up to Tazio, cautiously not saying a single word more than necessary; Nuvolari was wary because he was also engaged in negotiations with Auto Union, careful not to prematurely discard a possible opening on the part of Ferrari, whom he both loved and hated. Meanwhile, as newspapers filled with rumours, Nuvolari was receiving letters from admirers and supporters who asked him the reason for his rumoured move to a German team.[3]

Alfa Romeo contributed in a decisive way when it came to channelling the negotiations towards a successful outcome. More specifically, Vittorio Jano took the situation to heart and led 'long, laborious and delicate negotiations' separately with each player.[4] It is unclear whether Jano's intervention was spontaneous or in any way solicited by Alfa Romeo, which had previously contacted Nuvolari, but had not been able to offer him a contract for more than two races and some testing sessions.[5] Nor is it clear whether the Milan company was requested to act by Italian sporting or political bodies.

In any case, Jano finally convinced the two rivals to meet. A neutral location was chosen, roughly between Modena, Mantua and Milan. And so the three of them met in Piacenza on the last Thursday in January 1935.

In Piacenza the cold soon melted. Ferrari and Nuvolari may have been prima donnas, but they were also pragmatic. It did not take them long to leave behind their accusations and quarrels and plan their future together. If there was one thing they had in common, it was an almost maniacal desire to win. Despite the accusations of the previous 18 months, their mutual esteem had remained strong since the first day they had met, more than 11 years before.

A private agreement between the parties that buried the ancient grudges was soon drafted, signed by all three: Nuvolari, Ferrari and Jano. The text clearly spoke of a new beginning.[6] After a year and a half of separation, Enzo Ferrari and Tazio Nuvolari were joining forces once again. They did it in the name of Italian motorsport and of their old friendship, with Alfa Romeo as a sponsor, and under the auspices of Italian fans. But they also did it because they had come to the conclusion that although both could stand on their own two feet – especially Nuvolari, of course – they were formidable only when they stood together.[7]

Having reached the agreement, Ferrari quickly announced it. A brief statement was immediately dictated by Enzo, approved by Tazio and issued to major Italian media outlets that very afternoon, from Piacenza.

As expected, the agreement sparked a great deal of enthusiasm in Italy. The press immediately labelled it the 'Treaty of Piacenza', praising the fact that Ferrari and Nuvolari had 'amicably resolved their personal disputes'.[8]

Newspapers used exaggerated language in the rhetoric of the time: 'The Nuvolari-Alfa combination, so dear to the hearts of all Italian sportsmen,' wrote Baron Guzman in Rome's morning paper, 'the duo that made us tremble with joy and enthusiasm in so many ardent battles gallantly fought and triumphantly won, forms again today thanks to Tazio's great spirit of patriotism, and thanks to the sagacity and firmness of purpose of Enzo Ferrari, a racer of never-forgotten value and a first-rate organizer today.'[9]

Happy and proud about the return of Nuvolari, in the next issue of the Scuderia weekly bulletin Ferrari let his writers flow without restraint, even paraphrasing Dante's *Divine Comedy*: 'Your black shadow, once departed, comes back.'[10]

The modified P3 tested by Nuvolari at Monza was one of two units trucked to Pau for the opening race of the 1935 season. The other P3 was going to be driven by René Dreyfus, a 29-year-old French talent that Ferrari had grabbed from Bugatti. Alongside them, the Scuderia Ferrari driver lineup included only Chiron, Trossi, Brivio and Comotti, all confirmed from the previous season. Gone were the gentleman drivers who had meant so much in the early years of Scuderia Ferrari. Despite the independence claimed and publicized by Ferrari, his Scuderia looked more and more like the racing department – external though it was – of Alfa Romeo. Which was exactly what Ferrari had wanted from day one.[11]

At Pau, Nuvolari and Dreyfus finished first and second. Despite its age, the P3 was a powerful car and both drivers had a glorious day right from the start. Nobody was fooled by the great result, however, since it did not escape anyone's attention that the Germans' cars, absent at Pau, were far superior and that once the season was in full swing, Auto Union and Mercedes would dominate. Nonetheless, it was good for both Ferrari and Nuvolari that their new life together started with a win.

A break of seven weeks separated the Pau Grand Prix from the next race – the Mille Miglia, scheduled for 14 April. Over this long period, the Scuderia Ferrari workshop in Modena saw nonstop activity while technicians and engineers hastily worked on developing the car on which Ferrari placed the only real hope of opposing German technical superiority in 1935 – the twin-engine *Bimotore*.

The idea of building a car with two engines had arisen during a meeting that Ferrari had held with his closest advisers on 16 December 1934. That Sunday, Ferrari had meant to analyse the new technical situation they faced following the superior performance by German cars in the grand prix events of the season that had just ended. All the men in the meeting were aware that the main reason – or at least, the most obvious one – for the Germans' supremacy was the huge engine displacements of both Mercedes and Auto Union.[12]

The problem was not trivial. While Jano was developing the new car at Portello, in Modena they were supposed to continue for quite some time with the old one. But then the audacious Bazzi spoke and told his colleagues of an old idea – namely, to mount the P3 with two engines instead of one. It was a bold concept, designed to address their lack of financial means with Italian ingenuity. But Ferrari agreed that it just might work, and approved the project.

When, thanks to Jano, approval from Alfa Romeo was granted, Bazzi immediately got to work.[13] The car was designed by Arnaldo Roselli and made exclusively of Alfa Romeo parts. Attilio Marinoni carried out all the tests. These were weeks of intense activity in the Viale Trento Trieste workshop. Under the direction of workshop chief Stefano Meazza, the Scuderia's 50 men worked virtually around the clock in 2 shifts[14] for 3 full months: nights, Sundays and holidays included.[15]

On 4 April 1935, the Bimotore was ready for its first test drive. The car was loaded onto a truck and taken 15km (9 miles) from Modena, into the countryside. At the wheel of the twin-engined monster, Marinoni went back and forth several times between the towns of Formigine and Maranello. On the narrow road bordered by trees and ditches, Bazzi's favourite tester did not push the car to its limit, but still touched 288km/h (179mph), a considerable speed indeed.[16]

Ferrari was pleased. The Bimotore was ready for the first real test.[17] Six days later it was introduced to the world.

Ferrari invited a handful of journalists, Alfa Romeo executives, representatives of the racing committee of RACI, Alfa and Pirelli technicians and, of course, Vittorio Jano was there too. It was Wednesday 10 April, a beautiful spring day. At the Brescia exit of the Brescia–Bergamo highway, under the watchful eye of Bazzi and Meazza, Marinoni started the Bimotore and launched it down the long straight heading for Bergamo. At kilometre 78 he stopped and got out of the car. Then Tazio Nuvolari took the wheel and drove the same stretch of road but in the opposite direction.

The Flying Mantuan drove the distance several times both ways. The highest speed reached was 338km/h (210mph), 50 more than in the first test in the Modena countryside. Tazio was excited, and predicted that, with higher gear ratios, the Bimotore could easily exceed 360km/h (224mph).

But there was more. Above the radiator, where it would be logical to find Alfa Romeo's circular logo, Ferrari placed the yellow shield with the black prancing horse in the centre. It was an unequivocal statement: despite the fact that the components of the car were almost entirely from Alfa Romeo, the Bimotore was a Ferrari – the *first* Ferrari.

Electrified by the first encouraging steps of the Bimotore, a few days later Ferrari tackled the Mille Miglia with great enthusiasm and energy. Without the services of Nuvolari – who had decided to concentrate on grand prix races, a decision that Ferrari had not disputed – Enzo fielded drivers in three cars who, compared with Nuvolari, were of a relatively modest skill level. Two were paired in Alfa Romeo 6C 2300 B sedans, touring cars that the Portello management gave Scuderia Ferrari with the obvious intention of promoting them commercially. The third car, entrusted to Carlo Pintacuda and Marquis Della Stufa, was a P3 Grand Prix with a modified body.

The choice not to question Nuvolari's decision to sit out the Mille Miglia – the race of races, as far as Italians were concerned – demonstrated the new course the relationship between Ferrari and Nuvolari had taken after the latter's return. In order to have the Flying Mantuan with him, Ferrari had given him total autonomy. If from the outside the two seemed equal, Ferrari had readily accepted a secondary position.[18]

Considered the car to beat, the Maserati soon betrayed Varzi. The victorious march of Pintacuda was slowed in the first part of the race by an Alfa Romeo prepared by Scuderia Ferrari, but raced as a privateer by Mario Tadini, who had just had a fight with Enzo and had momentarily left his Scuderia. Pintacuda won hands down.

The success in the Mille Miglia was a welcome confidence boost. But the real challenge started the following week in Monaco. Auto Union and Bugatti may have decided not to go to Monte Carlo, but Mercedes showed up in force with four sleek 4.0-litre W25s entrusted to Caracciola, Lang, Fagioli and von Brauchitsch. Ferrari could try to beat them with the talents of Nuvolari, Dreyfus, Chiron, Brivio and Trossi – the entire lineup, that is – but little else.

At Monaco, Ferrari's Alfa Romeos were never in the heat of the race. The end result was more generous than the race itself had been: Dreyfus in second place, Brivio in third. The finishing order would have been very different if Caracciola's Mercedes and Etancelin's Maserati had finished the race. 'To analyse the reasons for our defeat and that of Maserati is futile,' Ferrari said on his return to Modena. 'To see and recognize instead the degree of efficiency of others is wise, fair and useful.'[19]

Although Enzo felt alone, he was as combative as ever. Feeling alone against everyone was a situation that stimulated him as few other things in the world did.[20] 'Today there are cries for revenge, talks of lost supremacy and other such jokes,' he courageously stated. 'But whoever dared, except for us, to recognize after the victory at Montlhéry in June, 1934, that the days of our supremacy were over? Who answered our alarm call at that time?' His accusation was detailed and precise: 'In motor racing,' he admonished, 'there are no miracles; we need technicians, drivers, mechanics, material and, above all, the tools.'[21]

After a couple of days in Modena, Ferrari set off for Palermo and the Targa Florio. The race remained one of the most demanding on the international scene, but the interest of the big manufacturers had now moved elsewhere. Scuderia Ferrari's Alfa Romeos were the only real contenders for the victory. But Ferrari, despite his personal memories from the great Sicilian classic and the affection for Don Vincenzo Florio, sent to the island in the Mediterranean only Brivio, Chiron and Pintacuda, granting his two team heavyweights a weekend of rest in view of the upcoming trip to Africa and the two grands prix of Tunis and Tripoli.

Chiron led in the first lap, Brivio in the remaining five. On the finish line, seven minutes divided the two; the Monegasque had valiantly solved some of the troubles experienced in the second lap, recovering some of the ground lost, but had stopped short. Between Chiron and the third-placed driver there was an eleven-minute gap. The expected success was precious for Scuderia Ferrari in terms of prize money. But from a purely sporting point of view, the result was worth little, and Ferrari knew that very well.

Held seven days apart in the first half of May, the two African races established once and for all the superiority of Auto Union and Mercedes, and marked the beginning and, at the same time, the end of the very short life of the Bimotore in the world of grands prix. Varzi won in Tunis, Caracciola in Tripoli. Scuderia Ferrari did not go beyond two fourth places, with Comotti in Tunis and Nuvolari in Tripoli. In Tunis, the Bimotore was not even entered; at Tripoli the power of the two engines disintegrated tyres at an impressive rate, and forced Nuvolari and Chiron to make an endless series of pit stops. Tazio finished the ordeal almost eight minutes behind the winner; Chiron, more than ten.

At the end of the month, the fifth running of the Avus-Rennen was seen as a sort of last chance for the Bimotore. The car had quality on a technical and mechanical level; its real problem was its gigantic tyre wear. Avus was an atypical circuit: two long straights connected by only two turns. Perhaps here the Bimotore could keep up with the German cars, some of which raced in streamlined versions for better aerodynamic flow – perhaps.

The Avus race gave mixed answers. Thanks to careful race conduct and especially to some fragility problems experienced by the fast but still too young German cars, Chiron finished second.[22] Nuvolari, however, delayed by a long pit stop to replace his tyres, did not even qualify for the final stint.

Fast circuits like Tripoli and Avus had unequivocally shown that the Bimotore could not aspire to be a grand prix car. The power of its two engines just pulverized the tyres. The car was fast on the straights, but it was unusually slow when turning; it *had* to be, to stay on the track. At this point all Ferrari had left to do with the Bimotore was to try to clinch new world speed records, attempted on long straights with no turns.

To do so, Ferrari chose the same stretch of highway on which, on 16 February, the Auto Union of Hans Stuck had broken the 1-mile speed record that Mercedes' Caracciola had set at Avus in the winter.[23] And he used different tyres, preferring Dunlops to the Pirellis the Bimotore had used up to that point.[24]

On the morning of Saturday 15 June, at the Altopascio exit of the highway connecting Florence to the sea, in its quest for top speed, the Bimotore sported an aerodynamic fin behind the driver's seat. At 5am[25] Enzo Ferrari himself directed the unloading of the car from the Scuderia's yellow and blue truck.[26]

Under the supervision of chief mechanic Meazza, whose overalls sported a black prancing horse on a yellow background, the mechanics of the Scuderia set up a field workshop. Around them soon gathered the usual crowd: journalists, Alfa Romeo engineers, Party officials, fans and the curious. Also attracted by Nuvolari's endeavour – setting new Class B world speed records on the Flying (meaning that, whereas Stuck had started his trial at 0km/h, Nuvolari would pass the start line already at top speed) Kilometre and Mile, set in 1930 by Michel Doré in a Panhard – was His Royal Highness, the Duke of Spoleto, son of the king of Italy and chairman of the RACI, who chatted with Ferrari while Bazzi and the mechanics prepped the car.[27]

The first to sit behind the wheel of the Bimotore was Bazzi, who drove the distance between the Altopascio and Lucca airfield highway exits, from kilometre 56.910 to 58.600 – the exact straight on which Stuck had set his own record four months earlier. At 9.50am, it was Nuvolari's turn to climb into the Bimotore. His was supposed to be just a trial test, but when he realized that the car was responding perfectly to his technique, the Flying Mantuan launched into a first attempt.[28] That first run gave him the new world record, despite the wind that twice threw the Bimotore sideways as he was speeding from Altopascio towards the sea, and a gust that almost sent him off the road while he was picking up speed before the timed section started.

The sum of the times recorded in the ascending and descending timed sections gave the Bimotore of Scuderia Ferrari and Tazio Nuvolari new world records on the Flying Kilometre and Mile – respectively 11 minutes 0.2 seconds, and 17 minutes 0.93 seconds. The average speeds were 321.428km/h (199.7mph) and 323.125km/h (200.7mph).[29] The Doré record was trashed, as was Stuck's (however, his belonged to another record class and, for this reason, still officially stood even though it had been beaten).[30] The maximum speed reached by Nuvolari was 336.252km/h (208.9mph); in the world, the only one faster than Nuvolari and the Bimotore was Malcolm Campbell and his Blue Bird, the design of which had very little to do with a car, being more of an ingenious blend of a plane and a missile.

The two world records of Altopascio had an enormous echo in Italy. In the press there was glory for all – 'Bazzi, the brilliant inventor, Ferrari, who has courageously promoted the construction, and Tazio Nuvolari, who drove it to victory with superb determination'.[31] While they did not cancel out the technical deficit against German cars, the world records aroused true enthusiasm among fans and patriotic fervour – 'Italian machine, Italian driver, flying over a road created by Fascism'.[32]

If it was true that the German teams had invested a huge amount of money to get where they were, the achievements of Nuvolari and Scuderia Ferrari appeared to have come almost naturally, if not with ease,[33] and certainly with an investment based more on intuition, improvisation and sweat than financial assets.

Despite the prancing horse that adorned the radiator of the Bimotore, Ferrari let Alfa Romeo take the credit for the endeavour. Even those journalists who were aware of the development of Bazzi's car spoke almost exclusively of the 'Alfa Romeo Bimotore fielded by Scuderia Ferrari'.[34] So did the accessories manufacturers in ads that crowded newspapers in the days following the setting of the records, all depicting the Bimotore as an Alfa Romeo model. Yet there were some who, without knowing it, anticipated the future and spoke of 'a racing car marked by Ferrari's prancing horse'.[35]

For Enzo Ferrari the summer of 1935, which began with these Bimotore records, continued with victories in races not entered by the German teams and anticipated bloodshed in those where Auto Union and Mercedes decided to participate – which were, of course, the most important races.

The German Grand Prix at the Nürburgring, the temple of German motorsport, was scheduled for 28 July. It was going to be a titanic clash, with Auto Union and Mercedes set to fight for the overall win, with Ferrari's Alfa Romeos and some Maseratis in supporting roles.

As usual, in the weeks before the race Ferrari had received from the event organizers the race money offer. Despite the expected presence of Nuvolari, the proposal was strangely lower than what European organizers normally sent Ferrari when Tazio was scheduled to race. Surprised at first by a strikingly low proposal, it did not take long for Ferrari to grasp the true reasons for such odd behaviour. The Germans hoped to discourage Nuvolari from participating. History had taught them not to trust a driver like Nuvolari, and the 1935 Grand Prix of Germany was too important in terms of German sport and industry propaganda for the Nazi regime to take even the slightest chance of risking the triumph of either Mercedes or Auto Union.[36]

Thus, for this time only, and of course in agreement with Nuvolari, Ferrari accepted much lower race money than it was logical to expect.[37] It is unclear whether Ferrari and Nuvolari hoped to make up for the low fee with the prize money if they won – which was very unlikely, given their record in the season. It is more plausible to believe that they decided to go for the priceless satisfaction of trying to derail the plans of German party bureaucrats, who feared them to the point of trying to prevent their participation.

Ferrari sent to Germany three Alfa Romeo P3s for Nuvolari, Chiron and

Brivio. The Germans had never before lined up two teams so large and strong: five Mercedes for Caracciola, Lang, von Brauchitsch, Geier and Fagioli; four Auto Unions for Stuck, Rosemeyer, Pietsch and Varzi. The Grand Prix of Germany was a race like no other for them. To even think of earning money at the expense of the German teams seemed pure utopia.

Instead, thanks to massive tyre wear on all German cars throughout the race, in the last miles Nuvolari and his tiny and by-now outdated P3 recovered the ground lost for a prolonged pit stop and overtook von Brauchitsch's Mercedes, the only Silver Arrow left. It was possibly Nuvolari's greatest career win. It was certainly the most prestigious as a Scuderia Ferrari driver.

The sporting German crowds bestowed upon the Italian champion the ovation he deserved. The head of the Reich's motorsport programme, however, Major Hunhlein, left the podium so as not to be forced to compliment the man who that day – and that day only – had defeated the German automobile industry. Ferrari, who was becoming more selective over which races he attended and had chosen to stay in Modena, missed all of this.[38]

The following week Ferrari travelled to Livorno for the Circuit of the Montenero. The race, dear to the increasingly powerful Ciano family, was an important showcase in mid-1930s Italy, and the pragmatic Ferrari knew how important it was to be there in person. When German cars were not racing, Scuderia Ferrari had no rivals, and so it was at Livorno: four cars at the start, four cars in the top four places in the final standings – with Nuvolari naturally the winner.

The music was different when Germans participated in the races. In Pescara, in mid-August, the six P3s of Scuderia Ferrari all came behind the invincible Auto Unions of Rosemeyer and Varzi, the young sensation of German motor racing. Even though it could not be considered a surprise, the disappointment was great for Ferrari and his drivers – but while Ferrari kept it to himself, his drivers voiced their displeasure in public.

Ferrari's reaction was immediate. Back from Pescara he sent his drivers an intra-company communication, commanding all of them to behave more correctly and to abstain from making negative statements in public in the future.[39]

Despite Nuvolari's win at the Nürburgring, it was clear that the P3 no longer had anything to offer. With the Bimotore definitely out of the picture, Alfa Romeo had to accelerate as much as possible the development of the new car designed by Jano, the Type C.[40] 'One swallow,' wrote Filippini after the victory in Germany, echoing Ferrari's thoughts, 'does not make a summer, and in order to win – now more than ever – we need new cars.'[41]

The first two 8Cs were available for the Italian Grand Prix, scheduled for 8 September at the Monza Circuit. Ferrari entrusted them to Nuvolari and Dreyfus. Louis Chiron, who had crashed two weeks earlier in Bern, was left to rest.

The debut of the 8C, if not memorable, was still encouraging. Although he had been forced to use the sister car that Dreyfus had raced until then, Nuvolari took a good second place behind Stuck's Auto Union and ahead of Rosemeyer's.

With the German cars away, the 8C won again in Modena in the middle of the month, and took another second place in Brno at the end of September – needless to say, with Nuvolari. Auto Union and Mercedes remained ahead, but the 8C was showing great potential.

On Sunday 6 October, Tonino Brivio won at the wheel of the P3 at the Cosenza Circuit, Scuderia Ferrari's final race in the 1935 season. In an attempt to catch up with the Germans, Ferrari ordered that testing for the following season start immediately. On 29 October, therefore, Nuvolari and Dreyfus were summoned for a day of testing on the twisty Montenero Circuit in Livorno. Taking turns with Marinoni, the two drivers tested the two 8Cs built up to this point, along with a P3, which was used as a benchmark.[42]

Another season had come to an end – the sixth since Scuderia Ferrari had started operations. 'The story of the 1935 racing season,' Ferrari could say at the end of the year, 'showed that the Scuderia can keep its ground and often knows how to win, even with mismatched rivals.'[43]

It had been a difficult season, one in which the Scuderia men had to 'work hard', to quote the words of its owner, 'to overcome the initially inadequate tools and address the nearly complete renewal of engines and cars while many foreign manufacturers have, for a number of reasons, enjoyed multiple and significant benefits'.[44]

Although destined to have no future, Bazzi's Bimotore, proudly suggested Ferrari, had been a 'particularly honourable experiment, and an original and bold initiative at a time when it seemed there was no technical way to make up for the initial disadvantage with wealthy foreign manufacturers, rich in materials and means, and for the outstanding achievement that rewarded the tenacious project'.[45]

The eight-cylinder Type C was off to a good start, while at Portello Jano was also developing the twelve-cylinder version. Ferrari knew that the pivot around which the fortunes of Scuderia Ferrari would turn in the following season was Tazio Nuvolari, whom Enzo had not hesitated to call 'immortal' for his multiple achievements in 1935.[46]

In mid-November Enzo wrote a 'Personal and Confidential' letter to Alfa Romeo managing director Ugo Gobbato, appealing to their 'mutual interests' and asking for Gobbato's direct intervention in negotiating the contract renewal for the Flying Mantuan.[47] Ferrari's fears were not unfounded, because even if Nuvolari still faced the ostracism of the Auto Union racing drivers, he was nonetheless being courted by Maserati, which, having obtained external funding, strongly wanted Nuvolari on its works team.[48]

'We would be sincerely grateful to Your Excellency,' Ferrari wrote, 'if you would kindly lend us a hand, either directly or through the person of *Commendatore* Jano, to encourage *Commendatore* Nuvolari to renew our contract for the next season.'[49] It was not going to be easy, because the economic terms would, out of necessity, be lower than in the previous season. 'We would hope that Your Excellency,' Ferrari continued, 'would let him know the necessity of adapting the conditions of the new contract at the particular moment we are living, given the scenario of the next racing season, when activity will likely be quite limited.'[50]

Though flattered by the energetic yet courteous appeals made by Maserati, Nuvolari never really considered the Bologna team's offer and, in the first days of January, renewed his contract with Scuderia Ferrari for the 1936 season.[51] In Modena on the day of the signing, Enzo Ferrari breathed a sigh of relief. He had once again secured the services of the greatest talent of his generation for the following season.

The End of Illusions

'He is the most popular racing driver that has ever existed in the world. His name is synonymous with legendary exploits that move and excite crowds. Fifteen years of experience and uninterrupted activity has not turned him into one who merely expends energy and takes risks. It has made him the strongest racing driver there ever was, and the most indomitable fighter' – *La Scuderia Ferrari* weekly magazine.[1]

The first season after the reconciliation with Nuvolari had provided more than honourable results in an atmosphere of collaboration without any particular tension. The second season would probably bring similar satisfaction, although the struggle against Auto Union and Mercedes would inevitably be an uphill battle.

Before Nuvolari's signing, Ferrari had been presented with two defections. The first was Louis Chiron's. The Monegasque had declined to renew his contract and had signed with Mercedes instead. His move had assumed geopolitical ramifications because it seemed certain that Chancellor Hitler himself had given the green light to the hiring of Chiron to send a signal of détente to the French government.[2]

Then it was René Dreyfus's turn. He feared that, due to the international political situation – Italy had invaded Abyssinia (which is now Ethiopia), and European nations were threatening to boycott Italy in various forms –he would be denied the opportunity to participate in races held outside Italian borders. He had received a good offer from another manufacturer and decided to accept it. He asked Ferrari to release him from his contract, which Ferrari had already signed. Ferrari had expressed surprise, but had been accommodating.

Two days after the mid-December meeting with Dreyfus, Enzo Ferrari presided over the annual board meeting of Società Anonima Scuderia Ferrari. During the meeting Count Carlo Felice Trossi resigned from the position of president that he had held for four years. The count's decision was said to be motivated by 'personal reasons'.[3] In reality, the reasons were very different: Trossi was a gentleman driver who was not at ease anymore within an organization more and more pledged to professionalism.

As much as he was fond of and in debt to him, Ferrari had never fully understood the fascinating and complex personality of Carlo Felice Trossi. Above all, he had never shared Trossi's ability to live 'as an amateur, content to merely skim the surface of the problems, to savour the passions'.[4] Ferrari did not lose his composure. He accepted Trossi's resignation, along with the board's vote electing him the new president, which immediately took effect.

After six years of racing and having needed first Caniato's and then Trossi's money, Ferrari was finally in an economic position where he did not need to depend on anyone else's financial backing. He had come full circle: he now was where he had wanted to be from the very moment he had conceived the idea of his own team. Scuderia Ferrari was all his.

Conscious of how his organization needed excellent protection in a country becoming increasingly politicized, Ferrari facilitated the election to the board of Eugenio Sillingardi,[5] an active member of the Modena Fascist Party. Thanks to his connections, in all likelihood the new board member would help to shield Scuderia Ferrari from the attacks of those, even within Alfa Romeo itself, who continued to ask for the return of manufacturers to racing.

Two months later Ferrari's Machiavellian plan could be considered successful when Sillingardi was appointed the representative of the Italian teams in the new Racing Commission of the RACI.[6]

In addition to the single-seater of 1935, suitably modified and updated, in the new season Scuderia Ferrari would be able to field the new 12-cylinder Alfa Romeo Type C. These were the cars on which Vittorio Jano had worked for months. Ferrari was certain that they would 'prove worthy of the fame of their creator'.[7]

The real variable of the season was represented by Italy's position in Europe, and by the possible adoption of continental sanctions against the country. In the winter of 1936 the defection of Dreyfus was just the tip of the iceberg, the first sign of Europe's turn against Italy.

But Ferrari also cultivated a dream to race in the United States, an endeavour he knew the Fascist state would support.[8] 'For several years,' he said, 'I have nurtured the idea of a trip to America.'[9] This dream was strengthened by the fact that the Indianapolis 500 had long been the goal of Tazio Nuvolari. The problem had always been the regulations, which differed greatly from those governing the races in Europe. But something, or someone, had told him that the situation was about to change. 'I'm waiting,' he said, 'for a concrete proposal, and if, as I was informed,

American racing regulations will sanction the admission of supercharged cars, then it is very likely that we will go there.'[10]

The moment he received confirmation of the change in regulations, Ferrari would be ready. 'The organization of a trip to America has already been planned and studied in its outline a few months ago,' he said.[11] He would choose between two races: the Indianapolis 500 at the end of May or the Vanderbilt Cup in mid-October.

Back in Europe, however, it would not be an easy season.

The first race of 1936 was the Pau Grand Prix on Sunday 1 March. On 20 February Ferrari had assembled his drivers at Monza to get to know the new Alfa Romeo Type C.[12] The two cars were then loaded on the yellow and blue Scuderia trucks and started on their way to France. When they arrived at the Italian–French border at Ponte San Luigi, however, the trucks were stopped.

Ferrari's winter presentiment had proved correct. The nightmare was materializing. Since the Paris government had agreed to economic sanctions against Italy, which had since left the League of Nations, the Mussolini government had frozen all relations with the Republic of France as a sign of retaliation. Arriving at the border, the Scuderia Ferrari party received a direct order from Rome to stop. That same day, men, trucks and racing cars were forced to return to Modena.

The international situation soon calmed down, and the about-face at Ponte San Luigi remained a unique episode. Therefore, after the Mille Miglia, in which Ferrari had won the top three places, the grand prix season began in Monte Carlo, and Ferrari was able to send four Alfa Romeo 8Cs to the Côte d'Azur.

Starting from the front row between the two Mercedes of Chiron and Caracciola, in the deluge of rain that made the street course treacherous, Nuvolari led for 30 of the race's 100 laps, before brake troubles demanded a more prudent pace.[13]

*   *   *

The invasion of Abyssinia, the war in Africa, the withdrawal from the League of Nations, the sanctions, the donation of gold to the Fatherland campaign and the proclamation of the Empire had made the single party popular in Italy as it had not been in years. In the spring of 1936, the regime's rhetoric pervaded the whole country. And in his public statements Enzo Ferrari himself was not immune – could not remain immune – to the exasperated nationalism that pervaded Italy.

Enzo's Scuderia was of course tied hand in glove to a state-run industry, Alfa

Romeo, and, like it or not, the situation had certain advantages. The regime saw it as a valid propaganda tool. His was an organization, as he himself had stated some time before, which in 'the industrious tranquillity created by the *DUCE* [rendered in all capital letters, as the ancient Romans did, and as the Ministry of Popular Culture requested] could be created, lives and thrives.'[14]

Here, then, was a total willingness on Ferrari's part to accept – not being free to do otherwise – the government's decision on whether to participate in events abroad: 'very pleased,' he had said, 'to feel more intimately, even in our activities, the influence of those directives that guide Fascist Italy in all her deeds'.[15] Or the commitment to face the challenges of the new season 'with the conscious audacity which is a way of life in Fascist Italy'.[16]

The appointment of Eugenio Sillingardi to the Scuderia board of directors was of course a sign of the increased attention that Ferrari had chosen to pay to the Italian political situation and the subtle equilibrium that held it up; likewise, his comments that winter on Nuvolari's choice to remain with his Scuderia: those who had always appreciated the Flying Mantuan for his racing skills, Ferrari said, 'will also be pleased to ascertain his Fascist devotion'.[17]

Being Italian – and therefore, Fascist – was becoming a recurring theme in Ferrari's prose and oratory in this historic time of nationalistic euphoria, during which, in the short space of a few months, two presidents of the Royal Automobile Club of Italy – appointed by the National Fascist Party – had succeeded one another, and the members of its racing committee had all been replaced.

*   *   *

At Monaco victory had gone to Caracciola's Mercedes. Behind had come the Auto Unions of Varzi and Stuck. Nuvolari was only fourth. Controversy aside, the expedition to the French Riviera had been a partial failure. Ferrari thus looked with anticipation to the debut of the Alfa Romeo 12C in Tripoli on 10 May, four days after the proclamation of the Empire and the final disappearance of any political or economic retaliation against Fascist Italy.

The 12C immediately proved fast. But in practice, on Saturday, a burst tyre caused Nuvolari to crash. The same problem had occurred a few days earlier, during a practice session at Monza, to the sister car of Farina, who had therefore skipped the trip to Africa. Nuvolari came out battered, but determined to race nonetheless. He was given first aid, disregarded the doctors' ban and on Sunday took the start of the race.[18]

The 12Cs of Nuvolari, Brivio and Tadini – who raced with the car that Nuvolari had crashed the day before, which had been put back into shape by Ferrari's mechanics during the night – fought on equal terms with Mercedes. But not with Auto Union. The major drawback encountered by the 12Cs was tyre wear. Forced to make several pit stops to replace tyres, they ended up sixth, seventh and eighth behind Pintacuda's 8C, which was less powerful and slower, but not plagued by tyre troubles.[19]

Auto Union had dominated the race and Varzi and Stuck took the top two places. The switch in the lead between the two drivers had been dictated by a precise order from Berlin that was intended to pay homage to Fascist Italy, in view of the Empire's proclamation – a decision that generated a lot of controversy within the team, and contributed from that moment to innocent Varzi's isolation within Auto Union. Such was the political importance that car races had in Europe during the mid-1930s.

A week later they met and raced again at Tunis. This time Ferrari sent only two cars: an 8C for Pintacuda and a 12C for Brivio. Nuvolari, his ribs broken, had gone back to Italy. In Tunis the problem for the Scuderia's Alfa Romeos was with gasoline. The Dynamin fuel prepared by Shell and normally used by the Scuderia units had not arrived from Italy. So Ferrari's men did what they could with a surrogate sent in haste from Tripoli. It worked only partially.[20]

With the Auto Unions sidelined by a variety of problems, the race was won by Caracciola's Mercedes. Pintacuda finished in second place, but by the appalling gap of two laps. Brivio had withdrawn on the eighth of thirty laps. Due to his Alfa's reduced power because of the poor quality of the gasoline, he had never been in the thick of the race.

Scuderia Ferrari was on its knees. Enzo Ferrari was beside himself. He complained of little or no attention from the sport's governing body and from Italian institutions. He accused the national car industry of taking no interest in motor racing and of leaving him alone to fight against the German car industry, which was more cohesive and supported by the Reich.

He thundered in public and in private. Because in Italy there were those who had accused his Scuderia – Ferrari, that is – of being responsible for the crisis situation, they immediately revived the old theme of returning racing to car manufacturers, rather than private teams. This was the issue that most annoyed Ferrari, because it undermined all the good work he had patiently done over the previous seven years. Consequently, he launched into counteraccusations against the whole system that was supposed to oversee motor racing in Italy, and which, instead, stood by with folded hands.

Ferrari thus threatened to withdraw from motor racing, or at least from participating in events on fast race tracks, which were home to the most important international races. 'With great sadness,' he said, 'we see the futility of perhaps persisting in an effort that is beyond our capability.'[21]

Of course, he was just confusing his audience, because races were his whole life. And he did it deliberately, in an attempt to prevent the attacks that he knew would be aimed at him. Anticipating his detractors, he added: 'If a higher duty exists in this defence of sporting prestige, it is logical that the torch be passed on today to those who think that car manufacturers should directly participate in motor racing.'[22]

Consummate actor that he was, he was bluffing. On one thing, however, he was genuine: 'Illusions,' he said, 'have disappeared with the tenth Grand Prix of Tripoli.'[23]

Enzo had in the meantime made his choice for the expedition to the United States and had decided not to go to Indianapolis, which was scheduled too close to the first European races; rather, his Scuderia would participate in the Vanderbilt Cup in October, when the motor-racing season in Europe came to an end.

Ferrari had a very different driver lineup in mind for the Vanderbilt Cup, beginning with Tazio Nuvolari, who, despite his desire to race at Indianapolis, had accepted Ferrari's decision without any problem. To Mike Boyle, the Chicago mobster with a passion for racing cars and the owner of a renowned racing team, who had personally invited him to race for him at Indianapolis, and who, in addition to providing a car, had also offered him a million francs, Nuvolari had simply said, 'Get in touch with *Signor Commendatore* Ferrari, who can dispose of my racing activities throughout 1936.' The peace between the two giants was holding. Their friendship was as deep as it had ever been.

The same day that Pintacuda and Marinoni raced in Rio de Janeiro, in what was the first event contested by Scuderia Ferrari outside Europe, Nuvolari, Brivio and Farina were in Barcelona, on the Montjuic Circuit, in the Grand Prix of the Penya Rhin. Ferrari had entrusted an Alfa Romeo 12C to Nuvolari, who won with a certain ease. Not everything, therefore, was rotten at Alfa Romeo. On mixed circuits like the one in Spain, the 12C was in fact extremely competitive. Nuvolari had been the only driver who raced that day to set a lap time below two minutes.[24]

The Alfa Romeo 8C and 12C might not have had the power and speed of the Auto Union Type C or the agility of the Mercedes W25K, but on mixed circuits – that is, on the vast majority of European race tracks – they had some shot of winning. In mid-June Nuvolari finished second in the Eifel Grand Prix; ahead of him came only Bernd Rosemeyer's Auto Union. Before the end of the month Tazio had clinched two consecutive victories in Budapest and Milan. And if it was true that in Milan the only Auto Union in the race was Achille Varzi's, in Hungary the German teams were present in full force.

On 9 July, Enzo Ferrari met at Portello with Gobbato and Jano for a sort of midsummer summit. Despite the latest victories, Alfa Romeo was receiving pressure from the state to counter German manufacturers with even greater strength. Of course, what was needed, first and foremost, was a contribution on the part of the state, but it was much easier to put pressure on those who were at the forefront rather than take responsibility and provide some substantive financial support.

The meeting produced the resolution on the part of both Alfa Romeo and Ferrari to make even greater efforts, although only those who knew nothing of motor racing, or had other purposes, could have accused either of them of not trying hard enough already. One should also not forget that, although it was present through Scuderia Ferrari in international motor racing, in 1936 Alfa Romeo was anything but a fully fledged car manufacturer. A company committed wholeheartedly to the production of aircraft engines, it would build during the entire year only 10 cars – exactly half of the production of 1910, the year it had been founded.

'Stressing the need to have more-efficient cars,' summed up Gobbato at the end of the meeting (stating the obvious, which must have annoyed Ferrari), 'Scuderia Ferrari will agree with *Commendatore* Jano on a programme in which they will participate in a number of races during the year.'[25] A sentence which officially – and politically – placed responsibility on the shoulders of Vittorio Jano and Enzo Ferrari.

Meanwhile, despite multiple wins, Tazio Nuvolari's summer was not serene. His son Giorgio had been ill for quite some time, and now his health worsened. By mid-June the situation seemed desperate. Sensing the drama of the moment, Ferrari had immediately telegraphed Tazio, who had rushed back home from Germany before going to Budapest for the next race. In his telegram, Ferrari wrote with sympathy, affection and elegance, avoiding direct mention of the delicate topic: 'We wish to inform you that if for any reason you would prefer to stay in Mantua, we would replace you for this race, or even renounce the participation of a car, without any problem.'[26]

Giorgio Nuvolari seemed to recover and Tazio continued to race, and to win. On 2 August he won for the fifth time in his career the Coppa Ciano on Livorno's Montenero Circuit, shortened to just 7km (4 miles), with the loss of the climb to the Sanctuary of the Madonna del Montenero and the subsequent steep descent to the Tyrrhenian Sea and the old Aurelia road. And he did so in one of those daring ways that were rapidly elevating him to the rank of living legend – in Pintacuda's car, which he'd climbed into after the Florentine driver had brought it back to the pits.

For personal PR reasons, Ferrari never missed going to Livorno, where, during the race, the notables of Italian motorsport would gather around Galeazzo Ciano. Therefore, he heard with his own ears Nuvolari imprudently talking to journalists, who were wondering how he could have won in Pintacuda's car, with brakes that were in poor condition. Brakes were not needed to go fast, Nuvolari said, 'A phrase,' Enzo would say afterwards, 'that haunted Pintacuda for a long time.'[27]

The three Auto Unions of Varzi, Rosemeyer and Stuck failed to finish. Ferrari placed three cars in the top three positions; behind Nuvolari came Brivio and Dreyfus, who had returned to the Scuderia starting with the Grand Prix of Deauville on 19 July. The return of the Frenchman once again revealed Enzo Ferrari's great pragmatism: he was able to forgive what he perceived as Dreyfus's personal wrongdoings over that torn-up contract, to secure one of the best possible driving resources. During a period of fervent nationalism, in which Fascist Italy was getting closer and closer to Nazi Germany, and conceiving racial laws that would be announced a year later, Ferrari could have prevented the hiring of a Jewish driver such as Dreyfus.

September brought Nuvolari's second place in the Italian Grand Prix behind an invincible Rosemeyer, and a victory, again clinched by the Flying Mantuan, at the Circuit of Modena. Still coping with an inexorable disease, Giorgio Nuvolari was hospitalized during those days in Modena, and had watched the race from his hospital-room window. Lap after lap, his father had taken one of the most challenging turns of the circuit with one hand gripped on the steering wheel while waving at his son with the other.[28] This was Tazio's third consecutive win in Modena and at the end of the day he was once again crowned Champion of Italy – a success that naturally reflected on Scuderia Ferrari yet another triumph on the national scene.

And then the time finally came to cross the Atlantic. The destination this time was New York, where, on 12 October, three Alfa Romeos driven by Nuvolari, Brivio and Farina would fight a myriad of American cars, a couple of Bugattis and a few private Maseratis for the gigantic Vanderbilt Cup trophy. Ferrari, who remained in Modena, had sent three 12Cs and an 8C by sea. With them, in addition to the three designated drivers, he sent Attilio Marinoni as reserve driver, Luigi Bazzi, *Maestro* Ugolini and four mechanics: Meazza, Stefani (who had already been to Brazil that summer), Mambelli and Bai.[29]

The Vanderbilt Cup was returning in 1936 after a long absence. It had been

20 years since the last one was run – there had been 11 races from 1904 to 1916, one of the fixed appointments in the pioneering days of motor racing. The 1936 event would be raced on a winding dirt track near the Roosevelt Field airport on Long Island, a few miles from New York City – the airfield from which, 9 years earlier, Charles Lindbergh had begun his historic solo Atlantic crossing. It was not a particularly technical circuit, and it was immediately clear that, unless something unexpected happened, Nuvolari could easily take home the trophy.

After setting aside the 8C with which he had got to know the circuit, with the 12C Nuvolari set the fastest practice time. In the race, he immediately took the lead, and was never really challenged by the other 42 drivers, including his 2 teammates. After a little over four and a half hours of racing, he passed the finish line with an almost embarrassing advantage over the second-place finisher: twelve minutes on Wimille's Bugatti. Third came Brivio, with the second Alfa Romeo, after another minute. The third Ferrari car, in the hands of Farina, had stopped on lap 17 with steering problems.

Nuvolari's win secured the Italians prize money of $20,000, equal to a quarter of a million lire. Brivio's second place earned another $5,000. And all Scuderia drivers, especially the Mantuan, of course, collected thousands of dollars during the race, since the leader had earned $100 each time he passed the finish line.[30] By contract, half of all the earnings went to Scuderia Ferrari.

If the regime had encouraged the participation of Scuderia Ferrari for obvious propaganda reasons, Ferrari's real reason for the American trip was the fabulously rich prize money. Mission accomplished.

Nuvolari's victory in America caused a huge stir in Italy, from which Alfa Romeo and Ferrari benefited as well. Enzo personally went to Genoa to meet his champion when he returned to Italy. The crowd was so huge that he was unable to manage more than a quick handshake. So, back in Modena, he wrote Nuvolari a letter of congratulations. 'I wish to express,' he said on 4 November, 'my deepest pleasure that you have in the final race of the season obtained well-deserved gratification, and my deep gratitude for the valuable cooperation you have given to the Scuderia this year.'[31]

Ferrari had wanted to speak to Nuvolari the moment he returned to Italy primarily to avoid any surprise. Having obtained a glittering win in America, he feared that Nuvolari might consider his stay in Modena over. 'I dare to hope,' Enzo wrote, 'that your relationship with my organization in the course of the year has been one of satisfaction, and that you can adhere to our desire to renew our agreements for next year.'[32]

To keep him on the team, Ferrari was now willing to let Nuvolari choose the other team members. 'I would like to speak with you as soon as possible,' he wrote, 'to decide on the future composition of the team, and especially, the confirmation of those drivers who were your teammates last season, and on the possible recruitment of others.'[33] On Ferrari's part, this was a connection that he had never previously had with any other driver, and that he would never repeat in the future – testimony of the esteem he had for the Mantuan but, also, a clear sign of Ferrari's willingness to accept a less-powerful role in their relationship in order to retain him.

A few days later Ferrari and Bazzi met Nuvolari to discuss the programme for the following season. Nuvolari approved the confirmation of Brivio, Farina, Pintacuda and Dreyfus, and the sporadic use of Tadini, Severi, Clemente Biondetti and Emilio Villoresi. The announcement of the 1937 lineup was made during the traditional end-of-year dinner, organized as always in Modena in mid-December. Although he made no mention of it that evening, with Nuvolari's approval[34] Ferrari was negotiating the return of Count Trossi, which would be announced in January. Achille Varzi had come to the dinner, too, and his presence had bewildered the journalists who were present.[35] Not knowing that Ferrari had left to Nuvolari the last word on the choice of his drivers, the press began to speculate on Varzi's presence.

The 1936 season had not been all negative, even if the gap between the Italian and the German automotive industries and racing teams had only increased. To defend his performance, in those early winter days Ferrari kept stressing that the German manufacturers had staked everything on what he labelled as exploding meteors 'expressly suited to one type of circuit and competition'. Alfa Romeo, on the other hand, had continued to develop – and his Scuderia would continue to use – 'racing cars',[36] with a particular emphasis on the word *cars*, to imply their closeness to everyday passenger cars.

It was true. But it was also, on the part of Ferrari, a blatant attempt to sugar the pill, because he was the first to realize that Auto Union and Mercedes, by so doing, were the only ones competing for victory in the most prestigious events.

For once Ferrari was not defending only Alfa Romeo; in the winter months of 1937, he was chiefly defending himself and his organization. He was being criticized for the slow pace and seemingly low quality of the job done by his Scuderia in developing and tuning those cars that Alfa Romeo sold him. In part he was paying for the efficiency he had shown in earlier seasons, when the level of opposition was not as high, and the Scuderia staff compensated for the work that it was not possible to carry out at Portello. But now the Germans had raised the technical bar, and an organization that remained fiercely small could no longer keep up with them.

If illusions had ended with the summer of 1936, in the winter of 1937 the illusion of Enzo Ferrari remaining independent was also coming to an end. In Milan, Ugo Gobbato had clearer ideas about the future of Scuderia Ferrari – a future less and less autonomous. In the very pages of the Ferrari bulletin, no more than one year ago, Gobbato had revealingly stated that 'wonderful companies went bankrupt when, without changing the internal structure, they expanded beyond the limits of their boss's imagination'.[37]

Bad Habits

In mid-February 1937 came proof that the die was cast.

On 19 February, Enzo Ferrari received a registered letter from the office of Alfa Romeo's general manager, containing a copy of the agreement between Alfa Romeo and Scuderia Ferrari for 'the management in partnership of all racing activity', and 'a letter regarding his appointment as racing director' of the new organization.[1] The agreement would be in effect from 1 January 1937 (meaning it had already been in place for a month and a half) until 31 December 1940, when it would automatically expire unless renewed by 30 June of that year.[2]

After months of negotiations and no response to his idea of creating a Scuderia Italia made up of Alfa Romeo, Scuderia Ferrari and Fiat,[3] Enzo Ferrari had sold 80 per cent of the shares in his company to Alfa Romeo. While on the one hand he had renounced – had been *forced* to renounce, because of the situation – the yearned-for and long-defended independence, on the other he had obtained a direct commitment from Alfa Romeo, which would now cover four-fifths of the Scuderia's operational costs.[4] The stated purpose of the new association was to 'make ever more efficient the participation of the Alfa Romeo brand in international motor-racing events'.[5]

Enzo had naturally asked for and received precise guarantees. 'Annually, or at every change in the international sports formula, or in national and international programmes,' he had wanted written in the agreement, 'Alfa Romeo's general manager, after consulting with the sales department and examining the technical and building capability of the workshop, will decide, in agreement with the management of Scuderia Ferrari, on a construction programme and on a racing schedule, taking as a reference the volume of activity done in the past' – Ferrari had always been delighted to compete with his Scuderia every single Sunday, in places far apart from each other – 'and in line with Alfa Romeo's sporting tradition.'[6]

In exchange for the interference to which he would now have to adapt, he was made the exclusive racing representative of Alfa Romeo; cars and spare parts, which remained the property of the Milan company, would be provided solely and exclusively to Scuderia Ferrari.[7] For his part Ferrari was required to field from now on only Alfa Romeos, which had until then represented the vast majority of the cars entered by his Scuderia, but with notable exceptions, of which Enzo – fond of Alfa Romeo, but in his own way – had always been proud.

Alfa Romeo pledged to invest half a million lire in Scuderia Ferrari, excluding the cost of racing cars. Scuderia Ferrari would draw its income from the race and prize money, from the reimbursement of expenses recognized by race organizers and from sponsor fees paid by automotive suppliers. For its part, the Scuderia would take care of all costs inherent in race participation – travel expenses for drivers, mechanics, staff and support vehicles, 'maintenance, repair and eventual reconstruction of racing cars', drivers' remuneration, to be taken from the race money of each event, and administrative costs.[8]

As president and general manager, Enzo Ferrari would receive 8,000 lire a month, for a total of 96,000 lire a year, a pretty lavish sum. The stroke of genius was the 25,000 lire a year that Alfa Romeo would pay him from now on to rent the building and workshop in Viale Trento Trieste,[9] a structure that Ferrari had been using since 1930.

The new agreement was not advertised,[10] the public not informed. Insiders such as Canestrini and Filippini probably knew, but did not disclose the information. At least on the outside, the credibility of Ferrari had not been undermined.

At Portello, Vittorio Jano was working on the 12C, completely refreshing it for the 1937 season, which would begin in April. Although he had already started in autumn 1936, the development was proceeding at a slow pace due to a chronic lack of components and lack of cooperation, despite initial assurances, from the Portello management. Moreover, after some of its men had been relocated to Modena, Jano's experimental department in Milan numbered only a dozen people.[11]

For all of these reasons, the 1937 season did not look all that promising in terms of racing results. But if Enzo Ferrari had realistically anticipated a transition year, the same could not be said for the Alfa Romeo management. Under pressure from the Fascist regime, because theirs cars were soon expected to return to play the leading role, Alfa Romeo executives poured out their frustration on Jano and Ferrari.

The racing season began on 4 April with the Mille Miglia. Ferrari lined up seven Alfa Romeos. He took home first-, second-, fourth- and ninth-place finishes. April continued with two other Italian races: the Turin Circuit on 18 April and the Princess of Piedmont Cup the following Sunday.

Against weak opposition, Scuderia Ferrari and Alfa Romeo clinched two more easy and expected wins.

But on the Thursday before the Turin race, Nuvolari was injured. During the first tests on the Valentino Circuit, having only just avoided two century-old trees, he had ended his run upside-down between the road and the footpath. Tazio had emerged shaken but relatively unscathed. The doctors, however, sidelined him for the next two races.

He returned on the second Sunday in May at the Tripoli Grand Prix, where the music – and it could not have been otherwise, given the participation of the Germans who had not contested the first Italian races – changed dramatically.

In Africa the six Alfa Romeo 12Cs entered by Scuderia Ferrari never had a hope of victory. They were merely sad extras in a race where Auto Union and Mercedes monopolized the seven positions in the front two rows of the starting grid, and the first eight final positions.

For Alfa Romeo and Scuderia Ferrari, the North African trip was a complete disaster. Despite warnings that were clearly visible the night before, the utter manifestation of helplessness at Tripoli was a heavy blow for all. At Portello Jano was pushed to complete the development of the new car as fast as he possibly could, and Ferrari himself began to feel the pressure.

Expected wins in races of moderate importance, such as the Parma–Poggio di Berceto or the Circuit of Superba, did not help to raise morale. Neither was the situation ameliorated by Pintacuda's win and Brivio's third-place finish in the Grand Prix of Rio de Janeiro, in which the only Auto Union at the start, driven by Hans Stuck, finished between the two Alfas. Fearing a massacre like at Tripoli, Ferrari convinced the Alfa Romeo management not to participate in the Avus race.

But naturally, Ferrari could not recommend – nor Alfa Romeo accept – a refusal to participate in all of the international races before the season's debut of the new car designed by Jano. So in mid-June, in an attempt to limit the damage, Ferrari sent only two cars for the Eifelrennen – two 12Cs entrusted to Nuvolari and the ever more promising Farina.

The Nürburgring proved to be less disappointing a race than Tripoli, even though the two Alfas never battled for the lead. On the day of Bernd Rosemeyer's third consecutive win, Nuvolari finished fifth, with four German cars in front of him and as many behind. The following week Tazio easily won yet another Italian race – the Milan Circuit – and prepared to leave with Farina for New York, where Ferrari had planned the (unsuccessful, as it turned out) defence of the win clinched at the Vanderbilt Cup the previous October.

With Nuvolari still on a ship on the Atlantic, on 11 July Ferrari fielded two Alfa Romeo 12Cs for Sommer and Trossi in the Belgian Grand Prix. Despite limited participation on the part of the two German teams, the Scuderia did no better than a fifth place.

The Flying Mantuan returned to European racing at the Nürburgring on 25 July for the German Grand Prix, an event once again dominated by German cars. At the wheel of a 12C, Nuvolari took home an honourable fourth-place finish, highlighted by the ovation he received from the German crowd,[12] who had not forgotten his great feat two years earlier. In all likelihood, the fans wanted to show him their support at a time of great personal sorrow for the recent death of his beloved first-born son Giorgio.

At Portello all efforts were by now concentrated on the new Jano car with a tubular frame. On 3 August, a first unit was finally ready for testing.

The test was not fully satisfactory. As Jano knew perfectly well, the car needed further development. But the only real ally Jano had left was Enzo Ferrari. They had become men of great racing experience who were not listened to any longer by managers who knew nothing about motor racing in a company that nonetheless called all the shots. As if this state of confusion was not enough, now politics had set in.

On 15 August the Coppa Acerbo was held in Pescara. Secretary Acerbo of the Mussolini government had personally asked Nuvolari, in the name of their old friendship, to press the Alfa Romeo management to have the new 12C at *his* race.[13] The natural and justified opposition of Jano and Ferrari was easily worked around, and the first two 1937 12Cs were trucked to Pescara to be fielded in the thirteenth running of the Abruzzo ace.

Ferrari had clearly been bypassed by the Alfa Romeo management, but the surprises were not over. The two new cars were going to be raced not through Scuderia Ferrari but directly by Alfa Corse, which, with these two cars and in this race, officially returned to racing after an absence of five years.

The fragile balance within Alfa Romeo had been broken. Deprived earlier in the year of a large part of his kingdom, Ferrari had now become a king without a crown. Despite what was specified in his contract, Alfa Romeo was doing what it wanted with Scuderia Ferrari, strengthened by the fact that the company controlled 80 per cent of the property. For the first time in eight years, Enzo Ferrari was no longer central to the Alfa Romeo racing project, a manufacturer to which he had linked his professional career since 1920.

At Pescara the modest technical quality of a car still short of development was dramatically exposed to all. On lap 7 Farina was called back to the pits and the new 12C was withdrawn from the race. For Alfa Romeo it was a public failure of enormous magnitude. The old 12C fielded by Scuderia Ferrari and entrusted to Sommer ran a few laps before being forced to retire, too.

The debacle was total. At Portello the situation would soon explode, but for now Gobbato decided to wait and ponder.

To avoid diluting the energy needed to develop the new car before the ever-important Grand Prix of Italy in mid-September, Alfa Romeo withdrew the new works 12Cs from participating at the Swiss Grand Prix of 22 August. In their place they sent two old 12Cs entered by Scuderia Ferrari, which had returned to act as a stopgap, as in 1930 and 1931.

Meanwhile, to further increase tension and fuel uncertainty, Nuvolari had raced in the Swiss Grand Prix with an Auto Union. This move – he had a contract with Scuderia Ferrari and another directly with Alfa Romeo, but still felt authorized to race with a third party – had caught Alfa Romeo executives off guard and shocked the Italian public.

So, when on 12 September the Italian Grand Prix held in Livorno turned into yet another embarrassing defeat, the first head to roll was Vittorio Jano's. On 28 September he was fired. The second head would be Ferrari's, although it would not roll for quite some time.

To save himself and his dream, Ferrari had by now realized that he had only one way left to survive: he had to hang on to Nuvolari. After the traumatic escape to Auto Union, Tazio returned to the ranks, finishing the 1937 season at the wheel of a Scuderia Alfa Romeo; however, it was far from certain whether he'd stay with the Italian manufacturer. Ferrari knew that Nuvolari's presence would make his (Ferrari's) position at Portello, if not necessary, at least strategic; after Jano's dismissal, he was the only one whom Nuvolari truly respected. In essence, his future – or at least his place at Alfa Romeo – depended on Nuvolari.

For this reason Ferrari tried to speak personally with Nuvolari, as soon as possible. He wanted to know the Mantuan's real intentions, and to try to convince him to stay with Alfa Romeo. Between mid-October and early December he wrote three letters in succession to invite Nuvolari to Modena, to discuss the future. From Mantua, however, no reply came. Time began to run out. Ferrari clearly spoke out: 'I absolutely need to have elements in order to make a decision that I cannot delay any further.'[14]

While Nuvolari was taking his time, in Milan Ugo Gobbato had already made a decision about Ferrari and his Scuderia. He had never been convinced of the validity, or even the need, for Alfa Romeo's direct participation in motor racing.[15] But even he could not indefinitely withstand the continuous pressure of the regime.

On 27 December 1937, Scuderia Ferrari ceased to exist. Gobbato had surrendered.[16] Within Alfa Romeo those who – whether they believed it or not – argued that direct engagement would increase the chances to do well had won. They were only illusions, unjustified from a technical point of view, fruit of much inexperience and equal presumption and, what was more, motivated by politics and ideology. To absorb Scuderia Ferrari in the Alfa Romeo bureaucratic machine was more of a political statement than a real step forward, toward greater racing achievements.

From one day to the next, Scuderia Ferrari disappeared. For Enzo Ferrari, who had invested eight years of his life in the Scuderia, it was a bitter day. He could not say that the decision had come as a surprise, but it was still pretty much a stab in the back. In 8 years, Scuderia Ferrari had participated in 225 races, with a total of 715 cars; it had obtained 144 victories and 171 podium finishes.[17] It had played an important part in European motorsport, and had for a long time shaped the Italian racing environment. Now it was being shut down without any public word of gratitude. The only satisfaction Enzo received was that it made him rich.

The liquidation of the Scuderia in fact provided him with more than a million lire. At the same time Enzo was named 'head of Alfa Corse',[18] a new department that he would help to create. The consultancy contract was valid for three years, from 1 January 1938 to 31 December 1940. At least on paper, the new contract promised autonomy. He would report 'directly and solely' to Alfa Romeo general manager Ugo Gobbato.[19] His place of employment would be Milan, in a new two-story building erected in the fall adjacent to the Portello factory,[20] but Ferrari was expressly 'relieved of any residence requirement, office hours and presence'.[21]

In the winter of 1938 the personal future of Enzo Ferrari was a difficult puzzle to decipher. In some ways the previous eight years had been annulled. On 18 February he turned 40 – an age at which a man could begin to see his life in some perspective, or at least a part of it. And if on the one hand he could be proud of what he had done, on the other he couldn't help but realize that the past 18 years had been wiped out by what seemed to him to be an irrational decision that had little or nothing to do with motor racing.

In the meantime Nuvolari had continued to buy time. On 24 January Gobbato himself had urged the renewal of his contract with Alfa Romeo: 'I trust' – the Alfa Romeo general manager had written with sincere hope – 'that you will come to an understanding with *Commendatore* Ferrari.' A Ferrari then, who – at least theoretically, and certainly in the triangle with Nuvolari – seemed to have maintained a substantial place in Gobbato's consideration.

Four days later Bernd Rosemeyer was killed trying to set a new speed record when a gust of wind blew his streamlined Auto Union off the Autobahn. He and Tazio were close friends, and his death seemed to cause Nuvolari to falter. The real possibility of honouring his friend by taking his place at Auto Union was appealing. He asked for more time, but eventually signed a new contract with Alfa Romeo – with how much conviction, everyone would see soon enough.

The 1938 season began on 10 April with the Grand Prix of Pau, and the Flying Mantuan's great fear of a crash materialized. During the race, his Alfa Romeo 308 – a transformation of the 8C 2900 A, one of the cars built during 1937 in Modena by Scuderia Ferrari,[22] which had impressed in practice for its speed – suddenly caught fire. Nuvolari parked it on the side of the road, where it was soon engulfed in flames, burning some of the surrounding bushes, as well. He was able to jump out right away, escaping with minor burns. But although he was almost unscathed from a physical point of view, apparently his morale was destroyed. He had never encountered fire in a race before and the experience seemed to traumatize him.

The following week, Nuvolari wrote to Gobbato, saying that he had decided to retire from racing.[23] Nuvolari's decision bewildered Gobbato, Ferrari and the whole world of motor racing. In reality it was all part of his plan to leave Alfa Romeo, which had cars that were no longer competitive and had as a company plunged into frightening managerial chaos, and go to Auto Union, which duly happened when summer came.

To try and have a collegial look at the general state of things, Gobbato summoned Enzo on 16 July to a strategy meeting in his Facen di Pedavena summer house in the Belluno Dolomites. But Alfa Romeo's general manager waited in vain all that Saturday. Ferrari did not go, and did not even bother to inform Gobbato that he wasn't coming.[24]

The situation was rapidly deteriorating. How, under such conditions, the relationship between Ferrari and Alfa Romeo could go on for another year remains a mystery, certainly not explained by the significant salary that Ferrari regularly received nor the indispensability of a man who did nothing to smooth over the edges and who, indeed, seemed to find every pretext to worsen his personal situation.

Alfa Romeo finished far from the podium in the Grand Prix of Switzerland on 21 August and watched helplessly as Tazio Nuvolari won the Italian Grand Prix at Monza on 11 September at the wheel of an Auto Union. The victory of the Mantuan was unreservedly hailed by the Italian press. Now that Italy and Germany were allies, Tazio's defection was much less controversial than Varzi's had been a few years earlier, but it hurt the Alfa Romeo management.

At the end of the race, Nuvolari was 'hoisted on the shoulders and carried in triumph by the enthusiastic crowd',[25] who, divided on the eve between an Italian car and an Italian driver, had picked the driver, relegating Alfa Romeo into a corner despite the extraordinary second place scored by Nino Farina with the Type 312. That same indifference greeted Emilio Villoresi and Severi, who, with the 158, had seized victory and second place in the Grand Prix of Milan, the voiturette race (for smaller cars) during the Italian Grand Prix weekend.

In the winter of 1939 the engine designer Gioacchino Colombo returned to Milan.[26] Ferrari could not have asked for anything better, since he had worked with Colombo in Modena and their relationship had been splendid. But there was a third wheel, a Spanish engineer, a consultant just like Ferrari, who, exactly like Ferrari, reported directly to Gobbato, enjoying his full confidence. His name was Wifredo Ricart.

Ricart had arrived at Alfa Romeo in October 1936 after fleeing from civil war-torn Spain. Hired as a consultant for testing and technical issues – including aeronautical matters[27] – he had eventually designed a six-cylinder diesel engine for passenger cars.[28] In theory, his path and Ferrari's should never have crossed. In reality, by virtue of the faith Gobbato had in him, Ricart began to meddle in the technical issues of Alfa Corse, going so far as to join Colombo at the helm of the technical department.[29]

Ferrari had never liked Ricart. He was unnerved by his arrogance and pomposity, and now by his repeated attempts to intrude upon the technical management of Alfa Corse. Ferrari was even bothered physically by the Spaniard[30] and did nothing to disguise his contempt. For his part, Ricart had no consideration for the technical depth of Ferrari, whom he considered a self-taught man devoid of the level of experience Ricart himself had.[31]

The conflict between Ferrari and Ricart became fierce when, in spring 1939, the first drawings of the new Type 512 – a rear-engine, 12-cylinder, 1500 single-seater – were presented. That day Ricart not only praised the new car, but derided the 158, which Scuderia Ferrari had built in Modena in 1937, calling it 'an outdated machine, good for demolition or museum exhibition'.[32] The open disagreement between two people who were supposed to work together would not help to solve Alfa Romeo's competitiveness problem. Despite mutual respect, Enzo Ferrari and Ugo Gobbato had two antithetical conceptions of how a racing team should operate. Unlike Ferrari, who grew up with motor racing, Gobbato believed neither in 'improvisation' nor in 'quick decisions'.[33] Indeed, he ensured that everything was arranged in advance down to the last detail – which, in the world of motor racing, was not always possible. Ferrari knew this; Gobbato did not.

From the point of view of the company man that he was, Gobbato considered a racing car the synthesis of all the departments that made up a company, the fruit of the work of many organizations, even if they were seemingly far apart. Ferrari, on the contrary, based on his experience, argued that race cars were to be 'the compendium of the work of a small auxiliary workshop, with excellent resources and its own special and flexible staff, ready to quickly translate ideas and projects into an ever-changing final product'.[34]

Even without the role played by Ricart, the disagreements would have escalated. But it was when Gobbato began to take Ricart's side more and more often that the relationship between the general manager of Alfa Romeo and Ferrari reached a critical stage. The heated discussions which, according to Ferrari, 'testified at least to a common passion',[35] became vitriolic battles. Animated by his usual fire, Ferrari asked Gobbato for a clarifying meeting.

The interview turned into a violent verbal confrontation. Ferrari shouted his rebellion in the face of the general manager. 'Along with the 158 units and the liquidation of Scuderia Ferrari,' he said, 'I have not abdicated my way of thinking.'[36]

Gobbato was just as crude and honest. 'At Alfa Romeo,' he said, verbatim, '*I* am in charge, and I cannot get rid of an employee to whom I gave my trust, nor can I agree to always follow your advice, Ferrari, without reservation, and in any case, without discussing it.'[37]

Ferrari sensed that he had gone too far. He apologized 'for having solicited such a harsh response'.[38] He added that 'the issue was not to discuss or accept in whole' what he said, but that he was displeased by 'the way' all the suggestions coming from Ricart 'were accepted'.[39] Despite the apology, as he was leaving Gobbato's office, Ferrari knew that he had lost. Now it was only a matter of time.

The 158 that Ricart wanted retired had in fact, at least in part, saved a season that was compromised from the start. With Mercedes and Auto Union calling the shots in the grand prix category and winning the four main events of the year – the grands prix of Belgium, France, Germany and Switzerland – thanks to the 158 Alfa Romeo had won both the Coppa Ciano and Coppa Acerbo, two races that, in 1939, were open only to voiturettes.

Pre-race practice for the Coppa Acerbo had given Ferrari another great sorrow. Giordano Aldrighetti, who in the first part of the 1930s had been one of the top drivers in the motorcycle department of Scuderia Ferrari, had a terrible accident. At first it looked like he would survive. Instead, he died the following night. Ferrari strove, as he always did in these cases, to provide familial support, meeting Aldrighetti's mother in Pescara, accompanying her on the journey back to Rome and organizing the funeral. In Livorno, on 30 July, the winner was Nino Farina.

In Pescara, two weeks later, four 158s finished the race in the first four places. But it was too late. Enzo Ferrari's stay at Alfa Romeo had come to an end.

On 28 August Ugo Gobbato asked the personnel office for details of the contract between Ferrari and Alfa Romeo. A typed sheet arrived on his desk. A few sentences: 'Contract terms: from January 1, 1938, to December 31, 1940 . . . notice of termination to be given through letter within 30/06/40 . . . annual compensation: 190,000 lire payable quarterly . . . annual remuneration up to a maximum of 60,000 lire on the sale of racing cars, contributions from suppliers, etc . . . car in use.'[40] Termination required six months' notice; however, Alfa Romeo wanted to terminate Ferrari's contract nearly a year and a half ahead of time. Gobbato was aware that firing Ferrari would cost him a lot of money. And this would be in addition to what Alfa Romeo had already paid him on two separate occasions: in 1937, when they had acquired 80 per cent of Scuderia Ferrari, and in 1938, when they had liquidated it. But he had made up his mind.

Remarkably, Enzo Ferrari and Alfa Romeo parted on good terms.

On 6 September 1939, Ugo Gobbato wrote a few lines to Ferrari to officially inform him of the termination of his contract, a short but friendly letter that contained a polite lie and appreciation – certainly sincere – for the job that Ferrari had done on behalf of Alfa Romeo since well before the present company leadership had come in.

'The current international situation,' wrote Gobbato six days after the German invasion of Poland, which had sparked a new continental war, 'has determined the cessation of the racing activity that you headed as our consultant. While we express our regret that circumstances have prevented us from continuing to require your assistance, we would like you to know that we appreciate the work that you have done for Alfa Romeo in the last twenty years, and are pleased that your liquidation came about in a friendly and fair way, and with mutual satisfaction.'[41] Two days later Italian sports fans became aware that some changes were being made at Portello. 'From a good source we learn that the Alfa Romeo leadership,' the *Littoriale* reported almost casually, 'will soon be making a new arrangement at Alfa Corse. In particular,' said the sports daily, without naming names, 'it appears that there will be some changes in the management positions of the racing department.'[42] Confirmation came about ten days later, without fanfare, without titles, in the context of a general update on the world of motorsport: 'Ferrari [no first name, only the last], after a mutual agreement with the management of the make, resumed his freedom with respect to Alfa Corse, and is now setting up, in the premises that were already home to the Scuderia, a workshop for repairing cars. The workshop will be ready at the end of the month. Racing is for the time being set aside.'[43]

Nineteen years had passed since the summer of 1920, when 22-year-old Ferrari had first entered the gates of the Alfa Romeo Portello factory in Milan. The road travelled together had been a long and profitable one. Ferrari had become a major actor in European motor racing. But his personality had never been an easy one and he had acquired as many foes as friends. In September 1939, Enzo Ferrari had not abandoned his personal way of thinking. 'I,' he proudly said as he was leaving, 'keep my bad habits and go back home.'[44]

In autumn 1939, while World War II broke out in Europe, Enzo Ferrari returned to Modena. His attachment to his city and its territory had always been nearly visceral. 'I am attached to my land, I daresay, in a fierce way,' he would confess with pride years later. It was a 'flat, monotonous, foggy land, with an exaggerated summer heat, no lakes, no beaches, with small hills on the horizon',[1] but he loved it deeply.

In his return to Modena as an Italian motor-racing celebrity, there was a kind of subtle revenge, 'a kind of moral revolt, because when I left in my youth,' he would recall years later, 'I did not enjoy but the tiny reputation of a quite strange young man, passionate about cars and motorsport, who did not possess particular skills'.[2] Now, as an established man in the sport, his return meant 'not only concluding a cycle', which he did not hesitate to define as 'almost biological', but also the challenge 'to show others and myself that at Alfa Romeo I had not lived only on borrowed light'.[3]

At 41 Ferrari wanted to 'persuade' the outside world, as well as his fellow Modenese, 'that the degree of celebrity that I had achieved was the legitimate consequence of my stubborn work and of my attitudes'. In essence, he concluded, 'it was time to show how far I could get on my own'.[4]

When he had left Alfa Romeo, Ferrari had accepted a clause under which he renounced 'for four years, from today, every technical and racing activity'.[5] He had accepted it because he thought that the war unleashed by the German invasion of Poland only days before would in fact put an end, at least temporarily, to motor racing. But nothing really prevented him, if he wanted to, from building a car to which he could give a name other than his, which could be raced by a different organization than Scuderia Ferrari.

Since he could not use his trademark 'Scuderia Ferrari' name, on 2 October 1939 Enzo chartered a one-man company that he named Auto Avio Costruzioni.[6] The name conveyed one of the two stated purposes of the new company: the construction of mechanical parts for aviation, because the aeronautics sector was growing rapidly, especially in light of the international situation.

In establishing a new company, Enzo remembered what he had learned from his father and did not seek a partner. When he had founded Scuderia Ferrari, ten years earlier, his financial situation had prevented him from being the only shareholder. Now, however, thanks to the severance pay received from Alfa Romeo – provided three times in three years, in 1937, in 1938 and, again, in September 1939 – he was in the privileged position of being able to go it alone.

On 6 November, two months after being fired from Alfa Romeo, Ferrari was already at work. Not being allowed to use Alfa Romeo components and inevitably having to rush, Ferrari had bought two Fiat 508C chassis – a very popular car in Italy in the late 1930s – that would serve as the basis for his two cars. No stranger than this choice of chassis was Fiat's decision to offer a 5,000-lire prize for the best-placed Fiat car or chassis in each of the classes into which the 1940 Mille Miglia would be divided.[7]

It took a remarkable amount of time to complete the design and the subsequent construction of the engine. The workshop in Viale Trento Trieste quivered with excitement. Despite the news coming from the east, where Poland had fallen into the hands of the Nazis, and the west, where England and France were waiting for a possible German attack in the spring, everyone's thoughts were focused on the 1940 Mille Miglia. In his daily journal Ferrari had highlighted a date: Sunday 28 April, the 17th anniversary of his wedding – but also the day the great race would be held. The two cars had to be ready at all costs – and running – on that day.

In the meantime, Ferrari had already come up with a name for his first car. His rationale was simple: a 1.5-litre, 8-cylinder engine. The result: *815*. He was no stranger to naming cars this way for, as logical as it was, he must have thought that the same procedure had been used to name his other car, built entirely in Modena: the Alfa Romeo 158 ('15' for the displacement of 1.5-litre, '8' as the number of cylinders) that he had first built and later defended from Ricart. The message could not be clearer: the 815 was not only the car with which Ferrari began his manufacturer career, but also, and above all, the weapon with which he was challenging Alfa Romeo.

The three numbers – 8-1-5 – were not just the 'acronym' identifying the model, but also the actual name of the car. Unable to give the car his own name, by virtue of the clause with Alfa Romeo, Ferrari did not even remotely consider calling the car Auto Avio Costruzioni.[8] The car was simply named 815 – a number that could be read on the engine head.

The body of his first car would be designed elsewhere. And Enzo had no doubt about who should dress the chassis of the 815 – Carrozzeria Touring in Milan.

Although he had assigned to others the design of the body of his car, Ferrari had well-defined ideas about it. He knew exactly what he wanted. During the first meeting with Felice Bianchi Anderloni, owner and founder of Carrozzeria Touring, he was very clear. He wanted a car, he said, that stood out from the others, one that would be instantly recognizable and unlike any other. At the same time, he wanted the Carrozzeria Touring trademark style – sporty, eye-catching, but always elegantly understated – to be immediately acknowledged. In short: a sports car that was, at the same time, a luxury car.[9]

On Valentine's Day 1940, the *Gazzetta dello Sport* printed the news of a rumour that Enzo Ferrari was planning to build a dozen units of a sports car of his own. The paper did not know its name, but indicated – incorrectly – the 1100cc engine displacement and, this time correctly, the engine: 8 cylinders in line.[10]

For once the leak had not come from Ferrari, who actually rushed to deny the news.[11] Under the agreements signed on parting, Ferrari had pledged not to compete against Alfa Romeo for the next four years.

It was true, however – not only that Ferrari was building a car of his own, despite his agreement with the management of Alfa Romeo, but also that he was thinking of building a small series of ten cars, with the same body designed by Carrozzeria Touring, slightly different from the sport version that was being built in those days.[12] Enzo was already thinking about how Italians would resume everyday life at the end of this 'phony' war that had worried the nation and immobilized Europe.[13]

Despite his denials, the whole world was aware of Ferrari's new car. Indeed, Ferrari was proclaimed a positive example for his initiative. 'At a time that is certainly not the best to deal with the uncertainties and risks of the construction of a sports-car model,' it was said in the Italian press, in those months during which the entire country looked with apprehension at a European war and an uncertain future, Ferrari 'has drawn the impulse to realize what has always been his never-hidden ambition.'[14]

The magazine pointed out Ferrari's great continuity of purpose: 'Since the now-distant time of the Scuderia, and more so today, when he is free from other commitments and can be considered the leader of a small but well-equipped and experienced group of men, the issue of making the type of sports car that can attract young drivers to motor racing has always interested and attracted Ferrari.'[15]

So, in spring 1940, no one was surprised to learn that 'in less than six months after the reorganization of the small workshop in Modena, Enzo Ferrari is able to announce his first construction'.[16] Despite Gobbato and Alfa Romeo.

In mid-April, the two 815s were ready. Ferrari had long since found two people interested in buying them. The luxury model with leather upholstery had been ordered by Marquis Lotario Rangoni Machiavelli,[17] a Modena aristocrat whom

Ferrari had known for a long time, and for whom, when he was director of Alfa Corse, he had custom-made a short-wheelbase version of the Alfa 2300, with which Rangoni had won some races in the 1939 season.[18]

The second car, with a much sportier configuration, had been ordered by Alberto Ascari, the son of Antonio, the never-forgotten Maestro and fraternal friend of Ferrari's youth.[19] Alberto, who was already active with motorcycles, had decided to start racing cars and had turned to his family friend.

The Mille Miglia was now only a couple of weeks away. Ferrari took Rangoni's 815 to the Via Giardini – a long straight flanked by centennial trees that started in Modena and cut the plains like a blade until the foothills of the Apennines, then went along the ridge of the hills up to Serramazzoni, on which the car had already scooted countless times over the winter.[20] Ascari took delivery of his 815 directly from Carrozzeria Touring at the Via Ludovico di Breme Milan showroom before having his photo taken in front of the Certosa di Garegnano Basilica, then tested it on the Milan–Lakes highway.[21]

Ferrari was pleased.

On Sunday 14 April, he wrote to Castagneto, one of the organizers of the Mille Miglia, to confirm that two 815s would be participating in the Mille Miglia.

Less than two weeks before the race, Ferrari was moving with great circumspection. In the letter to Castagneto he took care to stress that Auto Avio Costruzioni would take care of 'the registration and all aspects concerning their participation' in the Mille Miglia, but that the competitors' licences were 'in the name of the drivers' – as if to say that it was the two drivers who had decided to race, and everything that he was doing (apart from having built the two cars, of course!) was to help them from a logistics point of view. This subtlety, Ferrari said, was due to 'various reasons, including one that I will explain to you verbally'.[22]

It is all too easy to see the clause he had signed with Alfa Romeo as the reason for such secrecy. If he had been cornered by the Portello management, Ferrari would have protested that the clause he had signed was valid only for *official* activities with *professional* racing drivers, while what he was doing now was simply an *unofficial* commitment to two *amateurs* who had turned to him for assistance.[23]

But Ferrari was also moving cautiously because even though the tests conducted with the 815 so far had proved satisfactory, the cars had not yet been tested on the actual course of the Mille Miglia. This test was scheduled for the end of the week, and only at that point would Ferrari finally make up his mind.

In a letter that he had sent Castagneto back in November, there had been no sign of the prancing horse that had been Baracca's, and which from 1932 to 1937 had adorned the cars of Scuderia Ferrari. But now, in spring 1940, the letterhead of Auto Avio Costruzioni was embellished with a big black prancing horse, under which the name of the company was secondary.

A few days later, Ferrari went with his two 815s to Cremona for the last tests. Sitting on a bollard, with a hat pulled down over his forehead and a turtleneck shirt under his jacket, Ferrari silently watched his cars as they tested. Rangoni Machiavelli and Ascari took turns at the wheel with the company testers. Top speed was not an issue. What began to trouble Ferrari as the hours passed was the fact that the engine had difficulty in maintaining high revs. The traction also seemed not to be up to expectations. And, of course, the reliability of the cars in a race nearly 1,000 miles long was far from certain.[24]

The day of practice ended at sunset. Although the 815s could definitely have benefited from a few more weeks of development,[25] Ferrari had decided: the following Sunday they would both take part in the first Gran Premio Brescia delle Mille Miglia, the 1940 edition of the most popular of all Italian races.

Enzo Ferrari arrived in Brescia on Tuesday 23 April.[26] It was the first time that he had appeared in public in his new role – the first time in 20 years that he had gone to a race without an Alfa Romeo hat. Few people, if any, were surprised to find him back on the racing scene so soon.

On Friday 26 April, the two 815s showed up at scrutineering in Brescia's Piazza Vittoria. On the long hoods were painted the race numbers: 65 for Rangoni Machiavelli, 66 for Ascari. The cars had a red livery, which was traditional for Italian cars. But it was a darker red than the one used by Alfa Romeo and Maserati, a red that could be mistaken for maroon.

The yellow rectangular shield with the black prancing horse did not appear on top of the radiator, as it had when the cars had left Carrozzeria Touring, and with which Ascari's 815 was photographed in Milan. (This image actually appeared in the special booklet that the Mille Miglia organizers had printed for the race.[27]) It is unclear whether Ferrari had been warned by Alfa Romeo about using the prancing horse that had once branded the Scuderia cars, or if Enzo had decided on his own not to further antagonize Alfa Romeo.

The two 815s were among the last cars to go through the technical scrutineering.[28] The following day, Saturday 27 April, the two cars tested repeatedly on the long straights near Cremona. Their top speed was respectable; the reliability remained unknown. Ferrari had never lied to himself, and he certainly was not about to start doing it at the age of 42. Beyond the race itself, he saw in the Mille Miglia the first real test of his first car.[29] What he really hoped for was to avoid looking bad. Consequently, he advised his two drivers to run a cautious race the following day.[30]

On Sunday 28 April, Rangoni Machiavelli's 815 took the start of the Gran Premio Brescia delle Mille Miglia at 6.21am. A minute later it was Alberto Ascari's turn.[31] The first cars had left at 4am, almost 2.5 hours earlier. It was a gloomy and overcast morning, and the forecast did not rule out a wet race.

Ferrari was waiting for his cars in Cremona. The first to speed past him was Rangoni Machiavelli's. But Ascari came right after, a clear sign that, of the two, the son of Antonio was the fastest. However, he was also the first to withdraw. Despite Ferrari's instructions, his two drivers had driven as fast as they could from the moment they had started the race – against time, against opponents, but especially against each other.

Between Cremona and Mantua, during the first lap, Ascari passed his teammate's 815 and took the lead of the 1500 class – or National Sport category, as it was called.[32] In Mantua he sped under the watchful eye of Nuvolari, who for once was on the sidelines. On that same stand were seated the three Maserati brothers – Ettore, Ernesto and Bindo.[33] But on lap two, a suspension component on Ascari's 815 suddenly broke, and the Ascari–Minozzi pair was forced to withdraw. At that point, the two 815s had been first and second in class, and twelfth and thirteenth overall.[34]

The class lead was then taken by the second 815. Confident at the wheel of his car, Rangoni Machiavelli maintained the lead lap after lap, steadily increasing his margin over the car behind, to a maximum of 33 minutes. Though still short of development, the 815 seemed to withstand the gruelling marathon. On lap three he was eleventh overall. On lap four, he was tenth. But on the penultimate lap, the only 815 left in the race started to experience handling problems. Against the advice of his expert race mechanic, the marquis decided to continue his run, even though he was left with only third gear. It was the prelude to a withdrawal, which came at Manerbio, at the beginning of the last lap.[35]

The outcome did not please Ferrari, who, despite having been realistic the day before about the possibility of doing well, during the race could not help but hope to bring home a well-deserved class win – a dream that faded a little more than 100km (62 miles) from the finish. Rationally he identified the 'haste with which this car had been built' as the main reason for the double mechanical failure.[36]

However, Ferrari did take the fastest lap record in his class, set by Rangoni Machiavelli at an average speed of 122km/h (76mph), and with a top speed of 172km/h (107mph).[37]

The press was favourable in its reporting, regarding both the outcome of the 815's first trial and the car itself: 'The 815 has convincingly shown its good potential,' Ferrari read in *Auto Italiana* in the following days. 'Not all of the components, in

1. Targa Florio, 1919. A young Enzo Ferrari, accompanied by Nino Berretta, is pictured at the wheel of the 15/20 CMN, with which he participated in his second career race. After more than ten hours of a long and gruelling race, Ferrari reached the finish line out of time.

2. Enzo Ferrari, the racing driver: 'Growing up at the school of a champion like Antonio Ascari, of a stylist like Sivocci, of a rude champion like Campari, Ferrari has now been able to craft his own style.' (*La Gazzetta dello Sport*, 18 August 1923)

3. To formalize the gift of the prancing horse that was on the aircraft fuselage of their fallen son, the parents of Francesco Baracca gave Ferrari a black-and-white photograph of the hero in his Italian Royal Air Force uniform, next to his biplane. Years later, Ferrari would ask the Bolognese painter Ettore Graziani to make a colour painting from this photo.

4. On the evening of 29 August 1924, a dozen Modenese 'friends and admirers' organized a dinner to celebrate Enzo's appointment as Knight of the Italian Crown, held at the Hotel San Carlo in Modena's city centre.

5. Vittorio Jano, talented engineer and a faithful associate of Enzo Ferrari from the days of the Scuderia, seen here in a famous photo portraying him alongside one of his creations: the Alfa Romeo P2 Grand Prix car.

6. The official Scuderia Ferrari newsletter devoted great attention to the great feat accomplished by Nuvolari at the Nürburgring on 28 July 1935.

7. Franco Cortese, the first driver to take one of the Prancing Horse's cars to victory in the Circuito di Caracalla in the May of 1947, poses alongside his 125 S, which he drove in the 1948 editon of the Mille Miglia.

8. Mille Miglia XIV, 1947. The first 'real' Ferrari, the 125 S entrusted for the occasion to Franco Cortese, is being prepared to take part in the famous race. It will be forced to withdraw in Fano because of the failure of a cylinder head gasket.

9. Mille Miglia XV, 1948. Nuvolari repaid Ferrari's confidence with an extraordinary performance. Leading in Rome halfway through the race, he held the lead until his car gave out on him on the outskirts of Reggio Emilia, at the Villa Ospizio checkpoint, where Ferrari was waiting for him. The latter convinced the Flying Mantuan to bow out.

10. Mille Miglia XV, 1948. Although Nuvolari did not make it all the way to Brescia, Ferrari won his first Mille Miglia with Clemente Biondetti and Giuseppe Navone, driving a 166 Berlinetta Allemano.

11. Mille Miglia XVII, 1950. Prompt as always, Ferrari showed up in Brescia for the scrutineering operations ahead of the race. Together with journalist Corrado Filippini, he watches the inspection of one of the 11 166 MM Barchetta units that will take part in that year's Mille Miglia.

12. The first Ferrari 250 in history, the S of Bracco and Rolfo at the start of the 1952 Mille Miglia, a race disputed in terrible weather which the two Ferraristi made their own after an epic battle with Kling and Klenkin in the Mercedes-Benz 300 SL.

La Gazzetta dello Sport

SUL CLASSICISSIMO CIRCUITO CHE GIA' VIDE LE PRODEZZE DEL PADRE

ALBERTO ASCARI trionfa nel G. P. d'Italia e si consacra campione del mondo 1952

PIÙ COMBATTUTA DEL PREVISTO
CORSA BELLISSIMA

Anche nell'Inter-Europa vince Ferrari con Sterzi

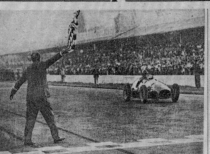

13. The headline that *Gazzetta dello Sport* devotes to this triumph is most eloquent.

14. Mille Miglia XXI, 1954. Enzo Ferrari walks around Piazza della Vittoria Square in Brescia on the eve of the race. Ironically, to have access to the 'pit area', he could not get better than a mechanic credential!

15. Alberto Ascari's death on 26 May 1955, at Monza, at the wheel of a Ferrari Sport that his friend Castellotti was testing, caused great commotion throughout Italy. The last photo ever taken of the champion appeared on the cover of the *Settimo Giorno* magazine.

16. Ferrari had met Juan Manuel Fangio in 1949, in Modena. As a driver, he had liked him immediately; as a person, even years later, he was not entirely sure. In the 1956 season, the relationship between the two was far from simple, and ended – albeit, with the conquest of the world title – at the end of that year.

17. Here is what remains of Eugenio Castellotti's car after the tragic crash that cost him his life on the Modena airfield track, on 14 March 1957. For Enzo Ferrari, the death of the young driver from Lodi was a source of great pain.

18. The Ferrari (number 531) of De Portago/ Nelson, protagonists of a terrible accident that, in the last stages of the 1957 Mille Miglia, would claim the lives of both drivers and nine spectators, leading to the end of the race.

19. The absolute silence that reigns the next day at the table where Ferrari and his guests sit (his wife Laura, right; Peter Collins and his girlfriend, left) speaks volumes about the difficult moment.

20. At the first round of the world championship on 10 May 1959 at Monte Carlo, the team from Maranello entered three updated 256s for Tony Brooks (No. 50), Jean Behra (No. 46) and Phil Hill (No. 48) as well as a Dino 156 for Cliff Allison (No. 52). In the background can be seen the technical director Carlo Chiti in a shirt and tie . . . as was the done thing at Monte Carlo.

21. The Monaco Grand Prix (29 May 1960) was an important moment in Ferrari's history as it saw the debut of the marque's first rear-engined single-seater. The 246 P was driven on the Monaco street circuit by the American Richie Ginther (No. 34), who finished in sixth place.

22. Monza, 1961, Italian Grand Prix. The key race for the world drivers' title: von Trips or Phil Hill (pictured together, with Richie Ginther). Despite the importance of the moment, the Ferrari pit is serene. In addition to engineer Chiti in the foreground, talking with young Pedro Rodríguez, Ferrari entertains Prince Bernhard of the Netherlands; in the background (right) is Romolo Tavoni. Unfortunately, everything changed the next day, with the death of von Trips after a terrible crash that killed several spectators. Phil Hill is the new world champion.

23. 'The Red Army', 1962, in the literal sense of the word, to which Scuderia Ferrari will entrust its fate in the new season. In front is the F1 car, then a sequence of six- and eight-cylinder sports cars and, at the end of the line, a Berlinetta that would participate in Gran Turismo races. It did not have a name yet, but the body was among the most beautiful Ferrari had built up to that point – the 250 'GTO'.

24. Modena airfield track, 1963. Enzo Ferrari did not want to miss the tests of his new 158 F1 single-seater, a car that in the 1964 season would take John Surtees (observing the car) to the world title.

25. In early March 1963, the Monza race track was the stage for the press introduction of the new 250 P sports car (left), the first Ferrari equipped with a V12 engine in rear-longitudinal position, and of the 330 LMB, a splendid Berlinetta directly derived from the 1962 GTO. From left: Mike Parkes, Lorenzo Bandini, Lodovico Scarfiotti, Nino Vaccarella and, on board the 330, Willy Mairesse.

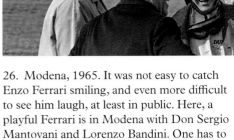

26. Modena, 1965. It was not easy to catch Enzo Ferrari smiling, and even more difficult to see him laugh, at least in public. Here, a playful Ferrari is in Modena with Don Sergio Mantovani and Lorenzo Bandini. One has to believe that the exchange that made them all laugh must have been in Modenese dialect, a preferred language when the interlocutors were from his hometown area.

27. With motorbike champion John Surtees – in the cockpit of the 512 F1, before the 1965 Italian Grand Prix – Ferrari went back to his roots, and to the drivers of his youth. Like Nuvolari and Varzi before him, Surtees had made a name for himself on a bike before he switched to cars.

this very first experimental edition, could be proportionate to the effort of a race like the Mille Miglia. With initial laps at an average of 146km/h [91mph], no one could expect to see it reach the finish line. But the testing has been convincing and satisfactory.'[38]

'The brand-new Ferrari 815s,' echoed Canestrini in *Gazzetta dello Sport*, 'not fully developed, had a good debut, even if they failed to finish.'[39] Generously – but possibly correctly – Canestrini wrote that Ascari's race could have been more satisfying, and certainly longer, if he had not preferred to sacrifice 'a suspension to the satisfaction of overtaking Rangoni'.[40] So much for Ferrari's specific requests for a cautious race the night before. But, concluded Canestrini, who knew what he was talking about, the 815 'is very stable and easy to handle. With the necessary adjustments it will become a brilliant sports car.'[41]

War and Peace

Apart from the positive press reviews, which naturally pleased him, Ferrari knew that with some clever fine-tuning and further development carried out without an impending deadline, as had been the case with the Mille Miglia, the 815 could win over the sports clientele he had patiently cultivated in the previous ten years. Moreover, as soon as Germany, England and France had reached some kind of armistice, the war in Europe would end and things could go back to normal – motor racing included.

Thus, Ferrari wasted no time in printing a small brochure to advertise his first car. Target audience: race-loving gentleman drivers scattered throughout Italy. The first two cars had quickly found buyers, but his goal was to build another eight.

On the cover of the brochure he proudly displayed the Scuderia Ferrari prancing horse, although Enzo had been careful not to make any reference to either the team or its symbol in the text. The horse appeared from behind the nose of a car that recalled the Scuderia Alfa Romeos of the 1930s more than the new 815. At the bottom of the rectangle Ferrari had placed the type: *Auto Avio Costruzioni – Modena, Italy.* The upper part was bordered by the three colours of the Italian flag.[1]

The intended construction of the remaining eight 815s went up in smoke at dawn on 10 May 1940, however. That Friday morning Hitler's army invaded Belgium, Holland and Luxembourg. The 'phony' war had ended – and the Battle of France had begun. Exactly one month later, Mussolini declared war on France and England, and Italy too entered the conflict that would very soon go from being European to global.

In an effort to make ends meet, Ferrari finally began to look at opportunities in the other stated activity of his company, the aviation sector, which he had ignored until then. So he looked up a contact he had at the Compagnia Aeronautica aviation company in Rome that built small four-cylinder engines for planes employed in the preparation of future pilots at pilot-training schools.[2] The transition from building automobile engines to (small) aeroplane engines was apparently painless.

The outbreak of the war had not brought any special excitement to Modena.

Like most Italians, Enzo's fellow citizens were convinced that the war would be short, and would be won. Just as had happened 25 years earlier, the military academy saw a steady increase in the coming and going of young officers for training before they were sent to the various war campaigns. In town the rest of life's activities continued as usual, although in most of the major city squares work on air-raid shelters had immediately begun, and brick walls now protected the marble lions of the cathedral.

Enzo, Laura and Dino were living in the first-floor apartment of the building on Viale Trento Trieste. In the first autumn of the war Ferrari had actually made some changes – mainly aesthetic – to the construction, transforming the windows from vertical to horizontal and making them wider. A few months later he expanded the building in the direction of the Via Emilia by building a foyer, staffed by a doorman. For the first time since moving in ten years earlier, there would be two separate entrances – one for the workers, at number eleven, and one for the showroom and his apartment, at number thirteen.

With the Alfa Romeo severance pay, in the first year of the war Ferrari purchased the Palazzo dei Cento Caproni, a simple four-story building on the southern side of Largo Garibaldi. For the time being he decided to rent the dozens of apartments in it and did not think of moving in with his family. He hadn't forgotten his father's credo – to stay close to the shop – although no more than 100 yards separated the new building from the Scuderia Ferrari structure, where the Auto Avio Costruzioni workshop was now located, and where Enzo lived.

*   *   *

The war had not weakened Enzo's interest in a young woman he had known some time before, and with whom, for some years now, he had woven a romance. The name of the girl was Lina, and her family – Lardi degli Aleardi – one of the most prominent in Modena. They had met when Lina was working at Carrozzeria Orlandi, which Enzo had used for years for the bodywork of those Alfa Romeo chassis that he would then sell to his Modena customers. Truth is, he had noticed her a long time before, when she was only 14. It was the summer of 1924, and she was taking a stroll on the side of a road in the Apennines, just south of Modena, when a car had come from the opposite direction. The car had slowed down and the driver had saluted her. It was clear to the girl that the man at the wheel had reduced the speed of his car to see her face. To him she was a total stranger, but she had recognized him instantly as Enzo Ferrari; after all, he was known in Modena as a sportsman of some distinction.

A few years later, when she was 19, they had met again. One morning she was walking out of the Carrozzeria Orlandi gate as he was driving in. He quickly broke the ice with quite a bold sentence for the time: 'How did you become so beautiful in so short a time?' He asked this with the confidence of a man who knew his business.[3] Then, without giving her time to react, he offered to give her a ride to the post office, where she was headed.

The thing could have ended there; there was the age difference to consider, along with the fact that all in Modena were aware that Ferrari led an uninhibited life. But the young lady had ended up falling in love with the famous driver, and he had long before ceased to resist temptation. Their story had begun. It was 1929.

The early times had been rough. Laura did not know anything, but it didn't take long for Lina's parents to find out. The family was naturally opposed to Enzo. They tried to convince the young woman that it was a story without a future. It was useless. Lina was in love and had accepted that she would live in his shadow. What is perhaps even more revealing of Ferrari's personality is that, before long, Enzo managed to win to his side both of Lina's parents, who soon accepted their daughter's love for him.

A few years later Scuderia Ferrari hired Lina as a secretary. And it was she who, often three times a week, accompanied Enzo to Milan when he needed to go to the Alfa Romeo headquarters at Portello. On the Sundays the Scuderia's cars were racing, now that Laura stayed at home with young Dino, it was Lina who followed Enzo to the circuits, always in the background but constantly at his side. The members of the noisy group – drivers, engineers, mechanics, journalists – were always in such conspicuous number that if on the one hand she had become indispensable, on the other her presence almost disappeared amid all of those people.

Now, in 1940, the time of the business trips to Milan was long gone, and the outbreak of the war had put an end to all forms of motor racing. But their relationship continued stronger and, necessarily, more clandestine than ever.

Auto Avio Costruzioni had about 40 employees, a number that with the arrival of the war had not grown, but nor had it diminished.

On 17 July 1941, the Auto Avio Costruzioni – 'Scuderia Ferrari' – Modena workshop was declared 'auxiliary' to the war effort. According to this status, all company employees became mobilized civilians, subject like all soldiers to military law. Put simply, anyone who was absent from work without a written permit or who failed to return from a vacation without a just cause would be considered a deserter.[4]

The second year of war went by with Ferrari in frantic pursuit of business opportunities. The work for the Compagnia Aeronautica in Rome had not fallen short; in the Viale Trento Trieste workshops, they had added a night shift,[5] but the profit was modest. And of course, no one spoke of cars anymore.

Then, in 1942, came a turning point.

Enrico Nardi, the trusted tester who had developed the 815, introduced Ferrari to a businessman from Turin named Corrado Gatti, a trader in machine tools for the manufacture of ball bearings. During their meeting, Gatti suggested that Ferrari produce machine tools for him in the Auto Avio Costruzioni workshop in Modena, for hydraulic grinding machines. All he had to do was duplicate German machinery the way Gatti was doing in Turin.[6] After two years of war, and with the prospect of at least that many more, it was a matter of survival. Ferrari accepted – and he never regretted it. So, in those rooms where a few years before the Alfa Romeo Bimotore that had set world speed records was born, those same people began building machine tools.

But Ferrari was always Ferrari and finding himself forced by the situation to manufacture banal objects probably injured the pride of a man born with, and for, motor racing. So, on each of those machines he affixed a tag with Baracca's prancing horse and the words *Scuderia Ferrari – Modena*. And because they were not cars, Alfa Romeo could not object.

Rare visits from old friends gave Ferrari a little peace of mind and, perhaps, hope, as when in the third year of the war, he received a visit from Trossi, elegant in his officer uniform. They enjoyed a cheerful break that lasted a whole day, in which the small group of friends pushed away thoughts of war and replaced them with talk of the exciting, glory-filled days of motor racing, in hopes that, sooner or later, they would return to those days.

This was something Ferrari never doubted. During the war he confided to a friend: 'If I save something, if they do not take everything away from me, the time will come, I'm sure, when I will dedicate myself only to the construction of racing cars, an activity that will allow me to see my cars race each Sunday simultaneously in two or three different parts of the world.'[7]

With Allied bombing looming, and with the passage of the law on industrial decentralization, which would facilitate the purchase of land in the countryside, in 1942 Ferrari started to think of transferring his business – or at least the production side of his business – outside Modena. He therefore began to look around for opportunities, and soon found a suitable place in a small town less than 24km (15 miles) north of the city, which had a special meaning for him. It was Carpi, the town where his father was born.

In Carpi Ferrari had eyed some abandoned warehouses. After some restoration work, he thought that he could transfer the production of the hydraulic grinding machines there, while leaving in Viale Trento Trieste the employees who could provide assistance, now more and more sporadic, for the old Scuderia customers. But the local authorities rebuffed his offer.[8]

With Carpi no longer an option, Ferrari continued to look, this time south of the city. At a similar distance, he found an area that could be right for him in Formigine, a small village on the road to the Abetone Apennines pass. But again he met opposition from the local authorities; this time, the mayor stopped the purchase.[9]

The third attempt paid off. The area he chose this time was in the town right after Formigine, going towards the Apennines. The place was named Maranello, a small municipality where the plains met the first hills. Maranello would be perfect. Ferrari already owned a good piece of land in nearby Fiorano, which he had bought with the severance money received from Alfa Romeo.

The Maranello mayor proved more farsighted, facilitating the purchase of the 'Cavani Fund', a portion of land owned by the Colombini family, adjacent to the plot owned by Ferrari. Ferrari moved there in September 1943.[10]

When Ferrari moved his business to Maranello, Auto Avio Costruzioni was a healthy company with 160 employees, almost all of them working on hydraulic grinding machines of German patent. The new location was right on the outskirts of Maranello, coming from Modena. The factory was on a much larger property than Viale Trento Trieste ever was, despite the several additions Ferrari had made over the years to his town property. On the left of the main road Ferrari erected a long and narrow building with yellow walls, as in Modena, and red roof tiles. The building formed a sort of triangle, with two sides entirely occupied by offices, workshops and a warehouse, and a third side, along the road to Abetone, which gave access to the large inner courtyard, with a much smaller structure.

Ferrari did not move his residence to Maranello. And when petrol rationing forced him to leave the car at home, he had no trouble covering the distance on his bicycle.

Like all auxiliary factories, the Maranello factory was occupied by the German Army immediately after Italy's 8 September 1943 armistice with the Allies. The officer in charge of inventory was impressed by the quality of the machine tools produced by Auto Avio Costruzioni. 'Mr Ferrari,' he said one day, with some irony, 'I know that you make some good grinding machines, and, for this reason, all that you are producing will from now on be confiscated.'[11]

It seems certain that the grinding machines never actually reached Germany. The underground Resistance movement managed to stop the trains on which the machines were loaded – in Formigine, because the railroad did not reach

Maranello then – and hid them. Those loads that made it to Modena never reached the Brenner Pass and Germany.[12]

The move to the foothills of the Apennines did not spare the plant, however, which was bombed twice: first on 4 November 1944, and again in February 1945.[13] In both cases, there were no casualties, but considerable damage to the premises.

The 8 September 1943 armistice had changed everything in Italy – and Emilia was no exception. The enemy was now domestic as well. In addition to the Nazis, who felt betrayed, there were those Fascists loyal to Mussolini who had sided with the new state, the so-called Republic of Salò, from the town on Lake Garda where the new regime had its headquarters. In Modena, the Republicans took control of the Palazzo Ducale, and from there established and conducted a gruesome reign of terror.

But there was also an invisible enemy, desperate and exasperated, an enemy that in Emilia – a land passionate as few others are in Italy – was more enraged than elsewhere: those Resistance *partigiani* who, in their struggle to survive, often chose to make no distinction between those who had supported the Fascist regime or, worse, the Republic of Salò, and those who, more simply, had pragmatically accepted the situation and had tried to cope with it.

Ferrari had never been a Fascist; he had always been a realist. He had not taken up membership until the day he had needed it to go abroad, and had not received special favours from the regime. His friends – some of whom were members of the Fascist Party of some importance, though mostly at a local level – were not responsible for the success he had known in the 1930s, or even for the livelihood that his company was able to provide for the Ferrari family and three hundred other families, many of whom had become his employees at Maranello during the war years. Indeed, if he had had connections or godfathers of some sort within the Party, or a way of thinking and acting differently from that personal stubborn individualism of his, the story with Alfa Romeo could have had a very different outcome.

When Fascism ruled and Italians believed in that *place in the sun* advocated by Mussolini, Ferrari had fought his own battle, which had never been political, but rather private, against what he saw as gratuitous persecution. For example, he had helped his friend Enzo Levi, the Jewish lawyer who had suggested that he give the Scuderia his name instead of the Latin name of Modena. Having found out that the Fascists were waiting for Levi at the Bologna train station to beat him up (and who knows what else), Ferrari had parked his car near the tracks, helped Levi on board and dashed off for Modena, never caught by the Fascist squad that was not able to keep up with his professional racing-driver level of driving.[14]

Like so many other entrepreneurs, Ferrari knew he could not change a political environment that in Italy had enjoyed the favour of the population for a long time. One should not forget, as Ferrari lucidly analysed it years later, that Fascism was 'condemned' on 25 July 1943, by Fascism itself (when the government turned against Mussolini and the Germans and started negotiations with the Allies), not by others.[15] He had accepted the status quo and had turned to work. But he had never married a cause, either before or after 8 September.

Actually, after the armistice, while his factory was occupied by the German Army, he allowed some of his workers, who were members of the Resistance, to work at night in one of the Maranello warehouses, where they built three-point nails that the *partigiani* employed to stop the Nazi truck columns.[16] Ferrari was aware of it and let them do it, well knowing that if those men had been discovered the Nazis would not only execute them; he himself would also be in danger. He also knew that during the small hours of the night, in one of the more-secluded rooms of the Viale Trento Trieste building in Modena where he lived, some of his workers repaired the rifles that the *partigiani* used by day.[17] In one of the ground-floor apartments in the Largo Garibaldi building that he owned in Modena, he had taken in the mother of Sandro Cabassi, a *partigiano* killed by the Republicans. He knew that in that same apartment anti-Fascists and members of the clandestine Italian Communist Party met regularly.[18] In the Maranello factory he offered asylum to Luigi Ranuzzi, a *partigiano* better known by his battle name of 'Caminito', who was wounded by the Nazis, medicated inside a Ferrari warehouse and kept hidden there for months.

Indeed, before he was wounded, Ferrari had often allowed Caminito to use one of the Auto Avio Costruzioni trucks to shuttle back and forth to his comrades, who had taken refuge in the mountains. It was only thanks to the safe conduct pass that the German Army had issued Ferrari, allowing his trucks to move about even after curfew time, that one night Ranuzzi – and in the end, Ferrari himself – had his life spared. Thanks to the pass, the truck was not searched and Caminito went on his way and took arms and ammunition to the *partigiani* hidden in the woods above in Montefiorino.[19]

In addition to the Resistance, Ferrari had also helped the Jews, even more concretely than he had helped his friend Levi before the war. He hid a Polish woman and her three children in a barn on the plains between the city and the hills, personally taking care of the four fugitives. He quietly fed and clothed them until the end of the war,[20] out of his own pocket, risking his own life.

As if this was not enough, he buried a case containing the money of the Communist Party under a tree on his Fiorano property, not far from the Maranello factory, and in his Modena apartment he'd agreed to conceal the archive of that same outlawed party. Finally, Ferrari was among those who actively contributed to the *partigiani* cause, giving the Resistance half a million lire in 1,000-lire bills.

And yet he ended up on the Resistance proscribed list[21] – or so it seems. There are several versions of the story, and there is no way to know for sure.

In spring 1945, with the war finally over, the Resistance *partigiani* brigades took command of the situation. Taking advantage of the institutional chaos, the Gap brigade killed Edoardo Weber – the carburettor manufacturer and Enzo's friend – who was wrongly considered a collaborator. Some people claimed 40 years later that the next name on the list was Ferrari's. The man who is said to have saved Ferrari was in charge of collecting money for the Resistance, Giuseppe Zanarini, known as 'Altavilla'. The Gap leaders went to Zanarini for the final decision on whether Ferrari should be killed or spared.

Zanarini's recollection – on which, it must be said, the official Resistance sources do not all agree – seems at the very least inaccurate. Speaking of when the *partigiano* had asked him whether Ferrari should be allowed to survive, just before he was to visit Enzo, Zanarini said that the man had come out of thick fog. Then he went on to describe the state of shock in which he found Ferrari, a few minutes later. According to Zanarini, Enzo was devastated by the news of Weber's death, and certain that he'd be next. Weber was killed on 17 May and Zanarini's visit took place a few days later. But it's hard to believe that there could be so thick a fog as to hide a person in Modena in mid-May.

Is Zanarini's recollection flawed? Had he confused people and situations? Or perhaps he magnified his own role? In subsequent years, given Ferrari's success and fame – and knowing that Ferrari's death would have been a burden hanging over their heads – other members of the Resistance said that no decision to eliminate Ferrari was ever made at a leadership level. It is possible that disbanded groups of Resistance combatants may have wanted to kill Ferrari and that if it had happened it would have been an autonomous decision never vetted by the high command.

Adding confusion to an already-confused situation, the year before he died, Ferrari responded to Zanarini, who had sent him a copy of the book in which he had reconstructed the incident. Ferrari cryptically wrote: 'I pretty much knew some of these things. Others I have learned which surprise me.'[22]

The fact remains that Ferrari was not killed. Actually, members of the Italian Communist Party had never been reticent in stating that 'as an anti-fascist and a democratic, he played his part' in the liberation war.[23]

Ferrari celebrated the arrival of peace with a bonus of 1,500 lire to each of his employees, the only one among Modena entrepreneurs to do so.[24]

The 'Ferrari'

That same month of May 1945 that brought distress over his fate also gave Ferrari the joy of becoming a father for the second time. Dino now had a brother – of whom he would not know anything for several years. The mother of Enzo Ferrari's second son was not his wife Laura, but Lina Lardi degli Aleardi, the woman with whom he had been involved since 1929.

When, the previous autumn, she had found out that she was pregnant, Lina had not been completely sure how Enzo would react. The couple was certainly well matched; their love was real. But in addition to his having a wife and another son, they were in the midst of a world war whose end was not yet in sight. Enzo's reaction had been one of joy, however; he had pulled Lina close and hugged her. An already difficult situation had just become even more complicated, but he would think about that another time. Ferrari had learned to deal with things one at a time. And now was the time for happiness. The first thing Enzo said to Lina was, 'What are we going to name him, if it's a boy?'[1] Lina suggested Piero, the name of her brother, who had died two years earlier – and Piero it was. Piero was born in Settecani, a cluster of houses located near Castelvetro, on 22 May 1945. The war had ended in Italy less than a month earlier. Dino was 13. If we are to believe Altavilla's story, Enzo had had his life spared less than a week before.

Ferrari did not choose a relative to serve as godfather for the child, but rather a longtime associate from the days of the Scuderia. His name was Mario Barozzi – better known to Ferrari and the *partigiani* of the Resistance by his battle name of 'Sereno'.[2]

A few days after the end of the hostilities, Enzo dusted off the old drawings and began to look for those who, among the technicians he had known and worked with before the war and during a part of it, were still alive. He was lucky: Gioacchino Colombo, the brilliant engineer who had played an important part in Enzo's life during the second half of the 1930s, was among the survivors. In August, Ferrari summoned him to Maranello and enlisted him to his cause. Since Colombo was still an employee of Alfa Romeo, he did not move to Emilia, but went straight to work in his home in Milan.

Ferrari had been clear with him. His first car – a racing car, of course – would have a 12-cylinder engine. This was the engine that had always fascinated him. He had first seen it on cars driven by American officers during the Great War, and it was the engine placed under the hood of the American car that Antonio Ascari had bought in 1919. Even 20 years after his death, Ferrari still regarded Ascari as his *Maestro* and role model.[3]

Colombo, who had the task of translating Ferrari's vision into reality, immediately set to work. On 15 August 1945 – *Ferragosto*, a secular and religious holiday in Italy, celebrating summer and the Catholic feast of the Assumption of Mary – he began to sketch the first drawings. Before the end of month, the initial drawings of what would become the first engine in the history of Ferrari were ready for the new manufacturer from Maranello to see.[4]

In September Colombo continued his work. In October he showed Ferrari the four-colour views of the new car.[5] The drawings carried the letter 'C', for Colombo. Alfa Romeo and Ferrari had buried the hatchet and forgotten the ancient grudges. In fact, the Milan company now looked magnanimously at the beginning of Enzo Ferrari's new adventure and agreed to send to Modena a young man named Luciano Fochi to help Colombo.

In the summer of 1946, the Maranello factory was operating like a well-oiled machine. Rebuilt after the partial destruction of the two bombings in the waning months of the war, the workshops and offices looked modern and well-equipped. The technicians were at work on their drawing boards, lit by large windows. A good number of the three hundred workers, many of whom had been with Ferrari since before the war, were already working on the new twelve-cylinder to meet the tight schedule that Enzo Ferrari had set months before; those who were still working on the hydraulic grinding machines would soon be moved on to car duties.

By July Ferrari felt so proud of his factory and so sure of the development of his first car, he invited his old friend Giovanni Canestrini of *La Gazzetta dello Sport* for a visit. The journalist was impressed by what he saw.

Before the factory tour, Ferrari explained that what he was building was not simply an 'exceptional' car 'that honours our technique and our work', but also 'a car within the reach of a large customer base, and thus affordable'.[6] Ferrari assumed a double use for the car: official, on the part of Scuderia Ferrari's racing drivers, and private, on the part of all those drivers, both gentleman and professional, to whom he would sell it.

The war had not taken away anything of the old Ferrari spirit. At the age of 48 he was ready for a new challenge. That evening Canestrini left Maranello believing that 'Ferrari will not only want to win the battle of becoming a manufacturer, but he will also want to become an industrialist.'[7]

While the programme Ferrari had in mind was certainly formidable, his true ambition was to build a car a day, exactly the quantity that Alfa Romeo had been producing the day he had first walked through their doors a quarter of a century earlier.[8] One car per working day, a pace that in 1946 Italy could appear daring, made less than three hundred cars per year – quite a few, but still a (small) manufacturer figure.

When the time came to find an identity for this first car, Ferrari did not hesitate. The first Ferrari would be named 125. The number indicated the displacement of each cylinder (125cc x 12 = 1500).

It's likely that Ferrari had been thinking of this naming method for some time, because it pleased him to the point of defining a sort of tradition that he would often implement in the future. He also thought of the possibility of adding one or more letters of the alphabet to the 'acronym'. In the case of the 125, Ferrari was thinking of 'S' for Sport, 'C' for Corsa and 'GP' for Grand Prix.

In the early days of December, Enzo perfected the contract with the man who was going to be the new Ferrari's first racing driver, Franco Cortese. They had known each other for quite some time, and Cortese, born in 1903, had raced with Scuderia Ferrari in 1930. He was not an exceptionally fast driver, nor was he particularly loved by Ferrari, but he was reliable and had great experience – all qualities that Ferrari valued immensely at this stage. Enzo saw in him 'talent, style and technical ability'. In other words, he was 'the right man for the debut of a new car that had never raced'.[9]

Certainly gratified by his appointment as official Ferrari driver, Cortese was to lose the income he had created for himself when, the year before, Ferrari had granted him the mandate to sell his machine tools. The gentleman driver had tried to convince the constructor to continue in the manufacture of those machine tools for which, in a country under reconstruction, there was great demand.[10] But Ferrari had been unyielding: his destiny was to build racing cars, not machine tools, despite the income that they produced.[11]

At the end of the year Ferrari was in a position to announce to the world the construction of the first automobile to which he could finally give his name. To the press he sent a series of illustrations of the engine, some details of the chassis and a transparency view of a sedan, showing the interior mechanics of the car. He also included a sheet with the technical characteristics – those of a three-seater *berlinetta* with an interactive central steering wheel (which would not in the end be built), 4,500mm (177in) long and 1,500mm (59in) in height and width. The weight was indicated as 800kg (1764lb).

The winter months of 1947 saw frenetic activity in the small factory at the foot of the Apennines. Ferrari's men were completing the puzzle, each working on the part that concerned them. Ferrari had not set a specific deadline,[12] but he was anxious to see the work completed. The racing season would start in the spring, and, unlike the previous one, the first after the war, would be full of events that he did not intend to miss.

Meanwhile, he named Federico Giberti, who had been with him since 26 December 1934, as team manager.[13]

Finally the great day arrived.

On Wednesday 12 March 1947, around 4pm, the first 125 was pushed from the workshop into the central courtyard, next to the entrance of the Maranello factory. The car had no body. Technicians and mechanics frantically checked every component one last time. In the crowd was Busso, the man who had completed the project, started a year and a half earlier by Colombo and Bazzi, who had returned home to Milan when Alfa Romeo had finally restarted operations after the war. In the crowd was also Nando Righetti, the tester, who from that moment on would carry out the on-road development of the car ahead of its race debut.

Wearing a suit and a tie, with hair that was now more white than grey, Enzo Ferrari silently watched his men check every item again and again, down to the smallest detail. Then, at an agreed signal, Ferrari walked through them and sat behind the wheel. When he started it, the engine seemed at first to cough. Then the 12-cylinder with Thin Wall bushings began to gain confidence, gradually increasing in intensity to climb to 'levels never heard before in the area',[14] according to those who were there.

After warming up the engine for a few minutes, Ferrari decided that the moment had come. He shifted into first gear, drove a few metres and stopped at the factory gate. Then he again pressed the accelerator, took a right turn and passed the factory gate. Shifting gear after gear, he gradually increased the speed on the asphalt strip framed by trees that led to Modena.

When he arrived in Formigine, about two miles from the factory, he stopped. He turned the car around and came back to Maranello with the same confidence. He reached the entrance of his factory, turned left and stopped not far from the spot that he had left only minutes before. Waiting for him were his men, eager to know the outcome of that historic first test.

The test had been quite satisfactory. The road ahead would be long, but what he'd experienced greatly pleased Ferrari. For the body, Ferrari had thought of an open car, which he had commissioned from a local craftsman named Giuseppe Peiretti. Although he was not employed at Ferrari, Peiretti worked on the body inside the Maranello factory gates. The second chassis would have a slightly different body, more similar to a single-seater and with small removable fenders, personally designed by Busso.[15]

As his men were working on the cars, Ferrari picked the debut race, in Piacenza, not far from home. And of course there was no time to waste, because the Piacenza Circuit event was scheduled for Sunday 11 May. To finish the car in time, the trustworthy Ferrari mechanics Meazza and Marchetti spent sleepless nights in the workshop[16] – just like in the old days.

On the hood of the 125, ready to face competition for the first time, Ferrari placed a glazed ceramic rectangle. 'As a trademark,' he recalled years later, 'I continued to use the prancing horse that had adorned the cars of the old Scuderia Ferrari.'[17] As in the 1930s, the horse remained black. Yellow – the colour of Modena – stayed as the background in which it was framed. What had changed was the shape. The shield that was the symbol of Scuderia Ferrari was now joined by a rectangular logo. It was placed on the nose of the car, in the same spot where the circular emblem of Alfa Romeo had been located in the 1930s; it also became the logo for the new company, which, without the reluctance of 1929, he had long since decided to name 'Ferrari'. Just as on the shield, which remained the symbol of Ferrari's racing activity, he topped the rectangle with the three colours of the Italian flag: from top to bottom, green, white and red.

On the bottom part of the shield, to the left and right of the horse, there had long been the two letters 'S' and 'F', for Scuderia Ferrari; in the lower part of the rectangular logo, he wrote the word 'Ferrari' in black. Typographically, it was rendered with the extended upper arm on the 'F' running above the rest of the letters, as he had done in the catalogue of hydraulic grinding machinery a few years earlier. The inspiration for the typography had come from the long 'P' of Pirelli,[18] a company with which he had always had excellent relations.

Encouraged by the sporting press, which had always had great respect for Enzo Ferrari, Italian motor-racing enthusiasts were awaiting the debut of the first Ferrari-built car with great interest.

Ferrari actually made the decision to go only at the beginning of the week before the race, when he also decided to field not one but two cars. He would entrust the 125 S, nicknamed by Gioachino Colombo 'Thick Wing', to Cortese, while Giuseppe Farina – who was no longer the young prodigy of the 1930s, but remained reliable, like Cortese, and much faster – would drive the 125 S Competizione, with its cigar-shaped car body and separate fenders.

The man and car to beat were Luigi Villoresi and his 1500 Maserati, the fastest in qualifying. In the less-powerful 125 S (90hp), Cortese set the second-fastest time, while Farina, with his 125 S Competizione, experienced one problem after another. Always mindful of the paramount importance of the engine, Enzo had increased the power of the 125 S Competizione, but the additional 30hp coaxed through development had made the car much less docile and Farina experienced two separate incidents during qualifying. This greatly annoyed Farina, who went to Ferrari and demanded Cortese's car for the race. Ferrari refused, and Farina said he would not race the next day. The discussion continued through Sunday morning, but neither gave in.[19]

So only Franco Cortese started Ferrari's very first race. Having posted the second-fastest time in qualifying, he dashed off from the front row of the grid. As the starter lowered the flag, the exhaust pipe of his 125 – naturally painted in red, like all Italian cars – let out a long and not very auspicious smoke trail.

Cortese complied with Ferrari's instructions – that he not force the pace – because, taking the long view, aside from the race result, it was important to give the 125 a comprehensive test in a real race environment. In the early stages Cortese kept the power of his car at bay. But once the early problems of lubrication were solved, he launched into a 'masterful pursuit' of the two 1500 Maseratis driven by Angiolini and Guido Barbieri, who had taken the lead.[20] His march from mid-race onward was impressive, reducing the gap to the race leader by three to five seconds per lap.[21] The power of the Ferrari engine and the handling of the 125 S were so impressive that Cortese took the lead, overtaking both Maseratis in a turn.[22]

With just four laps remaining, a technical failure suddenly stopped Cortese's ride, clipping the wings of Ferrari's dream. 'Without a trivial incident to the pump,' Canestrini wrote the next day, 'Cortese would have won with clear superiority.'[23] Ferrari was very pragmatic: 'A failure, then, but promising.'[24]

Despite the missed win, the debut of the Ferrari 125 S had been satisfying. Had Farina raced in the second car, reporters wrote in the following days, 'Ferrari could probably have recorded a victorious debut, instead of having to settle for a satisfactory, but unlucky, trial.'[25]

But the comments on the first car of Enzo Ferrari the constructor were all largely positive. 'What matters,' wrote the *Gazzetta* reporter, 'is the fact that this new product has been very stable and easy to handle, and with wonderful brakes.'[26]

Two weeks separated the Ferrari debut race from its next trial, scheduled for Sunday 25 May: the 9th Grand Prix of Rome on the street circuit of Caracalla.

Ferrari sent the same car and the same driver to Rome as had raced in Piacenza on the second Sunday in May. With Villoresi sitting out the race, the cross-town duel between Maserati, driven by Barbieri, and Ferrari soon resolved in favour of the latter. After Fernando Righetti's Fiat was delayed by a long pit stop, the race interest focused intently on the significance of what was about to happen: the first historic success of a car named 'Ferrari' – written in quotes, because readers and fans were used to a name that, until then, had been that of a first-rate racing driver, of the owner of a victorious racing team, of the manager of Alfa Corse . . . but not of a car manufacturer.

For the Ferrari pit crew, Cortese's race, 'an inspired and intelligent race',[27] was not as smooth as it looked from the grandstands: the 125 S was troubled by carburettor problems until the 20th of the race's 40 laps, and by an alarming binding of the steering wheel in the last.[28] But on the finish line Cortese's 125 preceded Barbieri's Maserati by more than 20 seconds, and this, in the end, was the only thing that mattered. At its second race, a Ferrari car had won. Enzo, who had remained in Modena, learned of the victory from the radio, and later complimented Cortese by phone.[29]

On 1 June, Cortese and the 125 S won the Vercelli Circuit in a race without real opposition, which was viewed by Ferrari as a further full test in the car's development process. In mid-June Ferrari fielded the 125 S Competizione in the Circuit of Vigevano. It was the car that had won in Rome, with the addition of fenders and an electrical system on board. Cortese won handily, and his success was seen as a good omen for the next race on the calendar: the Mille Miglia, which was being contested for the first time since the end of the war.

Ferrari went to Brescia for the start of the race.

With number 219 painted on the red body, the 125 S of Cortese, who confided he was confident despite the difficulties he knew he would face in the race,[30] left the starting platform 19 minutes after 2am. After a very fast start, in Padua he was seven minutes ahead of Villoresi, who had started the race three minutes after him. But in Fano he was forced to withdraw by the failure of a cylinder head gasket.

Back in Maranello, technicians disassembled the 125 S while Ferrari sent the 125 S Competizione to Varese, where Cortese won again. But the real news at this point was the reconstitution of the Ferrari–Nuvolari pairing. The historic day was Sunday 6 July; the occasion, the Forlì Circuit, the race named after Luigi Arcangeli, the never-forgotten 'Leone di Romagna', whom both Ferrari and Nuvolari had known well.

Just like old times, Nuvolari won hands down. At the end of the race Ferrari waited for him in the pits with a bottle of mineral water in one hand, as he had so often done in the golden years of the Scuderia.

Nuvolari won again the following week in Parma, on a day when, for the first time, Ferrari fielded two cars: the 125 S Competizione for Nuvolari and the 125 Integral S for Cortese. Two cars at the start; two cars in the top two places in the final standings. It was the first double in the nascent history of Ferrari the constructor. Of course, first came Nuvolari, whose engine had actually shut off at the start of the race. He had restarted it, and when he finally got under way he was 15th. But he was Nuvolari, and he eventually overtook all 14 drivers ahead of him.

A month later, in mid-August in Pescara, Ferrari introduced his second model. It was the 159 S, the natural evolution of the 125, whose engine displacement had been increased to 1900cc for maximum power of 125hp. At the wheel was Franco Cortese, who immediately took the lead but dropped out of contention early – once again, the consequences of limited development. After three laps he was forced to pit to repair the oil cooler. He lost twenty minutes and, despite a stirring second part of the race, could not do better than second place.

After Pescara, Livorno. For Ferrari the summer of 1947 was an endless journey down memory lane. He had raced in these towns and on these circuits in the 1920s, and fielded his Scuderia Alfa Romeos in the '30s. In Livorno in a race which of course was no longer called Coppa Ciano, but rather Coppa Montenero, from the name of the circuit, he again entered his friend Nuvolari.

There should have been two cars, one for Nuvolari, one for Cortese. But during testing before the race, Luigi Bazzi crashed the car that should have been Nuvolari's. Bazzi broke a leg and some ribs, and the car suffered even more damage. Ferrari gave Tazio the other car and excluded Cortese.[31]

On Sunday, Nuvolari withdrew after just three laps due to technical failure. Tying together the brief and unsuccessful race of the Flying Mantuan and Bazzi's disastrous accident the day before, the press said: 'It looks like luck has deserted Ferrari lately – but he is accustomed to much harder complications, and he will certainly get where he deserves to be.'[32]

If luck seemed to have abandoned Ferrari – even though he always claimed that he didn't believe in luck, either good or bad[33] – nothing had prepared him for what was about to happen.

The Modena Circuit was on the last Sunday in September. For Enzo it was both the home race and the stage for a cross-town battle with Maserati, the other Modena manufacturer. He prepared for the race with extra care, deciding to field two 159s, which he entrusted to Cortese and, once again, Nuvolari. Nuvolari bowed out before the race because of illness, and Ferrari replaced him with Righetti. Then, during a test run before the race on the hills south of Maranello, Righetti crashed. He was thrown from the cockpit, but escaped 'miraculously unscratched'.[34] Righetti was rescued, but the car ended up in the ravine below.

At the start of the race the Maseratis of Villoresi and Ascari went into the lead. Cortese tailed them and, after a brief duel that ignited the enthusiasm of the spectators, took the lead. On lap 16 he pitted to change a spark plug. Shortly afterwards, he was forced to stop again, this time for ignition problems. But as he was reentering the circuit he ended up obstructing Giovanni Bracco's Delage, which was launched at full speed. In his efforts to avoid the Ferrari, Bracco lost control of his car. When he realized he was headed directly into the crowd of spectators, he chose to drive his car towards a tree instead.

The results were tragic: 17 spectators injured and 5 killed; among the latter was a 9-year-old boy.

On lap 24, the race was stopped. Victory went to Ascari and Maserati.[35] That evening Cortese was questioned by the police. After the interrogation, the police let him go.[36]

After questioning both drivers – Bracco had been hospitalized because he had purposefully directed his car towards a tree in his attempt to avoid spectators – the conclusion was that there was no evidence to blame either driver. 'It was,' the authorities declared, 'a fatal circumstance of superior strength [rather] than the will of the men involved.'[37]

A day of mourning was proclaimed in Modena. Forty thousand people attended the funeral service, cramming the cathedral, the square in front of it and the adjacent Piazza Grande, before unwinding in a long procession through the streets of downtown. Among them was Enzo Ferrari.

By a fortuitous coincidence, that same day, Wednesday 1 October 1947, Ferrari's plan to change the official name of his company took effect. Auto Avio Costruzioni ceased to exist.

On this first day in October, a new company named Ferrari was officially born: Auto Costruzioni Ferrari, to be exact.[38] Shaken by the carnage in Modena, Ferrari pondered at length whether to participate in the next race, the Grand Prix of Turin, held on the Valentino Circuit.

With the exception of the Mille Miglia, it was the most important Italian race of the season. But the controversies following the tragic accident in the Modena race had hurt him personally, and Ferrari could not make up his mind. He decided to participate only when he realized that, after the unfortunate problems of the early races, his indecision had been interpreted as a sign of a difficult technical situation; for his team, it was a sort of early end of the racing season, with the sole purpose of continuing the development of the car for the following season.[39]

Having arrived in Turin at the last moment in the pouring rain, delayed by Ferrari's prolonged indecision, Sommer's 159 S set only the seventh-fastest time in qualifying. But looking at the race, Ferrari was confident: the car had good potential, he had a first-rate driver at the wheel and the 2.0 Maserati was a new model that could possibly experience some sort of mechanical trouble.

The day of the race – Sunday 12 October, 11 years after Nuvolari's win at the Vanderbilt Cup – the weather was beautiful. The start came at 11.10am. The only attacks to Sommer's lead came from Ascari and Villoresi, and only in the early part of the race. Struggling with new cars with still-limited development, the two Maserati drivers wisely decided to let up on their assault on Sommer's Ferrari, preferring to spare their cars' mechanical strengths for the second half of the race.

When, on lap 18, Ascari withdrew due to gearbox problems, Sommer had a lead of 9 seconds over Villoresi. Ten laps later, when Villoresi also stopped, the Frenchman had already established the fastest race lap. With the withdrawal of the second Maserati, the race of the Ferrari driver became almost a formality. On lap 40 his lead over 2nd place had increased to 1 minute and 12 seconds.

The second part of the race became almost boring for the large crowd thronged along the elegant boulevards of Turin. With race conduct deemed 'extraordinarily safe',[40] and without serious competition, after 105 laps and 504km (313 miles), Sommer took the chequered flag. The moment he got out of his car, he was embraced by Busso, the designer of the 159 S. More composed, Ferrari rejoiced in silence. Bazzi, who had played his usual gigantic role in this conspicuous Ferrari win, was naturally there with them.

In the moment of triumph, once the celebration had ended and there were no more compliments to receive, the last interview over and notebooks closed, away from prying eyes, there was one last thing that Enzo Ferrari wanted to do before leaving the never-loved Turin. There was a precise spot where he wanted to go, not far from the finish line of a race that had meant so much to him, and that represented a milestone in his professional life.

Nearby, there was a bench in Valentino Park, like all others, made out of wood and wrought iron. For almost 30 years that bench had represented a starting point for him, and, now he knew, a goal. On that bench he had found comfort on that day in November 1918 when Fiat had denied him a job. Today, on the day of the first prestigious win by a car that bore his name, Enzo Ferrari came to pay a debt to himself.

He left his men and ventured into the park. Alone, as he had been 30 years earlier – although this time he had sought and welcomed the solitude with its underlying melancholy that he liked so much, and in which he recognized himself – he searched for that specific bench that for three decades had populated his nightmares. He found it, sat on it and wept, just as he had wept out of despair in autumn 1918. 'The tears of that day' in October of 1947, of course, 'had a very different taste.'[41]

It was a melodramatic gesture, the kind that he loved almost to excess, and could not resist – and one that he had probably planned long in advance. Tears were included, because only the complete replication of what he had done and suffered 29 years earlier would set him free. For Enzo Ferrari, this rather awkward ceremony marked the end of the first part of his existence.

The Chase

In 1947 Enzo Ferrari had built three cars. With these cars he had participated in 14 races, taking home 7 overall or class wins. Despite a considerable economic investment – largely derived from the Scuderia income in the 1930s, the various liquidations from Alfa Romeo and important loans from three of Modena's largest banks[1] – earnings had come only from the race and prize money, which had been divided 50–50 with the drivers.

It was clear that to prosper – and Ferrari never had any interest in mere survival – it was necessary to start building cars to be sold to the many gentleman drivers who had returned from World War II. So, if on the one side he decided to increase the company's direct participation in races within and outside the Italian borders, on the other, he began to put in place a clear strategy for sales to the wealthiest amateurs.

'After a long break imposed by world events,' Enzo wrote in the editorial of the first newsletter that he published that spring, along the lines of what he had done in the 1930s, 'Scuderia Ferrari has come back to racing. It is a fundamental, complete return,' he emphasized. '[We are] no longer just a sporting organization for the dispute of races around the world, or a preparer of automobiles and men, but first of all, a manufacturer of racing cars.'[2]

The first goal on Ferrari's agenda for 1948 was the Mille Miglia, held the first weekend in May. Seen by the press as the favourite for the overall victory,[3] Ferrari fielded six cars – the entire company production up to that point. And he reserved a 166 Inter Sport for Tazio Nuvolari, with whom he had reached an agreement before the start, beating Alfa Romeo.

Fearing Ferrari's new cars and irritated by an explicit reference to the 158 that Ferrari had made a few days earlier when he had said that the 158 had been built in his Modena workshop and not in Alfa's Milan headquarters, Alfa Romeo had decided to offer a car to Nuvolari, who, to quote *Gazzetta dello Sport*, was 'desperately looking for a car to compete in this race so dear to his heart'.[4] But Ferrari got there first. Having heard of Alfa Romeo's intentions, he had immediately gone to Brescia, where he knew Nuvolari was a guest at the race scrutineering. They met and quickly made a deal.[5]

Nuvolari had participated in his last race seven months earlier and, due to the condition of his heart and lungs, his doctors had prohibited him from racing again. But he wanted to participate one last time in the Mille Miglia, and had decided to do so at the wheel of a Ferrari.

Nuvolari repaid Ferrari's trust with an extraordinary race.

When he reached Rome he was in the lead, which he kept while his car remained intact. He surrendered only when the car failed him, just outside Reggio Emilia, at the Villa Hospice refuelling, where Ferrari waited for him. The breaking of a spring bolt persuaded Ferrari to order Tazio to stop. Nuvolari wanted to continue, but accepted the decision. Things had changed; now, in 1948, the stronger man in the Ferrari–Nuvolari combination was the former.

In Bologna, a few miles before the surrender, Nuvolari and Scapinelli – his onboard mechanic, personally chosen by Ferrari[6] – were 29 minutes ahead of Biondetti's Ferrari, in second place. When he withdrew, at about 4pm, Nuvolari asked the hospitality staff for a priest, whose church was nearby. He was drained and asked to lie down.[7]

Later that afternoon, Ferrari went to check on Tazio. When he arrived at the Villa Ospizio vicarage, he found his friend sleeping on a cot. When he awoke, Ferrari saw a man exhausted from a physical point of view and disappointed at being forced to give up a triumph he knew was at hand, and one which he sensed was, in all likelihood, the last of a remarkable career. Enzo tried to comfort him with words that he knew were not true, but that he believed suitable to the circumstances. He told him to cheer up, and promised him that he could win the following year.

Nuvolari looked him in the eye and said with all sincerity: 'Dear Ferrari, at our age, days like these are rare. Remember that, and try to enjoy them, if you can.'[8] Although the Flying Mantuan could not suspect it, for Enzo Ferrari, at the age of 50, the best was yet to come.

Nuvolari had not won the Mille Miglia, but Ferrari had. The race had been won by a 166 Berlinetta with a body designed by Allemano, driven by Clemente Biondetti, with Ferrari chief tester Giuseppe Navone at his side. It was Enzo Ferrari's first great victory as a manufacturer. In a burst of generosity, Ferrari wrote a 100,000-lire cheque for Navone as a reward for the win.[9]

On 30 May Biondetti, this time without Navone, took another win, in Stockholm, collecting for Enzo Ferrari's new company its first victory outside Italy.

Two weeks later Mantua staged the last act in the long partnership between Enzo Ferrari and Tazio Nuvolari, one of the longest and most successful in motorsport history. Ferrari made a car available to Tazio to compete in the race named for his two sons, who had both died at 18 of the same disease, Giorgio in 1937, and Alberto in 1946. Nuvolari led the race in the first four laps amid the excitement and commotion of his fellow citizens but his frail health forced him to withdraw. He would never again sit behind the wheel of a Ferrari race car.

Despite the dramatic workforce escalation – which managed an increase in manufacturing, from 140 units in 1947 to 255 in 1948[10] – the development work on the Formula 1 car was quite slow. When the F1 car did reach completion, it was Sommer, the driver on whom Ferrari had decided to rely in view of his great manner, judgement and international fame, who drove it in its debut race.

The new car's debut occurred at the Italian Grand Prix on Turin's Circuito del Valentino on 5 September. Ferrari said that the single-seater raced that day – derived from the 1500 Sport, the model used in non-grand prix races – embodied 'the road we have chosen to create: a car easily usable by our customers, on nearly all circuits'.[11]

On this first Sunday in September 1948, Ferrari fielded three F1 cars. Sommer fought on, and in the end clinched a precious third place, giving Ferrari a boost in optimism in a time when his many efforts seemed to drain him emotionally.

'The debut of Ferrari's F1 model is unquestionably an exceptional proof of efficiency and preparation by Enzo Ferrari and his men,' said Canestrini. 'It must be concluded,' he went on, unconsciously answering the question that Ferrari had asked himself before the race, 'that Ferrari is therefore on the right track.' Canestrini's prediction: 'On the horizon looms a Ferrari threat which Alfa Romeo engineers should immediately start to take into consideration.'[12]

The Turin race was a turning point.

The following week Luigi Chinetti took the Ferrari 166 to its maiden win at the 12 Hours of Paris. On 24 October, Nino Farina won the Circuito del Garda with a 125 C. But above all, again in France, and always on the Montlhéry circuit, before the end of the season Chinetti and his 166 set three international speed records on the hour and on the 100 and the 200 miles, at more than 200km/h (124mph) – despite the rain and the wind.[13] For a company founded only a year earlier, these were no small feats.

'The expected results have been reached,' Ferrari declared. 'The merit belongs first of all to my men, who have placed in *us* [an archaic way of referring to oneself in the plural form, much like royalty, but here, with only one possible meaning: Enzo Ferrari], at all times, serene confidence. Without aid, but with the quiet certainty of a good cause, we have worked with artisanal and provincial obstinacy.'[14]

In the meantime, in mid-September Enzo Ferrari had participated in his first motor show as a manufacturer.[15] The car that was introduced at the Turin Motor

Show would make history. It was the 166 MM, where the double Ms stood for Mille Miglia, in celebration of the victory clinched that spring. But right away the press came up with a different name that reflected the form, and would, in time, come to indicate this type of open car: *Barchetta* ('small boat' in Italian).

For Enzo Ferrari, the 166 MM Barchetta was a declaration of intent, a sports car with a sensual shape, as fast and powerful as it was beautiful and elegant. It was the foundation on which, from that moment on, he would build every road model: cars capable of winning races on circuits and roads all over the world and, at the same time, the protagonists of the most prestigious *Concours d'Elegance* in the four corners of the earth.

Strengthened by the successes obtained during the racing season, at the end of 1948 Luigi Chinetti went to Maranello to convince Ferrari to participate in the Le Mans 24 Hours. Chinetti had already won the classic French race twice, in 1932 and in 1934, both times with an Alfa Romeo. He had known Ferrari since those days, and he now asked Enzo for two cars and eight mechanics to race in the 1949 contest.[16] He would personally race one car and friend René Dreyfus, with whom he had fled to New York at the outbreak of the war, would race the other.

Despite Chinetti's insistence and analysis, and his spontaneous but valuable alliance with two such esteemed engineers as Colombo and Lampredi, he did not succeed in persuading Ferrari, who, at that time, was not entirely sure he was ready to participate in such events. The lesson of the Carrozzeria Emilia failure was not forgotten. Plunging into a new adventure too early was a mistake Enzo was not going to repeat. He would likely participate in the Le Mans 24 Hours, but in due course, once he felt he could honour the race and not make a fool of himself. If he really wanted to race at Le Mans, Ferrari told Chinetti, he could always purchase two cars from Ferrari. Which Luigi promptly did.

The year 1949 began early for Enzo Ferrari, who, instead of waiting for the resumption of racing in Europe, decided to send a car to South America to take part in the Latin American racing season that Argentineans and Brazilians called the *Temporada*.

Like the previous year, Ferrari's European season began in the spring, with the Giro di Sicilia. Also like the year before, Biondetti won at the wheel of a 166. He also triumphed in the Mille Miglia, at an incredible average speed of 131km/h (81mph), shattering his own record on the distance, set in 1948. 'Ferrari and Bazzi,' the press said, referring to the string of successes with which Ferrari had opened the season, and also praising Enzo's technical alter ego, 'deserve all of this satisfaction for the brilliance and technique of their work.'[17]

The quality of his cars allowed Ferrari to restore the post-race routine that had been so familiar in the days of the Scuderia. The Monday after a race was a quiet day, devoted to taking in Sunday's results and to recharging batteries. It was also the day when the cars that had raced on Sunday returned to the factory. Tuesday was the day on which the drivers who had raced over the weekend arrived in Maranello, where they received their share of the race and prize money – always divided 50–50 with the boss – and the day when, according to the importance of the victory, Ferrari offered either a luncheon or a dinner to celebrate.

Besides being particularly beautiful, the 166 MM was also fast and reliable. And in the capable hands of Luigi Chinetti – the other endurance race specialist – in late June it clinched victory in the Le Mans 24 Hours.

The 166 MM raced by Dreyfus, with co-equipier Jean Lucas, was forced to retire after crashing, due to problems with the steering. But Chinetti and Lord Selsdon, who had driven for just an hour or so – which meant that Luigi had raced for more or less 23 of the race's 24 hours! – won hands down.

That very Sunday afternoon, waiting for news from Le Mans, Enzo and son Dino, now 17, climbed up the steep ascent leading to the old medieval fortress of San Marino, whose pale stone bulk has been proudly silhouetted against the sky for centuries atop a rock of the Apennines. From the mountaintop, one could clearly see the Adriatic Sea. Despite being slightly overweight, thanks to his healthy appetite and fondness for the simplest pleasures of life, Enzo was an athletic man and his climbing was vigorous.

Dino was a good-looking young man, nearly as tall as Enzo, and probably slimmer than his father ever was. He shared his father's features and ambition, and the same determination in climbing. But he lacked his strength. Despite his efforts, he could not keep up with his father and lagged behind. Every few steps his father would stop, turn and wait for him. A few feet above Dino, Enzo stood watching his son following him with increasingly uncertain steps; he could hear his son's troubled breathing, which made it sound as though Dino might expire at any moment. Looking into the distance, beyond his son, Enzo could see the summer sky tinged with the burning colours of the approaching sunset. It was all so beautiful and, yet, so cruel.

At the age of seven,[18] Dino had started treatment for what doctors at first had called nephritis (inflammation of the kidneys), but which soon turned out to be something difficult to diagnose and impossible to cure: muscular dystrophy, a disease for which there is still no cure today, and the reason for Dino's valiant struggle on their climb that day. Ferrari carried a portable radio with him, one of those transistors able to pick up radio waves from antennas scattered over the peaks of the hills surrounding the fortress, whose range was rapidly increasing thanks to post-World War II technology. He planned to use it to check on the results at Le Mans.

Father and son shared a passion for racing cars. And if the father had long made this obsession the focus of his professional life, Dino had soon shown the same interest. He was about to get his diploma from Modena's Corni Technical Institute,[19] and had decided that he would go on to study engineering in college. In Maranello it was not uncommon to see Dino discreetly wandering around the workshop to see if his father's men were working on something new,[20] or sitting behind the wheel of a car that had just been finished and was parked in the factory yard.[21] The motor-racing press had got to know him, and sometimes mentioned his name as his father's companion.[22]

Once they reached the top of the hill, father and son switched on the radio and awaited news from France. The sky before them now had even brighter colours and the clouds were blazing red. When the news came it was good: one of his cars, the same colour as those June clouds, with a black prancing horse on the hood, had won the greatest race of all, the Le Mans 24 Hours, unequalled amid endurance competitions. For Ferrari and his factory, it was their first international win. For a racing-car manufacturer, it was a magic moment.

But for Enzo, his elation over the victory soon faded to anxiety, the feeling of anguish that had given him no rest since the day Dino had been diagnosed. 'The radio brought me a moment of great joy,' Enzo would say years later, '[but] all I could think of was that my son was slipping away from me. That I would soon lose him!'[23]

For an instant, and an instant only, Enzo entertained the appalling idea of a sublime act of love. It would only take a moment, the time required for a desperate act of courage. It would all be over in just a few seconds. 'In front of the cliff of the Marecchia,' he recalled years later, 'I told myself that I did not have the courage; otherwise, I would have hugged my son and I would have jumped into the gorge with him.'[24] He felt it was the best solution: a leap into the unknown, embracing his son, a leap that would spare Dino an inevitable and painful fate and himself the grief of surviving him. 'In that moment,' he would write in his memoirs, 'I realized that I was a coward, because man has come up with another term to defend himself from reality. The term is *bad luck*, but in reality, it only expresses what man has not been able to do or foresee.'[25]

The sun soon disappeared behind the clouds. A slight breeze blew in from the sea, and the heat of the day suddenly became a distant memory. Father and son began their descent toward the plains, and their respective fates.

* * *

The month before the 24 Hours of Le Mans, the single-seater that Enzo Ferrari wished to field in 1950 in the first season of the soon-to-be-introduced Formula 1 World Championship was finally ready.

The 125 F1 had faced its first test on 28 May. A tester left the factory in Maranello and launched the car down the road to Abetone. Ferrari waited at the usual turn near the village of Serramazzoni. He sat all day on a small brick wall in the company of Colombo and their men, in his shirtsleeves, with an out-of-fashion cap on his head to protect him from the late-spring sun. The sound of the engine cut the otherwise perfect silence of the Apennines, and every time the car stopped in front of him, he rushed over to speak to whoever was at the wheel, Navone, D'Angelo or Cortese.[26]

On 3 July, in this car – powered by a supercharged 1.5-litre engine – Ascari dominated the Grand Prix of Switzerland and, on 20 August, the International Trophy race. With a similar car Gigi Villoresi won the Dutch Grand Prix on 31 July. 'Enzo Ferrari,' the Italian press stated in the summer of 1949, 'can be satisfied with the results that the red cars built in the Maranello workshop are getting lately on all circuits.'[27] But of course, Ferrari was never satisfied; in September, at the Grand Prix of Italy in Monza, he intended to debut the new 1500 twin-compressor engine.

On Sunday 11 September 1949, Alberto Ascari brought the new car to victory in the Italian Grand Prix, featuring the latest version of the 12-cylinder engine that was 'the first new product of the postwar period, and the expression of the tenacity and work of this remarkable new industrial complex that Enzo Ferrari created at Maranello'.[28]

Despite the glory of the day at Monza, Ferrari knew it was not a true representation of the coming season and the fierce competition it would bring. None of the races won by the 125 F1 had been attended by the Alfa Romeo 158 that the Milan company intended to use in the F1 world championship in 1950. To make matters worse, on the only circuit where Ferrari could make a comparison – Monza, where the Alfas had lapped in pre-race practice – the 158 was six seconds faster than the pole position time set by Ascari.

At this point, Ferrari made a decision: while Colombo would continue to work on the development of sports racing cars and passenger cars, responsibility for the F1 project would be assumed by a young Livorno engineer who had until then reported to Colombo, Aurelio Lampredi. Of course, it was not just a matter of a simple division of tasks. Ferrari had always been convinced that pitting his technicians against each other was the key to success.[29] Above everyone was *Cavalier* Bazzi, who had been with Ferrari since 1923; this was never in question and Bazzi had long ago become Enzo's conscience from a technical point of view.

Despite the understandable importance placed on the upcoming inaugural F1 World Championship, the modern version of the grand prix racing series of his racing driver and Scuderia days, Ferrari had not forgotten the cars of the other formulas. The design he had in mind was clear: Ferrari would not focus on one type or category of racing, but would instead seek to honour commitments in as many categories and formulas as possible. He had made this promise to himself during the darkest days of the war, when the thought of racing again might have seemed like a mirage, and he had not changed his mind now that not only racing, but also success, had returned to his life.

Accompanied by Dino, in November he went to Monza for a practice session of the new F2 single-seater. Behind the wheel sat Felice Bonetto, a driver he particularly liked for the audacity and ruthlessness he showed in the race.[30] Back in Modena, that evening Ferrari penned in his journal: 'The car is really amazing and exciting.'[31]

Although the year 1949 had been an important one for Ferrari, 1950, with the first F1 World Championship, promised to be a possible turning point.

Revenge

In the winter of 1950 the small car manufacturer out of Maranello was the absolute star of the South American Temporada. This time Ferrari had gone the extra mile. Instead of the single car for Farina that he had shipped overseas the year before, he sent three 166 FLs – FL for Free Formula (Formule Libre) – for Ascari, Villoresi and Dorino Serafini. In addition to these, there were two cars that he had sold to the Equipo Argentino team, entrusted to local drivers Juan Manuel Fangio and Benedicto Campos, and Peter Whitehead's entry, a single-compressor 1500 Ferrari, personally owned by the British driver. Despite Maserati's fierce competition it was a Maranello triumph.

Ferrari won all four races he entered with Ascari and Villoresi, who won two each. As if this were not enough, the sports car support race of the Grand Prix of Mar del Plata was won by Argentinean driver Carlos Menditeguy, at the wheel of his own Ferrari 166 MM.

While Ferrari pressed Lampredi and his aides, who were frantically working on the new F1 engine, time quickly passed and winter gave way to spring. Before the direct confrontation with Alfa Romeo in the F1 World Championship, there was another event that could not be underestimated: the Mille Miglia.

Ferrari actually took the opportunity of the demanding race up and down the Italian peninsula to debut two examples of Lampredi's new engine – albeit not yet in its final configuration, and mounted on the two S 275s entrusted to Ascari and Villoresi.[1] But the real surprise – and success – unexpectedly came from the car of a gentleman driver who had faced the gruelling ride dressed in his elegant beige and maroon office suit.[2]

Giannino Marzotto was the archetypal Ferrari Sports customer: a gentleman with a talent for driving matched only by his love for life's strong emotions. Sitting in his bright blue Ferrari 195 S Berlinetta, he raced the event, marked by severe weather, with class and ease. And when the two Ferraris of Ascari and Villoresi withdrew, he inherited the lead, which he kept until the finish line in Brescia.

The Marzotto brothers actually entered four Ferraris in the 1950 Mille Miglia: in addition to the blue 195 S belonging to Giannino, there were Vittorio's red 195 S (which finished ninth overall), Paolo's red 166 MM and Umberto's white 166 MM (which crashed near the city of Peschiera). They had all been purchased by and were the property of the four children of Count Marzotto.[3] As before the war with the Scuderia privateers, Ferrari had simply organized their participation and provided assistance throughout the race. But for the public, and ultimately for Ferrari himself, it did not matter.

Despite the not yet fully reliable new engine mounted in the cars of his works drivers, thanks to the exploits of the 22-year-old Vicenza aristocrat the lord of Maranello proved that anyone – provided, of course, that he possessed Marzotto's talent – could win a race with a Ferrari.

The F1 World Championship dawned on Saturday 13 May 1950. That afternoon, on the English circuit of Silverstone, the king of England was present to solemnly inaugurate the series. Enzo Ferrari had chosen to remain in Maranello with his cars. Because of the still unsatisfactory development of the F1 car, Ferrari had decided not to participate in the first round of the new championship.[4]

Ferrari's debut in the F1 World Championship therefore took place on 21 May 1950, in Monaco. Ferrari fielded three 125 F1s for Ascari, Villoresi and Raymond Sommer. A fourth 125 F1, privately entered by Englishman Peter Whitehead, to whom Ferrari had sold it two years earlier,[5] took part in pre-race practice sessions.

The debut was positive in terms of results, with Ascari on the second step of the podium behind Fangio in an Alfa Romeo 158. But the outcome of the race was influenced by a giant crash during the first lap that had forced half of the cars to withdraw, including the other two Alfa Romeos of Nino Farina and Luigi Fagioli. Ascari, who in practice had been three and a half seconds slower than Fangio, finished an entire lap behind the winner.

In the attempt to give a world identity to the new championship, the Indianapolis 500 was included, but none of the European manufacturers participated. It was only on 4 June that all European teams and drivers met again at Bern's Bremgarten Circuit for the Swiss Grand Prix. The Scuderia lineup was the same as in Monaco, even though this time Sommer was at the wheel of a 166 F2. In practice Alfa Romeo's power was overwhelming: Fangio, Farina and Fagioli set the three fastest lap times. The race proved to be just as disappointing for Ferrari's drivers: Ascari broke the oil pump on lap four, Villoresi, the engine on lap nine and Sommer, a suspension component on lap nineteen.

Ferrari was furious. The Alfa Romeos were out of reach, the 125 F1 outdated. He angrily ordered that for the next race, pending availability of the final car (the one with the 4.5-litre engine), Lampredi at least arrange an engine with the biggest displacement he had obtained up to that point.

Two weeks later, in Belgium, Ascari took to the track with a car that for the first time mounted a Ferrari naturally aspirated engine; the displacement was 3300cc, the first stage in the growth towards 4500.[6] Lampredi had fitted a Type 275 engine on a Type GP 49 chassis, with a modified gearbox and differential. Even so, things did not improve. Ascari grabbed fifth place, behind not only three Alfa Romeos, but also, surprisingly, an old Talbot raced by Louis Rosier.

The situation was critical. Ferrari decided to sit out the 2 July Grand Prix of the Automobile Club of France. Then he demanded that in the following Grand Prix des Nations in Geneva, later that same month – a race not valid for the championship – his Scuderia would field at least one single-seater, with the next evolution of the naturally aspirated engine. Lampredi and his men worked the entire month of July by day, night and weekends, and prepared a Type 340 with a 4100cc engine that was trucked to Switzerland.[7] But even so, in practice Ascari trailed 2 seconds behind Fangio's 158. And in the race, the new engine just blew up.

On 30 July in Geneva, Villoresi was badly injured in a crash that put an end to his race seven laps from the chequered flag. Ferrari decided to take part in the next Italian Grand Prix at Monza with just two drivers: Ascari and Dorino Serafini. But at Monza, on the day of Alfa Romeo's apotheosis, with Nino Farina crowned the first F1 world champion, for the first time Ferrari went home with some positive feedback.

Lampredi and his team had made a miracle happen: at Monza, both drivers were at the wheel of the new Ferrari 375 model, equipped with the 4.0-litre engine that Lampredi had been working on for over a year. And the results were not long in coming. Ascari had set the second-fastest time in qualifying, breaking Alfa Romeo's monopoly for the first time, which had placed its three drivers in the top three qualifying spots in all the preceding races that season except one. During the race, Ascari even briefly went into the lead before experiencing technical problems that forced him to the pits, where he climbed into Serafini's car. Facilitated by Fangio's withdrawal, Ascari finished second, ahead of Luigi Fagioli's Alfa Romeo.

At the end of the year Enzo Ferrari could claim: 'After years of an unchallenged rule in F1 by supercharged vehicles, the work we have done' – meaning, the study and development of the naturally aspirated engine that now equipped the 375 – 'is bearing its first fruits.' As always, he knew that everything had a price in life, and that joy was never complete. 'Progress is difficult, and the path to conquest punctuated with blood: Our dear Raymond Sommer has left us,' he said, referring to his old friend's death in a racing incident earlier in the year, 'and we cannot but voice our pain.'[8]

Alberto Ascari and Luigi Villoresi were certain to have seats on the Ferrari F1 team for 1951. As for Serafini, who had replaced Villoresi when Gigi had suffered the crash that had sidelined him for a long time,[9] Ferrari was having second thoughts, thinking about replacing him with Piero Taruffi, who had already raced for him in the days of the Scuderia.

For the by-now traditional winter Temporada, Ferrari relied this time on Argentineans Froilán González and Oscar Alfredo Gálvez, who drove 166 FFs fielded by a local team, subsidized by the government of General Perón, who, like many political leaders before and after him, understood the importance of motor racing in terms of propaganda. González won the two races in which he participated, on 18 and 25 January 1951.

Before the F1 World Championship's opening act in late May, there was the Mille Miglia, which Ferrari had won three times in a row. And before that classic race on the streets of northern and central Italy was the Tour of Sicily, which for Ferrari, now accustomed to more-prestigious events, was losing importance every year. Nevertheless, it was still an event that he wanted to honour, if only out of loyalty to Vincenzo Florio, one of the men he respected the most in the motor-racing community.

As it turned out, the 1951 Tour of Sicily became the stage for a generational and cultural clash with the Marzotto brothers, especially with Giannino, the winner of the 1950 Mille Miglia. That winter Giannino had purchased two Ferrari 212 Export chassis. For the bodies of the two cars, instead of turning to any of the coachbuilders normally recommended by Ferrari, he decided to do things his own way. He thus commissioned a sculptor to design a revolutionary body for one of the cars, to be built by a craftsman who also designed the body for the other chassis, straight out of Giannino's imagination. The Marzotto brothers ironically christened the two cars *The Egg* and *The Little Spider* because of their unorthodox bodylines. Knowing that they could not do otherwise, they showed them to Ferrari before leaving for Sicily.[10]

Nothing had prepared the exuberant young men, heirs to a large textile empire, for the reaction of the sage of Maranello. At first Ferrari was puzzled. Then, in a fast crescendo, he became outraged and finally exploded. 'It's as if you had raped my daughter in front of my eyes,' he cried.[11] The Marzotto brothers were petrified. In the courtyard of the Maranello factory, Ferrari's screaming voice echoed in the late-spring afternoon.

The project was apocalyptic for its extravagance, he shouted, and completely wrong from a technical point of view. He pointed to the side bracket that was supposed to hold the spare tyre. 'That bracket there,' he barked, 'will collapse at the first hole.'[12] Giannino leaned on it to show its strength – and the bracket fell on the floor.

Ferrari felt challenged. It mattered little that the Marzotto brothers had purchased from him one car after the other, and that Giannino had won the Mille Miglia the year before. No one dared to challenge Enzo Ferrari – let alone young men in their 20s. While Ferrari screamed, he announced to the Marzotto brothers that he would officially run in Sicily with a 180hp, 3-carburettor 2560 that he would entrust to Piero Taruffi.

The four brothers were unimpressed. Back in Valdagno, Giannino decided to respond to Ferrari's outburst by further customizing his Little Spider. He called an artist friend and asked him to paint the face of a shark on the hood of the car and the body of a dragon on the sides. Any reference to Enzo Ferrari was not accidental. Painted in this fashion, the car caused a scandal on its arrival in Palermo. But while the race organizers and stewards spoke of a 'desecration of the seriousness of motor racing',[13] Sicilian sports enthusiasts were fascinated.

On Sunday 1 April 1951, Vittorio, the eldest of the Marzotto brothers, at 28, won the 11th Tour of Sicily. At the finish line in Palermo he preceded Piero Taruffi's works Ferrari by a little over a minute. Bombastic as only a handsome, 22-year-old millionaire could be, the day after the race Giannino Marzotto phoned Ferrari to maliciously comment on the race.

'As I had expected,' Ferrari cut him short, 'a Ferrari won!'[14]

And that was the whole conversation.

Four weeks later all the Marzotto brothers participated in the 1951 Mille Miglia. Together with Marco Crosara, and at the wheel of The Egg, Giannino led the race until he was forced to withdraw. The lead was then taken by Villoresi in one of the two 340 Americas that Ferrari had fielded.

He had never been particularly close to Ferrari, but when Ferrari said simply 'Bravo!' to him,[15] Villoresi felt galvanized by the unexpected encouragement, and flew all the way to Brescia. Although you might not necessarily like Ferrari, his personality was so overwhelming that sometimes a single word from him was enough to focus all the adrenaline in one's body. As always, Villoresi gave his race mechanic his own half of the prize money earned with the victory.[16]

A few days later Ferrari offered Villoresi a dinner to celebrate his victory at the Mille Miglia. Invited to the dinner that evening in Modena were the drivers, mechanics, engineers and some of his own friends. And Dino was invited, of course, more and more captivated by the world of motor racing.

The signs of the muscular dystrophy that had afflicted him for years were evident that evening, in all their devastating cruelty. Try as he might, Dino could not stand by himself and required constant support. Struggling to maintain his independence in terms of movement, he had refused to be overcome by the growing difficulties he faced when it came to walking, stoically refusing offers of help.[17] But that night, he had surrendered.

Overcome with anguish and concern, Enzo hastily decided to cut the dinner short and avoid further suffering for his son.[18] When he later spoke of 'terrible joys', he would also refer to incidents like this one, where he was unable to fully enjoy a sporting success because of life's cruel realities.[19]

*   *   *

Before the start of the 1951 F1 World Championship, Enzo Ferrari went to Tortona. The place had been chosen because it was (almost) equidistant between Modena and Turin. In this neutral territory, Enzo had finally decided to meet the coachbuilder Battista Farina, known to all by his nickname of *Pinin*, in the great Turin tradition.

Always focused on the design and development of new engines and mechanical components, Ferrari had never really sought a reference coachbuilder, preferring to leave his customers the choice of the craftsman to turn to, as had been standard practice in the 1920s when he himself had experimented in the role of coachbuilder, and then again in the 1930s. For him, what had always mattered most in a car had been the engine; everything else was less consequential. Count Marzotto's two bizarre creations had probably opened his eyes, however, convincing him that the time had come to also start worrying about what was over and around the engine.

There were good reasons why, of all Italian coachbuilders, Ferrari had decided to approach Pinin Farina, whom he had known from the early 1920s when they had found each other at the start of an Aosta–Gran San Bernardo hillclimb, and whose subsequent creations he had admired. Not wanting to give the impression of asking for anything, Ferrari had ruled out visiting Pinin in his Corso Trapani workshop in Turin. By now Ferrari was a king, and the king received in Maranello. By the same token, Pinin, who would benefit immensely from Ferrari's contracts, did not want to give Enzo the impression that he was looking for work. It was only through the mediation of Pinin's son Sergio and brother-in-law Renzo Carli that the two men agreed to meet, in as neutral a place as could be: a restaurant in Tortona.

When they finally met, it did not take them long to understand each other.[20] Ferrari, accompanied by commercial director Gerolamo Gardini,[21] said that he was looking for someone who could complete the mechanics of his cars with their body designs. Body and engine – elegance and power – had to go hand in hand, and had to be born and grow together. He said that he was not looking for a tailor, but for a coachbuilder who worked at his side and conveyed in the shape of the body the power and philosophy of his cars. The coachbuilder, he said, must be involved from the beginning of the project, not called merely to dress a finished product.[22]

Farina, who had never liked 'the body reduced to a matter of decoration, or as the packaging of a mechanical product', was immediately won over by Ferrari's 'clear ideas'.[23] He sensed that he and the man from Maranello spoke the same language and saw the car in the same way. Before the end of their lunch, Pinin had agreed to work with Ferrari.

Together, they determined to 'pull the car away from melodrama, from the monumental, even from the visionary, and quit forever the decorative',[24] as Pinin Farina would later sum it up. At lunch they had quickly gone beyond general topics and had spoken of specifics.[25] Their first joint project was to be a convertible that they agreed to introduce a year later.

On Sunday 27 May, the Swiss Grand Prix in Bern inaugurated the second Formula 1 World Championship. The optimistic impressions that had emerged from the last event of the 1950 championship proved to be correct. Although in qualifying Alfa Romeo's dominance was barely touched by Ferrari – Villoresi third, with two Alfettas in front and two behind – the race said something different. Taruffi came in second behind Fangio, after a long and successful battle with reigning world champion Nino Farina's Alfetta. In Maranello, Ferrari saw the result as an encouraging sign,[26] although the other three Alfa Romeos had finished the race behind Villoresi, and Ascari only came in sixth.

The Indianapolis 500 was scheduled three days later, once again on the championship calendar and once again snubbed by European manufacturers and teams – but not entirely by Enzo Ferrari. He had sent one of his men to Indiana to watch the race and take note of all the technical aspects that could prove relevant to possible future participation.[27]

Pressed by Chinetti, Ferrari had started to look at the US market as a huge reservoir of customers for his sports cars and road-going berlinettas; not surprisingly, the model that Villoresi had driven to victory in the Mille Miglia was called *America*. In addition, Ascari himself had expressed interest in one day participating in the Indy 500. And then, of course, one must not forget that it was the Indianapolis 500 that had stirred Enzo's imagination when he was a boy.

In mid-June the F1 championship returned to Europe when the Spa-Francorchamps race track hosted the Belgian Grand Prix. With the third-fastest time in qualifying, Villoresi started from the front row of the grid, next to the two Alfa Romeos of Farina and Fangio. Thanks to the lower consumption of the normally aspirated 12-cylinder engines mounted on their 375 F1 models, Ferrari's drivers clinched second- and third-place finishes.

Once again all that glittered was not gold, since Ascari and Villoresi had finished three and four minutes behind Farina, and if Fangio had not experienced problems with a wheel during a pit stop for refuelling, he would probably have finished second. But it was a fact that, despite the delays, Lampredi and his men were finally approaching the level of competitiveness at which they had aimed for months, and which looked even nearer at the next race, the Grand Prix of the Automobile Club of France, where, after qualifying, reporters observed: 'You have the distinct impression that the 4500 model out of Maranello has come close to its adversaries and can now threaten them very closely.'[28]

Ferrari, who had always had an eye for young talents, had before the race offered one of his cars to 23-year-old Stirling Moss, who had declined.[29] And so, in France, the third works Ferrari was raced by Froilán González – the vigorous driver from Argentina who had won two of the Temporada races at the wheel of a Ferrari – replacing Taruffi, who was engaged that same day in a motorcycle race. A few days after the French Grand Prix, his friend Fangio took him to Maranello. Fangio personally introduced him to Enzo Ferrari, and González walked out of the meeting with a contract to race with Ferrari until the end of the season.[30]

The next event was the Grand Prix of Great Britain and Europe at Silverstone, where the previous year the World Championship had held its maiden race. It was scheduled for Saturday 14 July 1951 – a date that would enter Ferrari history.

The race weekend started well, with Froilán González setting pole position over Fangio, one whole second slower. It was the first time in a season and a half that an Alfa Romeo driver did not capture the first position in qualifying. And, of course, it was the first pole position in F1 in the history of Ferrari.

On Saturday afternoon, González lined up his 375 Ferrari on the far right of the front row of the starting grid. Next to him were the two Alfettas of Fangio and Farina. At the far left, Ascari closed the front row with his 375.

González was in a state of grace today and the Ferrari 375 was in top shape. The Alfetta's engine was still more powerful than the 375's 12-cylinder, but the engine to which Lampredi had dedicated 2 years of his life was providing power in a more balanced and smooth way, enormously benefiting González in his chase.[31]

Shortly before half distance, with a stunning manoeuvre at Becketts, one of the most challenging corners of the ultra-fast Silverstone, the pupil passed the master. González took the lead, which he held until the end, despite Fangio's stubborn persistence.

It was a historic moment. Not only was it González's first F1 victory, but it was also the first time that an Alfa Romeo did not win a race valid for the modern F1 World Championship. The victory of the 375 also meant the first defeat for the supercharged engine, and the first success of the normally aspirated. And it was also, of course, the first victory of a Ferrari in an F1 World Championship race.

Scuderia Ferrari team manager Federico Giberti rushed to the phone and immediately informed his boss of what had just happened.[32] On hearing the news in Modena, Ferrari said that he wept with joy.[33]

The great moment had finally arrived. Revenge was accomplished. He, the small-town craftsman who had been kicked out unceremoniously after 20 years of loyalty and dedication by an ungrateful and politicized management, had beaten the big carmaker that for a year and a half had dominated the top category of motor racing. Enzo Ferrari had founded his company partly to show the Portello leadership the mistake they had made when they had done away with him.[34] Now the enormity of their mistake was there for all to see.

And since *his* 375 had defeated *his* 158, that afternoon Ferrari reached a conclusion which only he and his contorted emotional complexity could have produced: 'I have defeated my mother,'[35] he confessed in a moment that should have been one of far-reaching joy for accomplishing what he had set out to achieve 12 long years earlier – but was not. 'Victory,' he learned, from the strange mix of satisfaction and frustration that his success had unexpectedly aroused in him, 'did not give me the joy I hoped.'[36]

But there was very little time for celebration. Two weeks later they would all meet at the Nürburgring for the German Grand Prix. For Alfa Romeo it was a chance to try to halt history; for Scuderia Ferrari, the opportunity to prove that the wind had changed.

But the wind *had* truly changed in F1, and Ferrari dominated the event from the first day of practice. Ascari set pole position with a time that was over three seconds quicker than Fangio's third place. González set the second-fastest time, a second and a half faster than Fangio. And the Sunday race indeed heralded the dawn of a new day.

In view of technical problems experienced by all the Alfa Romeos in the race, the four Ferraris flew unimpeded. The only Alfa Romeo that put up some opposition was Fangio's, whose class on a circuit like the 'Ring could still make the difference. But Ascari's 375, with the lowest fuel consumption, also played in favour of Ferrari's driver, who pitted for refuelling only once. At the chequered flag, the Italian and his Ferrari beat Fangio's Alfa Romeo by half a minute. But while the Alfetta of the Argentinean was the only one that finished the race, behind it came the other three Ferraris: González, third; Villoresi, fourth; and Taruffi, fifth.

It was the end of an era. Enzo Ferrari had forced Alfa Romeo to its knees. In Maranello, that evening, Enzo Ferrari stated: 'It's over. Today, Alfa Romeo,' said the man who had tied his name to the Portello company for 20 years, 'started the downward cycle already made, all the way to the final surrender, by Fiat.'[37]

The next race was the Italian Grand Prix at Monza. Twelve months earlier Alfa Romeo had celebrated its first F1 world title on this track. Now it had to struggle to stem the firepower of the Ferraris. Things went well for Alfa Romeo in qualifying, with the two Alfettas of Fangio and Farina ahead of everyone. The race was a different story, however, with Ascari and González finishing in first and second place. The first Alfa Romeo – Bonetto's, which Farina had driven – was only third, a whole lap behind Ascari and followed by the other two Ferraris of Villoresi and Taruffi. By the time Ascari took the chequered flag, Fangio had been in the pits for more than 40 laps, with the engine of his Alfetta blown up.

For Enzo Ferrari, Monza was a day of true glory, but for Italian motor racing as a whole it was bittersweet. Giovanni Canestrini, who for 30 years had been chasing Italian race cars on tracks all over Europe and beyond, said: 'If this total Italian victory, which crowns the efforts, work and intelligence of that perhaps unique-in-the-world organization created by Enzo Ferrari, is exciting, the defeat of this car' – the 159 Alfa Romeo, evolution of the 158 model – 'is just as poignant, having for so many years given us wins and glories that have honoured our country.'[38]

If for Enzo Ferrari Silverstone had been the time for tears, and the Nürburgring the day that sanctioned the end of Alfa Romeo's historical cycle, Monza should have been the high point. In addition to having defeated Alfa Romeo on its home circuit, with the win in the Italian Grand Prix, Ascari and González had become contenders for the title of world champion. Instead, this complex sportsman did not allow himself to completely savour what he had achieved. It was as if, as journalist Gianni Brera tried to explain after interviewing Ferrari a few days later, he had been 'assaulted by the torment of someone who, not having thought of anything but victory for a long time, having achieved it, suddenly feels as if his life no longer has any purpose'.[39]

The second F1 World Championship title would be awarded with the last race, on the Pedralbes circuit on the outskirts of Barcelona, in late October. For this last and decisive grand prix, Pirelli suggested mounting larger tyres than those used so far, ideal, according to the Milanese engineers, for the long and fast straights of the Catalan circuit and the five sharp (and therefore slow) bends after each straight. Ferrari doubted the good faith of Pirelli – a Milan-based company like Alfa Romeo. Instead of their recommended 46cm (18-inch) tyres, he stuck with the 40cm (16-inch) ones, encouraged by the fastest time in qualifying set by Ascari.

The race told a different story. Ascari was forced to pit seven times to replace tyres that disintegrated incredibly fast. Fangio, whose Alfetta was fitted with the tyres recommended by Pirelli, won the race and the title.[40] Ferrari and Ascari had to settle for the second spot in the world championship standings. It was no small feat in light of how the year had started, but considering what had happened in the second half of the season both knew that they had thrown away a golden opportunity.

On Top of the World

Despite the bitterness of the results, the 1951 F1 season had seen Ferrari fill the gap that at the beginning of the year had still existed between them and Alfa Romeo. To limit the costs of F1 pending the entry of the new regulations, the Fédération Internationale de l'Automobile (FIA) had decreed that in 1952 and in 1953 the World Championship should be contested by Formula 2 single-seaters.

The decision did not change the fate of Alfa Romeo, which had decided to withdraw from motor racing because of the high cost involved, and which, to contain expenses, had never really renewed its racing equipment since 1938.[1] But ultimately it did not alter the fortunes of Ferrari, either; although they were damaged by the sports authorities' decision, they did have a brand-new engine ready for the new championship and the new rules, thanks to Enzo Ferrari's foresight. While he was closing the gap to Alfa Romeo, Ferrari had asked Lampredi to start working on a project that he had mentioned one Sunday morning in the spring of 1951.

With Alfa Romeo's withdrawal, Maserati represented the only real obstacle on Ferrari's road to his first F1 world title. But with Maserati experiencing big delays in the development of their new car, Enzo Ferrari began to turn his attention to motor racing on the other side of the Atlantic.

The first to advocate for Ferrari participation in the Indianapolis 500 was Luigi Chinetti, who had found two precious allies in Alberto Ascari and, as in 1949 for the Le Mans 24 Hours, Aurelio Lampredi. Chinetti was not the only American thinking of racing at Indianapolis in a car with the prancing horse on the hood. In early December 1951, Ferrari had met in Maranello with Tony Bettenhausen, to whom he had sold a 4500 model that the Illinois champion wanted to race at Indy in 1952 with his own team.[2]

On 18 February 1952, Enzo Ferrari turned 54 years old. Despite his hectic pace of work, his health was good. His days of depression belonged to a distant past, even if that sense of latent anguish never completely left him – an anguish now fuelled by the poor health of his son Dino, who too often lacked the strength to stand on his own.[3] Physically Enzo was still an imposing man, at 187cm (6ft 2in) and 120kg (265lb). His size elicited respect, his work, praise, the road travelled thus far, admiration. And everyone knew – or suspected or feared – that he had just started.

With the thin lips that Enzo had inherited from his mother,[4] his mouth seemed always 'bent to irony'. His 'big eyes' were now 'a little opaque'. His 'mighty' nose was curved 'on the subtly malicious cutting of his mouth', giving 'his face a look that was at once rapacious and sarcastic'. He could remind you of Voltaire, wrote journalist Gianni Brera in *La Gazzetta dello Sport* after meeting him – adding with mischievous approval 'that in a younger world they would have burned this provoker of demons'.[5] Ferrari maintained the unpretentiousness of those who were accustomed to having to fight to survive. He knew that he had become the best – or, at least, he knew that he was in the process of becoming the best – but he had not forgotten the nights when he'd gone to bed without dinner, the days when he was the last of the Alfa Romeo racing drivers, his firing and the bank loans. It was actually for this reason that he did not indulge in the luxury of owning one of his own cars: 'For someone who has a whole lot of debts,' he said, 'to own a six-million-lire automobile would be a tasteless extravagance.'[6]

He did not allow himself to be mesmerized by the throngs of admirers who had begun to court him when his cars started to defeat Alfa Romeos. Fiat and Lancia flattered him by offering to let him use his name together with theirs in the production of cheaper cars, available to everyone in an Italy that was rebuilding itself, and in which the automobile would soon become one of the symbols of the new prosperity. But he had not taken the bait.[7]

'I sell sports cars as a way to allow my workers to support themselves, and to find the means necessary to construct race cars. I have no other ambitions.'[8] Money only interested him to the extent that it allowed him to continue building new race cars. In 1951 he had built and sold 33 cars; the year before, 26. He knew that in 1952 he would inevitably build and sell a dozen more.[9]

To remind himself of who he was and, above all, where he came from, he had transformed a hidden corner of the large courtyard at the Maranello factory into a curious graveyard, where chassis, car bodies and engines that had not lived up to his expectations were scattered. Every day he would pause in front of this odd cemetery of twisted metal rusting under the elements to remind himself that the line between success and failure was thin, and that nothing happened by chance or without stumbling along the way.

Although he was the pivot on which turned an entire universe, he remained fiercely solitary, 'as befits his figure of a disdainful man possessed by a single passion',[10] one who 'can withstand bitterness and renunciations that ambition would not justify in any way', wrote Brera.[11]

Of himself he was fond of saying: 'I am a man who elbows his way through.'[12] He knew he was a difficult man, and he didn't really care. It was part of the legend that he saw rise almost involuntarily around him. But the creation of the legend demanded a price. 'Dear loved ones,' he confessed, 'come last.'[13] Perhaps it was for this reason that for some years now he had treasured Dino's company; when illness permitted it, his son rarely left his side.

Spring brought a great novelty. On 16 March, the four 500 F2s that raced in the non-championship Grand Prix of Syracuse that opened the European racing season bore the famed prancing horse shield that had adorned Scuderia Ferrari's cars from 1932 to 1937. Now, like then, Ferrari did it to differentiate his own cars from the others, though now the distinction was from the private Ferraris purchased and raced by those drivers to whom he had sold them.[14]

But as he waited for the World Championship to start – on 18 May with the Swiss Grand Prix – for Ferrari the spring of 1952 mainly meant preparing for Indianapolis.

From Malpensa, Milan's airport, five men flew to America: driver Ascari, team manager Nello Ugolini, technical director Aurelio Lampredi and two mechanics.[15] By now Ferrari was very sceptical of the success of the mission, had scaled down his involvement and was publicly talking of an 'unofficial technical expedition with scouting purposes', paid for by Chinetti, with the Italian distributor of the Champion spark plugs company that equipped the Ferraris paying for the flights of men and materials.[16]

In America, the small Italian contingent leaned heavily on Chinetti's team. In the official photograph that was taken of all participants, the 4500 with Ascari at the wheel bore the inscription 'Ferrari Special', while the label with the shield was white and without the prancing horse, as if to say that yes, it was a Ferrari . . . but not really.

It was, of course, all part of the subtle engagement–disengagement strategy designed by Enzo Ferrari for a race that could end in great disappointment[17] – as if sending the car that had put Alfa Romeo on its knees, the most serious candidate for the title of 1952 F1 world champion, his technical director and team manager could pass for a picnic in the industrial Indiana countryside.

Once in Indianapolis, the Italians did not lose their motivation and good humour. Despite various reinforcements to chassis and suspension,[18] Ascari's Ferrari proved quite unsuited to the circuit. On the long straights the car simply lacked speed.[19] But they had crossed the Atlantic to try, and so they did. Ascari set the 19th-best speed average on the 4 qualifying laps for a place on the 7th row of the starting grid.

The three American drivers were rather disappointed by the car that dominated European racing. Johnnie Parsons drove it in some practice sessions, but then discarded it when it came time to set the average speed to qualify.[20] Johnny Mauro failed to qualify and Denver did not even sit behind the wheel of his Ferrari.[21] In the end, of the four Ferraris that had arrived in Indianapolis, only one – Ascari's – started the race.

On race day, Friday 30 May 1952, no one on the Ferrari team nurtured any great illusions. Some tiny hope was placed in the fact that it only took the Maranello mechanics and their colleagues (provided by Chinetti) 30 seconds to refuel and change the 4 tyres of the 4500, instead of the nearly 2 minutes it took the Americans.[22] In a race of such a distance – 804km (500 miles) – this could be a remarkable advantage. Instead, however, on the 40th of the race's 200 laps, the spokes of a wheel bent. Ascari nonchalantly kept control of his car, but was forced to withdraw. And the dreams of glory ended there.

The Italian press gave no emphasis to Ferrari's expedition to Indianapolis, even though *Gazzetta dello Sport* had sent along its best reporter, Giovanni Canestrini. Enzo Ferrari behaved as if the race had never taken place, and refused to consider his team's participation in the 1952 Indy 500 official, either then or later. Ironically, because of team manager Nello Ugolini's signature on the required race documents, the participation of Scuderia Ferrari with Alberto Ascari at the 1952 Indianapolis 500 was recorded as official, however.[23]

While Ascari, Lampredi and Ugolini were in Indianapolis, in mid-May Ferrari's F2 single-seaters had dominated the opening race of the third World Championship. Ferrari had sent to the Bern 500 F2s for Nino Farina, Piero Taruffi and Frenchman André Simon, who made his debut that day with a works Ferrari, which he would race again only in the last race of the season.

In his maiden championship event with Ferrari, Farina, who had been the quickest in qualifying, did not have much luck in the race, despite swapping cars with Simon on lap 22. It was Taruffi, then, who gave Ferrari his first season win. Swiss driver and Ferrari client Rudi Fischer of Ècurie Espadon finished in second place.

When Ascari returned to Europe, he effortlessly imposed his rule on opponents and teammates. With an ease that could seem disarming – but which was, instead, the result of an innate sense of class coupled with constant training[24] – Ascari won the next six world championship races, one after the other.

He began on 22 June at Spa with a victory in the Belgian Grand Prix and ended on 7 September at Monza with a triumph in the Italian Grand Prix. Farina and Taruffi never worried him, nor did Villoresi when he returned to racing in Holland in the penultimate race of the year. To his teammates he left just one pole position at Silverstone – to Farina – and not a single race fastest lap.

To their opponents Ascari and Ferrari left only bits and pieces – a third place at Silverstone to Mike Hawthorn and his Cooper-Bristol; a second place at Monza to González in the new Maserati. But not even the new Maserati, when the A6G CM was finally available in Germany, worried the Ascari–Ferrari duo. And in three of the seven European races, three Ferrari drivers occupied the three steps of the podium.

Alberto Ascari had become world champion on 3 August, after victory in the German Grand Prix at the Nürburgring. There were still two championship races to go. Among the first to congratulate Enzo Ferrari was Alfa Romeo general manager Franco Quaroni, who sent his company's former driver and aide-de-camp a congratulatory telegram.

Ferrari was very impressed. He did not hesitate to describe his 20 years with Alfa Romeo as 'fabulous'.[25] Quaroni's telegram was the greatest reward he could imagine. He knew that his reply would in many respects close a circle, so he carefully pondered each of his words, which, without wasting any time, he wrote in a brief letter, that meaningfully began: 'Dear Friends of Alfa'.[26]

The text was a declaration of true love for Alfa Romeo and an ode to his youth. 'Your telegram of today,' he confessed, 'brought me a great breath of fresh spring air, and in the clear sky I read, with disconcerting clarity, the entire book of our memories. Twenty years I have lived with you; how many facts, events, people have passed! I have remembered everything and everyone today.'[27]

He closed the letter with the spontaneous declaration of a man who claimed that he elbowed his way through life: 'I still have for our Alfa, you may rest assured, the adolescent tenderness of the first love, the immaculate affection one holds for one's mom!'[28]

Since the days of Auto Avio Costruzioni and the 1940 Mille Miglia, Ferrari had always shown a particular fondness for Alberto Ascari. From him, Ferrari accepted things that other drivers would not dare say. Alberto knew how to handle him with his poise, his control in never raising his voice and his natural skill in exposing the facts in the smoothest, most judgement-free possible way. Returning from a race in which the gearbox had not worked as it should have, Alberto had said: 'Ferrari, the gearbox of your car is good and strong, but look what it did to my hand. Just think; after the race, there were beautiful girls asking me for my autograph, and I could not sign any.'[29]

None of Ferrari's other drivers could have been so direct in their criticism of a particular component of one of his cars. Alberto could. Ferrari had laughed at his joke about the beautiful girls and, when Ascari left, had ordered his mechanics to disassemble the gearbox and improve its functioning.[30]

But Ferrari, engaged as usual in nearly all categories of motor racing, had collected further accomplishments during the year. In the spring, for the fifth time in a row, a car that bore his name had won the Mille Miglia: the 250 S driven by Giovanni Bracco. But thanks to the cars that he had sold to customers scattered around the world, hardly a single Sunday would go by without one of his cars winning somewhere. Such was the importance that Ferrari was assuming in the motor-racing world – where large manufacturers either were about to leave or had not yet confirmed their future commitment – that at the end of the season the FIA, which had just launched the new Manufacturers' World Championship for 1953, awarded him the 1952 title for his many wins in that season's endurance races.

In the early days of October, at the Paris Motor Show, the fruit of the collaboration between Ferrari and Pinin Farina was publicly displayed for the very first time. What visitors to the Parisian *Salon* saw was the elegant Farina elaboration of the 212 Inter model originally crafted by Vignale. It was the second of two fashioned during the year – the first commissioned by, and sold to, Swiss gentleman driver Georges Filipinetti.[31]

At any rate, the collaboration had yielded its first fruit: a sleek convertible with stylishly sensual lines that were noticed by the car community. Referring to Ferrari and Pinin's difficult personalities, there were some who declared that despite the beauty of this first model, the Ferrari–Pininfarina partnership would not last long. Ferrari, who had immediately understood that Pinin's genius was exactly what he had been looking for, denied the false prophets: 'My relationship with Pinin Farina,' he thundered, 'will last.'[32]

An otherwise perfect world was darkened by Dino's health. On 1 October 1952, Dino began his fifth year at the Fermo Corni Vocational School in Modena. He was finding it more and more difficult to walk, and by now his hands and arms were ever more rigid. He had to be helped by schoolmates just to get up the steps into the school. But he was a generous young man, easy to love, and his friends helped him in any way they could, even in the school's lab when his hands could not properly handle the tools necessary for certain assignments. Aware of the enormous and selfless assistance provided by both teachers and students, without whom Dino's experience at school would have been hell, to repay their generosity (at least in part), Enzo invited them all to Maranello for a factory visit and a sumptuous luncheon, washed down with Lambrusco wine. It was 12 October and the first snowflakes were falling.[33]

At the end of the year the president of Italy bestowed on Enzo the honorific title of *Cavaliere del Lavoro*.[34] The Kingdom of Italy had knighted him when he was just 26 years old and, a little later, had named him *Commendatore*. The war and the Republic had taken away all the honours granted during the reign of Fascism, however. Unlike many, Ferrari had not worked at all to get them back, something that was possible within the new order in those cases where the honours had not been attributed because of, or through, the Fascist Party. Ferrari had been bestowed both honours for motor-racing merit, but had never considered wasting his energies for so little.

In planning for the 1953 F1 season, Ferrari confirmed world champion Alberto Ascari and his runner-up, Nino Farina. They were again joined by Gigi Villoresi, who lived and raced in perfect harmony with Ascari, a bond that in some ways was reminiscent of the one between Nuvolari and Borzacchini. In addition to the trio, quite surprisingly – but clearly with an eye toward the UK automotive market – Ferrari called to his court a young Englishman named Mike Hawthorn, who, with his Cooper-Bristol, had had some very interesting races in the previous season.[35]

Despite Maserati's massive participation, Ascari and Ferrari dominated the season from start to finish, and when Fangio's A6GCM was able, for the first and only time in the season, to put its nose in front of Ferrari's 500 F2, the championship crown was already in Ascari's hands. Alberto mathematically clinched the 1953 world title on 23 August in Bern.

Twelve days earlier, at 6.30am on Tuesday 11 August, in his home in Viale delle Rimembranze in Mantua, Tazio Nuvolari had passed away.[36] He was 61 years old, 6 years older than Enzo Ferrari. They had known each other for nearly 30 years – from the day, in 1924, when Ferrari had won his 2nd race in Ravenna.

In the three decades that had passed since then, they had perhaps never been friends in the deepest sense of the word, but they had certainly influenced each other more than either of them probably cared to admit. For Enzo, Tazio had been an example of style and courage as a racing driver, the ace up the sleeve of a very young Scuderia Ferrari, the great enemy at the time of his flashy separation from the team, his last resource against the German threat after his return, the great ally in the Alfa Corse stormy waters.

Together they had written important pages in motor-racing history. Grateful for the role that Nuvolari had played in his professional career, after the war, Ferrari – who, to rejoin his name to the Mantuan's, from 1935 to 1938 had accepted a subordinate role in their professional relationship – had given Nuvolari the possibility of attaining the last rewards of a long and unique racing career. The last time they had seen each other had been 11 months earlier, in September 1952, when Nuvolari had gone to Modena to watch Ferraris and Maseratis battle each other on the new airfield race track on the outskirts of town.[37]

On hearing of Nuvolari's death, Ferrari asked his wife to send a telegram on behalf of the company;[38] then he sent a second in his own name.[39] After that, he took the car and drove to Mantua to personally comfort Carolina, Tazio's widow, and to see Tazio one last time.

At 5pm he lost his way in the small, winding, history-rich streets of Mantua's medieval city centre.[40] Disorientated, he got out of his car to ask an old man for directions. It was a hot and steamy summer afternoon. Before he answered, the old man slowly walked around the car to read the licence plate. When he saw the Modena plate, he recognized Enzo Ferrari, warmly shook his hand and thanked him for coming. 'There will never be anyone like him,' the old man said, referring to Nuvolari.[41]

When he finally reached Villa Nuvolari, Ferrari walked past the tall concrete fences that Tazio had wanted built just like the pits of the old Nürburgring, painted in yellow, his signature colour. Standing on the sidewalk he saw dozens of people who had gathered outside Nuvolari's home to pay their respects to their larger-than-life fellow Mantuan. The local citizens looked suspiciously at outsiders, 'as if they were afraid of being robbed of their grief'.[42] Enzo was led to the room where Nuvolari kept his trophies, and where Carolina had brought the body of her husband to lie in state.

Ferrari did not return to Mantua for the funeral.[43]

A month later Carolina Nuvolari went to Modena for the grand prix. Before the start of the race, a minute of silence was observed in honour of Tazio,[44] who had won on the Modena Circuit three times.

Enzo Ferrari, who had in turn won the race twice, was present, but had not fielded any car in open conflict with the automobile club of his hometown.

And then there was the fact that at the end of August, Enzo Ferrari, at odds with the FIA – which had endorsed the concept of eliminating race and prize money from all events, and had joined with Italian authorities in not safeguarding Italian teams at the international level – had announced that he was withdrawing from motor racing after the Italian Grand Prix, which was now past.[45]

He was bluffing, of course, to win the attention of Italian sports and motor-racing bodies that were ignoring the needs of Italian teams but always ready to exploit to their advantage the many victories achieved with individual sacrifices by the likes of Ferrari, the Orsis or the Maserati brothers. The issue was all the more important because, eight years after the end of World War II, money was scarce in motor racing; technical suppliers were less and less inclined to spend; and on the horizon loomed large manufacturers such as Lancia, and especially Mercedes, which had budgets that small manufacturers like Ferrari, Maserati and Osca simply did not.[46]

On the airfield track, Ferrari's defection paved the way for Fangio's Maserati, the winner of the previous week's Italian Grand Prix. But by now, for Enzo Ferrari Modena was too small a stage anyway. The world had become his stage – a world that his cars and his beloved Ascari had conquered for the second year in a row.

In addition to the F1 World Championship, in autumn 1953 Enzo Ferrari was also about to secure the first officially sanctioned sports car championship world title. To some extent, a success in this new racing category could prove even more beneficial to his commercial activity, since events were raced and won not by prototypes, but by sports cars almost identical to those that he was selling to an increasingly passionate clientele.

Much as he had done three years earlier with the F1 World Championship's maiden race, Ferrari had sat out the first event of the new championship series. The reason had once again been purely financial: he had judged that a winter expedition to Florida for the Sebring 12 Hours would be too expensive for a company that remained small, and in which all expenses must always be carefully weighed. In Ferrari's mind, the money saved by not going to Florida could be put to better use in the Mille Miglia, the second round of the new championship. Ferrari had successfully participated in a race that he knew well, and that he had won in the five previous runs, with a fierce squad consisting of four cars entrusted to Farina, Villoresi, Hawthorn and Giulio Cabianca. Ascari did not particularly care for endurance races. Like three years earlier, Giannino Marzotto had saved the day at the wheel of his private 340 MM Ferrari, bodied by Vignale. It was Giannino's second Mille Miglia victory, and the sixth consecutive one for Ferrari; but, above all, as far as the sports car championship went, it meant precious points.

At Le Mans in June, there had been no private gentleman drivers to send points for the championship Maranello's way, apart from the few that Giannino Marzotto and his brother Paolo took home with their fifth-place finish – a brilliant result for two brothers who raced for fun, but a disappointing one for a car manufacturer with world title ambitions. The music had fortunately changed with the next event, the Spa 24 Hours, won for Ferrari by Farina and Hawthorn. There was no opposition from Jaguar, Aston Martin or Lancia – in 1953 Europe, no car manufacturer had a big budget, and each had to choose carefully which races to attend.

In late August, Ferrari had then entered three cars in the fifth race of the season, the Nürburgring 1000km. The battle for the championship was heated, and Ferrari had sent to Germany three 375s for the Villoresi–Hawthorn, Ascari–Farina and Maglioli–Carini pairs. But the dreadful German circuit in the Eifel forest had put a strain on the three cars. Hawthorn had destroyed the body of his, and the gearbox on Maglioli's had broken, as had the suspension on Farina's. Ferrari's mechanics tried all the tricks they knew but, in the end, of the three cars, only one made the start of the race.[47] Ferrari made the most logical decision, entrusting the event to his two world champions, Ascari and Farina, who on Sunday won the race and clinched the lead in the championship.

At this point, despite the need to defend their lead in the standings, Ferrari sat out the next race, which would have required a very long and expensive journey all the way up to Northern Ireland where, on the Dundrod Circuit, the Tourist Trophy was to be held.[48] Aston Martin won the race, but Jaguar collected enough points to move to the top spot in the world standings.

Now, in October, Ferrari knew that to win the first sports car championship he should, first of all, change his mind about withdrawing from any official racing activity, despite his announcement in August. But could he plan and finance a much longer trip than the one to Northern Ireland that he had already skipped? In the end, he concluded that official Ferrari participation in the Carrera Panamericana Mexico – the championship's final event – was out of the question because the budget required for the long trip and on-site assistance was far too big for his small company. And perhaps he had not yet obtained what he was hoping to get from the international and Italian federations when he had announced his withdrawal.

Enzo Ferrari was not the only one who decided to turn down official participation in the new championship's final event. From England, Jaguar's general manager William Lyons acknowledged that his company could not afford to race in Mexico, either.[49] Privateers who would take part in the Mexican race with their own Ferraris and Jaguars would thus decide the contest.

By this time, the network of personal contacts that Enzo Ferrari had woven throughout his life made the difference. By 1953 he could count on a number of passionate importers or dealers eager to please him by racing in his place. This was nothing new for Enzo, since it was exactly what he himself had done with his Scuderia for the best part of the 1930s. But it was only thanks to two of them, the omnipresent Luigi Chinetti and the equally active Franco Cornacchia, Ferrari's sales agent in Milan,[50] that Enzo Ferrari became world champion for the second time in one season.

The 1952–1953 season had been exhilarating for Enzo Ferrari and his company, which was now universally recognized as a towering player on the international motor-racing scene. Over the past five years, Ferrari had won every Mille Miglia and there was no endurance race, from the Le Mans and Spa 24 Hours to the Nürburgring 1000km and the Carrera Panamericana Mexico, that he had not won. For two years in a row he had clinched the F1 world title, and this year he had the sports car championship as well.

These motor-racing triumphs had provided extraordinary publicity for the small company at the foot of the Apennines, which, despite its bucolic setting, was becoming the destination of the world's wealthy and famous. It had all begun with Oscar-winning Italian director Roberto Rossellini, who had gone to Maranello with wife Ingrid Bergman. Ferrari had sold Rossellini a 166 and had fallen in love with Bergman's eyes, whose unique grey-and-gold colour combination he would later try to replicate as an exclusive car colour for his increasingly sophisticated clientele.

Rossellini had become a loyal customer and now bought one Ferrari model after another. But he was not the only member of the world's elite who, having once experienced the excitement of a Ferrari, became familiar with the road from Modena that led to the open countryside. Hollywood actors, actresses like Anna Magnani and entrepreneurs like Gianni Agnelli and Henry Ford II[51] were now queuing up to take possession of the few cars that Ferrari produced every year – just 57 in 1953.[52]

Perfectly mastering the art of creating an illusion to enhance the mystery around his person and his cars, Ferrari now carefully chose the customers with whom he would spend time, go for a personal factory tour and dine.[53] Among them were crowned heads such as Emperor Bao Dai of Vietnam and European monarchs like Bernhard of the Netherlands and Leopold of Belgium,[54] who, once admitted to the court of King Enzo, treated him as an equal.[55]

What is more, Ferrari's racing and commercial success had created a climate of serenity in Maranello and Modena that simply hadn't been there before. Enzo Ferrari remained the absolute master not only of his company, but also of the scene. Financial concerns were never entirely absent, as well as health ones,[56] intertwined with his own personal anxiety and restlessness with which he struggled to come to terms. But around him moved a multitude of workers, engineers, technicians, mechanics and, of course, drivers, who worked in harmony together.[57] There were evenings when he would surprise his men with dinner at Cavallino, or when he'd stop by the workshop late at night with his wife and son – not to check on his people, but to foster the sense that all of them were part of one large family.[58]

Despite the King's inclination to put his men in competition with each other, in the two years of Ascari's string of victories and of the conquest of the first sports car championship, at Ferrari all worked together with a rare unity of purpose. Lampredi was the undisputed head of the technical department. To him reported Rocchi, Colotti and Salvarani, with whom he had created an enviable sense of teamwork. Above them all was the priceless Bazzi, who had been working with Ferrari since 1923 and knew how to navigate the perilous waters around the Boss. *Maestro* Ugolini was the experienced team manager, another member of the Old Guard who knew Ferrari well and, like all the 'old-timers', knew that one should truly worry not when the Big Man shouted or raged, but when he remained silent. And then there was Romolo Tavoni, who managed Ferrari's agenda, the valuable secretary who was of course much more than that, and had become – against his own will – the shadow of the Boss.

But also among the drivers reigned a serenity that had no precedent in other situations and in other times. Ascari and Villoresi were also friends off the track, and the age difference meant they were never in real competition. Referring to this period with Ferrari, Villoresi would remember that the climate was that of 'a family; we had our arguments, at times', he would say, 'but we loved each other and worked side by side with pleasure'.[59]

This idyllic time would end all too soon, however.

High Treason

With Alfa Romeo gone, Lancia now loomed as a menacing presence on the horizon, a company that had decided to spend what was necessary, and perhaps more, to go back to its origins – motor racing.

Ferrari chose not to see (or perhaps just didn't believe) that Lancia was courting his world champion. True to script, despite the interest that he knew Ascari stirred, at the end of the extraordinary 1953 season Ferrari remained ambiguously capricious with his drivers about the racing programme for 1954 – a season when the rules would change again. F1 cars would once more vie for the title of a championship series in which, if one was to believe his August statements, Ferrari would not participate. Moreover, the contracts with the drivers did not expire until 30 April 1954, and Ferrari did not understand why Ascari and Villoresi seemed to be in such a hurry.

Hungry for an answer, Ascari and Villoresi – who, like Nuvolari and Borzacchini in the 1930s, now operated only as a pair – asked Ferrari for a meeting, whose stated purpose was to know his plans for the following season. Ferrari talked, talked and talked but did not reveal much about his future plans, including the F1 World Championship.[1]

The trip to Modena had been ineffective. Back in the car on their way home to Milan, Ascari and Villoresi spilled their hearts out. On one side was Ferrari, without a defined programme and with a new car – the 553 F1 – whose value was yet to be demonstrated. On the other was Lancia, with a car designed by Vittorio Jano, a well-defined programme and a substantial budget, including drivers' remuneration. Their decision made, they wasted no time: they stopped along the way and phoned Gianni Lancia to tell him they were ready to talk business.[2]

At the 12 December end-of-season annual lunch in Modena, and in front of about two hundred guests (including his drivers, of course) Ferrari announced that he would return to racing, happy about the attention that his dreaded withdrawal – now dismissed as the 'uncertainties of August'[3] – had aroused, and the pledge by Italian sports authorities to defend the interests of Ferrari and other Italian manufacturers.

On 20 December, Ascari and Villoresi took second place in the Casablanca 12 Hours, the race that concluded the 1953 racing season. Between Christmas and New Year's Eve, the two drivers were summoned to Maranello. With their contracts due to expire on 30 April, and given the fact that Ferrari had seemed to baulk when it came to renewing their contracts for the following season, they thought they were being called to receive instructions ahead of the Grand Prix of Argentina, which would open the 1954 F1 World Championship in three weeks.[4] Instead, after much beating around the bush, Ferrari now appeared to be in a hurry to close the negotiating game.

On Tuesday 29 December, Enzo Ferrari asked Alberto Ascari and Luigi Villoresi to sign immediately with him without waiting for the current contract to expire. He offered them a new contract starting on 1 January 1954, rather than 1 May. Ascari and Villoresi objected; after Ferrari had avoided their requests for so long, it made no sense to sign with him right away. What they did not know was that Ferrari feared if he waited until spring, the big manufacturers arriving on the scene would make everything more expensive.[5] Had Ferrari been aware of the delays that both Mercedes and Lancia were experiencing, he probably would not have tried to force his hand so early in the winter, and it's likely his two drivers would have stayed with him for at least another season.

The discussion soon became animated and moved to specifics: race and prize money. Ferrari told his two drivers that he could never equal the money that Lancia offered, whatever it was. While Lancia could offer money, Enzo said, Ferrari offered winning cars with which they could certainly make more money for themselves than Lancia could ever offer.[6] The two drivers countered with a proposal of their own, saying that if Ferrari would just match Lancia's economic offer they would stay with him. They knew that while Gianni Lancia had enthusiasm and money, Ferrari had experience and 1954, with the return of Mercedes, promised to be a challenging season.

Enzo Ferrari was not going to give in. He remained firm on his position, perhaps even annoyed by the fact that Villoresi – and especially Ascari – had gone that far in negotiations with Gianni Lancia. They either accepted his conditions, Ferrari said, or else they could just walk out his door right now, without waiting for the contract to expire on 30 April.

Night had nearly fallen by the time they left. As Ascari stopped to bid farewell to the guards, he burst into tears.[7]

The following day, Ferrari issued a press release to announce the end of a beautiful friendship that had benefited both Ascari and Ferrari, Ferrari's still-young factory, Italian motorsport and, ultimately, postwar Italy herself.

Although Ferrari's press release only mentioned Ascari's termination, of course Villoresi was leaving too. As expected, the two drivers signed with Lancia in Turin on 21 January 1954.[8] Eugenio Castellotti also left with them; he had never raced with a works Ferrari, but had already proven his talent with the many personal Ferraris he had purchased over the years.[9]

Having lost Ascari and Villoresi, Enzo Ferrari hurried to confirm Farina and Hawthorn, to call back González and promote Maglioli. Replacing Ascari was perhaps impossible, but Farina was an experienced champion, Hawthorn was one of the most talented young drivers of the new generation and González knew how to fight with the best.

The car for the new formula represented the real variable. Lampredi had been experiencing delays in the development of the new 553 F1, and for the debut race of the 1954 World Championship, in January in Argentina, Ferrari was forced to field four 625s, a car that had first raced three years earlier.

Ferrari was not the only manufacturer behind with his schedule, however; Ascari and Villoresi had a contract with Lancia, but Lancia did not yet have a car for them. Therefore, they remained in Italy. Mercedes, too, was behind in developing the car with which it was returning to motor racing after the glories of the 1930s. But Fangio, now under contract with the Germans, lived in Argentina and took part in the season's first race at the wheel of a Maserati.

The first event of the second sports car championship was also held in Argentina in January – the Buenos Aires 1000km, seven days after the F1 grand prix. Ascari and Lancia were forced to sit out this event while Ferrari, with the 375 MM entrusted to Farina and Maglioli, won the race. Lancia made its debut in March at the Sebring 12 Hours, where it was the fastest in practice, but showed a worrying fragility in the race. The Mille Miglia, on 2 May, was a whole different story: Lancia won the race with Ascari, while Ferrari experienced major problems. None of the official works Ferraris made it to the finish line, and Farina suffered severe injuries in a terrifying crash.

For the first time since 1948, Ferrari had not won the Mille Miglia – and success had ironically gone to Alberto Ascari. His fondness had remained, despite Ascari's departure and all that it had meant. After the race, Ferrari took pen and paper and jotted a note that was quite telling about their relationship: 'Although the circumstances of life have divided us,' he wrote to Alberto, 'you can rest assured that our friendship survives, its origins going beyond any other consideration.'[10]

The 500 Mondial that Ascari and Villoresi had driven to success the previous

December in their final race for Ferrari had marked the beginning of the cooperation between the Maranello factory and a Modenese coachbuilder named Sergio Scaglietti. Just like the now-famous Turin coachbuilder Pinin Farina, the almost-exclusive interpreter of the forms of road-going Ferraris, Scaglietti, who from now on would play a consistent role in making some of the most enduring Ferrari models, was also a self-made man. This unknown craftsman born on the outskirts of Modena had a gift when it came to shaping raw material.[11]

After the Mille Miglia, the racing season came alive. Lampredi had finally finished the 553 F1, but Lancia was still groping in the dark and Mercedes had once again postponed its debut. But on Ferrari's road to victory now unexpectedly stood the other half of Modena. In the second race of the season (apart from Indianapolis), Maserati had once again fielded Fangio, who had won the Grand Prix of Belgium. And when Mercedes had finished its car and Fangio had gone to the Germans, Maserati had offered the steering wheel to both Ascari and Villoresi.

Mercedes made its debut on 4 July 1954, at the Grand Prix of the Automobile Club of France held in Rheims. For Ferrari it was a debacle only partially mitigated by the third-place finish of Robert Manzon, a Frenchman who raced with a Ferrari entered by Ecurie Rosier. Ascari had also been unlucky, withdrawing on the first lap. Fangio and Mercedes, however, had shown in all their devastating power the potential of Mercedes-Benz. Severely wounded, Ferrari spoke without hesitation of an authentic 'Caporetto-style' defeat for his team, comparing his setback to the Italian army's humiliating rout in the Great War.[12]

Quite surprisingly, two weeks later Ferrari returned to victory. On Saturday 17 July, at the circuit where he had scored the first win for Enzo's team, Froilán González took the 625 to success. Mercedes experienced unforeseen handling problems, and Ferrari also took home second place. Looking at Ferrari's one–two finish and at Maserati's third with Onofre Marimon, the casual observer might be led to believe in a quick restoration of the old order. Ferrari himself spoke of a 'Battle of the Piave' resurgence at Silverstone that had avenged the Caporetto-style defeat suffered in Rheims.[13] Nothing was further from the truth, however. The France fiasco was only a coincidence and, at the end of August, after his victory in the Grand Prix of Switzerland, Fangio became the new world champion.

With the world title now lost, the Italian sports world mobilized. The Lancia D50 on which Jano had been working for so long was not ready yet. The Germans were dominating; the war had left many an open wound in Italy and Ferrari himself had used military metaphors when he had spoken of his defeats and wins against Mercedes, though he had looked to World War I rather than II. Maserati and

Ferrari strived, and the best Italian driver of his generation had been sidelined for much of the season.

Driven by public opinion, the Italian motor-racing establishment devised a solution that would need Enzo's active support – which could not be taken for granted. On Saturday 28 August 1954, eight days before the Italian Grand Prix, Ferrari met the president of the Automobile Club of Milan, Luigi Bertett, who had arrived from Milan with Alberto Ascari, in Salsomaggiore Terme. This get-together, on the gentle slopes of the Apennines behind Parma, produced the desired outcome. Ascari welcomed the news 'with enthusiasm'; Lancia gave it his 'full and cordial consent', so that 'his driver would not remain extraneous to the big event, in defence of Italian colours'. Ferrari said that he was 'happy to give one of his cars to the incumbent world champion'[14] for the Italian Grand Prix, scheduled for Sunday 5 September. The real winner was Enzo Ferrari, who welcomed back his favourite driver and, at the same time, was publicly acknowledged for the 'sporting spirit of the Maranello manufacturer'.[15]

Ascari did not disappoint. Back at the wheel of a Ferrari, he set the second-fastest time in qualifying and remained in the lead of the race for half the distance. He surrendered halfway through when his engine blew up. Fangio once again won the race.

The Italian Grand Prix was the first and only event that Ascari raced with Ferrari after their sensational separation at the end of the previous year. In the month and a half that separated the race in Monza from the last grand prix of the 1954 season, in Pedralbes, Spain, on 24 October, the Lancia D50 was finally finished. The new car was unquestionably fast, and Ascari set the Spanish Grand Prix pole position. But it was not yet reliable. Ascari led the race until he was forced out due to the poor operation of the clutch. Villoresi had withdrawn on lap one for problems with the brakes on his D50.

Mike Hawthorn won the race. For the 25-year-old Englishman, it was his second victory with the Maranello team. For Enzo Ferrari it was the second win of the season, which came too late to be useful for anything beyond the prize money.

Ferrari took some consolation in a second consecutive win in the sports car championship.

In the course of 1954 Enzo Ferrari had substantially expanded the Maranello plant. The most important addition was the construction of the foundry for light alloys,[16] which Ferrari considered the true heart of a racing-car factory for the timely innovation that it allowed.[17] With space limited to the west by the state road, the enlargement was to the east.

Ferrari had also wanted his own foundry to ensure greater privacy for his many projects, and to check the quality of materials and components. Despite the fact that production had grown in 1954 by only a single unit – from 57 to 58 – his plans called for a wider and ever more complete road-going range. At the October Paris Motor Show, Ferrari introduced the 250 Europa GT, designed by Pinin Farina and destined to be produced in small series by two different coachbuilders – Boano and Ellena[18] – for an increasingly demanding and sophisticated clientele who had found in the Maranello manufacturer and in his Turin tailor the response to their refined requests.

Although it had immediately been effective, the relationship between Ferrari and Pinin Farina was not a simple one: one was bad-tempered, the other, grumpy; Ferrari was loud and verbose, while Pinin Farina was quiet and reserved. They were both jealous of their own genius. 'What does Pinin Farina think?' Ferrari would sometimes complain. 'I make the man, he makes the clothing. And then he expects me to make the man the way he wants him, so that he can make the clothing in a simpler way.'[19]

But in his heart Ferrari knew that since he had never really cared much for the clothing, having found Pinin's vision had been a huge gift. For his part the Turin coachbuilder loved the 'realism without half measures, the workshop language and the background music that engines make on their test beds' that he had found in Maranello, and which he interpreted as 'the pulse of a new mechanical situation'.[20]

They had been looking for each other for a long time and, now that they had finally met, theirs had become a combination of energy not easily found elsewhere or in other situations. This, despite the fact that, due to the almost aristocratic character of Pinin and the overwhelming personality of Enzo, at the centre of the scene there was always only Ferrari – with Pinin Farina performing an almost inevitable bow every time Ferrari left the room.[21]

Despite the attention that his road-going berlinettas received from press and clients alike, 1955 opened with disturbing prospects for Enzo Ferrari, for whom success and the consequent sale of passenger cars was not an end in itself, but rather the means through which he could continue his racing activity. In addition to Mercedes, which in 1954 had shown a clear superiority, his 'minute make'[22] would now also have to confront Lancia. The duel with Ascari that he had feared 12 months earlier had just been postponed. In all the testing, the Lancias had proved fast, and reliability would soon come. And then there was the 250 F, the extraordinary Maserati single-seater of which everyone was saying only good things.

But Enzo had other reasons to be distressed.

Dino's illness had exploded in all its devastating brutality. For a long time the boy, now a man, had stubbornly resisted his condition, falling to the ground while trying to walk without aid, and struggling with all the strength in his body to rise, pushing away those who did not know him and hastened to help. Now Dino needed help to walk and had to be sustained when standing.

His visits to the factory had become much less frequent, as had his outings with friends. To avoid embarrassing him in front of strangers, Enzo had got into the habit of letting him organize small parties in the former Scuderia Ferrari headquarters showroom in Viale Trento Trieste, where old classmates, friends and his sweetheart Ines would spend many an evening. Here Dino was in a protected environment; everyone knew his condition and no one looked at him, wide-eyed, when he struggled to walk. To spare Dino the additional torture of walking up and down the stairs that connected the showroom on the ground floor to the apartment on the first, Enzo would now carry him up and down those steps in his arms.[23]

From the factory that he had built in the cornfields of the flat land between Modena and the foothills of the Apennines, Enzo had sought medical assistance for his son from every corner of the earth. Once he had exhausted the possibilities in Italy, he posted long letters to friends in the United States, asking for advice from his wealthy clients who came to Maranello, the capital of his world, to buy his red berlinettas. Thanks to them, thanks to who he was, he had been able to contact professors and university researchers working on this rare, virtually unknown and lethal disease of muscular dystrophy. He had always feared that he would not be able to find a treatment in time to save his Dino – and now, in winter 1954–1955, he knew that the time had almost come.

For many years he had thought that he could cure his son with the same devotion and determination that he had applied to racing cars for 30 years. He had monitored his son's disease in the same way that he had always monitored the development and tuning of his racing and road cars. He had even developed a series of charts in which he recorded, day after day, progress towards the longed-for recovery.

Each evening he had meticulously penned the number of calories that could prove beneficial to his son's failing health, and each day he had updated diagrams of his son's albumin levels, urine specific gravity, blood nitrogen and diuresis.[24] For years he had deceived himself into thinking that there was some progress. Now he finally understood that this was a battle Dino would never win.

Doctors had been probing in the dark. Although Enzo's life savings had allowed him to take Dino to the best specialists, none of the doctors had been able to understand the precise cause of the boy's inexorable decline. By the time they came up with a diagnosis, it was too late. Dino was being consumed by muscular dystrophy, for which – then, as now – there is no cure. His son, Enzo now knew, was condemned. Still, Dino maintained an astonishing serenity. He often comforted his father when the latter had some motor-racing or factory-related problem. 'Dad, don't get upset,' he would say. 'These are things that time will put back together.'[25] In his strong underlying optimism, the son echoed his father, who, when he was Dino's age, and the world had come down on him with Carrozzeria Emilia's bankruptcy, had never lost hope and had always looked at the bright side of the things.

Dino did not share his father's anger excesses – indeed, he was a sweet and kind young man. But he had the fortitude and stubbornness of the father he adored, who seemed to be at the very centre of his personal universe.[26] Like his father, Dino was a generous man who knew how to conceal his generosity. Over the years he had personally purchased textbooks for some of his classmates who did not have his financial means. For some friends who shared his own passion for racing cars, he had paid out of his own pocket for subscriptions to automotive magazines.[27]

* * *

As expected, Mercedes started the 1955 F1 season with a bang, Fangio winning the first grand prix of the year in Argentina. Yet, despite its manifest inferiority, in the most atypical of all races – the Grand Prix of Monaco – Frenchman Maurice Trintignant's Ferrari surprisingly won out over the fast and powerful Mercedes team, which in 1955 also featured the prodigious talent of 25-year-old Stirling Moss. Three weeks before Monaco, this emerging star of international motor racing, with the help of navigator Denis Jenkinson, had won the Mille Miglia ahead of Fangio in a peremptory Mercedes triumph. The first Ferrari, driven by Maglioli, had finished only third.

At Monaco, at the wheel of his works 625 Ferrari, Trintignant shrewdly took advantage of the mishaps that hit those who preceded him. After starting ninth on the grid – best of the Ferrari drivers – he inherited the lead when, one after the other, three leaders of the race were forced to withdraw: Fangio on the fiftieth lap, with suspension problems; Moss, on lap eighty-one, with engine failure; and Ascari, on lap eighty-one, dramatically plunging with his Lancia into the waters of the Monaco harbour.

In Love With Night

Enzo Ferrari learned of Alberto Ascari's death over the telephone. At the other end of the line was Luigi Bazzi, calling from Monza, where the team was conducting private tests with sports cars. Convalescing at his Milan home after the previous Sunday's crash at Monte Carlo, Ascari had shown up unexpectedly at the Ferrari pits. He confided that he wished to get back behind the wheel of a racing car as soon as possible to overcome the trauma of plunging into the waters of the Monaco harbour. He then asked if he could take a car for a few laps around the Monza track. He was given Eugenio Castellotti's 750 Sport. On the second lap, the two-time world champion was killed in the same spot where Ugo Sivocci had died in 1923.

Although he did not go to Milan for the funeral, which was celebrated in the central church of San Carlo Borromeo with huge attendance, Ferrari was shaken by the death of his friend. A few days later he wrote a long and tender letter to Alberto's wife. In addition to civil liability and the judgement of public opinion, every time a fatal accident occurred Enzo Ferrari also had to come to terms with his own conscience.[1] The burden was naturally greater now that a family friend had died – and death, thanks to Dino's illness, seemed almost to wait outside his own door.

Mietta Ascari replied: 'My grief,' she wrote, 'would diminish a little if I could openly speak with you, who were his close friend and played the role of a father to him all these years. I wish I could tell you how much Alberto loved and admired you, and how jealous I was because you were taking up so much of his time, which I feared too short.'[2] Knowing that her husband's love and admiration for Ferrari was mutual, Mietta ended her letter with comforting words: 'I know that you too are going through a period of anxiety, and I pray that you can soon put this bad moment behind you. I also know that these tears of mine will only add new sadness to yours, and that you don't need that now, but I need to pour myself out to you because I know that you will understand me better than anyone else.'[3]

Trintignant's victory in Monte Carlo remained an isolated feat. The deficit to Mercedes was significant, and difficult to make up for a small team that prided itself on remaining so. But if Enzo was forced to admit the overwhelming power of the German giant, that did not mean that he was ready to accept it.

Ascari's death caused Gianni Lancia to reflect. The Turin industrial leader allowed Castellotti to take part, as a privateer, in one last race – the Grand Prix of Belgium on 5 June, in which he set the fastest time in qualifying. But then he made the decision, final and irrevocable, to withdraw from competition. Ferrari wasted no time and offered a car to Castellotti, who raced the next Dutch Grand Prix in a Ferrari.

Lancia's decision left unused all of the D50 single-seaters that had been produced, and which, in their short career, had proven their enormous potential. Italian motor racing mobilized. Now that Lancia was sidelined, Mercedes ruled unopposed. After several meetings in Turin and Milan, it was decided that an exploratory phone call would be made to Modena, to test Enzo Ferrari's reaction to a certain idea.[4]

On 7 July, an announcement took the world of motorsport by surprise. Lancia had given all of its motorsport equipment to Ferrari, free of charge. The deal included six F1 cars, all spare parts and even the trucks that would transport the cars and the rest of the material to Emilia. The ceremony took place on the afternoon of 26 July in the courtyard of the Lancia headquarters in Turin. The team's technical director, Mino Amorotti, was Ferrari's highest official present.[5] Grateful but at the same time humiliated by such an important gesture, Enzo Ferrari had remained in Maranello so that he wouldn't be forced to personally and publicly thank Lancia for a gesture that had no precedent.[6]

Along with Lancia's technical equipment, Ferrari also took the first 50 of the 250 million lire that Fiat – the real architect of the Lancia operation, along with the Automobile Club of Italy – had promised over the next 5 years as a contribution towards Enzo's motorsport activity.

As he did every summer, Ferrari would spend most of his time at the factory in Maranello. Likewise, as they did every summer, his wife and son spent a few weeks in the Adriatic Riviera, in the modest house that Enzo had purchased a few years earlier in Viserbella. Enzo often visited them there, though never for more than 24 hours at a time except in the middle of August.[7] Because of Dino's increasingly frail health, the length of their stay had stretched from year to year.

In August, away from the factory but always immersed in the technical matters his father had encouraged him to pursue years before, Dino wrote to his father. In handwriting that his illness had made increasingly uncertain, Dino gave his father written advice about the new engines that Ferrari's engineers were studying at the time.[8] Like his father, Dino saw the engine as the heart of a racing car. But as much as – and perhaps even more than – his father, Dino also had an eye for the rest of the car. The year before Dino had talked Scaglietti into designing a headrest for a 166 MM that the Modena coachbuilder was rebuilding. Enzo had at first challenged the project, but then, finding out who was behind the idea, had approved it. The headrest detail, according to Scaglietti, not only had a certain aesthetic value, but also an aerodynamic one.[9]

Juan Manuel Fangio had become world champion in the middle of the summer with his second-place finish in the British Grand Prix at Aintree. Still shaken by a terrible accident during the Le Mans 24 Hours that had caused the death of 83 people and of French driver Peter Levegh, the organizers of the grands prix of Switzerland, Germany and Spain had decided to cancel their events. The only race that was not cancelled was the Grand Prix of Italy, scheduled for 11 September 1955, at Monza. Fangio won again there. The best of Ferrari's drivers was Castellotti, who finished third. Ferrari, who had started to test the cars he had received from Lancia in late July, had preferred not to use them in official races just yet.

At the end of the season Mercedes announced that it was withdrawing from motor racing. The carnage at Le Mans, caused by one of its cars leaping into the grandstands, was probably what convinced the Stuttgart manufacturer to leave. Mercedes preferred to declare that they had made the decision after realizing they had won all there was to win, which was true – Mercedes had snatched the sports car championship from Ferrari that year as well.

The withdrawal of Mercedes, together with Lancia's in the summer, and the latter's subsequent gifts from Turin, gave new energy to Enzo Ferrari. Now he could not only count on cars as good as the Lancia–Ferrari D50 – the term used by the press, not by Enzo, who never uttered the word *Lancia* in relation to those cars[10] – and the financing of Fiat, but also on three young and highly talented drivers: Italians Eugenio Castellotti and Luigi Musso, and Englishman Peter Collins. Ferrari had the capacity and the good fortune to flank these talented young drivers with an incumbent world champion, Juan Manuel Fangio, who, with the withdrawal of Mercedes, was now looking for a seat for the 1956 season. Ferrari had met Fangio in the spring of 1949 in Modena. As a driver, Ferrari had liked him immediately; as a person, he was still not entirely sure, even six years later.

Fangio's hiring gave new hope to Ferrari. But his renewed optimism about the upcoming 1956 season was also due to the return of Vittorio Jano, the great engineer that Enzo had stolen from Fiat in 1923, and who had played such a gigantic role in the glory days of Scuderia Ferrari. Now that the Lancia experience in F1 was over, Jano had gone to Modena, where Ferrari was waiting for him with open arms. Even more introverted and withdrawn than before, more rigid and inflexible with his subordinates than ever,[11] Jano set to work to upgrade the cars that he had designed with the Lancia name.

He was soon to undertake another task, too: together with Ferrari, Jano started to visit more and more frequently the apartment at 79 Viale Trento Trieste in Modena, which he knew well from the 1930s. Dino, whom he had known as a healthy child, was now almost constantly confined to his bed, his muscular dystrophy having reached its final stage. Jano had lost his only son, Francesco, ten years earlier, when he was a few years younger than Ferrari's son was now.

Tenacious and sharp as ever despite the further worsening of his disease, Dino, who had turned 24 on 19 January 1956, did not want to give up his contribution to the design of the new 1.5-litre engine. There were four solutions under consideration: four-cylinder, six-cylinder, six-cylinder at V and eight-cylinder. Dino received daily progress reports and technical memos from his father each evening. He would discuss the various possible solutions with Enzo and Jano, more and more voicing his preference for the V6 engine.[12] That winter Ferrari decided to go along with his son's choice, and his engineers soon started to develop a 65-degree V6 engine.

Fangio started the season behind the wheel of a Ferrari, with which he competed and won the first F1 grand prix of the year in Argentina. The race was not without its problems, and Fangio had to climb into Musso's car, which had been called back to the pits by new team manager Eraldo Sculati, to allow the Argentine driver – Ferrari's biggest pretender to the world title – to continue the race, catch Menditeguy's Maserati and engage in an all-out duel with former Mercedes teammate Stirling Moss.[13]

Fangio was displeased, however, when he discovered that, despite the favour from which he had benefited in Buenos Aires, when Musso had pitted to allow him to continue, Ferrari had not assigned him the role of 'team captain', to which the Argentine champion believed he was entitled by virtue of his three world titles.[14] Fangio was disappointed, but he kept his mouth shut. Speaking for him, and subsequently throwing fuel on the fire, would soon be the ubiquitous Marcello Giambertone, his personal manager. When his client began to experience repeated problems – in April, at the Mille Miglia; in May, at Monte Carlo and the Nürburgring; and in June, at Spa – Giambertone set out to plead Fangio's case directly with Ferrari. But Enzo's attention was elsewhere.

The winter and spring had been a long ordeal for Dino, and a terrible martyrdom for his parents.[15] To ease his suffering, one evening Ferrari had called some friends who, armed with guitars, serenaded him for a while outside his open window.[16] Dino's health had further worsened by mid-June, and the family lost all hope.

On Sunday 24 June, a few minutes after receiving news of Collins's victory in the Monza 1000km, with a smile on his face Dino said: 'Dad, it's over.' He had just suffered a cerebral haemorrhage. Shortly thereafter he slipped into a coma that lasted for several long and excruciating days.[17] His heart stopped at dawn on Saturday 30 June 1956. He was just 24 years old.

In that same journal in which he had diligently recorded the course of his son's illness, that night Ferrari found the strength to write the final words of his son's long odyssey: 'The match is lost,' he wrote with a heavy heart. 'I lost my son, and I have found nothing but tears.'[18] For years he would only wear black ties as a visible sign of his mourning.[19] The next morning, Sunday 1 July Modena stopped for the funeral.

Enzo's mechanics and Dino's friends had been seated next to the coffin during the long hours of the wake. It was a rainy morning. Shortly before 10am, a long procession set off for the Santa Agnese parish church. The coffin was carried on the shoulders of Ferrari's mechanics. The funeral Mass was celebrated by Father Alberto Clerici, the Benedictine from the Santa Maria del Monte monastery in Cesena, a longtime friend of Ferrari's who, in 1923, had officiated at his wedding. Then the coffin was transported to the cemetery of San Cataldo,[20] where Ferrari had years before built a family tomb in which he had laid to rest the remains of his father and brother,[21] and which now welcomed his son – three men who shared the same first name, Alfredo, whose lives had ended much too early.

On the card with which his parents announced Dino's death – 'from the Kingdom of the Righteous, where certainly the Almighty has placed you' – those who knew the dynamics of the Ferrari household and could read between the lines could not fail to see the promise that Enzo had made to his wife at their son's deathbed: 'Sustain all who mourn you and be of comfort to your mother, and vivid flame on the path that your father still has to walk, to honour that name *that was yours, and yours will remain.*'[22] Enzo had sworn to Laura that he would never give the name 'Ferrari' to the son that he had had 11 years earlier with Lina Lardi degli Aleardi,[23] a promise that he would keep all his life, and that he would deem rescinded only at the time of his own death.

That same afternoon in Rheims, wearing black armbands, the Ferrari drivers raced and won the Grand Prix of the Automobile Club of France. But for the first time in his life, Enzo Ferrari was unsure of what he would do next.

The Odd Couple

The victory of Peter Collins in the Grand Prix of the Automobile Club of France on Sunday 1 July, the day of Dino's funeral, consolidated Ferrari's grip on the 1956 F1 World Championship. But for Enzo Ferrari it was not a time to rejoice. Though he had known what was to come for a very long time, the death of his son had left him devastated. Ferrari was crushed – and he was alone.

In mid-July Enzo wrote to his longtime friend, Italian television journalist Gino Rancati, confessing his anxieties and future intentions. He shared a rare friendship with Rancati, and told him that he intended to 'go on to the end of this season', but that he had also 'decided to leave to others the honour of better defending the prestige of Italian work abroad'.[1] Ferrari was seriously considering a withdrawal from motor racing.

He ended his handwritten letter – a clear sign that no one from his office had seen it, and that it was thus a truly private confession – with the reason behind his decision: 'One must learn to give up something dear in one's life,' Ferrari said, 'and I think that, after having lost my son, I don't have anything more dear to me to give up'[2] than racing.

Motor racing was his whole life, but Ferrari was sincere. He had experienced a sort of symbiosis with Dino, and now that he had lost him, his life seemed meaningless. In his heart he knew that Dino, so absorbed by the Ferrari factory life, would never want him to take such a drastic step. But in the first weeks after Dino's death, Enzo's life seemed to him an empty shell, his company a minor detail, motor racing – for the first time in his life – a game in and of itself.

* * *

In the days of Ferrari's agony, Juan Manuel Fangio had plunged into an acute personal crisis. The main reason was his failure to obtain the status of team captain. Instead of calming him down, manager Giambertone had fired him up, telling him how Ferrari's behaviour could easily be explained with personal reasons. Two of his three teammates – Musso and Castellotti – were Italian, and it went without saying that an Italian team would give priority to home drivers. Collins, on the other hand, was English, and Giambertone pointed out that the British car market was much more appetizing than the Argentine one, which at the time was actually closed to foreign car imports.

Fangio was most likely convinced of the trustworthiness of his manager's words by what had happened in early June at the Belgian Grand Prix. Collins had won the race, whereas Fangio had experienced a technical failure in his car after starting from pole position and leading for the first 20 laps. Back in the pits, Fangio had learned from the mechanics who had examined his Ferrari after the withdrawal that the failure had been caused by excessive overheating of the differential, probably due to an oil leak. At that point Fangio had gone, with Giambertone, to survey the entire track – which at Spa was more than 14km (8.7 miles) long – in search of the patches of oil that his car was bound to have left.

The mere act of patrolling the track betrayed a lack of confidence in his own team, which turned into suspicion of sabotage or something like that when Fangio and Giambertone found no trace of oil.[3] After all, this was not the first 'strange incident'[4] that had occurred with Fangio's cars that year. Giambertone reminded his client of what had happened at the Mille Miglia in April, when a hole made by a Ferrari mechanic to cool the brakes – because of rain that had fallen over much of the road – had almost flooded the cockpit of his 290 MM.

Alongside these were other misfortunes – the gasoline leak in Argentina, the damaged suspension in Monte Carlo – and so Fangio had more than one reason to consider his a terrible season. By contrast, to cheer him up there was the thought that, on two separate occasions, team manager Sculati had ordered Musso and then Collins to swap their cars with him so that he could finish the race and rack up points for the world standings. Yet even this was more an isolated gesture than part of a definite strategy from a team that refused to officially confer on him the rank of captain.

The week Dino died, Giambertone had sent a telegram to Ferrari's commercial director Girolamo Gardini to report to the boss that Fangio resented his treatment and the poor quality of the cars that had been entrusted to him. If driver and manager had thought there was some sort of deliberate move on Ferrari's part to damage him, they did not say.

Despite the great distress over Dino's failing health, Ferrari had quickly replied. He had never understood why one of his drivers had to be represented by a third party. Nonetheless, Ferrari sent Giambertone another telegram to inform him that Fangio had in the end been made 'team captain'.[5]

Fangio was pleased,[6] but when in the next grand prix he saw Collins win while his own car had experienced other bizarre problems – this time a fuel leak that had forced him to pit for more than a minute – he went back into a state of depression.[7] At the suggestion of his manager, in early July Fangio went to see a neurologist, who found him suffering from 'reactive neurosis' characterized by a state of 'emotional anxiety'.[8]

For Ferrari all of this was of course very strange – not only because it took place in the days following the death of his son, but also because, for the first time in his life, he was dealing with a driver's problems through an intermediary, without actually talking to or seeing the driver in question. However, he agreed to another meeting – not with Fangio, but, once again, with Marcello Giambertone.[9]

In the course of the meeting, Ferrari gave in to the proposal that Fangio be assigned a personal mechanic – the only person who would be allowed to work on his car. Chosen by Ferrari, this mechanic would be totally at Fangio's disposal.[10] The request must have appeared strange to Ferrari, and in other times he would probably have fought it – not necessarily because he thought it was wrong, but for the simple reason of not wanting to give in to one of his drivers' requests. But in the first week of July 1956, Ferrari's mind was elsewhere, and so was his determination to fight.

Whether it was coincidence or not, once he got his own mechanic and the confirmation of his role as team captain, in mid-month Fangio won the British Grand Prix. With eight points for the victory, he climbed to second place in the world championship standings, a single point behind teammate Collins.

On 5 August Fangio won again – this time, the German Grand Prix at the Nürburgring, where he even succeeded in lowering the fabulous lap record that had been set by Hermann Lang in his prewar Mercedes 18 years earlier.[11] With Collins forced to withdraw, that night Fangio passed his teammate in the world championship standings.

With just one race before the end of the season, thanks to his two consecutive victories in the span of three weeks Fangio had put his hands on his fourth world title, which for Ferrari would be the first since Ascari's two.

Beyond the personal tragedy, Dino's death meant the loss of Ferrari's heir. Now even the future of Ferrari the company was at stake. Piero was too young, and, in mid-1950s Italy, where divorce and double lives happened only in the shadows, it was impossible for Enzo to consider a son born out of wedlock as the future leader of his company. He had always planned for Dino, that son 'born in, and with, motor racing', the one he'd allowed occasionally to drive his cars at the Modena airfield track, to fulfil this role.[12]

Looking for certainties, in August Ferrari went to Turin. In the offices at the Mirafiori plant, he met Vittorio Valletta, the man behind the great industrial miracle called Fiat. They had known each other since the spring of 1922, when Valletta was already one of the leading Fiat executives and Enzo was an ambitious racing driver. Thirty-four years later, Ferrari had in turn created a company that was now the flagship of Italian motorsport production, and which, in international motor racing, had taken the place that Fiat had held in the first two decades of the century.

Valletta had been the architect of the cost-free transfer of all the Lancia equipment to Ferrari. Enzo wanted to talk to him about the future. In the course of a private meeting, Ferrari informed Fiat's top man of the situation that had developed in his company with the death of his son. He confessed that Dino's death had thrown him into a state of 'deep despair [and] crisis'. For the first time in his life, the future didn't seem to interest him.

Ferrari was reassured. Valletta told him that 'a friend sits behind this desk, and this friend represents Fiat'.[13] Valletta said that Ferrari could always count on Fiat. Ferrari left without a definite arrangement, but with the understanding that the small Maranello manufacturer could always call on the Turin giant for any future need.

On Sunday 2 September the Italian Grand Prix at Monza was going to award the title of F1 world champion for the year 1956. Fangio was the natural favourite, but Collins could still become champion. The only one now out of the picture was Jean Behra in a Maserati.

Fangio dashed off from pole position with Castellotti and Musso next to him on the first row of the grid. But on lap nine Castellotti was forced to withdraw after a terrifying skid at the exit of the banked curve. Surprisingly, on lap 20 Fangio himself returned to the pits with a damaged wheel. At that point Collins, who continued his smooth race, was the virtual world champion.

According to Ferrari's pre-race arrangement, if Fangio was forced to stop prematurely De Portago would be called into the pits to swap cars – but he had been out of the race since lap six. Team manager Sculati had only one option left: stopping Musso. But when the Italian came into the pits to change his tyres, he refused to hand over his car to his teammate. Victory at Monza was too high a prize for Musso to relinquish, whatever the consequences at the end of the race. So for 18 long laps Fangio had to watch Collins come closer and closer to the world championship title.

Then, on lap 35, Collins came into the pits for a tyre change. It was a scheduled stop. With only 15 laps to go, by finishing the race Collins would become the new world champion. But the motor-racing world of the mid-1950s maintained a great element of chivalry. Collins was a gallant man as well as a very talented driver. Before Monza Ferrari had spoken to him. Enzo had not explicitly asked him for a 'waiver in favour of Fangio'.[14] He had been a racing driver himself and knew that such a team order would be repulsive to any driver. But Ferrari had wanted to know the English driver's opinion, had that opportunity come knocking on their team's door.

Collins had replied in his well-mannered and generous way – as Ferrari had probably expected, and certainly hoped. Although Enzo did not particularly love the Argentine, a man like Ferrari – who had been raised in the school of Antonio Ascari and Giuseppe Campari, and had worshipped Tazio Nuvolari for years – couldn't help but recognize Fangio's 'divine right' to the world crown, by virtue of his immense natural talent. 'I never thought that a young man of 25, like me, could take such a great responsibility,' Peter Collins had said.[15] The Englishman told Ferrari that a driver like Fangio deserved to be world champion again. And as for himself, he was young and had time to be crowned champion in the future.

One look was all it took for Collins to realize what was going on, and what he should do. Despite the grim look on his face, Fangio was still wearing his race helmet, as if hoping for some divine intervention. He stood alone, watching everything that was going on in the Ferrari pit lane. When he caught Fangio's eye, Peter gestured for him to come closer, and as the great champion walked the brief distance, the young lion got out of his car.[16] No words were necessary, and none were spoken. Fangio hugged and kissed Collins, got into the Englishman's car, adjusted his racing goggles and went on to a second-place finish and his fourth world championship.

After the race, Fangio generously acknowledged that if he was champion again, it was only 'thanks to Collins and his very English sense of sportsmanship'.[17] Collins downplayed the nobility of his gesture, then and later. Fangio never suspected that behind Collins's generosity was also a meeting between Peter and Ferrari until, six years later, the latter published his memoirs.[18]

Apart from Piero's mother, Lina, who officially did not exist, Ferrari now had only his mother. At 84, *mamma* Adalgisa was more active and present in the life of her son than ever. Just as after the Great War, when fate had spared only the two of them, now, in the summer and autumn of 1956, she was her son's true point of reference in what was left of her life. Adalgisa visited Enzo on a daily basis,[19] urging him not to give up, to seek in his work the antidote to his grief, to see in tomorrow a fresh start.

In October, with the F1 title in his pocket, Ferrari had not yet made a final decision about his future. He was thinking about it,[20] because the engine envisioned by Dino was due to arrive in November.[21] 'Witnessing the death of our loved ones,' he confided to a friend, 'it is natural to ask: What do we have left? But since man is a beast with a tremendous spirit of adaptation, I am convinced that you can learn to live without loving life and, especially, without understanding why one comes [in]to this world.'[22] So, when at the end of the yearly press conference he announced that he would actually stay in motor racing to honour the memory of his son, no one was surprised.

That day Ferrari presented all of his racing drivers with a gold medal in memory of the 1956 world championship season; in addition to the F1 title, Ferrari had once again won the sports car world title as well. The only one who did not receive his gold medal was, ironically, Fangio, the world champion, who had already returned home to Argentina for his winter holiday. Ferrari would never give Fangio this medal.[23]

Tragedy

On the Modena airfield track, on 2 December 1956, Enzo Ferrari watched the first tests in preparation for the new racing season. The whole F1 team was there.

Fangio, the world champion, had chosen to go back to the other Modena team, Maserati. Following this loss, Ferrari had promoted the young pretenders in his team: Eugenio Castellotti, Luigi Musso and Cesare Perdisa, Britain's Peter Collins and Mike Hawthorn, as well as international nobility, Spaniard Marquis Alfonso De Portago and German Wolfgang Graf von Trips.

Because these seven men were so young, representing the first generation of postwar racing drivers, the press quickly christened the new lineup *Ferrari primavera*,[1] to signify a sort of new beginning at Maranello. But fate would soon turn against these young, talented and gallant cavaliers.

Eugenio Castellotti was the first to die. Castellotti had long been a privateer, who raced with the Ferraris that he purchased. He had gone with Ascari to Lancia but then had won the 1956 Mille Miglia for Ferrari, under a deluge of rain. Ferrari valued Eugenio, even if he didn't see in him 'great class' or a 'perfect style'.[2] But for his generosity, Castellotti reminded him of Antonio Ascari and this was, of course, more than enough.

But in the winter of 1957 Castellotti was not serene. Two things made his life difficult at that time: the struggle with teammate Musso for Alberto Ascari's legacy, and his private life. Castellotti's fiancée, actress Delia Scala, wanted him to quit racing; he would oblige only if she would quit the stage, but she would not even consider that idea.

During a test session at the Modena airfield track in mid-March, Castellotti suffered a fatal crash, his Ferrari plunging into the chicane stands and disintegrating. Eugenio died a few minutes later as he was being taken to the hospital.[3] He had been going back and forth between Modena, where he would test alongside Musso during the day, and Florence, where Delia Scala was onstage and where he, night after night, tried to persuade her to reach a decision that would satisfy them both. That day he had seemed to Ferrari 'embittered' and 'distracted'.[4]

A few weeks later, on the eve of the Mille Miglia, Ferrari made a surprising public statement. It was during a ceremony honouring Castellotti, who had won the previous year's race. Still shaken by Dino's death, and evidently not at peace with his tormented idea of God, Ferrari said, 'I have a great burden on my conscience: I would like to know if *I* am responsible for the deaths of Castellotti and Ascari . . . *I*, who have put together those steel monsters.'[5]

Castellotti's death also made a great impression across Italy because it meant the sudden end of a love story that had electrified the whole country. But the echo of the young driver's death was nothing compared with the popular indignation that ignited less than two months later after the appalling incident that took place during the final stages of what would be the last Mille Miglia.

*   *   *

Ferrari was informed of the crash on the afternoon of Sunday 12 May by Renzo Castagneto, one of the Mille Miglia organizers, whom he had known for more than 30 years. Castagneto told him that car number 531 had suffered a crash at Guidizzolo after Mantua. The driver and co-driver (De Portago and Nelson) had both been killed, along with a still-unconfirmed number of spectators, including children.

Ferrari was devastated.

The judicial investigation began immediately. Ferrari was charged with murder. All of his Mille Miglia cars were confiscated. As a precaution, his passport was taken from him. Enzo immediately said that, notwithstanding the legal findings, he would personally compensate all of the victims' families. Then he quickly set things in motion with his company's insurance firm; if he'd had to pay everything out of his own pocket, he would have gone broke. But some members of the press, their behaviour exacerbated by a hatred for motor racing, strove to inflame public opinion and didn't waste any time in starting a witch hunt against Enzo Ferrari.[6]

Ferrari felt 'attacked from everywhere and everyone'. And betrayed. 'So-called friends and colleagues,' he would later remember, 'would speak of rebellion and refusing to go along with possibly fatal races on Monday, after they had praised my work and the work of my men on Sunday.' He remained silent while taking it all in, but he would never forget. 'I have a delicate skin,' he would say years later, 'and things like these wound me deeply.'[7]

Secluded in his Modena home, Enzo was torn by this new grief that had reopened the even deeper and more personal year-old wound of Dino's death. Alone with his own thoughts, Ferrari did not even go to the barber for a shave, which he routinely did every morning of the week.[8] He stayed in touch with the rest of the world only through the telephone or the occasional visit of a few of his men. He stayed inside his apartment for a whole week.[9]

Towards the end of May, Ferrari came out of his self-imposed isolation. One morning he picked up Tavoni and Peppino Verdelli and they sped down the Via Emilia toward Bologna and the Adriatic Sea. The passengers realized where they were going only when they saw in front of them the walls of the Santa Maria del Monte Benedictine monastery in the city of Cesena. In this moment of despair, Enzo Ferrari, who had always declared himself *unable* to believe, rather than a *non*-believer, was looking for answers in the wisdom of a religious man.

When they arrived, Ferrari asked for Don Alberto Clerici, the priest who had celebrated his wedding and who, 11 months before, had officiated at Dino's funeral.

Ferrari let it all out. He told Don Berto that he had had enough. As if the grief he felt at the loss of so many lives was not enough, the press had called him a monster and ferociously attacked him. Along with Castagneto, the organizer of the Mille Miglia, in that moment Ferrari was very likely the most hated man in Italy.[10] He wanted to quit motor racing. No more automobiles, no more races, no more crashes, no more deaths. He could go back to making machine tools, objects of some utility to people and incapable of bringing death.[11]

A few hours before the start of that last Mille Miglia, Ferrari had made some rather revealing statements. 'At my age,' he had said that evening in Brescia, 'after a whole lifetime spent in motor racing, I am tormented by a grave doubt; and, the small-town sinner that I am, I submitted it to the mayor of the city where the Mille Miglia was born. He is a man of profound faith, and will be able to say whether my determination to build ever more modern and fast cars is a mission of civility or [an offence] against my fellow man.'[12]

Don Berto patiently listened to him. What else can I do *this* well and with *this* passion? Enzo asked. The priest told him that he had been sent to this earth to build sports cars, beautiful, powerful and fast. If he quit, he would only hurt himself and those who worked with him. He told Enzo to continue, with the same passion, with the same determination, with the same honesty. This went on for 20 or more laps around the cloister.

When they were finally through, Don Berto called Tavoni and Verdelli and, together with Ferrari, all four knelt and prayed. Ferrari was crying as Don Berto recited the Pater Noster. The three men then climbed back into the car and headed for Modena. Ferrari was naturally behind the wheel, silent and thoughtful. No one dared to speak. It was Enzo who finally broke the silence as they entered Castel Franco, Emilia, where, past the Panaro River, they entered the Modena area.

'Well, it's easy for them,' Ferrari said, speaking of Father Clerici and the other priests. 'But they have faith.'[13]

The great moment of despair had passed.

*   *   *

Come summer, Ferrari was back in the office on a regular basis. In the meantime, Fangio and Maserati had won the first three world championship events: Argentina, Monaco and France. The Ferraris had disappointed: not a single podium finish in the first two races; a second and a third place for Musso and Collins in France. Fangio had 25 points in the standings; the best of Enzo's drivers, Musso, only seven.

There had also been a change in team manager: Ferrari had fired Eraldo Sculati for failing to call from Argentina at the end of the season's first race. Instead, Ferrari promoted to the team manager position his all-purpose personal secretary, Romolo Tavoni, who naturally kept his old position as well.

On 20 July, on the Aintree Circuit near Liverpool, victory went to Vanwall, the car that British industrialist Tony Vandervell had wanted to beat his client Ferrari at his own game. Despite the exaggerated reports in the press, there were elements of truth in the story that Vandervell's decision to race against Ferrari had come after an endless and pointless wait outside Enzo's Maranello office.[14] At any rate, Vanwall's victory, obtained by Tony Brooks and Moss together, signalled the end of an era: the absolute dominance of continental makes – Alfa Romeo, Ferrari and naturally Mercedes – in F1.

August brought nothing new: Fangio won at the Nürburgring and arithmetically clinched his fifth world title. Ferrari had to be content with Hawthorn's second-, Collins's third- and Musso's fourth-place finishes. But at Pescara, and then again at Monza, victory went once again to Stirling Moss's Vanwall in a sort of alarming prelude to the 1958 season. And to make things worse, Maseratis had consistently placed right behind Moss: three at Pescara and Fangio's at Monza. Ferrari had brought home only a third place in the Grand Prix of Italy with von Trips, the twenty-nine-year-old German aristocrat, in his best career performance to date.

After the end of the F1 championship, in September Ferrari was seen for the first time in public since the Mille Miglia tragedy. On that same track where Ferrari engineer and tester Fraschetti had been killed a few days earlier, the new 1500 6-cylinder V65 engine, developed with Dino's support, made its debut. Enzo had not wanted to miss it, despite the fact that his public presence would stir controversy on Modena's home turf.

This would be the last time Enzo Ferrari would ever attend a race. In the future, he would still be seen every now and then, at certain race tracks, but just for some quick testing sessions, never again for a race. He would never really explain his decision, even though he would later say that he no longer attended races because 'conceiving a car and then see[ing] it live and die – because in a race, a car always dies, even if it wins', was too much for him to stand.[15] Of course, this had never prevented him from going to races before.

Those who knew him well supposed that this change had to do with Dino, and perhaps with a promise that father had made to son on his deathbed – or that Enzo had made to himself on Dino's death. The engine Dino had wanted to develop had become a reality and now Enzo would walk away from the race tracks that Dino had been forced, by fate, to stay away from forever.[16]

* * *

The season was saved at least in part by a new sports car world title that Ferrari won, thanks to three wins in seven races. His cars and drivers – Masten Gregory, Eugenio Castellotti, Luigi Musso, Piero Taruffi, Peter Collins and Phil Hill – had won the Buenos Aires 1000km in January (Castellotti–Gregory, and Musso), the Mille Miglia in May (Taruffi) and the Venezuela Grand Prix in early November (Collins–Hill). But, naturally, 1957 had been a year in which sporting results, as important as they always were, had received much less attention than in the past because of the Mille Miglia tragedy, which had marked the end of a one-of-a-kind race and of Piero Taruffi's career. And Ferrari had played quite a significant role in Taruffi's retirement – Taruffi had promised his wife he'd retire if he won the Mille Miglia.

Despite the polemics and the accusations following the Mille Miglia, in the course of 1957 Ferrari had for the first time sold more than 100 cars in a year – 113, to be exact.[17] His models had reached and conquered all of the most important markets on earth. On 22 November, during the traditional end-of-year lunch with the press, Ferrari introduced the 250 Testa Rossa model that would go on to play such a great role in the company's racing history, and in the imaginations of generations of car lovers. The following month, he presented a new, incredibly elegant convertible built by Scaglietti, whose name revealed its destined market: the 250 Spider California.[18]

Inspired by the forms dear to Pinin Farina,[19] the California had been entirely conceived and built in Modena. The working relationship with Scaglietti had quickly consolidated with mutual satisfaction and now, in late 1957, the Modenese coachbuilder was the specialist to whom Ferrari would turn for the most extreme examples of his racing *granturismos*.[20] In Enzo's eyes, Scaglietti had a great advantage over the Turin-based Pinin Farina: geographic proximity.

Ferrari could visit Scaglietti every day of the week, including the weekend. On these occasions, he was free to adjust, suggest, ask for changes, try new solutions – in short, to build cars that differed from one another only in small details.[21] The great craftsman that he was, Scaglietti was also a realist, willing to accommodate the client, especially when the client was Enzo Ferrari, having understood from the very beginning of their relationship that his task was to compromise a car's beauty, not its performance.[22]

Pinin Farina himself, despite the worldwide fame, was actually more pragmatic than dogmatic, unlike other coachbuilders with whom Ferrari had worked in the early days, such as Boano and Bertone, men very proud of their stylistic intuition and much less inclined to compromise.[23] But compared with the old Pinin, whose genius Ferrari admired and, at the same time, feared, with the much younger Scaglietti he could be even more daring.

Then there was the fact that, within the Ferrari company, there were those who put pressure on the owner because he would go against his own nature and increase the number of units produced of each model to make business ever more profitable. And the relationship with Scaglietti, whom Ferrari visited alone in the morning on his way to Maranello, or in the evening before he went home, allowed him a certain freedom of movement in a company that was ever bigger, more prestigious, but with departments – commercial, purchasing, administration – that kept reminding him that his intentions for automobile production were extremely costly,[24] and perhaps downright archaic.

On 16 October 1957, Ferrari changed the legal denomination of his company, whose name for the last ten years had been Auto Avio Costruzioni Ferrari. The modification simply meant the loss of the word *Avio*. The new denomination thus became Auto Costruzioni Ferrari.[25] On 1 December, the rumour spread around Modena that Adolfo Orsi had been forced to ask for temporary receivership for Maserati.[26] Because of a loss of $1.5 million in another sector of the family's activities, Orsi was on the verge of bankruptcy. Filing for temporary receivership was the only way to try and save what could be saved.[27] Ferrari was informed over the phone by a journalist looking for his comment. His reaction was moderate. 'Too bad,' he said. 'It's a bad day for our world. Even for me and my company.'[28] Those who were with him at the time felt that perhaps Ferrari was not being completely sincere.

Ferrari had never cared much for Orsi, whom he considered an industrialist, in private a 'rags dealer',[29] and certainly not a car guy. In addition, he had always suffered the cross-town rivalry with Modena's other team, whose headquarters were ironically a few hundred yards from the historic Scuderia Ferrari building, and even closer to the house where Enzo was born.

And then there was the story of a bank loan for the construction of a new production line in Maranello that the Banco di San Geminiano e San Prospero had denied Enzo in 1952 because, he had been told, of Orsi's opposition.[30] A couple of months after the bank had turned him down, Orsi had called Ferrari and offered to give him money out of his own pocket in exchange for a share of Ferrari.[31] A few years had gone by, but Ferrari had not forgotten.

To save his car company, which in those years was in much the same situation as Ferrari's, Orsi was forced to close down his world champion racing department. He may not have been a car guy, but he certainly was a man who took care of his people, despite what the Modena unions thought following an incident back on 9 January 1950, when police officers had opened fire on workers outside the Maserati plant. Before informing his men that he was closing down the department, Orsi tried to find each of them a new job. Ferrari was among the first he called.

In an act of great humanity towards his men, and of generosity towards Ferrari – his motor-racing opponent, to whom he now offered men who had just won a world championship – Orsi asked Enzo if he would hire some of his race mechanics. Ferrari said yes; he would hire them for the same jobs and at the same pay.[32]

But Ferrari could be vindictive, if he so wished. A second phone call followed a few days later. This time, it was Ferrari calling. Remembering what he saw as Orsi's earlier duplicity, he cynically said: 'If you want to sell Maserati, I will buy.'[33]

The Church vs. Enzo Ferrari

In view of the 1958 F1 season, Enzo Ferrari decided to increase the displacement of the 65-degree 6-cylinder V-configuration engine advocated by his son and now called the Dino.

The three works drivers would be the young and talented Musso, Collins and Hawthorn. In place of Franchetti, the chief engineer and at times test driver who had died testing a new Ferrari, in late November 1957 Ferrari had hired as technical director a young Tuscan engineer who came from Alfa Romeo and was an aerodynamics expert. His name was Carlo Chiti. The first thing the new chief engineer did was build a 1:10 scale wind tunnel in which to test sports-car models of the same scale.[1] Although Ferrari wasn't particularly in favour of the idea, he went along with it. He was still of the opinion that the engine was the central component of any race car, but by now understood that the chassis was becoming ever more important.[2]

The victory scored by Stirling Moss in his agile rear-engined Cooper-Climax in the season opener Argentina Grand Prix sparked debate within Ferrari. Enzo's inner circle soon split. On one side there were those who thought that Cooper's innovation in putting the engine behind the driver was an anticipation of the future; on the other, those who believed that his win in South America was simply a coincidence. Among the former was the new man, Carlo Chiti; Ferrari appreciated his 'vast theoretical culture', but not his not-so-hidden 'anxiety to emerge'.[3] Among the latter was of course Enzo Ferrari, who, with the agricultural metaphor of the cows pulling and *not* pushing a wagon, was defending the historical legitimacy of the front-engine layout, and shut down all opposition – or so he thought.

The debate exploded again when, in mid-May, another Rob Walker Cooper-Climax, driven by Maurice Trintignant, won the Grand Prix of Monaco. One victory could be accidental, but not two. Ferrari therefore allowed Chiti to start working on a central, or mid-engined, car. Halfway through 1958, it was not clear whether Ferrari was actually convinced this was a good idea or, rather, as he had done with Lampredi a few years earlier, he simply wanted to test Chiti and then fire him.[4]

Thanks to two second-place finishes in Buenos Aires and Monte Carlo, Musso was now leading the world championship standings. Furthermore, despite the fact that victory had both times gone to someone else, Ferrari's drivers had placed second and third in each of the two races.

The next two races made it clear that the real obstacle on the path to the World Championship was not a mid-engined car, but one with the engine placed in the traditional front position. It was Vanwall, which won with Moss in the Netherlands and with Brooks in Belgium – which was also the first race in which a woman participated in an F1 event: Neapolitan aristocrat Maria Teresa De Filippis, in a Maserati, quickly christened by Juan Manuel Fangio as *Pilotino*.

After four races – five counting Indianapolis – Moss was leading the championship, but Hawthorn and Musso were right behind him. The next race was going to be held in the French region of Champagne, where Musso and Hawthorn thought they would battle for team leadership and, with it, the right to challenge the two Vanwall drivers for the crown. Fate would soon decide otherwise.

On Sunday 6 July 1958, Luigi Musso was fatally injured during the Grand Prix of France, while battling teammate Hawthorn for the lead. His Ferrari entered the ultra-fast turn at Gueux too quickly and bounced four times without flipping before ending up in a cornfield. In the last bounce, Musso was ejected from the car and landed on his head. He was immediately rushed to a nearby hospital, where he died at 7pm.[5] Musso's body arrived back in Italy on Wednesday. The funeral was held the next day in Rome. Ferrari remained in Modena and sent flowers.

The death of Musso reopened old wounds. Like the year before, the press started to attack Ferrari, and there were even those who stated that all car constructors were 'murderers'.[6] But this time the Church stepped in. On Wednesday 9 July, three days after the crash at Reims, the Vatican's official newspaper, the *Osservatore Romano,* printed a story under an eloquent headline: 'Industrial Saturn'.[7]

The attack on Enzo Ferrari – who was never mentioned by name – was in the opening paragraphs: 'A modern Saturn become industrial tycoon, he continues to devour his sons. As in the myth, so unfortunately in reality.' This referred to the myth of the Roman god Saturn who was said to have eaten his sons in an attempt to avoid a prophecy that his son would oust him. And then: 'Luigi Musso is the latest of his victims, around whom, once again, arises a widespread sentiment of solidarity that has only one fault: of never learning from experience; of not realizing how, from everyone's conscience, a sentiment and an invocation arise: Stop!'[8]

The article made it a 'question of morality', observing that while Ferrari spoke of 'science and progress', in reality he was hiding 'an industrial interest'.[9]

The Catholic Church had declared war on Enzo Ferrari and, with him, motor racing in general and what the Vatican's newspaper described as 'intentional suicides by great sports champions'.[10]

In virtue of the religious nature of the new great inquisitor, the Pope, the debate over motor racing acquired a new dimension and moved to an ethical level. Ferrari thus ended up at the centre of a diatribe on the moral reasons for motor races sanctioned by the Church. Worried by the influence and sanctity of the new interlocutor, Italian sports authorities decided not to speak up on behalf of either Ferrari or motor racing. Enzo was alone. How distant now seemed the visit that the president of the Republic of Italy, Giovanni Gronchi, had paid him three weeks before the crash at Guidizzolo, in spring 1957. Abandoned by those who had the obligation to protect him – specifically, ACI, the Italian Automobile Club, and CSAI, ACI's racing commission – Ferrari resorted to a tactic he had used in the past, and 'leaked' to the press that he was about to quit racing once and for all at the end of the year – or, at the very least, to limit his activity. Through friendly channels, he even spread the rumour that, if it had not been for the battle with Vanwall, he would have retired immediately from the F1 World Championship.[11]

The next grand prix, in England, strengthened Ferrari's lead in the championship, but the following race ended, once again, in tragedy. Peter Collins, the winner of the Grand Prix of Great Britain, was killed at the German Grand Prix.

On Sunday 3 August Collins went off the road with his Ferrari at one of the fastest turns of the insidious Nürburgring circuit, while battling with Tony Brooks in a Vanwall. His Ferrari flipped three times. Ejected from the cockpit, Collins landed on some bushes. Before he lost consciousness, a race steward heard him whisper: 'Like Musso.'[12]

At home in Modena, Ferrari was shocked. And even if the death of Collins, an Englishman, did not have the same impact on the Italian press that Musso's had had, once again Enzo was assaulted by doubts about his motor-racing future. He and his wife had both truly cared for Peter, and now felt as if they had lost another son. In the last months of Dino's illness, Collins had visited him quite often, and after Dino's death Enzo and Laura had insisted that Peter stay in their cottage when he was in Maranello.[13]

But the *Osservatore Romano* summer column had only been the appetizer. In early autumn, with just one race left in the F1 season, Ferrari was attacked by the mighty Jesuits. In the 4 October 1958 issue of *Civiltà Cattolica*, Father Leonardo

Azzollini revisited the issue of the immorality of motor racing with a long story titled: 'A Senseless Massacre: Motor Racing'.[14]

The Jesuit priest did not spare anyone, blaming 'the public authorities . . . [members of the] public that first . . . [go] to motor-racing events . . . then complain, but never allow its elimination; the spectators, the drivers' and, especially, 'the car manufacturers, whose product carries a terrible capability to trigger massacres and disasters'.[15] And here, without assessing any 'moral judgement', he was quoting Ferrari himself and the words he had used a year before, on the eve of the 1957 Mille Miglia, when, commemorating Castellotti, Enzo had asked if *he* was responsible for all those tragedies. Azzollini's conclusion was simple: 'All motor-racing events, either on [a] track or on [a] normal road, any way they are organized, should be stopped.'[16] This article, widely quoted by the national press, further fuelled the controversy.

There was only one race left to run in the 1958 world championship, the Grand Prix of Morocco. Hawthorn was leading in the standings, but if Stirling Moss won the race *and* set the fastest lap time at Casablanca, he could still have a shot at the crown depending on how Hawthorn did.

Moss did win and *did* set the race's fastest lap, but Hawthorn's second-place finish gave him the title, Ferrari's fourth.[17] Vanwall took home the first manufacturers' cup, which Ferrari failed to win primarily because his team of drivers had been so reduced that summer. Deeply affected by the death of his teammate and friend Peter Collins, back in London Mike Hawthorn announced his withdrawal from motor racing. He had never considered himself a professional racer; he'd achieved his goal and had no intention of taking any further chances.[18] Ferrari would remember him as a 'driver perplexing for his possibilities and for his discontinuity'.[19]

Although he failed to win the first F1 manufacturers' cup, Ferrari had won the Sports Car World Championship for the fifth time in six years. The role played by the 250 Testa Rossa in its first racing season had been fundamental. Peter Collins and Phil Hill had driven it to victory in the Buenos Aires 1000km and the Sebring 12 Hours; Musso and Jean Behra, in the Targa Florio; and Behra and Hill, in the Le Mans 24 Hours.

To better reply to the accusations concerning the ethical question, sparked by the stories published in the Catholic press – and there had been a third, in a magazine named *Orizzonti*, in which the author had tastelessly put the death of Enzo's drivers on the same level as Dino's[20] – Ferrari decided to change the format of his traditional end-of-year meeting with the press. On 9 December 1958, in place of the usual luncheon, whose origins went back to the years of the Scuderia, he organized a press conference with around a hundred journalists. They would have an equal chance of asking Ferrari all the questions they wanted, giving him the chance to fully address the so-called moral question.

'Once upon a time in Italy, motor races were glorified,' Ferrari said, answering one of the first questions on the main topic of the meeting, 'then they were accepted, then tolerated, and today they are under trial, while the Queen of England invites her World Champion driver to dinner, thus recognizing the value of motor racing.'[21]

'The moral condemnation that has been placed upon us,' he went on, 'has deeply touched me. I have asked myself, together with my technicians, if any action on our part could be the cause of such disasters.' But from this private examination, Ferrari and his men had 'reached the conclusion that we [had] done all that was humanly and technically possible to prevent any incident'.[22]

Stirred by another question on the ethical issue, Ferrari gave his personal version of the crashes in which Castellotti, Musso and Collins had been killed. He had very clear ideas on the subject: race organizers and those in charge of safety at every circuit were responsible. As far as Musso's crash went, he denounced the organizers, saying that 'the track was not in the best condition for a grand prix'. Similarly, 'concerning Collins's crash, you only have to look at a series of photos published in France to see that the terrain on the sides of the track was dangerous and could actually act as a springboard'.[23]

Finally, in Castellotti's case, he pointed the finger at the 'dangerousness of the forty-centimetre walls at the chicane'. He had drawn attention to this danger several times in the past, but, he said, he had been publicly told that those small walls would act as a deterrent for those drivers who may want to dare too much, and that therefore they had to stay where they were.[24]

After the Le Mans 1955 crash, in which no Ferraris had been involved, Enzo had written about – but not published – what he saw as the true cause of car crashes: 'The elusive desire on the part of many race organizers to make their events ever faster, as to be able to boast that theirs is the fastest circuit in Europe, or even in the world.'[25]

What he saw as the amateurish conduct of race organizers was thus, now as in the past, the core of Ferrari's defence. 'Car manufacturers,' he said, 'must meet the costs of building new cars; organizers should bear the cost of the modernization of their race tracks.'[26]

Having stated his unequivocal point of view, Ferrari confirmed that in 1959, his team would contest both the F1 and sports car championships. But he also declared that, because of the ethical question, he had decided not to field Italian drivers and, very likely, would not participate in any race held in Italy.[27]

With Hawthorn now gone, he announced the names of the drivers for the 1959 season. Among them were two Americans, a Brit, a Belgian and a Frenchman – but no Italians: Phil Hill, Dan Gurney, Cliff Allison, Olivier Gendebien and Jean Behra. And, the moment Wolfgang von Trips recovered from injuries suffered in his crash at Monza, Ferrari would also offer a car to him.[28]

Enzo left his master stroke for a few days later, after the Italian newspapers had given substantial exposure to his opinions. Ferrari had asked for, and obtained, a clarifying meeting with Father Azzollini, the Jesuit who had attacked him in October in *Civiltà Cattolica*.[29] Accompanied by a fellow priest, Father Gambigliani, in mid-December Father Azzollini came to Modena.[30] Ferrari went to the archbishop's palace[31] and met his critic for five long hours.[32] By the end of their meeting, Ferrari had convinced Father Azzollini of the soundness of his opinion, and enrolled him to his cause. He even persuaded the priest to write another article on the subject, this time in Ferrari's favour.

Leonardo Azzollini thus authored a second article, published in the 7 March 1959 issue of *Civiltà Cattolica*, under the neutral headline: 'Motor-Racing Events'.[33] With the same richness of documentation and detail as the first story, he elegantly and intelligently reversed the conclusion that he had reached in his first article, writing that he had 'instigated reactions not necessarily serene and objective, and some, actually, even prejudiced. For this reason, and not out of a desire for controversy,' he wrote, 'we deem necessary a few clarifications.'[34]

It was Enzo Ferrari's decision no longer to employ any Italian drivers and not to participate in any race in Italy in the future that had convinced the priest to return to the issue of motor racing and write this second article, he said. It was 'a decision so important', he told his readers, that Ferrari 'could not have taken it lightly . . . but only after various considerations, among which were ethical ones. We believe that one can differ with Ferrari on other points, but that one cannot but honestly recognize a moral sensibility in the way he conducts his activity as a car manufacturer.' The condemnation expressed in his first article, he now wrote, had not been 'a personal condemnation of Ferrari'.[35]

If Ferrari and, with him, sports-car manufacturers had been acquitted, it was necessary to indicate those who were guilty. Therefore, echoing what Ferrari had said in his December press conference, Father Azzollini placed the responsibility for the incidents and the multiple deaths 'entirely on race organizers, and those who have public authority over them. Car manufacturers,' he concluded, 'and especially Ferrari, have nothing to do with it.'[36]

The meeting with Father Azzollini was his masterpiece. With the new *Civiltà Cattolica* article, the Church had acquitted Enzo Ferrari.

The Ferrarina

A month and a half before the second *Civiltà Cattolica* story was published – the one that morally acquitted Ferrari – Enzo learned of the death of his new world champion. Mike Hawthorn was the fourth member of the *Ferrari Primavera* lineup to die, though this time not in a racing car. He hit a large tree while driving his personal Jaguar on a rainy evening, not far from London. It was 22 January 1959.

The day before, Ferrari had personally written to Tony Brooks to thank him for agreeing to meet in Maranello – the invitation had been made by telephone, in Ferrari's name, by team manager Romolo Tavoni on 18 January.[1] After learning of Vanwall's surprise retirement, announced by Tony Vandervell on 12 January, Ferrari had wasted no time. He decided to try and hire one of the two talented drivers who, the previous season, had taken from him the first F1 manufacturers' cup. In so doing he beat Colin Chapman who, on 20 January, offered Brooks a seat with Lotus.[2]

A few days later, Tony Brooks, accompanied by his wife Pina, an Italian girl from Pavia whom he had married the year before, arrived in Maranello. Elegant in a double-breasted grey suit – he was slowly learning to dress with a style that he'd never had before – Enzo outlined the various programmes for the 1959 season. There would be no team captain until the championship revealed which of his drivers would be the leader, he explained, and even then, this driver would still have to abide by his orders.[3]

Ferrari told Brooks that, in addition to F1, he also wanted him in sports cars. Brooks accepted, but asked that he be spared participation in the Le Mans 24 Hours.

On 6 April Enzo Ferrari went to Mantua to be deposed by examining magistrate Luciano Bonafini in the city courthouse. He had been called to give his statement on the crash that, 23 months earlier, had resulted in the death of 2 Ferrari drivers and 9 spectators during the last Mille Miglia. Because of the legal procedure following the Guidizzolo crash, the state still held Enzo's passport and his driver's licence, as if he had personally been driving De Portago's car.

Ferrari was concise and precise. 'In my opinion,' he stated, 'the puncture of the tyre on De Portago's car happened after the car hit the so-called "cat's eyes" reflectors in the centre of the road around the Volta Mantovana junction, just outside the village of Goito. It is possible,' he went on, 'that, because of the high speed, the thin tread, hitting the obstacle . . . provoked the rupture of the tyre.'[4]

The reconstruction of what Ferrari thought had happened had been validated by his technicians and by those at Englebert, the company that produced the tyres. Lastly, he said: 'The tyre blew up because of the impact that I think I have identified.'[5]

That was the extent of Ferrari's deposition that day.

*   *   *

The first F1 race of the 1959 season took place in Monaco on 10 May. Australian Jack Brabham won in his Cooper-Climax. The two wins in 1958 had convinced Climax to invest in F1 and, for the new season, the company from Coventry had built a new engine specifically designed for a racing car – rather than powering water pumps, which is what the Climax had originally been designed to do. As a consequence, Cooper had not only dominated from qualifying onwards, but had also placed Trintignant in third place and a very young Bruce McLaren in fifth. Ferrari and his front-engined single-seaters – the 1958 256 F1, with a dozen more horsepower[6] – had taken second place with Tony Brooks and fourth with Phil Hill.

This was a disappointment for Ferrari, but one that emphasized the superiority of mid-engine design. The old saying that it was sufficient to give his drivers 20 more horsepower than the opponents was becoming less and less true.[7] And at this point, despite his emphatic agricultural metaphors about cows, horses and wagons, and that the natural order was that the power source was always in the front, *pulling*, not behind, *pushing*, Ferrari really began to think that Cooper's arrangement was the solution of the future.

There was a second disappointment to come – one that hurt much more than the first. On 22 June 1959 Enzo Ferrari was charged for the 'Guidizzolo massacre'. The prosecutors and the experts who had conducted the technical investigation[8] had apparently convinced the judge more than Ferrari had been able to with his 6 April deposition.

In the distorted and confounding language of the Italian bureaucracy, Ferrari was accused of being a monster for causing the deaths of 11 people, and incompetent for having fitted – at least according to the prosecutors and the so-called experts – tyres that were not suitable for his cars. If it were not for the enormous legal and moral weight that it carried, after his 40 years in motor racing, the accusation would have been seen as ridiculous.

But Ferrari had no desire to laugh; he had to conceive a defence strategy. The Catholic Church had acquitted him in the spring. Now it was the Republic of Italy that was waging war against him.

When the summer of 1959 came, it was torrid.

Inside the cockpit of his Ferrari in the sun-drenched Champagne countryside, on 5 July, Tony Brooks fought more against the sweltering heat than against his opponents. For once, even the agile Cooper-Climax did not perform as expected, leaving to Ferrari's drivers the first two steps of the podium: Brooks, first; Phil Hill, second.

But Brooks's success unnerved Jean Behra, who from the beginning of the season had often felt, and behaved, as if he were the team captain, and had shown along the way some intolerance towards Brooks.[9] The victory at the Grand Prix of France had transformed Brooks into Ferrari's leading candidate for the world title, shattering the French driver's last hopes. At the end of the race, Behra got into a heated argument with team manager Tavoni before knocking him down with a well-placed punch. Two days later, on a steamy July afternoon, a very upset Ferrari summoned Behra to Modena and fired him.

On 17 July, following the instruction of his lawyer, Giacomo Cuoghi, Ferrari wrote to examining magistrate Luciano Bonafini. A rumour had spread that De Portago's mother had given one million lire to the Cavriana parish – the tiny village just outside Guidizzolo, where the Mille Miglia crash had taken place – to support the families of the victims, and that Ferrari, on the other hand, had not given anything to anyone.[10]

'While declaring myself entirely unconnected to the facts' and 'reserving the right to prove with the pertinent documentation that – as far as the eventual civil liability for damages to third parties goes' – he was 'fully insured and, notwithstanding the already stated non-involvement,' Ferrari wrote, 'I believe that it is my right to bring to [your] attention that ALL DAMAGES CAUSED TO THIRD PARTIES in the aforementioned incident have been [paid].'[11]

For once, Ferrari, who normally helped his fellow human beings without ever advertising it, had thought it wise to publicly disclose his donation.

The following day the Grand Prix of Great Britain at Aintree was scheduled, but Ferrari was forced to stay away because of a long strike that had shut down his factory and his racing department. Ferrari workers had gone on strike on 9 July – like workers throughout Italy – to demonstrate in favour of the renewal of the national contract. The following day, pickets had been organized in front of the

Maranello factory gates, preventing everyone from entering until 16 July. When they were finally removed, it was too late to prepare the cars for the British race.[12] Ferrari's personal attempts at negotiation, which had been so successful in the past, had led nowhere this time.

Thanks to yet another win in England, Jack Brabham and his small, agile and revolutionary Cooper-Climax were now ever more in control of the championship standings. But at the next race, on the ultra-fast Avus track in Berlin, which had taken the place of the Nürburgring after the controversy following Collins's death a year ago, Brooks and Ferrari experienced a day of true glory.

For the first and only time in world championship history, the Grand Prix of Germany was held in two separate heats, at the end of which the combined times would determine the winner. On a track where speed and power were the only prerequisites, Ferrari's 256 F1 had an easy day; at Avus, the potency of having 20 horsepower over one's opponent still remained.

Brooks won both heats, and the race, with an impressive 230km/h (143mph) average speed. Behind him came his two American teammates, Dan Gurney and Phil Hill. The first Cooper, Trintignant's, was in fourth place, an entire lap behind. Brabham's had withdrawn. With the nine points for the win, plus one for the race's fastest lap, Brooks shortened his gap to Brabham in the standings, making the union-induced nonparticipation in the British Grand Prix all the more relevant.

For Brooks and Ferrari that day at Avus was magnificent, even though the race was saddened by the death of Jean Behra in a Porsche the day before. But it was also their last win of the season. In the next two races – Portugal and Italy – Cooper-Climax dominated, and even though Brabham took home only a third-place finish at Monza, his lead in the standings increased.

On 14 September, the day after the Grand Prix of Italy, Ferrari's lawyer Giacomo Cuoghi sent a long letter to Mantua's deputy public prosecutor Mario Luberto, ahead of the questioning that the judge would soon have with his client. It contained details from Ferrari's memory – accurate, specific and aimed at proving Enzo's innocence. Cuoghi wrote that, '[These] reflections suggested by the examination of the procedure' would lead the prosecutor to dismiss the charges. Cuoghi was convinced that 'from the answers that Ferrari will give you, and by the thoughts contained in this letter . . . you will draw the evidence [you need] for a full [dismissal]'.[13]

Point by point, in great detail and with the aid of a scientific report authored and signed by a professor of the behavioural science department of the University of Genoa, Cuoghi tried to disassemble the entire prosecution.

'[There is] nothing else,' Ferrari's lawyer wrote in the final page of his long essay, 'we believe we should add, except [to] stress the point that Scuderia Ferrari has participated in the XXIV Mille Miglia with five cars. Of them (not considering De Portago's), three finished the race in the top three positions, travelling at higher speeds than any other competitor. None of these cars, despite the long distance travelled and the high speed sustained throughout, experienced any tread trouble, although three of them were of the same identical type [as De Portago's], and were fitted with tyres of equal pressure.'[14]

At the end of October, Enzo Ferrari purchased the Italian headquarters of Ford in the city of Bologna. This was mainly a public relations move. Ferrari had no need whatsoever of a branch office in Bologna, where he claimed that he wanted to move a few divisions of his company, such as the commercial and administration departments, and customer service.

As at other times in his life, this purchase was a message to various audiences: Italian automobile manufacturers, the public bodies governing the national automotive and motor-racing sectors and, last but not least, his fellow Modenese, who continued to love him in their peculiar and never-unquestioned way, and to whom he could now prove two things: first, he was so big he could afford to buy the building that had served as the Italian headquarters of the world's largest car manufacturer; and second, no one should take for granted that Enzo would forever keep his factory and his business in Maranello and in the Modena province.

*   *   *

The last race of the 1959 world championship was scheduled for 12 December in the warm, subtropical weather of Sebring, Florida. For the first time in F1 history, a real Grand Prix of the United States had been organized. Despite the rare ups and many downs of a difficult season, Tony Brooks still had a real chance of winning the world title, even though, of the three drivers in contention – the other two being Brabham, with the works Cooper-Climax, and Moss, with an identical car fielded by Rob Walker – Brooks was the one with the fewest points. Both Brabham and Moss qualified better than Brooks. Tony started from the second row with the fourth-best time. But at the very first turn after the start of the race, he was hit by teammate von Trips. The next lap, he pitted to have his mechanics check his car. The check took a couple of minutes, but it showed that the car was intact. Brooks went out again and fought like a lion, but in the end he could not do better than third place. He scored four points: enough to beat Moss but not Brabham, who was the new champion.

For Brooks, and for Ferrari, the final result was disappointing, but they both knew that the world title had not been lost in the last race but, rather, in the course of the season. The Grand Prix of Great Britain that they had been forced to miss because of the long summer strike was the prime suspect.[15] And since the Sports Car World Championship had also been disappointing, at the end of the year Enzo Ferrari had, for once, no new world titles to celebrate.

It was for this reason that on 29 December 1959, when the usual crowd of reporters met him in Modena for the traditional end-of-year press conference, they were certain they would find him in a bad mood.[16] As always, Enzo surprised them. To everyone's amazement, he started the meeting with a tribute to the British automotive industry that, at least this year, had defeated him twice.

No one was fooled, of course. He was not praising the British automotive industry per se, but rather delivering a subliminal attack to those Italian automobile notables who had, once again, left him alone in the arena.

The focus of the conversation remained on all things British when someone asked why, in the list of drivers that he had just provided – Hill, Allison, von Trips – he had not included the name of F1 runner-up Tony Brooks. 'Brooks,' Ferrari said, 'told me that, today, he wants to be a good husband, a great father and an even better dentist.' For this reason, Ferrari said, Brooks was retiring from motor racing.

Then, after a brief pause, he started philosophizing: 'Men have a curious destiny when they get married,' he said. 'If they are able to make it through the first year, all is fine; they go faster than before. If, instead, they don't make it through the first year, motorsport loses them.'[17] To stress his thesis, he offered the example of Tonino Brivio, although he could just as easily have offered himself as an example.

Ferrari had never appreciated a driver who lost his brio or motivation because of a woman. While he respected Brooks, it was clear that his decision to quit had disappointed Enzo greatly – even though, actually, Tony had made his decision not because he'd got married, but because of the birth of his first child, a baby girl named Caroline, that summer. Enzo himself had done the same thing when Dino was born, in January 1932.

But there was more.

Referring to the factory visit that had preceded the press conference, a reporter asked: 'We have seen an 850cc engine . . .'[18] This was true, since Ferrari had wanted it positioned where it was impossible to miss. That engine was a provocation, a gauntlet to Italian automakers, as well as a tangible demonstration that the experience gained through motor racing was also important when it came to developing small-engine technology.

Enzo explained that this was just a project, and excluded the possibility of ever producing a car with that engine – at least under the Ferrari name. He added that the project of developing a car for that engine had actually already been set in motion, even though he was not yet satisfied with the result. Finally, to confound everyone even more, he said: 'That car will probably bear a name very dear to me, but,' he confirmed, 'will not be produced by Ferrari.'[19] He could not have been more vague and misleading if he'd tried.

Many in the audience thought that the company in question was Fiat. Those who did not think so believed, on the contrary, that the small Ferrari – or 'Ferrarina', as it was quickly named – was a project designed to compete with Fiat. No one could have suspected that Enzo Ferrari was thinking of a small-engine car that he wanted to name after his son – an idea, at the time, that had aroused the opposition of most of his top men, beginning with his commercial director.[20]

Acquitted

In the winter of 1960, Enzo Ferrari was finally questioned by the deputy public prosecutor of the Mantua district court. Ferrari gave one of the best, and most misleading, performances of his life. Having already been deposed in front of the judge the previous spring, and after the long written statement presented by his lawyer, he behaved in such an extravagant manner – for those who did not know him – that poor Mario Luberto was taken by surprise, and fooled. After Luberto's first question, Enzo suddenly began to sob. Seeing a 187cm (6ft 2in), 118kg (260lb) man weep was not a pretty sight, especially when the man who was crying was famous and was considered by most to be ruthless. And when he began to speak, he spoke with the innocence of a child.

'I know nothing,' he said, sobbing. 'The only thing I know is that a tyre blew up, causing the tragedy. If it is technical explanations that you want,' he went on, 'you must speak with my engineers. I,' he insisted, 'don't feel any responsibility.'

The totally unexpected behaviour immediately produced the desired effect.

'*Ingegner*, calm down . . . Nobody wants to convict you or send you to jail,' Luberto said.

Embarrassed by this emotional display, the judge, a man still in his youth and with only a couple of years of experience, had fallen into the trap. He tried to calm Enzo down again and encouraged him.[1] How could anyone believe that a grown man who wept like a child for the deaths of all those innocents was a monster! Especially someone who clearly thought of his racing drivers as his own sons, weeping at the mere mention of their names.[2]

It was at this point that Luberto made his big mistake: he let emotions take over and linked Ferrari's public life – motor racing, the Guidizzolo crash, the death of his drivers – with his private life; with Dino's death, that is. In that moment, for Luberto, Ferrari became the 12th victim of the Mille Miglia incident.

It was all true, of course: the grief caused by the crash and by the massacre of all those innocents was real. Two years earlier, it had taken all of Father Alberto

Clerici's persuasive powers to urge Enzo to go on building and racing sports cars, and to convince him that he was blameless and must now concentrate on creating a better future. But that had passed, and Enzo had absorbed even the deaths of Musso and Collins, which had naturally wounded him.

Ferrari had put on an act for the young Mantuan magistrate – an act carefully planned and skilfully played. Enzo had known how to command tears all of his life.[3] It was not by coincidence that, in Modena, there were those who had maliciously christened him Zacconi, after a famous stage actor.[4]

An unrelated announcement came on 7 April.

'At the suggestion of the illustrious Professor Dore, dean of the engineering faculty, the University of Bologna, lecturer Professor Morandi,' a statement issued by the university said, 'the faculty has unanimously decided to submit to the approval of the Minister of Education the bestowal of an honorary degree in mechanical engineering to *Cavaliere del Lavoro* Enzo Ferrari. Minister Medici granted the required permission.' The reason for the honour? 'With his technical activity, [Enzo Ferrari] has honoured our country internationally.'[5]

While it was certainly true that, with his work, Enzo Ferrari had honoured the name of Italy in the world, behind the *honoris causa* degree was the purchase of the Ford Italiana building in Bologna, and Ferrari's interest in the deal. Whether Ferrari had a real interest in moving part of his activity to Bologna, or his purchase was simply an astute PR move, a short time after the purchase, Professor Morandi would pay him a visit in Modena and, on behalf of the dean of the oldest university in the Western world, bestow on him the honour.

Then, on 23 May, Enzo Ferrari went from being the sole owner of his company to one of its shareholders. Auto Costruzioni Ferrari would end its existence on 30 June, to be replaced, from 1 July, by Società Esercizio Fabbriche Automobili e Corse –SEFAC, pronounced 'sea-fak'.

It was a joint-stock company in which each of the five shareholders owned two stakes of 100,000 lire each, for a joint stock of one million lire. The five shareholders were Gianni Agnelli's brother-in-law, Carlo Caracciolo; food mogul Ugo Colombo; French industrialist and Ferrari client Michel Paul-Cavallier; coachbuilder Giovanni Battista Farina, who would be the vice president of SEFAC; and, naturally, Enzo Ferrari, the president.[6]

Enzo had wanted this new company structure not because he needed shareholders, but for two equally important reasons. The first was of a fiscal nature; the second, perhaps more important, was the desire not to be the sole person legally responsible if there were any future fatal incidents.[7] For even if he had tricked Mantua's young deputy public prosecutor, the judicial procedure for the Guidizzolo crash itself was still pending.

*   *   *

The last Sunday in May, Ferrari's first mid-engined single-seater made its debut. According to Ferrari's agricultural metaphor, the cows had been moved to the back of the wagon. American Richie Ginther drove it in the Grand Prix of Monaco, where it finished sixth overall, some thirty laps behind the winner. Things went better with the front-engined car that the other American, Phil Hill, drove to a third-place finish.

But if the F1 world championship was discouraging, things were going much better for Ferrari in the sports car series. After Phil Hill and Cliff Allison had won the Buenos Aires 1000km in January, on 26 June, Belgians Olivier Gendebien and Paul Frère won the most prestigious endurance race in the world, the Le Mans 24 Hours. Both wins had been taken by the front-engined 250 Testa Rossa.

The day of the conferral of the honorary degree, Thursday 7 July, 1960, finally arrived.

It was a hot and steamy summer afternoon. When Ferrari read, as protocol required, an essay on the activity that had won him the honorary degree, the crowd in the auditorium was quiet. He had written it together with the boyfriend of the barber's daughter,[8] a law graduate with a very Modenese last name (Franco Gozzi) and a rare gift for writing.

'Motor racing, which I consider . . . a sensational affair and a true show with a strong technical content,' he proclaimed to an audience hanging on his every word, '. . . offers satisfactory results only when the whole organization that governs the interactions with the drivers, with the technicians and with all those who work in the fiery environment of competitions are animated by a true *esprit de corps*. It is this *esprit de corps*,' he said, 'which, during the long years of our activity, has allowed Ferrari to clinch successes that have honoured Italian work.'[9]

Enzo ended his speech, 15 pages in all, by remembering 'those young people who, in their excitement for conquest, [made] the ultimate sacrifice.'[10] Tears began to roll down his face.

In mid-July the SEFAC shareholders met for the first time. Only the French stakeholder had not reached Modena. The meeting represented the second and final step in the shaping of the new company. The share capital went that day from 1 to 200 million lire. Enzo Ferrari had transferred to the new company all the property he owned, valued at a total of 199 million lire. By virtue of this transaction, Enzo received 1,990 new shares. Now he owned 1,992 of SEFAC's 2,000 stakes against 2 each for the other 4 shareholders, Caracciolo, Colombo, Paul-Cavallier and Pinin Farina. During the meeting, the new majority shareholder was elected president of the company.[11]

The summer of 1960 went by quickly.

September brought the only breath of fresh air to an F1 World Championship played in a minor key. At Monza, Ferrari took his first grand prix win of the year, placing three cars in the top three final positions.

But there was an explanation for this victory – or, rather, two. The first was the decision by the organizers to hold the race on the complete circuit, which also included the high-speed ring, to favour the power of the Ferrari engines. The second was the decision of the English teams to boycott the race – not so much because the decision to include the rarely used, high-speed, banked track was so blatantly favourable to Ferrari, but because of the suspected danger inherent in that high-speed part of the circuit, on which there were spectacular cracks in the asphalt. Phil Hill won the race, followed by Richie Ginther and the Belgian Willy Mairesse. It was the last F1 victory for a front-engined car.

In 1960 Ferrari production surpassed the 300-unit mark for the first time, with all cars selling well in advance. The employee count had passed this mark long ago.[12] After realizing that his customers went on purchasing his front-engined granturismos and berlinettas despite the new motor-racing trend that had moved the engine behind the driver, Ferrari was finally convinced that the mid-engine layout represented the future.

After confirming that he would once again employ only foreign drivers, in the spring of 1961 Ferrari decided to give one of his F1 cars to FISA – the Italian Federation of Motor Racing Teams – because they selected an Italian driver to whom to entrust it in certain races.[13] Wanting to avoid any new controversy in the event of fatal accidents, he had come up with a solution that would allow Italian sports fans to see an Italian driver at the wheel of a Ferrari, while escaping direct responsibility.

FISA selected a young driver from Milan named Giancarlo Baghetti, who, in his first race with the private Ferrari, won the Grand Prix of Syracuse. The race did not count for the championship, but all the drivers and cars that would battle for the world title were there. Baghetti confirmed his class three weeks later in Posillipo.

The 1961 F1 World Championship started in May in Monaco. As had happened the year before, it was Stirling Moss who won, this time in a mid-engined

Lotus-Climax. But this year, Ferrari also had the engine behind the driver and, with Ginther, Hill and von Trips, took second, third and fourth places. Victory had not come, but the Monaco race had confirmed to Ferrari and his drivers the potential of the mid-engined car.[14] Monaco was only the beginning of a splendid second part of the season. Between the end of May and mid-June, Ferrari won the grands prix of the Netherlands and Belgium with von Trips and Phil Hill – events during which Enzo's drivers had the chance to fully explore the great potential of their mid-engined cars for the first time.[15]

Then, on 21 June 1961, came what was in all likelihood one of the happiest days in Enzo Ferrari's life. The deputy public prosecutor of the Mantua district court asked that all charges against him for the incident on 12 May 1957 – which had caused 11 deaths in the 24th Mille Miglia – be dropped.

At the end of the investigation, and according to the conclusions of the experts, of the three hypotheses considered as possible causes of the incident, two had been discarded: 'incompetence' or 'lack of judiciousness on the part of the driver'; and 'incapability or negligence on the part of Ferrari, the company, in the construction and preparation of the car'. The cause of the Guidizzolo crash was determined to be 'unpredictable and imponderable factors'.[16]

De Portago was completely exonerated. 'From the findings there isn't the slightest [evidence that calls] into question the responsibility of the driver, whose expertise was known to all. Equally,' Mario Luberto wrote, 'one must exclude Enzo Ferrari's responsibility, supported solely by the findings of the first report, but not confirmed by the second, after the technical appraisal has shown with a wealth of scientific arguments that the quality and pressure of the tyres did not cause the accident.' The report continued: 'Even if, theoretically, one should believe correct the findings of the first experts, the responsibility could not be placed on Enzo Ferrari because the construction of the tyres that fitted his cars had been made by a specialized foreign company specialist, which had also sent to Italy [their] technicians, along with the tyres.'[17]

It was a victory on all fronts. And there was much of the Ferrari personal magic in it. After the deposition, complete with tears and sobs in the spring of 1960, Ferrari had invited Luberto to Maranello, where the judge had not only talked to technicians, who had explained how things must have happened in Guidizzolo, but had also been charmed by Enzo in the guise of a Leopold of Belgium (or Bernhard of Orange)-like ride in a Ferrari driven by the king himself, followed by lunch at the Cavallino Restaurant.

*   *   *

The 156 F1 seemed to have no rivals, regardless of the driver, which became most evident on 2 July, when Giancarlo Baghetti, in the Ferrari fielded by Scuderia Sant'Ambroeus on behalf of FISA, won the Grand Prix of France in Rheims.

On 26 July Enzo Ferrari was cleared of any responsibility in the Guidizzolo crash. The court had ruled that the cat's-eye reflector had caused the incident, when it had been hit in the Volta Mantovana turn by the tyre of De Portago's car, which had blown a few miles later. Consequently, Enzo Ferrari 'was acquitted of all charges'.[18]

As in the war against the Church a couple of years earlier, he had not only been acquitted, but – so to speak – sanctified. The verdict included a description of the man and entrepreneur who, after years of accusations, must have felt validated for all of his suffering: 'A man with a strong and incisive personality, gifted with above-average intellectual and moral qualities, through enormous sacrifices and driven by a passion for motoring, he has been able to create out of nothing, with his own strength, a wonderful industry and a perfect workshop, winning universal respect and admiration, building cars, both for competition and for tourism, for which the whole world envies us, triumphing in undisputed manner on tracks and roads on all continents.'[19]

*   *   *

The battle for the title between the two Ferrari drivers had set Italian fans and public opinion on fire. Within the team, the burden of an internal duel was beginning to be felt. The only one who did not want to talk about it was Ferrari, perhaps due to some sort of superstition – or so thought Phil Hill, one of the two contenders.[20] At any rate, if the German count had finished ahead of his American teammate at Monza, on 10 September, he would have been the new F1 world champion. Instead, on that day, Wolfgang von Trips – 'Taffy' to his friends and colleagues – was killed, along with 15 spectators, more than had died at Guidizzolo 4½ years earlier. Hit from behind by another car, von Trips's 156 took off on the bank beside the track and plunged into the crowd.

The race was not stopped.

The winner was Phil Hill, who became the new champion.

Headlines and controversy continued for days on end. Although it was nothing like what had happened after the Guidizzolo crash, or when Luigi Musso had been killed, perhaps it was a good thing that the acquittal for the Mille Miglia incident had come six weeks earlier.

'It ended in this tragic way,' a bitter Ferrari remarked at the end of the season, 'a glorious year for us,'[21] where, after a long delay, he had beaten the British at their own game or, rather, with their own weapons. He had gone to Monza, as usual in recent years, only for practice and qualifying, and had for the first time brought with him his son Piero, who was now 16.[22] And as a Scuderia Ferrari pit guest in what was supposed to be a weekend of celebration was none other than Prince Bernhard of the Netherlands.

But the real twist was yet to happen. With both the F1 and sports car world titles in his pocket – four wins, including the Le Mans 24 Hours, in a total of five races – in the last week of November, Enzo Ferrari turned on his management staff. Out of the blue, he fired eight directors – in short, all of the executives who reported to him.

The statement issued to the press said 'Eight SEFAC Ferrari executives ended their employment with the company, by sending a registered letter to the president and managing director, Enzo Ferrari, and to the board of trustees.'[23] The reason: 'overvaluation of marginal facts that have nothing to do with the normal business life of a company'. In reality, they had all been fired. There was indeed a letter, but it was not a letter with which the eight managers had informed Ferrari that they were leaving. Instead, it was a letter that had infuriated their boss and led to their dismissal.

The letter had been written by the lawyer the eight managers had chosen to represent them. In it, the managers – all of Enzo's first reports, the heads of all company departments – after carefully reconstructing various incidents, asked for their boss's intervention to stop the incursions being made by his wife in the professional matters of the company.

For years, Ferrari had allowed Laura to intrude at will in corporate matters. He had done it in part to keep her quiet, and in part to keep her away. It was not uncommon for her to go with the team to motor races, during which time she hovered suspiciously in the Ferrari pits, intervening even when she shouldn't.[24] This also meant that Ferrari's men still felt as though they were being watched, in the chief's absence. Terrified by the very idea of becoming poor again, as had happened after the failure of the Carrozzeria Emilia, Laura was almost maniacal in her efforts to ensure that not a single penny was wasted, something that Ferrari naturally appreciated.[25]

No one dared to talk to Ferrari about the excessive liberties that his wife took within the company or during motor-racing trips. Quite simply, Ferrari, who naturally knew all about it, refused to discuss the subject.[26] And so, knowing that there was no real way to speak with him, in order to be heard his eight executives had decided to communicate through a lawyer.

Although it was written in a gracious and polished fashion so as not to hurt Ferrari more than was strictly necessary, the lawyer's letter naturally infuriated Ferrari. He, who had always shunned any attempt to discuss the subject, now felt betrayed by the fact that his men had turned to a lawyer. He may have been right; however, the eight men had tried everything to get his attention, and the lawyer's letter was the last card played by professional managers embarrassed on a daily basis by their boss's wife.

The Tuesday meeting after Enzo received the letter was uneventful. Ferrari may have seemed a little more stiff than usual, but it looked like he had no intention of addressing the topic. Yet it was clear that he had read the letter, because he kept it folded in front of him, in the open page of his diary on the table around which the eight executives sat. When the meeting ended, Ferrari closed his agenda and said goodbye as he always did before returning to his office.

But a surprise awaited the eight men. As soon as they were alone, deputy personnel director Radighieri summoned them one by one, handing each man an envelope. Inside they found a letter announcing that they had been fired. Ferrari had not intended to discuss the matter even then; he had simply taken notice, felt betrayed and disposed of all of them. From behind the closed door of his office, he was heard shouting: 'They did not understand anything! What kind of men have I fashioned who send me a registered letter!'[27]

Along with team manager and press officer Tavoni, that night Enzo Ferrari fired commercial director Gerolamo Gardini, administration director Ermanno Della Casa, purchasing director Federico Giberti, personnel director Enzo Selmi, head of the foundry Fausto Galassi, head of experimentation Giotto Bizzarrini and chief engineer Carlo Chiti.

The lawyer's letter had triggered Ferrari's astonishing decision, but the truth is that he had long been suspicious of some of his top men. The press release spoke of 'an act of solidarity' on the part of seven of the eight men, 'with *Ragionier* Gardini invited not to return to the office after having made allegations deemed disrespectful toward Ferrari and spoken in a public place in the presence of *Signor* Luigi Chinetti, general manager for the United States of America of Ferrari cars'.[28]

The phrases overheard and reported by Chinetti had most likely ended up inside some folder that Ferrari must have placed in an office drawer, ready to use whenever necessary. Indeed, if he kept updated dossiers on the professional and personal lives of drivers and journalists,[29] he certainly could have had the same for his top executives. Wasn't it true that he had a phone on his desk through which, by pressing a special red button, he could listen in on any telephone call made inside his company?[30]

Since the company had changed its legal structure and Enzo Ferrari had shareholders at SEFAC, the company organization had also changed. For the first time in its history, Ferrari had a real organizational chart with well-defined positions and responsibilities, just like much larger companies. At this point, some of his employees – now managers and directors – had started to behave more independently than before. The members of the Old Guard, the people from Modena, like Tavoni, Giberti and Della Casa, had changed little or nothing in the way they went about their business.

But some of the newcomers had taken a lot more autonomy than Ferrari was willing to give them. And it was this new environment, in which it might look as if Ferrari was not in charge as firmly as he'd been before, that the conviction was born – which in earlier times, would simply have been unthinkable – that some of those high-ranking managers felt free to comment on their boss in public, at times voicing their dissatisfaction or, as in the case of matters concerning the boss's wife, showing a disturbing patronizing attitude.[31]

The mass firing of his top executives stirred pandemonium in the newspapers. Even those who knew how Ferrari operated had been caught off guard by this astonishing and, for many, incomprehensible move. But there were also those who stated, not without reason, that the 'eight, leaving, made him feel ten years younger. The angrier he gets, the younger he feels.'[32]

'My Terrible Joys'

One morning in mid-December 1961, Ferrari summoned to his office one of the most promising engineers of the new generation. He had been with the company for a little over a year, but Reclus, his father, was one of the members of the Old Guard, his association with Ferrari going back to the glory days of the Scuderia. The young engineer left his desk and walked towards Ferrari's office, wondering what the boss wanted from him.

'Forghieri,' Ferrari said, when the 26-year-old engineer stood before him, 'how do you feel about becoming the new technical director of the racing department?'

Despite his young age, the skinny, black-haired engineer had great talent and rare common sense. He thanked Ferrari, but said that he did not possess enough experience to manage the racing department of the F1 and sports cars world champion team. 'While I think I may have something to contribute in some engineering matters,' he said, 'I have doubts about my present ability to manage the racing activity of Ferrari as a whole.'

Enzo had already made up his mind, however; Mauro Forghieri was *the* man, one of his lieutenants that he was going to promote to general. 'You don't have to worry,' Enzo said. 'Go to work and get busy. I will take care of everything else.'[1]

Shortly after Christmas, two of the cast-offs – Giberti and Della Casa – returned. It is unclear whether Ferrari had forgiven them for committing the crime of showing solidarity with a colleague, or if he had realized how difficult it would be to replace them with men of equal competence in their respective roles – purchasing and administration.[2] At any rate, they were the only ones to return of those who had been fired in late November. Toward the others, whom he evidently considered more guilty or easier to replace, he would be inflexible and, in some instances, even vindictive.[3]

Some of the eight decided to seek justice in court. The idea was to demonstrate that Ferrari was out of his mind – a sound man, they argued, would not fire the entire top management of his company. After trying to show that his wife was crazy, they now set out to prove that the real madman was Enzo. They went to another

Modena lawyer with what they thought was an ace up their sleeve – Fiamma Breschi.

Breschi had been the fascinating girlfriend of Luigi Musso, who had left his wife and children for her. She was brilliant, young and beautiful, with long red hair and gorgeous eyes. Not long after Luigi was killed at Rheims, in July 1958, Enzo had taken her under his wing.

Annihilated by Dino's death, exasperated by the constant quarrels with Laura, forced to maintain his relationship with Lina and Piero without the freedom that he longed for, Ferrari soon started to see in Fiamma – just 25 when he met her – a breath of oxygen in a tremendously complex life. Thus, he had deliberately added complexity to complexity, starting a courtship that at first was veiled, and then became more and more insistent, composed of requests for advice, the sharing of some business situations, asking for her take on this or that driver . . .[4]

In Maranello, in 1961, there were many who knew of the relationship between Ferrari and Musso's girlfriend. Even if they did not know about the letters he wrote to her on an almost-daily basis, they knew of the long phone calls, which were much more difficult to hide. Alone in his office, Ferrari spent hours and hours on the phone with Fiamma, complaining about the unhappiness of his life, involving her in many business issues, making her feel important in an attempt to appeal to her vanity and convince her to move their relationship to a less-platonic level.[5]

Some of the managers who had been fired decided to use their knowledge of these phone calls to their advantage. Their intention was to demonstrate that a 63-year-old man who behaved like a boy, in love with a woman 36 years younger than him, had simply lost his mind – just as he had demonstrated when he'd fired the 8 of them for no substantial reason.

To prove their case, they needed to get hold of the record of telephone calls made within the company. The men located the staff member who checked the phone records each month for accounting purposes, but this person did not go along with their plan. He had been working with Enzo since before the company was named Ferrari. He would not tell Ferrari about their nefarious plan, he said, but he would not give them what they wanted to frame his boss. Therefore, thanks to the loyalty of this employee, their plan could not be put into action.[6]

At the 24 February 1962 press conference, in which he introduced the programme for the new season, Ferrari introduced the berlinetta that would participate in the grand touring races of 1962.

The elegantly shaped car, equipped with a 300hp 12-cylinder engine, had originally been designed by Bizzarrini and Chiti, two of the eight that had been fired, and completed by young Forghieri. It did not have a name yet, but its bodywork was the most beautiful that Ferrari had ever developed up to that point. And although none of the journalists suspected it, this body had never been sketched on paper, but rather had been created inch by inch by Scaglietti as he covered the chassis.[7]

In the course of the year, the elegant berlinetta would acquire a name – the 250 GTO, where the 'O' revealed the fact that the International Sporting Commission (CSI) had approved it for racing in the gran turismo category.[8] (The 'O' stands for *Omologato*, or 'homologated', which means the car was officially approved.) In 1962 and 1963, Scaglietti would build 36 of these cars, with 3 more in 1964.[9]

On 10 March 1962, Enzo Ferrari met in Maranello with F1's king without a crown.[10] Unhappy with the attitude of his new world champion, Phil Hill (who lacked the sense of adoration nearly all of his drivers had for him), and disinclined to deal with him, Enzo had decided to go ahead with Stirling Moss. He had always liked the British racer because he reminded Ferrari of certain drivers he had known in the 1930s.

An agreement was reached to the satisfaction of both.[11] Together, Ferrari and Moss chose their debut race: the Daily Express Trophy in May, a non-championship race, which would allow the British driver to get used to his new car. But then, during another non-championship race at Goodwood on Easter Monday, in which he had already been entered with a Lotus-Climax, Moss had a terrible crash, which put an end to his extraordinary career and, of course, to his adventure with Ferrari.

The 1962 season gave only sporadic gratification to Ferrari, who was busy reorganizing the technical department. The F1 World Championship, dominated by British teams, brought him only a few podium finishes with world champion Phil Hill, and Lorenzo Bandini's third place in Monte Carlo. The year before, Bandini had lost the battle with Baghetti for the car that Enzo had given to FISA, but both had been hired this season by the Ferrari works team after Enzo was acquitted for the Mille Miglia incident. Alongside them was the ever-reliable Mairesse and a 20-year-old Mexican, Ricardo Rodríguez, a driver Ferrari liked very much.

During the year, the atmosphere inside the team was never serene. Phil Hill, self-assured after winning the title, had started to show reluctance when it came to conducting the tests he had carried out in previous seasons. The team was now divided: on one side were Hill and Baghetti, drivers who did not go along with Forghieri, and made no secret of regretting Chiti's departure; on the other, Bandini, Mairesse and Rodríguez, who, instead, were in tune with the new technical director.[12] A further negative impact on the championship results was dealt by ongoing trade union strikes, which had forced Ferrari to work in fits and starts on the cars, missing participation in the French Grand Prix.[13]

Then Rodríguez lost his life in a crash during the last race of the season in his native Mexico, at the wheel of a Lotus, after Ferrari had decided not to race the last two championship races so that he could better prepare for the following season.

Meanwhile, the 1962 sports car championship was for the first time run by GT cars rather than the sports cars that had competed in the first nine seasons. Also for the first time, the championship was divided into classes. Ferrari competed with the 250 GTO, which won eight races hands down, clinching the world title in its class. And as for purpose-built racing sports cars, Ferrari took home the title in the new World Endurance Challenge, which had been set up by the organizers of the Le Mans 24 Hours, the Sebring 12 Hours, the Nürburgring 1000km and the Targa Florio – that is, the four most important endurance races in the world. Enzo thanked the 250 TR/61, the 330 TRI LM and the SP 246, the first mid-engined sports Ferrari, for the win.

Enzo's courtship of Fiamma continued throughout the spring, summer and autumn. The young woman had refused his proposal the first time, and continued to refuse all of the subsequent ones.

With each rejection, his infatuation became more intense, his letters more passionate, his proposals more tangible. Ferrari was confident that Fiamma would eventually agree to marry him. To have her at his side, he told her that he was willing to leave his wife, to whom he was prepared to give a settlement of 900 million lire. He even got to the point of asking his lawyer to study the possibility of drawing up a prenuptial agreement, as he had heard that this type of thing was done in the United States.[14]

Fiamma did not surrender – not in 1962, nor ever.

On the first day of December 1962, at the Hotel Palace in Modena, Enzo held his traditional end-of-year get-together with the press. Despite the unsuccessful F1 season, Ferrari could still celebrate a total of 163 victories earned by the works team, as well as those earned by the clients that he now had all over the world, who raced and won for him Sunday after Sunday.[15] Enzo also mentioned the fact that it had been impossible for him to compete on equal terms with his F1 opponents because of the trade union strikes.

Of course, he could always withdraw from motor racing, he said. After all, Alfa Romeo was still selling cars thanks to the sporting image that had been built a long time ago – that is, when *he* was at Alfa (although he didn't say this out loud). However, he added, 'I would consider withdrawing [from racing] desertion; worse, a betrayal of all those who have worked, suffered and died for racing, whose deeds have [led to] automotive advancement.'[16]

Ferrari would go on racing, but he knew it would do no good to sugarcoat things. 'We cannot continue to give you what you expect,' he warned the press, who would likewise warn Italian fans. 'We've done it while it was possible; we can't do that anymore.'[17]

Today's press conference, aside from the many themes treated in his always-peculiar fashion, had opened with two important announcements.

The first was the establishment of a journalism prize named after his son Dino, 'to be awarded', said Giovanni Canestrini, who would be one of the members of the jury, 'to the Italian journalist who writes, between January and October of each year, the article on motorsport that is judged the best among those submitted to the jury'.[18]

The second announcement was that Enzo had become an author.

Ferrari had titled his book *Le mie gioie terribili – My Terrible Joys* – and he couldn't have come up with a more appropriate title. 'In this book,' the publisher said to all present, including Ferrari, to whom he presented the first copy, '[you will find] all of Ferrari.'[19] And it was true – or, at least, it was true for that part of himself that Enzo intended to tell his readers about.

The volume, whose subtitle was *The Interview of a Lifetime*, retraced the life of Enzo Ferrari from birth to the end of the 1962 season. It was the first full account of his story, a story that fascinated millions, not only in Italy, of which, apart from insiders, most knew very little. People were familiar with his seemingly infinite string of victories and his splendid cars, but of Enzo Ferrari the man, very little was known. This book would fill in the gaps.

'In these years, more than once,' he wrote in the foreword, 'I was invited to write the story of my "case", but I never did. The sum of the daily tasks, which I judged could not be postponed, did not give me the time to reorder in my memory the men, the things, the events, which have characterized my life, and led me to build cars bearing my name, the last act of a progression begun with my adolescent dreams.'[20]

Everything had changed following the event that had saddened and marked his life forever. 'The death of my son Dino,' he confided, 'made me stop and think. And after such a [painful] journey, turning back, I was able to look at my entire existence. So I resolved to give vent to this conversation with myself, perhaps too long postponed. An interview in solitude, accompanied by the greatest sorrow of my life.'[21] A beautiful black-and-white photograph of a smiling Dino welcomed the reader. On the back of the page with the image of the young man, Ferrari had written these few words:

Dino Ferrari, my son Born January 19, 1932
I lost him on June 30, 1956.[22]

In that *I lost him* was all of the father's pain. Perhaps writing the book had helped to metabolize at least some of it, although he would never entirely overcome his grief. As one might expect, the book was dedicated 'To my son Dino'.[23]

In presenting the book to the press, small Bologna-based publisher Cappelli said it had been 'published with a speed equal to the speed of a Ferrari', revealing that the book had been completed 'in twenty days'.[24] This was true, in a way, although he was referring only to the time period that began with the day Enzo had turned in the manuscript and ended with the day the book was printed, just in time for the 1 December press conference. As for writing it, that work had been time-consuming and had started more than a year earlier.

The first to jot down Enzo's lifelong recollections had been Fiamma, in several small Emilia restaurants, during the summer of 1961. Sitting at a table with her, in the corner of many a brasserie with white plastered walls, or under a shady pergola when the weather allowed, Enzo's memories had come easily, one after the other.[25] While he probed his memory and dictated, she diligently took notes. As far as his personal correspondence went, Enzo typically wrote most of his letters by hand and, naturally enough, had never sat in front of a typewriter in his life.[26] He soon realized, however, that as pleasant as it was to spend time with a beautiful young woman, and as diligent as Fiamma was in keeping track of his flowing recollections, if he wanted to fashion a real book, he needed professional help. Despite his friendship with two gifted writers, Gino Rancati and Franco Gozzi – the latter, the barber's daughter's boyfriend, with whom he had worked on his honorary degree speech a year earlier, and who, in the meantime, he'd hired – he decided to turn to a young journalist from Turin.

Gian Paolo Ormezzano was a young reporter when, during the year of the Rome Olympics, he'd come to Maranello to interview Enzo for *Tuttosport*, the Turin sports newspaper. After the interview, Ferrari had invited him to write the story right there in Maranello, asking to read it before the journalist returned to Turin that evening. Ormezzano had complied and, back in his office in Turin, had turned in the text approved by Ferrari, from which, given its length, two articles had resulted. But then he had published a third article in which he'd told the story of the other two – namely, how Ferrari had wanted to approve their contents.[27]

Ferrari usually expected unquestioning obedience from all those who were admitted to his court but, at the same time, he often found those who dared challenge him irresistible – as long as the person in question had triggered something in him. Despite Ormezzano's impertinence in discussing Enzo's behaviour, Enzo had decided that this reporter was the one to help him write his book.

Tracking him down was not easy. Fearing Ferrari's wrath for that third, somewhat mischievous article, Ormezzano could not be found for days. But when he finally agreed to climb what felt like the steps to the gallows, he found that the executioner was offering him an extraordinary opportunity to help him in drafting his autobiography.[28]

Ferrari had been clear from the very beginning: he was not looking for a ghostwriter. He was looking for a professional journalist who would not only organize his recollections, but would also ask him the right questions to fully stimulate his memory and dictate its flow. For his autobiography, Enzo Ferrari had chosen the interview format.

Ormezzano asked his newspaper for a leave of absence and, armed with a small tape recorder and a lot of patience, he began to spend his days in a small room near Ferrari's office. There, he waited all day to be admitted to Enzo's presence and start recording his reminiscences. For hours, he only felt his presence. He would hear him scream, bark, always noisy – but he would never see him. Then, in the evening, or often even later, Ferrari would finally summon him to his office. Together, they would go to some restaurant where, between one dish and another, with personal chauffeur Peppino dozing off in a corner, one dictated and the other took notes, while the soft whirring of the recorder could be heard in the background.[29]

Ferrari's ability to dictate was extraordinary, as was his capacity for synthesis. His naturally slow speech allowed him to mentally compose sentences, to which Ormezzano simply had to add the punctuation. Listening to these tapes, one cannot help but marvel at Enzo's natural gift, for his words are uttered in the same order as they would appear on paper.

At one point Ormezzano realized that he had used up all of his leave, plus the vacation days that he was entitled to. With the end of the project not yet in sight, he reluctantly informed Ferrari that he was sorry, but he had to return to Turin if he wanted to keep his job. Ormezzano suggested a colleague and a friend, Gianni Roghi, who soon joined Ferrari and, in time, completed the job.

'My book [would] have to be published only after my death; otherwise, I would spend the last years of my life in jail,'[30] Ferrari had often said when, long before publication, the rumour had spread that he was working on his memoirs. In fact, his book was peppered here and there with severe judgements on drivers, organizers and public figures, but Gozzi, under whose scrutiny all proofs had passed before publication, had made sure that most of the rough comments had been softened, if not altogether removed.[31]

Enzo's most severe comments had been addressed to Fangio – but there was a reason. The year before, the five-time world champion had published his own memoir, in which he had implied that Enzo may have resorted to sabotage to make Fangio lose the 1956 world title. Ferrari had picked up the gauntlet, coldly dismantling Fangio's theory of sabotage – even though Fangio hadn't actually used that term – ridiculing the charges that the Argentine brought forth when discussing possible commercial strategies behind some team decisions. Ferrari had divided his book into six chapters: 'A Life for the Race Car'; 'Drivers, What People'; 'I Do Not Go to Races, But . . .'; 'Maranello: A Magnet'; 'Ah, Women!'; and 'Why?' He had told his personal story and the story of his company, but he'd also described a cross-section of the automotive and motor-racing worlds, and of Italian society.

'The way my personal story will be narrated,' he wrote in the initial pages, 'does not pretend to . . . tell the "history of the automobile". It will simply be an opportunity for me to reveal the thoughts, the ideas, the convictions, the feelings that have made up the tissue of my canvas. [I hope] the reader,' he almost begged, '[will] be generous with the "author", like many have been with the car manufacturer.'[32]

My Terrible Joys would have great success in terms of both sales and reviews. In the six months following its first edition, it went through two more printings. In a very short period, it would be translated and published in France, Belgium, Germany, Great Britain, Spain, the United States, Portugal, Japan, Czechoslovakia and the Netherlands.[33] The literary critic of the French newspaper *Le Figaro* loved it: 'Infallible eye, delicate heart in a chest made of steel, Ferrari the wizard of red sports cars, the Lord of Modena, Le Mans, Rheims and other circuits, is an author of the most authentic romantic tradition.'[34]

American Dream

The year 1962 had been a record year for Ferrari, which had built and sold close to five hundred cars. Italian customers bought about a third, but the portion going to faraway shores was continuing to grow, year after year.

On 12 January 1963, during his traditional gathering with customers and suppliers, along with the drivers of the previous season, Ferrari honoured Luigi Chinetti, his trusted point man in the US market and owner of the North American Racing Team (NART), and Colonel Ronald John Hoare, the Ferrari representative in the UK.[1]

Three months later, on an early spring morning, Franco Gozzi received a phone call. At the other end of the phone was Filmer Paradise, the president of the Italian branch of Ford Motor Company. In Italian, flavoured with a strong American accent, Paradise asked if he could speak to Enzo Ferrari. Gozzi said that he would take a message. Paradise insisted: Was Ferrari in his office or not? He wasn't interested in leaving any messages; he only wanted to speak with him.

Gozzi, who had a cup of coffee in one hand and a crossword puzzle magazine in the other, said that Ferrari had not arrived yet.[2]

'Tell him that I called to know if he is interested in meeting me,' the American manager said.[3]

Ferrari arrived at the office in the late afternoon. It was one of those days where he'd said he had some business engagement outside Modena, and only Peppino knew where he was really going.[4] Gozzi informed him of the phone call. Ferrari had met Paradise a couple of years earlier, and wondered what he wanted. They had seen each other at public occasions but had never met in private. Ferrari concluded that, in all likelihood, something was going on.

Consequently he asked Gozzi to arrange the meeting, giving instructions to organize it in Modena, in the old Scuderia Ferrari headquarters in Viale Trento Trieste, away from prying eyes. He also recommended the strictest confidence within the company ranks. Gozzi called Paradise, and the meeting was set for two days later, Friday 12 April 1963.[5]

When they met, Paradise got straight to business. He asked Ferrari if he was interested in discussing a possible collaboration with Ford, in Italy. He explained that Ford's sales were growing both in Italy and in Europe, and that a gran turismo designed by Ferrari and built by Ford in 'significant numbers for the European market' was something that would make sense for both of them.[6]

Ferrari was certainly interested but also quickly realized there must be more. The president of a national subsidiary didn't have the authority to discuss business plans with another manufacturer. Although Ferrari's interest was whetted by this first proposal, he was certain that Paradise had something else in store. He was not mistaken; he had an unfailing sixth sense for some things. Paradise played his cards, and asked if Ferrari was interested in a real 'industrial partnership'.[7]

Ferrari said yes, he was interested in an industrial agreement with Ford. He said that he had always seen himself as a small constructor, not an industrialist. He was building road cars only to finance his racing activity. 'The production growth' of his company, he said, 'interested him only if it was managed by others.'[8] The only condition that he set forth in order to engage in any discussion with Ford Motor Company, he said, was 'complete independence'[9] in the management of his motor-racing activity.

They parted with the understanding that they would soon meet again with a small delegation of Ford managers for an exact assessment of the economic value of Ferrari.[10]

That night Paradise informed the Ford headquarters in Dearborn, Michigan, that the meeting had gone well and that Enzo Ferrari was interested in the operation. Five executives prepared to leave immediately for Italy. The leader of the expedition was a 38-year-old British engineer named Roy Lunn. Having worked in the 1950s at Aston Martin, he was the only engineer at Ford with any real experience in European sports cars. If an agreement was reached, in all likelihood he would be the new technical director of Ferrari in Maranello.

When they arrived in Italy, Lunn and his four companions were greeted with curiosity rather than hostility. For three weeks, they and their colleagues, who joined them later on,[11] checked even the smallest detail with the heads of each department at Ferrari, a company that this year would produce roughly six hundred cars – that is, half of what the Ford plant along the Rouge River in Dearborn produced in a single day.

Every night Ferrari received the American delegation in his office. He was aided and flanked by administrative director Della Casa, commercial director Manicardi and his personal attorney, Cuoghi. Italians and Americans discussed, approved and then translated all of the paperwork.[12]

In the early days of May, a complete assessment of everything that existed in Maranello and its value was ready. The resulting figure was $18 million – a sum that Enzo Ferrari thought fit for concluding the operation. Henry Ford, whose personal wealth was equal to about half a billion dollars, gave his approval for the purchase. At this point Ford Motor Company's top executive in charge of the whole operation, Lee Iacocca, sent his deputy Don Frey to Maranello, to sign the agreement.[13] Meanwhile, Ferrari, to alleviate any doubts, and with 'an intimate feeling of patriotic fervour',[14] had investigated the three largest Italian car manufacturers. Before selling to the Americans, he wanted to be sure that he had no real alternatives in Italy. But the three answers that he obtained, although different, made him realize that the spirit of national unity that had been felt throughout the country only two years earlier at the celebration of the centennial of Italian unification had quickly faded.

At this point, Ferrari was convinced that if any criticism arose on the part of the Italian media or the wider public, he would be able to say honestly that no Italian company had been willing to help him. Ford was his only chance if he wished to stay at the top of motor racing and ensure a future for his company. Ferrari's racing licence would remain Italian and his cars would go on racing painted in red – and that, in the end, was all that mattered.[15]

When Don Frey arrived in Maranello and met Enzo Ferrari, he found him at peace with the idea of signing an agreement of that scale with an American manufacturer. In the course of several long meetings – made even longer by the inevitable continuous translation – Italians and Americans never found themselves in real disagreement. Ferrari even began to sketch possible logos for the companies that would be born from the union of Ferrari and Ford. This was the direction in which they were travelling: the creation of two new companies.

Therefore, when on Wednesday 15 May Frey and two colleagues sat down at the table with Enzo Ferrari and his men to start the final talks, everything led them to believe that only the time required to draft, read and sign the necessary documents separated the two companies from a landmark agreement. That day the Americans signed a brief note that Enzo Ferrari had personally handwritten, in which the creation of two companies was established: Ferrari-Ford and Ford-Ferrari. The first would have 'the purpose of creating prototypes and racing cars to compete in all professional motor races in the world'. The second 'would build touring cars for the Italian and European markets'.[16] Enzo Ferrari would own 90 per cent of the shares of the first company and would be its president, with full powers. Of the second, Ferrari would be the vice president and own a 10 per cent stake. As far as his duties in the Ford-Ferrari company were concerned, Enzo would limit himself to 'technical supervision of production'.[17]

On the evening of Monday 20 May 1963, on a desk in Ferrari's office, all of the typewritten documents that had been prepared by Ford's lawyers in the previous five days were laid out. One by one, all present reread each document before Frey and Ferrari signed them. A few times Ferrari mildly voiced his concern when he found 'modifications and variations to the pre-agreement signed five days earlier',[18] but he let it go, knowing that he was on the verge of an agreement that would solve any future problems for his company. But then, when he picked up attachment number 17, the one that dealt with the racing department budget, he suddenly realized that something was not right. 'It says here,' he said, raising his voice, 'that if I spend for racing more than' 450 million lire, which had been established on an annual basis, 'I will have to ask for authorization in America! Does it say the same thing even in the official text in English?' he asked Gozzi.[19]

The official text of the agreement in English confirmed that the presidency of Ferrari-Ford and 90 per cent of the shares did not guarantee the full and unrestricted autonomy that Enzo had indicated was his only and indispensable condition for any agreement, from day one. Seeing that his fundamental negotiation goal had been ignored, Ferrari exploded in anger. He had specifically asked to 'be absolutely free and independent' in the formulation and management of his motor-racing activity, 'free to determine programmes, free in the choice of means and men'.[20] What, then, were those restrictions?

The answer wounded him deeply.

'Mr Ferrari,' Frey said, 'you have decided to sell your company; do you still want to dispose of it at will?'[21]

Doing everything in his power to stop himself from knocking over the table,[22] Ferrari said that he had sold the *industrial* sector of his company, *not* the racing department.

He was about to detonate.

He looked at Frey and asked: 'How much do you think that I can commit to, without prior consent from Detroit?'[23] And when Frey replied that the maximum figure was ten thousand dollars, Ferrari's anger turned to despair.

At that point, he really began to scream. He shouted to the Americans that they had cheated him, deceived him and betrayed him. On the first page of attachment number 17, he underlined with his purple fountain pen the paragraphs that had infuriated him. Then, on the margin of the paper he wrote: 'No, this is not good!'[24] Complete with a huge exclamation mark. And while he was writing, he screamed, of course in Italian, yelling words that no one dared translate.

The members of the Ford delegation, who had a little earlier attempted to maintain a calm, unemotional reaction, looked at him, stunned.

Then, suddenly, Ferrari fell silent.

Looking at Gozzi, as if the storm had never taken place, with incredible self-control he said: 'Let's go eat something.'[25]

They left the meeting room, exited the building and crossed the street to enter the Cavallino Restaurant. It was 10pm.

The agreement with Ford was no more.

Thinking back over what had happened, Enzo Ferrari, who had strongly believed in a deal with Ford,[26] realized what a fool he had been. It had taken him until that last night to realize that the whole situation with Ford would have been but a repetition of what had happened in 1938, when he had sold Scuderia Ferrari to Alfa Romeo to become director of Alfa Corse, ending up in a gilded cage.[27]

Independence had cost him dearly: by cancelling the deal, he lost out on 12 billion lire, plus the two companies' shares.[28]

*   *   *

The 1963 F1 World Championship started the weekend following the agitated end of negotiations between Ford and Ferrari, with the Monaco Grand Prix. Earlier in the year, Ferrari had witnessed the departure not only of Phil Hill, but also of Giancarlo Baghetti, the young driver on whom he had placed so much hope. Both had gone to ATS, a new team created in nearby Bologna, whose technical director was none other than Carlo Chiti,[29] one of the eight executives he had fired in November 1961, thirsty for revenge.

On 4 August 1963, Ferrari won his first grand prix in nearly two years. Victory was not completely unexpected, as the potential of the 158 had already been established in the previous races, but it helped to restore confidence within the team. After the race and the ritual call to Maranello, team manager Dragoni gathered the whole team together to convey Ferrari's heartfelt thanks.

That same day, Mairesse had a crash that would leave him sidelined for the next races. Ferrari, who in the course of the year had fielded Lodovico Scarfiotti, put in another Italian driver for Mairesse. The substitute was Lorenzo Bandini, who had raced the first events of the season with a BRM entered by the small Scuderia Centro Sud team.

The rest of the season was a huge disappointment, however, which was not mitigated by two fifth-place finishes earned by Bandini in the United States and

South African Grand Prix. Surtees did no better than fourth place in the final standings, topped by new world champion Jim Clark.

Ferrari consoled himself with a victory in the 1963 International Manufacturers' Gran Turismo Championship, where the 250 GTO had no rivals, and with his second consecutive title in the World Challenge Endurance. The day of glory was 15 June, when the all-Italian Scarfiotti–Bandini pair, at the wheel of the P 250 prototype, won the Le Mans 24 Hours.

And, of course, further consolation came with the profits from the growing sales of his road cars: 598 units sold[30] – 100 more than the year before. In 1963, the Maranello plant had produced an average of two cars per day. With the line expansion that had been built in the course of the year, production would be increased to three a day in 1964.[31]

The never-signed agreement with Ford Motor Company had killed the possibility of access to significant sums of money. For this reason, and because he wanted to go on competing in all racing categories, during 1964 Ferrari could not afford more than two F1 cars until Monza, when he entrusted a third one to Scarfiotti. The Italian Grand Prix was right after Lorenzo Bandini's first career win in Austria in mid-August. Despite his victory at Zeltweg, the World Championship had until then been a race between Brit Graham Hill in a BRM and Scot Jim Clark in a Lotus, the 1962 and 1963 world champions, because, as always, Ferrari waited until after the Le Mans 24 Hours before he really put a hand to the new F1 car.[32] Monza, however, completely changed the face of the championship.

On 6 September John Surtees won hands down an Italian Grand Prix that he had dominated from qualifying. With the nine points for this victory, he was just two points behind Clark (in second place) and four behind Hill, who was leading in the championship standings. Surtees and Ferrari were thus well in contention for the title. Except that, immediately after the Monza race, Enzo Ferrari had returned his competitor's licence to the CSAI Italian Motor Racing Committee. With this gesture, he took himself out of the quest for the 1964 F1 world title. What led to such a controversial and unprecedented act?

At the 1963 Paris Motor Show, Ferrari had introduced the car that first joined, and then replaced, the 250 GTO in GT races. To celebrate the prestigious victory of two Italian drivers in the most famous endurance race in the world – the win by Scarfiotti and Bandini in June – he had named the new car the 250 Le Mans.

To acquire homologation for the GT championship, it was necessary to build at least one hundred units. The rule applied to all car manufacturers, from the world's largest to smaller ones like Ferrari. The apparent obstacle deriving from the construction of so many units and from the major financial commitment that it involved was normally bypassed by demonstrating that you were *able* to build a hundred of them; after homologation some manufacturers had not even gone on to build all one hundred. And even those that actually built a hundred cars did it step by step, financing the production of later cars with the money made selling the earlier ones.

In early July 1964, the head of the technical and sporting department of the CSI International Sporting Committee, the body in charge of homologating cars for all officially sanctioned world championships, had gone to Maranello. In the course of his visit, Mr Schild had counted seven finished 250 Le Mans units, six in the finishing stage at Scaglietti's Modena workshop, seven on the Maranello production line, four complete engines and gearboxes, nine cars being built at Scaglietti's and, last, four chassis being built at Vaccari's, Ferrari's chassis manufacturer. Schild had counted a total of 37 cars.[33] Sixty-three units were still needed to reach the planned one hundred.

Ferrari said that a good number of cars had previously been delivered to customers, who had already raced them on tracks such as Daytona, Sebring, the Nürburgring, Reims and, of course, Le Mans. At Schild's specific request to know the total number of cars built, and to see the documentation attesting to the number of those already delivered, Ferrari had said 'No,' adding that what was important was to have demonstrated that 'the car was being built in series, and earnestly'.[34]

Back home, Schild had confirmed in a written report that the 250 Le Mans model was 'really produced'.[35] But since he had counted only 37 units, and Ferrari had not wanted to indicate the total number that had already been built, the request for homologation was postponed to a later CSI meeting. The next meeting had been called for 2 September 1964, in Milan, the week of the Grand Prix of Italy. In Milan, Ferrari had been betrayed – as he saw it – even by the Automobile Club of Italy, which not only had failed to defend him, but, in spite of Fiat's Gianni Agnelli's pressure on its president, had also supported the refusal to homologate the 250 Le Mans.[36]

Thus, in open disagreement with the CSI, which, he said, was unfairly penalizing him, and with the Automobile Club of Italy, which had not defended him, the day after Surtees's win at Monza Enzo had returned his CSAI competitor's licence and his ACI membership card, which he had had for 43 years. 'I realized too late,' he would bitterly comment, 'that the belief the interests of my small factory could benefit not only myself, but also my country and the international prestige of Italian sports authorities, was just a presumptuous illusion.'[37]

There were now only two races left in the F1 World Championship – the Grand

Prix of the United States and the Grand Prix of Mexico. While protesting against the FIA and screaming his disappointment at the Italian ruling bodies made him feel better, Ferrari did not wish to throw away the opportunity to deal with those gentlemen from the privileged position of F1 world champion. Thus, he called his friend Chinetti in New York and then announced the solution.

Surtees's and Bandini's 158s were not going to be officially fielded by Scuderia Ferrari, but by the North American Racing Team. And, as cars of a US team, Ferrari would abandon Italy's red and paint his cars in the white-and-blue colours of the United States. To be sure that the message was loud and clear, Ferrari did not simply choose the colour normally used by Chinetti's NART – Ferrari-red with a white-and-blue centre stripe – but had the bottom of his cars painted in blue and the top in white, with a blue stripe running down the middle. To complete the work, instead of the shield with the prancing horse, he had Chinetti apply NART's rectangular sticker, which incorporated elements of the Scuderia's graphics.

It was thus at the wheel of a white-and-blue Ferrari that, on 25 October 1964, John Surtees became, because of a single point, the new champion, at the end of a grand prix that stirred many a controversy because of teammate Bandini's race conduct, which led to a crash that left Surtees's rival for the world title sidelined.

The next CSI meeting was held in Paris on 6 October. By then, even Ferry Porsche, son of the founder and general manager of Porsche, had personally voiced his solidarity with Enzo Ferrari, stating: 'All the manufacturers that have homologated GT models were outlaws. In this situation, the fairest of all was Ferrari, and therefore I am amazed at the decision that has been taken against him.'[38]

But even the influential intercession of a manufacturer such as Porsche did nothing to solve the issue of the homologation of the 250 Le Mans, which was finally rejected until Ferrari could prove that he had built all hundred units.[39] At the end of the year, looking ahead to 1965, Ferrari could only say that 'without the homologation of the 250 Le Mans, we will not be in a position to defend the title that for so many years, with the help and enthusiasm of our customers, was ours.'[40]

Although it was characterized by such unnerving and endless controversy, 1964 had been a year that also brought great satisfaction to Enzo Ferrari, beyond, of course, the conquest of the F1 World Championship with John Surtees. On 15 July Enzo Ferrari had, for the first time since September 1939, gone back to the Alfa Romeo headquarters at Milan's Portello.

A quarter of a century had passed since the company that was too politicized to understand the anxiety of continuous advancement that animated and tormented him had shown him the door. He must have savoured every step of that visit, every look, every scent. 'I walked into the old Via Gattamelata courtyard and, almost trembling, I looked around. Only a few things had changed. But I felt an air of impersonality that troubled me a little,'[41] he would recall.

Luraghi did not give him the time to finish his opening sentence. The Alfa Romeo top executive said that *he* was glad to have been in a position to do something for Ferrari, who, with his cars, was doing so much for Italian motor racing. For Enzo it must have been immensely satisfying to hear such words spoken by the president of Alfa Romeo, the make that he had adored and then hated, but to which, as he discovered when he'd begun to defeat it on international race tracks, he still felt incredibly close. 'Ferrari,' Luraghi said, 'you always stay in your factory and in your town, but if you went around the world as I do, you would quickly find out the reputation that you enjoy everywhere.'[42] The ice broken, Ferrari was assailed by memories. He had spent 20 years with Alfa Romeo, formative years preparatory to his later activity. He had known Luraghi since 1946, when he'd served as general manager of Pirelli, the other Milan company for which Ferrari had always had a soft spot.

In so many ways, Enzo had returned home. But in the excitement of the moment he missed a chance to test the waters. He had broken off negotiations with Ford 14 months earlier and had rejected, 6 months later, an attempt on the part of the Americans at reopening the talks.[43] At that moment, no other manufacturer was on the horizon. The idea of mentioning something to Luraghi did flash through his mind, but Enzo chose to defer it. Five years later, he would be sorry.[44] After handing over his Italian competitor's licence, Ferrari had said that, in 1965, his cars would be painted in the national colours of the private teams that he would designate to represent him.[45] 'We are out of the control of the C S A I,' Enzo warned everyone at the end of the year, 'and we will remain out. This does not mean that we don't want to get an Italian licence; it would be against our sentiments.'[46]

But before Christmas, he refused to confirm that in 1965 his racing cars would return to the familiar Italy-red.

David and Goliath

The day after the tumultuous end of the negotiations with Enzo Ferrari, Don Frey had gone back to Detroit. The following day, he had personally met Henry Ford II to report on what had happened. As he was describing the details of that fateful evening of 20 May 1963, Ford had become increasingly agitated.

'Very well,' Ford said when Frey ended his report. 'We will race against him, and we will defeat him.'[1]

The Americans had been quick. After briefly courting Colin Chapman, they had bought Lola and turned the English team's Slough workshop into the headquarters of Ford's European motor-racing operations.

The first round had gone to Ferrari. Frenchman Jean Guichet and Italian Nino Vaccarella had won the 1964 Le Mans 24 Hours at the wheel of a 275 P Ferrari. Enzo had not underestimated Ford's challenge, and had sent to France three 275 Ps, and as many 330 Ps. Result: Ferrari's drivers had occupied the entire podium.

The three Ford GTs had impressed everyone with their speed, but had all been forced to withdraw. Before Forghieri had left for Le Mans, Enzo had discussed strategy with him and ordered that Surtees be as quick as possible in the first phase of the race, to force Ford to send at least a couple of cars in pursuit. 'I am curious to see how long the Fords will resist at an average speed of 130 miles per hour [209km/h],' he had said.[2]

He had not been mistaken. Two of the three Fords had withdrawn with gearbox troubles.[3]

But 1965 promised to be a whole different story.

*   *   *

The first day in March 1965, Ferrari and Fiat announced a partnership for the construction of 500 units of a 6-cylinder, 1.6-litre engine. The construction of all engines would take place within a 12-month period so that the International Sports Committee could homologate the engine. From that engine – whose not-so-distant parent was Dino Ferrari's 65-degree 6-cylinder V-configuration – Enzo would derive a power unit for the F2 championship series,[4] and Fiat, the engine for an agile, high-performing sports car that was going to be named the Dino.

The agreement was, first and foremost, an important step on the road that would one day take Enzo Ferrari to Turin. Having missed the chance to talk business with Alfa Romeo when he had met Luraghi in July 1964, Ferrari knew that the only real prospect in Italy for his company lay with Fiat. This was because no one could predict where the duel on the track with Ford would take him, and a small manufacturer such as Ferrari needed an industrial giant at this point in the game. And then, there was a personal matter that was not at all secondary: after the signing, Ferrari did not hide from his men his excitement at the thought of the largest Italian car manufacturer building an automobile bearing the name of his late son.[5]

On 10 May 1965, Enzo Ferrari handed over the position of general manager to Piero Gobbato, the son of Ugo Gobbato, who'd fired him from Alfa Romeo in September 1939. Enzo would remain president of the company.[6]

As much as Ferrari continued to pride himself on being a small manufacturer, his factory had become an important industrial reality. After the firing of the directors at the end of 1961, the command structure had never really been reconstructed. The days of a single man at the helm were gone. Ferrari had built more than 650 cars in 1964, and in 1965 there was every intention to make well over 700.

What was needed now was a man to whom all company departments would report. A young man – Gobbato was 47 years old – who would oversee all company functions and report solely to Enzo Ferrari. Gianni Agnelli had suggested Gobbato to Enzo. He was one of his most brilliant executives who, in light of the spirit of cooperation, Fiat's boss had offered to Ferrari.[7]

With the appointment of Gobbato, who relieved Enzo from an important amount of work, Ferrari would also be freer to concentrate on racing activity.

*   *   *

The F1 World Championship had started on the first day of the year with the Grand Prix of South Africa in East London. Ferrari had naturally returned to the red, which he'd chosen for the two 158s of world champion John Surtees and Lorenzo Bandini. He explained that he'd done it because the CSAI, who had not defended him when the FIA had refused to homologate the 250 Le Mans, had at least homologated it for Italian races.[8] At times he could be satisfied with not having much, but the show of strength and the bombastic protest had been seen and heard by all, and nothing could make him abandon the red that had adorned the cars of Nazzaro, Campari, Ascari and Borzacchini. Surtees finished second behind Jim Clark, driving a Lotus-Climax.

On 30 May Bandini came second in the Monaco Grand Prix and Surtees finished fourth. But one morning a few days later, when Ferrari called Mauro Forghieri into his office, he wanted to talk about Surtees. Ferrari handed his chief engineer a copy of *Auto Italiana* magazine, opened to a three-page story titled 'Surtees's Hobby'. The article, written by British journalist David Phipps, explained that the 1964 F1 champion had such a passion for motor racing that he had created his own team with which to participate in the sports car championship races that Ferrari did not enter.

It was true: Ferrari had personally authorized Surtees to do so – something that had no precedent in his company's history. But Enzo held John in high esteem: he had been a motorcycle champion like Nuvolari, and Ferrari had always appreciated his deep technical background. What Ferrari had not imagined was that his driver could cooperate in the design and development of a racing car built by others.

Forghieri agreed that, yes, there were some similarities, especially in the front end. But when Forghieri said that, in light of the current regulations, it was difficult to build a completely different car from all the others, Ferrari replied: 'The Americans have done it. The Ford GT doesn't look like our cars, and not even like the others.'[9]

On 13 June, in the Belgian Grand Prix at Spa, the two Ferraris did not shine. But all eyes were by now fixed on the 33rd Le Mans 24 Hours of 19–20 June, the stage for the 2nd all-out fight between Ferrari and Ford.

Both contenders showed up in force. Ferrari lined up ten cars between those officially fielded by his works team and those entrusted to the private teams of Chinetti, Hoare and Swaters, on which Enzo knew that he could always count. Ford brought to France 11 Ford GTs and Cobra Daytonas. To these cars, one had to add the seven works cars entered by Porsche.

The race was exhausting as always, the pace even more hectic than usual given the fierce rivalry between the Detroit giant and the small Maranello manufacturer. As a consequence, no works Fords and no works Ferraris managed to finish the race. The last to surrender was the 330 P2 Ferrari of Parkes and Guichet, which withdrew after 315 laps. But since Ferrari could always count on his parallel network of teams operated by his importers, he managed to win the second round of the duel with Ford.

The 1965 Le Mans 24 Hours was won by the Ferrari 250 Le Mans – the car that the CSI had failed to homologate in the gran turismo category. It was entered by Luigi Chinetti's NART and entrusted by Chinetti to American Masten Gregory and Austrian Jochen Rindt. Thanks to his importer's teams, Ferrari actually conquered the whole podium: Belgian Gosselin and Frenchman Dumay finished second in the 250 Le Mans owned by the latter; in third was the Belgian pair of Mairesse and Blaton, in the 275 GTB entered by Jacques Swaters's Ecurie Francorchamps.

Success at Le Mans was once again complete.

But Enzo Ferrari was a man who had never deceived himself. He could read the results of a race better than anyone else, and if on the one hand the conquest of the podium by his importers' private teams made him proud, on the other hand it irritated him. The technical failure of all his works prototypes was not an encouraging sign for the future. In addition, the Ford GTs, despite not yet being reliable, were enormously powerful.

But the plot was thickening. To help it defeat Ferrari, Ford was now courting his men – not his engineers, but his importers. At the centre of attention was Colonel Hoare, the remarkable English importer of Ferraris and owner of the Maranello Concessionaires team. Ford wanted him as a dealer-importer for the UK of a special series of GTs built with English coachbuilder Radford. They were not asking him to give up importing Ferraris, but to add to his roster. While it was clear to Hoare that the economic benefit of a Ford partnership in an English-speaking country was of paramount importance, he had no idea what Ferrari's reaction might be.

The colonel personally went to Maranello to convince Ferrari to let him take the Ford contract. It was not an easy negotiation, but finally Ferrari was left with no choice but to accept.[10]

Two third-place finishes by Surtees in France and England were the best results the F1 team took home in the second half of the season. On 25 September, the British driver suffered a terrible crash on the Canadian circuit of Mosport while testing the Lola T70 that had made Ferrari and Forghieri suspicious in the spring, and his racing season ended there.

But if the F1 World Championship had given him little gratification, Ferrari could always take comfort in the wins of his sports prototypes. In addition to Le Mans, cars with the prancing horse on the hood had triumphed in all major 1965 endurance races – the Monza and Nürburgring 1000km and the Targa Florio – and they had won the International Prototype Trophy.

*   *   *

Well past the age of 90 now, Adalgisa Ferrari had lost little of her volcanic energy, although her visits to her son's office had become less frequent. They had gradually lost the fire that had animated many a stormy moment when, after loudly arguing with Enzo, she would leave the office, slamming the door and shouting at the first person she met: 'I pity you; you have to work with *this* guy . . . I don't know how you do it. I had two sons,' she would continue. 'The intelligent one died in the war, and all I was left with was *this* one . . .'[11]

On 15 October 1965, however, Adalgisa died in her Corso Canal Grande apartment. She was 93 years old. That afternoon Enzo went to her apartment to check papers and documents. He took 20-year-old Piero with him. Opening a drawer, he found some photographs. He came upon a framed one, and he unceremoniously passed it on to Piero. 'Keep this with you,' he said. 'This young man was your brother.'[12]

Enzo had long ago promised Adalgisa that he would find Piero a job at Ferrari. It would not be easy, because Laura continued to wander at will around the company. But he had promised and the time to keep the promise had come.

Looking at the future, and thus to 1966, he could see the clash with Ford on the horizon. The US manufacturer had a colossal budget. Ferrari had 160 men in all, who took care of the design, construction and development of racing cars for all categories, as well as assisting in all the series in which these cars participated.[13]

Like David in front of Goliath, Ferrari chose not to hide: 'In front of so much consideration' on the part of Ford, he said in December, 'we should just quit racing. But after spending a lifetime saying that races are useful to all of us, can we quit today, when everyone is returning to the roots, rediscovering motor racing as a decisive factor in human progress?'[14]

* * *

On 3 April 1966, old Pinin Farina died. He was almost 73. Since 1961, a decree of then president of the Italian Republic, Giovanni Gronchi, had changed his last name from Farina to Pininfarina.

Ferrari had quit going to funerals a long time ago. Whenever he could, he made a visit the day before instead. Pinin had died in Lausanne and was subsequently taken to Grugliasco, on the outskirts of Turin, for the funeral. Ferrari came from Maranello and stood ten minutes in silent prayer before the coffin. Then he turned to Pinin's son and said: 'Sergio, from now on, let's you and

I be on a first-name basis.' It was his very personal way of showing appreciation to father *and* son.[15]

*   *   *

The new F1 car had been unveiled on 11 December 1965. For the third year in a row, the drivers were John Surtees and Lorenzo Bandini. They were fast, reliable and, above all, in harmony with each other.[16] The new car made its debut with a win in a non-championship race at Syracuse, but as the championship got started, Surtees's stay in Maranello was coming to an end.

The misunderstanding about the Englishman's participation in the design of the Lola T70 that had irritated Ferrari and Forghieri in June the previous year had never really been resolved. And the crash that Surtees had suffered in Canada in September, which had prevented him from participating in the last two races of the 1965 F1 championship, had further upset Ferrari.

In Maranello there were some who threw fuel on the fire. Personal relations between Surtees and sports-car driver Michael Parkes had never been good, and the two Englishmen in King Enzo's court had gone to war with each other. Inside the factory, and especially inside the racing department, alliances were made. Parkes, who wanted to race in F1 as well as with the prototypes, had long realized that there was bad blood between Surtees and team manager Dragoni, and had fuelled the politics of suspicion.[17]

An already-tense situation exploded on Saturday 22 May in Monte Carlo when, during qualifying, driver and team manager had a war of words in front of the team, reporters and public. Dragoni accused Surtees of having wrecked the differential with deliberately brutal driving. And when Dragoni returned to Maranello, he tried to convince Ferrari to get rid of his former world champion.

On Monday afternoon, Ferrari called a meeting and asked Surtees to attend. He listened to the explanations of both driver and team manager, but did not make any decision. Then, after the meeting, he ordered Gozzi to call 25-year-old Italian-American Mario Andretti in the United States, to find out if he was free and interested in driving for him.

On Tuesday, Ferrari called a second meeting, this time without Surtees. On the agenda was the possible removal of their 1964 world champion. Ferrari did not express his views, but said that he was interested in the opinions of the other men around the table. Some were in favour, others were not. Concerning the drivers, Gozzi said that Bandini was not a number one; that Parkes was not as good in F1 cars as he was in prototypes; and that Andretti – whom he had talked with on the phone – was happy to drive for Ferrari, but was not available until the following year. Last to speak was Dragoni, who reminded all present that Surtees, when he visited the workshop, had always looked with great interest at the 330 P3. His deliberate allusion to the Lola issue convinced everyone, including Ferrari.[18]

Ferrari knew what he was losing by firing Surtees,[19] but he had never really got to the bottom of the Lola issue, and in his mind the idea of Surtees's involvement in a possible double-cross had grown. Therefore, he decided to announce Surtees's dismissal at the end of the next race, the Grand Prix of Belgium on 12 June.

To handle the situation in the best possible way – the conflict within the team was known to all – and to prove that the decision had been made directly by him, Ferrari sent Franco Gozzi, who'd just started to manage his company's and team's public relations, to Spa. But in a race characterized in the early stages by a violent downpour, Surtees won, and Gozzi, who at the end of the race had desperately looked for a telephone to inform Ferrari of the outcome of the grand prix and receive instructions, was stopped. The firing had been suspended.[20]

In fact, it was only postponed. On Wednesday 15 June, at Le Mans, Surtees did some test laps at the wheel of the 330 P3, with which he thought he was racing Sunday's 24 Hours. When he pitted, another argument broke out between him and Dragoni. The quarrel was once again violent and public, and almost certainly provoked by the team manager.[21] At the end of it, Dragoni announced that John Surtees was fired, as if the decision was a consequence of that dispute – something for which members of the press, including Italian reporters, harshly attacked him in the following days.[22]

The truth is that all had been arranged before the team reached France. Proof of this was the document that Dragoni had carried in his pocket since leaving the factory: a sheet of paper with names written on it, in red and blue pencil. It was a personal and reserved communication from Enzo Ferrari to his team manager, one of those that could not be disregarded. On that piece of paper, on which Ferrari had personally handwritten the pairs of drivers who would take part in the 34th Le Mans 24 Hours, the name of Surtees did not appear.[23]

In this turbulent way ended one of the finest, sincerest and warmest relationships that Enzo Ferrari had ever enjoyed with one of his drivers.[24]

But the real problem for Ferrari at Le Mans that year did not come from England, but rather from the United States. On Sunday 19 June 1966, the debacle was complete. Ford took first, second and third places with its 7.0-litre GT Mk IIs, which in the twelve months since its debut had become unbeatable. Behind the three Fords came four Porsches. All the Ferrari works cars had withdrawn. The first Ferrari to cross the finish line was Colonel Hoare's 275 GTB/C driven by Piers Courage and Roy Pike, eighth – and first in the GT class.

Guest of honour at Le Mans that weekend was Henry Ford II himself, who was granted the privilege of starting the race – and, 24 hours later, waving the chequered flag at his victorious GTs.

While it was not necessarily related to the firing of John Surtees, the rout at Le Mans caused a storm in the Italian press. As always, defending Ferrari was the privilege of a few, while attacking him seemed to be the duty of many. Three days after the race, Ferrari summoned the press – relatively unusual for him in late June, accustomed as he was to meeting journalists at the end of the season, and, when the two did not coincide, at the introduction of his new cars.[25]

But that day he felt the need to explain a few things. He addressed one issue after the other, and was even more uncompromising than usual. The firing of Surtees had been decided by him and not by others. The press should know better than to think that Dragoni, or any team manager at Ferrari, enjoyed so great a power as to decide the firing of a racing driver.[26]

Ford's supremacy at Le Mans was something quite obvious in light of the huge difference in the engine displacement: 7.0 litres for their GTs versus 3.0 litres for his 330 P3s. He had anticipated it. His cars had been defeated, but those were the rules of the game, and it made no sense to make a fuss about it. Ford was able to invest in motor racing at a level that he simply would never reach and, he said, Ford did not have to struggle with the unions, which even in the course of 1966 had dictated the pace with which his men could work on his racing cars, as well as his road cars.[27]

Three weeks later, because of yet another never-ending strike, Ferrari was forced to miss the British Grand Prix.

*   *   *

On 30 June, it was exactly ten years since the death of Dino. A few years earlier Ferrari had stopped wearing black ties, but he continued to go to the cemetery every morning, right after going to the barber in Corso Canal Grande where he shaved, before going to Maranello. This he did every single day of the week, every week of the month, every month of the year, no matter the weather.

'When I cross the cemetery gate, before coming to the factory, and I sit on my son's grave, I forget everything. Time,' he admitted, 'no longer exists. It's good for me to understand that I am nothing.'[28] In his office, the three plastic carnations in front of Dino's pictured remained lit throughout the night.[29]

For some time now he had stopped listening to the tape that Dino, unbeknown to him, had recorded, to leave Enzo the sound of his voice. The young man had also recorded himself reciting verses of Leopardi. Dino had studied engineering, but had also enjoyed literature. Enzo had listened to the tape for years, alone in the evenings, but lately could no longer find the courage to listen to the voice of his son. 'I think that a pain like mine,' he confessed, 'cannot be mitigated, although I have tried in many ways to soothe it, to size it to a proportion that, in time, should have allowed me to look with a less aching soul at my tragedy.'[30]

*　*　*

Ferrari had replaced John Surtees with Mike Parkes, the tall British engineer who was formidable in sports cars and aspired to drive in F1. In the first race after his promotion, Parkes took an encouraging second place behind Australian Jack Brabham in the Grand Prix of France. But at Monza, in September, Ferrari lined up a third car that he entrusted to Ludovico Scarfiotti, grandson of the first president, and one of the founders, of Fiat.

Monza had always been the most important race of the season for Ferrari, and this year there was the additional task of keeping John Surtees away from the podium. Surtees hadn't gone to just *any* team, but to Cooper, a team equipped with engines built by Maserati in Modena, and who had finished second in Germany in August.

Between mid-August and early September, Forghieri and his men worked without pause on a new version of their 12-cylinder engine,[31] and at Monza the 312 dominated the entire race weekend: Parkes on pole position, the front row entirely to Ferrari, fastest race lap and win for Scarfiotti and second place for Parkes.

The victory of an Italian driver in the Italian Grand Prix greatly pleased Ferrari,[32] but the glory days of F1 ended there that year. 'Finally,' Enzo Ferrari wrote at the end of 1966, 'we have been defeated at Le Mans. An event that we had expected, and that found us morally prepared. Humiliated and offended? No. We welcome sporting victory by those who have deserved it, after having tenaciously pursued it.'[33]

Was he sincere? Probably, albeit in his own peculiar way.[34]

'As crazy as it sounds, the Detroit–Maranello match continues, as far as we are concerned,' he promised.[35]

Turin

Après mois, le deluge . . .,' Enzo Ferrari said in French, quoting King Louis XV in the tone of an experienced stage actor while answering a question asked by journalist Gino Rancati on the future of his company.[1]

It was the last question at a round table with five reporters: Canestrini, Benzing, Bernabò, Boschi and Mariani, all chosen by Ferrari,[2] hosted by Gino Rancati and filmed and broadcast by Italian television on the evening of 13 December 1966. Ferrari had preferred this format to the traditional conference in Modena, which had reached giant dimensions – the one hundred journalists of seven or eight years before had now become two hundred, and sometimes more. Thus, the idea of a sort of debate to be broadcast on television, just like the political forums that he liked to watch.[3] As with Louis XV, Enzo's implication was that there would likely be chaos after his tenure was over. Would there be a Ferrari after him? Enzo Ferrari would turn 69 in just 2 months, in February 1967, and the question was legitimate. Rancati suggested that it was a 'dramatic subject'.[4]

'The tragedy,' said Ferrari, 'is in the answer.'

He had been asked the same question by the unnamed journalist – Ormezzano, followed by Roghi – in the closing pages of the first chapter of his memoirs, four years earlier: *You said: the future. What will happen to Ferrari after Ferrari?* And the answer, although worded differently, had been the same: 'I had my son. But in life, you make a lot of projects, which then fate, circumstances, fatality, turn upside-down.'[5] Dino had died ten years earlier. Piero had been working in his father's company for a little over a year but, officially, he did not yet exist.

After John Surtees, Eugenio Dragoni left Ferrari as well. He had become too unpopular with the press for Enzo to consider confirming him for another year. As a provocation against those journalists who had attacked Dragoni for months, Ferrari chose one of them as his new team manager.[6] Franco Lini may not have possessed the qualities of a great team manager,[7] but, as an experienced and talented journalist, he knew what made headlines.

A few minutes before noon on Sunday 5 February 1967, EDT, 6pm in Modena, Lini gave a specific order to the three drivers of the two 330 P4s and one 330 P3 that were leading the Daytona 24 Hours, the first round of the 1967 World Sports Prototype Trophy series. He asked them to wait for one another in order to parade together as they crossed the finish line at the stroke of the 24th hour. Lini the journalist knew perfectly well that that photograph would show the Ferrari supremacy at Daytona better than thousands of words.

He was right. The photograph of the Bandini–Amon, Parkes–Scarfiotti and Rodríguez–Guichet Ferraris parading down the final straight quickly went around the world. Daytona was not Le Mans, but Ferrari had defeated Ford in their home race.[8]

As Enzo himself had said, the future of Ferrari had yet to be written. But more and more evidence indicated that the future, sooner or later, would take him to Turin, where, on 25 February 1967, in homage to Fiat, which had produced the engine, Ferrari introduced the new F2 car – the Dino 166 F2.

'The relationship with Fiat,' Ferrari said that day, 'is one of cooperation, in perfect harmony and mutual understanding.' The core of that partnership was the engine 'that we have designed', he said, and 'that Fiat will produce in series'. Moreover, he added, 'whenever we need a laboratory test, we know that turning to Turin, we will find men and equipment to meet our needs'. But, he warned, no one should see in this cooperation more than there was to it: 'Other than that, we have no other company-related association with Fiat. Absolutely [none].'[9] By 1967 Ferrari employed 470 people and produced between 650 and 700 cars per year, at the rate of 3 per day. Until just a few years earlier, Enzo had known by name all of his workers and the villages where they lived – all so close that they could easily come and go by bicycle. Lately, he had begun to panic when he came across faces that he did not recognize.

For lunch he had a private room at the Cavallino Restaurant on the other side of the road but, from time to time, if he had no guests, he would go to the factory's canteen, as in days past, and maybe sit at the table with some of his mechanics. It was rare for him to show up before 1.30pm[10] and, in any case, the conversation always suffered: Ferrari was Ferrari, particularly within the walls of his factory, and if he'd once aroused fear, now his larger-than-life persona intimidated most of his employees.[11]

He ate little: dry rice, a little meat and maybe two slices of prosciutto. He liked mandarin oranges and drank dry wine, preferably white, and mineral water. He said that he did not smoke,[12] but in reality at times he puffed on menthol cigarettes – just a few, once in a while, to be enjoyed preferably away from prying eyes.[13] 'My medicine,' he said, 'is the daily shower I take in all seasons. I start it hot and finish it cold, before I face the outdoor weather.'[14]

He dressed with more sophistication these days, compared with just a few years earlier. His wardrobe revealed a woman's touch – Fiamma's. Although she would never marry him, she remained his muse. He preferred 'not bright clothes'[15] and took pride in never purchasing neckties, but instead wearing those he received as gifts from his friends. Among them were food tycoon Pietro Barilla and Tonino Brivio, who had raced for him in the now-distant years of the Scuderia. He bought his clothes at his father's tailor's son's store. From a pocket in his trousers, a gold medal with the image of a *carabiniere* peeped out – 'I think,' he said, 'that, in all times, Italy has benefited from the deeds of carabinieri.'[16] The medal was chained to a pocket watch that he had owned for 30 years and wound manually every night.

He confessed that he felt a stranger in his own home because he went out in the morning and never came back until late in the evening, when he was 'exhausted'. The furnishings were still those that he had purchased with Laura when they got married – 'The furniture,' he said, 'is that of a middle-class family on the verge of poverty from half a century ago.'[17] There were few paintings on the walls; the photographs on the bookshelves, sideboard and tables here and there were mostly images of Dino.

He slept alone, and often fell asleep with the television on. He said that he did not sleep more than four or five hours a night. 'When a man wakes up and feels healthy, robust, and, above all, impatient to do something new,' he said, 'it means that his age is still that of a teenager and that he still has dreams to realize.'[18]

*　*　*

On 25 April 1967, at the Autodromo Nazionale in Monza, Lorenzo Bandini and Chris Amon – a short New Zealander who had arrived that winter in Maranello – repeated the feat they had accomplished at Daytona and won the Monza 1000km. Everything indicated that the 330 P4 would be able to keep up with the Ford GTs at Le Mans this year, and that Bandini and Amon would fight for victory in a race that, on its own, was worth an entire season.

But before Le Mans, there were two F1 rounds. The first was scheduled for Sunday 7 May in Monte Carlo, where Ferrari made its 1967 world championship debut, having been forced to skip the first grand prix of the year, in South Africa in January, once again because of the ongoing problems with the trade unions – strikes that had compromised the preparation of the cars.

Second in qualifying behind Brabham, second in the race behind Hulme, on lap eighty-two Lorenzo's Ferrari swerved at the chicane leading to the harbour. In all likelihood, he was tired. His Ferrari struck some bales of straw on the side of the road, overturned and caught fire. From the port of Monte Carlo a sombre column of black smoke rose. Watching the images on his black-and-white television screen in his Maranello office, Enzo felt that it had to be Lorenzo.

Ferrari had loved Lorenzo.[19] He had never considered him a sublime driver, but had always appreciated the dedication with which he went about his work, and the loyalty he'd displayed to Ferrari and his company. Bandini felt the rivalry with Scarfiotti, the other Italian on the team, and Ferrari had understood that; driver and team owner had known that 1967 could be Lorenzo's year, and Enzo had moved Scarfiotti to sports cars, promoting to the F1 team Chris Amon, who was young and from the other side of the world, and therefore harmless in Bandini's eyes.[20] Thirty days after Bandini's death, on 10–11 June, three works Ferraris took part in the 1967 Le Mans 24 Hours, the fourth one since Ford had chosen it as a battleground with Ferrari. Only a single Ferrari made it to the finish line, the 330 P4 driven by Ludovico Scarfiotti and Mike Parkes. They finished second, four laps behind the Ford GT40 Mk IV driven by Americans Dan Gurney and A J Foyt. Third place went to the Ecurie Francorchamps 330 P4 Ferrari of Mairesse and Blaton, fielded by Swaters. Compared with 12 months earlier, Ferrari had at least saved face, but Enzo was the first to know that 'the runner-up is only the first of the losers'.[21]

At the Spa circuit, during the first lap of the Grand Prix of Belgium, Parkes suffered a crash; although it was less dramatic than Bandini's, it was equally conclusive for his career, which came to an end that day. In the remaining races of the season, Ferrari lined up only one single-seater for Chris Amon, who did not go beyond a few podium finishes for a final fifth place in the standings.

At the September Frankfurt Auto Show, Ferrari introduced the final evolution of the prototype whose first version had been shown at the 1965 Paris Salon de l'Automobile. It was the little Ferrari, the Ferrarina – 'almost a Ferrari', as one could read a few months later in the commercial brochure. 'Minuscule, quick, safe',[22] the Dino Ferrari was a small car with a six-cylinder engine, revealing the evolution of the powertrain once advocated by Enzo's son, positioned transversely behind the cockpit.

The body had soft lines, was sleek and looked compact. Entirely made in aluminium by Scaglietti in Modena, it had been designed by Pininfarina with the clear intention of lasting over time and inspiring later, and larger, Ferraris.[23] In place of the rectangular badge with the prancing horse, on the hood was a horizontal insignia with the word *Dino* written in blue, modelled after the young man's signature. The colours – the blue of the text and the yellow of the background – were the colours of the city of Modena.

On 28 November, and then again on 20 December, Gianni Agnelli and Giuseppe Luraghi met to discuss the future of Ferrari. Enzo naturally knew about the meetings, even if he had not been officially informed.[24]

Agnelli and Luraghi estimated the value of Ferrari at about four billion lire[25] – a figure that Francesco Bellicardi of Weber was asked to communicate to Ferrari just before Christmas.

Enzo Ferrari did his maths. On 18 January 1968, Bellicardi, in his role as the intermediary between potential buyers and the eventual seller, met Luraghi in Milan. To the president of Alfa Romeo he reported that Ferrari had judged their offer to be too low. Based on the assessment made by the Americans, the value of his company, Ferrari had said, was at least six billion lire[26] – two billion more than Alfa Romeo and Fiat were ready to offer.

The other obstacle on the path towards a possible joint purchase of Ferrari by Alfa Romeo and Fiat was the ownership structure proposed by Ferrari: one-third each to Fiat, Alfa and Ferrari himself. Luraghi was furious.

Torn between the desire to hold on and the need not to break ties with players who could ensure a future for his company, on 3 April 1968 Ferrari invited Luraghi to Maranello for a private meeting. During their chat, Ferrari assured him that he had not changed his mind. He was always interested in selling – indeed, he was even willing to sell to Alfa Romeo alone.[27]

The 1968 F1 World Championship had begun with the South African Grand Prix on the first day of the new year. Ferrari had confirmed Amon and hired two young and talented drivers: Andrea de Adamich, who behind his university researcher glasses hid the gift of speed; and Jacky Ickx, a young Belgian who was speed personified. Replacing Franco Lini, who had returned to his career as a full-time journalist, Ferrari had promoted to team manager his formidable press secretary, Franco Gozzi.[28]

The season's debut had been far from memorable. In late May, Ferrari decided not to participate in the Monaco Grand Prix. This was a protest at the poor safety measures at the circuit, and especially at the chicane that the year before had claimed Bandini's life.[29] The organizers had reduced the length of the race from one hundred to eighty laps, but Ferrari had said that this was not enough. Among the Italian press there were those who praised his decision and those who criticized it.[30]

But when, on 9 June, his cars took to the track at Spa for the Belgian Grand Prix, Ferrari introduced an innovation that would make history.

The idea was Mauro Forghieri's, who had supported and defended it for a long time. As usual, Ferrari had at first been puzzled by the concept; as with all new things, in order to accept it, Enzo first had to live with it a while. But by the spring of 1968 he had finally grown accustomed to the importance of aerodynamic issues, and had consequently given Forghieri the green light to mount on the 312 a rear wing above the rollbar.[31] With this wing, Amon took pole position and Ickx earned third place in qualifying, and in the race. And in France, the following month, the young Belgian won his first grand prix.

Amon's luck appeared to change with the British Grand Prix, in which he took second place. After that, he did not finish another single race, while Ickx, collecting podiums and systematically finishing in the points, remained in the quest for the title, until he suffered a crash at Mont-Tremblant, the weekend of the Canadian Grand Prix, and broke a leg, thus bidding goodbye to his world championship ambitions.

On 23 October 1968, Ferrari and Luraghi met again. The meeting put an end to the possibility of a joint purchase of Ferrari by Alfa Romeo and Fiat.

The meeting was cordial. For Enzo Ferrari, Alfa Romeo would never be a company like all others. Alfa withdrew and left the field to Fiat. Parting at the end of the chat, Luraghi shook hands with Ferrari and said, 'The day you cease your interactions with Fiat, my company will be honoured to bind its name to yours,'[32] suggesting that the real obstacle had been the deterioration of relations between Alfa Romeo and Fiat.

Hearing the parting words of Alfa Romeo's president, Ferrari recalled when they had first met, four years earlier. At the time he'd had no connection with Fiat, and Alfa had not yet returned to motor racing. He had really missed an opportunity. If he had taken it, he now thought, 'the history of Ferrari would have gone back to its roots'.[33]

Fiat, then.

Gianni Agnelli did not waste much time. On 11 December he informed Luraghi that Fiat had considered the purchase of Ferrari.[34] Agnelli and Ferrari met before Christmas.[35] Others would study and draft wordy and tedious documents. The two of them quickly agreed on the direction to take. Ferrari was not interested in the details; he didn't care what Fiat would do with the passenger-car side of his company. The only thing that he was interested in was full and unquestioned independence in managing the *Gestione Sportiva* – the racing department.

Agnelli agreed.

After victory at Le Mans in 1967, Ford had begun its disengagement from sports car and prototype races; Ferrari had done the same. On the one hand, Enzo had once again argued violently with the FIA for yet another change in the regulations that had retired the still-competitive 330 P4. On the other, he was seriously beginning to fear that the commitments to so many categories and formulas were just too much for his small company, as so many of his men had long been trying to tell him, beginning with Forghieri.[36] Thus, urged by Forghieri, he came up with the idea of a radical change at the technical level that also signalled a future revolution in Ferrari's approach to motor racing.

He asked Forghieri not to follow the race team on the track in 1969, but instead, to spend a year in the former Scuderia Ferrari headquarters in Viale Trento Trieste in Modena, to study far-reaching new solutions. Forghieri asked for and was given five designers.[37] The press, which did not understand the dynamics between the master and his chief engineer, spoke of a Forghieri 'exile'.[38]

Ferrari went to Turin twice in February and then in March 1969. He met only with Gianni Agnelli, and never really discussed the details of the operation, which did not interest either of them. Enzo left the details to his small and trusted team: Ermanno Della Casa and Carlo Benzi, who had been with him for over 20 years, under the legal supervision of the always-present attorney Cuoghi.[39]

In late April the agreement with Fiat was completed. Agnelli's role had been crucial for many reasons, and had been instrumental in overcoming some hostility demonstrated by Fiat's office of special affairs, to which the operation did not seem completely advantageous.[40] Ferrari was so sure of himself that he announced to an amused press – without explaining how – that his financial concerns, the same that had prevented him from building the required 25 units of the 512 S model necessary for homologation from the CSI, had been solved.[41] The proof was that he could now pick up the fight against Porsche in the 1969 Sports Prototype World Championship.

Racing had become incredibly expensive. In some ways, Ferrari lived in the past. He continued to give 50 per cent of race and prize money to his drivers, along with the reimbursement of expenses,[42] exactly as he had done with Nuvolari, Campari and Borzacchini in the 1930s. But the world had changed. The year before, Colin Chapman's Lotus had departed from its famous and celebrated British racing green and had the body painted in the yellow, white and gold of Gold Leaf, a prominent tobacco company. Although Ferrari continued to hold great allure for drivers, not all of them were willing to accept Enzo's conditions.

Chris Amon and Derek Bell, who had contested a couple of races at the end of the 1968 season, were the only two drivers that Enzo had confirmed for 1969, and that was because Firestone and Shell had taken on the burden of paying their salaries.[43] In the meantime, Enzo had lost the promising champion-in-the-making Jacky Ickx for economic reasons.

On Wednesday 18 June 1969, Enzo personally drove his Ferrari, a silver 330 with beige interior, to Turin. With him was Dino Tagliazucchi, who had recently taken the place held for 40 years by Peppino Verdelli, and who, of course, was sitting in the passenger seat.[44] When they arrived at the Fiat headquarters in Corso Marconi, Enzo took the stairs as usual, despite the fact that Agnelli's office was on the eighth floor – his relationship with lifts had never been a good one and had not improved with age. 'Ferrari,' Agnelli said when the man from Maranello was introduced in his office, 'I'm listening!'

Enzo Ferrari spoke at length of his factory, his past, his present and how he saw the future. He liked Agnelli. He sensed his preparation, 'the power of the modern man, of the politician and the business diplomat, the lively and synthetic observer'.[45] In some respects, Ferrari and Agnelli were natural opposites; in others, they were incredibly similar. And then, of course, Enzo had met Agnelli's grandfather, whom he considered 'a giant', a man who 'possessed the great vision of seeing automotive development, and the immense faith to make it happen'.[46]

When his turn came, the president of Fiat asked specific, short and precise questions. Gianni Agnelli was a direct and self-assured man. His attitude towards Ferrari, as in previous meetings, however, was positive, constructive and never patronizing.[47] It was true that one was selling and the other was buying, but he who was buying was not looking down at the other, because he knew that the man who that day was selling had been rejected by Fiat 50 years ago and, in the half-century that had elapsed since then, had created a company whose name had become synonymous with speed, power, elegance, beauty and success, a company that people on 5 continents immediately associated with Italy.

When the private meeting was over, Agnelli ushered in his aides. 'Well, Ferrari,' he said, 'isn't it true that we could have done this deal before?' Then, turning to his men, he said: 'Gentlemen, perhaps we have wasted some time. Now we need to make up for it.'[48]

Fiat acquired 50 per cent of Ferrari for a sum that a few days later the press speculated was about 2 billion and 150 million lire.[49] As for his 50 per cent, that evening Enzo signed a private agreement indicating that 40 per cent would be automatically acquired by Fiat at the time of his death, while 10 per cent was made out to his son, Piero – although, inevitably, this last part would remain secret for a long time.[50]

After the signing, Ferrari went back down the stairs and got into his car. He drove in perfect silence all the way to Maranello. He felt 'peaceful'.[51] He knew that he had made the best choice for his company, for the people working in it, for their families and, ultimately, for himself.

For some time now he had not been feeling well. Kidney trouble had kept him away from his office for some time in the second half of 1968, and continued to afflict him. Although the situation was under control, the fear of death had crept into his mind. Enzo Ferrari was afraid that his time was up, and this had been the main impetus behind selling a portion of his company to Fiat.

28. Ferrari in the pits during practice for the first run of the Monza 1000km race, 1965, an event dominated by his cars, with the Parkes/Guichet and Surtees/Scarfiotti pairs first and second at the chequered flag. Next to Commendatore Ferrari is renowned photographer Bernard Cahier.

29. The press introduction of the 312 F1, the car for the new 3000cc formula governing the F1 world championship from 1966. Ferrari showed the car to the press, first in the factory courtyard and then during the press conference. Next to him is the dean of automotive journalists, Giovanni Canestrini.

30. In the mid-1960s, Ferrari slowly moved from the production of many 'one-offs', which had characterized the previous decade, to a larger production of each model, as this image shows very well.

31. John Surtees talks to Enzo Ferrari's wife, Laura. This image reflects the difficult relationship Laura, a very complex woman, had with her husband's technicians and drivers.

32. Enzo Ferrari with Adolfo Celi, the Italian actor who played a character that resembled him very much in John Frankenheimer's 1966 cult movie, *Grand Prix*. Ferrari granted director and crew two entire days for filming inside the Maranello factory, and is said to have much appreciated Celi's performance.

33. Grand Prix of Italy, 1966. Lodovico Scarfiotti takes the chequered flag at the wheel of his 312 F1. It's the first win by an Italian driver in the home grand prix since Alberto Ascari, and Ferrari rejoiced for a very long time afterwards.

34. Enzo Ferrari and Lorenzo Bandini in Maranello, in the spring of 1967, the last year for the Italian driver. Ferrari appreciated Bandini for his dedicated work ethic and for his loyalty to him and his company, but never recognized him as a top-class driver.

35. Monaco Grand Prix, 1967. This is what was left of Lorenzo Bandini's Ferrari after the crash in the last phases of the race that claimed his life. The Italian driver hit the straw bales on the side of the road; his car flipped and then caught fire. Watching the grand prix from his Maranello office, at the sight of the smoke column rising from the Monte Carlo harbour, Enzo immediately sensed that it was Lorenzo.

36. In 1968 Ferrari staged the presentation of his new sports car in the ballroom of the Hotel Fini in Modena. Despite the beautiful shapes, in 1969 the 312 P failed to deliver what it had promised.

37. Italian Grand Prix, 1970. Swiss driver Gianclaudio (Clay) Regazzoni wins at Monza in his first F1 season. At the end of the year he is third in the world standings. With that first win, Ferrari fans fall in love with a driver who will spend a total of six years at Maranello.

38. A very young Piero Ferrari in the Monza pits watches his father's mechanics work on the 512 S, the prototype that Scuderia Ferrari will field in the 1970 World Championship of Makes.

40. Italian Grand Prix, 1970. While Ickx is returning to the pits, Enzo Ferrari visits his team on the day of qualifying. The next day, Regazzoni will win the grand prix in his 312 B.

39. Enzo Ferrari between Mario Andretti and Clay Regazzoni, at the press unveiling of the new 312 PB, in 1970. The car will debut in 1971, and win the 1972 world title.

41. Fiorano track, 1974. Enzo Ferrari during a break in the testing of the 312 B3 redesigned by Mauro Forghieri, together with his young assistant, Luca di Montezemolo, and their new, semi-unknown Austrian driver, Niki Lauda.

42. Bologna, 1972. Enzo Ferrari hands world champion Emerson Fittipaldi the Casco d'Oro award on behalf of friend Luciano Conti's *Autosprint* sports magazine.

43. Italian Grand Prix, 1975. One of many perfect days in the history of Ferrari. Regazzoni wins the race, while Lauda, third, is the new world champion. 'I think I deserve this win . . . which rewards everyone at Ferrari for their hard work,' says Niki Lauda, after bringing back to Maranello the first world title in 11 years.

44. The heir to the 1975 world champion car, the 312 T2 on the day it is unveiled to the press. Enzo Ferrari is with his two drivers, Niki Lauda and Clay Regazzoni, both confirmed for the 1976 season. After the first races with the old T, the T2 will immediately show its great potential with Niki.

45. Italian Grand Prix, 1976. On Friday 10 September, in pouring rain, Niki Lauda returns to racing after the terrifying August crash at the Nürburgring. He is back to defend his shot at a second world title. He will finish the grand prix in fourth place.

46. Luca di Montezemolo, together with Enzo Ferrari. Luca leaves Ferrari at the end of the victorious 1975 season, but will be back after Enzo's death in the early 1990s, as president of Ferrari.

47. Ferrari had mixed feelings toward Niki Lauda in 1977. On the one hand, he believed that the Austrian had asked too much from himself before the 1976 Japanese Grand Prix, in which he lost the world title. On the other, he felt indebted to him. In 1977 they won another world title, but the Austrian left Ferrari before the end of the season.

48. Ferrari announced the hiring of Canadian Gilles Villeneuve in 1977, explaining the many comparisons with the Niki Lauda he had hired in 1973. He said: 'I chose him after I had been told that he was talented and mature. We hope that he will not let us down.'

49. By the spring of 1978, Enzo Ferrari had many doubts about Gilles Villeneuve. The Canadian was fast and showed great character, but he was not yet reliable. It took Ferrari a whole year before he finally saw Villeneuve take his first F1 win, at the Grand Prix of Canada.

50. Ferrari uncorked a bottle of champagne before distributing a press release to journalists, announcing that the drivers for the 1979 season were Jody Scheckter and Gilles Villeneuve.

51. In 1980, the 312 T5 was not as good as the world champion T4. For Ferrari and his drivers, the 1980 season was an endless frustration.

52. On a hot July day in 1980, Enzo Ferrari went to Imola, where Villeneuve was testing the T5. The Grand Old Man went to the pits and was soon joined by his Canadian driver, *Autosprint* publisher Luciano Conti (left) and race-track director Roberto Nosetto.

53. On Saturday 13 September 1980, in practice for the Italian Grand Prix, Villeneuve tests the new supercharged 126. The car proved faster than the T5, but the debut was ultimately postponed to the following season.

54. By 1981 Enzo Ferrari was the recognized patriarch of international motor racing. He played a fundamental role in finding a solution to F1's many problems. The main goal was to rediscover lost unity. From left: Bernie Ecclestone, Jean-Marie Balestre, Marco Piccinini, Enzo and Piero Ferrari.

55. He used to call them 'Monday-morning quarterbacks', but he couldn't have lived without them. Although he'd wanted to be one in his youth, Enzo Ferrari maintained a love–hate relationship with journalists throughout his life.

57. The future knocks at the door with the arrival at Maranello, in 1986, of a new technical team led by John Barnard, and new drivers, with Gerhard Berger a works Ferrari driver from 1987. Together with these two, this photo also shows Piero Ferrari (first left) and Marco Piccinini (right).

56. Enzo Ferrari holds the traditional press conference ahead of the 1984 season, a year rich in novelties for the Scuderia, which fielded an innovative car, the 126 C4, finally after many years driven by an Italian, Michele Alboreto, who recorded his first win in red in the Belgian Grand Prix at Zolder. A relationship of great respect and reciprocal affections was established between Alboreto and Ferrari.

Colazione in fabbrica dei collaboratori
della Ferrari S.p.A.
per il 90° compleanno di
Enzo Ferrari

Maranello 18 febbraio 1988

Ristorante

Aperitivo Formula 1

Antipasto di prosciutto, salame, ciccioli, mortadella,
cipolline della nonna con gnocco ingrassato

Tortellini Cavallino alla panna

Lasagne alla Cardinale

Zampone di Modena con fagioloni

Nodino di vitello con purè e verdure al forno

Torta del compleanno

Caffè

Bianco Malvasia
Lambrusco Cà Berti
Riesling Spumante Martini

58. 'If one day I should die', Enzo Ferrari said to all of his employees on his 90th birthday, in 1988, 'you will go on with your loyalty and with the current executives'. It was his last public appearance.

Evening Shadows

The agreement between Ferrari and Fiat was announced on the afternoon of Saturday 21 June 1969: 'Following the meeting of Fiat's president Dr Giovanni Agnelli with engineer Enzo Ferrari, in order to ensure continuity and growth to Ferrari Automobili, it was decided that the technical collaboration in place with Fiat will be transformed within the year to [one of] "equal stakes participation".'[1]

The press reaction was of course positive. There were even those who considered Enzo's sale of 50 per cent of his company 'his greatest victory', a true 'masterpiece'. And recalling the door that Fiat had slammed in his face in November 1918, a journalist remarked: 'Half a century is long. The man from Maranello has spent it working hard, depriving himself of holidays and amusements. Exploiting his financial intellect, he has built an empire that is worth a few billion lire. Through motor racing he became rich, where others lost everything.'[2]

On the very day of the announcement, Chris Amon clinched a promising third place in the Dutch Grand Prix, but then his season continued with a series of withdrawals and, after the Grand Prix of Great Britain, the New Zealander left.[3] He was tired of waiting for a winning Ferrari. He knew he had the ability to do well and had decided to try his luck elsewhere. In the rest of the season's races, Ferrari fielded just Pedro Rodríguez, Ricardo's older brother, alongside Italian Tino Brambilla in the Italian Grand Prix.

The results of the sports-car races were equally disappointing, except for the second place clinched by Mario Andretti and Chris Amon at the wheel of the 312 P in the Sebring 12 Hours. The only real satisfaction, in 1969, was the enthusiastic reception the press and public gave to the 365 GTS/4 Spyder, the open version of the Daytona, which was introduced at the Frankfurt Motor Show in an unusual and eye-catching bright yellow. Born from the imagination of Pininfarina, the elimination of the hardtop made the convertible look even more slender, more aggressive and more elegant.[4]

As far as the 1970 season and the future were concerned, Ferrari had high hopes in a new beginning and confidence in the work that Forghieri and his six-man team – including Walter Salvarani and Angiolino Marchetti, Enzo's son Dino's old schoolmate – were carrying out in the Viale Trento Trieste workshop.

On 13 September 1969, engineer Giuseppe Dondo arrived in Maranello. He was the first general manager of Ferrari appointed by Fiat. The new board of trustees comprised Enzo Ferrari as chairman; Francesco Bellicardi as CEO; Sergio Pininfarina, Carlo Pelloni, Oscar Montabone and Piero Lardi as board members; and Ermanno Della Casa as secretary. Bellicardi and Montabone were Fiat men.[5] This was also the first official recognition for Piero Lardi, son of Enzo and Lina Lardi.

On 13 December 1969, Peppino Verdelli died. He had been with Ferrari for 49 years, as a race mechanic, assistant and personal chauffeur – even if he had rarely driven with Ferrari at his side, since Enzo hardly ever relinquished the steering wheel. For almost half a century he had been Enzo's shadow and the depository of the many secrets of his private life. He had retired in the spring, his position filled by Dino Tagliazucchi, a young worker that Ferrari had transformed into his new chauffeur.[6]

In spring 1970, Ferrari decided to field a second car alongside Ickx's – the Belgian had returned to Maranello after a year at Brabham. For the moment he did not make a final choice in terms of which driver, for he had two that he judged equally talented. Despite the recent entry of Fiat, the racing budget was still tight and the only solution was to alternate them from race to race.[7]

The two drivers were Ignazio Giunti from Rome and Clay Regazzoni from Switzerland. Ferrari had interviewed the latter in Maranello on Christmas Eve back in 1968, and kept him under observation for the entire 1969 season, when he was crowned Europe F2 champion at the wheel of a Tecno. The first to make his debut would be Giunti in the Belgian Grand Prix. Clay's debut would come in the following Dutch Grand Prix. Then, they'd do one race each until Austria and, finally, both would race together at Monza.

The start of the championship, with just Ickx, had not been easy. But when, shortly after mid-season, the tuning problems had finally been solved, the new 312 B began to demonstrate its full potential, which was huge.

At Zeltweg in mid-August, Ickx won the race ahead of teammate Regazzoni, who won the following race, the Italian Grand Prix at Monza. Accompanied by wife Laura in one of her by-now rare public appearances, Enzo Ferrari had gone to Monza for Friday's practice and Saturday's qualifying. With them that weekend was Gianni Agnelli,[8] Fiat tycoon and now Ferrari 50 per cent partner.

Just minutes from the end of the qualifying session, Jochen Rindt crashed his Lotus and died. Ferrari left immediately after being told of the Austrian's death.[9]

After Monza, Rindt had a lead of 20 points over his closest pursuer, 24 over Regazzoni and 26 over Ickx. There were still three races left in the championship; the way the drivers were performing and the superiority of the 312 B led Ferrari to think that the fight for the title – with Rindt unable to defend himself – was open to Ferrari's two drivers. As cruel as it might sound, that was how motor racing worked.

However, despite two victories and two second places scored by Ickx and Regazzoni in Canada and Mexico, due to less-than-stellar performances by both drivers at Watkins Glen in the penultimate race of the year, Jochen Rindt was posthumously awarded the world title. Ickx was runner-up and Regazzoni finished third.

* * *

Enzo Ferrari was hospitalized on 13 December 1970. His health had deteriorated to the point where hospitalization, which he had long resisted, could be postponed no longer.[10] Kidney failure, from which he had suffered for years, was now compromising his vital organs. He required medical treatment and total rest. Reluctantly, he accepted the diagnosis and started temporary dialysis treatments. The fear of death that had led him to conclude the agreement with Fiat had been real, and had never left him.

He spent both Christmas Day 1970 and New Year's Day 1971 in the Villa Laura clinic in Modena's Via Prampolini. His wife didn't visit him, but Piero came every day from the office, often with his wife Floriana, whom he'd married two years before. Just a handful of Ferrari's men were allowed to visit him, and all were advised to keep their work topics to a minimum, bringing them up only if necessary. Occasionally it was Enzo who called them on the phone to ask for updates, but above all to reassure them that he had not abandoned them.

He was released from hospital on 9 January 1971, but wouldn't return to the office until early March. The doctors prescribed a very strict diet. For months, in the evening he was allowed to eat only fruit, which he preferred to consume in the form of salad. Looking forward, the doctors said, the future was in his hands. If he followed their guidelines, he could live at least 15 more years, and possibly 18 to 20 years.[11]

While convalescing at home, on 18 February 1971 Enzo turned 73. Despite the many sorrows, despite the many *terrible joys* – 'When you live [your] joys,' he said, 'then you pay everything' – his had been an extraordinary life. He had lived longer than most men of his sport that he had known, and more intensely than most of the people he had met – first moving from race to race, from circuit to circuit, from motor show to motor show, and then almost secluding himself in his small but precious realm that had as its boundary the Via Emilia to the north and the first elevations of the Apennines to the south.

His last name – one of the most common in Italy – had become synonymous with racing cars. Abroad, *Ferrari* meant *Italy*. Maranello, the small town to which he had moved his business in the middle of World War II, had become one of the world's capitals of sports cars. When he had first arrived, the village had a population of less than four thousand; now, fourteen thousand people lived there and the town had a vocational school named after his son Dino, which he had financed.[12]

Thanks to him, Maranello continued to be visited by Hollywood actors such as Tony Curtis, directors of the world's most famous philharmonic orchestras, such as Herbert von Karajan, pianists like Arturo Benedetti Michelangeli, writers such as Françoise Sagan, European kings, queens and prince consorts like Leopold of Belgium and Bernhard of the Netherlands, the Shah of Iran and the Aga Khan. Fans who were not admitted inside the factory took photos of themselves in front of the gates, or waited for night to descend before removing the Maranello road sign to take home with them.

Ferrari was aware that he had already 'passed the top of the mountain', but his mind was 'pcacful'. His hope was to be able to work 'until the last day'. In his work, he said, 'I approached the mystery of the soul, but have never been able to discover my own.' He made no secret of considering 'those who have faith [to be] very fortunate; in it they find a welcoming shelter [for] their anxieties'.[13]

He remained what he'd always been: a loner. Despite all the people he'd met, the ones he'd loved or the ones who had turned him down, despite all those who had applauded him at every win or accused him at every failure, he was ultimately alone. He would say: 'After all these events, I feel lonesome and almost guilty for having survived. Sometimes' – he never tired of repeating, to himself as well as to others – 'I think that sorrow is nothing more than an exaggerated attachment to life in the face of the incredible fragility of existence.'[14]

When he returned to the office in March, he submerged himself in everyday work with that extra energy often felt by someone who has been away for too long. During the winter of 1971, he had renewed his contracts with Ickx and Regazzoni, and had reached an agreement with Mario Andretti, the Italian-American driver he liked so much, who he had chased for a long time. The day after his hospital discharge, 10 January, he had received the news of the death of Ignazio Giunti during the Buenos Aires 1000km. The absurd dynamic of the incident – French driver Jean-Pierre Beltoise was pushing with his bare hands his petrol-less Matra from one side of the track to the other in a crazy attempt to reach the pits – that claimed the life of his young and talented driver drove him mad.[15] 'He had talent and passion, and there were many of us who loved him,'[16] he would say.

The 1971 F1 World Championship began in the best possible way in South Africa, however, with an Andretti win in his first race with Ferrari. Regazzoni came in third. Ickx did not score points in that race at Kyalami, but began an impressive crescendo with the following race – second in Spain, third in Monte Carlo, first in the Netherlands – that projected him into the shadow of Jackie Stewart in the championship standings. But it was an illusion. The 312 B suddenly lost its edge and the drivers were shipwrecked along with it.

Ickx and Regazzoni had complained of strong vibrations on the rear tyres. The cause could have been a malfunction of the Firestones that Ferrari continued to use; many of the other teams had gone over to Goodyear. Forghieri had decided to modify the rear suspension of the 312 B, and did not change his mind even after Ferrari began to question his decision. Indeed, he continued to defend it in spite of the fact that its promised results were not forthcoming.[17]

As a consequence, Ickx and Regazzoni ran into an impressive series of withdrawals that exasperated the drivers, Ferrari and, of course, the fans, to the point where on the Friday of the 1971 Italian Grand Prix, Enzo was soundly booed by the crowd. Offended by the crowd hysteria, he would never return either to Monza or to any other circuit.[18]

In addition to the many technical questions the team faced, once more, Enzo's health came into play, affecting the manner and speed with which he dealt with issues. Despite ongoing treatment and strict observation of his diet, his kidney disease continued to trouble him and often kept him away from the office. For someone who already didn't attend the races, his absence from the office helped to widen the distance between Enzo and any problems that arose – along with, of course, any possible solutions.

By the winter of 1971–1972, it was clear even to Enzo Ferrari that if he wanted to continue to be a protagonist and not just a supporting actor, he had to make a choice. And since a Fiat man was now at the technical helm of his racing team, and Fiat, for a number of commercial reasons, seemed to prefer sports cars, the 1972 season was planned as a great crusade toward the Makes world title – naturally at the expense of the F1 championship. The irony was that the 312 PB had been designed and developed by Forghieri, who had to celebrate its great achievements from a distance.

As for the drivers, to the three who competed in F1 – Ickx, Andretti and

Regazzoni – others would gradually be added, like endurance race specialists Arturo Merzario, Tim Schenken, Sandro Munari and even Ronnie Peterson, the Swede who was widely regarded as the fastest racing driver of his generation, a sort of Stirling Moss of the 1970s.

Enzo lived the great season of the 312 PB mostly withdrawn, inside his house, struggling with the disease that gave him no rest. He savoured from afar ten wins out of ten races. In some events – like the Buenos Aires, Brands Hatch, Spa and Nürburgring 1000km, and the Daytona and Watkins Glen 6 Hours – the PB 312 finished first and second. At Zeltweg, where Ferrari exceptionally fielded four units, the 312 PB came first, second, third and fouth. And there was also time to win the glorious Targa Florio, which Enzo had raced for the first time in 1919.

So, despite the seclusion and concerns for his health, Ferrari was extremely pleased with the title – sports cars remained his first love.[19] Significant and opulent manufacturers like Ford and Porsche had come and gone, but he was always there. He could be bent, but never broken.

The 1972 world title was the 13th Ferrari had won since the Sports Car World Championship, then Prototypes, now Makes, had been established in 1953 – and he, of course counted 14 titles, because he always included the unofficial one he had been awarded in 1952.

The F1 season, by contrast, was a long and disappointing ride. The only joy came on 30 July, when Jacky Ickx won the German Grand Prix after starting from pole position and setting the race's fastest lap. Some podium finishes with young Italian newcomers Nanni Galli and Arturo Merzario were all the season brought.

And yet, while the 312 B2 limped along, in the Fiorano advanced research department, where Ferrari had placed him, Forghieri and his men were laying the foundation for the future by working on a new car in which the mass was concentrated at the centre, the radiators on the sides and the front air intakes placed in a wing with such an odd shape that, when they saw the car, Italian journalists maliciously called it a *snowplough*. Enzo kept in touch with Forghieri via telephone.[20] Colombo was the technical director chosen by Fiat – but Mauro was *his* man.[21]

'The relations between Ferrari and Fiat,' said Enzo Ferrari in December 1972, 'are very clear, although in recent times there have been elements and assumptions that could give the impression that there were discrepancies.'[22]

There *were* discrepancies. Struggling with a stagnant car market, Fiat intended to reduce the contribution that Enzo had requested for racing activity, which he had estimated at half a billion lire a year.[23] After less than three years, the first clouds were starting to darken the sky of the Fiat–Ferrari partnership. Ferrari was furious and stamped his feet, but in the end, he had no choice but to make the best of a bad lot. The relationship with Fiat had reached an all-time low.

The 312 B3 proved to be as disappointing as the cars that had preceded it. But when, in the early summer of 1973, Enzo Ferrari was finally able to put his long convalescence behind him, returning in better shape than ever, things finally began to turn around.

First, Enzo resumed full control of the racing department. According to the agreement signed in June 1969, it was rightfully his. But, taking advantage of his long absence, Fiat men had not only been incorporated in the *Gestione Sportiva* structure, but had also assumed a freedom of movement that would not have been granted to them in another situation or another time.[24]

The first decision Enzo made was to concentrate efforts on a single racing category. Starting in 1974, Ferrari would no longer race in the World Championship of Makes, instead focusing solely on F1. Then he went to Forghieri, who had been advocating this plan for years. Forghieri had been waiting two years for this moment and eagerly accepted his old position at the helm, planning to immediately modify the existing 312 B3 by building a 'pre-edition' of the car he'd had in mind for the following season.

But Ferrari also had other things in mind. His prolonged absence from the office had given him the chance to think, and from this introspection came the decision to instigate a revolution not just at the technical level; *Gestione Sportiva* must also be radically changed. Even if he did not particularly like the word, it must be *modernized*. In the time he had been away, he had shaped a precise idea of what he wanted.

At the age of 75, Enzo Ferrari chose as his new team manager a young man not yet 26, with a degree in international law. His name was Luca di Montezemolo. Ferrari had summoned him to Maranello three years earlier after listening to him on a live radio broadcast. On 2 July 1973, he hired him with the title of 'management assistant. His tasks,' the internal communication read, 'will be carried out through special assignments on the industrial side as well as on the racing side of the company.'[25]

Enzo had long since decided to do away with the current driver lineup. Ickx had by now reached breaking point, exasperated by three seasons in which he had achieved very little. And as for Merzario, Enzo thought he was better suited to endurance races than F1. He had always liked Clay Regazzoni; the Swiss driver had left the year before, but personal relations between the two continued to be good. Clay agreed to return to Maranello, and when they saw each other, Regazzoni spoke well of his teammate at BRM – an Austrian of few words and great talent, Niki Lauda, who was 24 years old. Ferrari, who was also considering French driver Jean-Pierre Jarier and Englishman James Hunt, did not reject Clay's idea, and told him that he would keep Lauda's name in mind.[26]

Ferrari discarded Hunt after meeting the wonderfully eccentric Lord Hesketh, who ran the team Hunt was currently racing for, in Maranello. At that point he sent Montezemolo to approach Lauda. Despite his lack of experience, the Austrian asked an astonishing sum to sign with Ferrari. But Regazzoni had spoken highly of him and Montezemolo was pressuring Ferrari to pick a young talent to flank an experienced man like Clay. Niki, he urged, was perfect for the role.[27]

At this point the team for 1974 was finalized: Forghieri, chief engineer; Montezemolo, team manager; and two cars for Regazzoni and Lauda. And while in August 1973 Forghieri was beginning to change the B3 that Regazzoni had tested incognito, because he was still under contract with BRM, Ferrari decided to split the mechanics into two teams, one for each car. The chief mechanic for Regazzoni's car would be Giulio Borsari; for Lauda's car, Ermanno Cuoghi.[28]

The 312 B3 of 1974 – which Forghieri would have liked to name the B4, because of the many changes he had made,[29] and to distance it from the previous management – proved to be fast and reliable. And in the B3, the pupil soon surpassed the teacher. In Spain, at the fourth race of the season, Niki Lauda took the first grand prix win of his career. And before Regazzoni won his first season's race in August, in Germany, Lauda had won a second time in Holland, in late June.

The team hierarchies had not flipped, but Lauda's quick growth was being observed by all. Ferrari watched, enjoyed and remained silent, a sign that things were going in the desired direction. Now that the big worries were behind him, he began to spend his days back in the office, resuming a relatively normal life.

On Saturdays he once again met his few friends and spent precious hours around lunchtime with them. They had stopped going to restaurants in the countryside around Modena and Reggio the way they used to do, just a few years earlier, but had returned to meeting on a regular basis. Despite the diet that he had to follow, on Saturdays he indulged in more delicious dishes – a slice of roast beef, a bit of Parmesan cheese, real coffee instead of barley coffee.

On those Sundays when grands prix were televised, he would watch them in his study on the ground floor of the little house in the middle of the Fiorano track that he had built two years earlier. He, who once waited alone for race results announced by the traditional phone call from the circuit, now watched the live television broadcast in the company of some of his trusted friends – Pietro Barilla and Sergio

Scaglietti, the physicians with whom he had developed sincere friendships; and Carlo Benzi, who had left Ferrari and now worked at Coca-Cola, but had gone on managing Enzo's personal finances.[30]

Now that his Fiorano cherry-tree fields housed a test track, which Fiat's money had allowed him to build, he had refurbished the whole area. He had transformed the old barn into a technical office and the stable into a garage, and had graced the farmhouse with a guest lounge, a meeting room, his study and a small room behind the study where he occasionally dined with special visitors.

Sitting comfortably in his study in a big leather armchair, he watched grands prix on two television sets placed side by side – one broadcasting the race in colour, with commentary from the Italian-speaking portion of Switzerland, the other, with black-and-white images and commentary from the Italian state network.

He changed his glasses when watching television, putting on a pair with lighter lenses. In his hand he held a bottle of fresh water from which he occasionally drank a few sips, placing it on a stool next to the phone. Forghieri would call him at the end of each race for his usual post-event debriefing. At the start of the race Enzo was usually still, silent, apparently emotionless. Only 'the recurring, continuous rhythmic movement of his right leg crossed over the left' betrayed his nervousness.[31]

After his victory at the Nürburgring, Regazzoni topped the world championship standings with 44 points. Behind him were South African Jody Scheckter in a Tyrrell-Ford, with 41; teammate Lauda, with 38; and Brazil's Emerson Fittipaldi in a McLaren-Ford, with 37. Only four rounds were left. Both Ferrari drivers had a shot at the title. In the last three years it had not happened. But Scheckter and Fittipaldi were pressing on and, perhaps, some in-house clarification was necessary.

In mid-August, after the Austrian Grand Prix in which Regazzoni had gained two more points on everyone, Lauda had asked Ferrari for instructions. Ferrari said what he normally said on this subject: that he relied on Niki's professionalism.[32] After the Italian Grand Prix, in which both drivers had withdrawn with blown-up engines, allowing Scheckter to close in on Regazzoni, and Fittipaldi to overtake Lauda, Ferrari still did not take a position: 'He who has raced knows,' he said, 'that no tactic is configurable except to appeal to the drivers' sense of responsibility.'[33]

With just one round to go, Lauda was out of the game, while Clay Regazzoni and Emerson Fittipaldi were tied in the lead of the standings. The 1974 F1 World Championship would be decided in the last race, the US Grand Prix at Watkins Glen. If one thought about how things had been a year ago, everyone at Ferrari should have been gratified. For this reason, before the race Enzo was focusing not just on Regazzoni's chances to win the title, but also on the progress that had been made in the past 12 months.

With Forghieri delayed by a problem with his passport, in practice at Watkins Glen the B3 did not shine, and engineer Caliri, after speaking to the drivers, modified the car set-up for the race.[34] The race was an ordeal for Regazzoni, who finished 11th and had to bid farewell to his world title dreams. But despite the disappointment of losing a title that he had not won in ten years, Enzo Ferrari did not appear particularly upset when his men returned from the United States.

'It is the bitter end to a good season,' he said. And, looking ahead as he typically did, he added: 'For Ferrari 1975 will begin this coming Thursday, October 10, at Fiorano.'[35] That day Forghieri's revolutionary 312 T would lap for the first time on Ferrari's private testing track. It was the F1 car on which the brilliant engineer had been working for more than a year, in which he and his boss had placed great hopes.

At the end of 1974, the future finally looked bright again for Enzo Ferrari. The long illness was behind him; the technical gap had been filled; he had two excellent drivers and a first-class technical department. And although he never forgot to remind himself and his men that 'when things go too well, there can be for many the momentary belief that a goal has been reached – a thing that I consider dangerous because in life you never stop learning',[36] he knew perfectly well that the wait was over. For the Grand Old Man, life really could begin again at the age of 76.

The Grand Old Man

The year 1975 dawned on a Ferrari that most observers saw, for the first time in years, as the legitimate favourite in the quest for the new Formula 1 world title. In the 90 days since the grim epilogue of the 1974 season, the engineers and technicians in Maranello had worked almost incessantly, putting the finishing touches on the old car while concomitantly developing the new one. There was at the moment only one prototype of the 312 T, but in all the tests the new car had lapped faster than the B3. What was more, given the different weight distribution, the 312 T seemed more at ease with the tyres – the discriminating factor in the previous year's battle for the world title.[1]

The 1975 racing season started early.

The two South American races in Argentina and Brazil were a huge disappointment for the Grand Old Man. Both grands prix went very differently from the way Enzo had expected, and his engineers had planned. In the brief winter break the B3s had lost their edge. By January, Shadow, Brabham and Hesketh had somehow closed the gap to Ferrari, while McLaren had remained at least as competitive as it had been in 1974. Watching the Grand Prix of Brazil on television in a Maranello covered with thick fog, Enzo was furious. There was only one solution: moving forward as quickly as possible with the debut of the new car, which at that point was planned for the Spanish Grand Prix in late April[2] – so great had been Forghieri's confidence in the qualities of the B3.

On Thursday 30 January, a beautiful, crisp, sunny day, Enzo Ferrari announced his daring decision. 'The 312 B3s have demonstrated real improvements, and the lap times set in qualifying and during the race [in the first two grands prix of the year] prove that,' said Enzo. But there was a problem: the unsatisfactory relationship between the B3 and the new Goodyear tyres, which were now the same for all teams. 'Unlike last year, when Goodyear gave us, for each race, temperature and weather condition, the tyres that best suited the B3,' Ferrari explained, 'this year, evidently for financial reasons, they have prepared only two kinds of treads.' Thus the decision to bring forward to the Grand Prix of South Africa on 1 March the debut of the 312 T, despite the 'implicit challenges posed by the shorter time to develop the car'.[3]

Less than three weeks later, on Tuesday 18 February 1975, Enzo Ferrari turned 77. His health was good, his spirits high, despite the disappointing start to the racing season. In spite of the general crisis in the automotive sector, Ferrari the company was in almost picture-perfect form with 750 employees – 25 times as many as Enzo's own father had had in the best of days. Deliveries to customers had lowered in 1974 by more than 300 units, to 1,436, but although there were markets that were underperforming, others had been opened that would soon make up for the units lost.

'While once the saying was true – "You don't buy a Ferrari, but you long for one" – and our clientele accepted deliveries in six, eight, twelve months, today's requests can be met rather quickly,' he said pragmatically. But Enzo wasn't worried: 'I believe that, for a production as irrelevant in terms of quantity as Ferrari's, despite the difficulties there will always be a market in the future.'[4]

After almost eight decades lived with rare intensity, he could profess that his love for the automobile and for motor racing, begun early in his youth, 'had not suffered from the insults of time'. He had watched his first race 69 years earlier, had been a driver for most of the 1920s, had created his Scuderia in 1929 and founded Ferrari in 1940. 'The secret of this *total* faithfulness, which I believe difficult to find in other types of relationships,' he confessed, 'springs from the possibility to do, year after year, new experiments, to find new solutions, to build new automobiles.'[5]

Again that word, *total* – whole, entire, full, unquestioned. He had used it to describe his departed son Dino, whom he had called a *figlio totale*, a total son – not to differentiate him from his other son, born out of wedlock, but to suggest Dino's total, unquestioned love for the automobile and motorsport – as if to state for posterity that nothing else mattered more in Dino's life, or in Enzo's.

Now he used the word again to describe his relationship with an activity that had defined the very essence of who he was. Perhaps at the risk of sounding blasphemous, he said: 'It is in the consciousness of this torment for technical renovation and in the resulting accomplishments that I have found, among infinite sorrows, my own *religion in life*.'[6]

At 77, Enzo Ferrari was serene. His black days were behind him; he had ensured continuity for his company with the agreement he'd struck with Fiat five years earlier, and his racing cars were competitive again. The future seemed full of promise once more.

*   *   *

Both Lauda and Regazzoni carried out nonstop testing at Fiorano, despite the typical February fog, rain and cold. Along with a 312 B3 spare car, two 312 Ts were flown to South Africa, where, on the first Saturday in March, they made their F1 debut. The new Ferrari was stunningly beautiful – the big air scope was white, with a stripe in the three colours of the Italian flag – and there was much anticipation felt by both the team at Kyalami and the old man in Maranello.

The car's first official performance was not what Enzo had hoped, however. In the qualifying sessions, Niki set the fourth-fastest time, and Clay, only the ninth. The race was just as disappointing. Regazzoni's 312 T experienced several technical problems and he ended the race seven laps behind the winner, local hero Jody Scheckter in the Tyrrell-Ford. Lauda finished fifth, half a minute behind Scheckter.

But despite the far from memorable finish and the open disappointment felt by Forghieri and Montezemolo, both Ferrari drivers were reasonably happy with the car. The 312 T still had some problems, but, said Lauda, 'it's as easy to drive as a bicycle'.[7]

There was a pause of almost two months between the South African race and the next official event on the calendar, scheduled in Barcelona on 27 April. Pleased with the positive feedback that his drivers had reported on returning from Kyalami, and delighted by the signals that had emerged from the testing session after the race, Enzo was cautiously optimistic. Forghieri, Bussi and Rocchi went back to the drawing board, while Regazzoni and Lauda spent most of March and April at Fiorano, developing new solutions.

By late April, when the new 312 Ts were trucked to Spain for the fourth round of the 1975 championship, Enzo was reasonably optimistic. In Barcelona the 312 Ts set the two fastest qualifying times, with both Lauda and Regazzoni starting the race, for the first time this year, from the first row of the grid.

Despite these positive signs, a misunderstanding between the two Ferrari drivers at the start jeopardized their chances to win the race. At the very first turn on lap 1, the two 312 Ts collided. Lauda, hit in the rear by Mario Andretti's Parnelli, which he hadn't realized was approaching, could not avoid his teammate. Both Lauda and Regazzoni were out of the race after some five hundred yards, each blaming the other for the debacle. The previous season had left scars.[8] Enzo's two drivers didn't trust each other anymore, and now they were openly fighting for the team's leadership.

Even with the lack of understanding that had nullified two months of testing, the 312 T had given an extraordinary performance in qualifying, as it had in South Africa. Both drivers had been impressed by the overall excellent quality of the 312 T. Coming back to Maranello and debriefing with his larger-than-life boss, Mauro

Forghieri was now confident. The next race in Monaco, where Ferrari had not won since 1955, could truly be the beginning of a new phase in the team's season.

The last Ferrari driver to win at Monaco had been Maurice Trintignant 20 years earlier. But it was clear from the first day of qualifying that, for Ferrari, it was finally morning again in Monte Carlo. On Saturday, Lauda set the fastest time and clinched the second consecutive pole position of the year. That night, from Modena, Enzo lingered on the phone much longer than usual with Montezemolo. He wanted to be reassured; he wanted to personally check every little detail with his young assistant. There were too many things that could go wrong; winning in Monaco, at this point in the season, with a car that was finally as competitive as any of its formidable opponents, was too important.[9]

On race day and in wet conditions, Niki took the lead from the start. Behind him the two Shadow-Fords of Jean-Pierre Jarier and Tom Pryce tried to keep pace with the number-12 Ferrari, but Niki soon flew away. When, after about 20 laps, the rain stopped and the asphalt started to dry, Lauda went to the pits to change his tyres. The Ferrari mechanics were perfect, and in just 23 seconds changed all 4 tyres. When Lauda went back onto the track, he was still in the lead, which he defended in the last laps from a late attack by Emerson Fittipaldi.

Monaco was a masterpiece of planning and execution. The 312 T was truly a superb car and Niki Lauda had proven how much he had grown as a driver. Now Enzo had a car as fast and reliable as any, and two drivers who could both aspire to the world title. To show the unity in the team – which did not exist any longer – Montezemolo had ordered Regazzoni, forced to withdraw, to come to the pit wall and personally show his teammate the sign that indicated there was one more lap to go.[10]

On Sunday evening, Enzo dictated a note to the press in which he thanked all Ferrari fans for the patience they had shown. It was the patience supporters had shown since the last Ferrari win at Monaco that he was addressing, though most commentators recognized that Enzo must also have been thinking of something bigger than the mere win of a single race, as significant and fascinating as the Monaco race had always been.[11] This Sunday night in May, Enzo knew that he had finally got a car – and a driver – that could win not just individual races, but the big prize.

Before the end of the month, Lauda and his 312 T won the Grand Prix of Belgium hands down. After six races, Ferrari and his young Austrian driver had become the main candidates for the title. Enzo tried to dampen the enthusiasm that he saw rising around him. He was not worried about his men, because he knew that experience had taught them to be cautious; nor for his driver, calm and steady as few he'd met in more than a half-century of racing. He was worried about his fair-weather friends in the Italian press, as easy with collective adulation as they were with brutal attacks when the weather changed.

Therefore, he greeted the second consecutive Lauda win with a lukewarm statement that ended with an unexpected look at the future. 'The championship,' he warned, 'is long and open to unknowns that we will try to predict. Our commitment now is to study and soon build a 312 T2.'[12] In referencing a new version of the T – the car that had just been introduced and was proving monstrously superior to the competition – it was clear that Enzo Ferrari had caught the unmistakable scent of victory.

Between early June and early July, Lauda laid the basis for his first world title. Of the three grands prix held in this period, he won two (Sweden and France) and took second place in one (Holland). Normally a taciturn man, when speaking of his formidable car Niki now used hyperbole – for him the 312 T was a 'wonderful car . . . Forghieri's stunning monument . . . a jewel disguised as a racing car'.[13] His teammate, whose contribution to the development of the 312 T had been just as important, could not put up any real opposition on the track. The state of grace Clay Regazzoni had experienced throughout the 1974 season was gone.[14]

Enzo wisely stayed in the background, letting Montezemolo manage the now somewhat awkward balance of power within his team, where the pupil was doing better than the master – a master who had actually talked his employer, two summers earlier, into choosing the young unknown who now outshone him. Somehow Clay had lost his touch. He scored podium finishes in Sweden and Holland, but always behind Lauda, whose supremacy was now complete, both inside and outside the team.

After four wins in five races, in the middle of the summer the 312 T unexpectedly lost some of its edge, but no one from the ranks of Lauda's antagonists came out decidedly against him – not even his teammate. As the Austrian did not go further than an eighth-place finish in Silverstone, a third at the Nürburgring and a sixth at Zeltweg, the three races produced three different winners. While Regazzoni continued to struggle, the only highlight in this period was Lauda's pole position on the old, celebrated and hazardous Nürburgring, where Niki was the first man ever to lap under the seven-minute barrier.

By the first week of September, the factory had reopened, though about half of the workers of *Gestione Industriale* – six hundred people[15] – were still at home, courtesy of an overstock that was about twice as big as normal.[16] If the staff working on the road cars were still not at full capacity, their co-workers in the *Gestione Sportiva* racing team were by now totally immersed in preparation for the next round of the F1 World Championship. The following weekend, at Monza, the Italian Grand Prix was going to be the defining moment of the 1975 season.

On Tuesday 2 September, Niki Lauda, the champion elect, was back at Fiorano prepping the 312 T that he was to drive on Sunday at Monza. That day he also met with Enzo Ferrari. With mutual satisfaction, the talk produced the renewal of his contract for 1976. The Grand Old Man had found, and shaped, a winner. Once again, he had been right: his choice of a virtually unknown Viennese driver had proven to be a good one. In the short span of one racing season, together, Enzo and Niki had become unbeatable.

The following day at Fiorano, it was Clay Regazzoni's turn to prep the car that he'd drive that weekend at Monza. He too met with Enzo, and happily emerged from the meeting to say that he was also very pleased to drive for Ferrari in 1976.

The contract renewals for both drivers did not tell the whole story. Although there was team harmony on the surface, the old wounds had not healed. Indeed, Lauda's imminent title had reopened them. 'I don't think that Lauda is the best driver of the pack,' Regazzoni said. 'He had luck on his side,'[17] he explained. Grossly underestimating the valuable development work and tuning Niki had done on the 312 T, Clay maliciously said: 'Lauda came to Maranello at the right moment, when Ferraris were once again very competitive.' Then, perhaps still thinking of the Niki of 1974, and not realizing how much his younger teammate had grown in only a few months, he added: 'One must still see if, under pressure, he will keep his cool.' Clay also had thoughts on Niki's 1975 season: 'He won four grands prix without real opposition. I could have been his only real opponent, but my car didn't help me. In Sweden and in Holland,' he specified, in case anyone had missed the point, 'I raced with drowsy engines.'[18]

On Thursday, three Ferraris were trucked to Monza. Enzo stayed behind, as always. Over the years, even when he had already stopped going to races, a quick visit to Monza on the Saturday of the Italian Grand Prix had become almost a ritual. However, after he was booed in 1971 he had never again considered going. He would remain in Maranello awaiting news through the telephone in his office. All week, he had been unusually nervous, almost as if Lauda's world championship were his first.

On Friday at Monza, Lauda and Regazzoni set the two fastest lap times, both lowering the previous track record. The following day Lauda took pole position and Regazzoni the second spot on the first row of the grid.

Luca di Montezemolo, the young team manager, kept the Grand Old Man constantly informed by telephone. Enzo wanted to know every little detail about his cars, drivers, mechanics and engineers. Despite the fact that his team's lineup had already been determined for 1976, he asked Montezemolo about the performance of various drivers from other teams, not necessarily those still battling with Lauda for the world crown. Perhaps looking further into the future than 1976, he was particularly curious about Tony Brise, the 23-year-old British driver with Graham Hill's Embassy-Lola team.[19]

Monza proved to be the ultimate Ferrari triumph. Regazzoni took the race, and Lauda, the world championship. 'I think I deserve this win,' Niki said the moment he climbed out of his Ferrari, besieged by hordes of fans who had invaded the track. 'This win,' he went on, generously sharing his brand-new world title with the whole team, 'is a reward for the hard work everyone at Ferrari put in.'[20]

Then he was handed a telephone. On the other end of the line was Enzo Ferrari. The Grand Old Man was unashamedly happy. He warmly congratulated and thanked Niki, who walked away with the impression that Enzo, alone in Maranello, had been truly touched by this triumph.[21]

One hundred and twenty miles away from the chaotic Monza celebration, in the quiet solitude of his blue-walled office, Enzo rejoiced.[22] He had waited 11 years but, at last, he was world champion again. Using cryptic phrases that, as usual, needed a good degree of interpretation, he said, 'This result is the demonstration of what one can do with hardworking faithfulness to an idea. And it comes as a reward to certain predestined human situations.'[23] In this moment of happiness, we are in debt' – he went on, using the ancient form of *we* instead of *I*, the *pluralis majestatis* that in Italy, apart from the Pope, only a few people still used 75 years into the 20th century – 'to Lauda, Regazzoni, the engineers, the mechanics, the suppliers and all the Ferrari fans that over the last 30 years have constantly provoked in us the determination to continue.'[24]

In Turin, Enzo's Fiat partner, Giovanni Agnelli, paid him tribute. 'For us' – and in his case, the choice of the word *us* implied that he was talking for Fiat *and* for himself – 'Ferrari is first and foremost a sentimental matter. If we are close to Ferrari today, it is because we have always believed in what this name means within the Italian automobile tradition.' Then he spoke directly of Enzo: '*Ingegner* Ferrari had faith in us and we in him – even in moments not as happy as this one. Today,' he concluded, addressing the future of the Fiat–Ferrari cooperation, 'the commitment to continue together is obvious.'[25]

Enzo had waited for 11 endless years, and now wasted no time. On Tuesday morning in Maranello, he spoke to more than one hundred journalists. Anticipating his customary end-of-season press conference by about three months, he wanted to set the record straight at this very moment: he was world champion again – for the first time since 1964.

He started by theatrically reminding his audience that he always dictated the rules of the game, not them. Lauda's, he said, was Ferrari's 21st overall world title, not the 7th, as they had all written in their papers over the past 2 days, counting only the times his drivers had prevailed in F1 racing. To the seven world crowns clinched since 1952 by Ascari, Fangio, Hawthorn, Hill, Surtees and now Lauda, he told racing journalists from all over the globe that they should add the fourteen world titles that his sports cars had won in a category that until yesterday had been as tough and as celebrated as F1.[26]

It was so typical of Enzo: now that he had finally obtained the long-sought-after prize, he somehow downplayed the value of it. But perhaps he was also sending a signal to Fiat: despite the fact that it had paid off almost instantaneously – renouncing competition in the Sports Car World Championship at the end of the 1973 season, a decision Fiat had strongly sponsored – it had been very painful for a man who was once proud to say that Ferraris could be successful in different racing categories on the same day, in all four corners of the world.

Having corrected everyone's maths, he was almost humble when commenting on his 21st title. 'We know how many sacrifices we have made to achieve this result,' he said unassumingly. 'We do not know how many sacrifices we will have to make to keep this supremacy.'[27] Again, it was quintessential Ferrari: I am the best, but becoming the best has a cost, and staying on top is the most difficult of things to do.[28]

Sitting at the head table with the new Fiat-appointed managing director of Ferrari, Piero Fusaro, to his right, Enzo thanked Giovanni Agnelli for his generous comments after the Monza race. 'Apart from the benefits from a financial standpoint,' he said of Fiat's role in his latest triumph, 'what helped us most was the chance to use the Fiat Group's computer system to obtain data whose acquisition would have otherwise required several days of testing.' He would only concede the bare minimum of praise to Fiat. While Fiat's role had been 'significant' in terms of budget, on the technological side the fruits of the cooperation with the Turin automotive giant were slower to come, he said.[29] When one of the Italian journalists impudently asked about Niki Lauda's secret, from behind his signature dark glasses Enzo unemotionally explained: 'He is a serious pro. He works according to a programmed plan. His secret' – he said, even though he didn't believe that drivers had particular secrets when they won at the wheel of one of his cars[30] – 'consists of meticulously preparing everything.'[31] The press had created an image of Lauda as a sort of racing computer, and Enzo, who didn't particularly enjoy Niki's driving style, and had historically been unhappy about having to share the success of his cars with the men who drove them,[32] had no intention of directing them elsewhere. The less the press and public appreciated Lauda, the more they would value his cars.

Ferrari could not plainly say so, but the real secret of Lauda's success, in his opinion, was the car that Niki had been driving. The secret, then, lay with his engineers: 'With the 312 T, we have built a car that works on 90 per cent of the tracks,' he said of the world champion single-seater. And part of the secret lay, of course, in the programme the team had planned and implemented: 'We have tested continuously,' he said, mentioning the second ingredient of the winning recipe.

Typically for Enzo, he didn't rest on his laurels; instead, he was already looking forward. Having paid tribute to the car that had dominated the 1975 season, he now looked ahead to 1976. 'We are working on a 312 T2 that, on paper, should be even more versatile than the T on all race tracks,' he anticipated.[33]

Enzo spoke with energy and enthusiasm for about two hours. In the sparkling question-and-answer session, he allowed himself to go back to the subject of sports cars. But Enzo also had a message to send to centres of power closer to home than the several British racing teams that competed against his cars in F1, and so he addressed the frenzy that had descended on Italy after he had clinched his new world title. 'I believe that, in this democracy of ours, the word *country* still holds a precise meaning, and one can honour his country even in sports.'[34]

He had never needed anyone else – he had always fought, won and lost battles alone. He had represented Italy for almost five decades, and had always done so on his own and on his terms. He wasn't really interested in the fair-weather excitement he was now seeing around his name and his company. One thing he had noticed and appreciated, however – and he saved this comment for last: 'The automobile,' he said, right before the press conference adjourned for lunch in a different room of the Cavallino Restaurant, 'was born with racing, and now the automobile is returning to it.'[35] Though one would expect cars to be mentioned first, then racing, this 'reversed' order provides an insight into Enzo's competition-obsessed thinking process. Racing always came first in his mind.

The week that had started with his 21st world title ended in frustration, however. Perhaps to steal the scene from its longtime associate and later strenuous rival, Alfa Romeo announced that it would likely make its F1 debut at the next and concluding event of the 1975 season, the US Grand Prix, scheduled for 5 October at Watkins Glen.[36] Carlo Chiti, one-time chief engineer at Ferrari and one of the eight executives Enzo had abruptly fired in autumn 1961, was now managing director at Autodelta, Alfa Romeo's racing department. He was going to London to make the final decision, along with Bernie Ecclestone, the owner of the Brabham racing team, on an eventual early debut of a new Anglo–Italian partnership.

More than the now almost-certain return of Alfa Romeo as a supplier of engines to one or more British teams, what troubled Enzo the most was the probable return of Alfa Romeo to F1 racing in the form of direct participation: car *and* engine. In June, Alfa Romeo had clinched its first Makes world title in the sports category, and its potential, although untested in F1 for the previous 24 years, could be destructive – especially in the capable hands of *Ingegner* Chiti, a man who had longed for revenge against his old boss from the very day he was asked to leave Ferrari.[37] For the Grand Old Man, it was the worst of all nightmares.

On 5 October, at Watkins Glen, Alfa Romeo did not return to F1 racing, postponing its debut as engine supplier to Bernie Ecclestone's Brabham to the first race of the 1976 season. What the US Grand Prix produced was another Lauda pole position and win, respectively the ninth and fifth of his extraordinary season.

Provoked by the press about the Alfa Romeo-powered Brabham, and after stating 'I was born at Alfa Romeo, and I have no envy' of the engine that would equip the British car in 1976, Ferrari mischievously said: 'Their boxer engine is a 12-cylinder like ours. Let's hope it's a good imitation.'[38]

The controversy surged the next day with Alfa Romeo's legitimate response. Chiti chose irony, and sarcastically replied that 'We, at Alfa, have been building boxer engines since 1940.'[39]

And, for once, that was all that was said on the subject.

In early October, at the Paris Auto Show, the new Ferrari 308 GTB premiered in front of the world press. Enzo had decided to skip the mid-September Frankfurt Auto Show in favour of Paris – a choice mostly dictated by sentimental reasons:[40] the three international auto shows normally chosen by Enzo for the worldwide premieres of his cars had historically been Turin, Geneva and Paris.

The car industry situation was still quite challenging, and Ferrari was in no better position than most of his fellow players. 'Today we have a production potential for two thousand cars,' explained Enzo, 'but the market can absorb only thirteen hundred.' Certain traditional Ferrari markets, such as Lebanon and Brazil, were at present closed to imports for reasons that had nothing to do with the car industry. 'In the former,' said Enzo, 'people shoot at each other in the streets; in the latter, they recently passed a new 207 per cent tax'[41] on imported luxury cars.

'Until a couple of years ago,' Ferrari had revealed that summer, 'you would [only] desire a Ferrari, not necessarily buy one. Today, instead, the client must only specify what colour he prefers.'[42] Still, he was positive. 'We have a lot of faith in the 308 GTB,' he said. 'It is a true Ferrari with an engine derived from the 1964 world champion unit.'[43]

Before the end of October, Ferrari once again summoned the press to Maranello.

The occasion was twofold: the presentation of the 1976 season and the departure of Luca di Montezemolo. With an F1 team in full health and a 312 T2 that was, it was assumed, as beautiful and competitive as the world champion T, the surprise farewell of the young team manager made headlines.

Ferrari explained the change at *Gestione Sportiva* – Montezemolo was being replaced by Lancia's team manager Daniele Audetto – as a normal move between the companies. Luca was going to Turin to work for Fiat but, Ferrari said, he would most likely still go to European races on Ferrari's behalf. The presence of the old and new team managers would naturally cause confusion. But, very cleverly, before someone asked the inevitable question, Ferrari jokingly used the fact that Luca was getting married in December as a way to respond: he defined Montezemolo's future presence at grands prix as 'an escape from married life'.[44] In so doing, he got rid of the hot issue without facing it.

Sending Montezemolo to Turin was a masterpiece of tactics.[45] On the one hand, his young and valuable adviser, who had helped Ferrari win a world title, succeeding where more experienced men had failed in 11 long years, would represent Ferrari within Fiat like no other person in the world could – and Enzo knew how much he needed a friend in Turin. On the other, although he naturally did not say so, the Grand Old Man was getting rid of a person who, with his enthusiasm, know-how, charisma and achievements, had for an entire season nearly obscured him.

While none of the journalists present that day dared to say anything during the press conference, after time to think about the change at the top, a few weeks later one of them wrote a column with a telling headline: 'Agnelli's Favours to Ferrari'. Though the story had no byline, it didn't take much for Ferrari to realize that the author was good old Lorenzo Pilogallo, who had had no problem writing that Enzo Ferrari had 'sighed with relief' when 'Agnelli took Luca di Montezemolo away from him'.[46]

'It's strange,' Ferrari said in a surprisingly conciliatory tone – now that he was world champion again, in all likelihood, the controversy amused him – 'that you accuse me of a jealousy that never existed, given that my recurring controversy [with the press] arises precisely from my refusal to appear or speak.'[47]

But if it was true that, during the following year, Montezemolo would find the time to go to some European grands prix, Ferrari would soon realize that it was not the same thing. All in all, encouraging Montezemolo to go to Turin was a huge mistake.

Interlude

On 18 February 1976, Enzo Ferrari celebrated his 78th birthday. 'He looks like the invincible [warriors] who conquered the Far West plains, leaving behind fresh graveyards as [they] advanced,' journalist and author Enzo Biagi had said only a few months earlier.[1] In 1975, the year that saw the return of the F1 title to Maranello after 11 endless seasons – 'a title that rewarded our work, the passion of all our employees, the expectation of our supporters'[2] – had been better than 1974, even from a commercial perspective. Sales had increased by a hundred units and, as far as the upcoming year was concerned, Enzo was optimistic enough to say 'There are problems because they are created by the general situation, but Ferrari is in a position to announce an encouraging forecast for 1976.'[3]

As the incumbent F1 champion and wise old man of modern motor racing – his 'moderating and conciliatory deeds'[4] had become increasingly valuable in the tug of war between grand prix organizers and the teams – he could even dwell in dreams. So, he – the only one who still had the livery of his cars painted in his country's national colour – romantically fantasized about an improbable collegial return to national colours, 'regardless of advertising'.[5]

Despite his age, Enzo was as energetic as ever and in great shape. The king was firmly on his throne. He believed until the end that he would live to be at least 93, like his mother.[6] He was making plans for the future,[7] impatiently waiting for the new racing season to start. 'I know the freedom that cars have given me. Could I do without it?'[8] he wondered. Even his spirit remained as fiery as ever. He had hailed the dawn of the new year with an internal memo to his closest aides in which he called them to order. His two drivers, talking to reporters over the Christmas holidays, had loosened up more than discretion would advise, especially Clay Regazzoni, who had basically told the press that all was not well in the house of Ferrari: 'Our shack squeaks,' the Swiss driver had said, providing a thankful journalist with a great headline.[9]

In 1974 Clay Regazzoni had lost a title that he had practically already won because of some decisive incongruity on the part of the team, which had sided with Lauda until it was too late to realize that only the more-experienced Swiss driver could bring home the world crown. Never one to let hard feelings and recriminations get in the way, Clay had taken it all in, convinced that 1975 would do him justice. Now, it was time for all to hear his story. 'Lauda,' he said, 'had been lucky to come to Ferrari when things were good. Had he come in 1971,' at the time of Clay's first stay at Maranello, 'he would not have won any world title.'[10]

Clay had very specific ideas about his world champion teammate and the reasons why he had risen to the top. He told the press plainly that Luca di Montezemolo, always 'a sponsor of Lauda', had contributed a great deal to 'the creation of the Lauda legend'.[11] Regazzoni maintained that Montezemolo, in 'his position as *Deputy* Ferrari', had enjoyed 'an unprecedented independence', accentuated by the fact that 'he knew that behind him was *Avvocato* Agnelli',[12] Fiat's tycoon.

'Although drivers are perfectly free to talk about their programmes and their activity,' Ferrari dictated in a letter, 'in order to avoid confrontational situations that may arise for casual or misquoted statements, it is necessary to invite them to understand that first, such a degree of freedom should respect what has been contractually agreed upon in terms of confidentiality' – Regazzoni had also confided that the 312 T2 was not as fast as the T – 'from a technical, organizational, business and racing point of view.' In addition, 'they must not mention the names of managers under any circumstances that could be interpreted in a way that may generate controversy, dualism or any misinterpretation'. This communication, along with a 'firm recommendation to make drivers aware of it', was sent to new team manager Daniele Audetto, Fiorano race-track head Sante Ghedini, chief press officer Franco Gozzi and Enzo's son Piero Lardi, who was more and more involved in the management of *Gestione Sportiva*, though still very much in the background from a public exposure point of view.

Despite all this, the new 1976 season started as Enzo had hoped: with his cars still faster and more reliable than all the others. Niki Lauda seemed just as hungry for success as he had been in 1975. The new champion won the first two grands prix of the year in Brazil and South Africa. The 'old' 312 T was still ahead of the pack, and Clay Regazzoni drove it to the last success of its 12-month racing history in the first US Grand Prix West, held at Long Beach, California, in late March.

Yet, underneath the apparent invincibility of the car and the unity of the team, things were not as good as they looked on the surface. Watching his new world champion closely, it didn't take Enzo long to realize that Niki was not devoting himself to testing with the same passion and almost maniacal attention to detail that he had shown the year before.[13] When lapping at Fiorano, Lauda was as cooperative and precise with the team's engineers as ever, but he no longer craved never-ending sessions the way he used to in the winter of 1974–1975. Now, whenever he could, he would fly away to meet his wife in their new seaside villa in Spain.

The first sign of tension within Ferrari surfaced in late April, a few days before the Spanish Grand Prix at Jarama. While driving a small tractor around the garden in his new Salzburg home, Niki flipped the vehicle and was pressed underneath, cracking two ribs. All in all, it could have been much worse.

Ferrari was understandably disturbed by the incident[14] – what he saw as more evidence that Niki was not the totally committed driver he'd once known. The Italian press, who had never loved Niki in the first place, began to publicly demand that Ferrari sideline him for the next race in favour of the young Italian driver Maurizio Flammini, who was making a name for himself in F2.[15]

In spite of his pain and bandages, Lauda did race in Spain, and brought the 312 T2 that made its debut that day to a second-place finish. When, at the end of the race, Hunt's McLaren was disqualified for irregularities in the size of the rear wing, Lauda and Ferrari were moved up to first place. So, the injured world champion returned from Spain with yet another victory, the third in four races.

The Sunday after the Spanish Grand Prix, a story in *Il Corriere della Sera* caught Enzo's attention. The quarrels that had followed the race at Jarama had by now died down in the press, and although the article – titled 'Down with the Winner' – dealt with his world, it was a peculiar story.[16] The 'winner' was not Enzo Ferrari, or anyone in particular, though as examples of the idea behind the story, the author mentioned the recent troubles experienced by motorbike ace Giacomo Agostini and F1 world champion Niki Lauda. By not dominating the way they used to, and by having to measure themselves against others, and fate, the story went, both Agostini and Lauda had suddenly become more loved by the public. Italians, the story said, never liked to side with the winner[17] – a thought personally shared by Enzo.

The story was by Alberto Bevilacqua, a journalist and author of national fame from nearby Parma. At 41, he was one of the leading members of the intellectual community from which Enzo was excluded (due to his education and background), but to which he felt fatally attracted.

Fascinated by the 'paradox of the title', Enzo read and reread the story. He pondered it on Monday and then, on Tuesday, he penned his reply, which was published in *Il Corriere della Sera* the following day, with the title: 'Ferrari Replies to Bevilacqua'. Carefully worded as always when he set his thoughts down in written form – a form he had by now come to prefer – the thrust of his argument lay in the fact that it revealed some of the most personal inner convictions of the Grand Old Man.

'Is it possible,' wrote Enzo, 'that Italians are so unconventional and self-destructive as to side with the loser and loathe the winner?' This was a general reflection that came from the experience he'd gained throughout his lifetime. He knew Italians, he felt very much Italian and, everywhere in the world, he was seen as a symbol of Italy, but, ironically, there was very little in his character and determination that could be deemed 'Italian'.

'Psychology, desecration of privileges, envy, a quest for solitude?' he asked, referring to what Bevilacqua had written. 'All correct,' he said, 'all so terribly true – by all means, all so Italian.'[18] There was more to it, of course. And there were other reasons behind the decision to put pen to paper and reply to the Sunday story. Enzo wanted to set the record straight, letting not only Bevilacqua but the whole country know how he saw the often bitter attacks that were regularly levied against his company and, especially, his racing cars.

Enzo went on, directly addressing Bevilacqua: 'I share your thesis, like the examples you used, agree on the causes and have for this reason felt a strong desire to let you know how much I feel that Ferrari is the living expression of your philosophical hypothesis.'[19] The phrasing may have been a little contorted, the choice of words antique, but the message was crystal clear: he was a winner in a land full of losers who resented the winner's success. Over the years, he had always maintained, and stated, that Italians can forgive anything but success.

In his reply to Bevilacqua, Ferrari at one point quantified a precise percentage past which, in his educated opinion, his fellow Italians began to detest the winner. That figure was 51 per cent. After a whole life dedicated to motor racing, Enzo had reached an age at which he loved to draw from his experience and formulate teachings that he would then distribute the way an old sage would. If anyone wanted to 'cultivate the illusion of success',[20] he said, he should not win more than one race – one match, one game, one event – out of every two.

Of course, Ferrari had never cared much about pleasing anyone when it came to racing, and in spite of the wisdom that he seemed to dispense in his reply to Bevilacqua, he had always tried to dominate the competitions in which his cars raced, trying to win as many events as possible. His cars had so far won all four races of the 1976 F1 season, and Ferrari would not have given up a single one of them to appear more sympathetic. But at the same time, he had not resisted the temptation to appear fair-minded – he who had never been fair-minded when it came to his chosen profession in life – and had come up with the surreal 51 per cent theory.

This theory produced two reactions; or, more precisely, two answers.

The first one naturally came from Bevilacqua. 'You – and this we must acknowledge – were able to create and preserve your company within the dynamics of mythology – all the more in times of scepticism.' Then Bevilacqua put it all in perspective: winners, losers, Italians, and this Italian who was so different from all others. 'Here, now, come together, along with the thesis of my story (that the winner is always hated), the message of your own life: that, in our country, the winner always remains standing – perhaps even when they throw rocks at him – and always pays a very high price. [This is especially true] when he did not emerge from bureaucracy and corruption, but became what he is through the work of his own hands.'[21]

The second reaction came from the odd man out – motorsport reporter Lorenzo Pilogallo – who, knowing Ferrari far better than Bevilacqua, smiled, or perhaps was horrified, on hearing the Great Old Man theorize that 51 per cent was the ideal percentage of winning. 'In this whole 51 per cent story,' he wrote, 'I feel like I am catching a glimpse of a gigantic lie. Because the real Ferrari, the most intimate [part of him]' – which Pilogallo certainly knew better than Bevilacqua – 'remains a tireless devourer of victories. What we see in newspaper interviews is someone who disguises himself as a man on a diet, and who finds comfort for his sufferings in the world of culture.'[22]

What sort of man was Enzo Ferrari, then, two years shy of his eightieth birthday? A Ferrari who, while his cars ruled on the world's race tracks, was about to start updating his autobiography – who was working in secret on a book about automobile journalists and, in the meantime, philosophized in the pages of major newspapers with successful authors? Was he the captain courageous that had bewitched Bevilacqua or the old sea dog described by Pilogallo?

No doubt he was one of the very few Italians respected on the international scene, like Federico Fellini and Gianni Agnelli, possibly closer to the former than to the latter, despite sharing with Fiat's tycoon a love and an interest and passion for the automobile. 'I watch movies from a distance,' he said, 'on television. I have not gone to a movie theatre in twenty years.'[23]

He was a man surprised by the political involvement of Gianni Agnelli's brother Umberto – 'I spoke to him twice in my life, eighteen years apart,' Enzo confided, but 'he does the right thing in trying to personally confront the challenges posed to our industry, rather than wait for professional politicians to try to solve problems they simply don't understand.'[24]

Of his own relationship with politics Enzo said: 'I never thought to engage in politics for two main reasons. First of all, I never had the time. Secondly, I read that politics is the art of lying at the appropriate time, which strongly contrasts with my brutal frankness.'[25] On three separate occasions he had been offered a safe seat, but every time he had refused – almost scornfully but, all in all, happy, or maybe just amazed, that shrewd politicians had thought of him as a way to gain consensus.[26] Of the climate of heated civic protest in which Italians had been living for years, and of the extra-parliamentary movements that had rejected dialogue in favour of violence, Enzo said: 'These are young people who cannot find in their original political parties the revolutionary force that comes instinctively at their age. I too,' he added, with a certain dose of realism and, perhaps, paternalism, 'have been young, and remember a certain temperament that led me to rebellion, before reaching an age, [in my] forties, when one begins to assimilate the mentality of the fireman,'[27] cooling down the fiery enthusiasm of youth with the perspective that comes with age and experience.

And, quoting a personal confidence received from historic Italian Communist leader Palmiro Togliatti – and unsuspectingly echoing Thomas Jefferson – he liked to emphasize the near inevitability of violent reaction. 'Thirty-five years have passed since the last war,' he said, 'and we should conclude that, historically, certain uncontrollable forces cyclically detonate, leading men to wars and revolutions.' But he had a conviction: 'That the laws that govern the economy of our country must be proposed, discussed, elaborated and voted on in the intended institutional bodies, and not elsewhere.'[28]

At nearly 80 years of age, Enzo was still the avid and disordered reader that he had ever been. The first author he remembered having an interest in was Stendhal, but he continued to be 'an admirer of Leopardi and D'Annunzio, Einstein's writings and Kafka'. He loved the rebellious soul and refined prose of Giovannino Guareschi, and confessed that he had 'a fondness for biographies'.[29]

He shared with an increasingly weak and distant wife the apartment on the first floor of the Cento Caproni building overlooking Largo Garibaldi in Modena. The apartment was spacious, relatively austere in its furnishings and certainly more comfortable than elegant. He had lived there with Laura since 1960, though each slept in a separate room and he, at night, locked the door to his.

For breakfast he drank a bowl of *café au lait* while munching the bread left from the day before. By breakfast time he had read the major national newspapers, the local and the sports press. He read *La Stampa* – the Turin newspaper owned by Fiat – to know what to expect from his cumbersome equity partner; and he leafed through the Communist newspapers – *Unità* and *Paese Sera* – because he wanted to know what the enemy was thinking.

Then he went to the barber, where he always sat in the same red-leather chair – the first as you entered, next to the window – where Massimo shaved him as his uncle Antonio had shaved him before that. It was his morning ritual of the past 40 years, every day of the week except Sunday. Then Dino Tagliazucchi, who seven years earlier had taken Peppino Verdelli's place, accompanied him to the cemetery for Enzo's daily visit to his son's tomb.

Despite the years that were beginning to become a burden, and the mayor's offer to let Enzo drive into the cemetery in his car, had Ferrari wished to do so, Dino Tagliazucchi parked outside the cemetery and then, side by side, they walked along the gravel paths and up the steps to the chapel. The chauffeur handed him a chair and then exited, leaving Enzo alone with his thoughts and the dead – his son Dino, of course, but also his mother, father and brother. They were all around him behind dark-red gravestones. He bowed his head, stared at the floor, his hands through his now completely white hair as if to hold up his head. He never said a word.[30]

The chauffeur reentered the chapel a while later, and it was time to go. Together, they quietly walked back to the car and rode to Maranello, through those small towns that Enzo had driven through for more than 30 years. He'd seen them grow little by little, and then faster and faster. By mid-morning he was at Maranello. He always met first thing with Franco Gozzi, who had married the barber's daughter, had been with him for 15 years and was a lot more than his chief press officer. When Gozzi walked out of Enzo's office – he'd never go far; he'd be back and forth several times during the next ten hours or so – Enzo's day began. A day made up of a few meetings, many talks and a lot of phone calls, the device through which he remained connected with the rest of the world.[31] He would break for a frugal lunch in the private dining room at the Cavallino, usually with Gozzi, always with Dino Tagliazucchi, sometimes with a few guests. Then, he would make a second visit to the production line, having already been there once in the morning. And if the F1 cars were testing that day, he would cross the street to Fiorano.[32] In the middle of all of this, he continued to update his original memoir. One could hear screams, yells, quarrels and outbursts as Enzo shared his thoughts with Franco Gozzi, along with long and lucid soliloquies, the precious search for episodes that emerged from his private and infinite memory archives, the reappearance of a familiar face, an anecdote about Nuvolari and Campari or Don Vincenzo Florio, as if he had talked to them just the day before.

When evening set in, Ferrari began to feel the grip of loneliness that he had come to detest.[33] And when it was time to go home, he tried to put it off as long as he could. Once, only a few years earlier, he would have found among his men a sacrificial lamb with whom to go to one of the many restaurants that he knew in the countryside. But now his age and health – good, certainly, but he had to be careful to keep it under control – called for an organized personal schedule and an unbending diet. All he could do, then, was to call Dino and ask him to drive him back home.

At home, Dino's wife had prepared a light dinner for Enzo. Laura had already had her supper and, at any rate, she had stopped cooking for him years ago. Then, some television; every Thursday he watched his favourite quiz show hosted by American-Italian Mike Bongiorno, whom Ferrari adored. Then a book, never the newspapers, many thoughts, much loneliness – once perhaps sought, now endured. Then to bed, never early,[34] with a thought – not necessarily a prayer, but a thought – for all of his loved ones, now gone, especially Dino.

*   *   *

In the second half of May, while Ferrari was philosophizing with Bevilacqua, Lauda won the grands prix of Belgium and Monaco, bringing his tally to five victories out of six races – and Ferrari's tally to six out of six. Then, unexpectedly, something happened. In mid-June, Lauda finished only third in Sweden, behind the two revolutionary six-wheeled Tyrrells. And in France, on 4 July, the engines of both T2s blew up. The team officially informed the world that electrical problems had caused the withdrawal of both cars – for Ferrari, the engine was never responsible for anything that was not a victory – but the pale blue cloud that had wrapped the two red cars left little to the imagination. So much so that, two days later, Ferrari was forced to admit that 'the two engines in both Lauda and Regazzoni's cars experienced the identical breaking of the crankshaft'.[35]

On the same day that Ferrari was forced to admit the fragility of his engines (it would not end here), the FIA reversed its previous ruling and returned to James Hunt the victory in the Spanish Grand Prix. The Grand Old Man was furious, but said nothing. He only broke his silence after the next grand prix, of Great Britain, where his drivers had nearly thrown each other out at the first corner and victory had once again gone to Hunt – a controversial one because Hunt's car had been damaged on the first lap and, if the rules had been correctly applied, he would not have taken the restart.

Ferrari finally lost his patience and decided to file an official complaint. 'Ferrari has never filed any complaint,' he said, 'but faced with situations that outside of Italy are readily defined [as being] "mafia-style" when they happen in Italy, I thought that enough is enough; the time has come to defend our interests with all available means.'[36]

It was not just the behaviour of the English race stewards at Brands Hatch that had made him lose his temper. That was the last straw. What had really infuriated him was the reversal of the Jarama decision. 'It all sounds like a fairy tale,' he said, with a good dose of sarcasm. 'They have disqualified a car at the end of a race to which this car should not have been admitted in the first place. This was followed by a controversial decision. Then, the paradox of the appeal to the FIA.'[37]

Ferrari knew that F1 had been in British hands since the early 1960s. But what he could not understand was how the Italian federation never managed to take his side. 'The CSAI,' he cried, 'limited itself to a [bland] statement of dissent, conceived with the clear [intention] of not taking any position. After all,' he said mockingly, 'which position could ever be taken by a sports body that is conspicuous for its absence at races since manufacturers [started] refusing to pay for their trips? As if Italian teams and drivers were not entitled to a diligent and effective support in the international arena.'

He'd lost the battle and he knew it.

'For my part,' he thundered, threatening to take drastic action, 'in the absence of a return to the letter and spirit of the law in our sport, I do not want to go on.'[38]

But there was more.

Ferrari had not appreciated the attitude of self-destruction his drivers had shown in England.

'I can understand human anxiety overcoming both drivers, but having to first protect the sporting interests of the team, I would like to remind them that both of them are employees who must cooperate in order to once again win the world championship title.'[39] He no longer understood Regazzoni and had come to the conclusion that he liked the new Lauda a lot less than he'd liked the old. 'Regazzoni's conduct leaves me puzzled, and I am also sorry for Lauda's,' he said, adding, 'And it's not the first time this year.'[40]

Having given up on Regazzoni,[41] Enzo directed his criticism towards Lauda, attacking the driver to defend the car and the team – Ferrari, that is. Lauda, he said, had been given 'a completely new T2' for the Grand Prix of France. 'On this new unit, in the *brief* tests conducted by Lauda at Fiorano' – and here, the word 'brief' was the real key to the sentence, and the situation as a whole – 'an oil temperature anomaly was discovered, and the cause was attributed to the engine. But since the driver wanted to leave immediately on his private plane for personal commitments, there was no time to replace the engine and try the car again, which,' he ruled, 'would have shown that it was not the engine, but the electrical system.'[42]

In essence, Ferrari suggested, it was the driver's attitude that had caused the problems encountered on the track. With the *old* Lauda, the problem would have been resolved earlier, the engine would not have blown up and Ferrari would have won in France.

'It is clear,' Enzo said maliciously, thinking about the long winning streak that had begun last season, 'that the 18 races completed by Lauda without any mechanical failure are the result of everyone's work, including the time that he devoted to testing.[43] I believe Lauda to be an intelligent and serious professional, [who will] understand the spirit of my comments,'[44] he said.

But the punch – hard, direct and unequivocal – had been delivered.

The Long Hot Summer

In the intolerable heat of a midsummer afternoon, the first day of August, the phone rang in Enzo's office. His cars were racing in the grand prix on the old Nürburgring that day, the legendary race track on which Tazio Nuvolari, in July of 1935, had scored one of Scuderia Ferrari's finest wins.

On the phone was team manager Daniele Audetto. Niki Lauda had had a terrifying crash on lap two, Audetto reported. His car had caught fire, and Niki had been saved by the prompt action of four fellow drivers, Harald Ertl, Brett Lunger, Guy Edwards and Arturo Merzario. Audetto and Lauda had reached Mannheim via helicopter after stops at hospitals in Adenau and Ludwigshafen. The situation, Audetto said, was desperate. Niki Lauda was in a coma and might not live to see the sun rise the following morning.

Enzo was appalled. Death had always been a component of motorsport, but every time it came knocking at his door, it was as if it were the first time. The Grand Old Man knew that he must not stop to think about death, its mystery and its consequences. He never had. He must look ahead.[1] He must put death behind him – and quickly. Therefore, although shaken by the unexpected and dramatic news, he ordered an astounded Audetto to go back to the track and contact Emerson Fittipaldi.

The order he gave Audetto was unequivocal: offer Emerson Niki's place on the team. Despite what had happened, Enzo could still think clearly. At this point in the season, few top drivers would leave their teams to drive for him. But Fittipaldi had left a top team like McLaren a few months before, and he surely couldn't be happy with the racing results he had obtained so far with the all-Brazilian team of Copersucar. He unemotionally directed Audetto to offer Fittipaldi a contract for the rest of the 1976 season, and for both 1977 and 1978.[2] For Ferrari the solution was simple: he would substitute one world champion with another. He had never concealed his belief from anyone: drivers were but a component of his cars.

Enzo isolated himself from the rest of the world, waiting for Audetto to call with either the news of Lauda's death or of Fittipaldi's decision. Perhaps both. The most daring among his journalist friends placed calls to Maranello. Enzo did not take most of them – but he did take some.

Those rare conversations were filled with long silences, interrupted by desperate efforts to find the right word that would make sense out of this situation.[3] It was so unexpected; up until that morning, Lauda had been safely cruising towards his second world title, and now he was possibly on his deathbed.

On Monday morning the news was not good. Niki Lauda was still alive and had come out of his coma, but the gravity of his burns, and especially the severity of the damage caused by inhaling the burning fumes while being rescued, left little hope. His lungs and bronchial tubes had been severely damaged. Doctors warned that complications could ensue at any moment. Even if his life was spared, no one would bet on his chances of ever returning to racing.[4]

In Maranello, Enzo was informed that Emerson Fittipaldi would remain with Copersucar.[5] From a racing point of view, it was a huge setback for Enzo. With Lauda out, his other driver, Clay Regazzoni, was 30 points behind James Hunt, who was now the potential heir to the leadership in the standings. In the past Clay had enjoyed the unquestioned confidence of his boss, but Enzo had already decided to let Regazzoni go at the end of the season. Something had been lost long ago in Enzo's affection for the Swiss driver he had once compared to Nuvolari.

Another night and another day passed. Niki was still alive, although doctors refused to raise anyone's hopes. Lauda had also fractured his legs and doctors still hadn't excluded the possibility of amputations to save his life. Niki was communicating with his brother and his wife Marlene, who were at his bedside, but, in two days, doctors said, they would know whether Niki would survive.

With his world champion seemingly on his deathbed in Mannheim, and the search for his substitute open, Enzo now found himself caught up in a controversy over the causes of the crash. It was nothing new, of course, but every time it came as a hard blow.

Niki Lauda's 312 T2 had been trucked back to Italy on Sunday night and was now in the Fiorano quarters of Ferrari's *Gestione Sportiva*. The organizers of the German Grand Prix, representatives of the German Automobile Club, who had examined it in the late afternoon of Sunday, and on Wednesday 4 August, announced their verdict. According to their findings, the incident had occurred when a suspension component broke on lap two. Tyres had been changed and fixed properly at the end of lap one; however, according to their report, Ferrari had not equipped its cars with automatic fire extinguishers and, thus, there had been no way to put out the fire.[6]

Enzo took in the verdict and, for the moment, did not comment. As Luca di

Montezemolo went to Adenau to visit his injured friend, doctors began to speak with some cautious optimism of the possibility that Niki might make it, although his chances of survival were still at 50 per cent. A crisis could still occur, and bronchial infections could strike suddenly, but the overall situation, compared with Sunday night, had improved dramatically.

In the afternoon of Thursday 5 August, the world of motor racing was taken by surprise by Enzo's sensational announcement. In a long and carefully articulated press release, Enzo Ferrari announced that he was abandoning F1 racing indefinitely.[7]

He had been toying with the idea since Tuesday and, despite his total independence in any question concerning his racing activity, had thought to inform Fiat of the possibility.[8] The situation had degenerated on Thursday morning, when the outcome of the Grand Prix of Great Britain was reversed and James Hunt was awarded the victory. (At issue was whether Hunt had completed a lap following a crash he was involved in; Ferrari protested, and was joined by three other teams. The decision was later overturned and Lauda awarded the win.) But it was at this early judgement point that the decision of the Grand Old Man had become irrevocable.

Enzo Ferrari was protesting the FIA's latest decision, but there was more to it – much more. He was raising his voice against what he saw as an anti-Ferrari front that had the international body at its centre, but also included the organizers of most of the races held so far in the season.[9] Few years had seen as many controversies as 1976, and a ruling unfavourable to Ferrari had solved most of the issues. Enzo wouldn't take it anymore; if F1 kept ruling against his team, why should Ferrari continue racing? Often at odds with the sports authorities, Enzo had threatened to quit before, but had never actually done so. This time, or so he said, he was going to do it.

Included in Enzo's sights was the Italian racing establishment, which, in his eyes, was guilty of not defending him on the international scene.[10] It was an old story, of course. The diatribe had never died out between the old man in Maranello and the Italian executives who every time Ferrari was in the spotlight, as after Monza 11 months ago, seemed to be the first to jump on the bandwagon, but, anytime he might need anything, were as elusive as they could possibly be.[11]

Theatrical moves had always been in Enzo's repertoire. By taking actions of a magnitude often greater than the cause to which they were a reaction, Enzo had usually won back the edge.[12] If the international rulings this year had always gone in favour of Ferrari, Lauda would now have 64 points; Hunt, 26. And 38 points, with 6 races to go before the end of the season, was a far larger gap to fill for the British champion of McLaren.

Alone against the rest of the world. It was a familiar theme in Maranello, and one the old man loved. He had always considered his life and career a personal crusade against the established powers and conventions of society. It was a struggle that he had never disdained, and that had ultimately made him who he was. At 78, it was perhaps also a way of feeling young again.

Of course, Enzo never really considered abandoning F1. His announcement was a superb *coup de théâtre,* staged to bring world attention to his position. Everyone – including Enzo – knew that F1's appeal would be totally different without his red cars, and too many people and organizations had too much at stake to let this happen. At the same time, it was obvious to all that for Enzo Ferrari, it was simply inconceivable to live and work without racing. He had never made a secret of this, to the point that, when in 1969 he had signed an agreement with Fiat, he had kept for himself *Gestione Sportiva* and all racing activity. Without racing there would be no more Enzo Ferrari and, by now, racing – in terms of technical content and popularity – was only F1. Therefore, all of his next moves were aimed only at staging his grand comeback.

First he invited the CSAI, the Italian racing commission, to inspect the remains of the wrecked 312 T2 that Niki had crashed at the Nürburgring. A delegation came diligently to Fiorano on Saturday, and the following day headlines all over Italy loudly declared that Ferrari had no responsibility in what had happened. Contrary to the German Automobile Club's findings, there had been no technical or mechanical failures. Responding to a precise point that had been raised in the report, released a few days earlier by a commission of the German Automobile Club, the CSAI made sure to certify that there had indeed been an automatic fire extinguisher on board the Ferrari; it had been built and installed correctly, and had, in fact, worked.[13]

By Wednesday, the CSAI executive board was openly begging Enzo Ferrari to reconsider his decision and go back to racing. In return, the highest Italian racing body publicly assured the Grand Old Man of all the support he might ask for from now on.[14] For Enzo, on the national front, it was a total victory.

As the Austrian Grand Prix approached, race organizers were busy calculating how much the absences of both the Ferrari driven by local hero Niki Lauda and the other Ferrari of Clay Regazzoni would impact the financial outcome of the event.[15] Regazzoni had tested at Fiorano earlier in the week and rumours were now seriously indicating that Ronnie Peterson was the most likely substitute for Niki Lauda[16] – but from the Old Man there were no signs. After his astounding announcement, Enzo had spoken no more.

Trying to predict the outcome of this crisis between Enzo Ferrari and the world of motorsport, some observers were now guessing that Ferrari would return to F1 only in 1977.[17] Others, more optimistically, were indicating Monza in September as the race that would see Ferrari's return.[18] Still, there were no indications whatsoever that Enzo Ferrari would ever reconsider his decision.

At last, on Saturday 14 August, almost two weeks after the accident at the Nürburgring, and eight days after announcing his withdrawal from F1, on the eve of the Austrian Grand Prix in which his cars would not take part, Enzo Ferrari made his position known. He sent a letter to Carpi de Resmini, the president of the Italian Automobile Club, the highest motoring body in Italy, which chief press officer Franco Gozzi quickly forwarded to all media.[19]

In his letter, the Grand Old Man thanked de Resmini for the support the national automobile club had voiced for his decision to withdraw from F1, and for the promise of different, more aggressive behaviour towards the FIA.[20] On the home front, it was a second home run. Enzo was not alone anymore; one of his goals had been achieved. The official recognition of his daring move and the position now assumed by the Automobile Club of Italy were beginning to pave the way for his return.

'My return,' Enzo warned, however, 'cannot be a personal act out of my love for this sport, but rather the rational prospect of defending the image of an automobile manufacturer belonging to the Fiat Group, and to the affection of all Italian fans.'[21]

The mention of Fiat was another hint of his intention to return. In the past, when he had been alone, he could have gone on indefinitely in his war with the powers that oversaw international racing. But now he, too, was part of a larger scheme and could not decide only out of instinct. He had other factors to consider.[22]

He left the toughest sentence for the last paragraph of his letter, in which he said that he might indeed return to F1, but also that in the future he may decide to put a definitive stop to his racing activity. 'If then, in the evolution of this modern world of racing, barter, corruption and blackmail should find a place in it, I believe that there will no longer be room in this world for me.'[23]

Enzo Ferrari had rarely used such strong language in an official document or statement. Could his rage be directed not just at the FIA and those F1 teams that, in his opinion, were not only cheating, but also influencing the power-holders? Could there be more to it than anyone assumed?

The moment Emerson Fittipaldi turned down the offer to take Niki Lauda's place, the Grand Old Man had had only one other driver in mind – Ronnie Peterson. The Swede was unanimously considered the fastest driver currently racing, a sort of 1970s Stirling Moss, and an enormously talented man whose career had been tormented until now by misfortunes of various natures that had prevented him from becoming world champion.

Ronnie Peterson was, however, one of the few drivers with whom Niki Lauda – who was friends with his current rival for the world crown, James Hunt – had had quarrels in the past when they were both racing in junior categories. Not certain of his own recovery, Niki would accept anybody in his car but Ronnie Peterson. Luca di Montezemolo's visit on 4 August in Mannheim had not been merely an act of friendship. Or, rather, it *was* an act of friendship on the part of the young former Ferrari executive, but Lauda had seized the moment to ask Luca's intercession in stopping the hiring of Peterson. Montezemolo was by now out of Ferrari, but maintained direct access to Gianni Agnelli in Turin. And it was Agnelli who personally called Enzo Ferrari to ask him not to hire Ronnie Peterson.[24]

Exasperated by this overt interference in the management of Ferrari racing activity, which, by virtue of the 1969 agreement, should have been his exclusive prerogative, Enzo had made the decision to withdraw.[25] On the part of Enzo, who now felt like a prisoner in a golden cage, the unprecedented decision to withdraw was therefore also a gigantic act of rebellion. If he did not have the freedom to choose his own drivers, he would quit.

In Austria John Watson scored a historic first win for himself and for the American team of Roger Penske, during the same race in which Roger's longtime driver and personal friend, Mark Donohue, had died a year earlier. James Hunt was fourth and took home only three points. Regazzoni, sitting out of the race, could have contributed further to preserve Lauda's leadership in the world standings, but instead watched the grand prix on television in his Lugano home.

The middle of August was a time of reflection for Enzo Ferrari. Alone in his farmhouse in the heart of a silent Fiorano race track, with all his closest aides and Ferrari executives on vacation, he pondered, carefully planning his return. Now that he had the Italian automobile and racing bodies aligned behind him, and had made sure that everyone in Turin knew that he was still the king, he could allow his team to reenter F1. This was the key. Ferrari *the company* would decide to go back; Ferrari *the man* would acknowledge the decision and respect it. Thus, the resolution to entrust the Ferrari board of trustees with the pronouncement – which, strictly speaking, given his mandated total independence in all racing decisions, was incongruous.[26]

Three weeks to the day after he was almost killed in the fire that had devoured his 312 T2 on the Nürburgring, Niki Lauda announced that he would return to racing. The incumbent world champion, resting at his home near Salzburg, was recovering faster than anyone had predicted. He was eager to return and defend his world title; and although he didn't say it, he desperately wanted to put an end to Enzo's irritating attempts at finding his replacement.[27] The mere three points collected by Hunt in Austria had probably added to his confidence. He did not indicate a date or a grand prix for his comeback, but rumours were beginning to point in the direction of Mosport, the Grand Prix of Canada – Friday 1 October, the first day of qualifying.

Ferrari's board of trustees met in Fiorano on Monday 23 August to decide the future of the team's racing activity. In the course of the meeting, the causes and effects of Ferrari's withdrawal were discussed.[28] The unanimous conclusion was that Enzo's decision had not only received undivided approval, but had also directed everyone's attention towards the necessity of more integrity and honesty in the handling of racing matters at the highest level.

Through the support of both the Automobile Club of Italy and its C S A I racing committee, Enzo received assurances that a moralizing process would soon be undertaken that would lead to a profound change within the international racing committee. For Enzo it was more than enough to feel vindicated and happily return to F1 racing.[29] Ferrari the company would thus return to where it belonged, and participate in the next event on the calendar – the Grand Prix of Holland, on 29 August – albeit with just one car, driven by Clay Regazzoni.[30]

Despite Lauda's resolve to stage his own comeback as early as possible, now that his cars had returned to the race track Enzo intensified his search for a new driver – whether as a substitute for Lauda for the remaining races of 1976, or as a 1977 substitute for Regazzoni was not clear, perhaps not even to him, at this point.

With Ronnie Peterson out of the question, the shortlist had been reduced to just three names: John Watson, Jody Scheckter and Carlos Reutemann – Enzo had preselected the latter about a month earlier, before the Nürburgring, to replace Clay Regazzoni from 1977 on.[31] Negotiations were now under way with Reutemann to race for Ferrari, beginning with the Italian Grand Prix and for the rest of the schedule, alongside Regazzoni.

On Wednesday 1 September, Carlos Reutemann arrived in a rainy Maranello to meet Enzo Ferrari and sign the contract. The terms of the agreement, despite two press releases issued simultaneously by both Ferrari and Brabham, were quite vague. Reutemann's engagement was limited to the 'next races, starting with Monza', while Ferrari 'waited for Lauda to return'.[32]

Confused by the team's decision to hire Reutemann now that it seemed Lauda was on his way back to the team, Regazzoni at last asked to meet Enzo Ferrari. 'Until now nobody has told me anything that would lead me to think that I will be fired,' he said, somewhat changing his tone from the more-optimistic note of just a few days earlier. Perhaps now seriously worried about his own prospects for 1977, he talked explicitly of the 'unique and unrepeatable synergy with Lauda over the last three seasons. I am the driver with the most grands prix ever with Ferrari,' he said, almost as if to convince himself that Enzo could not decide to do away with him. 'I know everybody at Ferrari, and I get along with all of them.'[33]

If Regazzoni was confused, Lauda was furious. He couldn't believe that now that he had announced his intention to return, Enzo Ferrari had hired a new driver. From Ibiza, where he was recuperating in the sun, Lauda announced that the following Tuesday he was going to Maranello. He would speak to Enzo Ferrari and then drive a few laps at Fiorano. He now wanted to return to racing at the Italian Grand Prix at Monza,[34] where Ferrari had just announced that he would enter two cars for Regazzoni and Reutemann.

Despite his doubts, Enzo Ferrari was deeply impressed with Lauda's stubbornness. On a personal level he was almost fascinated by the courage that Niki was displaying. In private, and later in public, he began to put him side by side with Tazio Nuvolari[35] – which, on his part, was the ultimate compliment. 'Only Nuvolari was like him,'[36] Enzo said.

The meeting between Clay Regazzoni and Enzo Ferrari produced no results. Despite Clay's insistence that he should be told here and now what Ferrari intended to do with him, *Il Commendatore* was very elusive. All that Enzo was willing to discuss were small details, not the central issue of Regazzoni's contract for 1977. Clay's present contract was due to expire on 31 December 1976.

Enzo asked him for patience – at least until the end of the season, on 24 October.[37] What he could not tell Regazzoni was that Carlos Reutemann was, at this point, his only certainty for 1977. As for the second driver, all depended on the return and the true physical condition of Lauda, who had a contract with Ferrari until 31 December 1977.

On Tuesday morning, 7 September, as announced, Niki Lauda came to Maranello. He met with Enzo Ferrari, who tried to persuade him not to rush his return. Niki told his boss that he felt good, that he wanted to race and that he knew what he was doing. Listening to him, Enzo quickly realized that 'something extraordinary has happened: we have retrieved a man *and* a champion'.[38]

Enzo was horrified at the sight of Niki's wounds and burns, but also touched by his palpable courage. 'We are in front of a person touched by a miracle,' he said. Then he characteristically tried to rationalize: 'It is clear that Lauda has a gut love for this sport. I don't know if anyone else, after a similar incident, would have returned so quickly.'[39]

While confirming that on Sunday at Monza there were going to be three

Ferraris, Enzo said that he would decide only after the Italian Grand Prix how many drivers he would enter in the three remaining events of the season. But, he warned the throngs of reporters who had descended on Fiorano, and now wanted to know if his two teammates would eventually help Lauda during the Monza race, 'don't deceive yourselves into thinking that a driver will ever respect a team's orders. Human egoism, even during a race, presents you with a thousand solutions.'[40]

That night, thinking of the way Niki looked, coupled with his stubbornness about immediately returning to racing, Enzo Ferrari confessed that the whole day had been 'a surreal experience, almost a dream'.[41] But the day had also confirmed one of the few certainties that he had. 'In life, you always pay the bill,' he said. 'Now we have paid it.'[42]

On Sunday at Monza, Niki Lauda stunned everyone by scoring a fourth-place finish that gave him three precious points in his quest for a second consecutive world title. James Hunt ended his grand prix when he spun off on lap 24, having started from the back of the grid because his qualifying time had been disallowed due to alleged fuel irregularities. In the three races when Lauda had been absent, Hunt had scored twenty-one points, closing the gap – since Ferrari's appeal about the British Grand Prix had not yet been examined in court – to two single points. After Monza, Lauda widened his lead to five points.

Of the three Ferrari drivers, in qualifying Lauda had surprisingly been the fastest. In the race, Regazzoni had done better, finishing second behind winner Ronnie Peterson after aggressively overtaking both of his teammates, as if to show the old man in Maranello that his class was still intact and that he should not be discarded just yet.[43] Somewhat lost in the pack was Carlos Reutemann – seventh after qualifying, ninth at the end of the race – perhaps the only one of the team's three drivers with nothing to prove to Enzo Ferrari on this day. After the race, while the whole world applauded Lauda for his astounding courage and unaffected driving talent, the Grand Old Man remained incongruously silent.

Purple Rain

For more than a week after Monza, Enzo Ferrari kept out of the limelight. The world speculated on his next move and Regazzoni, Lauda and Reutemann impatiently awaited his decision. Then, on 23 September, the day before the international racing committee met in Paris to examine Ferrari's appeal concerning the British Grand Prix, Enzo spoke.

Ferrari would enter only two cars in the last three races of the championship, and the drivers would be the pair who had started the season: Niki Lauda and Clay Regazzoni. Carlos Reutemann would remain at Fiorano to develop the car for the 1977 season. Reutemann was implicitly confirmed for the following year; all decisions regarding 1977, Ferrari insisted, would be made, or at least announced, only after the last event of 1976.

Regazzoni, however, was going to be released from his contract with Ferrari on 26 October, the day after the Grand Prix of Japan.[1] Although Clay wasn't bitter, he openly admitted that he could not fully comprehend why Ferrari had wanted to substitute him with Carlos Reutemann, a driver of approximately his age.

The following day the FIA appeals court met in Paris for the hearing on the Ferrari protest over the British Grand Prix. The ruling was favourable for Ferrari: Lauda was at last awarded the win, and James Hunt was disqualified. It was very good news for the Austrian, and for Ferrari, since their lead over Hunt and McLaren had now widened from five to seventeen points. With only three races to go before the end of the season, if Hunt did not finish in the top six in the next event, Lauda would need only two points to be the champion again. The verdict in Paris provoked international pandemonium, yet again.

McLaren's team manager, Teddy Mayer, accused Enzo Ferrari of intentionally destabilizing the situation to turn things to his advantage. 'With the help of the Italian press,' he said mockingly, 'Ferrari will in the future win the world championship without even having to start – or finish – races.'[2] Yet the same Italian press that Mayer was accusing of playing Enzo Ferrari's game was accusing the Grand Old Man of foul play.

At this crucial moment of the season, the Ferrari team suddenly lost its edge. At Mosport, in the Canadian Grand Prix, both drivers finished far from the podium and James Hunt returned to victory, closing the gap to just eight points with two races to go. Lauda kept assuring everyone that he was well enough to race, and grimly said that the trouble rested with the cars. In his opinion, the real problem was that in the two months following his near-fatal accident at the Nürburgring, no real development had been accomplished on the 312 T2, which, by early October, was no longer the best car in the pack.[3] Even though only four days remained before the beginning of the US Grand Prix weekend at Watkins Glen, Ferrari asked for an early, extra day of practice. This was granted, and Lauda and Regazzoni lapped Watkins Glen on Thursday, but the problems did not go away. On Sunday 10 October, Hunt won again and Niki finished a disappointing fifth. Lauda's lead had now been reduced to only three points.

There was only one race left: the Grand Prix of Japan. It was the first ever F1 event in Japan and no one was familiar with the Mount Fuji circuit – which at this moment, for Ferrari and Lauda, was actually a blessing. Two weeks separated the two North American races from the last grand prix of the season. The Grand Old Man had taken refuge in one of his customary periods of self-seclusion from the world. Journalists kept calling, but he would not return their calls.[4] Perhaps Enzo *should* have spoken, cried out, yelled at this or that, as he had so masterfully done countless times in the past. He could have blamed Lauda, Regazzoni or Forghieri. He could even have blamed the Italian press, if this would have helped to change the situation, or just make him feel better.

Instead, Enzo chose another familiar way out – total isolation from the rest of the world. It was an old habit that he'd adopted often in situations of distress, even when he was much younger. Now and then, it had worked. This time, the only thing he accomplished with his silence was to leave his three drivers and the rest of the team wondering what he might be planning next. And, of course, the summer months had convinced everyone that Enzo Ferrari was capable of even the most improbable of decisions.

A profound sense of uncertainty reigned in Maranello while the incumbent world champion driver and team prepared for the last and deciding race of the year. While Ferrari refused even his closest aides access to his innermost thoughts,[5] Reutemann, who should have been at Fiorano developing the car for 1977, was relaxing at home in Spain because no testing sessions had been scheduled.[6] Regazzoni, for whom the Japanese Grand Prix would be his last race with Ferrari, went on the record saying again that the real problem in Maranello was that Enzo, by not going to the races, depended too much on what his men reported back to him. As a consequence, Clay said, all too often Enzo did not see things the way they really were.[7]

On 24 October Enzo Ferrari was watching the race on television in his Modena apartment. Shortly after 5.30am, along with all viewers in Italy, he was told by TV commentator Mario Poltronieri that Ferrari had very likely lost the 1976 world title due to an electrical problem that had forced Lauda's 312 T2 into the pits at the conclusion of the first lap. Enzo watched Lauda stand up in the cockpit of his Ferrari; someone offered him an umbrella as a shelter from the torrential rain as he spoke with Mauro Forghieri.[8] In the deluge that had overcome the Fuji circuit, James Hunt still needed four points to become the new world champion, but there was no opposition that Lauda, who had now walked away from his 312 T2, could put up.

It was only later, with the race still on – and Hunt on his way to a third-place finish that would make him the new champion – that Daniele Audetto told Enzo what had really happened over the phone. Understandably, Enzo did not like what he heard.[9] Niki Lauda had decided that he wouldn't take any chances in the pouring rain, and had abandoned the race. Forghieri had volunteered to cover this up, at least with the press and the public, but Lauda was adamant: he would stand by his decision. To reporters he had candidly said: 'Gentlemen, *this* is my level of madness.'[10]

It was only after he reached the airport in Tokyo about two hours later that Niki Lauda spoke with Enzo Ferrari. When the Grand Old Man came on the phone, Niki apologized for his conduct. His decision had caused the whole team to lose a world title for which everyone at Ferrari had been relentlessly working for a whole year. But the incessant rain had been too much for him that day and he'd decided not to continue.[11] He had not been a victim of a psychological block, he said, because, if that were the case, he would have quit at Monza, the Friday he had returned – another rainy day that could have reminded him of the weather conditions on the day of his August crash in Germany. Today, he said, he stopped because he rationally thought that it was pure madness to continue.[12]

Although upset about the outcome of the championship, and appalled by the way both Lauda and Ferrari had lost it, Enzo told Niki that he respected his decision.[13] He would have time to address the situation in full in the following days, but at this moment he could afford to be sympathetic towards his courageous driver. Enzo had been a driver himself and knew that it took guts to throw away a world title in such a fashion and then to take responsibility for the decision.

When Enzo spoke with Lauda, it was already Sunday evening in Japan. In Modena, it was the morning of yet another foggy day. While his former world champion flew west towards Europe, the Grand Old Man started to coldly assess the bizarre situation he was now confronting. A part of him could not help but feel intimate solidarity with Lauda – for his brave act, and his even more courageous decision to honestly state what had happened and why.

Yet, despite the admiration he felt for Lauda's courage, as the owner and manager of a racing team, there were other aspects he had to address. He had bet – or he'd been persuaded, convinced or forced to bet – everything on Lauda's full recovery as a first-class driver. Now his former champion's seemingly odd behaviour in Japan legitimized everyone who'd second-guessed his decision. Lauda had a contract until the end of the 1977 season, and every intention of standing by it, but no one could see into his head to really know whether his refusal to race in Japan was, as the Austrian claimed, a reaction to an absurd racing situation or, as Enzo feared, a psychological block resulting from his near-fatal accident in August. As a former driver, Enzo understood that Lauda could honestly be claiming it was the former, sincerely not realizing that it was, instead, the latter. Enzo knew very well that after Lyon, he had not been the same driver that he'd been before.

Frustrated by a deep sense of impotence at not being on top of the situation – a rather unusual circumstance for him – on Tuesday afternoon, on the premises of the old Scuderia Ferrari headquarters in Viale Trento Trieste in Modena, Enzo held a much-awaited press conference. It was one of the longest he'd ever held, and one of the more energetic. He appeared in front of the press that he had been eluding for weeks in an extremely good mood – certainly neither depressed nor perceptibly aggravated by the dramatic finale of the 1976 championship.

'Today I will tell you *everything*,' he started out, boldly encouraging them to 'take advantage of this opportunity'.[14] Characteristically, he told them only what he chose to reveal, skilfully playing with his audience for three hours. Some of the reporters had come straight to Modena from Japan. His decision to hold a critical end-of-year press conference just 48 hours after a race that had been contested on the other side of the world was yet another way of punishing journalists, and they knew it. He measured his answers, masterfully playing with pauses and crescendos, firing irresistible one-liners and ad libs, now caustic, now brilliant.[15] He wanted them to hear what he had to say. He and his team had been castigated by the press for weeks on end; today, it was his turn to speak.

'What do you *want* from me?' he asked, theatrically raising his voice. And then he answered on their behalf: 'Don't *you* worry: you will have me around until I die.'[16] After such an encouraging preamble, he reiterated his case. 'I am legitimately worried for all that has been said and written. For this reason, I would like to give you a written statement, so as to avoid ghastly misinterpretations of what I will say.' At this cue, Franco Gozzi went around the room handing each journalist a single sheet of paper. The text on it read:

He did the right thing by not racing if, thinking of what he felt on August 1, and of his present form, he was afraid of the weather conditions. The future will depend exclusively on what he will decide. I too felt it necessary to question myself when I was a driver – when my Dino was born, and I made the decision to retire. After I have spoken with Lauda, I will be able to tell you whether he has that motivation, which does not go hand in hand with willingly taking unnecessary risks.[17]

Despite his signature old-fashioned prose, a precise sign that Enzo had personally dictated the statement word by word, at least three distinct points clearly emerged from the brief statement.

First: Lauda had been afraid, but he, Enzo, was magnanimous and respected his decision. Second: The future of the Lauda–Ferrari relationship rested solely in the hands of the Austrian driver. Third: By recalling his own experience, it was evident that Enzo believed Lauda was finished as a first-rate driver, and openly suggested that he retire.

A thoughtful mind could also draw at least another pair of conclusions. Lauda was not mentioned by name until the last sentence, and then, only by his *last* name. Referring in the text to Niki's 'present form' was a subliminal way to state that, if Lauda had listened to his advice and had not returned as early as he had, he may have been in better condition for the last and decisive races of the season, and perhaps would not have made a fool of himself in Japan.

Enzo gave journalists a moment to quickly glance through the few lines typed on the page, and then immediately started to address the only point that was truly on his mind today: the end of Lauda's career. 'If Lauda wishes to retire,' he said of his former world champion – who had openly stated in the past 48 hours that he would *not* retire and that he actually expected to be at Fiorano testing his Ferrari this coming Friday[18] – 'I will respect his decision.'[19]

Next, he was the sympathetic patriarch: 'I cannot let him down now and put another driver in his place,' he explained. 'I can't do it even if it was in the best interest of the company – and not merely to avoid you saying that I am the usual opportunist or, worse, cynic.' Then he was cautious again: 'For the time being there is a contract that I intend to honour.' Finally he was noble: 'At Ferrari a handshake is worth more than binding papers,'[20] as if to say that Lauda should not be concerned about the 31 December 1977 expiration date on his contract; if he wanted to go now, he was free.

That Enzo Ferrari was diametrically opposed to Lauda and clearly preferred that Niki move out of his way was obvious with what he said next. 'I am waiting to meet with him, perhaps even before the end of this week, to try and understand what's inside him – presuming that he himself knows.' Using strong words that were wholly in contrast with those written on the statement that had been distributed to his audience moments before, and that eloquently betrayed his real thoughts, he explained: 'I do not intend to continue our working relationship, or to end it, without this clarifying meeting.'[21]

The love story between Enzo Ferrari and Niki Lauda – if there ever had been love between the two of them – was officially over. Ferrari clearly had strong feelings about Lauda and did not try to hide them. 'Lauda called me two hours *after* the end of the race, not *before*,' he said accusingly, as if to say that the decision to pull out of the race and the responsibility for it was Niki's alone.[22] He may have respected it, but that didn't mean that he agreed with it.

Furthermore, Enzo Ferrari was not just criticizing his former world champion for his behaviour at the Grand Prix of Japan. He was scrutinizing the whole two-month period between late August and the last race of the season. 'If there was a mistake on Lauda's part,' Enzo said, 'it was when he pretended to race in Monza.'[23] But this was not all, because Lauda had also pretended to have the final word on who should be hired as the team's new driver. Given the choice between Peterson, Scheckter and Reutemann, Enzo said, Lauda had chosen Reutemann, only to drop him when the decision was made to have two cars compete in the last three events of the season, Canada, the United States and Japan – another choice imposed by Lauda.[24]

By now he was on a roll. Lauda had made mistakes, said Enzo, well before the incident at the Nürburgring. The Grand Old Man pointed the accusing finger at the British Grand Prix – not at the embarrassing incident at the start, but at the way Lauda had prepared for the race. 'He had already stopped testing then,' he said, addressing yet another point – Lauda's accusation that the world title had been lost because Ferrari had stopped developing the car following the incident in Germany.[25]

After such a devastating and largely unexpected attack on Lauda, the best part of the day was naturally over. Still, Enzo had more in store for his audience.

Clay Regazzoni was next on his list. Holding the race report his men had filed after the event at Brands Hatch, Enzo bluntly blamed Regazzoni for the incident with Lauda at the first start of the British Grand Prix in mid-July, and for driving too slowly at the Dutch Grand Prix in late August. Reading from a document that was originally – and clearly – intended for his eyes only, Enzo commented: 'Regazzoni has manifestly demonstrated that he has always raced only for himself.'[26] (Despite this indictment, Enzo knew better than anybody else that a driver – any driver – drives first and foremost for himself.)

The press conference was at last drawing to an end. Journalists were by now more exhausted than their septuagenarian host, who notoriously sucked life from encounters of this kind. Those in the media who accused Ferrari of dispersing his energy on other racing categories rather than concentrating all his efforts on F1, Enzo howled, did not back up their opinions with any proof. Yes, Ferrari had been working on an F2 engine, but that project had not distracted anyone.

Now, it was time to go. Enzo Ferrari had spoken for three hours and taken dozens of questions, answering them all, albeit in a way that best served his version of the truth. Yet, the one question to which the hundred or so journalists convened in Modena on this Tuesday afternoon demanded a response, remained unanswered: was Niki Lauda going to race for Ferrari in 1977?

While Lauda did not make any comment, the following day brought to Maranello the echo of Clay Regazzoni's severe reply to the accusations Enzo had levied against him. 'If I raced only for myself,' said the disenchanted Clay, 'this past Sunday in Japan I would have abandoned the race, too – the way Lauda did.' He had been in Maranello for a total of six years, and thought that by now he deserved better treatment from the 'Old Man', as he'd always affectionately called Enzo Ferrari when the microphones were off. 'I have constantly worked hard without complaining. I played second fiddle when it was necessary, both to Ickx and to Lauda. But when the time came to help me win the world title,' he said bitterly, recalling the missed opportunity of 1974, 'nobody did anything.'[27]

Without naming any names, Regazzoni openly talked of a group of people at Fiat who were putting pressure on Enzo Ferrari. 'Reutemann,' Clay said, 'was hired through the Turin channel.'[28] Then he contradicted his former boss, who had said that Niki had personally chosen the Argentine over Peterson, Scheckter and, naturally, Regazzoni himself. 'It is absolutely not true that Lauda is fond of Reutemann,' said Clay. 'Actually, Niki can't stand him.'[29]

Regazzoni was not the only victim of the end-of-season purge. After a single year in Maranello, Daniele Audetto was going back to Turin. 'It is no longer the time for team managers,'[30] explained Enzo. In place of Audetto, described by Ferrari as nothing more than a 'diligent clerk',[31] there would now be a group of three people who would take upon themselves the duties that di Montezemolo had performed to perfection and his successor had not: Sergio Tomaini, Sante Ghedini and Roberto Nosetto. It was a *troika* in the style of the one that Enzo had created to head the *Gestione Sportiva* technical department. But unlike the Forghieri-Bussi-Rocchi trio, this was a largely untested group of men.

Enzo Ferrari had stated that everything now depended on his one-on-one meeting with Lauda. He had said that he hoped the meeting would take place before the end of the week. By Thursday, however, rumours were in the air of a probable postponement due to pressing medical examinations and possible eye surgery that Niki had to undergo in London. Off-the-record information, skilfully leaked to the press by Ferrari executives, was now indicating Tuesday of next week as the possible date for the summit, perhaps even later.[32]

It was a masterfully executed diversion, personally orchestrated by Enzo to deceive reporters.[33] The much-awaited meeting did indeed take place on Sunday, the last day of October and seven days after the Grand Prix of Japan. As Enzo had planned, there were no reporters or photographers around. The deception had worked.

What did not work so well was the outcome of the meeting.

Enzo had hoped to persuade his former world champion to stop, reconsider, stay away and completely recover in body, but also in spirit, and then, eventually, come back – and not necessarily with Ferrari. Perhaps the insinuation of a possible deal with another team, coupled with the brutal accusations that he had delivered to the international press the previous Tuesday, might convince Lauda himself to leave. That would have been by far the best solution. He had hinted at it on Tuesday: despite the contract, Enzo had said, he would let Lauda go without any penalty fee if he so chose. That week he had even offered Lauda Audetto's position as team manager, asking di Montezemolo's help to convince him. But Niki had turned it down.[34]

Niki came to the meeting determined to race in 1977, and to race for Ferrari. If he had doubts about staying with Ferrari, which by now he understandably did, it was for the part of his career that would start on 1 January 1978, not 1977. He had not changed as a driver, he told Enzo over and over again; he would not quit, nor would he go elsewhere. This was it, whether Enzo Ferrari liked it or not. Lauda had always been direct in his relationship with Ferrari, by whom he was not the least bit intimidated, and his behaviour was no different today. Ferrari was furious. He had let Lauda manage his comeback and defence of the title the way Niki had wanted. Despite palpable scepticism, Enzo had given him a car for Monza, had agreed that Reutemann would stay home in the last races of the season and had publicly stood by Niki's grand refusal to continue at Fuji. (Technically, the Grand Old Man could have fired a driver who had decided to walk out of a race, and throw away a world championship, for the sole reason that he considered it 'madness' to continue.) He had been patient and unusually obliging, but he couldn't take it anymore. He thought that Niki was finished as a top-class driver and told him so.

The two positions were clearly irreconcilable. At the end of the meeting, a simple press release summed up the situation. There were no joint appearances in front of the press, as had been the case in early September when Lauda had returned to Maranello for the first time since the Nürburgring crash, nor were any photos taken to mark the event. The release issued by Gozzi in the afternoon was eloquently impersonal, even by Ferrari standards:

> *Following today's meeting with Lauda, Ferrari [the company, not the man] informs that the driver will immediately start testing for the 1977 season in order to have the necessary time to undertake a plastic surgery operation to the right eye. The Make [again, the distinction between the company and the man who runs it – ed.] acknowledges Lauda's strong determination to resume his activity in the form and with the intensity of past seasons.*[35]

As always with Enzo Ferrari, one had to read between the lines, interpreting the words that were used – and those that were not. Deciphering Enzo Ferrari had become an art at which some of his friends in the press had become very proficient and nobody was fooled by such an icy statement. It was Lauda, not Ferrari, who had decided to continue in the relationship. Ferrari the company, the team, the 'Make' – but *not* the man – was only acknowledging its driver's 'strong determination' to race again. Tellingly, Ferrari the man was not even mentioned in the release.

Lauda would thus race with Ferrari in 1977, but he would do so in a house divided, despite the gracious lie that Enzo supplied to the press a few days later. 'If it will take Lauda some time to be again the driver that he used to be,' he said nonchalantly, 'we all will help him.'[36]

Paradise Lost

Some relief in a very tense period came from a visit by Hollywood star and car enthusiast Paul Newman. The great American actor was a Ferrari owner and, the following February, was scheduled to participate in the Daytona 24 Hours at the wheel of a Ferrari 365 GTB/4. More to the point, he had lately been thinking of creating his own racing team and wanted to ask Enzo for advice.

Newman's visit to Maranello was a very different affair from the customary stopovers of movie stars, who often knew little about the cars they were going to buy but were fascinated by the charm their host could emanate on such occasions. Newman was very much interested in hearing directly from Enzo Ferrari all there was to know about running a successful racing team. He was granted a full two days in Maranello, where he met with Ferrari top management and was shown the whole factory and the racing-team premises – a big privilege in Ferrari terms, because *Gestione Sportiva* was normally off limits to anyone. Newman went to the Imola race track to watch Carlos Reutemann test his 312 T2, and then lapped himself at Fiorano at the wheel of the 308 GTB of which he had just taken delivery.[1]

On the second day, he finally met Enzo. The two men spoke in the blue-walled office overlooking the central court of the factory. Despite the fact that they had to talk through an interpreter, their dialogue was a lengthy and lively one. The problem was that while one was asking all sorts of questions about how to run a racing team, the other was trying to know all there was to know about the feminine universe in Hollywood.

Perhaps choosing to ignore Newman's decision to live in Connecticut, and certainly unaware of his famous quip – 'Why go out for hamburger when you have steak at home?' – Enzo kept pressing him on Hollywood women. The American movie icon would each time politely reply that he was not that kind of man, and then fire off another question aimed at understanding how to manage a racing team. Enzo would quickly answer Newman's question and then ask him yet again about women in the movie industry.

Paul Newman had clearly not come to Maranello to answer Enzo's repeated questions on actresses, or provocations on eventual opportunities to betray his beloved wife. He didn't give in and refused to play the old man's game. Enzo finally saw that there was no way to distract his determined guest from the purpose of his visit and realized that the time had come to stay focused on managerial and technical questions. Once they both understood that business was to be their sole focus, they talked on and on, skipping lunch, with Paul Newman being served two cups of tea and Enzo being served sandwiches and a beer only after the actor had left.

At the end of their meeting, which despite the bumpy start had been very cordial, it was time for the customary exchange of gifts. Enzo, disappointed but now convinced of the fidelity of Paul Newman, presented him with a Ferrari scarf for his wife Joanne Woodward. Newman gave Enzo a black crystal prancing horse that he had especially commissioned in Venice. On an attached plaque, he'd had inscribed, in Italian: 'From a Silver Knight to a Great King.' Enzo immensely appreciated Paul Newman's gift and kept it on the bookcase behind his desk from that day on.[2]

On Saturday 20 November journalist and author Alberto Bevilacqua was awarded the Dino Ferrari prize for his 'Down with the Winner' story, which had been printed in *Il Corriere della Sera* the previous spring. A few months earlier, Bevilacqua had given his readers a brief but perfect description of the most famous Italian in the world: 'A great man – and you certainly are – needs constitutional flaws: He is selfish, perhaps prophetically capricious, an actor, never individualistic.'[3]

But today was a special day. Journalists had been invited not just to the award ceremony, but also to the introduction of Enzo's new book, which was no ordinary volume. For today the Grand Old Man was not going to present the latest revision to his famed autobiography, but, rather, a completely new volume wholly dedicated to his friends in the press.

Though some of them feared bloodshed, they had all come, and now filled to capacity the largest room that the Fini Restaurant in downtown Modena could offer. Enzo had never made a mystery of his love–hate relationship with journalists – and now he had written a book about them! He had titled it *Il Flobert*, from the light rifle that he had used to hunt mice in the ditch near his home when he was a kid. Hearing the title, some of the journalists sitting there prepared themselves for a literary slaughter. Playing with them and their fears, Enzo somehow reassured them. While he had chosen the name of a rifle for his title, it was a small one: mice could be killed by its bullets; grown-up men would only be scratched by them, he said, half-jokingly.[4]

With copies of *Il Flobert* in plain sight, but kept at a safe distance from the journalists – who would have to wait until the end of the presentation to read what Ferrari had written about each of them (there could be no crueller trick) – Ferrari briefly explained the rules of the game. He said that the book was made up of 'simple annotations' written 'during the long waits on those Fridays and Saturdays when the telephone and telex rang late' to bring him news from race tracks. 'Sheet by sheet,' he said playfully, 'they resemble those letters that kids usually put under their parents' plates on Christmas Eve. At 79,' he confessed, 'one is still moved by simple things, by facts and situations that seem irrelevant to most, but instead enclose in their simplicity the fragrance of purity.'[5]

The style of each portrait was sharp and concise. Ferrari did not waste much time in preliminaries, and went straight to the heart of the matter. After all, he'd already apologized in the preface for being irreverent, saying that this was his chance to retaliate against his enemy-friends in the same way they'd always treated him. With a few biting exceptions, the manufacturer-turned-author limited himself to whispers, innuendo and suggestions, yet hardly ever sinking the shot.

In mid-December, the newspaper for which he had worked in his youth paid tribute to the Grand Old Man's interest in journalism by publishing one of the letters that 16-year-old Ferrari had written in November 1914. It was a chronicle of the soccer match between Modena and Inter, which the sports daily offered as 'an eloquent and old testimony of [Ferrari's] vocation' for journalism.

That day *Gazzetta dello Sport* had casually printed, next to Enzo's 1914 story, a box of 20 lines or so describing a young driver who had just become Canadian champion. The driver, who answered to the name of Gilles Villeneuve, claimed that the following season he would be James Hunt's teammate at McLaren.[6] Given the proximity to his 1914 correspondence, Enzo Ferrari certainly saw it. And that information, that name, would soon come in handy.

For Enzo Ferrari, the year that had just ended had been a very peculiar one. Besides seeing a world title, seemingly already won, vanish, it was the unexpected sense of powerlessness and frustration that left deep scars. At 78, after a lifetime spent dictating, or otherwise affecting, the rules of the game, from August onward he had not been able to make a single decision. Fate and then the stubborn intransigence of his world champion had brutally reminded him that, after all, he too was mortal.

He continued to have ambivalent feelings about Lauda. On the one hand he accused him of having 'asked too much of his [own] physical and mental resources before the Japanese Grand Prix'. On the other, he felt 'indebted' to him for what he had done for Ferrari – hence, 'the obligation to show him our gratitude', meaning, to confirm Lauda as a team member for the next season. This, despite Enzo's sincere doubts that the Austrian had made a full recovery, and his repugnance – also sincere – at having been forced to accept, thanks to Fiat's complicity, a series of decisions made by others.[7]

The ever more tangible presence of Fiat in Ferrari's decision-making became evident in early January 1977, the day the new Formula 1 season started with the Grand Prix of Argentina. That Friday the 312 T2s of Lauda and Reutemann took to the track sporting the blue rectangular logo of Fiat. It was only the manifestation of a statement of fact, of course; but it was also the first time that Ferrari was forced to put the badge of another car manufacturer on his cars.

The first race of the new year, in Argentina, was a big disappointment, made even more distressing by the excellent performance of the Alfa Romeo-powered Brabhams. Reutemann did no better than third place and Lauda retired before half distance. Lauda was summoned to Maranello, and two days after the race he took part in a summit with Ferrari and Forghieri, who had not travelled with the team to Argentina, remaining at Fiorano to develop the new car. After the meeting, during which Niki agreed to do some extra testing, Ferrari said he was satisfied. And even though he knew that his technicians could not perform miracles every time his cars were tested,[8] he said that he had finally seen in Lauda the same determination he'd shown during his best days.[9]

Despite the odds, things went much better in the next race in Brazil, where Reutemann won and Lauda finished third. The victory of the new driver, however, ended up sharpening the tension within the team – a team not necessarily divided, but definitely not as unified as it had been in the past. To make things worse, Enzo was battling a viral pneumonia that would keep him away from his office for a whole month.

Lauda returned to victory in South Africa on the first Saturday in March. The day was marred by the tragic and absurd death of Tom Pryce, killed by his impact with a fire extinguisher that a young marshal was holding when he crossed the start/finish straight as Pryce's Shadow was speeding by.

On Saturday 19 March 1977, Enzo Ferrari resigned as president of Ferrari. He would remain as a member of the board of trustees, and 'at the disposal of anyone who may need me'. The name of his successor would be announced at a later date. His resignation was contained in a letter sent to all board members, in which he informed them that he felt he had 'completed [his] mission as president'. The reasons for his decision included his health and age, which 'suggested a necessary sacrifice'.[10] 'He, who has created Ferrari and wants continuity, development, success,' he wrote, 'feels today this obligation. It is without question that the new programmes require a commitment that I cannot continue as [I've done] in the past.'[11]

In fact, Ferrari was distancing himself only from the industrial management of his company, not from his racing team, to which, indeed, because of this move, he would now offer even greater energies. The new programmes he mentioned concerned the designing and marketing of new road-going berlinettas. Of Ferrari's racing division, he remained the supreme and responsible director.

With the 1977 Formula 1 championship in full swing, the two Ferraris seemed to lack the competitiveness of their main rivals – Brabham-Alfa, Lotus-Ford and the brand-new and very convincing Wolf-Ford. Lauda's second-place finish at Long Beach had not boosted the morale of a team plagued by the rumour that Ferrari wanted the Austrian to leave at the end of the year. Reutemann too, after his Brazil win, had not repeated his feat. And so, week after week, new rumours suggested that either Lauda or Reutemann was on his way out, to be replaced by Emerson Fittipaldi, a driver Enzo Ferrari had always liked but never hired.

When the rumours became deafening, Enzo Ferrari decided that it was time for so-called experts and public opinion makers to listen to what he had to say on the subject.

'I wonder who may have an interest in spreading uncertainty and disharmony within our team,' he said. 'Lauda has been, and remains, our champion. Reutemann deserves our trust.' Hoping that his would be the last words spoken on the issue, he added: 'We have no desire to deny or correct information designed to be sensational or to fill empty newspaper space.'[12]

The second Sunday in May, Reutemann came second in Spain, behind Mario Andretti's Lotus. Two weeks later Lauda and Reutemann placed second and third in Monte Carlo, behind Schechter's Wolf. Despite the fact that victory continued to escape them, the two Ferrari drivers were now second and third in the championship standings. Yet it was clear to all that the team was no longer what it had once been.

Apart from the lower performance level of the 1977 312 T2, what Ferrari lacked was harmony. The two drivers had never taken a liking to each other, and spent the race weekend ignoring one another. Additionally, between Lauda and Forghieri there was now a perennial state of war. What was missing was someone with the overall vision and power to intervene where and when necessary. And soon the press came to the conclusion that what Ferrari needed was the return of Luca di Montezemolo.

Ferrari was once again forced to issue a public statement. The Grand Old Man had greatly appreciated his young assistant, but in the last season that he had spent in Maranello, Enzo had become somewhat jealous of Montezemolo, a state of mind quite rare in a man like Ferrari. Well knowing that he could not afford to appear jealous of a man who was not yet 30 years old, Ferrari worked his way out of the awkward situation by referring to Fiat, which had required Montezemolo's service a year and a half earlier. 'It would be absurd now,' he said, 'to ask Fiat to give him back to me.'[13]

Ferrari next decided to get rid of Reutemann, and instructed his men to strike a deal with Mario Andretti. Enzo had had Andretti on his team early in Mario's career, and had since maintained a fondness for the Italian-born American driver. Andretti replied that he would gladly come back to Ferrari at any time, but not to play second fiddle to Lauda. Informed that second fiddle would indeed be his role, Mario declined.[14]

On Thursday 30 June, Lauda went on the record for the first time about the many rumours surrounding his future. In a sort of declaration of love for his second father, he said that he would not leave Ferrari. At the same time, he asked for 'a more compact and tight-knit team'.[15] Three days later, however, he began negotiations with Bernie Ecclestone to move to Brabham-Alfa.[16]

Two weeks later, Lauda came second in the British Grand Prix, behind James Hunt. One year after the terrifying crash at the Nürburgring, on 30 July, Niki Lauda triumphed in the German Grand Prix at Hockenheim, the faster but shorter track that had replaced the old and outdated circuit, changes made in large part because of the pressure Lauda put on authorities to do so. In the next race, the Grand Prix of Austria at Zeltweg, for the first time in 13 months Lauda took pole position. And with second place in the race behind the surprising Shadow of Australian Alan Jones, he now led the world standings over Jody Scheckter, by 16 points.

However, the following week, Lauda did not show up at a private Ferrari testing session at Monza. The team announced that Lauda was not feeling well. From Austria came the news that Niki was actually in excellent health and had left on a personal trip.[17] Lauda did not go to Monza, and showed up at Fiorano only the following week.[18] Meanwhile, once again the rumour started that Ferrari was seriously interested in Emerson Fittipaldi. If before Lauda's mysterious absence from Monza everyone had thought that Fittipaldi could take Reutemann's place, now everyone assumed that Emerson was about to replace Lauda.[19]

On Sunday 28 August, Niki Lauda took his third win of the season in the Dutch Grand Prix. His lead in the standings extended to 19 points, an almost-unbridgeable gap. The next day he finally went to Modena to talk to Enzo Ferrari about his future.

The Old Man knew one thing: he was going to meet the economic demands that Niki would certainly make.[20] He had never liked to pay his drivers ridiculous amounts of money, but he had always come to terms with such requests in the past when he felt the driver deserved it. And Lauda had recently proven that he was once again the top driver he'd been before the Nürburgring. Despite some irritation and mutual incomprehension over the previous months, Enzo Ferrari was reasonably certain that, notwithstanding the speculation on the part of the press, all Niki would ask for was more money.[21]

In the offices of the old Scuderia Ferrari on Viale Trento Trieste in Modena, the Grand Old Man spoke first. With him were Ferrari's deputy managing director Della Casa and Piero Lardi.

'What have you come here to tell me after all that has been said, and all that I've read in the papers?' he teasingly asked Niki.

Lauda was in a very different mood.

'I am embarrassed,' he said, 'because I told you that I would stay with you as long as you remained at Ferrari. Today I cannot stay any longer because I have lost my motivation.'[22]

Convinced that Lauda was bluffing to raise the stakes, Ferrari told him that if it was a question of money, he was ready to discuss it. He told Niki that he was willing to match any offer he might have received from any other team.

Lauda replied that it was not a question of money, but of motivation. After four years, he simply wanted a change. He did not wish to stay another season in a team where he no longer felt at ease.[23] He had experienced problems with the technical staff and, since Montezemolo had left, the team had lost its unity.[24] As if to stress this point, Niki had asked Montezemolo to be present at the meeting. A few minutes late, Montezemolo arrived after Lauda's announcement had already taken place.[25]

Lauda stopped after the first few sentences, saying that he couldn't find the right words in Italian. He asked to be allowed to speak in English. Piero prepared to act as interpreter, but Enzo thought differently: to say unpleasant things, he told Niki, the little Italian he knew was more than enough.

Ferrari had been caught off guard. It was he who decided when a driver ended his stay in Maranello. With malice he said: 'When you said you'd stay with me, you calculated my age and the illness that has been afflicting me for some time, right?' And without giving Lauda time to answer, he added: 'Because if you made these calculations, I understand the implication of your promise.'[26]

The meeting continued, briefly, with mutual accusations. Lauda was adamant, and Ferrari made no counteroffer. At the end, a brief press release was issued, stating that it had been 'decided that the working relationship begun in 1974' between Ferrari and Niki Lauda would end 'on October 30, at the conclusion of the present World Championship'. In the short communication, Ferrari thanked his driver 'for the invaluable cooperation given' and wished him 'the best for the continuation of his career'. In the same text, a few lines down, Lauda thanked 'Ferrari for four years of exemplary cooperation', and reserved 'a special grateful thought for Enzo Ferrari'.[27]

When they parted, Ferrari and Lauda agreed that neither would speak publicly about the end of their cooperation until the day the contract expired at the end of October. But naturally, in the motor-racing world, no one spoke of anything else. Regazzoni, who still had a grudge against Enzo, remarked with undisguised pleasure that 'Ferrari has received from Lauda the treatment that in the past he has reserved for others'.[28]

Niki, at Monza for the Italian Grand Prix, had received the usual applause and affection from Italian fans. He began to go on the record with accounts of what had happened at the meeting. Lauda's statements infuriated Ferrari – and a furious Ferrari knew of only one way to appease his anger.

The Tuesday after the race at Monza, the Grand Old Man presided over a crowded press conference on the premises of the old Scuderia Ferrari. Elegant in a grey suit, a colour he rarely wore, 'thinner but still imposing',[29] and protected from scrutiny by his traditional dark glasses, he poured gasoline on the fire that Lauda had ignited the week before. 'Truth and reason,' said Ferrari, 'are the most common of the world's prefabricated materials.' The press had in the previous days voiced Lauda's truth. 'Now,' he said to his guests, 'you're going to hear *my* truth.'[30]

After unveiling the details of the meeting in which Lauda had announced the separation, Ferrari took off. 'My mother,' he said, 'has left me three proverbs, one of which says that when two people leave each other, only the best days should be remembered.' Perhaps to explain his decision, Lauda had chosen to remember only the bad ones. 'Lauda,' he said reproachfully, 'accuses us of not having protected him after Japan, but you all know how much I defended him. Lauda,' he pressed on, 'said that Enzo Ferrari couldn't imagine keeping someone on his team stupid enough to risk suicide, because in that case, it would be worth hiring a monkey.'[31]

'In my memory,' he continued, in an attempt to disavow one of Lauda's achievements – that of making Ferrari unbeatable – 'I remember only Nuvolari and Moss who have been more important, percentage-wise, than the car they drove. In 1974 and '75,' he conceded, 'Lauda made notable contributions. But after that,' he accused, 'he has placed the search for new personal sponsorships before the interests of the team.' And at any rate, he added, 'I still have to find a driver who can suggest remedies in addition to identifying the problems of a car.'[32] Ferrari responded point by point to each of the attacks that Lauda had made against him in recent days. With a hint of malice, he closed his long verbal crusade against his now two-time world champion with a wicked quip: 'Lauda,' said the old man, 'will not dump Ferrari the way he dumped Mariella'[33] – referring to the longtime girlfriend Niki had hastily left to marry Marlene.

That same day, in Germany, Lauda announced that in 1978 he would race with Brabham-Alfa Romeo. Enzo's two-time world champion had defected to his lifelong nemesis.

With Lauda gone, Ferrari hurried to choose the driver who would replace him. He had been vague with the press: 'I'm considering four or five names.'[34] The truth was that, one after the other, the drivers he wanted – Fittipaldi, Scheckter and, especially, Andretti – had announced they were all remaining with the same teams for which they had raced in 1977.

Unable to hire a great name, Ferrari devised a different solution, 'just like we did in 1973 with Lauda', he said, giving a clear clue that the press totally missed. And so, with the forced end to negotiations with established drivers, the 'Lauda 1973 solution',[35] as he himself would call it a few days later, became the most viable alternative for replacing the Austrian champion.

There was a young Canadian driver with a single Formula 1 race under his belt who had stimulated Enzo's curiosity – the very driver named by *La Gazzetta dello Sport* next to Enzo's 1941 piece back in December. Ferrari had seen him race in the Grand Prix of Great Britain on television. Back from Silverstone, Forghieri, who had seen him race in person, had spoken of him with great enthusiasm. The Grand Old Man had then spoken to two people who knew the Canadian because they'd had him on their team in the Can-Am Championship series: Walter Wolf and Chris Amon, owner and team manager of the team, respectively.[36] Amon, who was one of Enzo's former drivers, had praised the 'incredible natural qualities'[37] of the young Canadian. At this point, Ferrari had ordered his men to secretly but immediately verify his availability.

At Enzo Ferrari's request, Gilles Villeneuve had been contacted by press officer Ennio Mortara in the last days of August, and had come to Modena on the same day on which Lauda had said goodbye[38] – Monday 29 August. Lauda had met Ferrari at 11am; Villeneuve had been received at 7pm.[39]

Up to that morning, the interview was just going to be exploratory, one of those conversations that Ferrari loved to have from time to time with promising young drivers, reserving for himself the right to call on them in the (more or less distant) future, if ever. But Lauda's departure, communicated in such a stormy way that very morning, had given the chat a decidedly different angle.

The interview lasted an hour. It was friendly, and ended with the understanding that Gilles would soon hear from Ferrari. The only obstacle to a possible agreement could come from the contract that Villeneuve had signed with McLaren for 1977, with an option for 1978. But before the young Canadian left, Ferrari told him there were many ways to get out of a contract.[40]

On 21 September Mario Andretti announced that he was staying at Lotus.[41] One day later, Jody Scheckter, who had met with Enzo Ferrari in Modena on 7 September,[42] announced that he was staying with Wolf for 1978.[43] And while the press insisted that Ferrari was now targeting either Alan Jones or John Watson, the Grand Old Man once again summoned Villeneuve to Modena.

The Canadian signed his contract with Ferrari at 10pm on Tuesday 27 September, on the premises of the old Scuderia Ferrari on the Viale Trento Trieste. He signed for one season, with an option for 1979. From an economic point of view, Ferrari did well: in his first season Villeneuve would receive $75,000, a figure that seemed irrational to him, but in the world of late-1970s Formula 1 was altogether modest.

Ferrari announced the surprising hiring of the unknown 24-year-old Canadian the next day. Comparing him to the young and unknown Lauda of 1973, Enzo said: 'I chose on the basis of indications that speak of a professionally mature and talented' racing driver. 'We hope,' he concluded, 'that his growth will be as expected.'[44] The Italian press responded as they had four years earlier, at the announcement of Lauda's hiring: they did not applaud the choice.

Gilles Villeneuve made his debut with Ferrari in the Canadian Grand Prix at Mosport, Lauda having decided to leave Ferrari ahead of time. It was anything but memorable. But what induced Ferrari to ponder on the wisdom of his recent choice was what happened in the next race, the Japanese Grand Prix that ended the 1977 season.

Graced with a naturally impulsive personality, in the first part of the race Villeneuve bumped into Ronnie Peterson's Tyrrell. The two cars plunged off the track and landed in a space prohibited to the public, but inside which there were bystanders, including a photographer. The result: two people dead and a sea of controversy, mainly aimed at Villeneuve – considered too young, too inexperienced, too impetuous – but also at Enzo Ferrari, accused of having committed a huge error of judgement when he had hired such an untested young driver.

In the days following the race in Japan, Ferrari questioned himself and his men about the validity of his choice.[45] To some journalist friends he confessed that even if he'd wanted to, he would not be able to replace Villeneuve with any other top-level driver.[46] And then there was his feud with Lauda, because of which he would never admit that he might have made such a gigantic blunder in choosing his replacement.[47] For all of these reasons he decided to give the Canadian the benefit of the doubt about the crash in Japan, and some additional time to fine-tune his natural talent.

But once again, hurt by vicious personal attacks from the Italian press, who derided him for choosing the small Canadian, he announced that he would withdraw 'in the hermitage of Fiorano, as small as it is noisy, and be a keen observer of events'.[48]

The Last Hurrah

In mid-November 1977 Enzo Ferrari introduced the first car of the post-Lauda era. It was the 312 T3, direct heir to the championship-winning T2. The tyres, French Michelin radials, represented the real news. Choosing a tyre manufacturer with very little Formula 1 experience was a gamble, and Ferrari knew that. But he had suffered for too long under the special relationship that Goodyear had established with several English teams, and had decided to follow a new path. Michelin had been the original equipment manufacturer (OEM) of tyres for road-going Ferraris for about ten years, and the Grand Old Man believed his gamble to be a calculated one.

For the launch of the new car, Enzo chose to go to the Maranello Civic Centre. And when the curtain that concealed the car from view was lifted, the press was surprised to see the car bearing the number '1' as its racing number.[1] In Formula 1 the numeral '1' had for some years been assigned to the driver who had won the world title the season before – thus, by rights, Lauda would sport it in 1978 on his Brabham-Alfa Romeo. But Enzo could not resist the temptation to stress one more time that the car that had allowed the Austrian to become the 1977 champion was one of his.

Enzo took the opportunity also to introduce to the press his new team manager. His name was Marco Piccinini, and although Enzo naturally did not say so, he was the answer to those who had invoked the return of Montezemolo or the arrival of a person with comparable characteristics. Like Montezemolo before him, Piccinini would soon be plenipotentiary on and off the track, reporting back to Enzo in Maranello all that was going on inside the Ferrari team and the F1 machine.

From his secluded retreat in Fiorano that winter, the Grand Old Man, who would soon turn 80, looked ahead with disenchantment to the season that would open in mid-January with the Grand Prix of Argentina. After winning a second world title in three years, and the departure of Lauda, he knew that 'a four-year cycle in which our cars have been at the zenith of international motor racing' had come to an end. Now another cycle would start and, though staying at the top was all but certain, 'We will be ready to fight,' he thundered, 'for the sake of our tradition.'[2]

Apart from the yet-to-be-proven quality of the new T3, it was the drivers that troubled him. Though he had personally chosen both of them, he knew that Carlos Reutemann had had a far from memorable season in 1977 and had been confirmed only because of Lauda's defection. And then there was young Villeneuve, who lapped and lapped and lapped at Fiorano, but was unable to come close to the lap times of his teammate or those who had preceded him.

The first two races of the year in Argentina and Brazil would show what kind of season 1978 would be – a season in which Ferrari would struggle to find the right balance between the car and its new tyres but then, once that balance was found, would be unbeatable. In Buenos Aires the T2s – preferred to the T3, which was still short of development – both finished out of the points.[3] But in Brazil, on the new Rio circuit, Reutemann won hands down, leading from start to finish.

The tyres provided by Michelin had made the difference in performance in both races. In Argentina they had proved inadequate. In Brazil, however, they had made Reutemann's Ferrari fly; Villeneuve ended his race off the track from yet another contact with Peterson, now at Lotus. There was a month between the Brazilian Grand Prix and the following race in South Africa. During this month Enzo Ferrari's personal life was touched by two events. On 18 February he turned 80. Even though this was a momentous milestone, celebrations were kept very quiet. His wife's health had worsened seriously. She had been confined to her bed, and died in the Modena hospital nine days after Enzo's birthday.[4]

The contrasts between husband and wife had been harsh. Theirs had never been an easy coexistence, even when they were young. But their paths had never separated completely. What largely kept them together was the memory of their son, who had died at the age of 24 from a genetic disease that had been transmitted by his mother, and that had now ended her life, as well. In recent years, their increasing age and Laura's worsening illness had taken away the bitterness of their past daily quarrels: 'Her smile and her always blue eyes,' Enzo said after her death, looking back at the last period of his difficult marriage with a feeling that came very close to tenderness, 'told me all her torment, and her great joy.'[5]

The passing of his wife was a hard blow. In his own peculiar way, he had always remained fond of Laura – certainly because of Dino, but also due to a sense of gratitude, personal, intimate and timeless, which Ferrari had always had, and which few suspected. To journalist friend Gino Rancati, who went to see him a few days after her funeral, he confided: 'Now that she's gone, I miss [having] a precise point of reference.'[6] Laura's death convinced Enzo to make two important decisions – one probably long planned, the other certainly long overdue. The first was to ask Lina and Piero to come and live in the Largo Garibaldi building. Piero, with his wife Floriana and daughter Antonella, could occupy the spacious apartment above Enzo's. Lina could live on the third floor. None of his intimate friends – that is, the very few who knew about Lina – were surprised that Enzo didn't invite Lina to move in with him.[7] They knew he would never have done that. This was not only out of respect for Laura, who had recently died, or out of devotion to his memory of Dino; with the death of Laura and the fading away of the last member of his *first* family, Enzo was now free to live with his second family. But the complexity of the man and his huge and troubled feelings would never allow him to start an entirely new life. At most, they would allow him to begin a new phase of that same life that he had led for 80 long and tormented years, and from which nothing or no one ever completely disappeared.

The second decision was to finally give his son his last name.

Enzo had long desired to give his surname to the son he had had with Lina, who had simply been known by all as Piero Lardi. Despite gigantic quarrels with Laura and bombastic moves, such as when he'd lived for a period of time in a hotel, or when he'd offered her a billion lire in exchange for a divorce to marry Fiamma, or, the same amount of money to give Piero the Ferrari last name,[8] the complexity of their relationship had always prevented him from leaving her or prevailing on certain issues – Piero's last name being the major one. Always a realist, Enzo had willingly surrendered and given up his crusade as long as his wife had been alive.

But even now that Laura was dead, Enzo did not completely achieve his goal. Piero would henceforth be called Piero Lardi Ferrari. He would become Piero Ferrari only after Enzo's death, so as to fully honour the promise he had made to his wife – or, more exactly, to Dino's mother – that the only *other* Ferrari in this world would always and forever be their child.[9]

*   *   *

In the early days of April, the 312 T3s of Reutemann and Villeneuve started from the front row in the US Grand Prix West at Long Beach. Villeneuve remained in the lead until he crashed with Clay Regazzoni's Shadow – yet another of his spectacular shunts, for which the Italian press had ironically labelled him 'the Aviator'. But victory did not escape Reutemann, who, with the winner's nine points, tied with Mario Andretti for the lead in the standings.

The Long Beach win remained an isolated feat. The season went on with mixed results for the rest of spring and for most of the summer, with Ferraris competitive only when the Michelin tyres played along. So, while Andretti took off in the standings, the two Ferraris alternated positive results with very disappointing ones, falling behind in the quest for the world title.

Enzo, who, true to his word, had truly secluded himself within the Fiorano fences this year, communicating little with the outside world, began to come under pressure to swap tyre suppliers. His relationship with the French company executives, and particularly with Francois Michelin, was personal and long-standing, and Enzo never actually considered abandoning the French supplier.[10] In his view, it was experience that would come in handy in the future.[11]

When Reutemann won again at Brands Hatch in mid-July, the fight for the world title was already largely compromised, as were relations between Ferrari and his number-two driver.

Even if he had never second-guessed his commitment to Michelin, Enzo had long had second thoughts about Villeneuve. While he valued his speed, determination and character, he'd also come to realize that his growth process would be slower than Lauda's.[12] So he decided to pursue a placement for him at Wolf – although through Michelin, he had also opened a negotiation channel with Renault;[13] it looked like Wolf would most likely take him back in 1980.[14]

Enzo's idea was to swap Villeneuve with Scheckter, and have the South African driver he'd always liked, and had wanted to sign the year before, team up with Reutemann. Except that the Argentine had different plans. Frustrated by the unreliability of his T3, annoyed by rumours that Scheckter would join him at Ferrari in 1979 and knowing that the Andretti–Peterson duo at Lotus would part at the end of the season, in the middle of the summer Reutemann struck up a deal with Colin Chapman. And so it was that Enzo Ferrari was forced to confirm Gilles Villeneuve for 1979.

Two days after announcing that next year he would race for Lotus, Reutemann showed up at Ferrari to tell Enzo what he had already learned from the press. Annoyed by the unexpected departure of Carlos, Ferrari did not wait for the Grand Prix of Italy, as the Argentine had insisted, and revealed to the press that very day his driver lineup for 1979.[15]

Immediately after lunch he asked the small band of journalists that normally patrolled the Maranello main gate or the entrance to the Fiorano track to join him in his private dining room at Cavallino. After asking the restaurant owner to open a bottle of champagne, as if to celebrate the event, he personally handed each journalist a typewritten text prepared that morning by Gozzi – present at the impromptu press conference, together with Piero and Piccinini – with which, 'conforming with the needs of the press,'[16] he communicated the names of Ferrari's two drivers for the 1979 season, Jody Scheckter and Gilles Villeneuve.

On the tragic day at Monza that cost Ronnie Peterson his life, his teammate Mario Andretti clinched the world title. That left two races before the end of the season. Reutemann won the first one at Watkins Glen. It was his fourth win of the season and secured him third place in the championship standings. On 8 October, Villeneuve finally took his first Formula 1 win at the Canadian Grand Prix, raced for the first time in Montreal. Knowing how much patience his employer had shown during his first full season, at the end of the race Villeneuve paid tribute to Enzo Ferrari and thanked him publicly.[17]

Although he had not won the world title, Enzo Ferrari could not be completely disappointed by the season that had just ended. His cars had won five races out of sixteen, and only the superlative Lotus 79 – plus the few ups and many downs of the Michelin tyres – had denied at least one of his drivers a fair chance to fight for the title. Not to mention the fact that Lauda had won only two races, and had placed fourth in the final standings.

On 20 February 1979, representatives of the national association of Resistance fighters went to Maranello to personally award Enzo the Gold Medal of the Resistance.[18] Although he rarely spoke about it, his role in the Resistance had been anything but marginal. Members of Modena's political parties and unions had always recognized his contribution, and now he was being acknowledged at the national level.

The presentation of the new car took place in the early afternoon of Monday 15 January 1979. Ferrari once again chose the Maranello Civic Centre, recently renovated and now featuring a round central hall that would act as a perfect stage. As expected, the new Ferrari was a ground-effect car in the fashion of Chapman's Lotus.

The press was not particularly impressed by the form of the new T4, a car not necessarily as streamlined as most of the others. There were those who said that it looked like a 'slipper', and others who stated that the front of the car reminded them of the 'nose of a hippopotamus'.[19] In a cartoon, motorsport magazine *Autosprint* wryly suggested that, in designing it, Forghieri had been inspired by a sack of potatoes.[20] Ferrari was uninterested in all of the witticisms. 'Let's hope,' he said, 'that the ugly T4 becomes a beauty on the track!'[21]

While the T4 lapped at Fiorano to smooth out its edges, Ferrari shipped the reliable T3 to South America for the first two races of the 1979 season. Both ended in huge disappointment. The new enemy now was French manufacturer Ligier, which won both races, in Argentina and Brazil, with Jacques Laffite. Forghieri rushed the development of the new car and sent two T4s to South Africa for Scheckter and Villeneuve, where, on 3 March, they made their debut at Kyalami.

On the African highlands, the superiority of the T4, derided for its unconventional form until the day before it ran, became evident to all. As did the growth of Villeneuve. In a race marked by rain and two starts, the Canadian proved fast and reliable, and won the South African Grand Prix.

Watching the race on television as usual, Ferrari soon realized that the race could be won. 'The way my drivers went about the track, the cornering behaviour of the cars and their acceleration' had 'inspired confident expectation' from the very early laps.[22] It was a Ferrari triumph, with Villeneuve first and Scheckter second. It was the 22nd 1–2 finish for Ferrari in Formula 1.

Villeneuve's first words as he got out of his car were once again for his boss: 'I dedicate this success to Enzo Ferrari, who has always had confidence in me,' he said. From Fiorano, the Old Man echoed, 'I am happy for this winning debut that has definitely made the T4 more beautiful, and will please many Ferrari fans.'[23]

A month later at Long Beach, Villeneuve won again over his teammate. With this second win in a row, he took control of the world championship standings with a lead of seven points over Scheckter. Between the two was Jacques Laffite's blue Ligier.

But Enzo needn't have worried. The second consecutive win did not change the Canadian in the least. Revealing himself to be not only a rapidly improving driver, but also a loyal man, to those who pestered him in hopes of triggering a controversy within Ferrari Gilles replied: 'It's good to lead in the standings. But Scheckter will come out in due time.'[24] Villeneuve had been kept on during the previous autumn to cover Scheckter's back and nothing, at least at this stage of the season, would change either his mind or the team's strategy.

Despite two consecutive one–two finishes and the apparent decline of Ligier, Enzo remained cautious. 'The result at Long Beach under the California sun,' he said, 'confirmed the good we had seen in the South African rain at Kyalami. To continue in this fashion,' he said, 'will not be easy.'[25]

Of course, he knew what he was talking about. When the championship series reached Europe, Ligier returned to success. With a win in Spain, Patrick Depailler tied Villeneuve for the lead in the standings. But Enzo was not just concerned about the racing results at Jarama.

A few days later, Alfa Romeo conducted the first public test of its new racing car, which the press had dubbed Alfa-Alfa, to distinguish it from Bernie Ecclestone's Brabham-Alfa Romeo. The occasion was a pre-race test session at Zolder, the stage for the mid-May Belgian Grand Prix, the race Alfa Romeo had chosen for its return to Formula 1 27 years after its last participation. Lapping for the first time alongside other cars, the Alfa-Alfa driven by young Italian talent

Bruno Giacomelli set the third-fastest time, right behind Depailler's Ligier and Scheckter's Ferrari.

If this was not enough, a very irritated Lauda went public, stating that, displeased with his present situation at Brabham, he was not ruling out a future move to the Milan-based Alfa Romeo team.[26] For Enzo it would be the worst of nightmares: his former world champion competing for his lifelong nemesis.

Serenity soon returned thanks to Jody Scheckter and his two consecutive May wins. Hired by Enzo with the stated goal of winning the world title,[27] the South African took back-to-back wins in Belgium and in Monte Carlo. 'More than for me,' he said at the end of the race at Zolder, 'I'm happy for Enzo Ferrari, for whom I have a debt of gratitude.'[28] Aided by two unfortunate performances by Villeneuve, Scheckter took the championship lead, never again to leave it.

On the first day of July, in the last laps of the French Grand Prix at Dijon, Ferrari's second fiddle fought a battle for the ages against Renault's René Arnoux. Enzo watched the showdown on TV and was captivated.[29] The small Canadian was made of champion material, no doubt. To his old friend and associate Luigi Bazzi, who two days after the Dijon race had sent him a letter of congratulations, referring to Villeneuve, Enzo asked: 'Doesn't he remind you of young Nuvolari?!'[30]

Two weeks later, Clay Regazzoni returned to success. At 40, the Swiss driver gave Frank Williams his first Formula 1 win. Enzo did not release any public statement, but in private he did not hide his satisfaction in Clay's triumph.[31]

In late July, the president of Italy, Sandro Pertini, awarded Enzo the honorary title of Knight of the Grand Cross. It was the highest honour the Italian Republic could grant one of its citizens. The president had intended to recognize 'his industrial and sporting feats'. Enzo was naturally gratified by the honour, but declined the invitation to go to Rome and be personally knighted.[32]

No one was surprised when Ferrari announced that he would not go to Rome. It was well known that he was not drawn to the spotlight and that he didn't like long trips. But there was more.

That summer there was something bugging Enzo, and it wasn't Alan Jones's Williams menacing Jody Scheckter's quest for the world title. Enzo Ferrari was indeed getting old. He had been on the sidelines for much of the year and was now restless. Health came and went, and his diet was even more rigid than it had been in the past.[33] He was working with Gozzi to update yet another edition of his autobiography, and he felt the urge to devote a few lines to the memory of his late wife.[34]

He knew that at age 81, this edition of his famed 'notebook of a lifetime'[35] could be his last, and he wanted to do it the right way.[36] The words he would choose to describe the woman with whom he had shared a long and turbulent relationship would in all likelihood be the way Laura would be remembered for posterity. Perhaps he missed Laura, despite her inconsistencies. Hadn't he confessed that, with her passing, he had lost a precise reference point?

The last Sunday in August, thanks to his third consecutive win, Alan Jones was just ten points behind Scheckter. Jody's lead in the world standings had narrowed dangerously. With three races to go before the end of the season, the 312 T4's performance seemed to have lost the many certainties of its extraordinary spring.

But the Dutch Grand Prix had also offered the televised images of Villeneuve driving a full lap with his three-wheeled T4 in a desperate and pointless attempt to reach the pits and replace the tyre that had frayed. Fans went wild, but not everyone in the Formula 1 establishment appreciated the feat, which was deemed heroic or foolish depending on one's point of view. And so, after more than a year, the little Canadian found himself once again at the centre of a heated controversy.

To his rescue unexpectedly came Enzo Ferrari himself. Ferrari, who had not commented on the incident in its aftermath, made his voice heard two days later – in so doing, incidentally, breaking a public silence that had lasted since the previous April. 'I have examples to offer,' he thundered from Maranello, 'not to defend Villeneuve, but because I would like [to ensure] that reality [is] not distorted.'[37]

He continued, mentioning Nuvolari who, in a grand prix in the 1930s, had done exactly as Villeneuve had done the previous Sunday, reaching the pits on three wheels. Nuvolari, Enzo said, 'was a driver who could end up off the track, but then he won like no other. Sure, he could make mistakes, but he then made up for them. Gilles, too,' he said, conferring on the brave Canadian the distinctive qualities of the Flying Mantuan, 'is made of that stuff, and sometime takes excessive risks. But if he didn't do it, he would not be Villeneuve, just like Nuvolari would not have been Nuvolari if he had behaved in a different way.'[38]

Ferrari had rarely spoken in public with such appreciation for one of his drivers. But the little Canadian, who in the beginning had elicited doubts so great as nearly to make Enzo change his mind, had conquered him with his driving as well as his conduct. 'Villeneuve,' he concluded, 'is like Nuvolari, and should be taken as he is.'[39]

With three races to go, Alan Jones was a real threat. Scheckter was still leading in the standings, but Villeneuve could no longer arithmetically win the title. Jody had therefore asked his teammate for help, and Gilles had immediately agreed. He had been a loyal teammate all season long and he promised that he would from then on watch Jody's back.[40] Which he masterfully did two weeks later at Monza, when he finished second, right behind Scheckter, who with the race brought home the world title.

Two years after the end of Lauda's era, Enzo – who had watched the race on television in his Fiorano study, next to a telex machine through which he spoke with his men in the Monza pits[41] – had won his personal battle with the Austrian, and was once again world champion.

Very sportingly, Lauda sent a congratulatory note. Enzo pondered his response,[42] and then dictated a text that spoke volumes of the consideration he still maintained for the Austrian. Niki's words, he said, had 'sparked a bitter reflection: if Lauda had stayed at Ferrari, he may have already equalled Fangio's record.'[43]

The Patriarch

The moment he climbed out of his championship-winning 312 T4 at the end of the Italian Grand Prix, Jody Schechter's first thoughts were for the Grand Old Man. 'This title is for Enzo Ferrari,' he said.[1]

But from Fiorano that day, and from Maranello in the following week, no words of appreciation came from Enzo to his new world champion. Not a word, not a line, not a thank you note. And when the press realized the incongruity, they all went to his gate to demand an explanation. 'There will not be any statement from *Ingegner* Ferrari,' said Enzo's press secretary, 'and, as far as I am concerned, no press release.'[2]

Still unsure of the reasons for Enzo's unfamiliar behaviour, the press next moved to Imola where, the weekend after Monza, a non-championship race was going to be held on the track that now bore the name of Enzo's fallen son Dino. The press didn't know that it was this very race – or, to be precise, this very track – that had created a divide between Enzo Ferrari and his new champion.[3]

Ferrari had long pushed for a world championship event to be held at Imola. On 2 August, Bernie Ecclestone – who, in addition to being the owner of Brabham, was also the representative of all F1 teams – of the Formula One Constructors' Association (FOCA) had reached an agreement with the automobile clubs of Milan and Bologna according to which, in the following four years, the Italian Grand Prix would be alternately held at Monza and at Imola. In September 1979, a rehearsal event was to be held at Imola, ahead of the 1980 grand prix. Enzo's role had been significant, and Ecclestone had publicly praised him that summer by saying that 'we owe it particularly to Enzo Ferrari if F1 has come to Imola'.[4]

But there was a problem, overlooked by the organizers but not by the drivers. Imola's track had been designed primarily for motorcycles. Cars had not raced on it for years, and modern F1 had never done so. In other words, according to F1 drivers, the Imola track was not safe enough to host a championship event. Jody Scheckter, as president of the Grand Prix Drivers' Association, had served as the spokesman for a drivers' crusade against a track that, unfortunately for him, bore the name of his employer's dead son.[5]

The tension between Ferrari and Scheckter had an emotional basis, and no real reason whatsoever to exist. It would remain secret for another 45 days. The new champion raced at Imola and the last few events of the season as *persona non grata* as far as the larger-than-life boss of his team was concerned.

Ironically, the winner at Imola was Lauda, who a few days later announced his retirement from motor racing.[6]

Although 23 years had passed since Dino's death, Enzo's son was constantly in his thoughts. 'Every morning,' Enzo had said some time earlier, 'I get up with death in my pocket.'[7]

Ferrari had no way of knowing that he would soon see his son again.

On Wednesday 9 October, two days after Villeneuve's win at Watkins Glen in the last race of the 1979 season, a little after 9am, appalling news reached Enzo. The night before, someone had broken into the Modena San Cataldo cemetery, opened the door of the Ferrari chapel and tried to steal Dino's corpse.[8]

Enzo prepared for the worst. The year before, someone had stolen Charlie Chaplin's corpse, asking an astronomical ransom for its return. In his heart Enzo knew that he would pay any sum, should someone ask for money in return for Dino's remains.[9] He was immediately reassured. Dino's corpse had not been taken. Something, or someone, had evidently disturbed the grave robbers before they could finish their grisly job.

Enzo rushed to the graveyard, arriving at around 10am. When he appeared at the door of the chapel, he was left alone and entered in silence, 'shocked by grief, almost dumbfounded'.[10] On the ground he saw a chisel and a couple of plastic bags next to the broken gravestone.

Then he looked up, and saw Dino.

His body was intact – probably because of the massive amount of medicines that had been injected into his body since the age of seven, in an attempt to cure him of his disease.[11] His face, hands, body – all intact, like the day of the funeral, a rainy day in July 1956. The flowers that Laura had put in the breast pocket of his jacket were still there, too. 'After all these years, I would never have thought that I would see my son again,'[12] was all he said.

He stood there for a few minutes. Then, pressing his forehead with his right hand to cover his face, he left. With his chauffeur next to him, he went back to the car and rode to Maranello, where he cancelled all of his appointments for the day.

The investigators concluded that the most probable hypothesis was indeed that someone had wanted to steal the corpse and then demand a ransom for its return. There was speculation that the thieves had probably aborted the attempt when they realized that Dino's body was intact and that, instead of a few scattered bones, they would have had to carry away an entire corpse.[13] The investigation led nowhere, and the case was closed, with no suspects.

Enzo always maintained a personal theory about what had happened. There was a legend in Modena that said a golden candelabrum had been buried next to Dino's coffin. It was not true, of course, but 23 years after the funeral the story still circulated.

Attracted by the possibility of finding gold, some 'fools' – the exact word used by Enzo to describe them – had probably broken into the chapel in hopes of walking away with the spoils.[14]

Still shaken by the desecration of Dino's tomb, but aware of the need to react quickly, ten days later Enzo presided over the traditional end-of-year press conference. He invited just 24 journalists, carefully selected among the hundred or so who normally attended these events. Obviously those excluded were frustrated, but this was part of the game that Enzo played with the press, and they knew it. Despite what had just happened, he was in top shape, ready to quarrel with his guests. 'As you can see,' he told a journalist who had criticized him all season long, 'this *lemon* factory managed to survive, and to win something this year.'[15]

He praised Villeneuve, but almost ignored the driver who had just given him his first world title since Niki Lauda. 'In him,' he said of the Canadian, 'I admire the courage, the will to win that annuls even some mistakes.' But significantly he also added: 'Another thing that I admire him for is his honesty. Villeneuve behaved loyally with Scheckter once he realized that he no longer had any hope to win the title.'[16] There was naturally a component of self-gratification in his appreciation of Villeneuve, a 'gamble', he told his audience, that he had won against all odds.[17]

Regarding his new world champion, he said only that 'Scheckter proved a wise administrator of his possibilities. He took risks when he had to, and saved his energy when he saw fit.' After all, he polemically told his guests, who had long doubted his choice of Villeneuve, 'when we needed someone to lead the charge, we had the "Snowmobile Man", the "Aviator".'[18] Again, he employed the words the press had used to describe Villeneuve, to tweak their noses. (The nicknames referred to Gilles's early days racing snowmobiles in his native Canada, as well as the fact that at the start of his F1 career the Ferrari cars he was driving took flight so often.)

Noting the evident disparity in Enzo's treatment of his two drivers, the press decided they wanted to know more, and maliciously started to ask questions about the crusade against Imola that Scheckter was leading. Enzo decided to play along, and didn't try to hide anything. 'If Scheckter has done something that goes beyond the contract he has with our team,' he said, 'we will intervene. If Scheckter, on the other hand, as president of the GPDA, intends to wage war against Imola,' he thundered, 'he will have to bring forward reasons that we presently do not see.'[19] The *we* naturally implied only Enzo Ferrari.

The die was cast. Enzo had publicly repudiated his new world champion. And if during the press conference he had managed to speak fairly diplomatically, later on, at the luncheon that followed, he was more direct. 'Scheckter,' he accused, 'has sided against a circuit bearing the name of my poor son Dino. I did not like that, because it is as if he sided against me.'[20]

Ferrari 80 was Enzo's Christmas present to friends, associates and journalists in 1979. It was the third edition of his memoirs, in a printing of just one thousand copies, not for sale.[21] It was a smaller book than its immediate predecessor – *Le Briglie del Successo* – and there were no photographs. The titles of the various chapters had also disappeared, though the text was still divided into the same sections. The beginning was also the same: 'In these years I have been invited more than once to write my "case history", but I have never obliged . . .'[22]

There were only a few differences in the text. As always, he had included a few negative things – he maliciously called Montezemolo a 'great friend' of Lauda's 'rather than a team manager'[23] – and had updated others, such as the chapter devoted to racing drivers, in which he had, as expected, included the newcomers, beginning with his own. He described Scheckter as 'predestined' and a 'bold fighter', but also a 'rational calculator of intermediate results'.[24] For Villeneuve he predicted a future as 'a great champion, if he will be able to do away with some naiveté'.[25]

The most important differences in the text had to do with Laura and Dino – Laura, who had died since the previous edition, and Dino, whose tomb had recently been desecrated. And if the desecration of Dino's tomb had taken place when Enzo and Gozzi were already reviewing the finished book, Enzo had wanted to publish *Ferrari 80* primarily to revise his thoughts on Laura.[26]

Missing from the revised text in *Ferrari 80* was Piero; even though he now went by Piero Lardi Ferrari, was more and more active in the company and was trusted by his father, he had once again been excluded from Enzo's official memoir.

Ferrari 80 also contained what Enzo called a 'parable'. The tale did not have a religious meaning, but rather a mathematical one. It focused on the drivers who had lost their motivation, a category in which Scheckter was the last example, and Lauda, the next to last, even though the parable had been inserted right after a brief profile of James Hunt, who had retired from motor racing the previous spring. This parable revealed Enzo's 'personal convictions' about what he considered the 'parabolic curve of a champion'.[27]

'The champion,' Enzo wrote, 'takes form and grows until the desire for human improvement prevents him from fully evaluating the risks and the economic advantages of his chosen profession. He is motivated, determined to win. He even compensates for eventual mechanical shortcomings with his total drive. He aims only at victory. The crowd's applause is the best reward. Having reached the zenith of his career,' he added, 'the champion confronts new necessities in life, new environments, new interests. The metamorphosis is complete: born is the public relations man, the owner of companies that have nothing to do with motor racing, the guest star of many a glittering event. The champion now does not win on the track as much as he used to, and tends to blame other people and situations, acquitting himself.' Enzo's lucid and cruel conclusion: 'The truth is that *he* is the preeminent cause of the decline. Gone is the fighter. The champion is now a supporting actor, and only his intelligence can spare him from a pathetic finale.'[28]

Given these ideas, it should come as no surprise that by late January 1980, after just two races in the new season, Enzo was vigorously looking for a new driver to pair with Villeneuve in 1981. The first to appear on his radar was Didier Pironi, a young Frenchman who set the second-fastest time in qualifying at the Brazilian Grand Prix. After the race, watched as usual on TV, Enzo asked Piccinini to contact Pironi.[29] The contract would be signed in the summer, but by 6 March Pironi had signed an agreement with Ferrari for 1981.

Now that Enzo had chosen the driver for the following season, the time had come to focus on the new car. It was at this point that Ferrari decided on the turbocharged engine. The new car – bearing the code number 126, which broke with the six-year series of T models – was tested for the first time on 10 July at Fiorano.

At the wheel was Villeneuve, who had renewed his contract with Ferrari at the time of the Monaco Grand Prix, and embodied the future.[30] Enzo watched every move through the closed-circuit television monitors installed in the small office behind the pits.[31] Although there was speculation on the part of the press about a debut in mid-August at the Austrian Grand Prix, Enzo knew that the 1980 season was compromised and it was worth waiting for the new season.

Proving Enzo's intuition as contained in the parable correct, a week later Jody Scheckter announced his retirement at the end of the season. Three days earlier at Brands Hatch, he had started the British Grand Prix from the last row of the grid. Two days later he had met Enzo at Fiorano to inform him of his decision ahead of the public announcement. The meeting had been cordial. Scheckter had told Enzo that he had new interests outside motorsport, including family and business. Enzo had assured him that it was the right thing to do, omitting to mention that he'd been so sure of this that he'd already found Jody's replacement.

When the time came to say goodbye, Scheckter shook Enzo's hand and told the Grand Old Man that the only regret he had was arriving at Ferrari a year later than originally planned. If he'd stuck to his original schedule, he would have won two world titles, and not just one[32] – a remark that must have enormously pleased Enzo, ever convinced that the T3 had had the potential to win the world title, and only the still-untested Villeneuve and the 'tormenting and tormented' Reutemann had let it go.

During the last week in July, Enzo bent a self-imposed rule and, for the first time in nearly ten years, made a quick visit to a track that was not Fiorano. The exception was made for Imola, the circuit named after his son Dino, soon to be the home of the 1980 Italian Grand Prix. Enzo arrived at around 12.30 in a Lancia Delta driven by Dino Tagliazucchi. Despite the heat, he got out of the car as fresh as a spring rose and clearly good-humoured.[33] Villeneuve was testing the T5 alongside the two Renaults of Jabouille and Arnoux. Enzo went to the Ferrari pits where, when testing stopped for the lunch break, his Canadian driver joined him. Sitting on two folding chairs, they chatted in French for a few minutes. Enzo was in a great mood and clearly enjoying the company of his cherished champion. Then he met the press for an impromptu press conference.

He was visibly happy to be at Imola and made no secret of the fact he was glad this track would host the next Italian Grand Prix. His love for a track bearing the name of his dead son was 'ancient and known to all'.[34] He skilfully ducked the compliments of those crediting him with the successful resolution of the dispute over holding the Italian Grand Prix at Imola, but said that, with everyone's contribution, it could become 'the most beautiful circuit in Europe'.[35]

On Saturday 13 September Gilles Villeneuve debuted the new Ferrari 126 turbocharged F1 car in practice for the Italian Grand Prix at Imola. The car proved faster than the T5, but the next day the Canadian took the start of the race at the wheel of the car he had driven all season long. Enzo did not return to Imola for qualifying, or for the grand prix.

On lap six, Villeneuve disintegrated his Ferrari in a terrifying crash at the Tosa bend. He walked away without a scratch amid the thunderous applause of a crowd of relieved, adoring *Ferraristi* (who are known outside Italy as the *Tifosi*). Ferrari himself was undoubtedly relieved when, the next day, he saw and publicly hugged his cherished champion.[36]

The meeting took place at Ferrari's 15 September press conference, in a room filled to capacity with journalists. Surprisingly, a smiling Didier Pironi walked in alongside Villeneuve. After Enzo unashamedly embraced his Canadian driver, Marco Piccinini introduced Pironi to Ferrari. Enzo hadn't personally met the driver he had wanted so badly until that day.[37]

Confident as could be for a man who'd won his personal gamble when he had hired Villeneuve three years earlier, Enzo had no problem revealing to his audience that he had chosen Pironi purely on the emotions he had felt while watching him race on television. 'I am an emotional man,' he said, 'and in life I have realized how often we end up making decisions not based on cold, rational reasoning but, rather, on the emotions we feel.'[38]

Someone pointed out that by hiring Pironi he would now have two ultra-fast and tempered drivers who could soon be competing for attention. 'I don't worry at all about possible quarrels within the team,' he said. Then, almost prophetically, he added: 'We will intervene only if the antagonism between Villeneuve and Pironi should damage the interest of the team.'[39]

Two days later, on Wednesday 17 September, Enzo presided over a top-secret *Gestione Sportiva* meeting centred on the activity for the next season. He gave precise directions to the eight men in charge of the racing team's different aspects: son Piero, Forghieri, Materazzi, Caruso, Poncini, Marchetti, Tomaini and Gozzi. The 'priority' was fine-tuning the turbocharged engine, but 'the T5 was not to be done away with right away', the hope being that by making it lighter, the Michelin tyres would perform better.[40]

According to Enzo, 'a lighter T5 without the miniskirts, with better aerodynamics and a further-tuned naturally aspirated boxer engine' could be 'competitive on all those circuits where the turbocharged unit could meet difficulties'.[41] All agreed on making the fine-tuning of the turbo car the priority, and on the opportunity not to throw away the T5 just yet, although Forghieri realistically pointed out that making the T5 lighter was a tough task, and all knew quite well how utopian it was to think that they could alternate cars depending on the race track.[42]

But despite the thoughts regarding the T5, the decision had been made to go turbocharged.

Didier Pironi had signed a contract for a year with an option for the next one, but he was still a Ligier driver until the end of the current season. At the end of September, at Montreal, Scheckter failed to qualify for the Grand Prix of Canada. It was the first time this had ever happened to a reigning world champion. It was the seal of a season that Enzo had no reticence in describing as catastrophic: 'Not so-and-so,' he said, 'but completely negative.'[43] Having admitted this, he angrily remarked: 'No one has the right to write, or to say on the radio, that Ferrari makes wheelbarrows and not cars. No one has the right to say that the prancing horse is red out of shame.'[44]

That winter Enzo Ferrari turned 83. 'I am still around,' he remarked, 'because I believe in the automobile, a conquest of freedom for man.'[45]

The challenge of delivering a winning turbo engine made him feel at least ten years younger. He was as active and enthusiastic as ever. He knew that the new season would be a good one, and therefore there was no time to rest: 'At my age,' he had said the previous summer, 'I have only one Boss, the good Lord. He alone will decide when I retire.'[46]

But before the 1981 season could get under way, it was necessary to solve once and for all the tension between the Fédération Internationale du Sport Automobile (FISA, which was authorized by the FIA to run F1) and FOCA that was tearing Formula 1 apart. The autumn had been a hot one, with the FOCA-affiliated teams speaking of secession and FISA countering with a threatened ban, and race calendars changing with each new week. It was clear that Formula 1 had no future unless some form of agreement could be reached. Therefore, after countless meetings that had not produced any real outcome, on behalf of FOCA Brabham's Bernie Ecclestone asked for help in mediation from the most improbable of all negotiators, a man who had spent most of his long life quarrelling with institutions and federations, who had made arguing a way of life, but whose immense experience could now benefit all.

On Monday morning, 19 January 1981, the key players in Formula 1 met in Modena to try and find some unity before facing Jean-Marie Balestre, who led the FIA, for the final showdown.

The FOCA front was made up of Bernie Ecclestone, Colin Chapman, Frank Williams and Alex Hawkridge, of the Toleman team. Representing the teams lined up with FISA's broad strategies were Carlo Chiti and Pier Luigi Corbari for Alfa Romeo, Enzo Osella and Gianfranco Palazzoli for Osella, Gérard Larrousse and Jean Sage for Renault, and Gérard Ducarouge for Talbot-Ligier. Sitting at the table representing Ferrari were Marco Piccinini and Piero Lardi Ferrari.[47] And then there was Enzo Ferrari, the patriarch of international motorsport, in the unprecedented role of great conciliator.

The summit was hosted in one of the meeting rooms on the ground floor of the old Scuderia Ferrari building on Viale Trento Trieste. It started at 10am and lasted for more than 13 hours. The participants were fed sandwiches at lunchtime and tea at 5pm. They remained cut off from the rest of the world until 11.30pm.[48]

It was a vibrant and hard-fought meeting that only the brilliance and personal charisma of Enzo Ferrari could help to steer in a conciliatory direction. During the heat of the debate, when no solution seemed in sight, Enzo came out with a request that could have sounded naive, but which was, instead, a tactical masterpiece. He turned to Ecclestone and Chapman, the two front men of FOCA, and simply asked for . . . a birthday present. He told them that he would soon turn 83, and that the best birthday present they could give him was to 'smooth out the difficulties that still existed'.[49]

Ecclestone and Chapman agreed, and through the mediation of Alex Hawkridge, whose Toleman team was the only British team aligned with the pro-FISA French and Italian teams, an arrangement was finally reached. At 11:30pm, they all emerged, visibly happy to have found the necessary unity to face Balestre and FISA. Most people quickly left, and it was Enzo Ferrari who met an anxious press.

Radiant and in a good mood, he sat in front of a microphone and uttered: 'Listen, it's almost midnight and I haven't had anything to eat since last night.'[50] After more than 13 hours of heated discussions, he was as sharp as ever. 'We have sanctioned the very important principle that FISA will continue to manage the rules, while someone else will take care of the economic part,' he said.[51]

Franco Gozzi read and then handed out a brief press release that said, 'a general agreement on the future of Formula One' had been reached, and that a 'steering committee will arrange the final text of a four-year global solution that will be submitted to the international federation'.[52] Renault's Sage, Alfa Romeo's Corbari and Ferrari's Piccinini would form a steering committee to write a text that had to be submitted for approval to FOCA before it was sent to FISA for evaluation, which was already set for 30 January. 'I hope,' said Enzo, 'that there will be no more complications and that FISA will accept our proposals.'[53]

Then, as if to distance himself from both the economic aspects of the story and the inevitable beatification process the Italian press would soon start, commending his valuable role in the process, he said: 'I want to say once again that all I have done is to make sure that we go on racing – all together. The rest, I don't care.'[54]

There was actually at least one other thing that he cared about, and it was a second birthday present from Colin and Bernie – especially Bernie. 'I am very happy,' he said, 'that the first San Marino Grand Prix will be held on May 3 at Imola, on a circuit very dear to my heart.'[55]

It was his fee for the mediation – a second Formula 1 race in Italy, and on the track that bore the name of his son Dino. Also thanks to Enzo, all of the proceeds from this new race would be donated to the population hit by the earthquake that two months earlier had struck southern Italy.

On 30 January, FISA rejected the proposals agreed in Modena. But it was only a pretext to save face, because it was clear to all, including Balestre, that an agreement with FOCA was the only plausible solution. Before the signing of the agreement – the famous Concorde Agreement, signed in Paris on 5 March – Ferrari and the rest of the non-FOCA teams sat out the first event of the year, the South African Grand Prix, which ended up not counting for the world title. The 1981 Formula One World Championship thus started on 15 March, at Long Beach.

Twenty-Seven Red

On 3 May, Gilles Villeneuve started the San Marino Grand Prix from pole position. This was the fourth round of the 1981 season. The previous Thursday Enzo Ferrari had briefly visited the circuit. He had paced the pits and had briefly spoken with his mechanics before being briefed by Forghieri. After less than 30 minutes, he had left and gone on to a private luncheon at an Imola restaurant.[1] He did not return for either qualifying or the race.

On Sunday, Villeneuve kept the lead for the first 15 laps before pitting to change his wet tyres for slicks. At that point it was the other Ferrari – Pironi's – that took the lead. But after these early fireworks, both Ferraris slowed their race pace: Pironi finished fifth and Villeneuve, seventh.

If the car was still not fully developed – the engine was fine, but the chassis was clearly still a work in progress – Enzo could be happy with the harmony between his two drivers. Villeneuve and Pironi had established a close relationship both on and off the track. Enzo's doubts about the possibility of a peaceful coexistence between two drivers of equal stature – which he'd felt during the winter, despite his public declarations – had faded. Without retracting his love for Gilles, Enzo now seemed particularly fond of Pironi, whom he'd started to affectionately call *Didì*.

On the last day in May, Gilles Villeneuve won the Monaco Grand Prix. It was Ferrari's first win in nearly six hundred days. Four laps from the end, Villeneuve passed Alan Jones's Williams and went on to take the most unexpected of wins. The moment he got out of his car, Villeneuve dedicated his win to Enzo Ferrari.[2]

'Thanks to all the members of the Ferrari family, and to all of our fans,' Enzo said the next day.[3] 'I had not expected a victory at Monaco,' he honestly acknowledged. 'We were defeated at Imola in a San Marino Grand Prix that we should have won. This,' he philosophically concluded, 'is the law of our sport.'[4]

The confirmation that the new turbo engine was good, and – if any proof was still needed – that Villeneuve's talent was rare, came three weeks later in Spain, when the little Canadian took an epic win after fending off for sixty-six seemingly endless laps the attacks of four cars that seemed glued to one another – and to his car. The next day, once more referring to the greatest driver he had ever known, Enzo said: 'Last Sunday Gilles Villeneuve made me relive the legend of Tazio Nuvolari.'[5]

After the Spanish Grand Prix, however, Villeneuve and Pironi suffered one withdrawal after another. His third place in his Canadian Grand Prix home race did little to boost Villeneuve's morale, for it was the penultimate round in the championship. Despite having extended his contract with Ferrari as early as the Monaco Grand Prix, Villeneuve almost accepted the courtship of McLaren, which offered a ludicrous amount of money. Then, thinking about Enzo's reaction, Gilles decided to keep his word and remain at Ferrari.[6]

At the end of the season, Enzo spoke words of authentic admiration for his Canadian driver. 'Both at Jarama and at Monaco,' he said with surprising candour, 'we won because of Villeneuve's skills, and for no other reason.'[7] And to those who still attacked Gilles for his predisposition to crash in races, he said: 'I like Villeneuve the way he is, with his exuberance and his incomprehensible risks.'[8] According to Enzo, although it had been far from the season that 'our fans expected', 1981 'had not been all that bad'.[9]

The new car was introduced on 6 January 1982. Enzo told the journalists who had gathered in Maranello that this car was a present to him from all his men, starting with chief designer Harvey Postlethwaite.[10]

Villeneuve took it to the track the very next day and immediately crushed the old Fiorano lap record, which had been standing for over a year.[11] Postlethwaite had managed to create a car whose chassis quality finally matched the power of the engine.

On 18 February, Enzo Ferrari turned 84.

He was still the owner and ruler of his factory's racing department, although the days of the absolute monarchy were in the far-distant past. 'It has been written and said that I am a man who personally makes all decisions and listens to no one. The truth,' he confided, 'is quite different. I have the habit of consulting with my closest aides, of learning their moods, of smelling – given the proportions of my nose – the air. When I found indifference, sometimes even hostility, I took steps back.'[12] And to those who asked for an example of Enzo listening to his aids, he named Alan Jones, whom he had wanted to hire, only to desist when he realized that no one else within his inner circle wanted him.

In Italy Enzo's popularity was at an all-time high. Italians loved him as they had never loved him before. Part of this affection, he knew, was due to his little Canadian driver.[13] 'I adore Villeneuve,' he remarked that winter, 'because he is a driver who races for the crowd.'[14] And the crowd, reciprocating Gilles's consideration, honoured the man who gave the Canadian the cars he raced.[15]

The Grand Old Man was peaceful. Thanks to Fiat, his company would have a prosperous future even after his death. He was serene enough to indulge in provocations: 'I have made my time,' he said. 'We'll see what happens next.' It sounded as if Enzo was uncertain about whether his company would continue racing after his demise: 'If, after I am gone, Ferrari will still race,' he said, 'I cannot say.'[16]

* * *

Like the year before, the fight between FISA and FOCA made for a rocky start to the Formula One World Championship.

After the cancellation of the 7 March Grand Prix of Argentina, the teams convened in Brazil on the first day of spring. Villeneuve started from the first row of the grid, but neither Ferrari did well on race day. The Canadian ended his day with a crash; Pironi did no better than sixth place. Despite the far from memorable results, the 126 C2 had nonetheless proved to be a very fast car.

At Long Beach, in April, Niki Lauda won his first grand prix after his return to racing following a two-year hiatus. 'When he suddenly retired [three years ago], I said that he had been honest and brave,' Enzo remarked after the race. 'Now he is showing great courage once again.'[17] But as far as Ferrari's cars were concerned, the US Grand Prix West had been another unfortunate race: Villeneuve, third, was disqualified for irregularities with the rear spoiler on his car.

When Formula 1 came to Europe for the second San Marino Grand Prix, the war between FOCA and FISA was at its peak. The pro-FOCA British teams showed up at the track, but in the end did not participate in the race. On Sunday, the grand prix was contested only by the Ferraris, Renaults, Alfa Romeos, Osellas, Tyrrells, Tolemans and ATSs – 14 cars instead of the 26 that normally lined up on the starting grid. But despite the odds, the cars that took the start of the grand prix battled each other to the end and, by the time the race was over, the Ferrari team was irreparably lacerated.

In the final laps, the two Ferraris of Villeneuve and Pironi overtook each other several times. Pironi had started the fratricidal battle by surprisingly passing his teammate after the two drivers had been shown the slow sign from the pits, indicating that they should hold their present positions. At first Villeneuve thought it was some kind of trick to amuse the all-Ferrari crowd in the stands. Soon, however, he realized that Pironi wasn't just playing a game for the benefit of Ferrari's fans, and responded fiercely to all the threats his teammate posed to his leadership.[18] Ultimately it was Pironi who won the grand prix, and Villeneuve swore eternal hatred to the friend who had betrayed him.

That afternoon Italy was divided: on one side was the multitude that believed, given his résumé with Ferrari, that Villeneuve had every right to consider himself the team captain. On the other were the few who had decided to side with Pironi, who, it must be said, had not realized the pandemonium that his race conduct and win had sparked, and had innocently dedicated his win to his new wife.[19]

In the middle, for the following 48 hours, was Enzo Ferrari, who no less than 5 weeks earlier had remarked: 'At Ferrari the team captain is the driver who wins on Sunday. It's the track that accounts for hierarchies.'[20]

On Sunday afternoon, right after the end of the race, the Grand Old Man confessed that he had feared some bad surprise towards the end. 'I am really pleased,' he had said, 'even though in the last laps I was afraid that the two drivers could damage each other and perhaps ruin their wonderful race.'[21] On Monday he remained silent. But then, on Tuesday, he spoke.

For the first time in his long life, Enzo sided with one of his drivers against the other – although in private he had doubts about the soundness of his position, since he knew that Gilles was on his way out and that, of the two, it was Pironi who would drive for Ferrari in 1983.[22] 'When at Imola the race result was already settled,' he said, 'Pironi underestimated the invitation to responsible conduct that the pits had constantly asked for, [indicated] with [the] sign [they held up] beginning at lap 45.[23] I understand Villeneuve's legitimate disappointment, and I share his frustration for the risks he took,' he said. 'I have been a driver myself, and I think that even in the modern age the feelings of those who race out of sheer passion have remained unchanged.'[24]

Here it was, at last – what had endeared Gilles to Enzo over the years: the passion that was at the core of the Canadian's love for motorsport, a passion that Enzo himself had shared some 60 years before. And just like Nuvolari, of course, the archetype on which he had always judged all drivers of all generations.

That week Enzo summoned them both to Maranello.[25] He preached judiciousness.[26] Pironi said he was sorry for Gilles's reaction, which he had not anticipated – at least, not in these proportions – when he had battled him at Imola.[27] But it was too late. Villeneuve would never forgive his teammate and, from that day on, he would race only to be faster than Pironi, both in qualifying and in Sunday's race.

On 8 May, eight minutes before the end of the qualifying session for the Belgian Grand Prix, the battle for pole position was at its height. Suddenly, frightening images appeared on the TV screen. A Ferrari hit the rear wheel of another car with its front wheel and was launched into a dramatic spin in the air. It came back to the ground, only to spin several more times. The driver was ejected from his car during the first spin, and ended up next to what remained of his disintegrated car. He was lying prone on the grass without his helmet, lost in the terrifying flight.

Enzo knew instantly that the driver, seemingly lifeless on the turf, was Gilles. And he knew – he just knew – that there was nothing anyone could do for him. 'If at Zolder my car were to skid,' Villeneuve had said the day before, 'the only thing I can do is call my mother for help and [make] the sign of the cross.'[28]

Enzo jumped up from his chair and rushed to the bathroom. He stayed there for a few minutes, and when he reemerged his eyes were red from crying.[29] He did not utter a single word. None of those present dared to speak. A few moments later Enzo was handed the telephone. From Zolder his men were telling him what he'd instinctively known: Villeneuve was still alive, but would not survive.

Enzo ordered his men to return to Maranello. Piccinini alone would remain in Belgium with Gilles.[30]

Quietly, Enzo's Saturday gang left, leaving him alone with his desperation. He had lived many such moments in his life. However much he had tried, he had never come to terms with this situation. And, of course, Gilles was special. Only for Peter Collins, a quarter of a century earlier, had he felt the same affection. And now Gilles, too, was gone. Enzo barricaded himself inside the Fiorano fortress, waiting for the news he knew would come sooner or later.[31] And when it came, he went on the record with emotional words that came from the bottom of his heart. 'He left us,' he said, 'for unintelligible reasons. Fate has deprived us of a great champion, a champion that I loved very much. My past is filled with sorrow and sad memories: my father, my mother, my brother and my son. Now, when I turn back, I see all those I loved. And among them there is also this great man, Gilles Villeneuve.'[32]

For a brief moment he hoped to replace Gilles with Mario Andretti, but from Pennsylvania the Italian-American driver replied that he could only make himself available for the North American races.[33] Enzo then chose Patrick Tambay, a Parisian he had been watching for some time, and who in the late 1970s he had considered before hiring Villeneuve. Tambay had then opted for McLaren, but at the same time had told Enzo that the day he needed him, he would be available.[34]

Tambay's debut in the car that had been Villeneuve's took place at the Dutch Grand Prix in early July. Pironi came second, only one point shy of the championship lead, which he took two weeks later. But fate had plans of its own for Didier, who, the morning of 7 August, during practice for the German Grand Prix, crashed in a way that was similar to Villeneuve's. He came out of it alive, but with both legs fractured and no hope of racing for the rest of the season – if ever again.

Deeply disturbed by this second frightening crash, Enzo remained distant from it all, alone with his men. Pironi had a modest lead in the championship, which could be defended, Enzo argued. There were four races to go before the end of the series – many, but not *too* many, and the 126 C2 had proved to be the fastest car around. The day after Pironi's crash, Tambay won the German Grand Prix, and he too was now in the fight for the title.

At this point, Tambay's history of back problems came into play, a consequence of his own terrifying crash at Monza in 1977. In the most shining moment of the season, and of his career, he was forced to sit out one race and to say goodbye to his world title hopes, as well as Pironi's. Two races from the end, Keke Rosberg took the championship lead away from Didier.

At this point Enzo played his hat trick and hired for the Italian Grand Prix at Monza his beloved and never-forgotten Mario Andretti.[35] It took Enzo a single phone call to convince the 1978 Formula 1 world champion to race a Ferrari at Monza. The next day Andretti climbed on board a commercial flight headed to Malpensa. At ten the next morning he met with Enzo and his engineers in Maranello. The Grand Old Man then invited him to lunch in his Fiorano hideaway and, in the afternoon, Andretti took the 126 C2 for a spin on Ferrari's home track.

Mario did 90 laps. On Saturday, amid the enthusiasm of the fans, the incredulity of the press and the satisfaction of Enzo,[36] he set the pole position. On race Sunday he finished third behind Tambay, who came second. If he had not experienced problems with the throttle pedal of his Ferrari, Tambay could have won.

Andretti's pole position and third-place finish at Monza convinced Enzo to ask Mario to race one more grand prix for Ferrari, at Las Vegas.[37] Mario accepted, but his second, and last, 1982 race for Ferrari was far less exciting than the first. At any rate, thanks to Mario's contribution, Enzo took home the manufacturers' title. In a cursed year – a year, Enzo would comment afterwards, 'when we could have won the title three times',[38] with Villeneuve, Pironi and Tambay – his team had at least taken home the consolation prize.

Michele

In the course of 1981, Enzo Ferrari had moved his office to Fiorano, as if to symbolically divide his universe: in Maranello, where the road-going car plant functioned, was Fiat; in Fiorano, it was Enzo and his racing team. The relationship with his partner remained a little bumpy. He had never really experienced any specific problem with either Giovanni Sguazzini or Eugenio Alzati, the Fiat-appointed president and general manager of Ferrari, or with the executives who had preceded them. And his personal relationship with Gianni Agnelli was fine: Agnelli acknowledged him publicly as a 'synthesis of genius, fantasy and technology'.[1] But, quite simply, Enzo missed the independence that he had enjoyed previously.

The tragedies and hardships of the previous year had made him reflect even more deeply than usual, and personal introspection had led him to revisit a forbidden dream[2] – distancing himself from the great mother Fiat and going on alone, like in the old days, with a small team totally committed to racing.[3] He was thinking of a sort of Scuderia Ferrari magically transported from the 1930s into the 1980s, with Fiat in the background to play the role that Alfa Romeo had played then. The dream soon vanished, though, because Fiat never allowed it any real chance.[4] Enzo took notice and confined himself to the self-imposed seclusion of the Fiorano city-state, going back and forth from the new *Gestione Sportiva* headquarters to the little mansion in the heart of the circuit, where he now had most of his lunches, preferring it for a number of reasons to his private and once-cherished dining room at the Cavallino: its location allowed him to bypass the curious masses who stood for hours in front of the factory gate just to catch a glimpse of him; he could more easily follow his rigid diet; and it fulfilled his desire to see as few Fiat executives as possible.

Enzo's new office was comfortable, spacious, bright and austere, just like the previous one. Behind his desk was the crystal prancing horse that Paul Newman had given him six years earlier. The walls were painted in a slightly brighter blue and a single oil painting hung from them, showing a racing Ferrari at high speed.

As expected, the black-and-white photograph of Dino with the little lamp and the three flowers in the colours of the Italian flag had also moved from the old Maranello office.[5] Despite his inner resentment of Fiat, at nearly 85 Enzo was content. 'Here it is always like a family. Here work the fathers, often the mothers, today the sons, sons-in-law, daughters-in-law, uncles. They all feel they are at home, and their lives [are at the heart of] the life of the Scuderia,'[6] Enzo would tell anyone who wanted to know what Ferrari was like in its 36th year: an avant-garde company, a top Formula 1 racing team but, especially, a big family made up of people from his own land, a land where the sense of belonging was very much felt, cemented by his towering personality.

These days Enzo woke up at 7.30am. After reading the usual bunch of newspapers, he went to the barber for a quick shave and then, if his health allowed, he would visit Dino's tomb. He no longer visited the cemetery every day, as he'd done just a few years earlier. He wanted to avoid catching a cold or, worse, the flu. If his health was good, the visit to Dino's tomb was his only stop on the way to Maranello.

The strict diet had made him slimmer and sharpened his face – 'my ill-mannered, provincial face'[7] – once round, now bony, lit by eyes brighter and livelier than ever. He drank barley coffee, keeping the 'real' coffee for Saturday's lunch, provided that the blood tests he took every week were good. Saturday was also the day he habitually sipped a small glass of whisky from a special bottle[8] that a Scottish admirer sent him year after year.[9]

His dinner was frugal, some fruit and not much else, consumed most often with Dino Tagliazucchi and his wife, and sometimes with Piero, Floriana and granddaughter Antonella.[10] After dinner he chatted with Lina, watched some television, read a book. He still went to bed later than most, usually after 1am.[11] And though he was isolated by choice from the rest of the world, he remained as curious as ever about anything that went on beyond the cornfields that covered the rich land between Modena and Maranello.[12]

Every word he uttered in public was taken as a final judgement, every memory, a dive into an unrepeatable past from which emerged faces and facts that at times went back to the dawn of a century that he'd travelled in its entirety with the passion, the flair, the loves and the hatred of few. 'Because I am considered a rather shrewd and complex man,' he loved to say with unconcealed pleasure, 'my words are regularly weighed, interpreted, discussed, so that in the end they often generate a confusion in which I take pleasure.'[13]

His love of quarrelling remained intact. If his arguing with FISA, FOCA, ACI or other Formula 1 teams was often vibrant, he could also bite more subtly, as when he stated that Ferrari should build no more than 2,000 cars a year, rather than the 2,500 units Fiat had wanted to build. 'A Ferrari,' he never tired of saying, 'must be desired, dreamed [of], and therefore waited upon, just like a celebrity.'[14]

Tambay and Arnoux began the new season in the best possible way. Starting from the same position on the grid that Villeneuve had occupied a year before, Tambay won the San Marino Grand Prix. The Imola crowd went wild.

At 9.30am on Sunday 29 May 1983, the president of Italy showed up at the Ferrari gate in Fiorano. Sandro Pertini was not the first Italian chief of state to visit Ferrari, but his arrival at the court of King Enzo had a very different significance from Giovanni Gronchi's visit in 1957. Pertini was the *other* Grand Old Man of 1980s Italy – a man who had come a long way, a founding father of the Republic who had been a Resistance hero during the war and had then navigated unscathed the muddy waters of Italian politics. He was perhaps the only living soul who was more popular – in Italy, at least – than Enzo Ferrari. The two had never met, which was probably not that odd, given that Enzo had last been in Rome in 1935 and Pertini had been a member of Parliament since 1946.

The visit started with a small diplomatic incident. The president arrived in his limousine, which was no ordinary state car, but a four-door sedan built by Maserati, Ferrari's cross-town nemesis. Pertini had personally wanted the fancy car in the presidential press fleet and was very proud of it. He couldn't have imagined the emotional turmoil he caused for Enzo when he passed through the Ferrari gate in a Maserati Quattroporte. When the limousine stopped, Enzo did not walk towards the car as he was supposed to according to the protocol and instructions that he had been given the day before.

The moments that followed were pure horror for the presidential party – a shock shared by Gozzi and Piero, who were also aware of the protocol. For a few, endless seconds, the president sat behind the car's closed door while Enzo stood motionless, with no apparent intention of walking towards his illustrious guest. The president solved the situation. Always pragmatic, and having realized that nothing was happening, Pertini opened the car door himself and started walking towards his host.[15] 'Dear Ferrari,' said the president, shaking Enzo's hand, 'I really wanted to meet you, and here I am!'

'Mr President,' Enzo replied, 'I am very honoured for this consideration, and for your gesture.'[16]

Enzo ushered the president inside the GES headquarters and, for the next half hour, hosted his guest in a thorough visit with Ferrari's famed racing team. Stressing the fact that Pertini's visit was first and foremost a tribute to Enzo Ferrari, the president visited only the racing-team premises where Enzo was still king, and did not cross the road to the *Gestione Industriale* side of the factory, where Fiat was in charge.

Enzo and the president chatted undisturbed for the whole time, speaking mostly of racing drivers and, especially, of the aces of their youth. Pertini was born in 1896, two years before Ferrari. They talked of Ettore Bugatti, Gastone Brilli-Peri and Tazio Nuvolari – particularly Nuvolari. But they spoke also of Lauda and Villeneuve, the death of the latter having touched the president deeply.[17]

Thirty-five minutes after arriving, the president bid Enzo goodbye with a warm handshake that became the embrace of two old friends.

'This,' Pertini told Enzo before departing, 'is a factory that honours Italy. It is incredible what you have been able to achieve with your capability, imagination and creativity.'[18]

Separately, both Gozzi and Piero later asked Enzo why, contrary to what he'd been instructed to do, he had not walked towards the presidential limousine. The answer was the same to both: Enzo Ferrari, he said, cannot walk towards a Maserati – no matter who's on board![19]

Tambay had won at Imola on 1 May. Arnoux won at Montreal, on the race track that had just been renamed after Gilles Villeneuve, in mid-June; at Hockenheim and then at Zandvoort, in early and late August. Both drivers were contenders for the title, but Enzo was not entirely happy with either of them. He did not particularly care for Tambay's slow starts and for Arnoux's overall race conduct, and he soon began to let his frustration be known. Regarding his two drivers, as early as late May, he'd told the president of Italy, 'One must [make] do with what one has.'[20]

Therefore, he started to look around, and despite the many drivers who were offering their services, he began to think more and more about Michele Alboreto in May.[21] The Italian driver's contract with Tyrrell was due to expire at the end of 1983, and Michele had told Enzo that he would be honoured to drive for Ferrari in 1984. On the last Monday in September, the Grand Old Man summoned Alboreto to Fiorano. At 7pm Enzo met Alboreto together with Piccinini and Arnoux. He told Michele that, if he wanted to, he could be a Ferrari driver in 1984. Alboreto immediately accepted.[22] As the presence of Arnoux at the meeting clearly indicated, Enzo had made his choice. Towards Tambay he was gallant: 'He is a great tester. He reminds me of Amon. He is a man who can tell you everything about a car. I know what I'll lose in not renewing his contract.'

If the press hailed the return of an Italian driver to Ferrari as the dawn of a new age, for Enzo the hiring of Michele represented a new beginning after the many thrills and devastating grief of the Villeneuve period. For Enzo, the post-Villeneuve era was beginning only now, 17 months after the Canadian's death. With Alboreto, Enzo was launching a new campaign: attempting to win the Formula 1 world title with an Italian driver for the first time since Alberto Ascari's two consecutive titles in 1952 and 1953.[23]

As he stood on the edge of yet another trial in his long life, Enzo Ferrari was as combative as ever. At 85, he still had the vitality of his younger years. Despite the manufacturers' title and third and fourth places in the drivers' standings, the press had given him a hard time all season long. It was nothing new, of course. He was used to the skirmishes with his friend–enemies in the press. When a reporter asked him why he was so often mocked by the press, he snapped: 'I am indispensable to all of you, because if I did not exist, you would invent me. You *need* Ferrari,' he said. 'In the end, what you all do does not surprise me, because [while] Italians forgive everything of thieves, assassins and kidnappers, they do not forgive success.'[24]

Enzo Ferrari's Christmas 1983 gift to friends and associates was a new book. With a print run of just 2,500 copies, which were not for sale, *Piloti, che gente . . .* was a brilliant dissertation on 8 decades of motor racing. The title, roughly translated, means *Racing Drivers: What People . . .* This book contained the central part of his famed memoirs devoted to the racing drivers he had met throughout his long life.

Along with the profiles of drivers who had raced both for and against Ferrari, Enzo had added those sections of his autobiography that dealt with his passion for motor racing and his own career as a driver. In the 21 years since the publication of *Le mie gioie terribili* (*My Terrible Joys*), he had more than once updated the original text by adding profiles of new drivers, but had never changed his opinion on his own modest talent at the wheel of a racing car. All he cared to say about himself in *Piloti, che gente* was: 'I don't think I was that bad as a driver.'[25]

He had grouped the drivers he had known into five generations. In Villeneuve's profile he had added the now frequently quoted comment about their complex relationship, which was, in fact, a postmortem tribute: 'He was a champion of combativeness and has gifted, has added, much glory to Ferrari. I loved him.'[26]

On his first day at Fiorano, Michele Alboreto set a new lap record. And in the first grand prix of the 1984 season, in Brazil, he started from the first row on the grid.

Alboreto led the Brazilian Grand Prix for the first 14 laps, before he was forced out by a mechanical failure. Michele's first win with Ferrari was only postponed to 29 April and the Belgian Grand Prix at Zolder, the circuit where Villeneuve had died two years earlier. But in his moment of triumph, Alboreto discovered the great complexity of his monumental employer.

Still in the Ferrari pits after the trophy ceremony, he was put on the phone to Fiorano. Michele was expecting to be congratulated. 'Well, *Commendatore*,' he said, 'what do you say?' Enzo chilled him. Without even hinting at the grand prix win, he said, 'I say that you made a colossal mistake that could have cost you the race. And then, in the end, you slowed your pace down without any reason.'[27] Michele was speechless. What he didn't know about Enzo Ferrari was that if there was one thing that truly distressed him, it was success.

'I don't know euphoria,' Enzo maintained. 'When I win a grand prix, I ask myself: Now, what will happen to me?' He was certain of just one thing: 'In life you pay for everything.' And since he believed that 'success has always come to me at a high price',[28] he could never fully enjoy any of the countless wins of his racing cars. Enzo Ferrari would never swap a victory for a podium finish – and yet, in his mind, a second or third place possessed the encouraging promise of success.[29]

Arnoux came in third in Belgium, second at Imola and third at Monaco. For Alboreto, on the other hand, a series of withdrawals began. Then Arnoux, too, started to underperform. The 126 C4 had lost its edge.

'The racing car today,' Enzo explained to his merciless detractors, in defence of his men, 'is no longer what it used to be in the days of Jano – the fruit of a superior mind. Today it is the compendium of many specializations. It is clear,' he was forced to admit, 'that in such a compendium of specializations, we lack something.'[30]

The situation was actually far more complex. Little by little Fiat's men had been placed in ever more significant positions within *Gestione Sportiva*. Most did not have a racing background but, because of their Fiat provenance, had influence and so jeopardized the power of the man who was solely, truly responsible for GES, Mauro Forghieri. Often on returning from a grand prix weekend, Forghieri had to undo what others, in his absence and against his directives, had done. Enzo had at least in part realized what was going on, but he no longer had the grit, the energy and perhaps even the will to step in.[31]

The Grand Old Man had confirmed both drivers for 1985 at the time of the Monaco Grand Prix in early June. Drivers were not the problem. 'I confirm my trust and keep Alboreto because he is Italian, a good driver and a good man,' he said that summer.[32] And though Fiat would have liked to see Arnoux replaced by Lauda,[33] Enzo kept repeating that he had no reason to be unhappy with his French driver.[34]

With the world title already in the hands of the McLaren duo, Alboreto scored two second places at Monza and the Nürburgring. Lauda became world champion, with half a point over teammate Alain Prost. Ferrari's drivers ended the season in fourth and sixth places.

At the end of the 1984 season, after 22 years at the helm of the technical direction of *Gestione Sportiva*, Mauro Forghieri resigned. Enzo Ferrari rejected his resignation. Moved by the gesture – Mauro's father had been with Enzo since the glory days of the Scuderia, and for Enzo, Mauro was like a third son – Forghieri accepted a position at Ferrari Engineering, a new and separate department where he would be in charge of researching aluminium chassis and four-by-four technology for road-going Ferraris.

For Enzo it was a bitter moment. For Forghieri it was a hard blow, made even harder by the realization that the tyrant-king he had served for more than 20 years was no longer either; tyrant no more, the king had lost his crown. In autumn 1984 Enzo Ferrari was a lonesome giant, a tired man and oblivious in the hands of Fiat men who did not keep him fully informed.[35]

The first winter without Forghieri to talk to, discuss things and argue with was a surreal period for Enzo Ferrari. By now the Grand Old Man had become a burden to the executive board of his company. In Forghieri, Enzo had lost not only a first-rate engineer, but also one of the few men who were still unquestionably loyal to him. From now on the Fiat men could do as they pleased without Enzo even suspecting their actions.

To the outer world he remained as brilliant as ever. Through statements such as 'I don't retire; the Lord Almighty will decide,' and 'acquiescent is someone who is about to die, but I have no intention [of dying] for the time being,'[36] he was showing his will to fight and, perhaps more important, he was projecting the image of someone who was still in charge. In reality, he was no longer centre stage, and was content to be briefed by Piero and Piccinini on a daily basis, and by Postlethwaite every now and then.[37]

But when, 2 days before his 87th birthday, the Formula 1 car for the 1985 season was shown to the press, his scepticism about the new course finally surfaced. 'It's a car born out of a different working scheme; now I expect it to win,'[38] he said.

After a single championship event in the 1985 campaign, Enzo let one of his two drivers go. The circumstances were – and remain – unclear. There were those who talked of a ferocious quarrel following the Brazilian Grand Prix, and others who spoke of problems of a more private nature.[39] Whatever the reason, René Arnoux was fired overnight and replaced by a young Swedish driver with little Formula 1 experience – Stefan Johansson, who, at Imola at the end of April, had come second in the San Marino Grand Prix.

The troubles with the new technical and managerial assets of Ferrari's *Gestione Sportiva* became evident in the course of the season. The 156-85 was unquestionably a good car. Thanks to several podium finishes and two wins, in Canada and in

Germany, Alboreto had taken the lead in the championship standings. But then two different problems surfaced, connected to each other and related to the new managerial situation.

The first was a good dose of anarchy within the Forghieri-free GES, where, despite the proven competitiveness of the car, there were those who decided to experiment with new solutions without the go-ahead of Postlethwaite, the man in charge – solutions that hurt the performance of the car. When he realized what was going on, a horrified Enzo asked Forghieri for advice. By this point Mauro had become somewhat removed from the racing team and didn't have a precise idea of what was going on. He did know one thing, however, and said as much to Enzo: a winning car was never to be touched in the course of a winning season.[40]

The second problem was Enzo himself, who chose the wrong moment and the wrong issue to show that, despite everything, he was still king.

When spring turned into summer, both 156-85s started to experience problems related to the motor power unit.[41] After a thorough internal investigation, the cause of the problem was finally identified: a small component made by a German manufacturer, which produced the same component for McLaren's Porsche engine (although McLaren hadn't experienced similar complications). Enzo ordered an examination of all relevant units that were already in-house, which proved that the components were not flawed; however, some Ferrari technicians pointed out that their overall quality had decreased in the course of the year.

Since Alain Prost in the Porsche-equipped McLaren was Michele Alboreto's only opponent for the 1985 world title, Enzo decided, without evidence, that it was a German conspiracy against Ferrari. He angrily raised his voice and ordered his staff to break the contract with the German manufacturer. Still screaming, he demanded that they get in touch right away with an American manufacturer that he personally knew. He asked for the phone number and opened his desk drawer to pick up his personal chequebook, a gesture he mechanically performed every time he was really upset and the only solution appeared to be doing something without any cost constraint.[42]

Piccinini tried to calm him down. He stated that, at this point in the season, it made no sense to start using components that had not been tested. But his team manager's observations only reinforced Enzo's resolution.

'What does it say here?' he shouted to Piccinini, pointing at the pin that he wore on his suit jacket.

'Well, *Ingegnere* . . . it says Ferrari.'

'Right,' cried the Grand Old Man, 'it says Ferrari. That's me, and *I* decide! The day it says Piccinini, *you* will decide.'[43] And so it was.

Ferrari changed supplier – and Alboreto did not finish any of the championship's remaining races. Alain Prost became world champion, with Michele the runner-up. The dream of winning the first world title with an Italian driver since the days of Alberto Ascari ended there.

There was one last dream, however: the Indianapolis 500. It was the grand race of his youth, the event that had won him over to motor racing because of Ralph DePalma's great feat. After becoming a manufacturer, he had never really given much consideration to the Indiana classic, except for the distracted semiofficial participation in 1952 and the engine he had provided in 1956. But surprisingly, 30 years later, Enzo Ferrari once more seemed to revive his own American dream – even though no one will ever know for sure with what degree of conviction.

The decision to build a Ferrari single-seater for the US Championship Auto Racing Teams (CART or Indycar) series was made in November 1985. Enzo asked that work immediately begin on designing a totally new chassis and engine according to CART homologation rules.[44] Responsibility for the chassis was entrusted to Gustav Brunner; the engine, to the Renzetti–Caruso–His trio. Postlethwaite was accountable for the overall Indycar project.[45]

By Christmas 1985 a small team of engineers and mechanics had started work on the new project, separate from the much larger team at work on the Formula 1 car for 1986. In the group were Antonio Bellentani, Scheckter's chief mechanic in 1979, and Angiolino Marchetti, Dino Ferrari's old schoolmate.[46]

The new Formula 1 car – named F1-86 – was officially launched on 10 March 1986. On that day Enzo revealed that, for once, the rumours were true: there would be a Ferrari for Indianapolis, and Andrea de Cesaris could be the designated driver.

'In regard to our American participation,' Enzo stated, 'after our debut race we will decide whether we will build two or three cars.'[47] That's as far as he went that day in talking about his American dream.

The car was ready that summer, and on 20 July 1986, a midsummer Sunday, the 637 Indy – this, the name of the car – was photographed in the inner courtyard of the Fiorano track, right in front of the red entrance door to Enzo's private retreat. Gozzi skilfully leaked the photo to the right journalists, along with the name of the US racing team – Truesports, led by owner Jim Trueman and driver Bobby Rahal. The latter had been used as an adviser, and would presumably race the car.[48] The past year had been a successful one for the team, with Rahal winning the Indy 500 and the CART championship.

A few days later news came from America that the Truesports team had entered the 637 Indy for the 12 October race at Laguna Seca – 50 years after the day Nuvolari had won his, and Enzo's, legendary victory at the Vanderbilt Cup.

Then, nothing else happened. At the end of September Enzo announced that participation in the CART championship series was 'no longer a priority'.[49] What had happened?

At least a couple of things. The first was direct intervention by Fiat, which called everyone back to reality and ended everyone's daydreaming. The cost of managing a Formula 1 team was too high to start thinking of racing in a second series, especially in the American market, where no Fiat cars were being exported.

The second was a step back by both Ecclestone, who led FOCA, and Balestre, who led the FIA, in their war over the management of Formula 1. Since the spark that had ignited Enzo's American dream had been his need to send an eloquent, powerful message to both men – that Ferrari could abandon Formula 1 and its politics, to F1's undeniable detriment, and compete instead in CART – a satisfied Grand Old Man immediately dropped his dream.[50]

Sunset

At the time of the debut of the new car for the 1986 Formula 1 season, the Grand Old Man had been cautious: 'It has not yet uttered a word,' he told those who said that the new F1 car was beautiful. 'I do not know how it will sing. I would be happy,' he confessed, 'if at the end of the '86 season we should again be the runner-up, 8 short points behind the winner, as in 1985.'[1]

For a man accustomed to looking forward, it was an extremely guarded statement. But perhaps Ferrari had realized ahead of anyone else that the managerial chaos that had engulfed his team would not lead to anything good.[2]

The Saturday before the introduction of the new car, he had played with his men like a cat playing with mice. He had invited 18 of them to lunch and, right before coffee, had handed out sheets of paper inviting his guests to secretly write the name of the driver and the team that would win the 1986 world title – and to sign the document.

To be fair, he said, he would do the same. Then he looked at Gozzi, who went around the table to collect each man's contribution.[3] 'Franco Gozzi will keep these papers,' he said. 'At the end of the year we will see who has guessed right.'[4] It was, of course, an extraordinarily subtle way to make his men face their individual responsibilities.[5] A month earlier, Enzo Ferrari had turned 88. 'I still like to fight,' he said, 'so I guess that I am fine.'[6]

Ten years after the release of *Il Flobert*, the book he had written about journalists, Enzo was planning a sort of follow-up, 'another book in which,' he said, 'I will make no judgements, but simply put together the verdicts that many journalists have written about me over the last few years.' And he had no doubt about the end result. 'It will be fun. If in life you lose the taste for revenge,' he said, chuckling, 'it's all over.'[7] Despite his infirmities – first and foremost, distressing back pain – he was not doing badly for a man of his age. He was still absorbed in the management of an automotive reality that had no equal in the world. 'Of the Ferrari team,' he said, 'I represent the past, I lead the present, and as far as the future goes, it's in the hands of the Almighty.'[8]

At 88, he also had less-earthly topics crowding his mind. 'Faith,' he held forth, 'is an energizing convenience that man created.' He remembered when he had said the same thing to a bishop friend, who had replied: 'If this convenience is offered to us by the Lord, why reject it? You, Ferrari,' the bishop had told him then, 'have more faith than you think.' Thirty years later Enzo was still living in hopes of finding that 'convenience' called faith.[9]

'At work,' he confided, 'I seek the cooperation of all. In my private life, I have always been a loner.'[10] To those who questioned his grip on events and his decision-making power, he replied: 'My son Piero and Piccinini, as long as I live, will do only what *I* authorize them to do.'[11] And as for the future, he had clear ideas: 'My son Piero will take my place the day that I am gone.'[12]

The 1986 Formula 1 World Championship proved to be a huge disappointment. The F1-86 seemed like a faded double of the previous year's car. The second place suggested by Enzo before the start of the season ended up looking like a mirage. Johansson and Alboreto had to settle for only a few podium finishes, and concluded respectively fifth and ninth in the championship.

At the end of the season, Enzo decided on a radical shake-up, which if on the one hand it confirmed that he still made the important decisions, on the other rejected the thinking and conduct of a whole lifetime. From 1 November 1986, Ferrari's chief engineer would be the immensely talented John Barnard, the key figure in McLaren's success, whom Enzo had met on 12 September in Maranello.[13]

'Barnard will have full powers, and he will work where he sees fit,' said Enzo Ferrari, announcing the hiring of the British engineer.[14] Barnard would not necessarily work in Maranello – he would spend most of his time in England, where Ferrari would soon build a sort of technical subsidiary. To get him on board, Enzo had accepted all of Barnard's conditions.

On 19 July, Enzo had signed an agreement with Nigel Mansell, who was currently driving for Williams. In the end, however, Mansell had second thoughts and stayed where he was. 'His behaviour surprised us,' Enzo said, 'and our lawyers will take care of the issue.' In Mansell's place, Enzo chose Gerhard Berger, the young Austrian driver who, although Ferrari did not say so in public, reminded him of Lauda.[15]

In mid-March 1987, accompanied by Dino Tagliazucchi, his faithful chauffeur who, like Peppino Verdelli before him, went *everywhere* with him, Enzo Ferrari went to the Modena Polyclinic. The new MRI machine that he'd recently bought as a gift for the city hospital was going to be officially introduced that day. He knew that he couldn't avoid some kind of ceremony, but had demanded something very simple and quiet. Protected by the dark-lens glasses he nearly always wore when he appeared in public, Ferrari said only a few words. 'I did not want any promotion,' he confessed, 'but only to help bring some benefit to those who suffer from muscular dystrophy, people destined to die, for whom medicine and technology can do so much.'[16]

The machine that he had chosen and paid for out of his own pocket was the most powerful in Italy; there was just one other machine similar to this in the country, in Milan. 'I am delighted,' he said, referring to the new hospital department that would house the MRI machine, 'to see a structure completed that makes Modena one of the most advanced research centres in Italy, and I would like to thank all those who contributed to the realization of this structure.'[17]

It was 31 years since Dino had died in June 1956 of muscular dystrophy, then, as now, an unforgiving disease. Since then, and almost always silently, Dino's father had donated billions of lire to research towards finding a cure.[18]

Three days later the new Formula 1 car for the 1987 season was introduced. It showed the hand of John Barnard, even though the British engineer stressed that this was not his first Ferrari – *that* would be the model that would race in 1988.

Spring saw Formula 1 return to Europe. Both Alboreto and Berger struggled. There was some progress at Imola and Spa, but the early-July Grand Prix of France was a rout. Ferrari summoned his top staff and put Barnard in the hot seat, asking his chief engineer for a detailed analysis of the disaster in France and demanding to know what he would do for the next grand prix, in England.[19]

The poor performance of the two cars in France was not the only charge against Barnard. Enzo also reprimanded and blamed him for the damage inflicted on Ferrari's image by some candid remarks printed in a London newspaper, and for wrecking the relationship with Michele Alboreto, who had recently renewed his contract with Ferrari for yet another year.[20]

Ferrari demanded that Barnard remain at Fiorano to work that week, instead of returning to his splendid isolation at Guilford in England. And while technical meetings chaired by Barnard were organized left and right at Fiorano, Ferrari disappeared into one of his traditional and most eloquent silences.[21] The performance of the two cars did not improve for the next race – at Silverstone, yet again, both drivers retired from the race.

On Tuesday morning, 21 July, Enzo went to the recently built Civic Centre in downtown Maranello for the invitation-only premiere of the car that Ferrari, the company – not the man – had wanted, with the purpose of celebrating 40 years of its activity. Nobody knew it at the time, but they would be witness to the last introduction of one of his cars ever attended by Enzo Ferrari.

The Grand Old Man sat at a conference table at the edge of a round internal court, at the centre of which was the new car. Wrapped in a brilliant Ferrari-red cover, the new model emerged from the otherwise darkened circular room only when it was hit by two spotlights that were in constant movement, like two nervous searchlights piercing the night sky.

The room was filled to capacity. Through the PA system, Enzo's slow words echoed through the darkness.

'This car,' he said now, with evident pride, 'is the compendium of the efforts made by all at Ferrari in [the past] 12 months. This car,' he said stressing the point, 'is the result of one year of studying and designing.'[22] Though he refrained from saying it, he had personally given a suggestion here, an indication there, while the car was being developed. Perhaps he instinctively knew that this was the last car he would ever see.

As he finished his brief remarks, the audience broke into deafening applause while Ferrari staff lifted the red cover to unveil their new crown jewel. It was going to be named the F40 Le Mans. The 'F' stood for Ferrari and '40' for the anniversary it marked. It had been suggested to Giovanni Razelli, Ferrari's president, by an old-timer, journalist Gino Rancati – 'F-Forty', Rancati had said, in English, well knowing that the largest share of these units would go to the United States. 'Le Mans' was a tribute to Enzo's original plan.

Despite the public show of unity, Enzo felt resentment towards the Fiat hierarchy, inside and outside his company, which only intensified as he grew older. His personal relationship with Gianni Agnelli remained on a high note – they shared mutual affection and respect. But Agnelli never intervened at the heart of matters and, after setting the broad guidelines for his company's dealings with Ferrari, typically let his men work out the details of day-to-day operations. Enzo had nothing personal against either Cesare Romiti (the CEO of Fiat) or Vittorio Ghidella; he simply resented the fact that half of his company was not in his hands any longer and that the once-total freedom he'd enjoyed in his own half was diminishing on a daily basis.

He had often confided to his close friends that, notwithstanding the incontestable help that Fiat had provided at a crucial time, for the survival of his company, if he ever had the opportunity he would buy back the 50 per cent he had sold to them. He had spoken very openly on the subject to Rancati in June: 'If I could,' he'd said, 'I would buy back the whole factory. When I sold it to Fiat in 1969,' he explained, 'I did it because I was afraid I was going to die. Fear made me do it.'[23]

The last day of August, Enzo sat down at his desk in Fiorano and wrote an unequivocal letter to Cesare Romiti. The tone was cordial, but firm. Referring to the stakes allotment, he proclaimed: 'I am either going to sell everything or buy it all back.'[24]

In his journal that night he reflected on this communication and commented: 'The letter to Romiti has been sent off. Now it's up to him: I will either buy his 50 per cent, or I will sell mine.'[25]

On 3 October, on the occasion of Ferrari's 40th anniversary, 3 generations of racing drivers met with Enzo in his Fiorano office. All those who were still alive had come: Froilán González, who had given him his first F1 win; Piero Taruffi and Phil Hill, Umberto Maglioli and Andrea de Adamich; Clay Regazzoni, Patrick Tambay and driver-importer-dealer Luigi Chinetti, who, in 1949, with his Le Mans victory, had given Enzo his first great international success. And Juan Manuel Fangio and René Arnoux were also there, the latter, dismissed suddenly two years earlier.

Along with the old drivers were two of the current lineup, and Mietta Ascari,[26] Alberto's widow, representing not just her own husband but all of those young men who had fallen in their quest to fulfil their motor-racing dreams. To each of them Ferrari gave a copy of his *Piloti, che gente* book – including Fangio, of whom Enzo still maintained a negative opinion, which had never been revised nor mitigated over the years.

The first day of November brought the first Ferrari win in F1 in twenty-seven months. Eight hundred days separated this win by Gerhard Berger in the Japanese Grand Prix from the victory Michele Alboreto had scored on the new Nürburgring the first Sunday of August 1985. As was customary when the race was broadcast during the night, Enzo watched in his Largo Garibaldi home with his son Piero. The moment Berger's Ferrari took the chequered flag, Enzo picked up the phone and called the other end of the world to compliment the team. It had been a long and hard road but, at last, one of his cars was again on top. There was only one more race left in the season, but success late in the year normally meant a head start in the new one.

The Italian press, which had attacked Enzo viciously in the previous two years, was now trying to reach him for a comment. He would have none of it – he would not play their game. After all the harsh criticism he'd received during the past two and a half racing seasons, he would make no statement on this day. He would speak only at the end of the year in his traditional press conference.[27]

Two weeks later, Gerhard Berger won again, in Australia, in the last race of 1987. Berger's win provided Ferrari with an opportunity to comment, not so much on the Austrian's second consecutive victory, but on a more general theme: 'When they say to me, you won a race, people don't realize that I am happy because I've paid a debt to all those who believe in me.'[28]

A few days later, he confessed to a friend: 'Everyone keeps asking me why I don't retire. But my work is my life, and I will work until the last day, because I am afraid of being alone.'[29]

*   *   *

By now autumn had arrived in Modena. In town, the echo of Enzo's generous donation of the M R I machine to the hospital, in an effort to help find a cure for muscular dystrophy, had not died out. Modena had never really understood this son of hers, who, despite the envy he could see but not understand, had never lost his love for his hometown. Talking again about the donation, almost annoyed by the incessant interest it had generated, Enzo was now almost brutal with himself.

'I have lost a son to muscular dystrophy, and I have since dedicated my life to this disease,' he said, echoing what he had said to local authorities and the city press a few months earlier. 'But,' he added, with cruel honesty, 'I want *this* to be clear: I have purchased this machine *because* I have lost my son. This shows you that what we do is always a consequence of something, never an act of generosity. Unless we are hit by a great grief,' he said, trying to explain his behaviour. 'Too often we underestimate what those who suffer really feel.'[30]

Twenty-one years after Dino's death, the sense of responsibility Enzo had felt since the first signs of the lethal disease had surfaced still suffocated him. He had experienced the most unnatural among the acts of life – surviving one's own son – and had never come to terms with it. At 89 he felt lonelier than ever. He had enjoyed a privilege his son had been denied: he had lived a long and full life, and now wanted to set the record straight. All the losses, all the mourning, all the suffering had not made him a better man – not better than he was when Dino was alive and life was full of promise, nor better than any of his fellow men. He should not be praised for what he'd done for those who suffered, and neither should he be pitied for the burdens he had borne.

*   *   *

At last he spoke to the press.

The 'luncheon of revenge' began at noon on Friday 11 December. Revenge in the sense that only a handful of journalists were invited and some of the absentees were, on purpose, among the top members of the Italian motor racing press, including the man from *La Stampa*, Fiat's controlled daily newspaper. Enzo was brilliant, sharp and charming with the lucky few who were present, and irresistibly polemic with the many who were not. He had invited only 14 journalists. Eleven were Italians, only three representing the international press. Of the Italians, one had been invited as a non-belligerent 'friend', three were from automotive magazines, six from national dailies. The 11th was the editor in chief of Modena's *La Nuova Gazzetta*, the only non-automotive publication. His 90th birthday was approaching, and Enzo had messages to deliver on this subject as well.

Enzo and his 14 guests took their seats in the small room adjacent to his office in the *Gestione Sportiva* building. It had been almost 30 years since he had gathered so few people to recap the year drawing to a close and speak about the upcoming one. In 1958, to openly address the fierce controversies that had resulted from the multiple fatal accidents of that racing season, he had for the first time opened his press conference to a multitude of a hundred or more journalists, who had since returned to Modena, Maranello or Fiorano year after year. Now, he spectacularly reversed that pattern, opting for the small lunchtime meeting that Gozzi had carefully prepared.

While the appetizers were being served, he began to address the F1 season that had just ended. 'We started the year with a car that was completely new, and without having done the necessary tune-up, which we were forced to do grand prix after grand prix. The car got better as we went along. We could have won in Mexico if we had not played down the fact that the race was going to be run on high ground, an inaccuracy that proved to be deadly for our engines. Then,' he said, 'in Portugal we lost because our driver made a mistake while he was leading the race. But at last,' he said, concluding his quick overview of the final racing season he would see through to the end, 'victory has come.'[31]

He clearly had mixed feelings about his drivers, which he did not attempt to hide from his guests.

'I like Berger,' he said, 'because he has a desire to win.' But when asked whether the Austrian reminded him of any drivers from earlier generations, an exercise in which he would normally have rejoiced, Enzo declined to name any, instead choosing the easy way out: 'In the past there were other tools, other cars,' he said. 'Comparisons between men are impossible to make.'

About Michele Alboreto, he was even less sympathetic. 'I remember when Alboreto, in 1985 at the Nürburgring, beat Prost,' he said. 'I only hope that, once his family anxieties [which were not explained] are over, he may return to being that kind of a driver.'[32] In spite of everything, he announced that both drivers were confirmed for the 1988 season – adding that a third driver might actually join the lineup at a later date, although only for testing.

He was as keen as he'd been in the old days. None of the journalists at his table would have said that this was a man of almost 90 years of age. His mind moved from subject to subject at an impressive speed. His quips were as sharp as they had ever been.

While risotto with truffles was being served, the conversation moved to John Barnard. The English genius had been his choice and, despite the exasperating delay, Enzo continued to defend his pick. He preached patience, a virtue he hardly appreciated. 'If Barnard [was able] to go to Indianapolis and win, if he won three F1 World Championships, we must be patient. I want to see what he can do for me.' He had chosen the man who had made McLaren invincible in the conviction that he would do the same for his cars. 'Before we judge him, we need to wait and see his new car,'[33] he added.

The lunch continued while the conversation ranged from Mikhail Gorbachev – 'to know whether or not he is credible as a great reformer, one must know which difficulties he encounters at home' – to Indianapolis. In 1986, in the midst of the latest controversy with the FIA, Enzo had threatened to leave F1 and race in the United States. He had even shown some reporters the car for the Indy 500. Now that project was all but abandoned. Yet he somewhat cryptically said: 'The car and the engines are ready. When, according to higher interests, we will be asked to go, we will go.'[34] He did not specify what *higher interests* he was talking about – nor did any of the journalists ask him. Clearly there were no other interests. The project had served the purpose of sending the right message to the right people, and that was that. The Indy car was now a museum piece.

Towards the end of the lunch, Enzo also found time to talk about his relationship with Fiat. The subject was introduced by talk of the wind tunnel and the three-year delay in its construction. 'If we'd had it before, I am sure that wins would have come at a much earlier date. I have full powers,' the Grand Old Man said, 'but even I cannot do it all by myself.' The implicit question was: who, or what, had slowed down the construction of the Renzo Piano-designed wind tunnel? Since the implicit answer was Fiat, Enzo now misled his guests by emphasizing that there were no problems with Turin. 'Ever since *Ingegner* Ghidella became the number-two executive at Fiat, I have always got along splendidly with him. I consult with him on everything, and we never have any problems,'[35] he volunteered.

The lunch ended with two different desserts being served before coffee. Enzo had shown a good appetite throughout; the only thing he hadn't touched was the wine. The journalist who was the least familiar with Enzo among those assembled, the editor in chief of Modena's local paper, asked him whether there was something special in store for his 90th birthday. Should Modena do something to mark the celebration? he asked. Even better, should Enzo do something in Modena involving his fellow citizens?

Enzo's answer was as brilliant and artfully impertinent as most of the answers he had given thus far. Well knowing that his relationship with his hometown had been rough at times, but perhaps sensing that the reporter wasn't aware of it, he sardonically replied: 'I do not want to add to the debts I already have towards my fellow Modenese citizens. They have already shown so much patience with me, tolerating me the way I am.'[36] An idea was already taking shape in his mind that he would outline to his closest aides in a matter of days.[37]

A couple of days before Christmas, two executives from the local branch of the Italian Automobile Club visited Enzo. They knew by now that the Grand Old Man didn't want his hometown to set up any special celebration for his 90th birthday, and had come to Fiorano to hear it from his own mouth. When they were printed in *La Nuova Gazzetta di Modena*, the closing remarks of his 11 December press luncheon had reverberated in town. The two officials still hoped they could somehow convince him. They had prepared a grand programme and had come to give him all the details. How little they knew him.[38]

Enzo listened courteously but did not change his mind. The more the two executives spoke of the flair and flamboyance of the event they were planning, the less interested he became. Modena had never loved him. His hometown had never forgiven him the monumental success he had achieved, of which its citizens had always been a bit envious. Now it was too late. He politely thanked them, but firmly asked that they abandon the project. He had other, more private, plans.

As always, Enzo Ferrari spent Christmas with his family. Granddaughter Antonella had entered the eighth month of pregnancy, and every celebration was marked by tranquillity.

On Thursday morning, 14 January 1988, after the customary early visits to the barber and then to Dino's grave, Enzo went to the municipal offices in Via Santi on the outskirts of Modena. At 11.30am he was going to be the guest star of a press conference that the mayor had called to reveal a new building project: the city of Modena was going to build its first public parking garage. Enzo had been invited because he had donated the land on which the parking garage would be built – no ordinary spot, since it had been home to Scuderia Ferrari since 1930. Always looking forward, Enzo had decided to tear down a building that, in its irregular shape, summed up the tormented but glorious history of his company. Perhaps no other construction contained so much of Ferrari, the man, than this unappealing yellow building standing on Viale Trento Trieste. Not only had it served as the initial nucleus of his company's activity, but for some 30 years he had even lived in it, on the 1st floor. In that building, in those rooms, his beloved son Dino had died. Nonetheless, Enzo had made the decision to demolish it, thus pleasing the public servants of his hometown, and today he was here as Modena officials informed their citizens.

Enzo showed up 15 minutes early, before the mayor and most of the other guests had arrived. While the mayor's press officer phoned his boss, asking her to hurry, Enzo sat in a small room near the main hall, reminiscing about the old days and what the building had meant to him. There was an unusual softness in his voice as he recalled anecdotes from 60, 50, 40 years ago. He spoke of the early days, when efforts were immense and satisfaction hard to come by. He proudly confessed that, like his father, in that building he had not only worked but also lived. He even explained that he had chosen the name *Scuderia* for his enterprise because real stables were actually located nearby.

Then the mayor arrived and Enzo left the warm and sheltered world of memories to come back to the cold January morning and the brutality of life at 90. Still wearing her fur, Mayor Alfonsina Rinaldi teased Enzo about the fact that he – a man of speed – had arrived well ahead of all others. For a few minutes they chatted amiably, the mayor still trying to change his mind about the public celebration the city of Modena wanted to throw for his birthday. He thanked her but, again, resolutely turned down the offer.

Enzo spoke briefly to the press, saying that the idea of demolishing the old building to create the space necessary for the public parking garage had come from a conversation he had had with the previous mayor, Mario Del Monte, about the many challenges posed by ever-increasing city traffic. The project had continued with Del Monte's successor and now a four-story building would be built to accommodate more than four hundred cars. The entrance would be from Viale Trento Trieste, the exit, on Via Malmusi. For 58 years these 2 streets had been the western and southern limits of his Scuderia. Ferrari the company would keep an office on the first floor to retain the historic 31 Viale Trento Trieste address.

'I am happy about the new purpose for this area, where Ferrari was born, and I hope that the building will be completed by the end of the year,' he stated, before saying goodbye. Then he rose and bade everyone farewell: 'I hope you will excuse me, but I have to go mind the store.'[39]

That night, reflecting on his bold decision to bulldoze what had been the pulsing heart of his life, and the true core of his chosen mission, in his journal Enzo wrote: 'Piero is with me, and approves my ideas.'[40]

Ferrari 90

On Monday 1 February 1988, the first day of the month in which he would turn 90, Enzo Ferrari was due in downtown Modena, where the academic world – and not just that – had convened for an official ceremony that would celebrate not his approaching birthday, but, rather, the accomplishments of a whole lifetime. Almost three decades after the University of Bologna had awarded him an *honoris causa* degree in engineering, the institution of higher education of his own hometown was going to bestow upon him a second honorary degree, in physics. That morning newspapers all over Italy had carried front-page stories announcing the Pope's visit to Ferrari. Pope John Paul II was scheduled to visit Modena on 3 and 4 June. The morning of the second day, a Saturday, he would visit the Ferrari factory in Maranello and meet Enzo Ferrari. Kings and presidents had all been guests, at one point or another, inside the Ferrari factory gates, but the Pope's visit was a first. It was seen not just as a tribute to a place of excellence within the borders of the diocese of Modena, but also as homage to the man who had inspired it all. For Enzo it was also a sort of personal and final absolution from the appalling accusations the Catholic Church had made against him in the late 1950s.

By the time Enzo, escorted by chief press officer Franco Gozzi and driver Dino Tagliazucchi, arrived at 11.30am, the San Carlo auditorium in downtown Modena was packed. Waiting for him there was the dean of the university, Marco Vellani, and Giovanni Galloni, Italian minister of education, who had arrived for the occasion from Rome. Hordes of reporters and photographers had descended on Modena from all over Italy, along with anyone in the town lucky enough to have obtained an invitation to the event of the year.

When Enzo walked in, the ongoing programme – which had repeatedly been disturbed in the past hour by photographers and cameramen moving around, in search of the best angle – came to an abrupt stop. The multitude murmured and gave the impression of physically moving towards Ferrari. The crowd burst into thunderous applause. Photographers' cameras started flashing, and journalists took their notebooks out, frenetically jotting down notes, recording everything they could see through the moving crowd.

Though protected by his customary dark-lens glasses, Enzo looked almost frightened by such conspicuous interest. Held up by Gozzi, he slowly walked towards the seat in the front row that had been reserved for him. Once he sat down, he faced the centuries-old yellow and blue standard of the University of Modena.

Advised by doctors and family that the programme needed to move along quickly to avoid tiring their illustrious guest, once the wild applause subsided, Dean Vellani immediately began to read a summary of the motivation behind this honorary degree. Being recognized today were the years of research, experimentation and development in the field of physics carried out by Enzo Ferrari and his teams of engineers. Particular attention was paid to the special alloys developed for Ferrari engines.[1]

Once he'd finished reading the official summary, Dean Vellani and Minister Galloni left their chairs behind the head table and solemnly made their way towards Enzo. The Grand Old Man, almost moved to tears, was too feeble to stand. Visibly annoyed by the fire of flashbulbs, he shook the dean's hand and accepted the rolled diploma, which he immediately handed over to Gozzi. Enzo's lips widened almost imperceptibly into a concealed smile. When he had accepted his first honorary degree, in July 1960, he was 62 years old and still vigorous. He had accomplished a great deal by then, and would do much more in the many years to come. Now, in 1988, he knew all too well that solemn moments like this resembled a eulogy in the presence of a breathing corpse – in this case, his own.

Next, Enzo shook the hand of the minister of education of the Republic of Italy. Holding Ferrari's hand, Giovanni Galloni solemnly said: 'The Italian people owe you this.'[2]

Normally the recipient of an honorary degree would at this point read a dissertation on the subject for which he was being honoured. This had been the case 28 years earlier when Enzo had entertained the dean, professors and students for a good hour on the subject of his cars and the reasons why he raced them, Sunday after Sunday, all around the globe. Enzo's age and health had suggested that he would probably forego the traditional speech this time. Nevertheless, after emotionally choking back tears, Enzo reached resolutely for the microphone that was hesitantly being offered to him. Despite his frail health, he wanted to thank the University of Modena for this honour.

His voice hoarse and weak, he travelled back in time, tellingly choosing to dwell on his past rather than looking forward, as he had always done. In the perfectly silent auditorium, he reminded his audience of the guilt he'd felt 28 years earlier.

'Forced to sit in the same chair where Guglielmo Marconi had sat,' he told them, 'I felt a sentiment of profound shame because I considered the honour bestowed upon my work and myself [to be] disproportionate. Today,' he continued, 'Modena has at last decided to confer upon me this further honour that I consider particularly meaningful, because it comes from my hometown.'[3] There was a certain emphasis in his voice when he pronounced the words *at last*, as if to say 'It took my own hometown 28 years longer than Bologna to honour me.' Despite his frail health, he could still bite.

He concluded his brief remarks by thanking 'all those who have wanted to remember a young man who, from the outskirts of Modena, walked into a new century of conquests – conquests not understood by anyone except that great precursor named Woodrow Wilson, the president of the United States, who predicted that the 20th century would be the century of the automobile.'[4]

Enzo had been 14 when Woodrow Wilson was elected president. Now, a few days shy of his 90th birthday, he was still looking back at those most formative years of his life – the 1910s – when most of his convictions had been formed. And, of course, only Enzo Ferrari, who had no particular interest in history, and had never visited the United States, could mention Woodrow Wilson in 1988 on receiving an honorary degree in physics from the University of Modena.

The crowd once again burst into tremendous applause, which did not fade until Enzo had left the auditorium. That night, reflecting on the way Modena had honoured him, in his journal he wrote: 'I have always felt special affection for my hometown, even though my fellow citizens have not always been on my side; I have never been fond of lukewarm loves.'[5]

In the following two weeks, finding ways to celebrate Enzo Ferrari's 90th birthday became something close to an Italian obsession. While thousands of birthday cards from fans and admirers started to pour into Maranello, the company in charge of the Italian highway system announced that a sculpture honouring Enzo and what he represented would soon be crafted and placed on the *Autostrada* near the Modena-North toll gate.

While private fans and public officials alike went about finding ways to honour him, Ferrari spent the days immediately before his birthday in an almost self-imposed seclusion. Most days he still rode from his home in Modena to his guarded office inside the Fiorano race track, but he would see few visitors, as his daily schedule was purposely kept very light. He declined to make any comment on all the excitement around him. The only official communication that reached the adoring multitude was that Enzo Ferrari would not take part in nor endorse any public event, and that the only affair in which he would participate would be the private gathering within the Ferrari plant that he had been planning for his 1,742 employees.

On the morning of Monday 15 February, yellow Ferrari flags were posted on two streetlights in Largo Garibaldi, right in front of Enzo's home. The flags were placed on poles on either side of the rectangular square by a direct order of the mayor of Modena. In so doing, the mayor fulfilled the dream of Sergio Donnini, a passionate Ferrari fan who owned and ran a car-repair shop a mile or so from Enzo's home, on the Via Emilia. The two flags facing Enzo's apartment building were crossed by a diagonal stripe with the green, red and white colours of the Italian flag. On one flag was inscribed a big 90 and the words 'the most beautiful victory'. On the other, '90 years and the race goes on'.[6]

By Wednesday 17 February, dozens of journalists had taken up temporary residence in Modena. Some were now stationed in front of Enzo's apartment building, which overlooked Largo Garibaldi.

Each morning that week, at 8am, they had watched Enzo's driver Dino Tagliazucchi pull up in front of the newsstand on the side of the square opposite the house. They had not dared to ask Dino directly, but they'd all spoken to Giulietta, the lady who ran the newsstand. Thus, readers throughout Italy were informed that each morning Enzo Ferrari would examine at least three national sports newspapers, his hometown daily *La Nuova Gazzetta di Modena*, Bologna's *Il Resto del Carlino*, Milan's *Il Giornale* and the Italian Communist Party official newspaper, *L'Unità*. Well knowing the importance of the Communists within Modena's city government and the unions that dictated the behaviour of most of his workers, the Grand Old Man had always wanted to know the party's official standing on a daily basis, so as never to be caught off guard.

On Wednesday afternoon Gianni Agnelli came from Turin to pay homage to Enzo in person. From Rome, the president of Italy sent a telegram wishing Enzo the happiest of birthdays. Speaking on behalf of an entire nation, President Francesco Cossiga thanked him for all he had done for Italy 'with such intelligence and passion'. The president of the Senate, Giovanni Spadolini, also sent a gracious note, praising a lifetime of 'constant, stubborn devotion to your work, a life in which your will to succeed was equalled only by your love for Italy'. Touching personal chords, Senator Spadolini added: 'You have been one of the towering pioneers of the new Italian society, and have kept your faith in life even in the darkest of days.'[7]

Thursday morning, 18 February, the day Enzo Ferrari turned 90, dawned sunny and chilly, the midwinter Modena air a little colder than expected. The throngs of journalists that had descended on the town to cover the event were, at the start of this morning, split into two groups of approximately the same size. Half were stationed in front of Enzo's apartment building in Largo Garibaldi. The rest were camped outside the fence of the Ferrari factory in Maranello.

At 10.30am, Enzo's personal barber Massimo walked through the building's main door and went up to the first floor. Like every morning that week, Enzo had asked Massimo to come to his home rather than going to his shop, which was besieged by reporters. When Enzo saw Massimo, he teased the barber about the interview he'd granted the previous day to a television crew. Never one to enjoy the limelight, Massimo was embarrassed at the thought of his famous customer watching him speak on national television about Enzo's daily routine, and said he hoped he had not said anything impertinent. The Grand Old Man reassured him.

His hair trimmed and freshly shaved, with a dark overall on to protect him from the cold, at 10.45am Enzo left with driver Dino and private bodyguard Vandelli from a secondary exit of the big apartment building; luckily, no one was patrolling this exit. The multitude of reporters who had been waiting in Largo Garibaldi since before 8am had been successfully deceived. It was not until he was already at his desk in Fiorano that the crowd realized they had been waiting in vain.

Onlookers hoping to catch a glimpse of the Grand Old Man were scattered along the 12-mile country road from Modena to Maranello. To ensure that Enzo had a smooth ride in his Lancia Thema, carabinieri patrolled junctions along via Giardini and then via Abetone Inferiore, through the small villages of Baggiovara, Formigine and Ubersetto. Dozens of red signs proclaiming 'Happy Birthday, Enzo' were everywhere along the familiar route – on telephone poles and traffic lights and in shop windows. From a lamp post not far from the main entrance of the Ferrari gate hung a handwritten sign that familiarly and affectionately said *Auguri, Vecchio* – Happy birthday, Old Man.

Having managed to enter his factory unnoticed through the Fiorano entrance, Enzo's morning was a busy one. Inside the *Gestione Sportiva* office, he briefly entertained one visitor after another.

Under Franco Gozzi's supervision and Piero's careful watch, Enzo spent a few minutes with each and every one of his many guests. Showing feelings in public had always been one of the things he hated most but, at 90, it was difficult to dictate his emotions the way he had managed to do so well, for so long. He saw the president of the Automobile Club of Italy, Rosario Alessi; the minister of sports and tourism, Franco Carraro; and Luca di Montezemolo – especially Luca di Montezemolo.

Enzo's two Formula 1 drivers called. Michele Alboreto phoned from Portugal, where he was carrying out some pre-season testing. Maranello would stop, if only for half a day, but for the *Gestione Sportiva* men, not even their boss's 90th birthday was a reason to stop testing, in light of the fact that McLaren, Lotus, Williams and all the others were certainly not observing Enzo's birthday. Gerhard Berger phoned his boss from Austria, where he was recuperating from the flu. Enzo's inner circle of friends called. They too, not being on the Ferrari payroll, had been excluded from the day's luncheon. But they would have a chance to see their old friend in a couple of days, during the ritual Saturday visits.

At around 12.30pm, holding their personal invitations, Ferrari workers who had finished the morning shift started to gather near the factory gate, on the inside. Their afternoon-shift colleagues joined them, dressed up for the occasion in elegant jackets and ties. Everyone would have the rest of the day off, although the afternoon-shift workers would make up for the hours lost today on Saturday. Some of the workers from the morning shift had decided against going back home to change, and instead began to make their way towards the lunch venue, still wearing their light-blue work overalls with the prancing horse on the breast pocket. The few who had gone home to change into more-formal clothes found it difficult to return because of the thick lines of journalists and fans who had amassed along the factory fences.[8]

Slowly the procession began. In less than an hour, a total of 1,742 Ferrari workers – mechanics, technicians, engineers, testers, employees and executives alike – would assemble around their legendary boss on a day that everyone knew was unique. Working at Ferrari, working for him, was something special. They had always known it – but it had never seemed as true as it did today. Standing in line on his way to the event, one of the racing-team technicians with the most seniority summed up what it meant to work for Enzo Ferrari: 'He always communicates a twofold feeling,' he said. 'The first thing you feel is that he is a simple man, very much like any of us, with the same curiosities we may have. But then you start feeling the silent strength of his charisma. In this sense, he is a myth even for us.'[9]

By 1.30pm, the production-line building had been turned into a huge dining hall for the occasion. It was packed. His employees had responded with enormous enthusiasm mixed with visible emotion to his personal invitation:

I shall see you at lunch
Thursday, February 18, at 13:30 pm
Inside the factory in Maranello[10]

Three lines – a command more than a conventional invitation. But their boss had never been a man of many words when it came to certain matters. More than the words written on the personal card that each and every one had received – the black prancing horse in the upper left corner, his tremulous purple-ink signature on the lower right corner – the message of unconditional affection had come from his stubborn refusal to let anyone else in but the people who worked *with* him. 'My employees are like my own family,' he had never tired of saying in recent weeks, to those objecting that he should also invite authorities, politicians, Fiat executives and VIPs. Along with the card, delivered by internal mail a couple of weeks earlier, all had received a silver medal with the inscription *Ferrari 90* on one side and the prancing horse emblem on the other.

Clustered together by company departments, they sat at tables covered with yellow tablecloths and yellow napkins that each accommodated 12 attendees,[11] all anxiously waiting for their larger-than-life boss to arrive. The employee with the most seniority had started working for Enzo on 1 April 1949 – almost 39 years earlier. The newest had been hired less than three weeks before. All were proud to work at Ferrari, but especially to work *for* Enzo Ferrari, because, said one of them, 'When you work for him, fatigue comes mixed with passion, and you cannot tell one from the other.'[12]

Like every year, come January, chief press officer Franco Gozzi had asked Enzo, on behalf of the handful of his closest aides, whether there was anything special he wanted for his birthday. In the past he had invariably replied that there was nothing he could possibly wish for. But this January the answer had been different. Yes, there was something he desired: he would like to see gathered together, for just one last lunch hour, all of his employees.[13] And here they were, all 1,742 of them. The decision had been his and his alone.

Most of the youngest had never seen him in person. In the last five years his presence around the factory had been limited. For the racing-team people it was a different story, of course, but since he had transferred his office to the Fiorano side of the road and had started taking his lunches in the white farmhouse in the centre of the race track, he had rarely gone to the other side, where the factory was located and where the vast majority of his people worked. 'What will it be like to see all of them once again?'[14] he had asked Gozzi the moment they left the *Gestione Sportiva* building in Fiorano, to cross by car the street that led to the factory in Maranello.[15]

At precisely 1.30pm, aided by driver Dino and personal bodyguard Valentini, Enzo walked into the huge dining room. The background noise made by almost eighteen hundred men and women casually chatting suddenly stopped. The air froze. Then, when they saw him, immense applause broke out.[16]

He wore a finely checked light-brown jacket over a white shirt, with a navy blue and gold striped tie. The familiar dark lenses protected his eyes. He slowly made his way to the round head table, acknowledging the tribute of his adoring employees.

He sat where everyone could see him, and where, with a simple glance, he could take in the whole dining area. While everyone else sat in white plastic chairs, he rested in a more comfortable white leather armchair.

At times taking his glasses off to better stress a point to his two closest tablemates – son Piero to his right, general manager Razelli to his left – Enzo ate little of the Modena-style lunch: tortellini, roast beef, his hometown signature pig's -trotter *zampone*. Opposite him sat Franco Gozzi, with team manager Marco Piccinini to his left and former general manager Della Casa to his right. Under the hot lights, with the distant music of a small orchestra in the background and in the incessant noise made by so many people assembled in a small area, conceived for a totally different use, he tired rather quickly. The service was, fortunately, as prompt as Beppe Neri of Cavallino Restaurant had promised, and, in less than 50 minutes, the time came for the big birthday cake. After the presentation of the cake and the formal toast, the Grand Old Man would be free to go back to Fiorano and rest.

When they received the signal, the waiters brought in a large cake with a yellow Ferrari shield and a dark-brown chocolate prancing horse on it. A single large red candle stood in the middle of the cake. Again, in the crowded production-line building, absolute silence set in. Those sitting in the back of the hall rose in an attempt to see better.[17]

Enzo gathered all the strength in his body and blew out the candle. All of the employees broke into deafening applause once again. Enzo was visibly touched. He motioned to Piero that he wanted to say a few words. Gozzi quickly handed him a microphone. Enzo made no attempt to rise, but removed his dark glasses as if to clearly state that he spoke from his heart – that, for this one time, everyone was allowed to look into his soul.

He said only a few words. Despite the microphone, his voice was barely audible in the back of the hall.[18]

'Let me thank all of you for accepting my invitation,' he said. 'But let me also thank you for *believing* in me.' The silence was by now total. It was one of those rare moments when human beings are confronted with history. He went on: 'If one day I should die,' he told them, 'you will faithfully go on with the present management.' It was a goodbye. These few words were his moral testament. His men and women had tears in their eyes. *He* had tears in his eyes. By now his voice trembled. He left them with his personal wish: 'Ferrari, as a company, will never die.'[19]

The intimates at his table got physically closer to him, as if to give him strength just by their presence. He was visibly touched, his lips tightly closed in an effort to stop any tears. He held strong for the few minutes necessary for the formal birthday toast. Eighteen hundred people rose and together chanted: 'Happy birthday,

Ferrari.' He drank to his and their health a small sip of champagne, not having touched the wine during the meal.[20]

Helped by Piero, Enzo rose. Now, again with the aid of Dino and Valentini, he left the room amid the thunderous applause of his people,[21] most of whom knew that they had seen him for the last time.

Enzo went back to his retreat in the heart of the Fiorano race track to rest. The emotions of the party and the strain of such a long public appearance soon took their toll. By the time he was ready to ride back home, in the foggy late afternoon, Enzo was not feeling well.[22]

Friday and Saturday, Enzo rested at home, awaiting news from the hospital. On Sunday the news came: at last, he had become a great-grandfather. At 7.30am his adored granddaughter Antonella had given birth to a 10-pound baby boy who had been named Enzo. The great-grandfather was too feeble to go and visit his granddaughter and great-grandson at the hospital, but was pleasantly surprised when son Piero brought home some pictures of the new baby boy for him to see.[23]

That evening he dutifully recorded the birth of his great-grandson in his journal: 'Enzo!' he wrote, crystallizing his happiness with a rare exclamation mark. 'I had never thought I would become a great-grandfather,' he wrote. 'Antonella made a good choice by deciding to name him Enzo, because it is a short name,'[24] he commented – almost too modest, or embarrassed, to admit that his granddaughter had wanted to honour him by giving the boy his name.

The next morning, the Grand Old Man was back in his office.

The next day it was the mayor of Modena's turn to go to Fiorano and pay homage. That same day, at 11am, two papal envoys came to Maranello to verify the premises in advance of the Pope's visit in June. They did not meet Enzo, but they visited the factory and took an interested look at the Fiorano area and race track, which they found to be a perfect venue for the Pope's Mass.[25]

On Wednesday, the Grand Old Man could not contain his happiness: he would meet his new great-grandson on this day! When Massimo arrived to shave him, he found Enzo in an incredibly good mood, impatient to finish the morning ritual and get ready to receive the infant. To Massimo he repeated what he'd confided in his journal: Enzo was a good name choice because it was a short one.[26]

Later that morning, Antonella and her husband Giacomo brought baby Enzo to the Largo Garibaldi apartment to meet his famous great-grandfather. When the baby arrived, Enzo insisted on walking to the door on his faltering legs.[27] A man with great respect for tradition, he wanted to physically welcome him at the door and personally escort him inside.

On Thursday 25 February, a week after his birthday, Enzo paid a surprise call on one of his greatest admirers in town. He had known about him for a long time – Modena was a small city, and certain news travelled fast. Not to mention the fact that both went to the same barber and Massimo (and Antonio before him) had repeatedly told Enzo about some of the extravaganzas of this particular supporter of his. Giancarlo Donnini was the one who had gone out of his way to honour Enzo on his birthday, convincing the mayor of Modena to raise the two yellow Ferrari flags in Largo Garibaldi, just in front of the apartment building where his hero lived.

Enzo decided the time had come to thank Donnini in person. Accompanied by chauffeur Dino and bodyguard Valentini, at around 11.30am, en route to Maranello, Enzo ordered Dino to stop the car along the Via Emilia, just in front of Donnini's repair shop. Dino stepped out of the car, crossed the road and went in to check the premises. Without giving him any hint of what was to follow, he told Donnini that he had a visitor. Dino then went back to the car from which, shortly thereafter, Enzo and Valentini stepped out.

The Grand Old Man crossed the street and entered Donnini's shop. There, against the back wall, he found a life-size picture of himself, from the late 1970s, the central piece of the repairman's collection of Ferrari memorabilia. Donnini was stunned when he saw Enzo. Tears came to his eyes. He had never met Enzo Ferrari, nor dreamed that one day the most famous Italian alive would stop by his workplace. But here he was, holding a book in his hand – a copy of *Piloti, che gente*, his volume on the various generations of drivers he'd known during his long life. It was a gift, Enzo's way of thanking Donnini for his support and personal consideration. Enzo inscribed and signed the volume for him,[28] and they stood and chatted for a few minutes.

Donnini was too excited, once Ferrari had left, to remember any of the topics of their conversation, recalling only the kindness of his larger-than-life visitor and, oddly enough, the fact that, in person, Enzo looked even more handsome than he did in photographs.

* * *

As winter gave way to spring, Enzo's visits to Fiorano became more irregular. On one of the rare mornings he was going to the office, Dino pointed at some trees that were blossoming in the fields at the edge of the familiar road.

'It's springtime,' Dino said casually.

'Yes, but it's wintertime for me,' was Enzo's reply.[29]

Only a few weeks earlier his mood had been much sunnier, and his reply, in a situation much like this one, had been more in line with the sort of man he had always been. Commenting on the colour of his new car, a beautiful, fiery red reminiscent of a sunset, barber Massimo had somewhat courageously teased him on whether Enzo felt near the sunset of his life.

When Enzo discarded the very idea of approaching the twilight of his existence, Massimo jokingly pressed on: was he still in the morning of his life? he asked.

'Let us not exaggerate,' Enzo had answered. 'Let's just say that I feel like it's around noon.'[30]

Heaven Can't Wait

The little strength Enzo had, he saved for the Pope's visit.[1] His relationship with priests had never been an easy one, but he particularly liked this Pope, whom he considered an 'exceptional man'.[2] There was something in John Paul II that appealed to Enzo's tormented Christian conscience. 'To him I could even confess my sins,' Enzo had once said to his intimates.[3]

Pope John Paul himself was not immune to Enzo Ferrari's magnetism. Talking to prelates during a papal stop in Imola a couple of years earlier, the Pope had specifically asked if Enzo Ferrari was there. When the Pope's enquiry was reported to him, Enzo was very much impressed.[4] It was from this unexpected show of interest in the Grand Old Man that the whole idea of a papal visit to the Ferrari factory and of a meeting between Enzo and Pope John Paul had originated. Despite all precautions and the doctors' constant attention, in the last part of May, as the warming Modena air was saturated by the intense and familiar scent of lime trees, Enzo's health began to seriously deteriorate. To the press it was reported that Enzo had suffered a minor attack of flu.[5] The truth was that the adrenal insufficiency that had haunted him in recent months was reaching a point where it could hardly be kept under control.[6]

On Wednesday 1 June rumours spread that a substantial technical and managerial revolution was about to take place at Ferrari. The gossip made it all the way to the front pages of newspapers throughout Italy. Those who were indiscreet talked about a divergence of opinion between father and son. The cause of the argument was the role of John Barnard within *Gestione Sportiva*. While Piero believed that the British engineer had wasted the unique opportunity and unprecedented mandate he had been given, Enzo was still willing to grant him more time. To make a critical situation more unpredictable, there was the latent conflict between the Fiat and Ferrari sides of the company, each ready to take control now that the end looked more and more imminent.

Perhaps to stop rumours and show everyone, inside and outside Ferrari, that he was still the king, Enzo decided to go to his office that day, to see and be seen. He was seen, all right, but his infirmity was now under scrutiny. He appeared extremely fatigued and frail to everyone he met.[7] If the plan was to show that he was still in control, the mission had failed.

The next day he rested at home. But on Friday 3 June, the day before the Pontiff's visit, Enzo went to the barber for the last time,[8] and then rode to Fiorano. Determined to meet John Paul II, he went over the protocol with members of the Pope's party.[9] The meeting was scheduled for 12.30pm the next day in Enzo's private office, inside the little white residence in the centre of the race track.

Soon after lunch, however, he began to feel unwell, and by 4pm his temperature had risen dangerously. He asked Dino to take him home. Dino drove him back to Modena and helped him to bed. One of Enzo's physicians, Dr Baldini, came and ordered him to stay in bed and rest. He would come back in the morning, and only then would they make a decision about whether Enzo could attend the yearned-for meeting with the Pope.[10]

No miracle occurred overnight; in the morning his temperature had lowered only by a fraction. Well knowing how important meeting the Pope was to his patient, Dr Baldini suggested that Enzo go, as long as he kept his activity to an absolute minimum. Always a realist, Enzo was more sceptical. He tried to stand up but could not. Realizing that he would not make it, no matter how hard he tried, he regretfully decided to stay home.[11]

At 9.45, 15 minutes ahead of schedule, the Pope's helicopter landed in the meadows by the Fiorano race track. Awaiting him were twenty thousand workers who, despite warnings from local branches of the Communist Party, had come from all over the diocese of Modena, including representatives from the old Ferrari rival, Maserati. Before he met them and before the papal Mass, to the delight of photographers and cameramen, John Paul II lapped around the race track with the Bishop of Modena in a red Ferrari Mondial convertible, driven by Piero Ferrari.

Once the official ceremony had ended, the Pope was invited inside Enzo's country retreat, where he privately met Piero and Floriana Ferrari and Giacomo and Antonella Mattioli, and was introduced to three-month-old baby Enzo.[12] Then the Pope remained alone in the room with Marco Piccinini, who, ironically, the Italian press had nicknamed *Monsignore* years before.

Enzo was lying in his bed in Modena. When the phone rang in his bedroom, his chauffeur Dino picked it up. On the line was Piccinini, calling from Fiorano.

'*Commendatore*,' Dino said, 'I have the Pope for you.'

Enzo took the phone and Piccinini, some 12 miles away, passed the receiver to Pope John Paul. Piccinini then excused himself and left Enzo Ferrari alone with his call.

When he heard the Pope's voice on the other end of the line, Enzo's eyes filled with tears.[13] He had always thought of himself as a sinner, and here he was, talking on the phone with the Pope. Sitting in his bed, with John Paul II on the other end of the line, he was surrounded by symbols of his torn relationship with religion and God: a wooden cross hung over the bed; images of the Virgin Mary and of Modena patron saint San Geminiano were on display on the bedside table, along with photos of his beloved departed family members: father Alfredo, mother Adalgisa, his brother – and, naturally, his son Dino.[14]

The conversation lasted only a few minutes and was somewhat one-sided. Enzo was visibly moved and could hardly hold back his tears.[15] To the Pope he said: 'I am not a good Catholic, and I have never prayed, but every night, before I go to bed, my thoughts go to the people who are dear to me, to those I have lost, and to those I have near me. Ever since I saw you stricken in St Peter's Square after the assassination attempt on your life, I have included you in my thoughts. I am sorry I did not have the chance to meet you.'[16]

Twelve minutes after entering the rustic residence in Fiorano, the Pope reemerged. Piero walked him to the helicopter, which he boarded to return to Modena and conclude his two-day visit.

On Wednesday morning, 8 June, the day of the Ferrari board meeting, on his way to Maranello Ghidella stopped by the Largo Garibaldi apartment in Modena to pay Enzo a visit. The Grand Old Man's health had not improved much from the weekend of the Pope's visit, but he nonetheless found the strength to meet with the Fiat-chosen president of his company.

They spoke of the latest developments, and agreed on the changes that were going to be approved during the meeting later that morning and announced at its conclusion. Piero would indeed leave *Gestione Sportiva*, as some papers had anticipated, becoming vice president of the company – a position created for the first time in the 41-year history of Ferrari – with a restricted range of action limited to the passenger-car production side of the company's activity.

Of Enzo and their private summit, Ghidella said: 'He opened the door to the future. He asked us to help him solve the problems. Now there is direct involvement with Fiat, which I represent.'

Ghidella left the decisive blow for the end. 'Companies,' he said wryly, 'must carry on even if the founder is not there. This is life.'[17]

The king had abdicated.

By mid-June Enzo's health had become a real concern. His renal failure had entered the final stage. Because he stubbornly refused to check into the hospital, he had to be treated at home. A haemodialysis machine was installed in his apartment.

The machine was so large that it could not fit through the doors, but had to be lifted up and pulled in through the wider window.[18] The treatment provoked painful itching that Enzo met stoically, never complaining, never feeling sorry for himself.[19]

The true scope of Ghidella's moves became manifest on Wednesday 22 June, when protégé Pier Giorgio Cappelli was entrusted with directly managing *Gestione Sportiva*. The official press release used all the right words: 'Notwithstanding Enzo Ferrari's supervision . . . Dr Cappelli will assist him in managing . . .'[20]

But the message was unequivocal: Enzo had been ousted from the last outpost of his once-monolithic empire. The king was now naked, without his kingdom.

The role of Marco Piccinini was also in question. Ferrari knew that his young right-hand man could hardly be relieved of his duties as long as he, Enzo, was alive. But he also knew that Marco's future was set. On a piece of paper, in the presence of Gozzi, Enzo scribbled a few words in handwriting so shaky as to appear at first sight almost illegible. He had so little strength in his body that the ink hardly imprinted on the sheet.

A few words: 'Marco, they will miss you . . .'

Then, before he handed the paper to Gozzi so that he could give it to Piccinini the first time they saw each other, Enzo added: 'Heaven, 28 October 1988.'[21]

That date, 28 October, was four months away. Enzo Ferrari knew that he didn't have much time left to live.

Three days later, on 27 June, Enzo went to his office in Fiorano. Despite the heat, on this Monday morning he wore a thick overcoat that made him look even thinner. Very frail already, the mechanical blood cleansing of dialysis made him feel cold. His face pale, he was assisted by driver Dino Tagliazucchi and by chief press officer Franco Gozzi. A photographer standing by took a couple of shots, the last ever taken of him.[22]

In his office, he talked mostly with Gozzi, primarily about chief engineer Harvey Postlethwaite, who – following Ghidella's shake-up – had as expected announced he was leaving Ferrari to go to the English Tyrrell racing team. John Barnard had been Enzo's choice and, despite the regrettable delay, Enzo still had faith in him. He hoped that the 1989 car would be the one to bring back to Maranello the Formula 1 title last won by Ferrari nine years earlier.

After two hours spent chatting with his most devoted adviser, he left. It was the last time he ever sat at his desk.[23] In the first part of July, Enzo's health continued to worsen. By now he was mostly confined to his bed.[24] Tellingly, it was Ghidella and not Enzo who took a firm stand with John Barnard. Frustrated by their manifest inferiority in comparison with McLaren this year (who won 15 out of the 16 grands prix in 1988), Ghidella ordered Barnard to immediately prepare a version of the

1989 car with a 'normal' gearbox, in place of the revolutionary electrohydraulic mechanism the British engineer was devising for the following season.

Barnard refused.

The second weekend of July, at Silverstone for the imminent British Grand Prix, Nigel Mansell confirmed to the press that he was going to drive for Ferrari in 1989. There were no comments from Maranello and Modena, but Mansell's arrival had been in the air for some time now, and nobody was particularly surprised. Of the present driver lineup, it was easy for all to see that the one who would leave at the end of the season was Michele Alboreto.

On Sunday 10 July 1988, Enzo watched his last Formula 1 race. It was that same Grand Prix of Great Britain which, 37 years earlier, had given him his first Formula 1 victory at the expense of Alfa Romeo. The day before, in qualifying, both Ferraris had done wonders. Thanks to handling problems for McLaren, the two Ferraris secured the front row of the grid, with Gerhard Berger setting the pole.

Soon after the start, too feeble to pay attention for long periods of time to the images on the television screen in his bedroom, Enzo fell asleep. About halfway through, he suddenly awoke. He instinctively turned to son Piero, who was watching the event next to his bed, and asked how the race was going. Piero said that things didn't look good for the Ferrari team. As always that year, McLarens were dominating the race, and, to further complicate things, Ferrari had to watch fuel consumption today.

'But at least we are ahead of the Alfa Romeos, right?' Enzo asked. Alfa Romeo had ceased to be a major factor in Formula 1 decades earlier, and had not competed in grands prix for three years. Yet this afternoon, on his deathbed, his first, almost subconscious, thought went to Alfa Romeo, his frantically adored and fiercely hated love of his youth.

These were the last words Enzo Ferrari ever spoke in the presence of son Piero about cars and motor racing.[25]

* * *

The summer heat was by now unbearable in Modena. Undergoing haemodialysis three times a week, Enzo was alternating between days in which he felt reasonably well and others when he could barely talk or move from his bed. Even Massimo, his barber, stopped coming every day.[26] At home, Enzo would no longer walk, Dino moving him from room to room in a wheelchair. Twice he collapsed during the treatment that had now become as vital to his survival as the air he was breathing.[27]

Besides Piero, Floriana, Lina, Dino, Dino's wife and his nurse and doctors, only a handful of people were admitted to Enzo's presence. Carlo Benzi and coachbuilder Sergio Scaglietti, old friends from his inner circle, came almost every day to keep him company. On those days when he felt reasonably well, they would even sip some champagne together. Enzo would ask Dino to uncork a bottle of Dom Perignon, the brand he had always preferred. Benzi and Scaglietti, who spoke only Enzo's native Modenese dialect, not contemporary Italian, would drink a glass, while Enzo would limit himself to a much smaller quantity.[28]

In the late afternoon it was Franco Gozzi's turn. Enzo would talk with him while sitting up in his bed. At times, flashes of the old energy still emanated from his debilitated body.

Then on Monday 25 July, the unimaginable happened. In the sweltering midsummer afternoon, Enzo went to Fiorano. He had wanted to go that morning, but his doctors had resolutely turned him down. After lunch, however, with the doctors away, Enzo had begged Dino to help him dress, insisting, until his loyal chauffeur of 22 years could no longer refuse to drive him to the office one last time.[29] Amid general incredulity, 20 minutes after secretly leaving the Largo Garibaldi apartment, Dino drove the red Alfa Romeo 164 down the driveway towards the *Gestione Sportiva* quarters in Fiorano. He stopped right in front of the office. Having seen the boss's car arrive, Franco Gozzi and Enzo's secretary Giuliana rushed outside to greet him. Enzo opened the door of the car and set both feet on the ground, still sitting upright in the backseat. In disbelief and unsure of what they should do next, Gozzi and Giuliana stood there waiting at the open car door.

Enzo's pale face was skeletal, his neck sunken inside the far too wide shirt collar. Inside untied shoes, his swollen feet seemed about to explode. His few, feeble words could hardly be heard by his press officer and secretary. They were mute with astonishment and anxiety, trying to understand the weak murmuring of their boss. Clearly in pain, he said only a few tearful, scattered words – never a whole sentence.[30] This most unusual of meetings went on for a few minutes. Then, more to himself than to his aides, Enzo said: 'I'm going back to Modena.'

Dino dried his boss's tears and pulled his legs back inside the car. Enzo motioned for him to drive away. Neither Enzo nor Gozzi or Giuliana actually said goodbye.[31]

Enzo went back home, never to leave again.

By early August, the Grand Old Man knew that the end was near. When he lost all hope, he lost all desire to voice his anxieties – and that was when silence set in. He now spoke very little, preferring the mute acceptance of the inevitable and the silent company of his thoughts. Intimates hearing the sound of his silence understood that the end would now come quickly.[32] He was not fighting any longer.

'I have suffered moral and material pressures, received subpoenas and stayed for years without a passport. I have been taken to court, I have been the subject of parliamentary inquiry and the Church compared me to a modernized Saturn devouring his own children. Time after time I fought and won countless battles,'[33] he had told Florentine writer Giuseppe Prezzolini a few years earlier. But after 90 years of battles, he had now surrendered.

It was infirmity that he had always feared, not growing old per se. Like so many times in the past, even the recent past, he had chosen not to go to the hospital, but instead, to be treated at home. This time he knew that he was staying at home to die there. To Massimo, on one of those now-rare mornings when his barber came to shave him, he confessed that he could not take it anymore. He was constantly in pain. At night he could not sleep for the itching, and now he had to undergo haemodialysis almost every day. He recalled his beloved Dino and the moment when he had given up all hope of saving him. To Massimo he simply said: 'In my journal, I had written then that the match was lost. Now,' he confided, 'I should write this about myself.'[34] Despite the worsening of his health, in the first week of August he found the strength to meet Michele Alboreto. For quite some time their relationship had not been the happy one of the first couple of years, but it was undeniable that the Grand Old Man maintained a soft spot in his heart for Michele. He wanted to reassure him. By now it was clear to all, Alboreto included, that there were two factions within the team, and Enzo's was not the one in charge anymore. But the old lion still had a roar in his heart – if not in his throat – and wanted to say as much to the young driver he'd once dreamed of transforming into a new Alberto Ascari.

Accompanied by Piero, Alboreto went to see Enzo in the Largo Garibaldi apartment. His once-formidable boss did all that he could to sit up in his bed, his voice feeble but his mind intact. He told his driver he knew that *the others* wanted to hire Mansell, but that he still had faith in him, and, if Michele so wished, he could still do something for him. Always a realist, Michele knew that, despite his personal reassurance, there was nothing that Enzo Ferrari could actually do for him. He took Enzo's hand in his, and thanked him. 'You now concentrate on getting better,' he told Enzo before leaving the room.[35]

Too feeble to rise from his bed, Enzo stopped eating lunch and dinner at the table with the faithful friends who never left him alone. By Wednesday, Enzo was too weak even to take the phone call that Maranello's vicar, Don Erio Belloi, customarily placed every 10 August – the day Catholics celebrated Saint Lorenzo, and Enzo enjoyed the closest thing to his name day. Dino took the phone call and told the priest that Ferrari was not feeling well and that it was better to let him rest. Enzo's condition, Dino said, was serious, but stable.[36]

A few hours later, however, the situation suddenly worsened and Enzo lapsed into a coma. Doctors were immediately summoned. When they arrived, they realized that it was now only a matter of hours.

By late afternoon, it seemed the end could arrive at any time. Son Piero sent for Don Galasso Andreoli, the Ferrari factory chaplain. Don Galasso came and, as the Catholic Church prescribed, administered Enzo the last rites *in articulo mortis*, along with a full pardon of his sins. Don Galasso anointed Enzo's forehead with oil in the form of the cross.[37] His relationship with God had always been a tormented one, but Enzo had never concealed the fact that he wished he had the faith that he confessed he did not possess. In the final moments of his long life, as he had asked,[38] he took comfort in the sacraments of God's church.

Enzo rested peacefully throughout the night, slipping in and out of the coma. Lina was constantly at his bedside, holding his hand. Piero and Floriana never left his sight. Carlo Benzi was there, along with Sergio Scaglietti and, of course, Dino and his wife.

Friday morning dawned.

His condition had neither worsened nor improved. Doctors were not relieved; they knew that this time, he would not pull through. It could happen today, tomorrow or the following week. But it would happen this time. The next cardiac crisis could be fatal.

Friends and family kept him company throughout Friday and Saturday while he continuously lapsed in and out of a coma. Dino would wet Enzo's lips with a handkerchief that had been gently soaked in champagne, and from which he seemed to take some momentary relief. Outside, the city was quiet. The normally high-traffic area of Largo Garibaldi was empty and still. It was the middle weekend of August, and everyone in town seemed to have left for the shore. By late Saturday night, doctors warned Piero and Lina that Enzo would not live to see the sun rise the next day.[39]

Throughout the night, the nightstand light was constantly on in Enzo's bedroom. Benzi, Scaglietti, Dino, his wife, Piero, Floriana and Lina took turns keeping him company. Doctors Baldini, Mattioli and Carano were there, too, even though there was nothing they could possibly do. Now and then Enzo would murmur, though none of those present could make out his words. For some reason he indicated – or they thought that he indicated – that he wanted a wristwatch to be given to Marco Piccinini.[40] His young team manager had been like a son to Enzo over the past ten years.

Lina held his hand throughout the night, never leaving his side, always finding words to comfort him.

Then the inevitable happened. Shortly after 6.30am on Sunday 14 August, Enzo Ferrari died.[41] He died peacefully, holding Lina's hand – a serene expression, almost a smile, on his face.[42] At last his 'long and wearing walk' – as he had famously described his life, stressing the burden he had felt throughout – had come to an end.

Carlo Benzi now took charge. He had already organized three funerals during Enzo's lifetime: Dino's, Adalgisa's and Laura's. The fourth would be the last. Enzo had personally asked him to take care of everything, including inviting the precious few who, by express desire of the Grand Old Man, would attend a funeral that he had designed to be as private as humanly possible. Enzo had personally given Benzi a list of those who should be admitted to the function. He wanted these people – no more, and possibly, no less.

Benzi immediately called the mayor of Modena, Alfonsina Rinaldi, to inform her that Enzo Ferrari had died. He had already called her earlier that week, on Thursday night, after the last rites had been administered. She would make sure that the news of Enzo's death did not leak to the outside world. Enzo had not only wanted a private function, but had also asked that the world not be informed until after the funeral had ended and he was peacefully resting behind a gravestone. The law prescribed that, whenever a death happened, the town's registry office be notified immediately. Having been informed, Alfonsina Rinaldi granted the special privilege of withholding the information from the public until after the service.

Next, Benzi placed the few calls that Enzo had thought necessary. He called Franco Gozzi and Marco Piccinini, both vacationing, and Sergio Scaglietti, who had spent most of the previous night in Enzo's bedroom, but was home at the time of his death. Piero called daughter Antonella, who was also vacationing with husband Giacomo and baby Enzo. Only a handful of additional phone calls were made. Even the majority of Enzo's closest advisers would not be told until after the funeral.[43]

The following night, the office of the mayor of Modena placed a phone call to Farri Funeral Home. The public official gave no details over the phone, but simply asked for an immediate appointment. Within an hour, accompanied by a small party, Mayor Rinaldi arrived at the funeral home. She was welcomed by owner Federico Farri and by his brother-in-law, Vasco Marinelli. With their help, the mayor personally chose a light-brown wooden casket, known in the industry as the styled ark model. Benzi's instructions to the mayor on Thursday night had been precise: nothing fancy, something simple, exactly like the Grand Old Man would have wanted it.

Then the mayor told Mr Farri when and where he would have to deliver the casket. It was only at this time that the owner of the funeral home realized who the casket was for.[44]

The news had not leaked; all had been prepared in great and unbroken secrecy. The Grand Old Man, dressed in his favourite dark-brown suit, lay in the bed where he had passed away.[45] In three short hours the casket and hearse would arrive. At 7am, the small procession would leave the Largo Garibaldi apartment and reach the cemetery, which, by direct order of the mayor, would be open at that hour to meet this most special party.

At 6am, as the day dawned, the hearse and the small team of workers from the funeral home pulled inside the courtyard of 11 Largo Garibaldi, right behind the building. This early on an August morning, they were not spotted by anybody. A lady staring out of a window in a house overlooking the courtyard did notice some activity, unusual for that hour of day, but did not realize exactly what was going on.[46] Upstairs, Enzo was placed inside the casket and a cross made of white flowers was positioned atop the coffin.[47]

Then it was time to go.

A little after 7am, the small procession made their way down the stairs. The only outsider was Giovanni Battista Razelli, the Fiat-appointed general manager of Ferrari. The rest were family and those, among the inner circle, who were in Modena at the time of Enzo's passing. The coffin was lifted inside the hearse and then, a few moments later, the courtyard gates were opened.

Modena was deserted on this Monday morning, 15 August, the day Italians celebrated *Ferragosto*, a Catholic holiday that had been transformed years before into a pagan mid-August celebration of summer. A dozen people dressed in black clothes boarded in perfect silence a handful of cars parked inside the gravel-paved courtyard. Then the cars left, followed by the hearse. In two minutes all had left the area.[48] The husband of the lady at the window, watering the flowers of his garden in the cool of the early morning, was the only witness to the scene. When the party passed him, he compassionately performed the sign of the cross, but kept the news to himself.[49]

Giorgio Ferri, Enzo's longtime personal secretary, had gone ahead to the San Cataldo cemetery. He had stopped by the house of the cemetery chaplain, part of the Madonna del Murazzo monastery structure, near the vast San Cataldo graveyard, to ask him to come to the Ferrari chapel at once. This early in the morning, Father Pier Paolo Veronesi did not understand the hurry. He knew very well, since he had often officiated himself, that Enzo Ferrari had a Mass celebrated in the family chapel for his departed son Dino every June, and thought that, for some reason, he wanted to have one this morning. Annoyed by Ferri's insistence, he told the secretary that there was no need to hurry – the cemetery would not open until 8am.

'No, no, you don't understand,' said Ferri. 'The cemetery is already open.'

The mayor had personally phoned the custodian at 2am, instructing him to open the gates at 7 for the early arrival of a coffin.[50] As agreed with Benzi the previous week, she had not revealed the identity of the corpse.

Father Veronesi took everything he needed to celebrate a Mass and followed Ferri to the octagonal Ferrari chapel. When he arrived and saw the coffin, he finally understood the reason for the hurry. Piero, concerned about being spotted by early risers, wanted to get the funeral service done as rapidly as possible. He asked for a quick Mass. Father Veronesi gently but firmly refused to hurry things further.[51] He performed the whole rite as the Catholic Church prescribed.

It was 40 minutes before the casket was placed behind a marble stone on the left side of the chapel. Enzo was laid to rest next to his father – surprisingly distant from Dino. His resting place was to be the first one to the left of the entrance door, behind a common gravestone already engraved, on the right half, with the words 'Alfredo Ferrari' and the dates '1859–1916'. In a few days, the left side would read: 'Enzo Ferrari' above the dates '1898–1988'.

No speeches were delivered, no official words spoken.[52] It was not necessary. For the dozen people assembled, it was the most private of functions. Others, in other places, would soon begin to celebrate the long and extraordinary life of the old man they had just buried. For those convened at San Cataldo this morning, he had been a father, a life companion, a father-in-law, a friend and a most unusual boss.

They all left as silently as they had arrived. Giorgio Ferri alone stayed behind until the masons had finished their job and the dark-red stone was cemented to the brick wall that sealed the grave.

The news of Enzo Ferrari's death broke at around nine o'clock that morning.

Having returned from the funeral, Sergio Scaglietti stopped by the usual café to have an espresso. Clearly out of place in the mid-August morning wearing his best dark suit, he attracted the inevitable question from the owner. With his friend resting at the graveyard, Scaglietti knew that there was no need for secrecy any longer. With moist eyes he confirmed the news.

'Yes, Enzo Ferrari is dead,' he said. 'He was buried at San Cataldo a short while ago.'[53]

Approximately 15 minutes later, Piero Ferrari issued a press release written with Franco Gozzi, officially informing the world that his larger-than-life father had died.

Post Scriptum

Piero Ferrari is still the deputy chairman of Ferrari, and a 10 per cent shareholder in the company.

Piero's mother Lina died in 2006 and was not buried in the Ferrari family chapel where Enzo rests with first-born son Dino, wife Laura, his parents and brother. Fiamma Breschi never married and died in 2015.

Luca di Montezemolo returned to Ferrari in 1991 and served as president and CEO for 23 years. Under his leadership, Ferrari won six *drivers'* and eight *manufacturers'* Formula 1 world championships.

For a brief period at the beginning of Montezemolo's tenure, Niki Lauda returned to Ferrari as personal assistant to the president.

Ferrari is still the only racing team to have participated in all Formula 1 racing seasons since 1950. Ferrari holds nearly all Formula 1 records, including *drivers'* and *manufacturers'* world titles, number of races run and won, podium finishes, pole positions and fastest race laps.

Ferrari builds over eight thousand cars per year – all of them made to order in the company's only factory at Maranello, with an average waiting list of two years.

There are two Ferrari theme parks in the world and nearly fifty Ferrari stores that sell not cars but licensed and branded Ferrari merchandise ranging from watches to fountain pens, from baseball caps to jewellery and men's and women's apparel. The flagship store is at the corner of Park Avenue and 55th Street in Manhattan.

Some of the most prestigious vintage Ferrari models are sold in worldwide car auctions at prices usually paid only for paintings by Picasso and van Gogh.

Because of the endless waiting list, Ferrari is the only company in the world where pre-owned cars of most new models are sold at a higher price than brand-new units.

Today, Ferrari is listed on the New York Stock Exchange. The company's Prancing Horse is one of the world's most recognized logos.

Endnotes

Modena

1. Author's conversation with Franco Gozzi, 19 May 2009.
2. Enzo Ferrari, *Le mie gioie terribili* (Bologna: Cappelli Editore, 1962), p. 12.
3. *La Nuova Gazzetta di Modena*, 10 March 2012.
4. Original document: Enzo Ferrari's birth certificate, 24 February 1898. Collection Museo Casa Enzo Ferrari, Modena.
5. Ibid.
6. Author's conversation with Don Sergio Mantovani, 19 February 2010. The church of St. Catherine is gone today. It was destroyed after Father Sergio Mantovani tried to tear it down by his own means to make room for a larger church, despite the contrary opinion of the Modena City Hall. Known in the world of motorsports as the 'chaplain of drivers', following this feat Enzo Ferrari dubbed Father Mantovani 'Father Caterpillar'.
7. Enzo Ferrari, *Ferrari 80* (Modena: Arbe Officine Grafiche, 1980), p. 12.
8. Ferrari, *Le mie gioie terribili*, p. 12.
9. Original document: Death certificate of Alfredo Ferrari, 26 August 1992.
10. Oscar Orefici, *Ferrari: Romanzo di una vita* (Milan, Italy: Cairo Publishing, 2006), p. 22.
11. Enzo Biagi, *Ferrari: The Drake* (Milan: BUR Biblioteca Univerzale Rizzoli, 2001), p. 107. In 1980 famed Italian journalist Enzo Biagi published a book on Enzo Ferrari. Biagi was not a car journalist, and had no interest or specific knowledge of that world. His book is a curious mosaic of quotes by Ferrari and a collection of sketches of Ferrari done by others. But it is also the result of what, in all likelihood, is one of the longest interviews ever given by Enzo Ferrari.
12. Ibid.
13. Original document: Letter by Alfredo Ferrari, 10 September 1905. Jacques Swaters Collection, Museo Casa Enzo Ferrari, Modena.
14. Ferrari, *Le mie gioie terribili*, p. 13.
15. Ferrari, *Ferrari 80*, p. 6.
16. Ferrari, *Le mie gioie terribili*, p. 13.
17. Biagi, *Ferrari: The Drake*, p. 109.
18. Author's conversation with Franco Gozzi, 19 May 2009.
19. Original document: Death certificate of Adalgisa Bisbini, 26 August 1992.
20. Author's conversation with Franco Gozzi, 19 May 2009.
21. Biagi, *Ferrari: The Drake*, pp. 108 and 109.
22. Ibid., p. 42.

23. Ferrari, *Ferrari 80*, p. 10. In his autobiography, Enzo Ferrari talks of a staircase made of pink marble. There is, of course, no such thing as pink marble; the staircase was made of Verona red marble. The author saw this staircase on 16 July 2010, before the reconstruction work on the house, and can testify that the red marble of the steps does look . . . pink!

24. Ferrari, *Ferrari 80*, p. 8.

25. Original document: Cresimati da Mgr. Natale Bruni nella Metropolitana, nella Pentecoste dell'anno 1903. Archives of the Santa Caterina Parish, Modena. Of the 65 boys and girls who were administered first communion and confirmation that day, Alfredo and Enzo Anselmo are listed as numbers 27 and 28.

26. Ferrari, *Ferrari 80*, p. 13.

27. Ibid.

28. Ibid., pp. 10 and 12.

29. Ibid., p. 9.

30. Biagi, *Ferrari: The Drake*, p. 107.

31. Ibid., p. 113.

32. Ferrari, *Ferrari 80*, p. 7.

33. Ibid.

34. Ibid., p. 108.

35. Ibid., p. 13.

The Spark

1. Ferrari, *Ferrari 80*, p. 11.

2. Biagi, *Ferrari: The Drake*, p. 96.

3. Alessandro Simonini and Michele Smargiassi, *Un sogno lungo un miglio* (Modena: Della Casa, 1992), p. 8. Printed locally in Modena in 1992, this booklet provides valuable information on the second racing event in the life of Enzo Ferrari, the Record del Miglio. All the information on the race and on how the culture of the automobile grew in Modena in the last decade of the 19th and first decade of the 20th centuries are taken from this source.

4. Ferrari, *Ferrari 80*, p. 10.

5. Ibid., p. 11.

6. Simonini and Smargiassi, *Un sogno lungo un miglio*, p. 42.

7. Ibid., p. 46.

8. Biagi, *Ferrari: The Drake*, p. 110.

9. Enzo Ferrari Press Conference, 15 September 1980 (original Ferrari transcription).

10. Ferrari, *Ferrari 80*, pp. 13 and 14. Mosquitoes must have been a real plague in the summer of 1915, because with this precise reference to mosquitoes, in the best style of a cheap novel, Enzo began the tale of his life in the first edition of his autobiography, *Le mie gioie terribili* (*My Terrible Joys*), 1962: 'Mosquitoes were really everywhere that night . . .'

11. Ferrari, *Ferrari 80*, p. 7.

12. Biagi, *Ferrari: The Drake*, p. 107. To Italian journalist Enzo Biagi, in 1980, Enzo Ferrari confided that his thought of someday doing what Ralph DePalma had done at Indianapolis was, at best, 'aïve'.

13. Ferrari, *Ferrari 80*, p. 9.

14. Biagi, *Ferrari: The Drake*, p. 109.
15. Ferrari, *Ferrari 80*, pp. 13 and 14.
16. Biagi, *Ferrari: The Drake*, p. 109.
17. Ferrari, *Ferrari 80*, pp. 8 and 9.
18. Original document (copy): Photograph with text on the back, handwritten by Enzo Ferrari, 19 July 1917. Adolfo Orsi private collection, Modena.
19. Ferrari, *Ferrari 80*, p. 14.
20. Biagi, *Ferrari: The Drake*, p. 115.
21. Ibid.
22. Ferrari, *Ferrari 80*, p. 14.

The Dream Comes True

1. Giulio Schmidt, *Le Corse Ruggenti : La vera storia di Enzo Ferrari pilota* (Milan: Edizioni della Libreria dell'Automobile, 1988), p. 20.
2. Author's conversation with Franco Gozzi, 19 May 2009. Forty-four years later, when he told for the first time the story of the interview with Diego Soria in his memoirs, Ferrari said nothing of the role played by his mother, referring instead to a letter of recommendation from one of the army officers under whom he had served during the Great War. In 1980, in the last revision of his autobiography, he had not changed his version of this story. On page 14 of *Ferrari 80* one reads: 'The military experience left me at least one letter of recommendation from my colonel that I used with Fiat.'
3. Schmidt, *Le Corse Ruggenti*, p. 18.
4. Ferrari, *Ferrari 80*, p. 14.
5. Ibid.
6. Ibid.
7. Author's conversation with Franco Gozzi, 19 May 2009.
8. Ferrari, *Ferrari 80*, p. 15.
9. Ibid.
10. Ibid.
11. Ibid., p. 16. Recalling the experience at CMN, and particularly this engine, many years later Ferrari wrote: 'Here's an engine that, in the crowd of acronyms and names with which my brain is saturated, has preserved in my memory a very special place.'
12. Ibid.
13. Schmidt, *Le Corse Ruggenti*, p. 24.
14. Ferrari, *Ferrari 80*, p. 17. In his memoirs, he continues: 'I say small compared to the vocation number two, which was to occupy, engulf, even dramatize my whole life: that of manufacturer.'
15. Schmidt, *Le Corse Ruggenti*, p. 188.
16. Ibid., p. 25.
17. *La Gazzetta dello Sport*, 4 October 1919.
18. Ibid.
19. Schmidt, *Le Corse Ruggenti*, p. 29.
20. Ibid., p. 30.
21. Valerio Moretti, *Enzo Ferrari pilota* (Rome: Edizioni di Autocritica, 1987), p. 13.
22. Schmidt, *Le Corse Ruggenti*, p. 31.

23. Ferrari, *Ferrari 80*, p. 17.
24. Ibid., p. 18.
25. Schmidt, *Le Corse Ruggenti*, p. 32.
26. Ibid.
27. Ibid., p. 34.
28. Ibid., p. 36.
29. Ferrari, *Ferrari 80*, p. 18.
30. Schmidt, *Le Corse Ruggenti*, p. 36.
31. Ibid.
32. Ferrari, *Ferrari 80*, p. 19.
33. Schmidt, *Le Corse Ruggenti*, p. 37.
34. Ferrari, *Ferrari 80*, p. 18.
35. Ibid., p. 19.
36. Ibid.
37. *Paese Sportivo*, 8 December 1919.
38. Enzo Ferrari, *Una vita per l'automobile* (Bologna: Conti Editore, 1998), p. 24.
39. Author's conversation with Franco Gozzi, 19 May 2009.
40. Ibid.
41. Moretti, *Enzo Ferrari pilota*, p. 77.
42. Schmidt, *Le Corse Ruggenti*, p. 44.
43. Ibid., p. 53.
44. Ibid., p. 44.
45. Ibid., p. 45.
46. Ibid., p. 46.
47. *La Gazzetta dello Sport*, 14 June 1920.
48. Ibid., 30 October 1920.
49. Schmidt, *Le Corse Ruggenti*, p. 46.
50. *La Gazzetta dello Sport*, 14 June 1920.
51. Schmidt, *Le Corse Ruggenti*, p. 47.

First Love

1. Author's conversation with Franco Gozzi, 19 May 2009.
2. Ibid.
3. Author's conversation with Piero Ferrari, 13 November 2012.
4. Adolfo Orsi, *Il ritrovamento archeologico*. The existence of Carrozzeria Emilia, one of the best-kept secrets in the life of Enzo Ferrari, was revealed by Adolfo Orsi, the Modenese historian and heir to the family that owned Maserati from 1937 to 1968.
5. Orsi, *Il ritrovamento archeologico*.
6. Original document (copy): Carrozzeria Emilia E. Ferrari & C. Charter, Adolfo Orsi Collection.
7. Schmidt, *Le Corse Ruggenti*, p. 48.
8. Biagi, *Ferrari: The Drake*, p. 119.
9. Schmidt, *Le Corse Ruggenti*, p. 50.
10. Ibid.
11. Moretti, *Enzo Ferrari pilota*, p. 20.

12. Schmidt, *Le Corse Ruggenti*, p. 50.

13. Ibid.

14. *AutoMotoCiclo*, 1–15 November 1920.

15. Schmidt, *Le Corse Ruggenti*, p. 52.

16. Ibid.

17. *La Gazzetta dello Sport*, 30 October 1920.

18. Ibid.

19. Schmidt, *Le Corse Ruggenti*, p. 53.

20. Ibid.

21. Ferrari, *Ferrari 80*, pp. 39 and 40.

22. Schmidt, *Le Corse Ruggenti*, p. 53.

23. Ibid., pp. 58 and 59.

24. Moretti, *Enzo Ferrari pilota*, p. 23.

25. Ferrari, *Ferrari 80*, p. 215.

26. Nunzia Manicardi, *Quel diabolico Ferrari* (Rome: Koinè Nuove Edizioni, 2000), p. 42.

27. Ferrari, *Ferrari 80*, p. 215.

28. Ibid. Curiously, in his memoirs Enzo Ferrari wrote that he married 'very young' in 1921. In fact, in 1921 he began living with his girlfriend. The wedding would arrive only in the spring of 1923. In his first book, *Le mie gioie terribili*, he was even less precise, and wrote 'around 1920' as the date of his wedding.

29. Ferrari, *Ferrari 80*, p. 215.

30. Manicardi, *Quel diabolico Ferrari*, p. 42.

31. Schmidt, *Le Corse Ruggenti*, p. 64.

32. Ibid., p. 65.

33. Moretti, *Enzo Ferrari pilota*, p. 28.

34. *Il Corriere della Sera*, 6 August 1921.

35. Schmidt, *Le Corse Ruggenti*, p. 70.

36. *La Gazzetta dello Sport*, August 16, 1921.

37. Schmidt, *Le Corse Ruggenti*, p. 65.

38. Ibid., p. 73.

39. Ibid., pp. 73 and 74.

40. Ferrari, *Una vita per l'automobile*, p. 32.

41. Moretti, *Enzo Ferrari pilota*, p. 31.

Laura

1. Author's conversation with Jacques Swaters, 4 October 2006. Among the extraordinary documents in a vast collection of Ferrari memorabilia, the former racing driver turned Ferrari dealer and importer for Belgium owned a part of the correspondence between Enzo and Laura, shown to the author of this book in the course of a long conversation in October 2006. While he continued to write with a fountain pen and black ink, in 1922 Ferrari began to use purple as the colour for the paper header of his personal stationery, including envelopes. He had at least two types: one with the header 'Enzo Ferrari— Modena' in English italic font; another with the header ENZO FERRARI written in capital letters and framed by a rectangle, also purple. It is clearly the first reference to

the memory of his father who, in the late 1920s, led him to use the purple ink for all his correspondence.

2. Ibid.
3. Schmidt, *Le Corse Ruggenti*, p. 76.
4. Ibid.
5. Ibid., p. 77.
6. Ibid., p. 79.
7. Author's conversation with Jacques Swaters, 4 October 2006. The newspaper quoted is the local Modena paper.
8. Schmidt, *Le Corse Ruggenti*, p. 81.
9. Author's conversation with Jacques Swaters, 4 October 2006.
10. Ibid.
11. *La Gazzetta dello Sport*, 26 July 1922.
12. Author's conversation with Jacques Swaters, 4 October 2006.
13. Ibid.
14. Schmidt, *Le Corse Ruggenti*, p. 85.
15. *La Gazzetta dello Sport*, 11 September 1922.
16. Ferrari, *Ferrari 80*, p. 21.
17. Moretti, *Enzo Ferrari pilota*, p. 33.
18. Ferrari, *Ferrari 80*, p. 20.
19. Ibid.
20. Ibid., p. 60.
21. Ibid., p. 59.
22. Ibid.
23. Ibid. The moment he realized he did not have the talent of Ascari and Campari, he turned to the example set by the former, who became his role model.
24. Ibid.

Victory!

1. Moretti, *Enzo Ferrari pilota*, p. 32.
2. Schmidt, *Le Corse Ruggenti*, p. 88.
3. Original document: Enzo Ferrari Press Conference, minutes, 15 September 1980. Private collection.
4. Moretti, *Enzo Ferrari pilota*, p. 33.
5. *La Gazzetta dello Sport*, 16 April 1923.
6. Schmidt, *Le Corse Ruggenti*, p. 90.
7. Original document: Wedding certificate of Ferrari Enzo Anselmo Giuseppe Maria and Garello Domenica detta Laura, 28 April 1923. Collection Museo Casa Enzo Ferrari, Modena.
8. Ferrari, *Ferrari 80*, p. 215.
9. Ibid., p. 214.
10. *La Gazzetta dello Sport*, Ferrari Racconta, Vol. I, p. 25.
11. Ibid., p. 37.
12. Luigi Fusi, Enzo Ferrari, Griffith Borgeson, *Le Alfa Romeo di Vittorio Jano* (Rome: Edizioni di Autocritica, 1982), p. 25.

13. *La Gazzetta dello Sport*, Ferrari Racconta, Vol. I, p. 37.

14. Ibid.

15. Moretti, *Enzo Ferrari pilota*, p. 36.

16. Enzo Ferrari, TV Interview, 1984.

17. *La Gazzetta dello Sport*, 14 June 1923.

18. Author's conversation with Franco Gozzi, 19 May 2009.

19. Ibid.

20. *La Gazzetta dello Sport*, 18 June 1923.

21. *La Gazzetta dello Sport*, Ferrari Racconta, Vol. I, p. 37.

22. Schmidt, *Le Corse Ruggenti*, p. 94.

23. Schmidt, *Le Corse Ruggenti*, p. 96.

24. Ibid.

25. *Il Corriere della Sera*, 9 September 1923.

26. *La Gazzetta dello Sport*, Ferrari Racconta, Vol. I, p. 25.

27. Ibid.

28. Ibid.

29. Enzo Ferrari, *Le briglie del successo* (San Lazzaro di Savena: Poligrafici Il Borgo, 1970), p. 32.

30. Gino Rancati, *Ferrari l'unico* (Milan: Giorgio Nada Editore, 1988), p. 20.

31. Ferrari, *Ferrari 80*, pp. 20 and 21.

32. *La Gazzetta dello Sport*, Ferrari Racconta, Vol. I, p. 38.

33. Fusi et al, *Le Alfa Romeo di Vittorio Jano*, p. 54.

34. Ibid.

35. Ibid.

36. *La Gazzetta dello Sport*, Ferrari Racconta, Vol. I, p. 38.

37. Schmidt, *Le Corse Ruggenti*, p. 98.

38. Fusi et al, *Le Alfa Romeo di Vittorio Jano*, p. 25.

The Champ

1. Moretti, *Enzo Ferrari pilota*, p. 47.

2. Author's conversation with Franco Gozzi, 19 May 2009.

3. Ferrari, *Una vita per l'automobile*, p. 51.

4. Schmidt, *Le Corse Ruggenti*, p. 103.

5. Ibid. The episode is reconstructed in the book, but the quotes are from *Auto Italiana* magazine.

6. Ibid.

7. Ferrari, *Le mie gioie terribili*, p. 171.

8. Schmidt, *Le Corse Ruggenti*, p. 107.

9. Moretti, *Enzo Ferrari pilota*, p. 51.

10. Author's conversation with Franco Gozzi, 19 May 2009.

11. Schmidt, *Le Corse Ruggenti*, p. 107.

12. Ferrari, *Una vita per l'automobile*, p. 46.

13. Schmidt, *Le Corse Ruggenti*, p. 106.

14. Moretti, *Enzo Ferrari pilota*, p. 48.

15. Schmidt, *Le Corse Ruggenti*, p. 110.

16. Ibid., p. 108.

17. Ibid., p. 110.
18. Author's conversation with Franco Gozzi, 19 May 2009.
19. Schmidt, *Le Corse Ruggenti*, p. 113.
20. *La Gazzetta dello Sport*, 2 June 1924.
21. Moretti, *Enzo Ferrari pilota*, p. 50.
22. Ibid, p. 86.
23. Author's conversation with Franco Gozzi, 19 May 2009.

Lyon

1. *La Gazzetta dello Sport*, 8 July 1924.
2. Federico Valeriani, *Coppa Acerbo: Circuito Internazionale degli Abruzzi* (Pescara: Asca-Res Imago, 2008), p. 34.
3. *Badische Presse*, 18 July 1924.
4. Moretti, *Enzo Ferrari pilota*, p. 20.
5. Ferrari, *Ferrari 80*, p. 21.
6. *La Gazzetta dello Sport*, 14 July 1924.
7. Ibid.
8. Valeriani, *Coppa Acerbo*, p. 22.
9. Schmidt, *Le Corse Ruggenti*, p. 119.
10. *La Gazzetta dello Sport*, 14 July 1924.
11. Valeriani, *Coppa Acerbo*, p. 13; letter by Enzo Ferrari to the author of the book.
12. Moretti, *Enzo Ferrari pilota*, p. 57.
13. *La Gazzetta dello Sport*, 19 July 1924.
14. Schmidt, *Le Corse Ruggenti*, p. 124.
15. *La Gazzetta dello Sport*, 23 July 1924.
16. Schmidt, *Le Corse Ruggenti*, p. 124.
17. *La Gazzetta dello Sport*, 23 July 1924.
18. Ferrari, *Ferrari 80*, p. 215. Ferrari chose the profession of bus driver to synthesize a job that was not dangerous and with an unabashed routine because it was the job of Laura's brother.
19. Author's conversation with Jacques Swaters, 4 October 2006.
20. Author's conversation with Franco Gozzi, 19 May 2009.
21. Ferrari, *Romanzo di una vita*, p. 62.
22. Author's conversation with Franco Gozzi, 19 May 2009.
23. Author's conversation with Jacques Swaters, 4 October 2006.
24. Ferrari, *Ferrari 80*, p. 22.
25. Schmidt, *Le Corse Ruggenti*, p. 124.
26. Author's conversation with Jacques Swaters, 4 October 2006.
27. *La Gazzetta dello Sport*, 4 August 1924.
28. Biagi, *Ferrari: The Drake*, p. 119.
29. *La Gazzetta dello Sport*, 19 August 1924.
30. Ferrari, *Ferrari 80*, pp. 22 and 23.
31. Moretti, *Enzo Ferrari pilota*, p. 83.
32. Schmidt, *Le Corse Ruggenti*, p. 124.
33. *La Gazzetta dello Sport*, Ferrari Racconta, Vol. I, p. 54.

34. Ferrari, *Le mie gioie terribili*, p. 52. It has been said and written that the prancing horse was given by Countess Baracca to Enzo Ferrari on the winner's platform of the Savio Circuit. It was actually given to him away from Savio, the autumn following Enzo's second win in Ravenna. Telling for the first time publicly how he came to possess Francesco Baracca's prancing horse, after describing the moment he made the acquaintance of Count Baracca, on page 52 of *Le mie gioie terribili*, Ferrari wrote: 'From that meeting another one came about, with his mother, Countess Paolina. It was she who one day said, "Ferrari, put the prancing horse of my son on your car. It will bring you luck."'

35. Cesare De Agostini, *Baracca: L'eroe del Cavallino* (Milan: Giorgio Nada Editore, 2008), pp. 16 and 17. Francesco Baracca was not the only Italian Air Force aviator to have adopted a personal emblem. In his squadron there were those who had painted on the fuselage of their plane a black star or a skull and crossbones. Even when, in the spring of 1918, the squadron adopted a group official emblem for all of the aircraft (a black hippogriff), each pilot kept his own personal emblem on his plane.

36. Ferrari Opera Omnia, Vol. 6 (Milan: *La Gazzetta dello Sport*, 2007), p. 34.

37. De Agostini, *Baracca: L'eroe del Cavallino*, pp. 14 and 15. This photograph was taken at Padua airfield on 10 April 1918, and was sent to his parents along with one of his letters, dated 27 April. The hero wrote regularly to his mother. In this letter Francesco explained that he had chosen the prancing horse as his personal emblem because it appeared in the arms of his regiment, the Piedmont Cavalry: 'I have here my horse and I started to ride with great pleasure; I will send you my picture on the horse soon, and meanwhile I send you this with the plane, and, on it, the horse, the emblem of the Royal Piedmont.'

38. Franco Gozzi, *Alla destra del Drake*, (Milan: Giorgio Nada Editore, 2007), p. 16. 'Cav.' is short for Cavaliere – Knight, the honorary title bestowed on Ferrari after winning the 1924 Coppa Acerbo, two months after his second victory at Savio. And in this abbreviation penned in ink by Baracca's mother is the unintentional but valuable solution to the question about the year Ferrari was given the use of the prancing horse – 1924 – an issue on which Ferrari contradicted himself many times.

39. Author's conversation with Franco Gozzi, 19 May 2009. Additional proof that the prancing horse was given to Ferrari by Countess Baracca in 1924, and not in 1923, comes from Franco Gozzi, the only person, apart from son Piero, to have access to the personal papers of Ferrari after his death. During one of the interviews granted for the writing of this book, Gozzi hinted at the greeting cards that the count and countess had sent Ferrari for Christmas in 1923 and 1924. While the 1923 Christmas card contained only the traditional wishes, on that of 1924, Countess Paolina spoke of the prancing horse that had been her son's, reminding Ferrari to paint it on his car.

40. Author's conversation with Adolfo Orsi, 19 April 2012. Among the papers of an extraordinary collection dedicated to the Modena world of motor racing, Orsi has a copy of the establishing chart of Cav. Enzo Ferrari Agente Generale Emilia e Romagna.

Exile

1. Author's conversation with Jacques Swaters, 4 October 2006.
2. Author's conversation with Gianni Rogliatti, 1 October 2009.
3. Ibid.
4. Ferrari, *Le mie gioie terribili*, p. 77.

5. Schmidt, *Le Corse Ruggenti*, p. 127.
6. Author's conversation with Gianni Rogliatti, 1 October 2009.
7. Author's conversation with Franco Gozzi, 21 June 2010.
8. Schmidt, *Le Corse Ruggenti*, pp. 127 and 128.
9. Author's conversation with Franco Gozzi, 21 June 2010.
10. Schmidt, *Le Corse Ruggenti*, p. 133.

Back to the Future

1. Schmidt, *Le Corse Ruggenti*, p. 132.
2. L'Auto Italiana, 30 May 1927, in *Le Corse Ruggenti*, p. 132.
3. Moretti, *Enzo Ferrari pilota*, p. 60.
4. Ibid.
5. Schmidt, *Le Corse Ruggenti*, p. 140.
6. Author's conversation with Franco Gozzi, 19 May 2009.
7. Moretti, *Enzo Ferrari pilota*, p. 60.
8. Schmidt, *Le Corse Ruggenti*, p. 144.
9. Moretti, *Enzo Ferrari pilota*, p. 60.
10. Ibid., p. 61.
11. Schmidt, *Le Corse Ruggenti*, p. 144.
12. *La Gazzetta dello Sport*, 10 September 1928.
13. *Il Littoriale*, 20 April 1929.
14. Schmidt, *Le Corse Ruggenti*, p. 155. On this page there is a chart originally published in the magazine *L'Auto Italiana*.
15. *La Gazzetta dello Sport*, 22 April 1929.
16. *Il Littoriale*, 22 April 1929.
17. Author's conversation with Jacques Swaters, 4 October 2006.
18. Ibid.
19. Schmidt, *Le Corse Ruggenti*, p. 151.
20. Ibid.
21. Ibid.
22. Adolfo Orsi, *Il ritrovamento archeologico*. The description of the typical working day of Enzo Ferrari in those years is by Enzo Levi, a lawyer friend who soon would play an important role in the life of Enzo Ferrari.

The Scuderia

1. *Il Littoriale*, 3 October 1929.
2. Ibid., 7 October 1929.
3. Luigi Orsini and Franco Zagari, *La Scuderia Ferrari: 1929–1939* (Firenze: Editoriale Olimpia, 1979), p. 14.
4. Ibid., p. 14.
5. Schmidt, *Le Corse Ruggenti*, p. 154.
6. Ferrari, *Ferrari 80*, p. 33.
7. Ferrari, *Romanzo di una vita*, p. 36.
8. Orsini and Zagari, *La Scuderia Ferrari*, p. 19.

9. Ibid., p. 23.

10. Gozzi, *Alla destra del Drake*, p. 18.

11. Franco Gozzi with Pino Allievi, *Ferrari: La storia di un mito* (Milan: *La Gazzetta dello Sport*, 1996), p. 12.

12. Biagi, *Ferrari: The Drake*, p. 127.

13. Author's conversation with Franco Gozzi, 18 December 2009.

14. Orsini and Zagari, *La Scuderia Ferrari*, p. 21.

15. Author's conversation with Franco Gozzi, 18 December 2009.

16. Ibid., 19 May 2009.

17. Ferrari, *Le mie gioie terribili*, p. 152.

18. Ibid., p. 153.

19. Author's conversation with Franco Gozzi, 19 May 2009.

20. Ibid., 18 December 2009.

21. Author's conversation with Jacques Swaters, 4 October 2006.

22. Orsini and Zagari, *La Scuderia Ferrari*, photograph on p. 29.

23. Author's conversation with Jacques Swaters, 4 October 2006.

24. Orsini and Zagari, *La Scuderia Ferrari*, pp. 25 and 26.

25. Schmidt, *Le Corse Ruggenti*, p. 164.

26. Author's conversation with Jacques Swaters, 4 October 2006.

27. Orsini and Zagari, *La Scuderia Ferrari*, p. 30.

28. Schmidt, *Le Corse Ruggenti*, p. 164.

29. Orsini and Zagari, *La Scuderia Ferrari*, pp. 26 and 33.

30. Ibid., p. 33.

31. Schmidt, *Le Corse Ruggenti*, p. 164.

32. Maurizio Tabucchi, *Nel Segno del Tridente* (Milan: Giorgio Nada Editore, 2003), p. 94.

Winning

1. *L'Auto Italiana*, No. 12, 30 June 1930.

2. Ibid., No. 13, 15 July 1930.

3. Orsini and Zagari, *La Scuderia Ferrari*, p. 39.

4. *La Gazzetta dello Sport*, 11 August 1930.

5. Schmidt, *Le Corse Ruggenti*, p. 165.

6. Ibid., p. 166.

7. Ibid.

8. *La Gazzetta dello Sport*, 8 September 1930.

9. *L'Auto Italiana*, No. 17, 15 September 1930.

10. Author's conversation with Jacques Swaters, 4 October 2006.

11. Ibid.

12. Ibid.

13. Ibid.

14. Schmidt, *Le Corse Ruggenti*, p. 168.

15. *Il Littoriale*, 17 October 1929. Modena, Bologna and Ferrara, the cities of the three leading members of the Scuderia. Of course, the only one who really mattered was Enzo Ferrari.

16. *La Gazzetta dello Sport*, 11 November 1930.

17. Ibid.

18. Schmidt, *Le Corse Ruggenti*, p. 168.

19. *La Gazzetta dello Sport*, 11 November 1930.

20. Orsini and Zagari, *La Scuderia Ferrari*, p. 61.

21. Gozzi, *Alla destra del Drake*, pp. 19–23. Curiously enough, Ferrari, who routinely collected autographed dinner menus, did not keep for himself this gift that marked the end of the first season of his team, and gave it sometime later to his doctor, Alvaro Magnoni. Magnoni years later bequeathed it to his barber, Antonio D'Elia, who was also Ferrari's barber. When he came in possession of the box and of its precious contents, the barber gave it in turn to the original owner, thinking it the right thing to do. But Enzo, who of course appreciated the gesture, handed it back immediately to Antonio, this time as his own gift.

22. Schmidt, *Le Corse Ruggenti*, chart on p. 167.

The Prancing Horse

1. Author's conversation with Franco Gozzi, 19 May 2009.

2. Orsini and Zagari, *La Scuderia Ferrari*, p. 87.

3. Author's conversation with Franco Gozzi, 19 May 2009.

4. Schmidt, *Le Corse Ruggenti*, p. 176.

5. *L'Auto Italiana*, No. 11, 20 April 1931, p. 203.

6. Ibid., No. 12, 30 April 1931, p. 56.

7. Orsini and Zagari, *La Scuderia Ferrari*, p. 95.

8. *Il Littoriale*, 15 June 1931.

9. Author's conversation with Franco Gozzi, 19 May 2009.

10. Ferrari, *Ferrari 80*, pp. 115–16. It is unclear whether the child, who would come after nine years of marriage and eleven years of living together, was an attempt to better the relationship between husband and wife. Some commentators, weighing the words Ferrari wrote 30 years later, and after the death of that son, believed they saw, in Enzo being confronted with a fait accompli, that perhaps Laura got pregnant without Enzo necessarily wanting a child. But this is only a hypothesis. All Ferrari intimates interviewed for this book, when asked for a comment, preferred to defer.

11. Ferrari, *Ferrari 80*, pp. 214–15.

12. Ferrari, *Le mie gioie terribili*, p. 123.

13. Ibid.

14. Schmidt, *Le Corse Ruggenti*, p. 176.

15. Ibid.

16. Orsini and Zagari, *La Scuderia Ferrari*, p. 108.

17. Ibid., p. 110.

18. Ibid., p. 149.

19. Author's conversation with Franco Gozzi, 19 May 2009.

20. *La Gazzetta dello Sport*, 8 November 1931.

21. Ibid., 22 November 1931.

22. *Il Littoriale*, 23 November 1931.

23. Orsini and Zagari, *La Scuderia Ferrari*, p. 116.

24. *La Gazzetta dello Sport*, 22 November 1931.

25. *Il Littoriale*, 23 November 1931.
26. *La Gazzetta dello Sport*, 22 November 1931.
27. *Il Littoriale*, 23 November 1931.
28. Ibid.
29. *Due anni di corse* (1931), p. 4.
30. Ibid., p. 18. Baron Giuseppe Federici di Abriola, chairman of RACI, wrote in a letter published on p. 18: 'Dear Ferrari: Your request for a photograph to be published with the report of the Scuderia's racing activity, "along with those of other authorities of the world of sports," embarrasses me also because I do not have any.'
31. *Due anni di corse* (1931), p. 6.
32. Ibid., p. 4.
33. Ibid., p. 3.
34. Ibid.
35. Ibid., p. 31.
36. Ibid., p. 32.
37. Ibid. Letter by Vincenzo Florio to Enzo Ferrari, 3 November 1931.
38. Schmidt, *Le Corse Ruggenti*, p. 176.
39. Ibid.
40. Interview of Enzo Ferrari, by Luciano Righi, Maranello, 27 December 1976. The quote is from Enzo Ferrari.
41. Ferrari, *Le mie gioie terribili*, p. 123.
42. Author's conversation with Franco Gozzi, 19 May 2009.
43. Orsini and Zagari, *La Scuderia Ferrari*, p. 163.
44. *Due anni di corse* (1931), p. 2.
45. Orsini and Zagari, *La Scuderia Ferrari*, p. 149.
46. Ibid.
47. *Il terzo anno di corse*, p. 5.
48. Orsini and Zagari, *La Scuderia Ferrari*, p. 116.
49. Ibid., p. 151.
50. Author's conversation with Franco Gozzi, 19 May 2009.
51. Ibid.
52. Orsini and Zagari, *La Scuderia Ferrari*, p. 175.
53. Author's conversation with Franco Gozzi, 19 May 2009.
54. *La Gazzetta dello Sport*, 18 November 1932.
55. Ibid., 20 November 1932.
56. *Il terzo anno di corse*, p. 31.

Tazio and I

1. *Il terzo anno di corse*, p. 31.
2. Cesare De Agostini, *L'antileggenda di Nuvolari* (Milan: Sperling & Kupfer Editori, 1972), p. 76.
3. Ibid.
4. *Auto Italiana Sport*, 1 February 1960.
5. Orsini and Zagari, *La Scuderia Ferrari*, p. 203.
6. Ibid.

7. *Il Littoriale*, 22 November 1932.
8. Author's conversation with Ermanno Cozza, 15 May 2012.
9. Original document: Letter by Prospero Gianferrari to Enzo Ferrari, 28 February 1933. Archivio Storico Alfa Romeo.
10. Orsini and Zagari, *La Scuderia Ferrari*, p. 208.
11. Ibid., p. 219.
12. Ibid., p. 217.
13. Valerio Moretti, *Quando corre Nuvolari* (Milan: Autocritica, 1992), p. 38.
14. De Agostini, *L'antileggenda di Nuvolari*, p. 82.
15. Author's conversation with Franco Gozzi, 19 May 2009.
16. Orsini and Zagari, *La Scuderia Ferrari*, p. 217.
17. Author's conversation with Franco Gozzi, 19 May 2009.
18. Giovanni Canestrini, *Una vita con le corse* (Bologna: Edizioni Calderini, 1962), p. 132.
19. Ibid.
20. De Agostini, *L'antileggenda di Nuvolari*, p. 83.
21. Ibid.
22. *La Gazzetta dello Sport*, 7 August 1933.
23. *Tazio Nuvolari fra storia e leggenda*, Round table organized at Milan's Museo Nazionale della Scienza e Tecnologia on 17 October 1992. Minutes from speech by Nello Ugolini, p. 24.
24. *La Gazzetta dello Sport*, 10 July 1933.
25. Orsini and Zagari, *La Scuderia Ferrari*, p. 219. That Sunday in Spa, a Maserati did race with the prancing horse painted on the hood. It was a 1500 owned by driver Ippolito Berrone, fielded and assisted – as a privateer – by Scuderia Ferrari.
26. Author's conversation with Franco Gozzi, 19 May 2009.
27. Moretti, *Quando corre Nuvolari*, p. 41.
28. De Agostini, *L'antileggenda di Nuvolari*, p. 84.
29. Author's conversation with Ermanno Cozza, 15 March 2012.
30. *Tazio Nuvolari fra storia e leggenda*, speech by Ugolini, p. 23.
31. De Agostini, *L'antileggenda di Nuvolari*, p. 85.
32. *La Gazzetta dello Sport*, 4 August 1933.
33. Ibid.
34. Ibid., 7 August 1933.
35. Ibid., 2 August 1933.
36. Orsini and Zagari, *La Scuderia Ferrari*, p. 220.
37. Orsini and Zagari, *La Scuderia Ferrari Settimanale Illustrato*, 17 December 1935.
38. La Gazzetta dello Sport, 4 August 1933.
39. Ibid., 5–6 August 1933.
40. Ibid., 7 August 1933.
41. Ibid.
42. Ibid.
43. Ibid.
44. Ibid.
45. Ibid., 8 August 1933.
46. Ibid.
47. Author's conversation with Cesare De Agostini, 22 October 2013.
48. *La Gazzetta dello Sport*, 5–6 August 1933.

49. Author's conversation with Franco Gozzi, 18 December 2009.

50. *La Gazzetta dello Sport*, 16 August 1933.

51. *Il Littoriale*, 20 August 1933.

52. Moretti, *Quando corre Nuvolari*, p. 176.

53. Orsini and Zagari, *La Scuderia Ferrari*, p. 232.

54. *Il Littoriale*, 11 September 1933.

55. Ibid., 12 September 1933.

56. Orsini and Zagari, *La Scuderia Ferrari*, p. 235.

57. Original document: Letter by Enzo Ferrari to Alfa Romeo, 18 June 1938. Archivio Storico Alfa Romeo.

58. *Il quarto anno di corse*, p. 16.

59. Ibid.

60. Orsini and Zagari, *La Scuderia Ferrari*, p. 238.

61. *Il Littoriale*, 5 December 1933.

62. Ibid.

63. Ibid., 1 December 1933.

64. Ibid., 5 December 1933.

The Moll Affair

1. *Il Littoriale*, 21 December 1933.

2. Ibid.

3. Ibid., 28 November 1933.

4. Ibid.

5. Ibid.

6. Ibid., 2 December 1933.

7. Ibid., 21 November 1933.

8. Orsini and Zagari, *La Scuderia Ferrari*, p. 241.

9. Ibid., 21 December 1933.

10. Ibid.

11. Ibid.

12. Ibid.

13. Ibid.

14. Author's conversation with Franco Gozzi, 18 December 2009.

15. Ibid.

16. Ibid.

17. Orsini and Zagari, *La Scuderia Ferrari*, p. 239.

18. Ibid.

19. *Il Littoriale*, 28 November 1933.

20. Ferrari, *Ferrari 80*, p. 207.

21. Orsini and Zagari, *La Scuderia Ferrari*, p. 241.

22. Ferrari, *Ferrari 80*, p. 71.

23. Ibid., p. 70.

24. Ibid.

25. Ibid.

26. Moretti, *Quando corre Nuvolari*, p. 180.

27. RACI, No. 17 (26 April 1934).
28. De Agostini, *L'antileggenda di Nuvolari*, p. 98.
29. Moretti, *Quando corre Nuvolari*, p. 182.
30. *Un ricordo di Guy Moll*, Centro di Documentazione del Museo Nazionale dell'Automobile di Torino, 2005.
31. MACS, 16 July 1934.
32. *Auto Italiana*, 30 June 1934.
33. Ibid.
34. Ibid.
35. Author's conversation with Franco Gozzi, 18 December 2009.
36. Ibid.
37. Author's conversation with Gianni Rogliatti, 1 December 2009.
38. Orsini and Zagari, *La Scuderia Ferrari*, p. 267.
39. Ferrari, *Ferrari 80*, p. 72.
40. Orsini and Zagari, *La Scuderia Ferrari*, p. 271.
41. Ferrari, *Ferrari 80*, p. 72.
42. Ibid., p. 71.
43. *LSF settimanale illustrato*, 7 February 1935.

Fighting the Silver Arrows

1. De Agostini, *L'antileggenda di Nuvolari*, p. 109.
2. Chris Nixon, *Racing the Silver Arrows: Mercedes-Benz versus Auto Union 1934–1939* (London: Osprey, 1987), p. 305. The letter was written by Auto Union press office director Richard Voelter, in French, since Voelter did not speak Italian and Nuvolari did not speak German.
3. De Agostini, *L'antileggenda di Nuvolari*, p. 108. Cesare De Agostini has collected, among others, a letter dated 25 October 1934, addressed to Nuvolari, which reads as follows: 'I am a comrade of yours from the war, a motorist; we met in Suzzara. If you saw me, you would recognize me. As I am an old comrade and a modest colleague, would you please tell me why you went over to German Auto Union?'
4. *La Gazzetta dello Sport*, 5 February 1935.
5. De Agostini, *L'antileggenda di Nuvolari*, p. 110.
6. *LSF settimanale illustrato*, 7 February 1935.
7. Author's conversation with Franco Gozzi, 19 May 2009.
8. *La Gazzetta dello Sport*, 5 February 1935.
9. *Il Messaggero*, 2 February 1935.
10. *LSF settimanale illustrato*, 7 February 1935.
11. Ferrari, *Le briglie del successo*, p. 49.
12. *LSF settimanale illustrato*, 11 April 1935.
13. Orsini and Zagari, *La Scuderia Ferrari*, p. 322.
14. *LSF settimanale illustrato*, 17 January 1935.
15. Orsini and Zagari, *La Scuderia Ferrari*, p. 278.
16. Ibid., p. 279.
17. *LSF settimanale illustrato*, 11 April 1935.
18. Author's conversation with Cesare De Agostini, 22 October 2013.

19. *LSF settimanale illustrato*, 25 April 1935.
20. Author's conversation with Franco Gozzi, 19 May 2009.
21. *LSF settimanale illustrato*, 25 April 1935.
22. *RACI* (newsletter), 30 May 1935.
23. *LSF settimanale illustrato*, 20 June 1935.
24. Orsini and Zagari, *La Scuderia Ferrari*, p. 300.
25. Ibid.
26. *LSF settimanale illustrato*, 20 June 1935.
27. Ibid.
28. Ibid.
29. Ibid.
30. Orsini and Zagari, *La Scuderia Ferrari*, p. 300.
31. *La Gazzetta dello Sport*, 16 June 1935.
32. *Corriere del Tirreno*, 16 June 1935.
33. *La Nazione*, 16 June 1935.
34. *Il Popolo d'Italia*, 16 June 1935.
35. *Corriere del Tirreno*, 16 June 1935.
36. Author's conversation with Gianni Rogliatti, 1 October 2009.
37. *Tazio Nuvolari fra storia e leggenda*, Round table at Museo Nazionale della Scienza e Tecnologia of Milan, 17 October 1992. Minutes of speech by Nello Ugolini, p. 13.
38. Author's conversation with Gianni Rogliatti, 1 October 2009.
39. Orsini and Zagari, *La Scuderia Ferrari*, p. 308.
40. Ibid.
41. *Il Littoriale*, 29 July 1935.
42. Orsini and Zagari, *La Scuderia Ferrari*, p. 310.
43. *LSF settimanale illustrato*, 5 December 1935.
44. Ibid.
45. Ibid.
46. Ibid.
47. Original document: Letter from Enzo Ferrari to Ugo Gobbato, 18 November 1935. Archivio Storico Alfa Romeo.
48. De Agostini, *L'antileggenda di Nuvolari*, p. 120.
49. Letter from Ferrari to Gobbato, 18 November 1935.
50. Ibid.
51. De Agostini, *L'antileggenda di Nuvolari*, p. 120.

The End of Illusions

1. *LSF settimanale illustrato*, 5 December 1935.
2. Ibid.
3. Ibid., 2 January 1936.
4. Ferrari, *Ferrari 80*, p. 75.
5. *LSF settimanale illustrato*, 2 January 1936.
6. Ibid., 24 February 1936.
7. Ibid., 2 January 1936.
8. *Tazio Nuvolari fra storia e leggenda*, speech by Nello Ugolini, p. 13.

9. *LSF settimanale illustrato*, 2 January 1936.
10. Ibid.
11. Ibid.
12. Ibid., 24 February 1936.
13. *RACI* (newsletter), 19 April 1936.
14. *Il quarto anno di corse*, p. 16.
15. *LSF settimanale illustrato*, 2 January 1936.
16. Ibid., 5 December 1935.
17. Ibid., 2 January 1936.
18. Orsini and Zagari, *La Scuderia Ferrari*, p. 340.
19. Ibid., p. 341.
20. Ibid.
21. *LSF settimanale illustrato*, 19 May 1936.
22. Ibid.
23. Ibid.
24. Orsini and Zagari, *La Scuderia Ferrari*, p. 342.
25. Original document: Letter from Ugo Gobbato to Enzo Ferrari, 9 July 1936. Archivio Storico Alfa Romeo.
26. De Agostini, *L'antileggenda di Nuvolari*, p. 122.
27. Ferrari, *Ferrari 80*, p. 75.
28. De Agostini, *L'antileggenda di Nuvolari*, p. 128.
29. Orsini and Zagari, *La Scuderia Ferrari*, p. 356.
30. *Tazio Nuvolari fra storia e leggenda*, speech by Nello Ugolini, p. 19.
31. De Agostini, *L'antileggenda di Nuvolari*, p. 131.
32. Ibid.
33. Ibid.
34. Ibid.
35. Orsini and Zagari, *La Scuderia Ferrari*, p. 356.
36. *LSF settimanale illustrato*, 5 November 1936.
37. Ibid., 10 October 1935.

Bad Habits

1. Original document: Registered letter from the office of the Alfa Romeo general manager to Enzo Ferrari, 19 February 1937. Archivio Storico Alfa Romeo.
2. Original document: Conference between S.A. Alfa Romeo and S.A. Scuderia Ferrari for the joint management of racing activity, 19 February 1937. Archivio Storico Alfa Romeo.
3. Ferrari, *Le briglie del successo*, p. 240.
4. Original document: Conference between S.A. Alfa Romeo and S.A. Scuderia Ferrari, 19 February 1937.
5. Original document: Letter by Ugo Gobbato and Enzo Ferrari to S.E. Guido Corni, 19 February 1937. Archivio Storico Alfa Romeo.
6. Original document: Conference between S.A. Alfa Romeo and S.A. Scuderia Ferrari, 19 February 1937.
7. Ibid.
8. Ibid.

9. Ibid.

10. Ferrari, *Romanzo di una vita*, p. 99.

11. Fusi et al, *Le Alfa Romeo di Vittorio Jano*, p. 20.

12. Orsini and Zagari, *La Scuderia Ferrari*, p. 392.

13. Ibid.

14. De Agostini, *L'antileggenda di Nuvolari*, p. 136.

15. Ferrari, *Romanzo di una vita*, p. 99.

16. Ibid., p. 101.

17. *La Gazzetta dello Sport*, Ferrari Racconta, Vol. I, p. 19.

18. Letter from the Alfa Romeo general manager to Enzo Ferrari, 18 June 1938. Enzo Ferrari was never an Alfa Romeo employee, but always an external consultant.

19. Ibid.

20. Orsini and Zagari, *La Scuderia Ferrari*, p. 395.

21. Letter from the Alfa Romeo general manager to Enzo Ferrari, 18 June 1938.

22. Luigi Fusi, *Le vetture Alfa Romeo dal 1910* (Milan: Editrice Adiemme, 1965), p. 467.

23. De Agostini, *L'antileggenda di Nuvolari*, p. 137.

24. Letter from the Alfa Romeo general manager to Enzo Ferrari, 21 July 1938.

25. *RACI* (newsletter), 15 September 1938.

26. Fusi, *Le vetture Alfa Romeo dal 1910*), p. 461.

27. *L'Alfa Romeo di Ugo Gobbato*, Monograph 92, Italian Association for Automobile History, 2 April 2011, p. 38.

28. Fusi, *Le vetture Alfa Romeo dal 1910*, p. 463.

29. Ibid.

30. Ferrari, *Ferrari 80*, p. 29.

31. Ferrari, *Romanzo di una vita*, p. 107.

32. Ferrari, *Ferrari 80*, p. 29.

33. Ibid., p. 28.

34. Ibid.

35. Ibid., p. 27.

36. Ibid., p. 30.

37. Ibid.

38. Ibid.

39. Ibid.

40. Original document: Alfa Romeo Personnel Department internal memo, 28 August 1939. Archivio Storico Alfa Romeo.

41. Original document: Letter from the Alfa Romeo general manager to Enzo Ferrari, 6 September 1939. Archivio Storico Alfa Romeo.

42. *Il Littoriale*, 8 September 1939.

43. Ibid., 19 September 1939.

44. Rancati, *Ferrari, l'unico*, p. 30.

815

1. Ferrari, *Ferrari 80*, p. 25.

2. Ibid.

3. Ibid.

4. Ibid.

5. Original document: Enzo Ferrari letter to Alfa Romeo engineer Paratone, 5 September 1939. Archivio Storico Alfa Romeo. Ferrari's letter is dated one day before the letter Ugo Gobbato wrote to inform him of the termination of his contract. Enzo Ferrari wrote verbatim on 5 September: 'As a result of our verbal agreement, I confirm that I give up for four years, from today, every technical and racing activity.'

6. Manicardi, *Quel diabolico Ferrari*, p. 126.

7. Franco Varisco, *L'anteprima Ferrari 815* (Milan: Ferrari World, 1990), p. 20.

8. Ferrari, *Le mie gioie terribili*, pp. 48 and 49. 'So I named it 815 because I could not give it my name, because of that clause with Alfa Romeo.'

9. Varisco, *L'anteprima Ferrari 815*, pp. 34 and 35.

10. *La Gazzetta dello Sport*, 14 February 1940.

11. Ibid., 15 February 1940.

12. Varisco, *L'anteprima Ferrari 815*, p. 36.

13. Author's conversation with Franco Gozzi, 21 July 2010.

14. Gian Paolo Maini, *La prima corsa di Enzo Ferrari* (Imprimatur Editore, 2013), p. 130. The quote is from *Auto Italiana*.

15. Ibid.

16. Ibid.

17. Varisco, *L'anteprima Ferrari*, p. 35.

18. Maini, *La prima corsa di Enzo Ferrari*, p. 107.

19. Varisco, *L'anteprima Ferrari 815*, p. 35.

20. Maini, *La prima corsa di Enzo Ferrari*, p. 124. To have an idea of the passion that pervaded the automobile world in those days, there are pictures of the early tests of the 815 showing the on-site presence of Ernesto Maserati, one of the founders of Maserati, which in 1939, after being purchased by Adolfo Orsi, had transferred its headquarters and workshops to Modena.

21. Varisco, *L'anteprima Ferrari 815*, p. 35.

22. Ibid., p. 46; Enzo Ferrari letter to Renzo Castagneto, 14 April 1940.

23. Author's conversation with Gianni Rogliatti, 1 December 2009.

24. Maini, *La prima corsa di Enzo Ferrari*, p. 124.

25. Author's conversation with Franco Gozzi, 21 July 2010.

26. Maini, *La prima corsa di Enzo Ferrari*, p. 129.

27. Varisco, *L'anteprima Ferrari 815*, p. 48.

28. Maini, *La prima corsa di Enzo Ferrari*, pp. 133 and 134.

29. Varisco, *L'anteprima Ferrari 815*, p. 54.

30. Author's conversation with Franco Gozzi, 21 July 2010.

31. Maini, *La prima corsa di Enzo Ferrari*, p. 137.

32. *La Gazzetta dello Sport*, Ferrari Racconta, Vol. I, p. 44.

33. Maini, *La prima corsa di Enzo Ferrari*, p. 140.

34. Ibid.

35. Ibid., pp. 140 and 141.

36. Ferrari, *Le mie gioie terribili*, p. 49. 'The experiment,' Ferrari wrote in 1962, 'did not have a happy beginning, albeit after a brilliant start [of the race], mainly for the haste with which this car had been built.' Despite Ferrari talking of the brilliant start, Rangoni Machiavelli's 815 stayed in the lead until the beginning of the last lap.

37. *La Gazzetta dello Sport*, Ferrari Racconta, Vol, I, p. 45.
38. Maini, *La prima corsa di Enzo Ferrari*, p. 144.
39. *La Gazzetta dello Sport*, 30 April 1940.
40. Ibid.
41. Ibid.

War and Peace

1. Varisco, *L'anteprima Ferrari 815*, p. 24.
2. Ferrari, *Le mie gioie terribili*, p. 49.
3. Orefici, *Ferrari: Romanzo di una vita*, p. 77. The story of how Enzo Ferrari met Lina Lardi was recorded by Oscar Orefici, an intimate friend of Ferrari's second son Piero, who had the opportunity to interview Ms. Lardi in 1998, 10 years after Enzo's death, on the occasion of the 100th anniversary of his birth. Orefici's interview is extremely valuable because there are no other known interviews with the woman who lived alongside Ferrari from 1929.
4. Manicardi, *Quel diabolico Ferrari*, p. 121.
5. Ibid.
6. Ferrari, *Le mie gioie terribili*, p. 49.
7. Rancati, *Ferrari, L'unico*, p. 12. The friend was Dario Zanasi, a journalist with *Il Resto del Carlino*, who described Ferrari at the time as 'mischievous, witty, subtly polemical. Hostile and friendly depending on the moment. Stubborn, unyielding courage, spirit almost prophetic.'
8. *La Gazzetta di Modena*, 18 August 1988.
9. Author's conversation with Franco Gozzi, 21 June 2010.
10. Author's conversation with Gianni Rogliatti, 1 October 2009.
11. Ferrari, *Ferrari 80*, p. 38.
12. Author's conversation with Franco Gozzi, 21 June 2010.
13. Ferrari, *Ferrari 80*, p. 38.
14. Author's conversation with Franco Gozzi, 21 June 2010.
15. Ferrari, *Ferrari 80*, p. 37.
16. Eliseo Ferrari, *Il 'padrone' Enzo Ferrari* (Modena: Edizioni Il Fiorino, 1999), p. 26.
17. Ibid., p. 25.
18. Ibid., p. 26.
19. Franco Gozzi, *Enzo Ferrari: La vita, il mito, le manie, le curiosità* (Bologna: Poligrafici Il Borgo, 2008), p. 53. On 20 February 1979, on Enzo Ferrari's 81st birthday, the Association of Italian Partigiani went to Maranello to personally award Ferrari the Gold Medal of the Resistance.
20. *Il Corriere della Sera*, 18 February 1986. Enzo Ferrari's recollection is contained in an interview with Luca Goldoni, published on the day of Enzo's 88th birthday.
21. Stefano Ferrari, *Ricordando 'Altavilla', l'uomo che salvo la vita a Enzo Ferrari* (Piacenza: Edizioni Pontegobbo, 2000), pp. 41–44.
22. Ibid., p. 87. The author has reproduced the letter that Ferrari sent him on 3 April 1987, in response to the letter that accompanied the book of war memoirs Zanarini had sent Enzo.
23. Eliseo Ferrari, *Il 'padrone' Enzo Ferrari*, p. 26.
24. Ibid., p. 24.

The 'Ferrari'

1. *La Storia siamo noi*, 'Passioni', TV series, Mediaset, 1998.
2. Gozzi, *Enzo Ferrari: La vita, il mito, le manie, le curiosità*, p. 54.
3. Ferrari, *Ferrari 80*, p. 40.
4. Author's conversation with Gianni Rogliatti, 1 October 2009.
5. *Ferrari: L'opera e il sogno*, Vol. 1 (Ferrari Spa, 2007), p. 21.
6. *La Gazzetta dello Sport*, 12 July 1946.
7. Ibid.
8. Ferrari, *Le mie gioie terribili*, p. 55.
9. Ferrari, *Ferrari 80*, p. 77.
10. Author's conversation with Gianni Rogliatti, 1 October 2009.
11. Author's conversation with Franco Gozzi, 21 July 2010.
12. Ibid.
13. Manicardi, *Quel diabolico Ferrari*, p. 126.
14. Author's conversation with Gianni Rogliatti, 1 October 2009.
15. Ibid.
16. Ferrari, *Una vita per l'automobile*, p. 136.
17. Ferrari, *Ferrari 80*, p. 39.
18. Author's conversation with Gianni Rogliatti, 1 October 2009.
19. *La Gazzetta dello Sport*, 14 May 1947. The Wednesday after the race, Canestrini revealed: 'Until a few minutes before the start everyone hoped that Giuseppe Farina could take the start with the second car produced in the Maranello workshop, which he had driven in practice. The argument between Ferrari and Farina had gone on until almost the moment of the start!'
20. *La Gazzetta dello Sport*, 12 May 1947.
21. Author's conversation with Gianni Rogliatti, 1 October 2009.
22. *La Gazzetta dello Sport*, 14 May 1947.
23. Ibid., 12 May 1947.
24. Ferrari, *Ferrari 80*, p. 42.
25. *La Gazzetta dello Sport*, 14 May 1947.
26. Ibid.
27. Ibid., 26 May 1947.
28. Ibid.
29. *La Gazzetta dello Sport*, Ferrari Racconta, Vol. I, p. 48.
30. *La Gazzetta dello Sport*, 22 June 1947.
31. Ibid., 25 August 1947.
32. Ibid.
33. Author's conversation with Franco Gozzi, 19 May 2009.
34. *La Gazzetta dello Sport*, 11 September 1947.
35. Ibid., 29 September 1947.
36. Ibid., 30 September 1947.
37. Ibid.
38. Manicardi, *Quel diabolico Ferrari*, p. 126.
39. *La Gazzetta dello Sport*, 8 October 1947.
40. Ibid., 13 October 1947.
41. Ferrari, *Ferrari 80*, p. 15.

The Chase

1. Author's conversation with Carlo Benzi, 25 November 2008.
2. *Ferrari Bulletin*, May 1948
3. *La Gazzetta dello Sport*, 1 May 1948.
4. Ibid.
5. Gino Rancati, *Ferrari, L'unico* (Milan: Giorgio Nada Editore, 1988), p. 44.
6. Ibid., p. 12. Interview with Sergio Scapinelli.
7. *La Gazzetta dello Sport*, 3 May 1948.
8. *La Gazzetta dello Sport*, Ferrari, la storia di un mito, p. 35.
9. Gino Rancati and Franco Varisco, *Ferrari, che gente. Un uomo, i suoi uomini* (Milan: Giorgio Nada Editore, 1996), p. 21. Interview with Giuseppe Navone.
10. *Ferrari: L'opera e il sogno*, Vol. I, pp. 20 and 38.
11. *La Gazzetta dello Sport*, 4 September 1948.
12. Ibid., 6 September 1948.
13. Rancati, *Ferrari, lui*, p. 47.
14. Ibid., p. 43.
15. Arnaud Meunier, *Tutte le Ferrari (1939–2014)* (ThisSideUp, 2014), p. 168.
16. Gozzi, *Enzo Ferrari: La vita, il mito, le manie, le curiosità*, p. 57.
17. *La Gazzetta dello Sport*, 25 April 1949.
18. Author's conversation with Dino Tagliazucchi, 2 December 2008.
19. Ferrari, *Le mie gioie terribili*, p. 55.
20. Ferrari, *Una vita per l'automobile*, pp. 140 and 141.
21. *Ferrari: L'opera e il sogno*, Vol. 1, p. 64.
22. *La Gazzetta dello Sport*, 26 April 1949.
23. Ferrari, *Le briglie del successo*, p. 64. Ferrari makes no mention of this episode in his first memoir, *Le mie gioie terribili*, published in 1962, but he talks about it from the second book on, *Le briglie del successo*, published in 1970.
24. Ibid.
25. Ibid. In the last edition of his memoirs, published in 1979 with the title *Ferrari 80*, Enzo would be less severe with himself, removing the word coward, writing only: 'In that moment I understood why man has come up with another word . . .'
26. Ferrari, *Una vita per l'automobile*, pp. 138 and 139.
27. *La Gazzetta dello Sport*, 5 July 1949.
28. Ibid., 12 September 1949.
29. Rancati, *Ferrari che gente*, p. 17. Interview with Giuseppe Busso.
30. Ferrari, *Una vita per l'automobile*, p. 142.
31. Ibid., p. 140.

Revenge

1. *Ferrari: L'opera e il sogno*, Vol. I, p. 69.
2. Cesare De Agostini, *La saga dei Marzotto* (Milan: Giorgio Nada Editore, 2003), p. 54. Marzotto's co-equipier was friend Marco Crosara.
3. Ibid., pp. 41 and 52.

4. *La Gazzetta dello Sport*, 3 May 1950. Scholars have always speculated about why Ferrari did not take part in the maiden race of the F1 World Championship. It seemed to be one of the many secrets of Enzo Ferrari's life destined to remain unexplained. Gozzi himself admitted to the author of this book that he had never known the reasons. But if you read the chronicles of those days in *Gazzetta dello Sport*, you will find the explanation: 'Ferrari has waived this race because his GP 1500 is not ready yet.'

5. Author's conversation with Gianni Rogliatti, 1 October 2009.

6. Rancati, *Ferrari, lui*, p. 54.

7. Author's conversation with Gianni Rogliatti, 1 October 2009.

8. Rancati, *Ferrari, lui*, p. 56.

9. Ibid., p. 55.

10. De Agostini, *La saga dei Marzotto*, pp. 62 and 63. The sculptor was Sergio Reggiani, the artisan, Paolo Fontana.

11. Ibid., p. 63.

12. Ibid.

13. Ibid.

14. Ibid., p. 68.

15. Rancati and Varisco, *Ferrari, che gente*, p. 37. Interview with Gigi Villoresi.

16. Ibid., p. 29. Interview with Pasquale Cassani.

17. Ferrari, *Una vita per l'automobile*, p. 149.

18. Ibid.

19. Author's conversation with Franco Gozzi, 19 May 2009.

20. Round table *Giovan Battista Pininfarina 1893–1993*, Museo dell'Automobile Biscaretti di Ruffia, Turin, 29 October 1993. Speech by Sergio Pininfarina, Minutes, p. 16.

21. *Ferrari: L'opera e il sogno*, Vol. I, p. 99.

22. Author's conversation with Gianni Rogliatti, 1 October 2009.

23. Valerio Castronovo, *Storia della Pininfarina 1930–2005: Un'industria italiana nel mondo* (Rome: Lazerata, 2005), p. 57.

24. Ibid., p. 58. The quotes are by Pinin Farina.

25. Round table, *Pininfarina 1893–1993*, p. 16.

26. Rancati, *Ferrari, lui*, p. 59.

27. *Ferrari: L'opera e il sogno*, Vol. I, p. 91.

28. *La Gazzetta dello Sport*, 1 July 1951.

29. Ibid.

30. Author's conversation with Gianni Rogliatti, 1 October 2009.

31. Rancati, *Ferrari che gente*, p. 33. Interview with Froilán González.

32. Ibid.

33. Ferrari, *Le mie gioie terribili*, p. 41.

34. Ibid. Ferrari wrote: 'I left Alfa to show the Alfa people who I was: an ambitious project, such as to ruin a man!'

35. *La Gazzetta dello Sport*, 14 October 1951. The phrase, as reported, was said to Gianni Brera in an interview published on the front page of *Gazzetta dello Sport* under the headline: 'The Devil among the Elms'. But since he must have loved the expression, Ferrari proposed it again, slightly modified, 11 years later, when for the first time he began writing his memoirs. On p. 41 of *Le mie gioie terribili*, one reads: 'When in '51 Gonzales, in a Ferrari, for the first time in the history of our direct confrontations, left behind the

158 and the whole Alfa team, I wept for joy, but I mixed tears of happiness with tears of sorrow, because that day I thought: "I have *killed* my mother." '

36. *La Gazzetta dello Sport*, 14 October 1951.

37. Ferrari, *Le mie gioie terribili*, p. 41.

38. *La Gazzetta dello Sport*, 17 September 1951. Quite significantly, the headline of Canestrini's story is: 'A Drama and a Triumph.'

39. Ibid., 14 October 1951.

40. Luca Dal Monte, *Il tedesco volante e la leggenda Ferrari* (Milan: Baldini & Castoldi Dalai, 2003), pp. 27 and 28.

On Top of the World

1. *La Gazzetta dello Sport*, 12 October 1951.

2. Ibid., 8 December 1951.

3. Author's conversation with Franco Gozzi, 19 May 2009. Franco Gozzi's wife, Gabriella, shared the particulars with the author.

4. Ibid., 18 December 2009.

5. *La Gazzetta dello Sport*, 14 October 1951.

6. Ibid.

7. Author's conversation with Gianni Rogliatti, 1 October 2009.

8. *La Gazzetta dello Sport*, 14 October 1951.

9. Author's conversation with Gianni Rogliatti, 1 October 2009.

10. *La Gazzetta dello Sport*, 14 October 1951. The quote is by journalist and author Gianni Brera.

11. Ibid.

12. Ibid.

13. Ibid.

14. Author's conversation with Gianni Rogliatti, 1 October 2009.

15. *La Gazzetta dello Sport*, 14 May 1952.

16. Gozzi, *Alla destra del Drake*, p. 49.

17. Author's conversation with Franco Gozzi, 26 May 2009.

18. Gozzi, *Alla destra del Drake*, p. 49.

19. *La Gazzetta dello Sport*, 23 May 1952.

20. Ibid.

21. Ibid., 28 May 1952.

22. *Ferrari: Mito, racconti, realtà: Sessant'anni dalla prima vittoria in Formula 1*, Monograph AISA 95, p. 15. Aurelio Lampredi reported the story.

23. Author's conversation with Franco Gozzi, 26 May 2009. The official race registration document of car number 12 read: 'car name: ferrari spl, driver: alberto ascari, entrant: enzo ferrari.' 'spl' is short for Special. (*Ferrari: L'opera e il sogno*, Vol. 1, p. 114.)

24. Author's conversation with Gianni Rogliatti, 1 October 2009.

25. Ferrari, *Le mie gioie terribili*, page 34.

26. Ibid., page 33.

27. Ibid.

28. Ibid.

29. Round table 'Ascari: Un mito italiano'. Automobile Club of Milan HQ, Milan, 28 May 2005.

30. Ibid.

31. Leonardo Acerbi, *Il nuovo Tutto Ferrari* (Milan: Giorgio Nada Editore 2015), p. 39.

32. *Storia della Pininfarina: 1930–2005*, p. 58.

33. Author's conversation with Franco Gozzi, 21 June 2010.

34. Rancati, *Ferrari, lui*, p. 69.

35. Ferrari, *Le mie gioie terribili*, pp. 105 and 106. When Hawthorn came to Maranello to confer with him, Ferrari realized that the young driver's father, who had accompanied his son to Italy, was a man he had met at Brooklands race track some 30 years earlier.

36. *La Gazzetta dello Sport*, 12 August 1953.

37. Ibid.

38. Ibid.

39. Ibid., 13 August 1953.

40. Cesare De Agostini, *Nuvolari: La leggenda rivive* (Milan: Giorgio Nada Editore, 2003), p. 8.

41. Ferrari, *Le mie gioie terribili*, page 89.

42. *La Gazzetta dello Sport*, 13 August 1953. The quote is by journalist Luigi Gianoli.

43. Author's conversation with Cesare De Agostini, 14 December 2015.

44. *La Gazzetta dello Sport*, 21 September 1953.

45. Ibid., 27 August 1953.

46. Ibid.

47. Author's conversation with Franco Gozzi, 21 July 2010.

48. Author's conversation with Gianni Rogliatti, 1 October 2009.

49. Gozzi, *Enzo Ferrari: La vita, il mito, le manie, le curiosità*, p. 62.

50. Ibid.

51. *Ferrari: L'opera e il sogno*, Vol. 1, p. 135.

52. Ibid., p. 126.

53. Rancati, *Ferrari, lui*, p. 73.

54. *Ferrari: L'opera e il sogno*, Vol. 1, p. 135.

55. Author's conversation with Franco Gozzi, 18 December 2009.

56. *La Gazzetta dello Sport*, 27 August 1953.

57. *Ferrari: Mito, racconti, realtà*, Monograph AISA 95, p. 15.

58. Rancati and Varisco, *Ferrari, che gente*, p. 131. Interview with Angiolino Marchetti.

59. *Ferrari: Mito, racconti, realtà*, Monograph AISA 95, p. 15.

High Treason

1. Rancati, *Ferrari, lui*, p. 72.

2. Ibid.

3. *La Gazzetta dello Sport*, 13 December 1953.

4. Ibid., 1 January 1954.

5. Ibid.

6. Ibid.

7. Author's conversation with Gianni Rogliatti, 1 October 2009.

8. *La Gazzetta dello Sport*, 22 January 1954.

9. Rancati, *Ferrari, lui*, p. 71.

10. Ferrari, *Le mie gioie terribili*, p. 137.
11. Author's conversation with Franco Gozzi, 21 June 2010. Scaglietti was born in 1920 in the tiny village of Tre Olmi, near the Secchia River, on the outskirts of Modena.
12. Dal Monte, *Il tedesco volante e la leggenda Ferrari*, p. 33.
13. Ibid.
14. *La Gazzetta dello Sport*, 29 August 1954.
15. Ibid.
16. *Ferrari: L'opera e il sogno*, Vol. I, p. 156.
17. Paolo Marasca, *Ferrari contro Ford* (The V12 Motor Company, 2009), Vol. 1, p. 28.
18. *Ferrari: L'opera e il sogno*, Vol. I, pp. 155 and 156.
19. Round table *Giovan Battista Pininfarina 1893–1993*, Museo dell'Automobile Biscaretti di Ruffia, Turin, 29 October 1993. Speech by Giovanni Agnelli, Minutes.
20. *Storia della Pininfarina: 1930–2005*, p. 57.
21. Round table *Giovan Battista Pininfarina 1893–1993*. Speech by Gino Rancati, Minutes.
22. *Ferrari: L'opera e il sogno*, Vol. I, p. 151. Ferrari's words come from the opening page of the 1954 Yearbook.
23. Author's conversation with Franco Gozzi, 19 May 2009. Courtesy of Franco Gozzi's wife, Gabriella, who was regularly invited to Dino Ferrari's parties.
24. Ferrari, *Le mie gioie terribili*, p. 58.
25. Ibid., p. 56.
26. Author's conversation with Franco Gozzi, 19 May 2009. Franco Gozzi's wife Gabriella confided to this author that Dino Ferrari often talked about his father, but rarely mentioned his mother.
27. Ferrari, *Le mie gioie terribili*, p. 58.

In Love With Night

1. Author's conversation with Don Sergio Mantovani, 19 February 2010.
2. Ferrari, *Le mie gioie terribili*, p. 202.
3. Ibid., pp. 202 and 203.
4. Author's conversation with Gianni Rogliatti, 1 October 2009.
5. *Ferrari: L'opera e il sogno*, Vol. I, p. 171.
6. Rancati, *Ferrari, lui*, p. 77.
7. Author's conversation with Carlo Benzi, 25 November 2008.
8. Ferrari, *Le mie gioie terribili*, pp. 56 and 57.
9. Franco Gozzi, *L'è Andèda Acsè: Sergio Scaglietti, una leggenda modenese* (Modena: Artioli Editore, 2008), pp. 70 and 71.
10. Author's conversation with Gianni Rogliatti, 1 October 2009.
11. *Una vita dai toni forti: la storia di Vittorio Jano*, by Donatella Biffignandi, Centro di documentazione del Museo Nazionale dell'Automobile di Torino, 2005.
12. Ferrari, *Le mie gioie terribili*, p. 57.
13. Juan Manuel Fangio, *My Twenty Years of Racing* (London: Temple Press Limited, 1962), p. 176.
14. Ibid., p. 177.
15. Rancati, *Ferrari, lui*, p. 83.

16. Author's conversation with Franco Gozzi, 19 May 2009. Once again, the story was narrated to the author by Franco Gozzi's wife, Gabriella.

17. Original document: Enzo Ferrari's taped interview for his first book, *Le mie gioie terribili*, 27 October 1961. Private collection.

18. Ferrari, *Le mie gioie terribili*, p. 58.

19. Rancati, *Ferrari, lui*, p. 84.

20. *La Gazzetta dello Sport*, 2 July 1956.

21. Author's conversation with Carlo Benzi, 25 November 2008.

22. Original document: Card announcing the death of Dino Ferrari, 30 June 1956. Private collection.

23. Author's conversation with Carlo Benzi, 25 November, 2008.

The Odd Couple

1. Rancati, *Ferrari, lui*, p. 83. Gino Rancati's letter is dated 16 July 1956.

2. Ibid., pp. 83 and 84.

3. Fangio, *My Twenty Years of Racing*, p. 180.

4. Ibid.

5. Ibid.

6. Ibid.

7. Ibid., p. 181.

8. Ibid.

9. Ibid.

10. Ibid.

11. Ibid., p. 182.

12. Ferrari, *Le mie gioie terribili*, p. 58.

13. Ibid., p. 46.

14. Ibid., p. 114.

15. Ibid.

16. Author's conversation with Gianni Rogliatti, 1 October 2009.

17. Luca Dal Monte and Umberto Zapelloni *La Rossa e le altre* (Milan: Baldini & Castoldi, 2000), p. 53.

18. Author's conversation with Gianni Rogliatti, 1 October 2009.

19. Author's conversation with Carlo Benzi, 25 November 2008.

20. Rancati, *Ferrari, lui*, p. 85.

21. Ferrari, *Le mie gioie terribili*, p. 57.

22. Giuseppe Allievi, *Il secondo è il primo dei perdenti: Enzo Ferrari in parole sue* (Milan: Rizzoli Libri, 2014), p. 97.

23. Fangio, *My Twenty Years of Racing*, p. 183.

Tragedy

1. Rancati, *Ferrari, lui*, p. 88.

2. Ferrari, *Le mie gioie terribili*, p. 101.

3. Lorenzo Montagner, *De Portago: Il pianto del Drake* (Mantova: Editoriale Sometti, 2007), p. 46.
4. Ferrari, *Le mie gioie terribili*, p. 103.
5. *Visto*, 19 May 1957.
6. Rancati, *Ferrari, lui*, p. 92.
7. Ferrari, *Le mie gioie terribili*, p. 150.
8. Montagner, *De Portago: Il pianto del Drake*, pp. 72 and 73.
9. Rancati and Varisco, *Ferrari, che gente*, p. 50. Interview with Romolo Tavoni.
10. *Il Corriere della Sera*, 16 December 1959.
11. Rancati and Varisco, *Ferrari, che gente*, p. 50. Interview with Romolo Tavoni.
12. *Civiltà Cattolica*, Anno 110, Vol. I, 7 March 1959, Quaderno 2609.
13. Rancati and Varisco, *Ferrari, che gente*, p. 50. Interview with Romolo Tavoni.
14. Author's conversation with Franco Gozzi, 21 June 2010.
15. Ferrari, *Piloti, che gente*, p. 357.
16. Rancati, *Ferrari, lui*, p. 96.
17. *Ferrari: L'opera e il sogno*, Vol. I, p. 204.
18. Gozzi, *L'è Andèda Acsè*, pp. 96 and 97. Ferrari had initially wanted to sell the 250 California only in the US market, but the model's huge success led him to sell it to European clients, as well.
19. *Ferrari: L'opera e il sogno*, Vol. I, p. 210.
20. Ibid.
21. Ibid., p. 211.
22. Gozzi, *L'è Andèda Acsè*, p. 80.
23. Ibid.
24. Author's conversation with Franco Gozzi, 21 June 2010.
25. *Ferrari: L'opera e il sogno*, Vol. I, p. 209.
26. Rancati, *Ferrari, lui*, p. 96.
27. Gianni Cancelliere, Luca Dal Monte, Cesare De Agostini and Lorenzo Ramaciotti, *Maserati: Un secolo di storia*, (Milan: Giorgio Nada Editore 2013), p. 63.
28. Rancati, *Ferrari, lui*, p. 96.
29. Author's conversation with Franco Gozzi, 18 December 2009.
30. Ibid.
31. Ibid. According to Gozzi, this was a favourite Ferrari story.
32. Cancelliere, Dal Monte, De Agostini and Ramaciotti, *Maserati: Un secolo di storia*, p. 64.
33. Author's conversation with Franco Gozzi, 18 December 2009.

The Church vs. Enzo Ferrari

1. *Ferrari: L'opera e il sogno*, Vol. I, p. 209.
2. Author's conversation with Gianni Rogliatti, 1 October 2009.
3. Ferrari, *Le mie gioie terribili*, p. 62.
4. Author's conversation with Franco Gozzi, 21 July 2010.
5. *La Gazzetta dello Sport*, 7 July 1958.
6. Ibid., 10 December 1958.

7. *L'Osservatore Romano*, 9 July 1958. The two-column story was printed on the fourth and last page for a total of ninety-six lines, and had no byline.

8. Ibid.

9. Ibid.

10. Ibid.

11. *La Gazzetta dello Sport*, 13 July 1958.

12. Ibid., 4 August 1958.

13. Author's conversation with Franco Gozzi, 21 July 2010.

14. *Civiltà Cattolica*, Anno 109, Vol. IV, 4 October 1958, Quaderno 2599.

15. Ibid.

16. Ibid.

17. Mike Hawthorn, *Champion Year* (Harvest Hill: Aston Publications, 1959), p. 181.

18. Ibid.

19. Ferrari, *Le mie gioie terribili*, p. 106.

20. Ibid., p. 233.

21. *La Gazzetta dello Sport*, 13 December 1958. As Hawthorn tells in *Champion Year*, regarding his 1958 world title, Queen Elizabeth and Prince Philip invited him for a luncheon at Buckingham Palace on 6 November 1958 (p. 184).

22. *Civiltà Cattolica*, Anno 110, Vol. I, 7 March 1959, Quaderno 2609.

23. *La Gazzetta dello Sport*, 13 December 1958.

24. Ibid.

25. Rancati, *Ferrari, lui*, p. 79.

26. Ibid.

27. *La Gazzetta dello Sport*, 10 December 1958.

28. Ibid.

29. Rancati and Varisco, *Ferrari, che gente*, p. 66.

30. Rancati, *Ferrari, lui*, p. 100.

31. Cesare De Agostini, *Don Ruspa* (Milan: Giorgio Nada Editore, 2015), p. 95.

32. Ferrari, *Le mie gioie terribili*, p. 232.

33. *Civiltà Cattolica*, Anno 110, Vol. I, 7 March 1959, Quaderno 2609.

34. Ibid.

35. Ibid.

36. Ibid.

The Ferrarina

1. Tony Brooks, *Poetry in Motion* (Croydon: Motor Racing Publications, Ltd, 2012), p. 175.

2. Ibid., p. 221.

3. Ibid., p. 175.

4. Montagner, *De Portago: Il pianto del Drake*, p. 86.

5. Ibid.

6. Author's conversation with Gianni Rogliatti, 1 October 2009.

7. *Ferrari: L'opera e il sogno*, Vol. I, p. 253.

8. Montagner, *De Portago: Il pianto del Drake*, p. 90.

9. Brooks, *Poetry in Motion*, p. 177.

10. Montagner, *De Portago: Il pianto del Drake*, p. 87.

11. Ibid.

12. Brooks, *Poetry in Motion*, p. 201.

13. Montagner, *De Portago: Il pianto del Drake*, p. 89.

14. Ibid., p. 94.

15. Brooks, *Poetry in Motion*, p. 219.

16. *Il Corriere della Sera*, 30 December 1959.

17. Original document: Enzo Ferrari Press Conference, Minutes, 29 December 1959. Private collection.

18. Ibid.

19. Ibid.

20. Rancati, *Ferrari, lui*, p. 104. A long time before the Dino was built, Ferrari managed to get the attention of Italian automaker Innocenti in regard to a small sports car powered by a small-displacement Ferrari engine. The project came to nothing because of the Alfa Romeo opposition.

Acquitted

1. Montagner, *De Portago: Il pianto del Drake*, pp. 80 and 81. The direct quotes come from Lorenzo Montagner's book, written after long interviews with former deputy prosecutor Mario Luberto.

2. Ibid., p. 83.

3. Author's conversation with Carlo Benzi, 25 November 2008.

4. Author's conversation with Ermanno Cozza, 15 October 2008.

5. Rancati, *Ferrari, lui*, p. 105.

6. *Ferrari: L'opera e il sogno*, Vol. I, pp. 275 and 276.

7. Rancati, *Ferrari, lui*, p. 106.

8. Author's conversation with Franco Gozzi, 21 July 2010. Ferrari had not hired Gozzi yet.

9. Ferrari, *Le mie gioie terribili*, pp. 67 and 68.

10. Rancati, *Ferrari, lui*, p. 7.

11. *Ferrari: L'opera e il sogno*, Vol. I, pp. 276 and 277.

12. Ibid., p. 270. The cars produced were 306; the employees were 367.

13. Rancati, *Ferrari, lui*, p. 109.

14. Lamm, *Phil Hill's 1961 Championship Season in His Own Words*. Notes expressly given by Mr. Lamm to the author for this book, p. 2.

15. Ibid.

16. Montagner, *De Portago: Il pianto del Drake*, p. 96.

17. Ibid.

18. Rancati, *Ferrari, lui*, p. 7.

19. Ferrari, *Le mie gioie terribili*, p. 238.

20. Lamm, *Phil Hill's 1961 Championship Season in His Own Words*, p. 4.

21. Ferrari, *Le mie gioie terribili*, p. 117.

22. Lamm, *Phil Hill's 1961 Championship Season*, p. 5.

23. *La Gazzetta dello Sport*, 1 December 1961.

24. Author's conversation with Giulio Borsari, 16 February 2009.

25. Author's conversation with Carlo Benzi, 25 November 2008.

26. Rancati and Varisco, *Ferrari, che gente*, p. 80. Interview with Romolo Tavoni.

27. Ibid.
28. *La Gazzetta dello Sport*, 1 December 1961.
29. Rancati, *Ferrari, lui*, p. 98.
30. Author's conversation with Franco Gozzi, 21 July 2010.
31. Author's conversation with Gianni Rogliatti, 1 October 2009.
32. Rancati, *Ferrari, lui*, p. 122.

'My Terrible Joys'

1. Marasca, *Ferrari contro Ford*, pp. 43 and 44. Interview with Mauro Forghieri.
2. Author's conversation with Carlo Benzi, 25 November 2008.
3. Rancati and Varisco, *Ferrari, che gente*, p. 80. Interview with Romolo Tavoni.
4. Author's conversation with Fiamma Breschi, 6 April 2011.
5. Ibid.
6. Author's conversation with Franco Gozzi, 21 July 2010.
7. Author's conversation with Gianni Rogliatti, 1 October 2009.
8. *Ferrari: L'opera e il sogno*, Vol. I, p. 303.
9. Gozzi, *L'è Andèda Acsè: Sergio Scaglietti una leggenda modenese*, p. 115.
10. Ferrari, *Piloti, che gente*, p. 355.
11. Author's conversation with Stirling Moss, 18 June 2014.
12. Ibid., p. 61. Interview with Mauro Forghieri.
13. Author's conversation with Franco Gozzi, 21 June 2010.
14. Author's conversation with Fiamma Breschi, 6 April 2011.
15. *Ferrari: L'opera e il sogno*, Vol. I, p. 315.
16. Original document: Enzo Ferrari Press Conference, Minutes, 1 December 1962. Private collection.
17. Ibid.
18. Ibid.
19. Ibid.
20. Ferrari, *Le mie gioie terribili*, p. 11.
21. Ibid.
22. Ibid., p. 6.
23. Ibid., p. 7.
24. Original document: Enzo Ferrari Press Conference, Minutes, 1 December 1962. Private collection.
25. Author's conversation with Fiamma Breschi, 6 April 2011.
26. Author's conversation with Franco Gozzi, 19 May 2009.
27. Gian Paolo Ormezzano, *Pronto, qui Enzo Ferrari* (Milan: Limina, 2012), pp. 21 and 22.
28. Ibid., pp. 23 and 24.
29. Ibid., pp. 25 and 26.
30. Marasca, *Ferrari contro Ford*, p. 77.
31. Author's conversation with Franco Gozzi, 19 May 2009.
32. Ferrari, *Le mie gioie terribili*, p. 7.
33. Ferrari, *Le briglie del successo*, p. 2.
34. *Le Figaro Litteraire*, 9 July 1964.

American Dream

1. Original document: Ferrari Press Release, 12 January 1963. Private collection.
2. Author's conversation with Franco Gozzi, 21 July 2010.
3. A. J. Baime, *Go Like Hell* (Boston: Mariner Books, 2010), p. 104.
4. Author's conversation with Franco Gozzi, 21 July 2010.
5. Ibid.
6. Ferrari, *Le mie gioie terribili*, p. 205.
7. Ibid., p. 205.
8. Ibid., pp. 205 and 206.
9. Ibid., p. 206.
10. Ibid.
11. Ferrari, *Le mie gioie terribili*, p. 206.
12. Marasca, *Ferrari contro Ford*, p. 90. Interview with Mauro Forghieri.
13. Baime, *Go Like Hell*, page 107.
14. Ferrari, *Le mie gioie terribili*, p. 207.
15. Ibid., p. 206.
16. Ibid., pp. 207 and 208.
17. Ibid.
18. Ibid., p. 208.
19. Gozzi, *Alla destra del Drake*, p. 79.
20. Ferrari, *Le mie gioie terribili*, p. 208.
21. Ibid., pp. 208 and 209.
22. Author's conversation with Franco Gozzi, 21 July 2010.
23. Ferrari, *Le mie gioie terribili*, p. 209.
24. Gozzi, *Alla destra del Drake*, p. 77.
25. Author's conversation with Franco Gozzi, 21 July 2010.
26. Ibid.
27. Ferrari, *Le mie gioie terribili*, p. 209.
28. Gozzi, *Alla destra del Drake*, p. 79.
29. Marasca, *Ferrari contro Ford*, pp. 61 and 62. Interview with Mauro Forghieri. In addition to Carlo Chiti, four other of the eight executives who had been fired in 1961 had ended up at ATS: Bizzarrini, Gardini, Selmi and Tavoni.
30. *Ferrari: L'opera e il sogno*, Vol. I, p. 326.
31. Original document: Enzo Ferrari Press Conference, Minutes, 11 January 1964. Private collection.
32. Danilo Castellarin, *Temerari* (Milan: Giorgio Nada Editore, 2014), p. 265. Interview with John Surtees.
33. Original document: Enzo Ferrari Press Conference, Minutes, 12 December 1964. Private collection.
34. Ibid.
35. Ibid.
36. Ibid.
37. Ferrari, *Le briglie del successo*, p. 239.
38. Original document: Enzo Ferrari Press Conference, Minutes, 12 December 1964. Private collection.

39. Ibid.
40. Ibid.
41. Ferrari, *Le briglie del successo*, p. 240.
42. Ibid., p. 240.
43. *Il Corriere della Sera*, 23 March 2009.
44. Ferrari, *Le briglie del successo*, p. 241.
45. Marasca, *Ferrari contro Ford*, p. 160.
46. Original document: Enzo Ferrari Press Conference, Minutes, 12 December 1964. Private collection.

David and Goliath

1. Baime, *Go Like Hell*, p. 110.
2. Marasca, *Ferrari contro Ford*, pp. 149 and 150.
3. Ibid., pp. 150 and 151.
4. Original document: Ferrari Press Release: 1 March 1965. Private collection.
5. Marasca, *Ferrari contro Ford*, p. 187.
6. Author's conversation with Franco Gozzi, 21 June 2010.
7. Author's conversation with Carlo Benzi, 25 November 2008.
8. Author's conversation with Franco Gozzi, 19 May 2009.
9. Ibid., p. 224.
10. Ibid., pp. 239 and 240.
11. Author's conversation with Franco Gozzi, 19 May 2009.
12. Piero Ferrari with Leo Turrini *Ferrari, mio padre* (Reggio Emilia: Aliberti Editore, 2007) p. 31.
13. Daniele Buzzonetti and Mauro Forghieri *Mauro Forghieri: 30 anni di Ferrari e oltre* (Florence: Giunti Editore, 2008), p. 63.
14. *Ferrari: L'opera e il sogno*, Vol. I, p. 379.
15. Round Table *Giovan Battista Pininfarina 1893–1993*, Museo dell'Automobile Biscaretti di Ruffia, Turin, 29 October 1993. Speech by Sergio Pininfarina. Minutes.
16. Castellarin, *Temerari*, p. 272. Interview with John Surtees.
17. Ibid., p. 271. Interview with John Surtees.
18. Gozzi, *Alla destra del Drake*, pp. 80 and 81.
19. Original document: Enzo Ferrari Press Conference, Minutes, 13 December 1966. Private collection.
20. Author's conversation with Franco Gozzi, 21 July 2010.
21. Author's conversation with Giulio Borsari, 27 August 2009.
22. *La Gazzetta dello Sport*, 18 June 1966.
23. *Ferrari: L'opera e il sogno*, Vol. I, pp. 391 and 392.
24. Author's conversation with Franco Gozzi, 21 July 2010.
25. Ibid., 18 December 2009.
26. *La Gazzetta dello Sport*, 23 June 1966.
27. Ibid.
28. Allievi, *Il secondo è il primo dei perdenti*, p. 118.
29. Ferrari, draft of an article by Giorgio Torelli, 1967.
30. Ibid.

31. Buzzonetti and Forghieri, *Mauro Forghieri: 30 anni di Ferrari e oltre*, p. 84.
32. Ibid., pp. 84 and 85.
33. Original document: Enzo Ferrari Press Conference, Minutes, 13 December 1966. Private collection.
34. Author's conversation with Franco Gozzi, 21 July 2010.
35. Original document: Enzo Ferrari Press Conference, Minutes, 13 December 1966. Private collection.

Turin

1. Original document: Enzo Ferrari Press Conference, Minutes, 13 December 1966. Private collection.
2. Rancati, *Ferrari, lui*, p. 150.
3. Ibid.; Author's conversation with Dino Tagliazucchi, 2 December 2008.
4. Original document: Enzo Ferrari Press Conference, Minutes, 13 December 1966. Private collection.
5. Ferrari, *Le mie gioie terribili*, p. 68.
6. *La Gazzetta dello Sport*, 14 December 1966.
7. Author's conversation with Franco Gozzi, 18 December 2009.
8. Ibid. Few knew, and even fewer would remember it, but Lini's idea was to demonstrate not only the superiority of Ferrari, but of the European automotive industry at large, and he had therefore asked Porsche's team manager to align two German cars in fourth and fifth place just behind the three Ferraris.
9. Original document: Enzo Ferrari Press Conference, Minutes, 13 December 1966. Private collection.
10. Ferrari, draft of an article by Giorgio Torelli, 1967.
11. Author's conversation with Giulio Borsari, 27 December 2009.
12. Ferrari, draft of an article by Giorgio Torelli, 1967.
13. Author's conversation with Dino Tagliazucchi, 2 December 2008.
14. Ferrari, draft of an article by Giorgio Torelli, 1967.
15. Ibid.
16. Ibid.
17. Ibid.
18. Ibid.
19. Author's conversation with Dino Tagliazucchi, 2 December 2008
20. Ferrari, *Le briglie del successo*, p. 132.
21. Private conversation between Enzo Ferrari and Pino Allievi, 20 November 1987.
22. Acerbi, *Il nuovo Tutto Ferrari*, p. 197.
23. Author's conversation with Gianni Rogliatti, 1 October 2009.
24. Ferrari, *Le briglie del successo*, p. 240.
25. *Ferrari: L'opera e il sogno*, Vol. I, p. 422.
26. Ibid., p. 435.
27. Ibid., pp. 437 and 439.
28. Author's conversation with Franco Gozzi, 18 December 2009.
29. Original document: Enzo Ferrari Press Conference, Minutes, 14 December 1968. Private collection.

30. Ibid.
31. Buzzonetti and Forghieri, *Mauro Forghieri: 30 anni di Ferrari e oltre*, pp. 95 and 96.
32. Ferrari, *Le briglie del successo*, p. 241.
33. Ibid.
34. *Ferrari: L'opera e il sogno*, Vol. I, p. 437.
35. Author's conversation with Franco Gozzi, 18 December 2009.
36. Buzzonetti and Forghieri, *Mauro Forghieri: 30 anni di Ferrari e oltre*, p. 94.
37. Ibid., p. 102.
38. Ibid., p. 111.
39. Author's conversation with Carlo Benzi, 25 November 2008.
40. Ibid.
41. *La Stampa*, 30 April 1969.
42. Original document: Enzo Ferrari Press Conference, Minutes, 14 December 1968. Private collection.
43. Ibid.
44. Author's conversation with Dino Tagliazucchi, 2 December 2008.
45. Ferrari, *Le briglie del successo*, p. 245.
46. Ibid., p. 242.
47. Author's conversation with Franco Gozzi, 21 July 2010.
48. Ferrari, *Le briglie del successo*, p. 245.
49. Rancati, *Ferrari, lui*, p. 148.
50. Author's conversation with Carlo Benzi, 25 November 2008.
51. Ferrari, *Le briglie del successo*, p. 245.

Evening Shadows

1. Rancati, *Ferrari, lui*, p. 147.
2. Ibid.
3. Buzzonetti and Forghieri, *Mauro Forghieri: 30 anni di Ferrari e oltre*, p. 117.
4. Acerbi, *Il nuovo Tutto Ferrari*, p. 207.
5. *Ferrari: L'opera e il sogno*, Vol. I, p. 457.
6. Author's conversation with Dino Tagliazucchi, 2 December 2008.
7. Author's conversation with Franco Gozzi, 26 May 2009.
8. Ibid.
9. Author's conversation with Dino Tagliazucchi, 2 December 2008.
10. Ibid.
11. Ibid.
12. Ferrari, draft of an article by Giorgio Torelli, 1967.
13. Ferrari, *Le briglie del successo*, p. 249.
14. Ibid.
15. Author's conversation with Dino Tagliazucchi, 2 December 2008.
16. Ferrari, *Ferrari 80*, p. 105.
17. Buzzonetti and Forghieri, *Mauro Forghieri: 30 anni di Ferrari e oltre*, pp. 122 and 123.
18. Author's conversation with Franco Gozzi, 26 May 2009.
19. Buzzonetti and Forghieri, *Mauro Forghieri: 30 anni di Ferrari e oltre*, p. 137.
20. Ibid., p. 125.

21. Author's conversation with Franco Gozzi, 26 May 2009.
22. Original document: Enzo Ferrari Press Conference, Minutes, 2 December 1972. Private collection.
23. *Ferrari: L'opera e il sogno*, Vol. I, pp. 531 and 533.
24. Author's conversation with Carlo Benzi, 25 November 2008.
25. *Ferrari: L'opera e il sogno*, Vol. I, p. 535.
26. Author's conversation with Franco Gozzi, 26 May 2009.
27. *Ferrari: L'opera e il sogno*, Vol. I, pp. 549 and 551.
28. Author's conversation with Giulio Borsari, 27 August 2009.
29. Buzzonetti and Forghieri, *Mauro Forghieri: 30 anni di Ferrari e oltre*, p. 142.
30. Author's conversation with Carlo Benzi, 25 November 2008.
31. *Il Corriere della Sera*, 9 September 1974.
32. Ibid., 11 September 1974.
33. Ibid., 18 September 1974.
34. Buzzonetti and Forghieri, *Mauro Forghieri: 30 anni di Ferrari e oltre*, p. 145.
35. *Il Corriere della Sera*, 8 October 1974.
36. Ibid., 9 September 1974.

The Grand Old Man

1. *La Gazzetta dello Sport*, 4 January 1975.
2. Dal Monte, *La Rossa e le altre*, p. 166.
3. *La Gazzetta dello Sport*, 31 January 1975.
4. Ibid., 11 January 1975.
5. Ibid.
6. Ibid.
7. Dal Monte, *La Rossa e le altre*, p. 168.
8. Author's conversation with Giulio Borsari, 27 August 2009.
9. *La Gazzetta dello Sport*, 11 May 1975.
10. Author's conversation with Giulio Borsari, 27 August 2009.
11. Author's conversation with Franco Gozzi, 21 July 2010.
12. *La Gazzetta dello Sport*, 27 May 1975.
13. Dal Monte, *La rossa e le altre*, p. 168.
14. Buzzonetti and Forghieri, *Mauro Forghieri: 30 anni di Ferrari e oltre*, p. 190.
15. *Il Corriere della Sera*, 14 August 1975.
16. Ibid., 2 September 1975.
17. Ibid., 5 September 1975.
18. Ibid.
19. *Il Corriere della Sera*, 7 September 1975.
20. Ibid., 8 September 1975.
21. Ibid., 9 September 1975.
22. Author's conversation with Franco Gozzi, 21 June 2010.
23. *Il Corriere della Sera*, 8 September 1975.
24. Ibid.
25. Ibid.
26. Ibid., 10 September 1975.

27. Ibid.
28. Author's conversation with Franco Gozzi, 18 December 2009.
29. *Il Corriere della Sera*, 10 September 1975.
30. Author's conversation with Franco Gozzi, 19 May 2009.
31. *Il Corriere della Sera*, 10 September 1975.
32. Author's conversation with Franco Gozzi, 19 May 2009.
33. *Il Corriere della Sera*, 10 September 1975.
34. Ibid.
35. Ibid.
36. Ibid., 12 September 1975.
37. Author's conversation with Franco Gozzi, 19 May 2009.
38. *Il Corriere della Sera*, 26 October 1975.
39. Ibid., 27 October 1975.
40. Author's conversation with Franco Gozzi, 21 July 2010.
41. *Il Corriere della Sera*, 26 October 1975.
42. Ibid., 14 August 1975.
43. Ibid., 26 October 1975.
44. Ibid.
45. Author's conversation with Franco Gozzi, 21 July 2010.
46. *Il Corriere della Sera*, 20 November 1975.
47. Ibid., 21 November 1975.

Interlude

1. *Il Corriere della Sera*, 9 September 1975.
2. Ibid.
3. Ibid., 9 December 1975.
4. Ibid.
5. Ibid.
6. Author's conversation with Carlo Benzi, 25 November 2008.
7. Author's conversation with Franco Gozzi, 21 July 2010.
8. *Il Corriere della Sera*, 9 December 1975.
9. Ibid., 31 December 1975.
10. Ibid.
11. Ibid.
12. Ibid.
13. Author's conversation with Giulio Borsari, 27 August 2009.
14. Author's conversation with Franco Gozzi, 18 December 2009.
15. *Il Corriere della Sera*, 29 April 1976.
16. Ibid., 9 May 1976.
17. Ibid.
18. Ibid., 12 May 1976.
19. Ibid.
20. Ibid.
21. Ibid., 27 May 1976.
22. Ibid.

23. Ibid., 9 June 1976.
24. Ibid.
25. Ibid.
26. Author's conversation with Carlo Benzi, 25 November 2008.
27. *Il Corriere della Sera*, 9 June 1976.
28. Ibid.
29. Ibid.
30. Author's conversation with Dino Tagliazucchi, 2 December 2008.
31. *Il Giornale*, 10 September 1976.
32. Author's conversation with Franco Gozzi, 18 December 2009.
33. Author's conversation with Dino Tagliazucchi, 2 December 2008.
34. Ibid.
35. *Il Corriere della Sera*, 7 July 1976.
36. Ibid., 20 July 1976.
37. Ibid.
38. Ibid. C S A I was the Sporting Committee of the Automobile Club of Italy.
39. Ibid.
40. Ibid.
41. Author's conversation with Giulio Borsari, 16 February 2009.
42. *Il Corriere della Sera*, 20 July 1976.
43. Ibid.
44. Ibid.

The Long Hot Summer

1. Author's conversation with Franco Gozzi, 18 December 2009.
2. *La Gazzetta dello Sport*, 27 August 2009.
3. *Il Giornale*, 3 August 1976.
4. *La Gazzetta dello Sport*, 3 August 1976.
5. *Il Giornale*, 3 August 1976.
6. Ibid., 5 August 1976.
7. Ibid., 6 August 1976.
8. Author's conversation with Franco Gozzi, 18 December 2009.
9. *Il Giornale*, 6 August 1976.
10. Ibid.
11. Author's conversation with Franco Gozzi, 18 December 2009.
12. Author's conversation with Gianni Rogliatti, 1 October 2009.
13. *Il Giornale*, 8 August 1976.
14. Ibid., 12 August 1976.
15. Ibid., 8 August 1976.
16. Ibid., 12 August 1976.
17. Ibid., 7 August 1976.
18. Ibid., 11 August 1976.
19. Author's conversation with Franco Gozzi, 18 December 2009.
20. *La Gazzetta dello Sport*, 15 August 1976.
21. *Il Giornale*, 15 August 1976.

22. Author's conversation with Franco Gozzi, 18 December 2009.

23. *Il Giornale*, 15 August 1976.

24. *Autosprint*, X-Files. Daniele Audetto.

25. *Il Giornale*, 17 August 1976. Journalist Enrico Benzing wrote in the columns of the Milanese newspaper: 'It is said that Peterson was at the origin of the post-Nurburgring decision, and that he created so strong a contrast between Ferrari and the managers at Fiat [that it led to the decision on] withdrawal.' Franco Gozzi confirmed this version of events to the author on 18 December 2009.

26. *Il Giornale*, 22 August 1976.

27. *La Gazzetta dello Sport*, 27 August 1976.

28. Original document: Ferrari Press Release, 23 August 1976.

29. Author's conversation with Franco Gozzi, 18 December 2009.

30. Original document: Ferrari Press Release, 23 August 1976.

31. *La Gazzetta dello Sport*, 27 August 1976.

32. Original document: Ferrari Press Release, 1 September 1976.

33. *Il Giornale*, 2 September 1976.

34. *Il Corriere della Sera*, 4 September 1976.

35. Author's conversation with Franco Gozzi, 18 December 2009.

36. *Il Corriere della Sera*, 8 September 1976.

37. Ibid. Enzo's behaviour would cost Clay a seat on a prominent team in 1977. Ronnie Peterson had just signed with Tyrrell, and Jody Scheckter with Wolf. At that moment, Clay could still have taken Reutemann's place at Brabham. But in the absence of certainty, Bernie Ecclestone would soon sign John Watson.

38. Ibid.

39. Ibid.

40. Ibid.

41. *Il Giornale*, 8 September 1976.

42. Ibid., 10 September 1976.

43. *Il Corriere della Sera*, 13 September 1976.

Purple Rain

1. *La Gazzetta dello Sport*, 24 September 1976.

2. *Il Corriere della Sera*, 26 September 1976.

3. Ibid., 13 October 1976.

4. Ibid., 18 October 1976.

5. Author's conversation with Franco Gozzi, 19 May 2009.

6. *Il Corriere della Sera*, 18 October 1976.

7. Ibid., 8 October 1976.

8. Ibid., 26 October 1976.

9. *La Gazzetta dello Sport*, 26 October 1976.

10. *Il Corriere della Sera*, 25 October 1976.

11. Ibid.

12. Ibid., 26 October 1976.

13. Ibid.

14. *La Stampa*, 27 October 1976.

15. Ibid.

16. Ibid.

17. *Il Giornale*, 27 October 1976.

18. *Il Corriere della Sera*, 26 October 1976.

19. *Il Giornale*, 27 October 1976.

20. Ibid.

21. Ibid.

22. Ibid., 28 October 1976.

23. Ibid.

24. Ibid.

25. Ibid.

26. Ibid.

27. Ibid.

28. Ibid.

29. Ibid.

30. *La Stampa*, 27 October 1976.

31. Ibid.

32. *La Gazzetta dello Sport*, 30 October 1976.

33. Ibid., 1 November 1976.

34. Niki Lauda, *I miei anni con Ferrari* (Florence: Editoriale Olimpia, 1979), pp. 63 and 64.

35. *La Gazzetta dello Sport*, 1 November 1976.

36. Ibid., 21 November 1976.

Paradise Lost

1. *La Gazzetta dello Sport*, 11 November 1976.

2. Gozzi, *Enzo Ferrari: La vita, il mito, le manie, le curiosità*, pp. 75–80.

3. *Il Corriere della Sera*, 27 April 1976.

4. *La Gazzetta dello Sport*, 21 November 1976.

5. Ibid.

6. Ibid., 11 December 1976.

7. *Il Corriere della Sera*, 31 December 1976.

8. Ibid., 9 January 1977.

9. Ibid., 12 January 1977.

10. Ibid., 20 March 1977.

11. Ibid.

12. Ibid., 8 May 1977.

13. Ibid., 17 May 1977.

14. Ibid., 23 September 1977.

15. Ibid., 1 July 1977.

16. Ibid., 30 August 1977.

17. Ibid., 19 August 1977.

18. Ibid., 23 August 1977.

19. Ibid., 28 August 1977.

20. Author's conversation with Piero Ferrari, 13 November 2012.

21. Ibid.

22. *Il Corriere della Sera*, 15 September 1977.
23. Author's conversation with Piero Ferrari, 13 November 2012.
24. *Il Corriere della Sera*, 30 August 1977.
25. Ibid., 15 September 1977.
26. Ibid.
27. Original document: Ferrari Press Release, 29 August 1977.
28. *Il Corriere della Sera*, 30 August 1977.
29. Ibid., 15 September 1977.
30. Ibid.
31. Ibid.
32. Ibid.
33. Ibid.
34. Ibid.
35. Ibid., 28 September 1977.
36. Gerald Donaldson *Gilles Villeneuve: La vita di un pilota leggendario* (Milan: Giorgio Nada Editore, 1990), p. 115.
37. *Il Corriere della Sera*, 28 September 1977.
38. Donaldson, *Gilles Villeneuve*, pp. 109 and 110.
39. Author's conversation with Franco Gozzi, 26 May 2009.
40. Donaldson, *Gilles Villeneuve*, p. 110.
41. *Il Corriere della Sera*, 22 September 1977.
42. Ibid., 11 July 1978.
43. Ibid., 23 September 1977.
44. Ibid., 29 September 1977.
45. Ibid., 25 October 1977.
46. Ibid. When journalist friend Nestore Morosini asked about replacing Villeneuve, Ferrari said: 'With whom?'
47. Author's conversation with Franco Gozzi, 26 May 2009.
48. *Il Corriere della Sera*, 13 November 1977.

The Last Hurrah

1. *Il Corriere della Sera*, 13 November 1977.
2. Ibid.
3. *La Gazzetta dello Sport*, 16 January 1978.
4. *Il Resto del Carlino*, 1 March 1978.
5. Ferrari, *Ferrari 80*, p. 214.
6. Rancati, *Ferrari, l'unico*, page 180.
7. Author's conversation with Carlo Benzi, 25 November 2008.
8. Rancati, *Ferrari, l'unico*, p. 129.
9. Ibid.
10. *Il Corriere della Sera*, 19 June 1978.
11. Author's conversation with Franco Gozzi, 26 May 2009.
12. Ibid.
13. Rancati and Varisco, *Ferrari, che gente*, p. 199.
14. *Il Corriere della Sera*, 29 August 1978.

15. Ibid., 7 September 1978.
16. Ibid.
17. Ibid., 10 October 1978.
18. Gozzi, *Enzo Ferrari: La vita, il mito, le manie, le curiosità*, p. 53.
19. Gianni Cancellieri and Cesare De Agostini, *33 anni di Gran Premi iridati* Vol. 2 (Bologna: Luciano Conti Editore, 1983), p. 277.
20. *Autosprint*, 23 January 1979.
21. Cancellieri and De Agostini, *33 anni di Gran Premi iridati*, p. 277.
22. *La Gazzetta dello Sport*, 6 March 1979.
23. Ibid., 4 March 1979.
24. Ibid., 10 April 1979.
25. Ibid.
26. Ibid., 4 May 1979.
27. Ibid., 11 September 1979.
28. Ibid., 15 May 1979.
29. Author's conversation with Franco Gozzi, 26 May 2009.
30. Nunzia Manicardi, *Pionieri dell'automobile: Lancia, Bazzi, Ferrari* (Kindle Edition, 2014).
31. Author's conversation with Franco Gozzi, 26 May 2009.
32. Rancati, *Ferrari, l'unico*, p. 181.
33. Author's conversation with Dino Tagliazucchi, 2 December 2008.
34. Author's conversation with Franco Gozzi, 26 May 2009.
35. *La Gazzetta dello Sport*, 1 December 1979.
36. Author's conversation with Franco Gozzi, 26 May 2009.
37. *La Gazzetta dello Sport*, 29 August 1979.
38. Ibid.
39. Ibid.
40. Ibid., 30 August 1979.
41. Ibid., 11 September 1979.
42. Author's conversation with Franco Gozzi, 26 May 2009.
43. *La Gazzetta dello Sport*, 20 October 1979.

The Patriarch

1. *La Gazzetta dello Sport*, 11 September 1979.
2. Ibid.
3. Author's conversation with Franco Gozzi, 26 May 2009.
4. *La Gazzetta dello Sport*, 28 August 1979.
5. Ibid., 20 October 1979.
6. Ibid., 29 September 1979. 'I am like a painter who has lost his inspiration,' said Lauda. 'I don't paint any longer.'
7. Ferrari, *Le mie gioie terribili*, p. 277.
8. *Il Resto del Carlino*, 10 October 1979. The desecration of Dino's tomb was discovered by a woman who happened to walk in front of the Ferrari chapel a little before 9am.
9. Author's conversation with Dino Tagliazucchi, 2 December 2008.
10. *Il Resto del Carlino*, 10 October 1979.

11. Author's conversation with Dino Tagliazucchi, 2 December 2008.

12. Ibid.

13. *Il Resto del Carlino*, Modena edition, 10 October 1979.

14. Author's conversation with Carlo Benzi, 25 November 2008.

15. *Il Resto del Carlino*, 20 October 1979.

16. *La Gazzetta dello Sport*, 20 October 1979.

17. *Il Resto del Carlino*, 20 October 1979.

18. Ibid.

19. *La Gazzetta dello Sport*, 20 October 1979.

20. Ibid.

21. Author's conversation with Franco Gozzi, 18 December 2009.

22. Ferrari, *Ferrari 80*, p. 5.

23. Ibid., p. 108.

24. Ibid.

25. Ibid., p. 109.

26. Author's conversation with Franco Gozzi, 18 December 2009. On the final page of *Ferrari 80* Enzo wrote: 'I could not have imagined that in the prize for notoriety that I have always paid in my life there was also the destruction of the tomb in which, twenty-four years ago, I buried my son Dino.'

27. Ferrari, *Ferrari 80*, p. 113.

28. Ibid.

29. *La Gazzetta dello Sport*, 16 September 1980.

30. Ibid.

31. Ibid., 10 July 1980.

32. Ibid., 16 July 1980.

33. Ibid., 23 July 1980. The next day journalist Athos Evangelisti wrote that Ferrari was an 'eighty-two-year-old young man.'

34. *La Gazzetta dello Sport*, 23 July 1980.

35. Ibid.

36. Ibid., 16 September 1980.

37. Ibid.

38. Original document: Enzo Ferrari Press Conference, Minutes, 15 September 1980. Private collection.

39. *La Gazzetta dello Sport*, 16 September 1980.

40. Original document: Transcript of a Ferrari Gestione Sportiva meeting, 17 September 1980. Internal communication from EF to UD/DT/UT/US/UE/GES/USP, 9/17/80. Private collection.

41. Ibid.

42. Author's conversation with Franco Gozzi, 18 December 2009.

43. Cancellieri and De Agostini, *33 anni di gran premi iridati*, p. 301.

44. Original document: Enzo Ferrari Press Conference, Minutes, 15 September 1980. Private collection.

45. Ibid.

46. *La Gazzetta dello Sport*, 23 July 1980.

47. Ibid., 20 January 1981.

48. Ibid., 21 January 1981.

49. Ibid.
50. Ibid.
51. Ibid., 20 January 1981.
52. Joint press release, 19 January 1981.
53. *La Gazzetta dello Sport*, 20 January 1981.
54. Ibid., 21 January 1981.
55. Ibid., 20 January 1981.

Twenty-Seven Red

1. *La Gazzetta dello Sport*, 1 May 1981.
2. Ibid., 1 June 1981.
3. Ibid., 2 June 1981.
4. Ibid.
5. Ibid., 23 June 1981.
6. Donaldson, *Gilles Villeneuve*, pp. 288–90.
7. Ibid., p. 295.
8. Original document: Enzo Ferrari Press Conference, Minutes, 23 October 1981. Private collection.
9. Ibid.
10. *Ferrari: L'opera e il sogno*, Vol. 2, p. 97.
11. Ibid., p. 98.
12. Original document: Enzo Ferrari Press Conference, Minutes, 15 September 1980. Private collection.
13. Ferrari, *Piloti, che gente*, p. 323.
14. *La Gazzetta dello Sport*, 19 March 1982.
15. Original document: Enzo Ferrari Press Conference, Minutes, 23 October 1981. Private collection.
16. *La Gazzetta dello Sport*, 19 March 1982.
17. Original document: Enzo Ferrari Press Conference, Minutes, 23 October 1981. Private collection.
18. *Ferrari: L'opera e il sogno*, Vol. 2, p. 106.
19. *La Gazzetta dello Sport*, 26 April 1982.
20. Ibid., 19 March 1982.
21. Ibid., 26 April 1982.
22. Author's conversation with Piero Ferrari, 13 November 2012.
23. *La Gazzetta dello Sport*, 28 April 1982.
24. Ibid.
25. Ibid., 29 April 1982.
26. Author's conversation with Franco Gozzi, 18 December 2009.
27. Donaldson, *Gilles Villeneuve*, p. 314.
28. Ibid., p. 319.
29. Author's conversation with Carlo Benzi, 25 November 2008.
30. Donaldson, *Gilles Villeneuve*, p. 321.
31. *Il Corriere della Sera*, 9 May 1982.
32. Donaldson, *Gilles Villeneuve*, p. 327.

33. Author's conversation with Franco Gozzi, 18 December 2009.
34. Original document: Enzo Ferrari Press Conference, Minutes, 23 October 1981. Private collection.
35. Author's conversation with Franco Gozzi, 18 December 2009.
36. Ibid.
37. *Autosprint: Legends*, 12 March 2013.
38. Original document: Enzo Ferrari Press Conference, Minutes, 29 August 1984. Private collection.

Michele

1. *La Gazzetta dello Sport*, 17 February 1985.
2. Author's conversation with Franco Gozzi, 18 December 2009.
3. *Ferrari: L'opera e il sogno*, Vol. 2, pp. 111 and 112.
4. Author's conversation with Franco Gozzi, 18 December 2009.
5. Rancati, *Ferrari, l'unico*, p. 189.
6. Ibid., pp. 190 and 191.
7. *La Gazzetta dello Sport*, 22 October 1983.
8. Rancati, *Ferrari, l'unico*, pp. 191 and 192.
9. Author's conversation with Franco Gozzi, 19 May 2009.
10. Author's conversation with Dino Tagliazucchi, 2 December 2008.
11. Rancati, *Ferrari, l'unico*, pp. 191 and 192.
12. Ibid., pp. 189 and 191.
13. *La Gazzetta dello Sport*, 22 October 1983.
14. Rancati, *Ferrari, l'unico*, p. 191.
15. Author's conversation with Piero Ferrari, 13 November 2012.
16. *La Gazzetta dello Sport*, 30 May 1983.
17. Ibid.
18. Ibid.
19. Author's conversation with Franco Gozzi, 19 May 2009; and author's conversation with Piero Ferrari, 13 November 2012.
20. *La Gazzetta dello Sport*, 30 May 1983.
21. Ibid., 22 October 1983.
22. Ibid.
23. Author's conversation with Franco Gozzi, 19 May 2009.
24. Original document: Enzo Ferrari Press Conference, Minutes, 21 October 1983. Private collection.
25. Ferrari, *Piloti, che gente*, p. 23.
26. Ibid., p. 303.
27. 'Alboreto: I sogni di un appassionato tra Monza e Ferrari,' by Paolo Ciccarone, www.automoto.it, 31 August 2015.
28. *Il Corriere della Sera*, 18 February 1986.
29. Author's conversation with Franco Gozzi, 21 June 2010.
30. Original document: Enzo Ferrari Press Conference, Minutes, 29 August 1984. Private collection.

31. Buzzonetti and Forghieri, *Mauro Forghieri: 30 anni di Ferrari e oltre*, pp. 201, 202 and 207.

32. Original document: Enzo Ferrari Press Conference, Minutes, 29 August 1984. Private collection.

33. Rancati, *Ferrari l'unico*, p. 194.

34. Original document: Enzo Ferrari Press Conference, Minutes, 29 August 1984. Private collection.

35. Buzzonetti and Forghieri, *Mauro Forghieri: 30 anni di Ferrari e oltre*, pp. 205 and 206.

36. Original document: Enzo Ferrari Press Conference, Minutes, 29 August 1984. Private collection.

37. Author's conversation with Franco Gozzi, 19 May 2009.

38. *La Gazzetta dello Sport*, 17 February 1985.

39. Author's conversation with Franco Gozzi, 19 May 2009.

40. Buzzonetti and Forghieri, *Mauro Forghieri: 30 anni di Ferrari e oltre*, pp. 209 and 210.

41. Dal Monte, *La rossa e le altre*, p. 249.

42. Rancati and Varisco, *Ferrari, che gente*, p. 191.

43. Ibid. Enzo's quote comes directly from Michele Alboreto, who was present.

44. *La Gazzetta dello Sport*, 11 March 1986.

45. Ibid., 24 September 1986.

46. Ibid., 25 September 1986.

47. Ibid., 11 March 1986.

48. Author's conversation with Franco Gozzi, 26 May 2009.

49. *La Gazzetta dello Sport*, 25 September 1986.

50. Author's conversation with Franco Gozzi, 26 May 2009.

Sunset

1. *La Gazzetta dello Sport*, 11 March 1986.

2. Author's conversation with Franco Gozzi, 26 May 2009.

3. Ibid.

4. *La Gazzetta dello Sport*, 11 March 1986.

5. Author's conversation with Franco Gozzi, 26 May 2009.

6. *Il Corriere della Sera*, 18 February 1986.

7. Ibid.

8. *La Gazzetta dello Sport*, 25 September 1986.

9. *Il Corriere della Sera*, 18 February 1986.

10. Ibid.

11. *La Gazzetta dello Sport*, 11 March 1986.

12. Ibid., 25 September 1986.

13. Ibid.

14. Ibid.

15. Author's conversation with Franco Gozzi, 26 May 2009.

16. *La Nuova Gazzetta di Modena*, 14 March 1987.

17. Ibid.

18. Ibid.

19. *Il Corriere della Sera*, 8 July 1987.

20. Ibid.
21. Ibid.
22. *La Nuova Gazzetta di Modena*, 22 July 1987.
23. Rancati, *Ferrari, l'unico*, p. 195.
24. *Ferrari: L'opera e il sogno*, Vol. 2, p. 210.
25. Ferrari, *Una vita per l'automobile*, p. 354.
26. Ibid.
27. *La Nuova Gazzetta di Modena*, 3 November 1987.
28. Ibid., 17 August 1988.
29. Allievi, *Il secondo è il primo dei perdenti*, page 26.
30. *La Nuova Gazzetta di Modena*, 17 August 1988.
31. Author's conversation with Franco Gozzi, 26 May 2009.
32. Ibid.
33. Ibid.
34. Ibid.
35. Ibid.
36. Ibid.
37. Ibid., 19 May 2009.
38. *La Nuova Gazzetta di Modena*, 27 December 1987.
39. Ibid., 15 January 1988.
40. Ferrari, *Una vita per l'automobile*, p. 354.

Ferrari 90

1. *La Nuova Gazzetta di Modena*, 2 February 1988.
2. Ibid.
3. Ibid.
4. Ibid.
5. Ferrari, *Una vita per l'automobile*, p. 360.
6. *La Nuova Gazzetta di Modena*, 16 February 1988.
7. Ibid., 18 February 1988.
8. Author's conversation with Claudio Ricardi, 27 November 2008.
9. *La Gazzetta dello Sport*, 19 February 1988.
10. Author's conversation with Claudio Ricardi, 27 November 2008.
11. Ibid.
12. *La Gazzetta dello Sport*, 18 February 1988.
13. Author's conversation with Franco Gozzi, 19 May 2009.
14. Ibid.
15. *La Nuova Gazzetta di Modena*, 19 February 1988.
16. Author's conversation with Claudio Ricardi, 27 November 2008.
17. Ibid.
18. Ibid.
19. *La Nuova Gazzetta di Modena*, 19 February 1988.
20. Author's conversation with Dino Tagliazucchi, 2 December 2008.
21. Author's conversation with Claudio Ricardi, 27 November 2008.
22. Author's conversation with Dino Tagliazucchi, 2 December 2008.

23. *La Nuova Gazzetta di Modena*, 23 February 1988.

24. Ferrari, *Una vita per l'automobile*, p. 364.

25. *La Nuova Gazzetta di Modena*, 24 February 1988.

26. Lycia Mezzacappa, *Il mio Drake* (Modena: Edizioni 11 Fiorino, 1998), p. 92.

27. Author's conversation with Dino Tagliazucchi, 2 December 2008.

28. Ibid.

29. Ibid.

30. Mezzacappa, *Il mio Drake*, p. 60.

Heaven Can't Wait

1. Author's conversation with Dino Tagliazucchi, 25 January 2011.

2. *La Nuova Gazzetta di Modena*, 4 June 1988.

3. Ibid., 17 August 1988.

4. Ibid., 4 June 1988.

5. Ibid.

6. Author's conversation with Carlo Benzi, 25 November 2008.

7. *Nuova Gazzetta di Modena*, 4 June 1988.

8. Mezzacappa, *Il mio Drake*, p. 99.

9. Author's conversation with Dino Tagliazucchi, 2 December 2008.

10. Ibid.

11. Ibid.

12. *La Nuova Gazzetta di Modena*, 5 June 1988.

13. Author's conversation with Dino Tagliazucchi, 2 December 2008.

14. Ibid.

15. Ibid.

16. Ferrari, *Una vita per l'automobile*, p. 373. Ferrari's quote is taken from the book, but Dino Tagliazucchi, who was with Ferrari, confirms it is accurate.

17. *La Nuova Gazzetta di Modena*, 18 August 1988.

18. Author's conversation with Dino Tagliazucchi, 2 December 2008.

19. Ibid.

20. *La Gazzetta dello Sport*, 23 June 1988.

21. Original document: Enzo Ferrari's handwritten note, June 1988. Private collection.

22. Author's conversation with Franco Gozzi, 19 May 2009.

23. Ibid.

24. Author's conversation with Dino Tagliazucchi, 2 December 2008.

25. Piero Ferrari, *Ferrari, mio padre*, p. 199.

26. Mezzacappa, *Il mio Drake*, p. 104.

27. Author's conversation with Dino Tagliazucchi, 2 December 2008.

28. Author's conversation with Carlo Benzi, 25 November 2008.

29. Author's conversation with Dino Tagliazucchi, 2 December 2008.

30. Author's conversation with Franco Gozzi, 19 May 2009.

31. Gozzi, *Alla destra del Drake*, p. 233.

32. Author's conversation with Dino Tagliazucchi, 2 December 2008.

33. Allievi, *Il secondo è il primo dei perdenti*, p. 120.

34. Mezzacappa, *Il mio Drake*, p. 104.

35. Rancati and Varisco, *Ferrari, che gente*, p. 191.
36. Author's conversation with Dino Tagliazucchi, 2 December 2008.
37. Ibid.
38. Author's conversation with Carlo Benzi, 25 November 2008.
39. Ibid.
40. Orefici, *Ferrari: Romanzo di una vita*, p. 191.
41. Author's conversation with Carlo Benzi, 25 November 2008.
42. *La Gazzetta dello Sport*, 17 August 1988.
43. Author's conversation with Carlo Benzi, 25 November 2008.
44. Ibid.
45. Author's conversation with Dino Tagliazucchi, 2 December 2008.
46. *La Nuova Gazzetta di Modena*, 17 August 1988.
47. Author's conversation with Dino Tagliazucchi, 2 December 2008.
48. Author's conversation with Carlo Benzi, 25 November 2008.
49. *La Nuova Gazzetta di Modena*, 17 August 1988.
50. *La Gazzetta dello Sport*, 17 August 1988.
51. Ibid.
52. Author's conversation with Carlo Benzi, 25 November 2008.
53. *La Gazzetta dello Sport*, 17 August 1988.

Index

About the Author

Luca Dal Monte, born in 1963 in Cremona, Italy, is an accomplished author and automotive industry veteran. After graduating with a degree in US history and political sciences, Luca served as the first Chief Press Officer for the Province of Cremona. He was enlisted for military service, and then worked for Cremona's *La Provincia* newspaper, before securing a job at the Italian branch of the French carmaker Peugeot in 1991. This initiated a fantastic journey into the automobile industry, and consequent roles with Toyota, Pirelli, Ferrari and Maserati. His automotive and writing experiences culminated in the publication of his debut fiction novel *La Scuderia* in 2009. Today, *Enzo: The Definitive Biography* stands as Luca's long-cherished project, offering a unique angle on a towering 20th-century figure.